Imagining Asia in 2030

Published by Academic Foundation
in association with the
Institute for Defence Studies
and Analyses (IDSA), New Delhi

Imagining Asia in 2030

Trends, Scenarios and Alternatives

Editors
AJEY LELE
NAMRATA GOSWAMI

ACADEMIC FOUNDATION
NEW DELHI

First published in 2011
by

ACADEMIC FOUNDATION
4772-73 / 23 Bharat Ram Road, (23 Ansari Road),
Darya Ganj, New Delhi - 110 002 (India).
Phones : 23245001 / 02 / 03 / 04.
Fax : +91-11-23245005.
E-mail : books@academicfoundation.com
www. academicfoundation.com

in association with :

Institute for Defence Studies and Analyses, New Delhi
www.idsa.in

Imagining Asia in 2030: Trends, Scenarios and Alternatives
Editors: Ajey Lele and Namrata Goswami

ISBN 10: 81-7188-870-4
ISBN 13: 978-81-7188-870-2

Typeset by Italics India, New Delhi.
Printed and bound in India.

Contents

III
Demography, Migration and Urbanisation

IV
Society, Identity, Religion and Governance

V
Transformational Technologies and their Impact on Society

VI
WMD and International Security

VII
Asian Militaries and the Future of War

VIII
Geopolitics in Asia: Country Perspectives

IX
Alternative Scenarios

About the Editors/Contributors

Editors :

Ajey Lele is a Research Fellow at the Institute for Defence Studies and Analyses (IDSA), New Delhi, India. His areas of research include: space security, strategic technologies and weapons of mass destruction (WMD).

Namrata Goswami is a Research Fellow at the IDSA, New Delhi, India. Her areas of research include: international relations theory, ethnic and intra-state conflicts and the theory and practice of conflict prevention, management and resolution.

Contributors :

Steve Aiken is lead author and desk office for geopolitics for the United Kingdom's MoD's Development, Concepts and Doctrine Centre (DCDC).

Sarita Azad is Project Associate at IDSA, New Delhi, India.

Judith M. Brown is Beit Professor of Commonwealth History, Balliol College, Oxford, United Kingdom.

Nayan Chanda is Director of Publications and the Editor of Yale Global Online Magazine at the Yale Center for the Study of Globalization, New Haven, Connecticut, USA.

Chien-Peng (C.P.) Chung is Associate Professor, Department of Political Science, Lingnan University, Hong Kong.

Martin van Creveld is Professor Emeritus at The Hebrew University, Jerusalem, Israel.

David P. Fidler is the James Louis Calamaras Professor of Law and Director of the Center on American and Global Security, Indiana University, Bloomington, USA.

Aaron L. Friedberg is a Professor of Politics and International Affairs at Princeton University, Princeton, USA.

David E. Fuente is Programme Head for Infrastructure and Governance at the Centre for Development Finance, Chennai, India.

Sumit Ganguly is the Rabindranath Tagore Chair in Indian Cultures and Civilizations, Professor of Political Science, Director of the India Studies Program, and Director of Research for Center on American and Global Security, Indiana University, Bloomington, USA.

John P. Geis is Director, Center for Strategy and Technology, United States Air Force, Montgomery, Alabama Area.

Adrian V. Gheorghe is the Faculty of Power Engineering at the Bucharest Polytechnic Institute, Romania.

Mohan Guruswamy is the Director the Centre for Policy Alternatives, New Delhi, India.

Yong-Sup Han is Professor of Korea National Defense University.

Stephan Harrison is Associate Professor of Quaternary Science, University of Exeter, Penryn, United Kingdom.

Roland Heickerö is Deputy Research Director at the Swedish Defence Research Agency, FOI, Stockholm.

Pervez Hoodbhoy is Professor of Physics, Quaid-e-Azam University, Islamabad, Pakistan.

G. John Ikenberry is Albert G. Milbank Professor of Politics and International Affairs, Woodrow Wilson School and Department of Politics, Princeton University, USA.

Makoto Iokibe is the President, National Defense Academy, Japan.

Ali Karami is Associate Professor of Molecular Biology at the Research Center of Molecular Biology, Baqiyatallah University of Medical Sciences, Tehran, Iran.

Catarina Kinnvall is Associate Professor, Department of Political Science, Lund University, Sweden.

Konstantin K. Khudoley is Dean, School of International Relations, Saint Petersburg State University, Russia.

Nabanita R. Krishnan is currently the Director, Management Information System and Technologies (MIST) at Defence Research and Development Organisation (DRDO) Headquarters, New Delhi, India.

Li Li is an Associate Research fellow at China Institute of Contemporary International Relations (CICIR), Beijing, China.

Phillip Longman is Senior Research Fellow at the New America Foundation, a public policy institute in Washington, D.C.

Vijay Sakhuja is Director Research, Indian Council of World Affairs (ICWA), New Delhi, India.

Uttam Kumar Sinha is a Research Fellow at IDSA, New Delhi, India.

Bilveer Singh is Associate Professor, Department of Political Science, National University of Singapore.

Narendra S. Sisodia is Director General of IDSA, New Delhi, India.

Ted Svensson is Assistant Professor at the Department of Political Science, Lund University, Sweden.

Stanislav Tkachenko was an Associate Professor of the Department of European Studies at the School of International Relations, Saint Petersburg State University, Russia.

Angela Woodward is Programme Director, VERTIC, United Kingdom.

Preface

Predicting the future is a hazardous enterprise. And yet, those nation states who aspire to shape their future must make some informed assessments of the plausible futures. The drivers affecting the future may vary in their intensity and impact. It is therefore prudent to imagine not just one future, but a range of alternative futures. Prudence also requires that even when well-informed and intelligent forecasts have been made, one is prepared to expect a wholly unanticipated surprise. However uncertain the possible futures, they must be imagined and to the extent possible, should be planned for. This is the essential task of strategists. Strategy is relevant only if there are possible futures to plan for.

It is in this backdrop that the Institute for Defence Studies and Analyses (IDSA) undertook two major exercises over the past several months. One was to assess South Asian futures in 2020 and the other, a somewhat more ambitious exercise was to forecast Asian futures for 2030. The exercise was enriched by perspectives of some of the best known domain experts assembled for the Asian Security Conference 2010. They addressed a whole array of relevant themes ranging from economic growth to climate change, from demographic trends to technological developments and from geopolitics to proliferation of weapons of mass destruction. The objective was to develop a rich and holistic view of the emerging futures.

Given the range of themes and diversity of perspectives, the exercise was the first of its kind for the Institute. Following the deliberations in the conference, the authors have also reviewed their contributions.

We believe that this volume would be particularly useful for policy-makers who can hardly spare any time from their operational pressures to think systematically about the future. Yet their current policy decisions must avoid knee-jerk reactions and keep the long-term developments in view. The book should be equally useful for scholars of the subject and an interesting read for the general readers.

— Narendra S. Sisodia

Director General,

Institute for Defence Studies and Analyses.

I

Climate Change, Environment, Energy and Water

1

Climate Change and Implications for Security

An Indian Dimension

STEPHAN HARRISON

Climate Change

With a scientific consensus (Oreskes, 2004) that human-induced global warming has now driven the climate beyond natural variability, much debate is now concentrated on the implications of continued warming for earth surface systems, the biosphere and human systems. Clearly, continued warming will have important consequences for a range of earth systems (including the atmosphere, cryosphere, oceans, hydrological systems and the biosphere). The consequences of this temperature rise have been well documented, and include rapid recession of mountain glaciers, rising sea levels, changing patterns and intensities of rainfall and drought events and latitudinal shifts in ecological systems. Policymakers and strategists are grappling to understand these impacts and the adaptation and mitigation strategies that follow. What seems clear is the likelihood that climate change will trigger migration and conflict over increasingly scarce resources and this chapter discusses some of the security implications of future climate change and the challenges that exist.

I will argue that climate change poses severe problems for those planning future strategic initiatives. There are at least three reasons for this. First, there is the possibility that future climate change will be non-linear and very abrupt, as it has been in the past, and that this will overwhelm the capabilities of the military and other security organisations and create threats in regions of the world where planners had assumed that such threats did not exist. The second issue concerns the variations in vulnerability to climate change that different regions will experience and the changing nature of the risks.

The third barrier to successful security planning is the dislocated nature of information transfer between climate science and planners in the military and foreign policy spheres (see Harrison 2005; 2008).

Vulnerability of India

For many geographical, political and cultural reasons India is vulnerable to the effects of future climate change. With a large and growing population, India is reliant on the monsoon rains and its river systems for agriculture and industry. Its long coastline interacts with important climatic belts and is vulnerable to shifts in the magnitude and frequency of tropical cyclones. Many of its water resources rise in the Himalayas and are fed by glaciers which are melting rapidly, or are transboundary with headwaters in neighbouring countries with which India has profound political differences. While there are many accounts of the significance of many of these factors (e.g., Kumar *et al.*, 2001; Parikh and Parikh, 2002; O'Brien *et al.*, 2004; Kumar *et al.*, 2006) the purpose of this study is to assess some of the wider implications of climate change for military planners and policymakers and to outline the continuing challenges.

Issues for Strategic Planners

Non-Linearity in Response

Non-linearity is an important characteristic of all global environmental systems. It occurs at a range of temporal and spatial scales and controls the climate, and human responses to it. Implicit in such non-linear systems are the existence of multiple equilibria and thresholds (so-called tipping points); these force the system to exhibit rapid and unpredictable change. The interactions between the non-linear atmosphere, hydrosphere, biosphere and geosphere, and society are complex and form one of the main sources of uncertainty in our predictions of future climate and environmental change. It is clear that such uncertainty is of intense interest to human society as rapid change would impose a very severe burden on the stability of cultural, economic and political (as well as ecological) systems. There are plausible system thresholds that could overwhelm the capabilities of humanity to respond. However, policymakers are only partly aware of the nature of threshold responses in the climate, the non-linear feedbacks that these create and the probabilities of rapid change.

Landscape Response is Poorly Modelled

The issue of landscape response is linked closely to non-linearity displayed in the outcomes of continued warming. As a result, developing credible strategies to adapt to climate change or mitigate its effects requires a sophisticated understanding of the nature of landscape response to climate change. For instance, understanding how river regimes will respond in a rapidly changing climate, or the impact of rainfall variations on soil erosion are non-trivial questions. Typically, there is the assumption that climate change will produce an identifiable and largely predictable landscape response which can then be embedded into adaptation and management plans. However, over the past few decades there has been growing evidence from geomorphology and earth system science that the response of landscape systems to climate change may be highly non-linear and unpredictable (e.g., Wolman and Gerson, 1978; Wells and Harvey, 1987), setting up difficult challenges for policymakers and adaptation specialists. New advances in the modelling of non-linear and dynamic geomorphological systems has begun to provide the tools by which better assessments of landscape response to climate change can be developed.

Transbounday Water Issues

Rapidly increasing demands for transboundary water resources have the potential to magnify pre-existing political tensions between nation states. Such issues are exacerbated by climate change causing reduction in glacier mass in mountain regions and the consequent long-term reduction in water supply. While the rapidity with which the Himalayan glaciers are melting has been recently exaggerated to some extent, the long-term trend for Himalayan glaciers under conditions of continued warming is clearly that they will continue melting. In the short-term this will liberate melt-water which can be used for agriculture and industry, but deglaciation also produces rapid destabilisation of mountain slopes, causing catastrophic landslides, rockfalls and mudslides, which have important implications for development in mountain valleys.

Regional Climate Change can be very Rapid

One of the important lessons from past climate change is that the climate system has undergone significant and rapid shifts, and these changes have been especially noticeable at the regional scale. When used to model past climates our global climate models (GCMs) do not recreate these rapid climate shifts and this should be seen as a considerable and dangerous failing in their ability to prepare policymakers for future changes. The past record of climate change has shown that the climate can be regionally and globally liable to rapid shifts when the forcings have increased rapidly; the implications of this are that recent rapid atmospheric forcing by greenhouse gas (GHG) emissions makes rapid climate change more likely, and this will be something too abrupt when measured on the timescale of human economic, cultural and political systems and global ecosystems (NRC, 2002).

Many instances in the past of rapid climate change have probably been the result of interactions between ice sheets and oceans during deglaciation and under conditions of positive climate forcing, conditions which are beginning to operate today. As a result, the study of past climate may be critical in identifying the characteristics and behaviour of systems just before they undergo rapid shifts, and in testing the ability of GCMs to predict such changes. The importance of this can hardly be exaggerated and the results so far show that our capability of predicting rapid climate change is far from adequate.

The last 11,000 years (ka) (the Holocene epoch) have so far been a period of relative climatic stability (at least on a large scale), but there has been no change in climatic forcing comparable to the doubling of atmospheric $C0_2$ concentrations over pre-industrial levels which we are likely to see by the middle of this century. Ice core records reveal that atmospheric $C0_2$ concentrations are now higher than for at least the last 650 ka (IPCC, 2007). As a result, the human influence on the global climate is very profound, posing possibly very severe future risks, although the exact nature, impact and timing of these is likely to remain uncertain.

Model Uncertainty

While we have compelling evidence of the rapid nature of past climate change and the rapid response of earth surface systems to this, our ability to model these changes, and thus our ability to predict them is currently poor. Clearly, the pattern and extent of future warming has huge policy implications for governments and business. The only way in which such predictions can be made is through the use of GCMs and downscaling of these to regional climate models (RCMs).

Climate models have evolved enormously from the simple energy balance models of the 1960s and are now used to make predictions and projections of future climate change. GCMs were developed to include atmospheric and oceanic processes and the influence of land-use change, vegetation and ice sheets and these models have been further refined to form atmosphere ocean general circulation models (AOGCMs) and earth system models (ESMs). These contain sub-models within them to describe the operation of carbon fluxes and other processes. In certain ways, climate change is a more difficult problem than weather forecasting as verification and development of the models from real-world observation is restricted by the long time frame over which the models are forecasting. In addition, the complex nature of the global climate system means that even the most sophisticated GCMs are unable to always successfully model important elements of the climate including the location of certain storm tracks, regional responses and ice-sheet dynamics. These limitations are not always considered by policymakers.

Researchers have identified a number of sources of uncertainty in modelling attempts to explore future climate change (Collins *et al.*, 2002; Stainforth *et al.*, 2007) and these can be sub-divided into two major categories: theoretical limitations and practical limitations in model predictability. They can be further broken down into problems related to the uncertainties associated with the physical processes that drive the global climate. These include initial condition uncertainty, model uncertainty and model inadequacy, and the uncertainties inherent in attempting to predict the likely trends in the main drivers of present and future climate (GHG emissions and the changing nature of sinks and sources).

The former uncertainties include poor scientific understanding of the operation of processes that occur at small spatial scales. These processes are parameterised and include land-use change, hydrological and albedo variables and processes such as those forming clouds. Over the last couple of years, there has been a greater recognition of the nature and policy implications that follow from these uncertainties and limitations, and these issues have been explored in a number of papers (e.g. Stainforth *et al.*, 2007).

GCM projections are generally robust for global temperature in that they mostly agree that northern hemisphere land masses will warm more than the global average, that the southern hemisphere oceans will warm least and that the Arctic will undergo rapid and enhanced warming (this is called polar amplification). The uncertainties that do exist are magnified at the regional scale to the extent that different models will produce different regional climates, even when forced by identical emissions scenarios. This is partly because of the operation of regional feedbacks and partly a consequence of model inadequacy. This is clearly a problem for policymakers who wish to have credible climate projections for specific locations. The problem is exacerbated by the poor ability of GCMs to resolve large-scale elements of the climate system, such as the El Niño-Southern Oscillation (ENSO). This is important because these characteristics of the climate system are the ones which play a central role in determining the nature, location, amount and timing of precipitation and therefore water availability.

In addition, future trends in precipitation are more uncertain than those for temperature since precipitation is affected by features such as the position of frontal zones and wind fields whose future behaviour is not easily modelled, and projections from regional modelling show wide variance. As Douville *et al.* (2006) recognise, 'uncertainties in precipitation change are, like precipitation itself, very unevenly distributed over the globe, the most vulnerable countries sometimes being those where the anticipated precipitation changes are the most uncertain.' For example, projections for central and tropical South America range from increases in precipitation by 2020 of 5 per cent to decreases of -5 per cent. By 2050 projections are still more uncertain, ranging from around 10 per cent increases and decreases. Such uncertainties are a feature of projections from GCMs and Magrin *et al.* (2007: 594) caution that, 'the current GCMs do not produce projections of changes in the hydrological cycle at regional scales with confidence. In particular the uncertainty of projections of precipitation remain high.'

Two questions follow from this. First, does this mean that our GCMs are unable to account for the likely future evolution of the climate? Second, is their inability to mimic the rapid climate shifts of the past (and some broad scale elements of the present climate system) mean that they are not preparing us for threshold responses? Clearly, these questions have important policy implications as climate change can be both rapid and unpredictable. We know that climate change in the past has happened very rapidly; we therefore know that such changes are possible in the future. Highlighting the uncertainties in our climate projections is crucial if we are to prepare society for the climate change, the associated conflicts and societal and ecological upheavals to come. For a fuller discussion of these issues (see Harrison, 2007; Harrison and Stainforth, 2009).

Conclusions

The perturbation we are imposing on the global climate system is significantly larger than any plausible natural variability. Predicting the likely response of this, beyond saying that climate sensitivity to doubling C02 concentrations is likely to be around 3°C (IPCC, 2007) is difficult. As Rial *et al.*, 2004 caution: 'since the climate system is complex, occasionally chaotic, dominated by abrupt changes and driven by competing feedbacks with largely unknown thresholds, climate prediction is difficult, if not impracticable.'

It seems likely that the models will underestimate rather than overestimate the climate sensitivity over the long term, because they omit relevant variables. It is also likely that the regional response to GHG forcing will be beyond the current capability of GCMs and RCMs to resolve. This makes more urgent the study of climate change in the context of strategic analyses.

This work has partly evolved from discussions with my climate science colleagues; especially Drs. Dave Stainforth and Ed Anderson. A longer treatment of these ideas may be found in Harrison (2007) and Harrison and Stainforth (2009).

References

Alley, R.B., D.A. Meese, C.A. Shuman, A.J. Gow, K.C. Taylor, P.M. Grootes, I.W.C. White, M. Ram, E.D. Waddington, P.A. Mayewski and G.A. Zielinski (1993). "Abrupt Increase in Greenland Snow Accumulation at the End of the Younger Dryas Event", *Nature* 362(6420): 527-29.

Alley, R.B., J. Marotzke, W.D. Nordhaus, J.T. Overpeck, D.M. Peteet, R.A. Pielke Jr., R.T. Pierrehumbert, P.B. Rhines, T.F. Stocker, L.D. Talley and J.M. Wallace (2003) "Abrupt Climate Change" *Science* 299: 2005-10.

Broecker, W.S. (1999). "What If the Conveyor Were to Shut Down? Reflections on a Possible Outcome of the Great Global Experiment", *GSA Today* 9(1): 1-7.

Collins, M. Frame, B.D. Sinha and C.Wilson (2002). "How Far Ahead could we Predict El Niño?", *Geophysical Research Letters* 29(10): 1492, 10.1029/2001GL013919.

Douville, H. (2006). "Impact of Regional SST Anomalies on the Indian Monsoon Response to Global Warming in the CNRM Climate Model", *Journal of Climate* 19: 2008-24.

Emanuel, K.A. (2005). "Increasing Destructiveness of Tropical Cyclones over the Past 30 Years", *Nature* 436: 686-88.

Fischer, L. Kaab, C.A. Huggel and J. Noetzli (2006). "Geology, Glacier Retreat and Permafrost Degradation as Controlling Factors of Slope Instabilities in a High-Mountain Rock Wall: The Monte Rosa East Face", *Natural Hazards and Earth System Sciences* 6: 761-72.

Harrison, S. (2008). "Climate Change and Regional Security: Assessing the Scientific Uncertainties" *Journal of the Royal United Services Institute* 153(3): 88-91.

———. (2007). "Predicting Future Climate Change: Lessons from Palaeoclimatology". Institute of Actuaries, at *http://www.actuaries.org.uk/__data/assets/pdf_file/0018/24408/harrison_climatechange.pdf*

———. (2005). "Climate Change, Future Conflict and the Role of Climate Science", *Journal of the Royal United Services Institute* 150(6): 18-23.

Harrison, S. and D.A. Stainforth (2009). "Predicting Climate Change: Lessons from Emergence, Reductionism and the Past", *Eos, AGU* 90 (13): 111-12.

Huntington, T.G. (2006). "Evidence for Intensification of the Global Water Cycle: Review and Synthesis", *Journal of Hydrology* 319: 83–95.

Hutton, J. (1975). *Theory of the Earth.* 4 vols. Edinburgh.

Intergovernmental Panel on Climate Change (2007). *Climate Change 2007: The Physical Science Basis.* Summary for Policymakers. Geneva: IPCC.

Jones, P.D. and M.E. Mann (2004). "Climate over Past Millennia", *Reviews of Geophysics* 42: 1-42.

Kumar, K.S., K. Kavi and J. Parikh (2001). "Indian Agriculture and Climate Sensitivity", *Global Environmental Change* 11: 147-154.

Kumar, K.R., A.K. Sahai, K.K. Kumar, S.K. Patwardhan, P.K. Mishra, J.V. Revadikar, K. Kamala and G.B. Pant (2006). "High-Resolution Climate Change Scenarios for India for the 21st Century", *Current Science* 90(3): 334-45.

Mann, M.E., R.S. Bradley and M.K. Hughes (1999). "Northern Hemisphere Temperatures during the Past Millennium: Inferences, Uncertainties and Limitations", *Geophysical Research Letters* 26: 759-62.

Mann, M. E., and P. D. Jones (2006). "Global Surface Temperatures over the Past Two Millennia", *Geophysical Research Letters* 30(15): 1820, doi: 10.1029/2003GL017814.

Magrin G. *et al.* (2007). " Latin America Climate Change 2007: Impacts, Adaptability and Vulnerability", Contribution of Working Group II to the *Fourth Assessment Report of the Inter-Governmental Panel on Climate Change.* Cambridge, UK: Cambridge University Press, Cambridge University Press.

Moberg, A., D.M. Sonechkin, K. Holmgren, N.M. Datsenko and W. Karlen (2005). "Highly Variable Northern Hemisphere Temperatures Reconstructed from Low- and High-resolution Proxy Data", *Nature* 433(7026): 613-17.

National Research Council (2002). *Abrupt Climate Change: Inevitable Surprises.* Washington, D.C.: National Academy Press.

O'Brien, K., R. Leichenko, U. Kelkar, H. Venema, G. Aandahl, H. Tompkins, A. Javed, S. Bhadwal, S. Barg, L. Nygaard and J. West (2004). "Mapping Vulnerability to Multiple Stressors: Climate Change and Globalization in India", *Global Environmental Change*(A) 14(4): 303-13.

Oreskes, N. (2004). "Beyond the Ivory Tower: The Scientific Consensus on Climate Change", *Science* 306: 1686.

Overpeck, J.T., B.L. Otto-Bliesner, J.T. Kiehl, G.H. Miller and R. Alley (2006). "Paleoclimatic Evidence for Future Ice-Sheet Instability and Rapid Sea-Level Rise", *Science* 311: 1747-50.

Parikh, J.K. and K. Parikh (2002). *"Climate Change: India's Perceptions, Positions, Policies and Possibilities", OECD Climate Change and Development Report.* p.30.

Phillips, D., M. Daoudy, S.Mc Caffrey, J. Ojendal and A. Turton (2006). "Transboundary Water Cooperation as a Tool for Conflict Prevention and for Broader Benefit-sharing", *Global Development Studies* No. 4. Stockholm. p.249.

Rial, A., R. Pielkesr, M. Beniston, M. Claussen, J. Canadell, P. Cox, H. Held, N. De Noblet-ducoudré, R. Prinn, J.F. Reynolds and J.D. Salas (2004). "Nonlinearities, Feedbacks and Critical Thresholds within the Earth's Climate System", *Climatic Change* 65: 11-38.

Stainforth, D.A., M.R. Allen, E. Tredger and L.A. Smith (2007). "Confidence, Uncertainty and Decision-Support Relevance in Climate Predictions", *Philosophical Transactions of the Royal Society* A/365: 2145–61.

Wells, S.G. and A.M. Harvey (1987). "Sedimentologic and Geomorphic Variations in Storm Generated Alluvial Fans, Howgill Fells, Northwest England", *Bulletin of the Geological Society of America* 98: 182-98.

Wolman, G. and R. Gerson (1978). "Relative Scales of Time and Effectiveness of Climate in Watershed Geomorphology", *Earth Surface Processes* 3: 27-36.

2

Water Security in Asia 2030

A Look at Indus and Ganga-Brahmaputra-Meghna River Basins

UTTAM KUMAR SINHA

Introduction

Transboundary river basins[1] are a prominent feature of the Asian physical landscape cross-cutting political boundaries and as such will be of paramount importance to Asia's geopolitical stability in 2030. Transboundary rivers physically links upstream and downstream users and its uses offer ample opportunity for harnessing development benefits. While they can serve as a cornerstone for cooperation, they can equally be a potential entry for tension and strife. Adding to the complexity, transboundary rivers are neither seen exclusively as a 'public good' (defined as non-rival and non-excludable) or a 'private good' (defined as rival and excludable).[2] Such amorphous definitional demarcation subjects transboundary rivers to various interpretations. That said, there is, however, a general view to perceive it as 'collective goods' or 'common pool resources'. Rivers have many uses. Some are 'consumptive' in nature and some 'non-consumptive'. The non-consumptive uses, such as navigation and hydroelectricity generation are less problem-generating than the consumptive uses such as drinking water and water for irrigation. Because river uses are subjective in terms of the where, what and how they are being used, a water-tight riparian treaty seldom emerges.

---

1. According to the 1967 Helsinki Rules, 'Each Basin State is entitled, within its territory, to a reasonable and equitable share in the beneficial use of the waters of an international Drainage Basin'. The Helsinki Rules also defines the 'Drainage Basin' as 'a geographical area extending over two or more States determined by the watershed limits of the system of waters, including surface and underground waters flowing into a common terminus.'
2. Tir and Ackerman (2009).

The chapter focusses on two crucial river basins: the Indus and the Ganga-Brahmaputra-Meghna (GBM) and looks at the driving forces behind water demand, on the political obstacles that stand in the way of river cooperation and the behaviour of the riparians. It reasons that future assessments cannot ignore the hydrology of the region and its interplay with the political reality. It builds scenarios through the description of the factors likely to shape events than a prediction of what will actually happen.

The hydrological profile of the two basins includes the vast water resources of Tibet. This inescapably brings into observation China's water concern and its riparian approach. In realpolitik, the preciousness of water often translates into possessiveness and at times resource aggressiveness. 'Water insecurity' can be expressed in terms of availability, reliability and quality, while 'water security' can be described as insecurity arising from control of headwaters. The insecurity-security dynamics can be explained through upper-lower riparian relations and further examined through the claims of 'absolute territoral sovereignty' *versus* 'absolute territorial integrity'. With no binding watercourse treaty, the region's hydropolitics is set for interesting development.

Water Facts

It is nature's greatest irony that while water covers most of the planet only 3 per cent is freshwater, of which 2 per cent is held in ice caps and glaciers. A mere 1 per cent in the form of lakes, ponds, rivers, streams, swamps, marshes and bogs, is non-frozen, salt-free and accessible for human consumption. It is this amount that truly matters in sizing the future water challenge. More importantly, there is approximately the same amount of water on Earth today as there was when it was formed.[3] With population increase and consumption patterns, it is projected that two out of every three people on the planet will live in water-stressed conditions by the year 2030. In the last century the world population tripled and the use of water grew six times. By 2030 the demand for water will be 40 per cent more than

3. See Water Facts and Trivia. *http://www.lenntech.com/water-trivia-facts.htm*

it is currently and 50 per cent higher in the most rapidly developing countries that include India and China.[4] According to UN 2004 estimates, by 2030 the world population is projected to reach 7.5 billion (low estimate) and 9 billion (medium estimate) by 2050 from the current level of 6.7 billion people. The bulk of the population increase will be in countries already experiencing water shortages.

Asia has more than 60 per cent of world population and 36 per cent of river-runoff. In terms of per person availability it has less freshwater than any other continent, except Antarctica. Asia has 2/3rd of world's irrigated lands and uses 85 per cent of water for irrigation.[5] The continent has 53 transboundary river basins covering 39 per cent of land.[6] The Indian subcontinent/South Asia home to about 34 per cent of Asia's population (1/6th of world's population) has about 4 per cent of world's annual renewable water resources that flows through several river basins.[7] Almost 95 per cent of water in South Asia is consumed by the agriculture sector as compared to the world's average of 70 per cent. Except for Nepal and Bhutan, the per capita water availability is lower than the world average. Given the uneven endowment and development of water resources in South Asia the issues and challenges are large, diverse and complex.

These facts and figures tell a telling tale. First and foremost, water is indispensable and the ultimate renewable resource. Second, water is being severely impacted by global population increase and economic growth. Together they are extracting and polluting it faster than it can be replenished. Third, the ever-expanding gap between demand (in terms of growing population and economy) and supply (in terms of availability) will potentially make water a contested issue particularly in densely populated countries. Fourth, since disputes over water are inevitable because of the changes, as described above, understanding the processes of resolution and framing new mechanisms and approaches becomes a necessity.

---

4. Mckinsey Report (2009).
5. World Resource Institute, 1999. At *http://www.wri.org/map/contributions-to-global-warming* (Accessed on December 08, 2009).
6. IJWRD (1999).
7. UNEP (2008).

Interlocking Challenges

Water requirement is the mainstay of states and societies. Between now and 2030, Asia will have to juggle competing and conflicting food-energy-water (FEW) concerns, yielding a set of challenging consequences. A 'perfect storm' of FEW shortages by 2030 has already been predicted.[8] These set of critical drivers will present difficult-to-manage outcomes and will reinforce each other as never before. First, as population grows, competition for food, energy and water will correspondingly increase. Increasing demand for food grains among the growing middle classes in Asia will claim larger areas of cropland and greater volumes of irrigation water. Second, with the risks that climate change attaches, FEW will be subject to various stresses and strains. Over the next 20 years, rising concerns about the effects of climate change will take greater precedence over any physical changes associated with climate change. Perceptions of a rapidly changing ecosystem in all likelihood will prompt nations to take unilateral actions to secure resources and territorial sovereignty. Any willingness to engage in greater river basin cooperation will depend on a number of factors, such as the behaviour of other competing countries, the economic viability, and other interests that states are reluctant to either compromise or concede.

A Tale of Two Transboundary River Basins

The Indus Basin is an important geophysical of the Indian subcontinent. The Indus together with the Chenab, Ravi, Sutlej, Jhelum, Beas and the extinct Sarasvati forms the 'Sapta Sindhu' delta in the Sindh province of Pakistan. The Indus originates in the Tibetan plateau in the vicinity of Lake Mansarovar, runs through Ladakh, Jammu and Kashmir, Gilgit-Baltistan and Pakistan before it merges into the Arabian Sea. The total length of the river is 3,200 km. The river's estimated annual flow is approximately 207 billion m^3.

---

8. As noted by John Beddington, UK Chief Scientist on March 18, 2009. See *http://www.guardian.co.uk/science/2009/mar/18/perfect-storm-john-beddington-energy-food-climate*

Table 2.1

Indus Basin

Total basin area	1170838 km^2
Annual available waters	224 billion m^3
Country	**Basin Area (Km^2)**
Pakistan	632,954
India	374,887
China	86,432
Afghanistan	76,542

Source: UNEP (2008).
http://www.reliefweb.int/rw/lib.nsf/db900sid/ASAZ-7NZJEX/$file/unep_Dec2008.pdf?openelemen. P26

The Ganga-Brahmaputra-Meghna Basin (GBM) flows through the northern, eastern and northeastern parts of India. The river system is as much a blessing as a curse because of its water potential and destructive reality. The basin covers an area of about 1.75 million km2 with an estimated population of approximately 535 million (75.8 per cent in India; 20 per cent in Bangladesh; 3.5 per cent in Nepal; 0.2 per cent in Bhutan; and 0.5 per cent in China). The basin has huge development opportunities but is home to the largest concentration of poor in the world. The majority of the population (approximately 10 per cent of the global population) subsists on agriculture.

Table 2.2

Ganga-Brahmaputra-Meghna Basin

Total basin area	1745000 km^2
Annual available waters	2,025 billion m^3
Country	**Basin Area (Km^2)**
India	1,105,000 (62.9 per cent)
China	326,000 (19.1 per cent)
Nepal	140,000 (8.0 per cent)
Bangladesh	129,000 (7.4 per cent)
Bhutan	45,000 (2.6 per cent)

Source: UNEP (2008).
http://www.reliefweb.int/rw/lib.nsf/db900sid/ASAZ-7NZJEX/$file/unep_Dec2008.pdf?openelemen. P26

Riparian Relations

Riparian nations, are those nations 'across which or along which a river flows, have legal rights to use the water of river'.[9] Simple as it may seem, varied interpretations have resulted in claims and counter-claims between riparian countries. Though disregarded by the international water laws, upper riparian nations essentially base their claims on 'absolute territorial sovereignty', i.e., the right to use water of rivers the way they want it to be used regardless of lower riparian concerns. The lower riparian nations, on the other hand, base their claims on 'absolute territorial integrity', claiming that upper riparian can do nothing that affects the quantity and quality of water flowing downstream. Clearly, both the claims are extremely incompatible. To overcome such differing positions, riparian states work through the more accepted legal norms of 'equitable utilisation', 'no-harm rule' and 'restricted sovereignty' and frame negotiations and treaties accordingly.[10] However, all these norms in state politics and power politics are rendered meaningless. It is a vague notion that nations are entitled to 'reasonable share of water'.[11] Keeping in mind that there is no legal-binding international treaty on water sharing, how will riparian politics play out in the region? The future of conflict or cooperation in the Indus and GBM basins will revolve around the water 'insecurity-security' dynamics of the basin states. Here is an overview.

1. China and India will be critical players in the hydropolitics of the region. India is simultaneously an upper, middle and lower riparian, China's hydrological position, on the other hand, is one of complete upper riparian supremacy. India, unlike China, has

9. International Water Law, *http://www.waterencyclopedia.com/La-Mi/Law-International-Water.html*
10. The rule of 'equitable utilisation', is based on the concept that an international drainage basin is a coherent legal and managerial unit, and embodies a theory of restricted sovereignty under which each nation recognises the right of all riparian nations to use water from a common source and the obligation to manage their uses so as not to interfere unreasonably with like uses in other riparian nations.
11. While this is enshrined in the UN Convention on the Non-Navigational Uses of International Watercourses (1997), it is not binding because the convention is not in force with only 16 countries have ratified it. To come into force it requires 35 countries. The UNGA (General Assembly) approved the UN convention by 104-3 in 1997. There is also the 'no-harm rule' in the convention, which states riparian nations to take all 'appropriate measures' to prevent causing harm to other watercourse nations.

a high dependency on the headwaters of the rivers sources such as Indus, Sutlej and Brahmaputra which originate in the Tibetan plateau. 'Water insecurity' in China relates to the disproportionate availability of waters, the majority of which is in the south (Tibet Autonomous Region, TAR) with the north and west excessively water stressed. Also, pollution is a big worry with a vast majority of lakes and many of its largest rivers unsuitable for human use.[12] In terms of 'water security', China has no threat. It is probably, along with Turkey, the world's most independent riparian country.[13] This position gives it enormous flexibility in shaping larger political equations with its neighbours. India, on the other hand, given its longstanding commitment to bilateral river treaties (which China has none[14]) has to assiduously balance the anxiety and concerns of its lower riparians (Pakistan and Bangladesh) without compromising its own water requirements. For India, both 'water insecurity' (internal water management strategy and its nighbourhood approach) and 'water security' *vis-à-vis* China is high.

2. An evaluation of the other actors in the two transboundary river basins, particularly Pakistan and Bangladesh, suggest that 'water insecurity' in terms of per capita availability, reliability and quality are severe. But the bigger fear is in terms of 'water security'. Pakistan is dependent on the sources of rivers outside its boundary but fears India more as an upper riparian than China which it has allowed building-operating-transfer (BOT) of river projects in Gilgit-Baltistan (Pakistan Occupied Kashmir, POK) for hydroelectricity. For Bangladesh, being the lowest

12. Overall, in terms of per capita availability, China ranks among the world's lowest.
13. Independent in terms of sources of rivers originating in its territory and not being dependent on the sources of the headwaters from other countries.
14. Except for a basin cooperation on Lancang-Mekong River. The Lancang River begins in the northeastern side of Tanggula mountains in Qinghai province, flows through Tibet into Yunnan province, and is called Mekong River when it flows out of 244 boundary stone in Mengla county in Yunnan province. Mekong runs all the way through Myanmar, Lao People's Democratic Republic, Thailand, Cambodia and Vietnam and empties into the South China Sea near Ho Chi Minh in Vietnam. Lancang-Mekong River is 4,880.3 kilometres long; the section of Lancang River in China is 2,161.1 km long. So far, 25 major projects have been listed: 14 projects inside China, 4 inside Laos, 4 along the borders of Laos and Thailand and Laos and Cambodia and 3 projects inside Cambodia. These dams are estimated to produce 70 per cent of China's current electricity needs.

riparian in the GBM, its dependency is extreme *vis-à-vis* India with 94 per cent of the waters originating beyond its border including the 54 rivers, rivulets and streams. With both the countries water will increasingly become a political, emotional and a critical driver of the larger politics with India. However, there are treaties and mechanisms to address the issue like the 1960 Indus Water Treaty now in its 50th year and the 1996 Ganges Treaty till 2026. Nepal and Bhutan unlike the other basin countries have high per capita water availability and therefore 'water insecurity' is low. The issue, however, is how best to share the benefits of water with India. This has failed to achieve the required success in Nepal's case as political complexities, implementation of treaties and perceptions have undermined enormous potential for water cooperation. But with Bhutan water cooperation has been a win-win.

A snapshot of the riparian behaviour suggests that no country will like to be dependent on either India or China having control over an indispensable resource. The inherent lack of trust accentuates it. For the basin states other than China, being water independent is not an option. For India water issues will be far more political and strategic *vis-à-vis* Pakistan and China. Though politics cannot be discounted from India's water relations with Nepal and Bangladesh, there is a considerable scope to overcome and break political deadlocks through sensible water sharing arrangements and resource development. In building hydro scenarios (2030) three important variables have been identified: (a) water resources of Tibet, (b) China's rise, and (c) Indus water treaty between India and Pakistan. The brief description of the variables will follow before the scenarios are drawn.

Tibet: The Third Pole

The Tibetan Plateau, regarded as the 'Third Pole', is a storehouse of bountiful freshwater captured in its massive glaciers, large lakes and cascading waterfalls. After founding the People's Republic of China in 1949, the new communist regime sought reunification with Tibet and invaded it in 1950. Following its occupation it made extensive modifications in the borders of the provinces of Tibet. Amdo was made the new Qinghai province. U-Tsang and eastern Kham were designated as Tibet Autonomous Region (TAR) of China and the remaining parts merged into its provinces of Sichuan, Yunnan and Gansu.[15] With an area spanning 470,000 sq km, TAR is the second largest province of China after Xinjiang.

The plateau serves as the headwaters of many of Asia's largest rivers including the Yellow, Yangtze, Mekong, Salween, Brahmaputra, Indus and Sutlej. It is estimated that the net hydrological flows in Tibet total 627 cubic km per year.[16] This is roughly 6 per cent of Asia's annual run-off and 34 per cent of India's total river water resources. The availability of fresh water is 104,500 cubic metres per year, making Tibet the fourth largest waterhouse in the world after Iceland, New Zealand and Canada.[17] Various figures estimate about 1.5 to 2 billion people in South and Southeast Asia dependent on the watersheds of these rivers whose sources are in Tibet. These vast water resources are also vulnerable to climate change and a host of serious environmental challenges that require global attention. The impact of global warming on the glaciers is also alarming with glaciologists suggesting that the glaciers in the plateau are receding at a rate faster than anywhere else in the world.

Tibet's water resources raise difficult and contesting questions. Should China alone be the stakeholder to the fate of the waters in Tibet? China has rampantly exploited all the rivers from the Tibetan Plateau except for the Nujiang River which flows through Yunnan and enters Myanmar, where it is known as the Salween.[18] The north-south diversion plans on the Yarlung Zangbo (Brahamaputra in India), the only other river untouched, are afoot causing fears and apprehensions for India.[19] With historical disagreement over the territory, Tibet's

---

15. Bajoria (2008).
16. The hydrological data of Tibet varies and most of these figures are near estimates. See *http://www.tew.org/tibet2000/t2.ch2.water.html*
17. Ibid. Also see Caidan (2003): 13.
18. The National Development and Reform Commission (NDRC) had approved of the construction of 13 dams on the Nujiang River to generate 21,000 MW of power that would have been bigger than the Three Gorges Project. It was only because of Premier Win Jiabao's intervention (February 2004) that the massive projects were suspended. However, the possibility of restarting the project cannot be ruled out. See, *http://news.xinhuanet.com/english/2009-05/22/content_11419960.htm*
19. Reports indicate that Gezhouba, China's leading Construction Company, admitted to building a feedline for a dam on Yarlung at Zhangmu. See, *http://www.economist.com/blogs/banyan/2009/10/dammed_rivers.cfm*, October 19, 2009.

unresolved political status will be of direct consequence to ways to sustainably manage the water resources and ensure its rivers natural hydrological flow are not disturbed by Chinese artificial diversion plans. Lower riparian pressure and international attention to defining vital resource as 'commons' would be significant to preserving and sharing the waters of Tibet. While such redefinition is politically sensitive, as it clashes with national jurisdiction, it nonetheless, merits attention keeping in mind future water requirement of South and Southeast Asia and its dependency on water resources in Tibet.

China's Thirst can make Others Thirsty

China literally sits on the hydrological throne in Tibet (TAR) and is the undisputed monarch of the unsurpassable water resources. China's colossal water diversion plans[20] from the rivers in Tibet are essential for its water needs (it will face 25 per cent supply gap for expected water demand by 2030)[21] but the diversions also have an unintended strategic sharpness to it. China's water need brings in certain awkwardness to the overall riparian relations in the Indus and GBM basins. Water is critical for China but in attempting to solve its water crisis it can potentially create water shortage problem among its lower riparians and thereby increase their reliance and dependency. Amid the fervour to dam every river, the Nujiang and the Yarlung Zangbo in Tibet are the only rivers in China whose ecology has been left intact. Water thus becomes a strategic component for China. It's rise, whether peaceful or not, has an unmistakable orientation about it—military capability, economic pace and now water. This is bound to be worrisome for the lower riparians particularly India.

---

20. The idea of 'reverse-flow' (Shou-tian) was first mooted by hydrologist Guo Kai. Shou-tian canal along the 'Great Western Route' was the brainchild of Guo. He was intrigued by Chinese geologist Weng Winhao's theories on Tibetan hydrographic net. Thus the idea of diverting Tibetan rivers was planned. Guo calculated that if water from the Nujiang, Lancang, Jinsha, Yalong and Dadu rivers in Tibet were diverted through the Aba divide, a solution could be provided to the crippling water shortage felt in north and northwest China. In 1988, Guo's plan caught the attention of the military. In 1989 a committee headed by top generals was formed to study the proposal. The first field survey of furthering projects on the 'Great Western Route' took place between May 18 and June 22, 1999. Guo Kai was part of the expedition. It now has a wide support of the PLA (People's Liberation Army). In 2005, the book, *Save China Through Water From Tibet* by Li Ling further caught the attention of various ministries and planners. It has been reported that the Ministry of Water Resources alone bought 100 copies.
21. Footnote 4.

Indus Water: The Crux of India-Pakistan Relations

The India-Pakistan Indus Water Treaty (IWT),[22] now in its 50th year, has enjoyed unprecedented success in the midst of troubled relationship. The success of IWT, many would argue, is that India has shown remarkable upper riparian restraint and a willingness to respect the treaty. India can, if it wants, disregard the provisions of the Treaty and thereby deny low water flows to Pakistan. The treaty restricts it because India respects it. Pakistan's lower riparian fears though understandable are misleading, often deliberately. There is a strong opinion in India that the Treaty was extraordinarily generous to Pakistan.[23] Of the total water of the Indus river basin, 80 per cent flows to Pakistan via the Western Rivers while only 20 per cent flows through the Eastern Rivers. Thus, the Treaty gave 80 per cent of water to Pakistan.[24] Some Indian experts have calculated that India should have got 42.8 per cent of the Indus basin's water.[25] The Treaty paid no attention to the future requirements of the population of J&K. With coalition governments becoming a norm both at the Centre and the state, the views of the Kashmiri people, their aspirations and demands will be critical to the functioning of the Treaty.

The Shape of Things in 2030

Scenario 1: Tibet, from Autonomy to Complete Annexation— Tibetan Waters for China and China only

A supremely confident China with the second largest economy and a formidable militarily power takes centrestage in Asian politics. While

22. The IWT divided the use of rivers and canals between the two countries. Pakistan obtained exclusive rights for the three western rivers, namely Indus, Jhelum and Chenab. And India retained rights to the three eastern rivers, namely Ravi, Beas and Sutlej. The treaty also guaranteed 10 years of uninterrupted water supply. During this period Pakistan was to build huge dams, financed partly by long-term World Bank loans and compensation money from India. Three multipurpose dams, Warsak, Mangla and Tarbela were built. A system of 8-link canals was also built, and the remodelling of existing canals was carried out. Five barrages and a gated siphon were also constructed under this treaty. For readings on the negotiations that led to IWT see: Lilienthal (1951); Khosla (1958); Gupta (1960); Gulhati (1973); Biswas (1992).
23. For a critique of the Treaty, see Warikoo (2005).
24. Many in Pakistan feel that the territories that went to India after partition were historically 'using less than 10 per cent of the Indus waters and that the Treaty was generous to India in giving it 20 per cent of the waters.' Iyer (2008).
25. Warikoo (2005): 17.

being militarily strong and economically dynamic it is equally resource hungry. Thirst for oil makes it the largest importer of natural resources which it has, over the last three decades (since 2000), made viable and secure political linkages with African and Latin American countries. Its accessibility to the warm waters of the Arabian Sea through the Gwadar Port near Karachi and the development of the Karakoram Highway gives it enormous flexibility. Its infrastructural aid and assistance over the last few decades has helped it to build unmatched political and diplomatic connections with Islamabad and Yangon (Myanmar) irrespective of the type of regime. India, its strongest challenger, has been 'encircled' through Pakistan in the West and Myanmar in the East. China continues to be thirsty for water as well and considers it an unquestionable national priority. Tibet no longer remains an autonomous region and its complete annexation has been prompted by securing the water resources by completing many of the diversion plans initiated in the first decade of the 21st century and many more in the operational stages. China's plan of rapid economic development and encouraging influx of Han Chinese into Tibet (since 1990) has slowly but surely paid off. A new generation of Tibetans, aware of China's awesome dominance, is less inclined to struggle for freedom and has now learnt to coexist with the demographic changes. The resources of Tibet are now in full control and for the sole interest of China. The legacy of Hu Jintao, the paramount leader, and his mega projects inspires the current leadership, dominated by hydrologists and engineers, to build more transfer-of-water projects. Chairman Mao Zedong way back in 1952 had innocently remarked, 'The south has a lot of water, the north little...If possible, it is okay to lend a little water.' In fact Beijing's total control over Tibet in effect is the 'total' control of the water resources. 'Absolute territorial sovereignty' and 'hydro-egoism' dictate water relation with its neighbours. The classic lines, 'He who holds Tibet dominates the Himalayan piedmont; he who dominates the Himalayan piedmont, threatens the Indian subcontinent; and he who threatens the Indian subcontinent may well have all of South-East Asia within his reach, and all of Asia,'[26] has become a reality for the down

26. Ginsburg and Mathos (1964).

riparians. This reality has forced the lower riparians to 'live and let live' with a China unwilling to concede on water sharing and look within to improve water-use efficiency of irrigation projects and surface water system.

Scenario 2: Tibet, from Autonomy to Partial Independence—Tibetan Waters Embraces Basin based 'Conjunctive Use' than Single-country 'Water Management'

Chinese lopsided development policies and unrestrained exploitation of the natural resources has led to a shaky China crippled with mounting domestic challenges from income disparities, social pressures, corruption and environmental devastation. All this is further impeding its economic progress. The Communist Party is troubled and hard pressed to retain public acceptance of the party's dominant role. Chinese leaders are finding ways to bring in greater political pluralism and accountability in order to restore public confidence. The difficult situation is further compounded by heightened nationalism in Tibet where the radicals, after the death of the Dalai Lama, are pitching for complete freedom. The US and Congress now officially encourage campaign for independence. Beijing is in a bind. It had long feared that any concession towards Tibet, which it had to concede gradually, would result in more uncomfortable demands. With the Centre not so strong and the periphery revolting, its worst fears have come alive. The growing anti-dam lobby has pushed the Chinese leadership to cancel many of its projects. The saner voices in the leadership following on the lines of Wen Jiabao, who when as premier cancelled 13 dams project on the Nujiang in 2004, are in favour of sustainable development and wider consideration for social and environmental impact, have grown in number marginalising the Hu Jintao camp. Without complete independence but with full control of its domestic affairs, the Tibetans have an equal participation in the management of the resources (not just needs-based but rights-based development) with Mainland China responsible for defence and foreign affairs. The decontrol of water resources in Tibet has ushered into a new framework on 'water resources management' and 'hydrosolidarity' that includes multipurpose beneficial utilisation of the resource with active participation of the basin states of South Asia.[27]

Scenario 3: Ecological Concerns put the Spotlight on Tibet's Glaciers and Water Resources—China Responds Positively

The science of climate change is nearer to the truth as never before on warming and glacial melting. This has prompted unprecedented global pressure and action in areas where vulnerability is high. Tibet draws particular attention. The International Union for the Conservation of Nature (IUCN), the largest and the most powerful environmental pressure group along with the UN declares the entire province of Tibet to be a protected area.[28] China's initial resistance based on suspicion and interference gives way to a sensitive understanding of the ecosystem. This has widespread approval of the local Tibetans who consider the ecology a way of life and have for long derided Chinese blatant mismanagement of the environment. This refreshing development has come about from within China. The Chinese environmental activists, scientists and journalists responding to the science of climate change and global warming have, despite all odds, worked hard to sensitise the local people, the authorities and the world on Tibet's diverse cultural and ecological wealth. This growing and concerned constituency has become an effective lobby helping China's leaders steer the country towards sustainable development and better management of water resources. Domestic legal mechanism is strengthened with SEPA (State Environmental Protection Administration) ensuring that the highest standards are applied on meeting environmental impact assessment law (EIAL). An environmentally conscious regime in Beijing, concerned with the impact of global warming, makes conciliatory moves allowing for

---

27. The concept of 'water management' has historically meant the manipulation of water for specific uses and the development of water-based projects like dams, canals and other such structures. The concept of 'water resources management' regarded as 'rational' and 'integrated', embraces the 'conjunctive use' of 'surface and underground water resources, the control of their quality and harmful effects, their sustainable development for multi-purpose beneficial utilization and the administration of corresponding use rights.' Wohlwend (2001).

28. There is an example. The 7.1 million hectare in Yunnan province, where the upper reaches of Asia's three great rivers (Yangtze, Mekong and Salween) run parallel from north to south, was declared a World Heritage in 2003. The Convention concerning the Protection of World Cultural and Natural Heritage was adopted by the General Conference of UNESCO on November 16, 1972. China ratified it. See *http://whc.unesco.org/en/list/1083*

broad-based basin management of the Tibetan rivers as well as framing effective bilateral river treaties.

Scenario 4: A 'Coalition of Lower Riparians' Challenges China on Water Issues

Probably nothing thrills China more than water and nothing bereaves it more. A strong and confident China displays 'hydro-egoism' and a riddled and tentative China reconciles to 'hydro-solidarity'. Irrespective of China's rise, the thirst of the lower riparians has resulted in a cohesive South and Southeast Asian grouping built on lower riparian concerns and based on the principles of 'equity' and 'no-harm' and challenging China's unrestricted exploitation of the water resources in Tibet.[29] This has expanded in recent times to include Kazakhstan and Russia, who as downstream countries are grieved over China's diversions on the Irtysh and Ili rivers. There is much concern in Cambodia, Laos, Thailand and Vietnam over a large number of dams being built on the Lancangjiang River since 2020 which has considerably reduced the flow of the Mekong River downstream affecting agriculture, fishing and navigation. Myanmar is equally disturbed over the Salween River as the influential dam lobby in China has won the day and restarted building the 13 dams on the Nujiang River. Taking this as a big opportunity, India unshackles its middle riparian constraint, which for long had hindered its riparian equation with its neighbours and puts the spotlight on China as the actual riparian aggressor. China is undoubtedly perturbed and views India's role with great suspicion and nervousness. India as an important pole in the multipolar international system, serves as a political and cultural bridge between a rising China and the West and is driving toward building partnerships with many countries, which it calls its 'arc of interest'. These partnerships are based on shared concerns particularly on shared watercourses. India within its neighbourhood is now viewed with less suspicion. Building a riparian

29. The community of co-riparian states is an important principle in the waters of an international river. According to Salman MA Salman, 'The basis is that the entire river basin is regarded as an economic unit, and the rights over the waters of the entire river are vested in the collective body of the riparian states, or divided among them either by agreement or on the basis of proportionality. Clearly, this is an ideal principle that overlooks sovereignty and nationalism.' Also, 'equality' and 'no-harm' principles are based on 'limited territorial sovereignty' and 'limited territorial integrity' as opposed to 'absolute territorial sovereignty' and 'absolute territorial integrity'. Salman (2007).

coalition has helped raise Tibet's water resources, vital not only to the Indus and GBM Basin but also the Salween and Mekong, as a regional concern ensuring that its natural flow is not reversed by China's artificial diversion plans. A need to redefine a vital resource like water as a 'common' to preserving and sharing the waters of Tibet has gathered momentum. While defining 'common' has been politically sensitive, clashing with national jurisdiction, it nonetheless, has gained international credibility and sympathy. Sustained political and environmental pressure on China enables Tibet's water resources to become a 'common' under global protection and monitored as a sensitive ecosystem.

Scenario 5: Pakistan-China become a Riparian Friend-in-Need to Counter India

Water relations between India and Pakistan continue to affect bilateral relations. Pakistan, as a lower riparian, habitually raises the issue of water with India but finds little international audience. It has, however, found a new meaning to its relationship with China on hydro-cooperation. The two projects in Gilgit-Baltistan: the Diamer-Bhasha dam on the Indus and the Bhunji hydro-project on the confluence of the rivers Indus and Gilgit have added a new strategic dimension to the relationship and paved the way for other BOT projects. In spite of the fact that China has built its own storages and dams on the headwaters of Indus in the Ngari Prefecture of Tibet[30] and thereby manipulate the flows of the Indus waters, Pakistan considers its dependency on China less threatening than its water dependency on India. For Pakistan, India remains the perennial threat and is willing to compromise its riparian position *vis-à-vis* China to strategically counter balance India. The dam partnership between two of the world's biggest dam builders has led to serious ecological and societal concerns and the Pakistani regime is under pressure to rethink its approach to big structures on the rivers. Sindh bearing the brunt of its down riparian position is up in arms with widespread civil unrest making Pakistan an unstable and high-risk state. Pakistan's

30. Various news report captured Alice Albinia's book, *Empires of the Indus*, London: John Murray, 2008. The author describes a dam being built on the upper reaches of the Indus in Tibet. Reports have confirmed that Senge-Tsangpo Hydropower station on the Indus has a capacity of 6,400 MW.

dependency on China has come with a telling cost and countering India in its overall game plan has not worked.

Scenario 6: India takes the Burden out of the Indus Water Treaty and Evolves Pragmatic Approaches

Having observed carefully the strategic alliance of China and Pakistan, its own water needs and requirements, and the different constituencies within India with different perspectives on the Indus Water Treaty, the government of India has taken a middle path of exploiting the potential permissible within the treaty. The decision has not been easy given the popular pressure to abrogate the Treaty as Pakistan continues to abet and aid terrorist activities directed at India. By 2030, India's position as an upper riparian is one of pragmatism drawing international kudos. Prompted by China's own storage designs on the upper reaches of the Indus, India has already constructed storage capacity of 3.6 Maf on the western rivers that the Treaty allowed but which for over 50 years did not achieve. With this acquired capacity, India's stance on the Indus waters is stronger and firmer. India continues to 'talk' to Pakistan but not 'negotiate' and the talks centre on 'water needs' and not 'water rights'. By 2030, it has also factored in the needs and aspirations of the people of Jammu and Kashmir and completed the 330 MW Kishanganga hydropower project and the Tulbul Navigation Project. India's roboust economy and stability gives it the capability to use the 'priority principle' of the Treaty and complete other projects on the Indus basin. It has also taken into account the poor maintenance of the existing barrages that allowed for about 2-3 Maf of water flowing easily into Pakistan. Having not terminated the Treaty and having mastered the use of water as a political leverage, and with Pakistan's inability to reign in terror, India has forced Pakistan into agreeing to 'modification' of the Treaty thus allowing it to develop and harness the potential of the Western Rivers. Pakistan is now compelled to buy peace for water from India.

Conclusion

The scenarios described above are based on the understanding of the current events and trends and not intended to be biased. The scenarios clearly demonstrate that transboundary rivers have a high strategic content and are crucial to peace and stability in the region. The management of such a vital resource does not operate in a vacuum but rather in a complex political and economic framework. Any success on the Indus and GBM river basins will hinge on generating a level of trust and cooperation that has yet to be seen in the region. The uneasy marriage of politics and external drivers that govern most shared waters cannot be overlooked. The scenarios suggest that the water resource of Tibet is crucial to the Indus and GBM river basins and how China approaches it will not only determine the riparian politics but also the larger geopolitics. Water as an instrument and tool of bargain and trade-off will be predominant because the political stakes are high in the region. Countries in the basin region will have to live with transboundary river arrangements and consider the scarcity problem based on strategic rationality, hydrological effectiveness and economic viability.

References

Bajoria, Jayshree (2008). "The Question of Tibet", *http://www.cfr.org/publication/15965/*, December.

Biswas, Asit (1992). "Indus Water Treaty: The Negotiating Process", *Water International* 17(4).

Caidan, An (2003). *Travel Guide to Tibet of China*. Beijing: China Intercontinental. p.13.

Ginsburg, George and Michiel Mathos (1964). *Communist China and Tibet: The First Dozen Years*. Martinus Nijhoff.

Gulhati, N.D. (1973). *Indus Water Treaty: An Exercise in International Mediation*. Bombay: Allied Publishers.

Gupta, Sisir (1960). "The Indus Water Treaty", *Foreign Affairs Report* 9(12).

IJWRD (1999). "International River Basins of the World", *International Journal of Water Resources Development* 15(4). December.

Iyer, Ramaswamy (2008). *Stimson Centre Paper*. Washington DC, October 27.

Khosla, A.N. (1958). "Development of the Indus River System: An Engineering Approach", *India Quarterly* 14(3): 234-253, July-September.

Lilienthal, David (1951). "Another Korea in the making", *Colliers Magazine*, August 4.

Mckinsey Report (2009). "Charting our Water Future", November 2009. *http://www. mckinsey.com/App_Media/Reports/Water/Charting_Our_Water_Future_Exec%20Summary_001.pdf*

Salman, Salman MA (2007). "Helsinki Rules, the UN Watercourses Convention and the Berlin Rules: Perspective on International Water Law", *Water Resources Development* 23(4): 627-628. December.

Tir, Jaroslav and John T. Ackerman (2009). "Politics of Formalised River Cooperation", *Journal of Peace Research* 46(5): 623. September.

UNEP (2008). *Freshwater under Threat: South Asia*.

Warikoo, K. (2005). "Indus Water Treat: View from Kashmir", in *Himalayan and Central Asian Studies* 9(3): 14-18, July-September.

Wohlwend, Bernard J. (2001). "Equitable Utilization and the Allocation of Water Rights to Shared water Resources", *http://www.bjwconsult.com/EQUITABLE.PDF.* p.2

II

Economic Growth, Globalisation, Poverty and Equity

3

Relative Growth of Nations

A View in the Mirror of History

NAYAN CHANDA

In this chapter, I intend to look at selected examples from the history of nations and territories to understand how they achieved growth and why others failed to grow. Predicting the future by extrapolating from the past is risky but can be a useful tool to divining the future. Angus Maddison's magisterial survey *Contours of the World Economy, 1-2030 AD: Essays on Macro-Economic History* (2007), among others, offers a valuable historical background for understanding long-term economic progress. Against a broad background of history, I will take a brief look at China and India's recent growth spurt and outline the scenario they are likely to face in the coming decades.

Of course, history is full of lessons about surprising new developments, upsetting well-laid plans or predictions of growth. It also offers plenty of examples of discovery and innovation that take a country or a continent in a whole new direction. The Black Death or bubonic plague pandemic of the 14th century, which killed a third of Europe's population, was one such episode that derailed many countries' growth and helped others. The arrival of Brahmagupta's work and the concept of zero in Baghdad in the 9th century, and its introduction to Europe through Arabic and Latin translation was, in retrospect, a turning point for European science. Christopher Columbus stumbling upon San Salvador in the Caribbean in 1492 was another such unforeseen event that changed the course of history, leading to the rise of new powers and decline of many regions, especially Africa. The Industrial Revolution, the discovery of fossil fuel and the invention of the microchip are other of unforeseen developments that altered the growth trajectories of nations.

Despite all the imponderables, history does throw up some common patterns in the rise of human societies. The first human civilisations to emerge—in Mesopotamia and the Indus Valley—provide interesting insights into the factors that allowed their economic and civilisational rise. Resources for successful agriculture and artisanal activities and trade can be seen as factors that enabled growth throughout history. Successful agriculture in the fertile valleys of the Tigris and Euphrates in Mesopotamia and in the Indus River basin allowed for production of surplus food, enabling the rise of urban centres and crafts. Manufactured goods—from clothes to ornaments—provided tradable items and the existence of urban civilisations in same neighbourhood promoted 'international' trade. The availability of abundant wood in the Indus region fostered the development of boat-building and consequently the efflorescence of trade. Judging by the archaeological evidence, the urban centres of Mesopotamia and the Indus valley stood out as islands of prosperity in the surrounding areas of subsistence agriculture. Natural resources, skilled human resources and technological skills needed to manufacture consumer items, build ocean-going vessels, infrastructure like docks and above all urban planning and construction enabled the rise of these civilisations. Historians speculate that perhaps environmental degradation brought about by large-scale deforestation for urbanisation and boat-building led to the silting of the river basin and eventual decline of these very civilisations.

While one can argue that most countries are perhaps endowed with the same human and natural resources, the growth pattern of each waxes and wanes depending on management and policy framework and the differing international context. The disappearance of the Harappa civilisation perhaps holds a lesson for today's world, engaged as it is in the frenetic exploitation of natural resources resulting in environmental degradation.

The phenomenal growth of China in the 10th and 11th century offers insights that illuminate developments in the modern period. Under the trade-friendly Tang dynasty (7th century) China had witnessed great prosperity and cultural efflorescence, but the country experienced its golden age under the Song dynasty (10th-13th century). The prime factors for this were a rising population backed by successful agriculture, and growth fuelled by industry and trade. Agricultural growth was given a spurt by the introduction of a high-yield variety of rice from Vietnam, leading in turn to a rise in population and the growth of manufacturing which could not have been undertaken by people surviving on subsistence agriculture. In the 10th century, cotton was introduced from India, creating the basis for a new industry. Buoyed by innovations in textile, porcelain, iron spheres, manufacturing took off. The Song government opened nine trading ports instead of the traditional one, to encourage trade and assisted in shipping by constructing infrastructure such as warehouses, beacons and lighthouses and other facilities along the coasts. Customs revenue was an important resource for the Song dynasty's coffers. In a celebrated comment, the Emperor rejected the advice of some mandarins to stop foreign trade by saying, 'the profit from maritime trade is very great and, if properly managed, would amount to millions of strings of cash. Would it not be preferable to promote this trade rather than to tax the people?'. It was perhaps no coincidence that this period of prosperity was also marked with great openness. The newly opened port cities attracted large communities of foreign merchants—Persians, Arabs, Turkish—who were granted a form of extraterritoriality for their activities. Many foreigners were even given official positions. An Arab served the Song emperor as superintendent of maritime shipping at Quanzhou. The Songs' interest in foreign trade led them to develop their own merchant marine—ocean going vessels which led to significant improvement in ship building and navigational technology. Songs laid the foundation for Admiral Zheng He's voyages to Indian Ocean and Africa in the 15th century. The Song period also provides an example of state-promoted industrialisation when the need for defending China from the northern nomadic tribes led to the setting up of its iron and steel industry. Historian Robert Hartwell estimated that iron production in China in 1078 was of the order of 150,000 tonnes annually—a remarkable amount as the entire production of iron and steel in Europe in 1700 was not much above this, if at all. However, the Ming emperor's decision in the mid-15th century to abandon seafaring and actually destroy knowledge of ship building also serves as an example of the ill effects of autocratic decision-making by unaccountable mandarins.

The Mughal period in India offers another example of a happy coincidence of resources and good governance to promote growth and prosperity. The Mughals, with their administrative organisation, fulfilled a major condition for economic growth. Aware of the value of trade for filling the imperial coffers, Mughal administration levied lower rates for land devoted to cash crops such as cotton and sugarcane than for land devoted to food grains. Encouragement to cotton and silk textiles and spice exports brought in substantial volume of silver bullion, allowing the empire to increase coined currency circulation. In order to increase the appeal of printed Indian fabrics, the Mughals encouraged the use of European designs and colours. India's long tradition of studying mathematics and its well-established *sreni* or guild system could develop into a sophisticated business practice boosted by the arrival of silver from the New World into the Mughal coffers. As historians Ronald Findlay and Kevin H. O'Rourke noted, 'The uniform silver coinage of very high purity, and a well-developed banking and credit system involving the use of sophisticated financial instruments such as the bill of exchange or *hundi,* facilitated the integration of commodity and capital markets.'

Before ending our brief peregrination in the past for identifying the factors behind successful economic growth, it is necessary to take note of some of the negative factors seen in history. If the accumulation and proper allocation of capital was a key element for growth, invention and the utilisation of technology has been a major driver. At a time when communication was difficult, accumulation and storage of knowledge and its dissemination played a key role. Papyrus in the Mediterranean world and paper in China helped to store knowledge. The renowned library in Alexandria (3rd century BC) with its manuscripts was an early example, followed many centuries later by the House of Knowledge in Baghdad under the Caliphate. Major scientific and technological advances during the early years of the Caliphate were directly related to this worship of knowledge. However, diffusion of stored knowledge was limited until the Gutenberg printing press came along in 1455 and opened knowledge up to a vast number of people. By 1500, 220 printing presses were in operation throughout Western Europe and had produced 8 million books (Maddison, 2005: 18). Both the Brahmanic tradition of India and

China's elitist system restricted learning to a privileged few. Though China had invented paper and printed books were available there five centuries before they were in Europe, literacy was restricted to serving Confucian education and bureaucracy. Indian Brahmanic elites too wanted to preserve their monopoly on knowledge by maintaining the 'oral' tradition and paid little attention to 'storing' knowledge on transferable material. Even after printing was introduced in India in the 19th century, it took time for it to be more valued than illuminated manuscripts. Imperial control over the diffusion of texts delayed its introduction in China. This was in addition to China's sense of superiority and pride which also stood in the way of the Chinese benefiting from Western technology. In 1792, the Qin emperor Qian Long expressing disdain about objects that the British envoy Macartney brought as gifts—from globes, mathematical instruments, chronometers, telescopes, plate glass etc., said, 'There is nothing we lack...we have never set much store on strange or ingenious objects, nor do we need any more of your country's manufactures.'

Maddison notes that both the Indian and Chinese elite were disdainful of materials and artifacts from other cultures. They treated lanterns, mirrors, telescopes, and eyeglasses from European as 'foreign curiosities and rarities,' and never attempted to replicate European mechanical clocks. It was not just the question of the mechanical engineering involved in making the clock, but the absence of curiosity and their lack of concern about keeping time to measure labour. The reason China slid back after a spectacular beginning, was that it failed to maintain its technological lead. From the wheelbarrow to water wheel irrigation, water power-driven spinning machines to gun powder and smelting, China's technological innovation was experience-driven. Because China had a large population, it had a substantial number of craftsmen and peasants. Because of this, China had the advantages in this aspect. However, that advantage was eroded as its growing population and the availability of a large labour force reduced the incentives to invent labour-saving machines. Besides, education was not directed towards invention and technology. Thus s technological innovations became rare and the economy became stagnant. In the Western countries, the scientific revolution occurred around the 15th-16th centuries. By the mid-18th century in Europe, the traditional experience-based technological inventions began to be replaced by science-cum-experiment based inventions based on learning. As Angus Maddison put it : 'From 1000 to 1820, investment in machinery and equipment [in Western Europe] was extremely modest. Investment in human capital was also modest, but the quality of human capital was transformed by the invention of printing, fundamental advances in science, and the spread of secular university education for the elites.' In China, education was designed to train the brightest minds in Confucian philosophy and classics. It took up to 20 years to pass the various exams to rise to the top of the officialdom—the most honourable and profitable occupation. Justin Lin (1992) writes that, 'They were so obsessed with the civil service examination that they had no time for the other branches of knowledge like mathematics and other useful techniques in real life. As a result, there were only a few scientists in China during the period.' Without Scientific Revolution, China could not overcome the barriers to productivity that Europeans managed to surpass. Its economy stagnated in relation to the West, which experimented with technology and improved upon inventions like gunpowder and the compass, which they inherited from China. It took the shock of British naval guns for China to realise the value of science and technology.

Asia also lacked secular educational institutions to promote scientific knowledge about natural science and encourage innovation. India's Buddhist Nalanda university was a pioneering place of learning but had a rather short life. In contrast with the lack of secular centres of learning in Asia, the first European university was created in Bologna in 1080. By 1500, there were 70 such centres of secular learning in Western Europe. As the rate of technological innovation accelerated, European economic growth picked up momentum. Lacking book-based knowledge and experiments to maintain its early technological lead, China fell behind. In 1820, its GDP still accounted for 32 per cent of the world total but by 1952 it amounted to mere 5.2 per cent.

The result of India and China's early scientific and technological lead, management skills and their later failure to keep up can be seen in the long range data and analysis provided by Maddison. His millennial economic history gives a sweeping view of the relative growth of nations over a long period of time. Maddison notes that during the second millennium, the world's population grew nearly 24-fold, per capita income 14-fold and GDP 338-fold. This is in sharp contrast with the previous millennium, when the world population grew six times and per capita income fell. Within this broad view of sharply rising populations and incomes in the past millennium, there have been significant variations over different periods and between regions and countries. During the past millennium, the economic gap between regions has increased from virtually nil in 1000 AD to an 18:1 gap ratio between the richest and poorest regions in the world at the end of year 2000.

In the early 19th century Britain's industrial revolution and successful use of energy—coal—turned the country into a world leader and doubled average per capita incomes within a couple of generations. However, in less than a century the United States, with its large territory, natural resources, growing infrastructure and innovations, overtook Britain in productivity. In the early 20th century, Japan, though resource constrained, invested massively in human and physical capital to catch up with the developed countries. The rapid rise of international trade in which Japan participated enthusiastically was another factor. The volume of export per head of population rose 103-fold in the UK, 114-fold in the US and even faster in Japan because it was closed to foreign trade for a long period earlier. One of the common features of these fast-growing countries was their human capital—as measured in number of years spent in higher education. Combined with technological innovations and growing stock of industrial machinery, the increasingly educated labour force propelled economic growth. While noting this endogeneous factor, let us not forget the exogeneous advantages Europe and the US gained from the discovery of the New World. Britain's Industrial Revolution and its cotton mills could bring in profit thanks in part to millions of African slaves working in America's cotton fields. Europe imported some 1,700 tonnes of gold and 73,000 tonnes of silver from the New World to finance its imports. About a third of the precious metal found its way to China and India as payment for their exports of silk, porcelain, cotton and spices.

In the 19th century, growth prompted by the discovery of the New World and extensive trading was substantial, but it reached a new high during the post-war years from 1950 to 1973 that Maddison termed 'the Golden Age'. The return of peace and massive investment in industry and infrastructure, the Marshall Plan for Europe, managed to relay the high growth momentum of the advanced industrial countries. Unlike Qing China, Meiji Japan had embraced Western education and in the post-war boom, Japan could leverage its higher education and familiarity with Western technology to participate in the growth. Japan's average level of education in 1950 was 9.1 years compared to 10.8 in the UK and 9.66 years in France. The rest of Asia was far behind Japan, with 1.4 years in India, 2.2 in China and 3.4 years in South Korea. This was also backed by Japan's high savings rate and favourable markets for its products pushed by the US. In this period Japan's per capita GDP grew at 8.1 per cent a year.

While the US, Europe and Japan were growing, a newly independent China virtually retreated from the world scene. During the first 28 years of its rule, the Communist Party pursued a self-defeating policy that economist Justin Lin has termed a 'comparative-advantage-defying strategy' (CAD strategy). It hoped to first develop advanced capital-intensive industries, which were the comparative advantage of developed countries. Politically directed misallocation of capital to heavy industry resulted in the construction of uneconomical enterprises and poor products. Not benefiting from their comparative advantages, the enterprises had to rely on subsidies and trade protections. Its isolation—and poverty—began to end with Deng Xiaoping's reforms. He partially removed the dead hand of government, freed the entrepreneurial spirit, and opened the door to capital, technology and trade. By opening the country's doors to foreign direct investment, China lured in much needed overseas capital—the bulk of it from its ethnic brethren in East and Southeast Asia. According to the World Bank (2007) while China absorbed approximately 18 per cent of world FDI inflows, as much as a third of that amount might have been 'round-tripping' (that is, it might be Chinese capital routed through Hong Kong so as to reap the tax benefits of foreign investment), and perhaps another third came from members of the Chinese diaspora.

Since the launching of reforms in 1978, the inflow of FDI to industrialise the country, privatisation of agriculture and opening of domestic market for private manufacturing, and efficient allocation of capital by stepped up expenditure in education had a miraculous effect. For over two decades China has maintained an annual GDP growth of 9.6 per cent. This year China is poised to overtake Japan as the world's second largest economy, after having dislodged Germany to become the top exporter of the world. It remains the world's biggest creditor to the US. Although China is far from the commanding position it held when it produced 32.4 per cent of the world's total GDP (1820), in two short decades it has grown from less than 1 per cent to account for 5 per cent of the output. One notable feature of China's surging exports has been technical upgrading—moving from low-tech to high-tech goods. China's rise has been made possible by the reversal of most of the policies that held China back—from the removal of fetters on the capitalist economy to end the country's isolation and return with a vengeance to learn from the West exemplified by the Qing emperor. Not only did the government allocate a large budget to strengthen the existing centres of higher education and build new ones, primary and secondary education facilities damaged during the Cultural Revolution were rebuilt. By 2000, China's literacy rate was 98 per cent and secondary school enrolment rate, 50 per cent. In 2005, China produced 3.4 million graduates a year, including 1,51,000 with postgraduate degrees. Doors were also open to travel abroad, sending tens of thousands of students to universities in the US, Canada, Europe and Australia. Special focus was given to train students in science and engineering who in 2006 constituted 21 per cent of the 4 million degree recipients in science and technology globally. Between 1995 and 2006, the number of Chinese researchers nearly tripled, from just over half a million to more than 1.4 million, boosting its global share from 13 per cent to 25 per cent. Not surprisingly, 23 per cent of China's GDP in 2006 was created in the knowledge and technology intensive sector and in 2008 China became the biggest exporter of high technology products. (National Science Foundation, 2010: 6-4)

Compared to China, India continues to lag very far behind in its attempt to get back to the position it once held when it produced 24 per cent of the world GDP—it now accounts for 2 per cent. India's phase of economic growth started with a trickle in the late 1980s but picked up speed in 1991, fully 13 years after China. The soft-socialism and bureaucratic red tape that straitjacketed the Indian entrepreneurial spirit and invested domestic savings in unproductive areas was loosened. A hesitant welcome mat was laid for FDI and tariffs reduced to engage India more fully in world trade. Although India was far behind China in literacy, the large number of graduates and engineers produced by Indian institutions, especially the country's premier technology and management schools could now be fully utilised. The country which invented the zero and had a long tradition of mathematics had a sufficiently large number of engineers to take advantage of the opportunity of the millennium bug scare. What started as a one-off consultancy grew into a bigger and more lucrative engagement in IT services. India emerged as the destination of information technology (IT)-enabled services for global companies, including call centres and software development, design, and maintenance. Software exports have grown from $5.7 billion to about $50 billion in 10 years. With increased trade, India was also able to exploit its comparative advantage in textiles (it had dominated the world textile market for 2,000 years before being dislodged by the Industrial Revolution and America's slave-grown cotton). Long-held skills and cheap labour allowed India to become competitive in textile and apparel. Its deep experience in traditional medicines (India once supplied doctors for the Chinese emperors) and its large pool of doctors trained in modern medicine enabled the country to emerge as an important player in pharmaceuticals. A country known for being one of the earliest producers of steel and with one of Asia's earliest steel mills, India could move aggressively into steel, white goods manufacturing and auto parts. With the deregulation of the telecom market, India has witnessed a phenomenal growth in mobile telephony. The number of mobile phone users has grown from less than 10 million in 1999 to 500 million and new mobile phone connections have gone from 0.1 million per month in 1999 to 10 million in 2010. Despite having been open since 1991, the Indian economy is still relatively closed compared to those of some of its Asian neighbours, where exports account for a much larger share of

GDP (33 per cent in China and 38 per cent in South Korea, as compared to 15 per cent in India in 2003). While this has somewhat shielded India from the global economic crisis, it has blocked the upgrading of Indian industry that comes through competition, thus effectively losing out in the world market.

The 2008 global crisis threw into sharp focus the relative strengths and weaknesses of India's and China's growth paths. As a country deeply integrated with the world economy, China was more exposed to the volatility of the global market. Chinese exports plunged 53 per cent from their pre-crisis September 2008 levels and some 15 per cent of export-oriented enterprises shut down or cut production by half within a few months. Nearly 20 million workers from export processing industry were laid off. In comparison, India suffered some losses in textile, gems and the tourism sector but its main loss was the sudden withdrawal of some portfolio investments causing temporary hardship. But India recovered quickly from both the export and capital outflow shock. Exports made a remarkable turnaround with growth of 18 per cent in November 2009. In 2009, India's FDI stood at $37 billion and the net portfolio investment at $24 billion.

Given the big shock that the crisis delivered to China, its recovery has been astounding. The Chinese government responded swiftly to the crisis by adopting a fiscal stimulus package over and above the large-scale investment it had already undertaken to reduce the gap between poorer interior and rich coastal regions. The package worth $585 billion amounted to 12-13 per cent of China's estimated 2009 GDP. China's massive trade surplus and high domestic savings had helped it to build a record $2 trillion reserve—nearly half of which was invested in US dollar instruments. Managers of China's sovereign wealth fund were also busy acquiring foreign assets, especially energy and natural resources. After the initial sharp drop in exports, China quickly recovered and has again begun building up a sizable trade surplus. China's projected 9 per cent growth reconfirms its position as the world's most dynamic economy—especially at a time when the US and Western economies are struggling to create jobs and emerge from the Great Recession.

In the light of this brief summary of China and India's economic growth paths against the backdrop of history, what can one expect of the future? It is difficult to predict the specific policies the two are likely to adopt but one can envisage the major issues they will face. A survey of the past shows that over the long run, economic growth primarily results from productivity growth rather than factor accumulation. Earlier in their history, India and China leveraged their factor advantage in resource and labour and their unique technological advantage (cotton, silk, porcelain and iron) to dominate the world economy. In the 21st century technology-intensive economic productivity growth rather than labour will determine economic growth. Availability of capital, technology, higher education, telecommunications and efficient infrastructure will be important drivers of productivity growth. As an ADB study (2010) looking at 2030 notes 'Given the greater availability of information and technology, what will differentiate countries is their ability to adopt these technologies—the skill level of their workforce, the appropriate capital and infrastructure, openness to trade and FDI, and more generally the investment climate.'

Transportation and telecommunications infrastructure, critical for the development of a knowledge economy, has been a priority in China in the past two decades. China's current stimulus package is being used to build a state-of-the-art bullet train network and a string of modern airports. Already China is linked by an extensive network of roads ready to be used by millions of Chinese buying a car for the first time. India's plans to build national highways and ports and airports will have to overcome myriad obstacles—bureaucratic and legal. As millions of Indian customers take to the roads in their Nanos and Marutis, traffic congestion will be inevitable if the government cannot quickly construct a road network. According to the International Energy Agency, 52 per cent of China's oil consumption comes from imports and it is projected to reach 80 per cent in 2030. India's share of oil from imports which is currently 70 per cent is projected to reach 92 per cent in 2030. If India and China's oil demand doubles in the next decade, as is expected, it would mean a world demand of an additional 9 million barrels of oil a day. With such a large rise in demand, the price of oil is certain to rise, placing additional burdens on their budget. China, with its large foreign reserves, is better positioned to meet these challenges than India.

According to the UN Population Division, the ratio of working population in the total population (15-64 years) will reach its peak in China in 2010 and in India in 2040. While China will thus have exhausted almost all its demographic dividend, India will have a window of opportunity to succeed China in becoming a manufacturing force in the world. A tightening of the supply of migrant workers in China's coastal areas resulted in wage increases and, as the impact of crisis dissipates and factories reopen, China will likely struggle to find the supply of cheap labour that contributed towards making it the factory of the world. India, conversely, will have an opportunity to leverage its comparative advantage if investment is made in both human resources and industrial development. From several perspectives, commercialisation of agriculture and rural industry will be the pivot for economic development. Failure in this area risks turning India's demographic dividend into demographic liability. Since agriculture provides 59 per cent of employment with only 16 per cent of jobs coming from industry (2000), job creation for rural labour will also be important for reducing the income gap. Given the large number of Indians living in poverty (456 million in India compared to 208 million in China in 2005) India's task in this area is more urgent. Employment generation in the rural areas would also be essential to prevent the agglomeration of slums around metropolitan areas.

There is concern that in pressing ahead for faster growth, China and India may be pushing against the limits of resource availability. Clearly, water shortage is becoming a major impediment in both countries. Approximately 400 of 660 major Chinese cities currently face water shortages, a third of them severe. Water shortage is already a problem in major Indian cities and a precipitous drop in the north Indian aquifer, as recent reports suggest, could have serious consequences for agriculture, threatening in particular the granary of the Punjab. In addition, global warming poses a serious threat to Indian agriculture. According to one estimate, climate change could reduce output by 30 to 35 per cent in southern regions of India and up to 60 per cent in the north (Cline, 2007).

The environmental cost of China's blazing growth has become evident. In 2009, China replaced the US as the world's biggest polluter, boasting of 16 of the 20 most polluted cities on earth. Around 6,00,000 Chinese die of pollution-related ailments every year. According to a World Bank report (2007), well over half the major lakes in China are severely polluted; 38 per cent of river water is drinkable; only 20 per cent of the population has access to unpolluted drinking water; and almost a quarter of the population regularly drinks water that is heavily polluted. A government research report in 2006 said that environmental pollution cost China 511.8 billion yuan (about $64 billion) in 2004, which amounted to 3.05 per cent of GDP that year. In the absence of serious measures, water shortage and environmental degradation will be exacerbated by the growth planned by both the countries. In recent years China has in fact emerged as a pioneer in adopting measures to reduce pollution and developing clean energy. But given the size of its economy, even low per capita emission has turned China into the world's biggest emitter of greenhouse gases. This has led to Western pressure on China to agree to a binding target on emissions cuts—a demand that both China and India have rejected. While the logic behind their refusal to accept hard targets may be reasonable from the point of view that they are latecomers to industrialisation, it may be unacceptable from the point of view of global stability. Over time, both India and China will face international pressure to join others in reducing the threat of climate change.

China may also be pushing against the limit of the world's tolerance for its relentless drive to dominate trade. By pegging its currency to a weakening US dollar, China has long been able to gain ever-increasing market share. That process has become even harder for its trade partner to accept, as China's stimulus spending has been creating massive overcapacities in steel, aluminium, cement, chemicals, refining and wind power equipment, thus increasing the possibility of dumping of Chinese exports. In a December 2009 report entitled 'Overcapacity in China', the European Chamber of Commerce warned of looming trade friction if China did not address the issue. By opening the credit tap under the stimulus plan, China has also been creating a property bubble. In just 11 months, Chinese agencies have disbursed new loans totalling RMB 9.3 trillion, almost twice the government's target. The consequence of a glut of credit could be an increase in non-performing loans and bank failures requiring further government intervention. China has been building up huge foreign exchange reserves (over $2 trillion) in order to keep the value of its currency low and its products competitive, but against the backdrop of high unemployment and recession this practice is creating resentment. Calls for protectionist measures against China are growing and unless Beijing revalues the RMB, the threat of widespread anti-dumping action and even protectionist measures will continue to grow. Nobel laureate, economist and influential *New York Times* columnist Paul Krugman recently wrote: 'The bottom line is that Chinese mercantilism is a growing problem, and the victims of that mercantilism have little to lose from a trade confrontation. So I'd urge China's government to reconsider its stubbornness. Otherwise, the very mild protectionism it's currently complaining about will be the start of something much bigger.'

India and China have astounded the world by their remarkably rapid growth over the past two decades. They have built on their human resources advantage, long historical experience in creating wealth by husbanding natural resources, and by achieving productivity growth through knowledge and technological invention. After two centuries of absence from the world stage when European colonialism held sway, they are back. How far they will grow and how long their pre-eminence will last will depend on how deftly they confront the new challenges they face in the coming decades.

References

Asian Development Bank (2010). "Human Capital Accumulation in Emerging Asia 1970-2030", *Economics Working Paper Series*, 216. At *http://www.adb.org/documents/working-papers/2010/economics-wp216.pdf* (Accessed on December 04, 2010).

Cline, William R. (2007). *Global Warming and Agriculture: Impact Estimates by Country*. p.49.

Lin, Yifu (1992). "The Needham Puzzle: Why the Industrial Revolution Did Not Originate in China", *UCLA Economics Working Papers* 650. UCLA Department of Economics.

Maddison, Angus (2005). *Growth and Interaction in the World Economy The Roots of Modernity*. Washington DC: The AEI Press. pp.55-60.

National Science Foundation (2010). "Overview", at *http://www.nsf.gov/statistics/seind10/pdf/overview.pdf* (Accessed on December 16, 2009).

World Bank (2007). *The World Bank Annual Report*. At *http://web.worldbank.org/WBSITE/EXTERNAL/EXTABOUTUS/EXTANNREP/EXTANNREP2K7/0,,menuPK: 4078239~pagePK:64168427~piPK: 64168435~theSitePK:4077916,00.html* (Accessed on November 05, 2009).

4

The Siamese Twins

How the USA and China took the World to the Brink of Economic Disaster

MOHAN GURUSWAMY

Imagine living on an island where one person alone has the right to set up a bank and print money. Soon all other residents of that island will be exchanging their surplus production with currency issued by the banker and will also keep surplus cash with him. With the money banked with him and with the unfettered ability to issue money (by his own mint), the banker can give himself the highest standard of living and the ability to buy goods without limits. Since the banker can buy his goods from anyone, it will soon so happen that the prices of produced goods will be pressured downwards and the producers will need to produce more and more to maintain their own living standards.

Now imagine that within this system the banker promises a fixed return on money deposited. Since he has the ability to print as much as he wants and borrow as much as the others want to lend, it would not be long before this system becomes a Ponzi[1] or now a Madoff. The world financial system, it seems, never learns any lessons. Otherwise how could Bernard Madoff have made off with over $50 billion by assuring fixed returns? Among those taken in by him were top international banks and high net worth individuals who should have known better.

Today almost 65 per cent of the world's reserves are held in US currency. Most of the rest are held in Euros. This clearly indicates that

1. Charles Ponzi (March 3, 1882–January 18, 1949) was one of the greatest swindlers in American history. His aliases include Charles Ponzi, Charles P. Bianchi, Carl and Carlo. The term 'Ponzi scheme' is a widely known description of any scam that pays early investors returns from the investments of later investors. He promised clients a 50 per cent profit within 45 days, or 100 per cent profit within 90 days, by buying discounted postal reply coupons in other countries and redeeming them at face value in the US as a form of arbitrage.

Table 4.1

Currency Composition of Official Foreign Exchange Reserves

	1995	1996	1997	1998	1999	2000	2001	2002	2003	2004	2005	2006	2007	2008
US dollar	59.0%	62.1%	65.2%	69.3%	70.9%	70.5%	70.7%	66.5%	65.8%	65.9%	66.4%	65.7%	64.1%	64.0%
Euro					17.9%	18.8%	19.8%	24.2%	25.3%	24.9%	24.3%	25.2%	26.3%	26.5%
German mark	15.8%	14.7%	14.5%	13.8%										
Pound sterling	2.1%	2.7%	2.6%	2.7%	2.9%	2.8%	2.7%	2.9%	2.6%	3.3%	3.6%	4.2%	4.7%	4.1%
Japanese yen	6.8%	6.7%	5.8%	6.2%	6.4%	6.3%	5.2%	4.5%	4.1%	3.9%	3.7%	3.2%	2.9%	3.3%
French franc	2.4%	1.8%	1.4%	1.6%										
Swiss franc	0.3%	0.2%	0.4%	0.3%	0.2%	0.3%	0.3%	0.4%	0.2%	0.2%	0.1%	0.2%	0.2%	0.1%
Other	13.6%	11.7%	10.2%	6.1%	1.6%	1.4%	1.2%	1.4%	1.9%	1.8%	1.9%	1.5%	1.8%	2.0%

Sources: 1995-1999, 2006-2008: International Monetary Fund, *Currency Composition of Official Foreign Exchange Reserves*, 1995-2010 at *http://www.imf.org/external/np/sta/cofer/eng/index.htm* and European Central Bank (2006). "Accumulation of Foreign Reserves", *Occasional Paper Series* 43, February. At *http://www.ecb.int/pub/pdf/scpops/ecbocp43.pdf*

the USA is the world's preferred banker (See Table 4.1). So the system we have in place now is one where countries like China and India produce goods and services at low costs for consumption in the USA, who pays us in dollars, and which we in turn deposit in US banks. More or less. Since money cannot sit still, this money in US banks is then lent to Americans, who already have the highest per capita indebtedness in the world, to further splurge on houses, cars, plasma TV's, computers and play stations which they can often ill-afford. This was well understood, but like the people who kept investing with Bernard Madoff, countries like China, Russia, Japan, Kuwait and India keep on investing in US securities at interest rates which are never more than 1-2.5 per cent. So in effect the rest of the world is plying the USA with cheap credit!

The Importance of being America

The US economy is still the principal driver of the global economy. Despite recent events one must emphasise the centrality of the US to global economic prosperity and stability. Figure 4.1 and Box 4.1 are the snapshots of the US economy which only underscore this centrality. The USA still accounts for about a third of world GDP with only about 5 per cent of the world's population. It is at the forefront of scientific and technological development, and it is unlikely that this will change even after countries like China and India edge closer to it in GDP terms. Consequently the value addition in manufacturing would for the foreseeable future be to its great advantage. For instance the value addition as a percentage on a passenger jet or an advanced microelectronic device would always be much higher than the value addition on a pair of shoes from China or a shirt from India. So the quantum of GDP, which is also related to size of population, alone is not an index of a country's place and power in the world, just as the size of its military is not.

The American Contagion

The current crisis is entirely of American origin and a consequence of the prolonged mismanagement and under-management of, both, the US economy and its financial system. When President Bill Clinton handed over the office to President George Bush in 2001, he left him with a budget surplus and a robustly growing economy. Since then the US government's finances have deteriorated sharply because of its vengeful and senseless war on Iraq and another misadventure in Afghanistan. Both wars are without UN sanction and due to US's delusions of omnipotence. As a direct consequence, financially, things ended up being worse than before Clinton took over from the earlier Bush (See Figure 4.2). In 2008 alone, the US had a budget deficit of about $455 billion.

Figure 4.1

USA Compared to the Rest of the World in the Year 2000

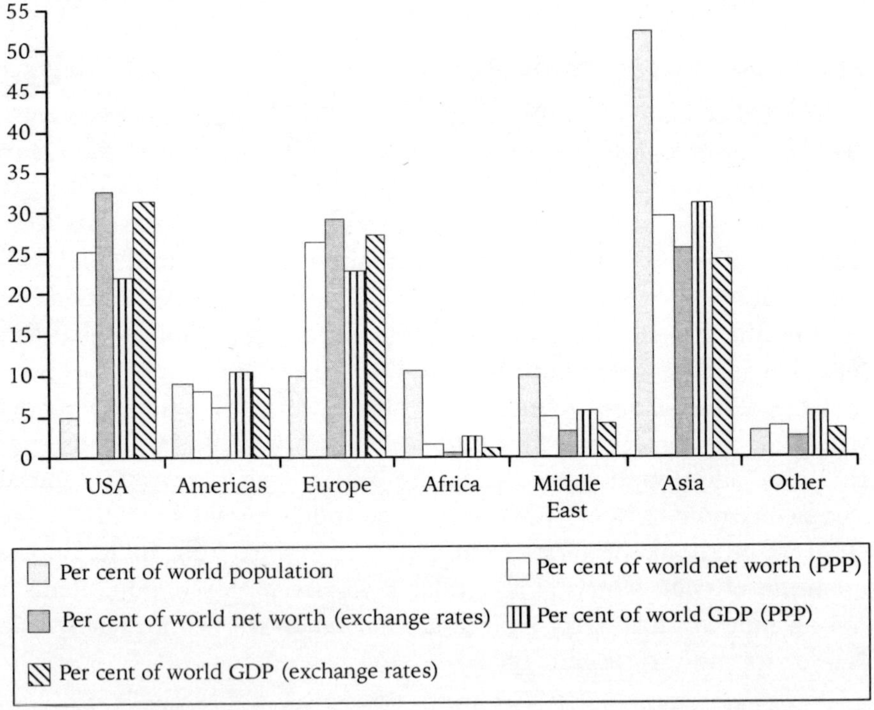

Source: *US Productivity Growth 1995-2000,* October 2001. At *http://www.mckinsey.com/mgi/publications/us/index.asp*

Box 4.1

The US Economy 1

- The US has the largest and most technologically powerful economy in the world, with a per capita GDP of $46,000.
- US firms are at or near the forefront in technological advances, especially in computers and in medical, aerospace and military equipment; their advantage has narrowed since the end of World War II.
- Soaring oil prices in 2005-2007 threatened inflation and unemployment, yet the economy continued to grow through year-end 2007. Imported oil accounts for about two-thirds of US consumption.
- The merchandise trade deficit reached a record of $847 billion in 2007. Together, these problems caused a marked reduction in the value and status of the dollar worldwide in 2007.

The US Economy 2

- **GDP (purchasing power parity):** $13.84 trillion (2007 est.)
- **GDP (official exchange rate):** $13.84 trillion (2007 est.)
- **GDP—real growth rate:** 2.2% (2007 est.)
- **GDP—per capita (PPP):** $45,800 (2007 est.)

The US Economy 3

- **GDP—Composition by sector:**
  Agriculture: 0.9%
  Industry: 20.5%
  Services: 78.5% (2007 est.)
- **Labour force:** 153.1 million (includes unemployed) (2007 est.)
- **Labour force—By occupation:** farming, forestry and fishing (0.6%), manufacturing, extraction, transportation and crafts (22.6%), managerial, professional, and technical (35.5%), sales and office (24.8%), other services (16.5%).
- **Distribution of family income—Gini index:** 45 (2007)
- **Inflation rate (consumer prices):** 2.9% (2007 est.)
- **Investment (gross fixed):** 18.8% of GDP (2007 est.)
- **Budget:**
  Revenues: $2.568 trillion
  Expenditures: $2.73 trillion (2007 est.)
- **Public debt:** 60.8% of GDP (2007 est.)

Source: "US Economic Recovery and Resurgence as of March 2007", at *http://www.sjsu.edu/faculty/watkins/recov2006.htm*, Also see International Institute of Management (n.d.). *The US Economy: US Economic Risks and Strategies for 2007-2017: A Policy White Paper.* At *http://www.iim-edu.org/u.s.economyrisks/*

Figure 4.2

Total Deficits versus National Debt Increases ($ billion)

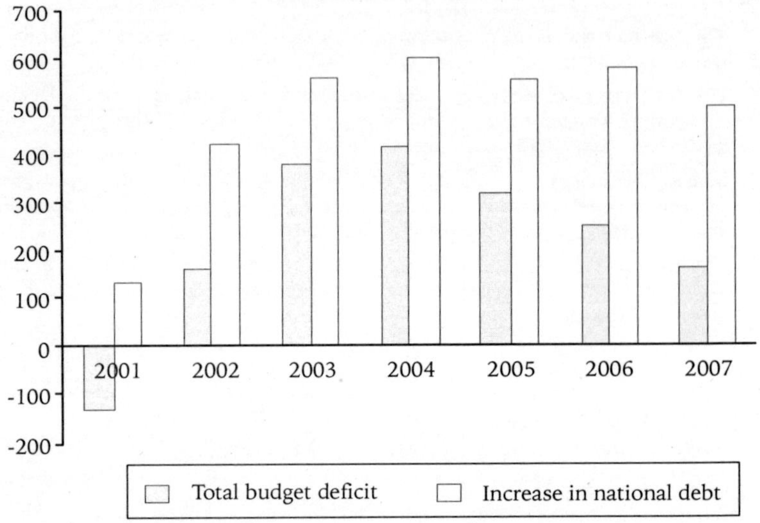

Source: "Historical Debt Outstanding Annual 2000-2010", at *http://www.treasurydirect.gov/govt/reports/pd/histdebt/histdebt_histo5.htm*

The US has had a trade deficit for decades now and this has grown to $847 billion in 2007 and is still growing (*Source:* "Best Countries for Business, No. 2, United States", at *http://www.forbes.com/lists/2009/6/bizcountries09-best-countries-for-business_United-States_CHI004.html)*. Traditionally it has been quite simple for the US to bridge the ever-widening gap because the rest of the world constantly hungered for US securities. China now has nearly $1.2 trillion in US Treasury as securities and India has about $150 billion. In the year 2007 alone China's investment in US Treasury notes increased by 52 per cent. Clearly there is little else you can do with huge piles of US dollars. The simple fact of the matter is that the US dollar is the preferred international reserve currency. This means that the US can print however many dollars it wants and can borrow endless amounts of them without facing the consequences, that is, as long as the pyramid does not collapse. There are other short-term consequences as well. For instance China is estimated to have lost about $80 billion due to the devaluation of the US dollar since the beginning of the crisis.

Well the pyramid did collapse and we are waiting with bated breath as the US attempts to put humpty-dumpty together again. President Barack Obama unveiled the biggest bailout plan in history and in the process effectively nationalised US business icons like General Motors, American International Group (AIG) and Citibank. There was a time when the chairman of General Motors could proudly say, 'what is good for GM is good for America!' That statement now has an ironic twist to it. The US seems to have stemmed the tide of 'red' that was threatening to engulf it, but few will agree that the Obama's intervention amounts to little more than putting a band-aid to staunch the bleeding from a wound that is much too big. The only true healing will take place when the US budgetary and trade deficits are covered. But that does not seem to be on the Obama administration's list of objectives. Living within its means would mean that the US substantially lower its standard of living and cut its coat according to the cloth. Thrift is not the American way anymore, it seems. So how long this situation will last is anybody's guess!

Contrary to popular perceptions the seeds of the US financial debacle were sown much before George Bush embarked on his two wars. It began with Bill Clinton's announcement in his acceptance speech as the Democratic Party's nominee, that he will make the great American dream of every family owning a home, come true. True to his word, soon after assuming office President Clinton announced a provision that allowed Americans to charge all the interest on a house loan as a tax deductable expenditure. So it made great sense to borrow to buy a home. Millions, many who could ill-afford it, went on a borrowing spree. Builders then went on a building spree. These were the Clinton boom years. In President Bush's second term the extension of this construction boom led to an oversupply leading to a sharp fall in valuations. Thus, loan portfolios became toxic and the toxicity spread. The Bush wars only exacerbated the condition and led to the present situation.

Consequently the US had an external debt exceeding $12.5 trillion in 2007 which had been growing by $500 billion since 2003. If you add future outgoes to its citizens like medicare, pensions etc., the US has another $42 trillion due for payment. The irony is that the world and even relatively poor countries like India saw lending to the US by buying US securities as a sound investment instead of the pyramiding scam it had actually become. That India still sees it as a sound investment is amply reflected by the fact that there have been no withdrawals from its dollar reserves even when the rupee came under pressure due to the flight of foreign institutional investor(FII) capital.

Box 4.2

US-World Trade Scenario

- Current account balance: $738.6 billion (2007 est.)
- Exports: $1.149 trillion f.o.b. (2007 est.)
- Exports—commodities: agricultural products (soybeans, fruit, corn) 9.2%, industrial supplies (organic chemicals) 26.8%, capital goods (transistors, aircraft, motor vehicle parts, computers, telecommunications equipment) 49.0%, consumer goods (automobiles, medicines) 15.0% (2003)
- Exports—partners: Canada (21.4%), Mexico (11.7%), China (5.6%), Japan (5.4%), UK (4.3%), Germany (4.3%) (2006)
- Imports: $1.965 trillion f.o.b. (2007 est.)
- Imports—commodities: agricultural products 4.9%, industrial supplies 32.9% (crude oil 8.2%), capital goods 30.4% (computers, telecommunications equipment, motor vehicle parts, office machines, electric power machinery), consumer goods 31.8% (automobiles, clothing, medicines, furniture, toys) (2003)
- Imports—partners: China (16.9%), Canada (15.7%), Mexico (10.6%), Japan (7.4%), Germany (4.8%) (2006)

Source: "World Trade: Possible Futures", at *www.bis.gov.uk/assets/bispartners/.../world-trade-possible-futures.pdf*

Box 4.3

US: Wealth and Debt

- Reserves of foreign exchange and gold: $70.57 billion (31-12-2007 est.)
- Debt—external: $12.25 trillion (30 June 2007)
- Stock of direct foreign investment—at home: $1.967 trillion (2007 est.)
- Stock of direct foreign investment—abroad: $2.627 trillion (2007 est.)

Source: "World Wealth Report 2007", *at http://majorgivingsolutions.com/de/Documents/World%20Wealth%20report.pdf*

What now compounds this problem is that the US still accounts for a large part of the gross world product (GWP) which is the sum of all national GDPs. So when the US sneezes many others catch a cold, which might even turn into pneumonia for some. If it was some third world country that was caught in this situation it would have been taken in hand by the IMF and the finances set right with all the attendant pains it would have entailed. If you did not accept the IMF conditionalities you were threatened with foreclosure and shut down, as happened with India in 1991. This has happened to Brazil, Argentina and even Great Britain in the past.

Now you can not do that to the US. It practically owns the IMF. And there is no country among the G20 which has the gumption or even the clarity of vision to tell the Americans that they can not go on spending and borrowing as usual, and that if the US does not set its house in order the rest will have to act. Not only is the US the world's greatest debtor, most of its citizens are also just as profligate borrowers. The credit card debt in the US is now in excess of $365 billion and of this $91 billion is considered as bad debt. This debt is bigger than the foreign debts of even good sized economies like India ($201.4 billion). This now threatens to be the next big blowback.

The US crisis is two crises morphing into one. The economic crisis which has been festering for long and the financial crisis which came to a boil a couple of months ago resulting in the failure of giants like AIG, Lehman Brothers, Merrill Lynch and Bear Stearns etc. The Chinese prime minister Wen Jiabao has succinctly described them as the crises in the real and fictitious economies. The largely unregulated US financial system began to tank when the bottom fell out of the US housing market. This was due to the downward spiral brought about by oversupply of housing, high interest rates and poor credit-worthiness of the borrowers. This turned into a severe liquidity crisis for the commercial and investment banks with huge exposures in the housing markets.

Box 4.4

The US Economy: National Debt

- As of September 2008, the total US federal debt was approximately $9.7 trillion, about $31,700 per capita.
- Of this amount, debt held by the public was roughly $5.3 trillion. If unfunded Medicaid, Social Security, Medicare, etc., promises are added, this rises to a total of $59.1 trillion.
- In 2007, the public debt was 36.9 per cent of GDP with a total debt of 65.5 per cent of GDP.
- The CIA ranked the total percentage as 26th in the world.

Source: "US National Debt and how it got so big", at *http://useconomy.about.com/od/fiscalpolicy/p/US_Debt.htm*

The Siamese Twins!

The spectacular economic rise of China in this century has so far been the dominant event of the times. China's economy was on an upward trajectory even before the advent of its economic reforms. This only provided the momentum for an even steeper growth after the reforms came into existence. The unfettered entry of foreign capital truly added to the sophistication and competitiveness of its industry. The winds of globalisation filled its sails as exports soared. Much of this export thrust was the result of foreign investment in China's coastal regions. But no export story can be possible without the huge US market with its insatiable hunger for all kinds of goods. Table 4.2 gives a vivid picture of how China's exports to the US soared in the last decade with its resultant huge accrual of trade surpluses. Ironically these surpluses fuelled even greater US consumption, the consequences of which are now obvious. This growing entwining of the US and Chinese economies is the underlying story behind the current global financial and economic crisis. In recent days many economists and commentators have taken to likening the two countries to siamese twins, with different personalities, but joined at the stomach. The USA and the PRC are two very dissimilar countries and economies. One is relatively poor and still has a command economy, while the other is a collectively and individually rich country with a free for all free market. Yet these two dissimilar nations have together taken the global system to the brink.

Table 4.2

China's Trade with the United States

($ billion)

	1999	*2000*	*2001*	*2002*	*2003*	*2004*	*2005*	*2006*	*2007*	*2008*
US Exports	13.1	16.3	19.2	22.1	28.4	34.7	41.8	55.2	65.2	71.5
% change	-8	24.4	18.3	15.1	28.5	22.2	20.6	32.1	18.1	9.5
US Imports	81.8	100	102.3	125.2	152.4	196.7	243.5	287.8	321.5	337.8
% change	14.9	22.3	2.2	22.4	21.7	29.1	23.8	18.2	11.7	5.1
Total	94.9	116.3	121.5	147.3	180.8	231.4	285.3	343	386.7	409.2
% change	11	22.6	21.4	21.2	22.8	28	23.3	20.2	12.7	5.8
US Balance	-68.7	-83.7	-83	-103.1	-124	-162	-201.6	-232.5	-256.3	-266.3

Note: US exports reported on FOB basis; imports on a general customs value, CIF basis.
Source: US International Trade Commission, US Department of Commerce, and US Census Bureau.

The huge US market also gave Chinese industry the economies of scale to make inroads into other markets as well. The resultant picture is seen in the following tables. Japan emerged as China's major trading partner as did Taiwan, apparently proving that good political relations are not a precondition for a mutually beneficial economic relationship (Table 4.5). Chinese bilateral trade with India has likewise been growing and in 2010 it is expected to cross $60 billion. In 2008, China emerged as the world's second largest exporting country, after Germany (Table 4.3). But Germany's trade is well balanced and it has not piled up surpluses like China has and deficits like the US has.

Table 4.3

Country-wise Export Data

Rank	*Country*	*Exports*	*Date of Information*
—	World (sum of all countries)	$ 16,280,000,000,000	2008 est.
—	European Union (minus internal trade)	$ 1,952,000,000,000	2007
1	Germany	$ 1,498,000,000,000	2008 est.
2	People's Republic of China	$ 1,435,000,000,000	2008 est.
3	United States	$ 1,291,000,000,000	2008 est.
4	Japan	$ 746,500,000,000	2008 est.
5	France	$ 601,900,000,000	2008 est.
6	Italy	$ 546,900,000,000	2008 est.
7	Netherlands	$ 533,200,000,000	2008 est.
8	Russia	$ 471,600,000,000	2008 est.
9	United Kingdom	$ 464,900,000,000	2008 est.
10	Canada	$ 459,100,000,000	2008 est.

Source: See World Trade Organization "World Export Data", at *http://www.wto.org/english/res_e/statis_e/its2009_e/its09_appendix_e.htm*

Table 4.4

China's Trade with the World

($ billion)

	1999	*2000*	*2001*	*2002*	*2003*	*2004*	*2005*	*2006*	*2007*	*2008*
Exports	194.9	249.2	266.2	325.6	438.2	593.3	762.0	969.1	1,218.6	1,428.5
% change	6.1	27.8	6.8	22.4	34.6	35.4	28.4	27.2	25.7	17.2
Imports	165.7	225.1	243.6	295.2	412.8	561.2	660.0	791.6	955.8	1,133.1
% change	18.2	35.8	8.2	21.2	39.8	36.0	17.6	20.0	20.8	18.5
Total	360.6	474.3	509.8	620.8	851.0	1,154.6	1,421.9	1,760.7	2,173.8	2,561.6
% change	11.3	31.5	7.5	21.8	37.1	35.7	23.2	23.8	23.5	17.8
Balance	29.2	24.1	22.5	30.4	25.5	32.1	102.0	177		

Note: PRC exports reported on an FOB basis; imports on a cost, insurance and freight basis.
Source: PRC National Bureau of Statistics and PRC General Administration of Customs, China's Customs Statistics.

Table 4.5

China's Top Trade Partners: 2008

($ billion)

Rank	*Country/Region*	*Volume*	*% Change**
1	United States	333.7	10.5
2	Japan	266.8	13.0
3	Hong Kong	203.7	3.3
4	South Korea	186.1	16.2
5	Taiwan	129.2	3.8
6	Germany	115.0	22.2
7	Australia	59.7	36.1
8	Russia	56.8	18.0
9	Malaysia	53.5	15.2
10	Singapore	52.4	10.5

Note: * Per cent change over 2007.
Source: PRC General Administration of Customs, China's Customs Statistics.

The growth of bilateral trade is not the issue. It is the imbalanced growth that is the problem. As China's trade surpluses keep growing it is difficult to see the wisdom in accruing them abroad. The accumulation of trade surpluses is in itself in breach of the spirit of the Bretton Woods consensus that suggested that countries will seek to balance their trade. China did not and it now runs the risk of the consequences. It cannot retrieve its overseas hoard quickly lest it cause a massive revaluation of its deliberately undervalued currency. Then what happens to Chinese exports?

One can speculate about the consequences of a Chinese foreclosure. Will it be possible for it to encash its securities at one go or even gradually within a foreseeable length of time? And then where can it take this money? It would seem that for the foreseeable future at least, this money will have to remain with the US treasury. Then what was the purpose of accumulating this hoard, especially given that China is still a poor country with huge domestic problems?

What Happened in India?

When the liquidity crisis hit the US's reckless domestic lenders they began to pull out their investments from emerging country share markets like India's. At the beginning of last year the quantum of FII investment in India's share market was around $66.5 billion. What should cause even more concern is that over half of this investment is through participatory notes better known as P-notes. This means that the brokers dealing with them do not have to be registered with the Securities and Exchange Board of India (SEBI). This also allows unknown entities and persons to invest in our share market and this was the previous BJP government's singular contribution.

Recently India's national security advisor warned that these P-notes were being used by terrorist organisations to multiply their funds and striking power. Not surprisingly this huge investment is being managed by no less than 1484 brokers making it almost impossible to track them to any purpose.

These FII investments had diminished by $11.1 billion between January 1 and September 15, 2008, and $8.3 billion of these were withdrawn after April 1, 2008. At the beginning of last year the Sensex index of selected shares stood at 20873 as the finance minister crowed approvingly. By the year end it was hovering around 8000 and he has reason to worry about that. This flight of institutional capital continued till the US liquidity situation improved. For a while it looked as though India was also looking down a deep well! The Sensex is now a little above 16000 and climbing. But that will only be till the next crisis hits US financial markets. This unfettered inflow and outflow of money is now seemingly inevitable in a globalised world.

The rapid exit of FII funds caused a spike in the demand for dollars that caused the Indian rupee to devalue by as much as 24 per cent. It is now around Rs.45 but it was a little more than Rs.50 to a dollar at the end of last year. Now the falling Sensex is not an economic crisis. But the rapidly devaluing rupee presents an economic challenge. Imports get expensive stoking inflationary fires. Simultaneously export markets contract thereby neutralising the main benefit accruing from devaluation. True world oil prices are also down but then even at these price levels petrol, diesel, kerosene and cooking gas still need to be subsidised in India. What the Indian economy urgently needs now is a strong infusion of money into critical development areas like infrastructure, which will not only create new demand but also jobs. That money has been hard to come by. The Indian government had announced what was a meagre $14 billion supplementary plan, which was far too little to make any significant difference.

The real Indian economy which otherwise was as robust as it ever was in the last few years, is naturally beginning to feel the pinch and it has begun to hurt somewhat. GDP growth dropped to around 6.5 per cent from the 9 per cent it was hovering around during the previous four years. Compounding this is the rapid contraction of consumer markets in the US, the world's most profligate spender whose humungous trade deficits we had all learned to love. China in particular, with its US trade surplus of over $300 billion is badly hit. In the past year hundreds of Chinese exporting companies have shut shop throwing an estimated 22 million out of work. India is a relatively small exporter of manufactured goods to the US and so was less badly hit. It is not as if India will not hurt because of the current US crisis. No economy is really immune from it unless it happens to be North Korea.

India's economy has been growing at over 9 per cent and even after the slowdown it dropped by just 2.5 per cent. In the overall view totality of things this is not at all bad for a country that had seldom seen more than a 3 per cent growth for the first half century of its independent existence. The GoI's finances are robust and the current account deficit very manageable. But the crisis seems to have seized our minds because of the precipitous fall of the Sensex. This is a real crisis for many and particularly those leaders of government and business who taking the P-notes route have salted away huge amounts in the share market. It is no surprise that all our recent policy initiatives are focused on lifting the Sensex. It is a futile exercise because the FII's can pull out far more money than the government's FI's can invest.

What India's government should instead be thinking about seriously is to bring back, say $100 billion or a third of our foreign reserves and launch a major infrastructure building programme to boost the economy. Unfortunately the government of India is pre-occupied with other and mostly trivial matters. Since Parliament is largely dysfunctional, the task of exploring and promoting policy options now seems to be devolving on trade and industry associations, who are but naturally more concerned with stock market indices rather than long-term strategies to put India on an even higher and more equitable growth path.

There is no Lord Keynes now

The Bretton Woods Conference of July 1944 took place under the fast receding shadow of the World War II and when the US was literally the last man standing. All other prewar powers including the victors were in shambles. The US was now the world's dominant economy and military power. The economists John Maynard Keynes of Britain and Harry Dexter White of the US led the teams to draft plans to set up a system of rules and institutions to regulate and manage the international monetary system. The immediate result was the establishment of the IMF and the World Bank.

Lord Keynes had in mind a more elaborate scheme that called for the establishment of an international reserve currency but this had to be shelved in the face of American obduracy. Keynes' proposal would have established a world reserve currency (he proposed it be called 'bancor') to be administered by a central bank. This central bank would have been vested with the possibility of creating money and with the authority to take actions on a much larger scale.

In case of balance of payments imbalances, Keynes recommended that both debtors and creditors should change their policies. As outlined by Keynes, countries with payment surpluses should increase their imports from the deficit countries and thereby create foreign trade equilibrium. Thus, Keynes was sensitive to the problem that placing too much of the burden on the deficit country would be deflationary.

But the US, as a likely creditor nation, and eager to take on the role of the world's economic powerhouse, baulked at Keynes' plan and did not pay serious attention to it. The US contingent was too concerned about inflationary pressures in the postwar economy, and White saw an imbalance as a problem only of the deficit country. Few then contemplated a continued build-up of surpluses as a problem.

Although a compromise was reached on some points, because of the overwhelming economic and military power of the US the participants at Bretton Woods largely agreed on White's plan. As a result, the IMF was born with an economic approach and political ideology that gave priority to controlling inflation and introducing austerity plans over fighting poverty. But the fact that the US has been the world's biggest deficit country for several decades and seemingly least concerned about it seems to have eluded the IMF. This and the fact that the US dollar has become the world's preferred reserve currency (63.9 per cent) is now the root of the world's economic problem.

This international system was unilaterally abrogated when in 1971 US President Richard Nixon US delinked the dollar from the gold standard. In the absence of a standard and a useful regulatory function for the IMF, coupled with the Reagan/Thatcher era that followed, the great private banks were given a license to run amok. We are now reaping the bitter harvest. The US dollar has become the world's preferred reserve currency. As long as that is how it is, the US and its citizens will have access to easy credit to fuel their consumption and the ever growing annual US trade deficit becomes the *de facto* engine of growth for many economies, such as China.

The G20 is getting institutionalised against this backdrop. It is a very different world now. For a start there is no towering visionary economist like Keynes on the scene. Keynes said after the Bretton Woods conference: 'We have had to perform at one and the same time the tasks appropriate to the economist, to the financier, to the politician, to the journalist, to the propagandist, to the lawyer, to the statesman-even, I think, to the prophet and to the soothsayer.' How can there be one like him when the world economic and financial elite lionised the likes of Alan Greenspan for so long? Or when the world's economic agenda making was privatised and handed over to dubious NGO's like the World Economic Forum (WEF)? There are no tall leaders like Franklin Roosevelt or Winston Churchill either.

A Very Different World to be

The gross world product (GWP) has been growing at a much faster rate over the past few decades. In 1985 it was growing at 2.76 per cent. In 2005 it grew by 3.56 per cent. Much of this is due to the changing of gears in countries like China and India which began their great leaps forward. China's growth in particular has been truly astounding.

Table 4.6

Growth of World Economy since 1980

Year	*Gross World Product (GWP) (trillion $)*	*Per capita GWP ($)*	*Annual Growth of GWP (%)*	*Annual Growth of P/C GWP (%)*
1980	26.8	6,042	--	--
1985	30.7	6,345	2.75	0.98
1990	36.3	6,867	3.4	1.59
1995	40.8	7,168	2.36	0.86
2000	48.6	7,985	3.66	2.18
2004	55.9	8,753	3.56	2.32

Source: World Watch Institute (2002) and IMF (2005). *World Economic Outlook Database*.

The growth trajectory of these countries has made people to review long held notions about how this century is going to shape up. It seems that in 2050 there will indeed be a very different world economic order. The firm of Goldman Sachs, the major survivor of the Wall Street shakeout has made projections of major GDPs and this is what the picture is: Only the US, China and India will stand tall. Even Japan, Russia, Brazil, Britain and Germany will be small in comparison with them. (See Figure 4.3). We are living in an age when economic power will be transiting from the western world to a more inclusive world economic order. This is the most difficult phase. While it is important to last this out, it is just as important to prepare for the future. Are we up to it?

Figure 4.3

The Largest Economies in 2050

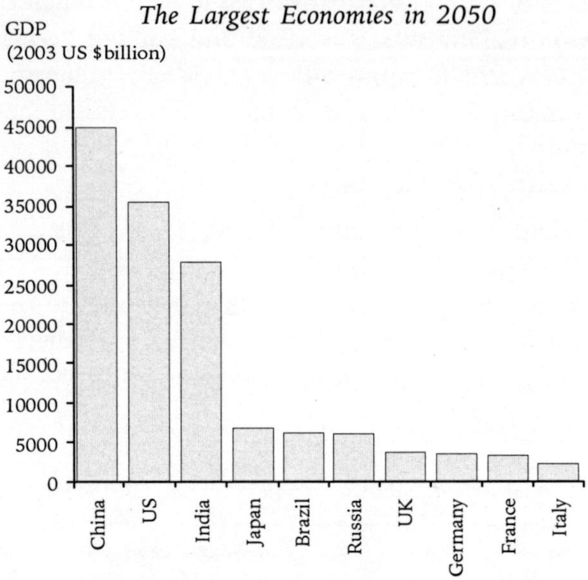

Note: GS BRICs Model Projections. See text for details and assumptions.

Source: *http://www2.goldmansachs.com/insight/research/reports/99.pdf*

Figure 4.4

BRICs have a Larger US$ GDP than the G6 in less than 40 Years

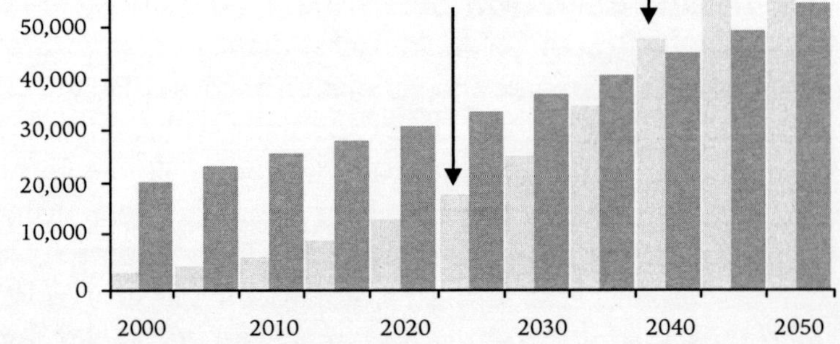

Source: GS BRICs model projections. See text for details and assumptions.

Figure 4.5

India Shows most Rapid Growth Potential of the BRIC

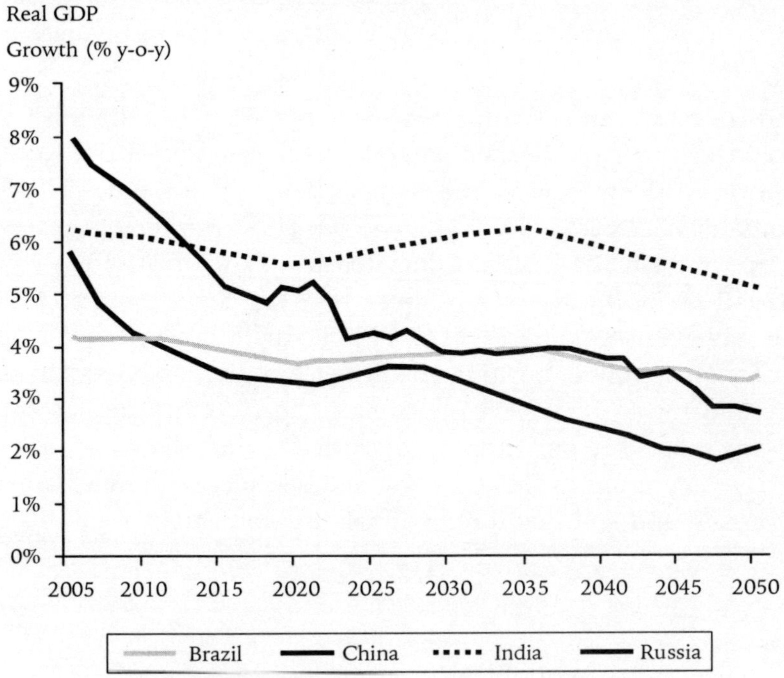

Source: GS BRICs model projections. See text for details and assumptions.

This may be or may not be. But the world is a rapidly changing place. The economic balance of power is shifting towards Asia. Like Communism, the ideology of the Washington consensus 'rammed down the world's throat' has been proved to be a failure. It is time we begin to think differently. The world's four fastest growing economies Brazil, Russia, India and China (BRICs) must now become the basic building bricks of the new order. They not only have the fastest growths but their share of GWP is also rapidly rising. It is expected that within the next quarter of a century the BRICs' GDPs will exceed those of the G6. This more than anything signals a power shift within the G20 (See Figure 4.4). So the question arises as to whether the BRICs are preparing for this eventuality?

These four growth engines must now seek to bring more order into the world system. Casino capitalism can no longer be the guiding ideology. It must be swiftly discarded and a more responsive and intelligent system best suited to all and not just the US is the need of the day. It is time we revisited Lord Keynes' proposal for a global reserve currency and consider establishing a system to regulate and manage it.

The US and even the Euro zone will not want to relinquish the duopoly they have established whereby 91.4 per cent of the world's foreign reserves are held in their currencies. While the dollar alone accounts for 63.9 per cent of reserves, the US's own foreign reserves stand at a measly $74 billion. Compared to this the rest of the world has $7910 billion in reserves. China's reserves alone stand at $1905 billion while Russia's are at $485 billion. India is way behind here with only $253 billion, but this is still twice of those of Germany and France and three times that of Britain. Clearly the time has come when we must put our money to work for ourselves and not be vulnerable any more to the gambling and speculative predilections of the overpaid and so-called professionals in Wall Street.

5

State of Critical Infrastructure

ADRIAN V. GHEORGHE

Critical Infrastructures and Emerging Risks

Part of the problem with understanding the behaviour of infrastructures (e.g., electric power system, transportation, information and communication systems, etc.) is that most of these systems were not designed as integrated systems, but gradually evolved over time. Most infrastructures originate from local networks. Over time, municipal networks evolved. In the Netherlands, for instance, city networks for electric lighting were established in the first decades of the 20th century. Interconnection of city networks and network expansion to rural areas were forged through the intervention of the provincial authorities. Provincial networks thus emerged in the first half of the 20th century. The national grid was not fully established until the second half. Over time, the density of end-user connections increased. Transport functions in the infrastructure were intensified (increasing throughput) to serve a steadily increasing number of users and a steadily increasing demand per user. To improve the security of service, the national grid was interconnected across national borders. At the moment, most national grids in Europe are interconnected. In the course of about one century the system's dimensions have grown by several orders of magnitude.

As illustrated by the case of electricity infrastructure evolution in the Netherlands, infrastructure networks generally do not grow randomly. New nodes added to the existing network are linked to specifically selected nodes. In the natural gas infrastructure, for instance, new urban areas will be connected to existing main pipes. In the world-wide-web (www), new pages usually link to pages that already have a large number of links to them. The advantage of such a 'preference' or 'associative' network is that the network becomes very robust against multiple failures of random nodes. The disadvantage is that such a network is extremely vulnerable to targeted attacks. Eliminating just a few of the main hubs in the network may cause the network to become disconnected or stop functioning at all. Within infrastructures we are dealing today with critical infrastructures; this is in fact the story of how the building up of systems ended up in risky and vulnerable constructs, highly interdependent and lately integrated into systems of continental or world dimensions.

Critical infrastructures protection (CIP) is at the crossroads of politics, business, technologies and risks. During the last decade it has been the subject of much rhetoric, but not as much effective action. This policy field was initiated by the 1997 report *Critical Foundations: Protecting America's Infrastructures,* the US President's Commission on CIP, and has been the subject of debate, strategies, programmes and plans in a majority of Western countries. It was as if, all at once, every government began recognising the serious dependence of their societies upon a set of infrastructures whose robustness they were neither able to evaluate nor assure with their existing capabilities. One point was never fully recognised: that behind the term 'critical' lay the need to cope with a new brand of emerging risks. These risks are international by nature—but the risks management solutions proposed were a re-edition of old models. This is still the case with solutions often offered by civil defence, or the emergency management institutions.

Some infrastructures e.g., energy, water supply, and tele-communications, are so vital and ubiquitous that their incapacity or destruction would affect the security and social welfare of any nation, apart from cascading across borders. Not only are they exposed to multiple threats—such as terrorist attacks, natural disasters, or institutional changes—but any attack on them might put other interconnected systems at risk. There is an urgent need to address such problems with appropriate risk assessment and in-time policy analysis at the international level.

The first question that one may ask is about the changes that make these infrastructures and their possible failures more critical than ever before. First of all, the political perspective on security changed with the end of the Cold War, and a new significance was attached to the essential services needed for the functioning of civil society. On the other hand, several processes, both technological and market related, were mutating the configuration and reach of the infrastructures.

The main factors that have transformed the nature of infrastructures, i.e., how these systems are designed, developed, deployed and operated, are:

- liberalisation of markets, mainly affecting the electric power and telecommunications industry which caused previous monopolies to cede their position and compete with other players;
- networking among infrastructures, that require each other for fulfilling their functions, resulting in an intertwined mesh of interdependent systems;
- increase in cross-border interconnections, justified by the need share capacity in case of major malfunctions; and
- technological changes brought about by the evolution of information and communication technologies and all their pervasive exploitation for improving the control of systems, interaction with the industrial and business sides of companies, and the relations among the players in the supply chains.

It was as if all were caught by surprise by the recognition of the fragility yielded by those changes. Infrastructures have been developing and playing an ever more important role in society since the industrial revolution in the last part of the 19th century. The evolution of technology since then has ensured a continual improvement of means, and the reliability of systems was only jeopardised by technical faults or by natural phenomena.

The above listed transformations also increased the possibilities of new risks:

- The liberalisation of markets has diluted responsibilities with regard to potential shortcomings. All operators of an infrastructural system look to protect their own business interests. The countermeasures for countering the risks respond to their individual judgment of costs and benefits, in the context of the rules and constraints defined by the authorities. Typically, infrastructural services are recognised as basic public services and for that reason they are subject to governmental regulation. Nevertheless, the risks are still managed piecemeal, without any overall consideration of the compound effectiveness of these single risk management approaches.

- The interdependencies among infrastructures means that the potential origins of system failures might stem from external systems. The normal method for dealing with risks considers systems within clearly defined interactions with their environment. But the complexity of interdependent infrastructures precludes the comprehensive knowledge of potential threats without a deeper understanding of the connected systems. But the most that can be expected is the defining of service levels among the individual operators of the systems.
- The increase in cross-border interconnections has made national infrastructures dependent on the proper functioning of those in other countries. Some of these interconnections are part of long and complex international infrastructural corridors (e.g., energy, transport, telecommunications, etc.), that need to be considered in their entirety. Most of them will lose much of their functionality and usefulness if disconnected. In addition, this interaction means that each interconnected system is at the same time a provider of services as well as a potential source of risk.
- The great changes in information and communication technologies have extended the channels connecting the systems, but most of them are open public networks. This fact further increases the possibility of malicious attacks. Open networks, now have a worldwide reach, and are as accessible to a user with legitimate objectives, as to those with vicious intent. Thus the greater the technological development the more the vulnerability.

Some of these problems were anticipated at the very beginning, but it remains doubtful whether the policies put in place have provided any effective answer. This is partially due to the many disciplines involved in the problem. These include legal and market issues, technologies, international relations, national security etc. There is no simple answer. A first consequence of this situation are the conjunction subjects previously treated separately: industrial policies for the regulation and development of services and the companies offering them, civil defence and emergency management for dealing with the negative consequences of potential accidents, law enforcement for coping with organised crime and national defence for responding to external threats. The nature and the challenges posed by critical infrastructures, therefore necessitates a convergence of all these issues.

However one question remains open: how to make decisions about the risks in critical infrastructures? This is outside the realm of governments, as infrastructures are operated (almost exclusively) by private companies. But leaving risk management decisions to the discretion of individual companies is unlikely to provide answers for global risk situations. The need for an apposite answer becomes imperative if this issue is given an international dimension. There is a new trend worldwide for addressing risks to complex systems, and this leads to the concept of risk governance.

Critical Electricity Infrastructures: The European Case

Europe witnessed a number of significant power contingencies in the last years. Some of them had the potentiality of a vast impact on the welfare of society and triggered pressing questions on the nature and reliability of electric power systems. Society has incorporated electricity as an inherent component, indispensable for the required quality of life. Therefore, any breakdown in the continuity and properties of the electricity services would be cause of great distress to society as a whole, affecting individuals, social and economic activities, other infrastructures and essential government functions. It would be possible to hypothesise that in extreme situations this could even upset national security.

Several notable lessons can be drawn from the blackouts and near misses that occurred in the last few years. These are:

- There are hints of some inadequacy. Heavy workloads and limited reserve generation capacities make systems vulnerable to widespread disruptions. Protection systems have been found to play a key role in the majority of catastrophic failures. Power systems have not been designed to cope with the concurrent outage of two or more critical components.
- Incidents were aggravated by other factors, including the lack of a comprehension by control room operators of potentially far-reaching failures and short-term emergency requirements.
- The recent liberalisation of the European electricity market has led to increased cross-border trade, which the power systems were not originally designed for.
- European TSOs (transmission system operators), who have only limited system monitoring capabilities and limited influence on international power trading, confront more and more unanticipated congestions on the tie-lines.

Europe has during the last decade developed a comprehensive energy supply policy, unbundling the previous monopolies and opening the generation and distribution markets.[1] This policy has radically changed the business and regulatory landscape of the electric power infrastructure. From the consumer point of view the effects have been positive: there are more potential suppliers, and prices follow market rules.

But the immediate economic effects of the new policy have not been accompanied by changes in the underpinning physical systems, whose evolution demands at least medium-term investment and planning. For the time being, the power infrastructure has showed an appropriate reliability level, but new threats can be seen on the horizon. Some of these threats are internal to the infrastructure mainly due to the increasing complexity of the many technical and market elements; some of them are external, for instance, the menace of terrorism.

1. European Commission (2000).

Therefore the security of the evolving European electric power infrastructure deserves a cautious and thorough reconsideration.[2] Electricity is a 'common good', central to the security and welfare of almost half billion people and the stability and future economic development of more than 30 countries. For this reason, although local contingencies can be tolerated up to a given degree, but if the power system becomes unreliable at the continental level, it will be a matter of major concern. Europe cannot afford systemic failures in its power infrastructure, which could eventually lead to the weakening of the citizens' trust in societal institutions.

The various national European electricity systems after the transformation of the last few years, have now united to form a unique and integrated, European Critical Electricity Infrastructure (ECEI). This is the result of a process of evolution that has unfolded over decades, which has been determined by two main driving forces: namely, market liberalisation[3] on the continental scale, and the high interconnectivity among regional systems. This has been made possible by the incorporation of information and communication technologies.

This infrastructure, a socio-technical artefact, tends to function as a unity, although it encompasses several jurisdictions, operators and markets. It derives from the interconnectivity between national and regional systems, but at the same time it behaves as a single, compound system-of-systems. It is decentralised; but any disturbance can propagate all through it, and risks have to be coped with in a coordinated way. The passage from a set of individual electricity systems to the ECEI is not just a question of more elements or actors, it represents a qualitative leap. ECEI, an infrastructural system-of-systems, is intrinsically different from a set of weakly connected power systems, where energy flows among different systems are marginal.

The materialisation of ECEI presents clear advantages, but also creates vulnerabilities which may threaten its efficiency. The fact that

---

2. A comparative analysis of policy and regulation in Western Europe has been earlier provided in Midttun (1997).

3. European Commission (2004).

these shortcomings are beyond the capabilities of individual parties means that there is a need for new and more effective instruments for managing risks.

The following picture depicts this evolution: national electricity power systems (EPS) being embedded into ECEI (see Figure 5.1). This chapter outlines the implications of this development, and studies the positive and negative effects of the extensive interconnectedness and digitalisation (i.e., the ubiquitous application of information and communication technologies).

Figure 5.1

The European Critical Electricity Infrastructure Concept: Trends and Driving Forces

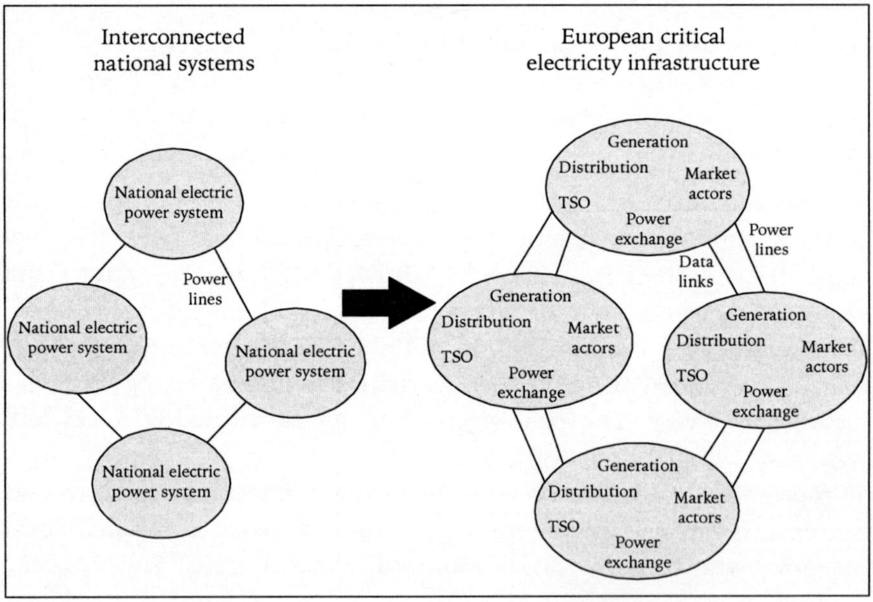

The liberalisation of the European electricity sector has replaced centralised control by regional monopolies with a complex decentralised market structure, in which many different agents control each part of a technically highly integrated ECEI infrastructure. The distribution of the many functions in the electricity supply industry among numerous different actors coordinated through national market mechanisms and grid codes has greatly increased the management complexity of the sector.

This *de facto* decentralised control can only work efficiently in the long term if all the different agents in the system institute the required incentives and comply with compatible rules all through the European infrastructure. Technical reliability, which used to be the goal for gauging the performance of electric power systems, is not enough for the ECEI reality. Many other factors, including environmental compatibility, market practicality and national security, have to be factored into the decision-making process. These factors

Figure 5.2

The Organisational Structure of the Electricity System before Liberalisation

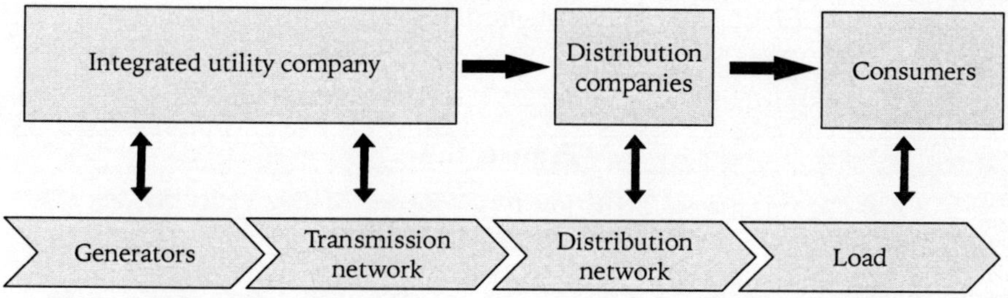

can be structured in five ranked layers (where the upper one comprises the lower ones):

Security: Sustainability: Economic efficiency:

Reliability: Technical performance:

Security can be used as the overarching concept, inclusive of all the other objectives.

With respect to this notion of security, all stakeholders need to have a common understanding of the overall system goals and be willing to work towards them, during normal operation and in case of contingencies. If not, the pursuit of their own private ends, although legitimate, may enter into conflict with public objectives such as availability and affordability. Whereas the regional monopolies of the past required only a relatively simple regulation of their performance and tariffs, the complex decentralised system that is the result of liberalisation requires careful crafting of its institutional structure to ensure that the multiple, and sometimes conflicting, public goals are met.

Figures 5.2 and 5.3 illustrate the organisational changes that liberalisation brought about. Figure 5.2 shows, schematically, the structure of a regional monopoly: nearly all functions are performed by the same agent—the electricity utility company. Often, distribution and end-user supply were managed by separate companies, but these were again regional monopolies. Figure 5.3 shows a simple model of a liberalised electricity system. The figure shows the different groups of actors who together control the physical system. In Europe many of these electricity systems are interconnected with each other. The operation is coordinated in several regional blocks (Union for the Co-ordination of Electricity Transmission/UCTE, Nordel, UK), leading up to the ECEI.

Figure 5.3

The Organisational Structure of a Liberalised Electricity System (Decentralised Model)

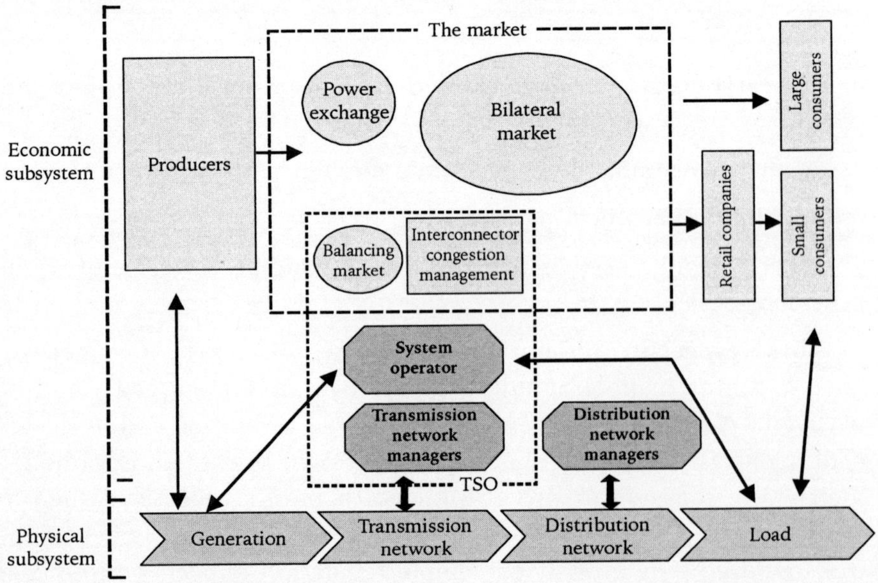

A second trend, which already existed prior to liberalisation but was further stimulated by it, is the internationalisation (i.e., interconnection among national grids) of the electricity system. The operation of the vast European power network is complicated by the many different jurisdictions. At a technical level, the transmission system operators cooperate with each other. At the economic level, large differences between the markets in different countries remain. In order to create an international level playing field, it is essential to have a synergy between economic factors such as transmission tariffs and network access rules prevailing in different countries. In practice, however, different countries liberalise at different speeds and implement different models—not always considering the global consequences of local measures. In addition, the differences in, for instance, environmental standards, taxes and subsidies also have to be considered.

The complexity that results from the combination of the liberalisation and the internationalisation of the ECEI poses a threat to the reliability of electricity services. A clear case is that of the difficulties in the coordination of the responses to wide area contingencies. The multitude of players and the many countries involved also complicate the achievement of a balanced development of the system in the long-term, which in turn may give rise to more contingencies.

A third trend, which we will call evolutionary unsuitability, is caused by the fact that electricity transmission networks increasingly are being used in ways for which they were not initially designed. Electricity systems are not just operated under high stress conditions, but also beyond the limits of their original design. The increasing development of wind power is already leading to stability problems in certain areas. The changes in the electric output of wind parks is leading to fast and significant changes in the way the electricity network is used. The network was not designed for such rapid operational changes. Distributed generation, which means the generation of electricity (and often also heat) in small units close to consumers, may also change the way the networks are used. Whereas large-scale wind energy mainly impacts the transmission networks, distributed generation would change the nature of distribution networks. This trend is unavoidable in an ECEI scenario. It is impossible to foresee the many uses that the infrastructure will be subject to. This will require a new approach to the engineering, deployment and operation of the infrastructure, which includes several non-engineering aspects. It is a 'science and art' issue that requires continuous collective learning for the production and management of complex systems.

A fourth significant trend is the wide-scale application of information and communication technologies in electricity systems, from the level of individual switches up to the operational control of entire electricity networks, and from customer databases to automated spot markets. While the use of information and communication technologies provides many opportunities, the huge increase in connected devices and information flows also increases the vulnerability of the ECEI to failures of the information infrastructure and to deliberate harm through the use of it. Therefore there is a double effect: on the one hand there is an increase in the functional capabilities due to the availability of information; but on the other there is an exposure of the system to cyber threats. All stakeholders have access, in one way or another, to the information components of the infrastructure—but at the same time it is also accessible to illegitimate intruders.

This amalgamation of electric power systems and information and communication technologies produces a new construct: 'Electricity plus information' (or E+I). The ECEI is co-natural to this E+I paradigm, where all electricity functions (i.e., production, trading, transmission, distribution, billing, customer interaction, etc.) are dependent on information. Electricity (the physical dimension of the infrastructural services) coexists with data (the digital dimension of the same infrastructural services). The first dimension is composed of tangible assets: generators, transmission lines, transformers, control and protection equipment, etc. Tangibles are the traditional objects for the valuation of the power business. The second dimension corresponds to intangibles: knowledge, transaction relationships, customer information, contracts, consumption profiles, security culture, etc. The perceived value of intangibles is overtaking that of tangibles. This happens in a continuous process that transforms the electric power infrastructure, leading to the formation and establishment of the E+I paradigm.

When assessing security, this E+I reality cannot be ignored because it determines the vulnerabilities and threats that have to be taken into consideration; the measures to be taken for solving the problems; but also how the risk can be managed. The wealth of information and the easy access to data sources, have to be factored in when designing the risk governance process.[4]

Threats and Vulnerabilities

The transformation of the electric power infrastructure indubitably a favourable fallout in terms of diminishing prices for consumers, more competitive markets which encourage innovations, apart from more alternative sources of electric power supply. But it might also generate conditions that are not very conducive for the overall security of the infrastructure.

The risk prone situations can impact many facets of the infrastructure. These include the organisation of the power market, the regulation of the interconnections to the power grid, its topology, and the technological solutions applied. In addition, it is necessary to consider the perception and reaction of society to those risks.

The liberalisation of power markets has fragmented investment decisions (mainly on the generation side) and now involves many industrial players. The relatively long time required for developing new installations raises uncertainties whether the combination of individual decisions will guarantee the security and adequacy of the infrastructure.

This situation can be complicated by the dependence of investments on environmental considerations, fuel prices and availability. A key fact is that the growth of transmission capacity, and in some places of generation, falls too short of the growth in consumption. The main obstacle in the way of new power lines and generation plants is the difficulty in obtaining the necessary permits,

---

4. COM/2004/702 final-Communication from the Commission to the Council and the European Parliament, "Critical Infrastructure Protection in the Fight Against Terrorism", Brussels, October 20, 2004.

mainly because of environmental considerations. The fuel aspects are obviously determined by geopolitical circumstances. Market dependence means that all new power plants make use of the same cheapest available fuel. The transition to liberalised markets has brought additional uncertainties provoked by changes in the regulatory frameworks.

The central question is whether competitive markets, even in a stable phase after liberalisation, provide adequate and timely investment incentives. The new regulation of power systems in Europe has a strong cost. Nevertheless, it is not clear if the reduction of costs can be balanced with the need to maintain security and expand the power grid in a timely and economically efficient manner

A key point is that different European countries have liberalised at different speeds and implemented different market models. This creates the significant risk of market distortions, which is further aggravated by the complexity of the institutional design.

Electricity generation has seen the development of power based on renewable energy. These are located where the resources are available, not where there is consumption. As a result, power transmission networks and international interconnectors are used in ways which they were not designed for, and their control and protection systems are put under stress.

These changes in power markets and in power generation and transmission are accompanied by a pervasive use of information and communication technologies. This has beneficial effects for the operation of power systems, and the integration of the industrial and business information systems within and between companies. But it has opened up the possibilities for new types of system failures, both of accidental and malicious origin.

First of all, information security was earlier never an issue for industrial systems, and therefore there was a lack of proper security-related standards and of specific security technologies. Only in the last few years, after becoming aware that interconnected information systems were open to electronic attacks, standardisation bodies (e.g., IEC, IEEE, NERC) have begun to work on appropriate security norms.

However, technologies change rapidly and the application of standards requires time. This opens up the possibilities for such risks.

The power grid is exposed to accidental failures and natural hazards similar to the ones endured in the past. The question is whether the new structure with multiple operators is as resilient as the more centralised one in the past. The complexity of the European power network topology creates the possibility of failures that escalate from local problems to broad disturbances, that propagate throughout the system, with the potential of causing cascading blackouts across international borders. This requires a well orchestrated safeguard, but also the coordination to restore services in case of widespread contingencies. As a matter of fact, many of the existing control and protection strategies and contingency defence plans are outdated. They were developed at a time when international flows were smaller, generation was dispatched by the system operator and the use of information and communication technology was much more limited.

Much attention is currently given to the risk of terrorist attacks. The chances of this are difficult to estimate, but it would require a sophisticated, well-coordinated attack to bring a large part of the European power system down. Failure of individual power plants or power lines is a contingency that the system is designed to withstand, but a complete assessment, considering the interdependencies with other infrastructures, has not been undertaken yet.

The Need for Risk Governance

The European electric power industry has been evolving rapidly in the last decade. The Electricity Directive 96/92/EC, adopted in 1996 set common rules for the EU internal electricity market. It established the basis for the opening of the national markets, for the unbundling of the vertically integrated electricity companies, and in general for the organisation of the generation, transmission and distribution business.

As a means for establishing a communication between the stakeholders, electric power systems and the decision-makers, the European Commission established a forum where the regulatory processes and the formation of the European internal electricity market were discussed. The first meeting of the forum was held in

1988, and it is commonly known as the Florence Forum. The normative context was complete in 2003 along with the new Electricity Directive no. 54,[5] complemented by Regulation 1228 on cross-border trade.[6] This Directive aimed at establishing by July 2007 the latest, an open European market for electricity, where consumers would be free to shop around across borders. At the same time, a set of regulators were instituted in all countries for ensuring the correct operation of the market and the regularity of the electricity supply especially in the public sphere.

The fundamental purpose of this policy initiative was the institution of a European internal market for electricity, and it is possible to say that up to now it has been successful and beneficial for the European citizen. Nevertheless, risk (and security) has not been considered to be major concerns. The security of supply is mentioned as one of the public service attributes to be guaranteed.[7] Specifically it is said that the goal is to achieve a 'competitive, secure and environmentally sustainable market in electricity' (Article 3). Some issues mentioned in the Directive are market mechanisms for ensuring sufficient electricity generation, long-term planning and the need to monitor the balance between supply and demand and areas left to the responsibility of each country. But no provision has been made for coping with the systemic risks that affect the European infrastructure as a whole.

Therefore, it is possible to observe a certain mismatch between the policy goal of developing a secure market and the lack of dedicated mechanisms for dealing with risks that might rise that are beyond the control of the single power company and the single country.

Would current instruments be effective for dealing with systemic risks threatening the infrastructure? The only group that brings

5. Directive 2003/54/EC of the European Parliament and the Council of June 26, 2003 concerning common rules for the internal electricity market; *Official Journal* L 176, 15/07/2003.

6. EC Regulation 1228/2003 of the European Parliament and the Council of June 26, 2003 concerning conditions for access to the network for cross-border exchange in electricity; *Official Journal* L 176, 15/07/2003.

7. COM/2003/740 Proposal for a Directive of the European Parliament and the Council concerning measures to safeguard security of electricity supply and infrastructure investment.

together all stakeholders (industry regulators, policy decision-makers, consumers etc.) is the Florence Forum. Could it be used for addressing risks to the infrastructure? The answer is negative, considering its current structure and working style. It is not a decision-oriented organisation, and is open to informal debates.

On the other hand, traditional methods of risk management (applied for instance by electric power companies) do not suffice for coping with the new challenges faced by the electricity infrastructure in its entirety. This chapter analyses these changes and proposes a new way for society[8] to handle them i.e., risk governance.

While the regional monopolies of the past were well-equipped to handle most challenges to the system, individually or in cooperation with each other, the scale and geographical scope of the potential security risks requires decision-making at many different levels: (i) by international bodies, such as the EU and associations of transmission system operators; (ii) at the national level by governments and regulators; (iii) at the company level by generation companies, network companies, system operators etc.; and (iv) finally perhaps also by end users themselves. As both the causes of the risks and the possible strategies for handling them often involve many different parties, this study proposes an approach of risk governance to arrive at joint solutions amongst all the involved stakeholders, in addition to the management of risks by individual parties.

The need for a new approach is partly due to the nature of the new risks, which range from terrorism and cyber attacks to international cascading blackouts, and partly due to the transformation of national electricity systems into a continental infrastructure. In addition, the changing nature of the European electricity markets creates new vulnerabilities that need to be addressed. Liberalisation has distributed the control over the system among many more parties than used to be the case before liberalisation, whereas the response to a contingency requires fast, coordinated action. The increasing internationalisation of the sector poses an additional challenge to contingency management across borders. In the near future, the European electricity

---

8. On a parallel line of work, in relation to CII (critical information infrastructures), one can consult Gow (2005).

infrastructure will be interconnected with North Africa, the Middle East, whole of the Balkans, and the extensive regions of Eastern Europe and Central Asia (from Lisbon to Vladivostok, and from the Arctic circle to the Maghreb). Not the least, the ubiquitous application of information and communication technologies in every part of the sector creates many new opportunities but also new vulnerabilities.

Past methods of managing risk in the electricity industry are no longer adequate given the realities of the current ECEI scenario. This is partly due to the emergence of new risks, but also to the restructuring of the electricity industry. In the past, utility companies with a regional monopoly could be held responsible for virtually every aspect of the delivery of electricity. Electric utilities managed technical risks as well as environmental and health risks. It was common practice to apply a cost-benefit analysis—to fulfill primarily the shareholder's concerns.

In the current decentralised nature of liberalised electricity systems individual actors cannot be held responsible for the way the system functions as a whole. This means that, more than in the past, issues such as reliability and resilience need to be addressed at the level of the whole system. This requires a new approach, which is risk governance, in addition to the risk management actions which were, and still need to be performed by the individual power companies. Risk governance admits the existence of multiple stakeholders, with their individual interests and viewpoints, along with the overall objectives relating to society as a whole. The decision-making process in general, and specifically that which is risk related has to take all these aspects into consideration. The diversity of objectives and actors has to be structured as a multi-criteria problem.

In the present system, all parties need to work together, along with parties who do not directly influence the physical system such as traders, brokers, power exchanges and retail companies. Through the risk governance process, the different affected actors (should!) cooperate to handle risks that exceed the boundaries of their own risk management processes. Risks that are (or should be!) the subject of the risk governance process are either risks that involve multiple actors or risks that originate outside the control of the actors involved.

Which issues should be dealt with through the risk governance process and which ones through the risk management process? If the solution is within the risk management loop, there is no need for governance of the issue. However, if the solution is beyond the powers of the actor that is affected, there is a need for risk governance.

Lessons Learned and Policy Recommendations

Some main lessons are as follows:

- The ECEI, a new kind of human construct of great technical and organisational complexity, which cannot be managed by a single entity. It is subject to risks that are critical for society. Those risks are of very varied nature, and have to be counteracted through a proper approach.
- The ECEI is evolving into an 'electricity plus information' (E+I) infrastructure. The operation of the power systems, the functioning of the markets, the links between industry, regulators and users—all are information-based. The efficiency of the system, the management of security, its adequacy, the market—all are E+I matters. The electric service is now an E+I compound product.
- The new risk landscape faced by ECEI can be split into three layers:
  - Technical layer: risks are caused by technical deficiencies (including failure of components, human errors, engineering flaws etc.). Solutions are mainly technical in nature (e.g., strict application of information and communication security measures, proper training of operators, review of protection mechanisms). Some problems can be addressed by single actors, or by the combined efforts of a limited group.
  - System layer: risks are caused by the interaction of several technical, organisational and market factors, with effects that are not always predictable (e.g., the discrepancy between electricity flows demanded by the market, and the available capacity of transmission lines). Solutions have to unavoidably combine different aspects (e.g., technical, financial) and actors—at times across national boundaries.

— Societal layer: risks have a society-wide resonance, potentially affecting the proper performance of a whole community, its security and survivability. Due to the interconnectedness of ECEI, these situations are transboundary in nature. Solutions have to address the infrastructure as a unity. This complexity calls for a European approach to risk governance.

Risk Governance

- ECEI's emerging risks with European-wide relevance have to be governed by means of a decision-making process tailored to its specific needs and requirements. Key features to be considered are: the multiplicity of stakeholders, the emergent security attributes of the infrastructure, and the dynamic nature of the system.
- In order to be successful, risk governance needs to take into account all risk factors and all threats that cannot be dealt with adequately by risk management processes of individual entities. Risk governance has to deal with them in a comprehensive and systematic way: e.g., bearing in mind among other power system dynamics, market incentives, information and communication technologies, and potential malicious attacks.
- Risk governance implies the involvement of all stakeholders, and clear rules for the deliberation and development of decisions. In Europe, due to the international nature of the problem, this situation will require the participation of national authorities; all business associated with the electric power infrastructure, international organisations, the European Union, and not the least—the end-users.
- Risk governance is a new discipline, and more research is urgently needed to develop it. However, this should not discourage the application of current solutions to such pressing problems as those presented by ECEI, because other alternatives are clearly less adequate.
- Risk governance needs to be supported by proper tools. Governance presupposes the participation of a multitude of actors, from a variety of fields (political, jurisdictional, technical, environmental, economic, etc.). The deployment of a risk

governance process for the electric power infrastructure will require the utilisation of advanced instruments (most likely based on digital platforms).

The implementation of a risk governance process leads to two possible alternatives:

a. The modification of the mission statements of the current organisations in Europe (such as the Florence Forum);

b. The institution of a European Council for the Security of Electric Power (ECSEP);

ECSEP will have the power to monitor and enforce compliance, but also to verify that the different organisations possess the appropriate capabilities. Compliance can be guaranteed by a set of different mechanisms: peer pressure, penalties, economic incentives, etc. The verification of capabilities can be linked to certification, auditing and other qualification procedures. Due to the increasing international interconnections of the ECEI with Central and Eastern Europe, Middle East and North Africa, ECSEP and its members will have to promote the adoption of its recommendations and standards in those regions. ECSEP will have to be granted regulatory powers by all countries falling under its regime and as considered appropriate by the European Union. The management of ECSEP as an independent authority will be guaranteed by a checks-and-control balance between an independent executive board (responsible for the planning and execution of ECSEP activities) and a stakeholders group (responsible for nominating the board members, setting the strategic objectives, and approving the financial statements etc.).[9]

---

9. This structure is similar to the one put in place for the North American Electric Reliability Council (NERC) and by several agencies of the European community.

References

European Commission (2004). *Towards a Competitive and Regulated European Electricity and Gas Market*. DG for Energy and Transport, Memo.

European Commission (2000). *Energy Infrastructures: Increasing Security of Supply in the Union*. DG for Energy and Transport, Memo. December.

Gow, Gordon A. (2005). *Policymaking for Critical Infrastructure: A Case Study on Strategic Interventions in Public Safety Telecommunications*. Hampshire, UK: Ashgate Publishing Company.

Midttun, Atle (ed.) (1997). *European Electricity Systems in Transition*. Amsterdam: Elsevier Science Ltd.

III

Demography, Migration and Urbanisation

6

The Geopolitical Implications of Global Ageing

PHILLIP LONGMAN

Introduction

In both hemispheres, in nations rich and poor, and under all forms of government, one broad social trend holds constant at the beginning of the 21st century: the world is undergoing a demographic transformation of historic and unprecedented dimensions.

Two major countries, Japan and Russia, are already experiencing absolute population declines. Due to a fall in birth rates, the working-age population of all developed countries except the United States will stop growing within five years. Thirty years ago, every developed country produced enough children to maintain a stable population from one generation to the next. Today, among developed countries, only the United States and France come close to producing the average 2.1 children per woman necessary to sustain population over time.

As births decline, life expectancy is also increasing, causing the population as a whole to age rapidly. Today in the developed world, persons aged 65 and above comprise 16 per cent of the population. According to projections from United Nations Population Division, by 2030, the numbers of the elderly are expected to rise to 23 per cent and by 2050 to 26 per cent.[1]

Yet the steepest drops in fertility and the most rapid rates of population ageing, are now occurring in the developing world where many nations are now growing old before they get rich. Iran, under the tight rule of a militant Islamic clergy, has slashed its fertility level

1. Unless otherwise noted, all population projections come from the UN 'median variant.' See: *World Population Prospects: The 2008 Revision,* Population Division of the Department of Economic and Social Affairs of the United Nations Secretariat, *http://esa.un.org/unpp*

by fully two-thirds and now produces barely enough children to sustain its population over time. Four Islamic countries—Iran, Turkey, Morocco and Lebanon—are now at, or below replacement level fertility. The one major exception to the worldwide trend is Pakistan, where, although birth rates have fallen by one-third since the middle of the last century, they still hover at 3.79 children per woman. India, by contrast, has a fertility rate of just 2.8 per cent, with its southern states already reproducing at below replacement rates. India's drop in fertility means that its population will be ageing at three times the rate of the US population over the next half-century.

China's low fertility, brought on in part by its one-child policy, has put the country on a course in which by 2015 its labour supply will be shrinking. In 20 years, its population as a whole will be in decline even as the number of elderly increases by more than two-fold. Because of falling fertility, Brazil, Chile and Mexico, may have older populations than the United States by mid-century. All said, some 59 countries, comprising roughly 44 per cent of the world's total population, are currently not producing enough children to avoid population decline, and the phenomenon continues to spread. By 2050, according to the latest United Nations projections, 75 per cent of all countries in even underdeveloped regions will be reproducing at below replacement levels.

How will the global distribution of power and geopolitical relations change, given current trends in fertility and population ageing? Below I offer three scenarios for both the short and the long term.

Best Case Scenario (2010-2020): Slower world population growth, to be sure, can offer many benefits—some of which have already been realised. Many economists believe, for example, that falling birth rates made possible the great economic boom that occurred first in Japan, and then from the 1960s in many other East Asian nations. As the relative number of children declined, so did the burden of their dependency, thereby freeing up more resources for investment and adult consumption. In East Asia, the working age population grew nearly four times faster between 1965 and 1990,than its dependent population thus freeing up a huge reserve of female labour and other social resources that would otherwise have been committed to raising children. Today, China's rapid industrialisation is aided by a dramatic decline in the share of dependent children in the population.

Over the next decade or so, the Middle East could benefit from a similar 'demographic dividend.' In every country of the Middle East, birth rates were falling, often dramatically, throughout the last two decades. The resulting 'middle ageing' of the Middle East will ease the overall dependency ratio, thereby freeing up more resources for infrastructure and industrial development, all else being equal. With young adults accounting for a declining share of the population, the appeal of radicalism may also diminish, as Middle Eastern societies become increasingly dominated by middle-aged people more concerned with such practical issues as health care and retirement savings. Because of population momentum from the past, there will still be considerable strains on water and other natural resources in the region, but much less than if the rate of population growth was not declining. It is also important to remember that the rate of population ageing will be much faster in the Middle East and other developing regions than seen in any other time or place in recorded history.

The population and GDP of the developed world as a whole will steadily shrink as a share of the world's total, causing the global influence of the developed world to decline. At the same time, however, the population and GDP of the United States will steadily expand as a share of the developed world's total, which should strengthen the influence of the United States within the currently developed world.

The three greatest strategic threats to the United States are its unsustainably high cost of health care, its energy dependence, and its under-regulated and oversized financial sector. In the context of current domestic politics in the United States, all three problems can seem intractable, but all can also be fixed through relatively minor changes in policy and technology. The example of other developed countries shows that the US could cut its per capita health care spending by half (thereby eliminating its fiscal deficits) without any adverse effect on population health. Switzerland enjoys a 70 per cent higher per capita GDP than the United States, and does so while using half the US's per capita energy consumption, primarily because of its reliance on an energy efficient 19th century technology—railroads. The essential solvability of the US's major problems gives it an edge over other great powers, such as Russia, Japan and the European Union, which face demographic declines for which there are no easy policy solutions or self-correcting mechanisms.

Theoretically, a highly efficient, global financial market could ease the challenges posed by population ageing. Japanese and European pension funds, for example, may be able to earn the high returns they need to cover their long-term deficits by investing in the emerging markets of comparatively youthful countries. These countries, in turn, may thereby be able to develop quickly enough to afford the looming cost of their own rapidly increasing numbers of dependent elders. By running persistent trade surpluses with the developed world, countries such as India and China may be able to acquire sizable foreign assets. This scenario requires continuing globalisation and integration of world financial markets, as well as underlying, sustainable balances of trade—trends that cannot necessarily be relied on to continue at the pace seen during the last two decades, due to factors such as resurgent protectionism, high energy costs, and fears of terrorism.[2]

Similarly, high rates of immigration from the developing to the developed world may help to smooth out existing imbalances in the age structures of the different regions of the globe. The United States, for example, has been able to avoid any prospect of population decline primarily due to it success in attracting and assimilating immigrants—a model that Europe and Japan may be able to emulate. Yet here, too, the flow of immigrants may be reduced due to security concerns and fears of a political backlash. On paper, ageing populations could benefit from higher infusions of youthful immigrants, but in practice ageing society also seem prone to increased 'nativism' as their majorities lose cultural self-confidence.

In developed countries, the challenge of population ageing may also be eased by the increased workforce participation of women and older citizens. Currently in the European Union, only 50 per cent of men and 40 per cent of women aged 60 are still in the labour market. The

2. Siegel (2007).

European Commission forecasts that participation rates for the 15-64 age group will increase in the EU25, rising from 65.5 per cent in 2007 to 69 per cent in 2020, primarily due to increased participation by women. If these targets are achieved, it will be possible for the European workforce to continue growing, albeit evermore slowly, through 2019. At the same, policies designed to ease the tensions between work and family life, such as family allowances and more flexible work arrangements, have had modest success in Scandinavia and France in maintaining fertility, even as working mothers become the norm.

Baseline Scenario (2010-2020): Many countries, notably Sweden, Germany, the United Kingdom and Japan have already made large prospective cuts in their pension promises to future retirees. However, enacting, or following through on plans to reduce spending on the elderly will be politically difficult and often threatening to social stability, due to a combination of factors that are threatening elderly populations around the globe.

In the United States, inadequate retirement savings, excessive consumer borrowing, poorly performing private pension plans, rising health care costs, and lost home equity will cause many members of the post-World War II 'baby boom' generation to face severely reduced circumstances as they age. According to a survey by Barclays Global Investors (BGI) released in April 2009, an astounding 58 per cent of American baby boomers, with retirement savings, say they expect to work until they die!

In the United States and increasingly throughout the world, the ability of delayed or cancelled retirement to solve the global ageing crisis is increasingly undermined by trends in public health. Life expectancy at older ages is generally still rising among the non-poor. But so are rates of chronic illness and disability. Just between 1995 and 2000, for example, the number of obese adults increased worldwide from 200 to 300 million, with 115 million of these living in developing countries. Over a billion people worldwide are now estimated to be overweight, creating a global pandemic of chronic conditions from heart disease to diabetes.[3] At the same time, we see

---

3. World Health Organization, *http://www.who.int/nutrition/topics/obesity/en/index.html*

a massive spread of 'Western' diets high in fat and unhealthy processed foods. The techniques of modern medicine have also proved to be remarkably ineffective in improving the health and productivity of older populations even when, as in the United States, they are widely available.

These trends are inconsistent with predictions of a coming golden era of 'productive ageing.' So too are trends in technology that make many job skills rapidly obsolete. We will continue to see increasing examples of individuals who make useful contributions through advanced old age, but on current trends they will constitute a fast vanishing small minority of their generation.

High rates of childlessness will also present elders with many challenges in old age. In the United States, about 17 per cent of those now approaching retirement age never had children. In many European countries, the number is (or will soon be) between 1 in 5 and 1 in 4. Even in countries with robust welfare programmes, navigating the health care system alone, or arranging for long-term nursing home care without the aid of family, is daunting. In countries lacking formal provision for the elderly, the cost of childlessness is often more extreme—at the start of this decade, elders living in urban China had an average of 3 grown children to share the burden of their care; by 2025, they will have just 1.3.

Throughout the 1990s and until the world economic crisis that began in 2008, the conventional wisdom at the World Bank and other leading global institutions was that financial provision for old age could best be accomplished through increased individual savings and investment in capital markets. So called 'pay-as-you-go' public pension plans, in which younger taxpayers who support older retirees, it was pointed out, can offer individual participants generous rates of return only so long as population growth remained strong. In the absence of population growth, returns are limited to underlying increases in productivity or its usual proxy, wage growth. In contrast, returns on capital, it was argued, could more than make up for the declining numbers of workers available to support each retiree.

Around the world, this thinking leads to rollbacks in conventional social security programmes, and the implementation of so-called 'individual accounts' in which workers effectively pre-fund their own retirement with matching contributions from their employers or sometimes government. The United Kingdom, Australia and Sweden for example, were leaders in taking this approach. Other countries such as Canada, have tried a hybrid approach in which government pension funds invest in the private economy.[4]

At the level of theory, it makes perfect sense in an ageing society for each generation to pre-fund the cost of its own retirement through investment in capital markets that ultimately raises each new generation's overall productivity. In practice, however, we have seen vast amounts of retirement savings wiped out by the world economic downturn that began in 2008. World financial markets were engaged in, what was clearly, excessive risk-taking. Moreover, rather than being investments that might improve the productivity of the next generation, much of the world's savings instead went to boost current consumption by lowering lending standards for home mortgages and credit cards. Though it is still too early to know how this crisis will play out over the next 10 years, a few trends can be confidently predicted:

- Banking and financial markets will become subject to much tighter regulation.
- Credit-financed consumption, particularly by Western consumers, will play a reduced role as an engine of world economic growth.
- Populations around the globe will look to government for more protection from financial risk and job loss.
- Stagnant or declining working-aged populations will retard economic growth in the absence of 'game changing' technological developments.
- The promise of unfettered capitalism and globalism will seem diminished, even as the limits of socialism and communism remain well remembered.

---

4. For a slightly dated, but still useful survey of pension reform efforts around the world, see: Capretta (2007).

Worse Case Scenario (2010-2020): During the '30s, many key observers of the Great Depression, notably John Maynard Keynes and his American counterpart Alvin Harvey Hansen attributed its root cause to the falling fertility rates in the western world at that time. Population growth creates more supply for the labour capitalists to buy, and more demand for the products and services for capitalists to sell, making it perhaps essential for keeping up the animal spirits of investors. John Hicks, in his famous review of Keynes' General Theory, went so far as to remark:

> Expectation of a continually expanding market, made possible by an increasing population, is a fine thing for keeping up the spirits of entrepreneurs. With increasing population investment can go roaring ahead, even if the invention is rather stupid; increasing population is therefore actually favourable to employment...One cannot repress the thought that perhaps the whole Industrial Revolution of the last two hundred years has been nothing else but a vast secular boom, largely induced by the unparalleled rise in population.

Today, the analysis of the world economic downturn has so far concentrated on the financial architecture—the growth of a shadow banking system, the complexity and synthetic nature of new financial instruments, problems with moral hazards, over-leveraging, etc. Yet stepping back from these details, one cannot repress the thought that the excess risk that infected the system had a root cause—it was ultimately driven by a quest to retain high returns on capital at a time when truly productive opportunities were diminishing, due at least in part, to slackening population growth.

Japan's economic stagnation began in the late '80s, just as growth in its working-aged population slacked off. Slow population growth in the western world is arguably a root cause of the excess capacity now found in nations dependent on it for export trade. For a long while, expanded consumer credit (financed by recycled foreign capital and asset inflation) could sustain high consumer demand in the US and most of Europe. But in the face of decelerating population growth, the trend becomes unsustainable due to exhausted consumer balance sheets and sheer satiety. There are only so many iPods and high definition television sets any given household needs.

If this analysis is correct, then averting a second Great Depression depends critically on raising effective consumer demand in those areas of the world where population is still growing and consumer needs are great. One might expect this to happen automatically, and so it may in the long run, but not before wrenching changes that can cause economic and social turmoil. Africa, Russia and much of the Middle East face problems of governance, from corruption to ethnic strife, that seem to stand intractably in the way of an expanding middle class. India, China and other export-driven countries must restructure their economies to stimulate domestic consumption. Yet they must somehow do so without creating a spike in global energy and food prices, without cutting off the United States from the credit it needs to continue as a strong export market, and all the while providing for domestic populations that are themselves ageing rapidly. The challenge of fostering a sustainable, worldwide middle class are even more daunting if one takes seriously the asserted relationship between increased greenhouse gas emissions and climate change.

The Challenge of the 2020s

As challenging as the remaining years of this new decade may be, it will be in the 2020s that the maximum effects of demographic change are likely to occur. In that decade, the post World War II 'baby boom' generations around much of the world will begin to experience, in mass, the infirmities of old age. At the same time, there will be reasons to worry about the return of 'youth bulges' in different regions of the Middle East. Birth rates there, to be sure, have been consistently falling. Yet because of the large numbers of people of childbearing age, even a decline in the average number of children can still create a so-called 'echo boom'. In the Arab world, for example, the growth rate in youth aged 15 to 24 is currently slowing down from 2.6 per cent per year between 1990 and 2005 to 0.9 per cent between 2005 and 2020. But then will come the 'echo boom' when the population of young adults will again accelerate to 1.9 per cent per year between 2020 and 2035.

Further, as geopolitical strategists Neil Howe and Richard Jackson of the Centre for Strategic and International Studies (CSIS) point out: 'The echo booms of the 2020s will be largest in precisely those countries where fertility has fallen the fastest over the past 20 to 25 years and youth populations are now declining most rapidly. In Iran, where the fertility rate plunged from 6.6 in 1980 to 2.1 in 2005, the number of 15-to-24 year olds will shrink by 34 per cent between 2005 and 2020. Between 2020 and 2035, however, the number will again swell by 34 per cent. Many other Muslim countries, from Libya to Pakistan, will also experience huge oscillations in their youth populations.'[5]

Most of the Central Asian republics will also face large 'echo booms' in the 2020s. For long the battlefield for major powers, from the Mongols and Persians to the Russians and the British, these newly independent states are once again the object of geopolitical competition due to their huge natural gas and oil reserves. The same is true of two of Latin America's most volatile countries, Peru and Venezuela, which will experience large 'echo booms' in the 2020s.

This decade will also see the consequences of today's imbalanced sex ratios in many parts of the world. In a normal population, there are roughly 105 baby boys born for every 100 girls. In India there are 110 boys born for every 100 girls and in China there are 117. These exaggerated gender imbalances have ominous implications. Today's 'missing girls,' as they are called in China, will become tomorrow's 'missing brides'. China is projected to have a surplus of some 30 million men of marriageable age by 2020, and the numbers in India are similar.

By the 2020s, military manpower shortages, along with fiscal constraints caused by population ageing are also likely to be playing a large role in determining how and whether wars are fought, and by whom. The US is the last remaining nation with enough manpower and hardware to deploy large, permanent military forces beyond its immediate boundaries. By the 2020s, however, the numbers of Americans fit for military service are likely be substantially reduced, while the 'greying' of the US federal budget will put pressure on military hardware spending. It may be that national power today is much less dependent than before on the ability to raise large armies and navies. Yet the technologies the United States currently uses to

5. Howe and Jackson (2008).

project its power—laser-guided weapons, stealth aircraft, navigation assisted by the space-based Global Positioning System (GPS), nuclear aircraft carriers—are all the products of massive and ongoing investments that the United States will not be able to afford if the cost of entitlements continues on its current course.

The same point applies to the US's ability to sustain, or increase its levels of foreign aid. If the war on terror is indeed a 'generational struggle', as some have warned, then the US will have a very difficult time sustaining its financing. Even within the US military budget, the competition between guns and butter is already becoming extreme. The Pentagon today spends 84 per cent on pensions for every dollar it spends on basic pay. Other nations that might challenge the US for military supremacy, such as China, are of course facing even more dramatic population ageing, so that the US's relative position may remain unchanged or even improve.

Viewed from afar, India's demographics present a mixed picture. Driven by the momentum of the past, India is poised to become the most populous nation on earth, eclipsing China for the first time in history. Falling fertility in the south is causing the country to age, but not as rapidly as China. India's population aged 65 and over is expected to increase from 60 million today to 221 million in 2050. More than 40 per cent of India's remaining population growth will come from increases in the ranks of the elderly. This is a substantial rise, but it still leaves only 13.7 per cent of the population over 65 by mid-century, which is a much smaller figure than what Japan and European countries are faced with today.

At the same time, India exhibits a wide differential in fertility rates among different segments of the population. This pattern is commonly seen in the western world, but not in Asia. Specifically, there are pervasive Muslim-Hindu fertility differences in India that remain evident even after adjustments to such possibly confounding factors such as socioeconomic status. According to the latest available 2001 census data, Muslim fertility in India was 3.06 children per woman, as compared to 2.47 per cent for Hindus.[6] Also, we see wide differences in reproductive behaviour between educated and illiterate

6. Census of India (2001).

women, and between city dwellers and those living in the country. An urban Indian woman with a graduate degree has only 1.6 children over her lifetime, while an illiterate Indian woman living in the countryside has an average of 4.1.[7]

Medium- to Long-term Scenarios

Best Case Scenario (20-50 years): Properly managed, the vast demographic transition now affecting nearly every corner of the world could lead to a new era of stability, prosperity, as well as cultural and political maturity, particularly in regions where birth rates are falling, but the labour force is still growing. The sub-replacement fertility rates now evident in nearly all developed nations may prove to be a temporary phenomenon, as societies take measures to reduce the cost of children to their parents, and to ease the tensions between work and family life. According to surveys, women aged 40 in 2000 in the United States and in every European nation, for example were coming to the end of their reproductive years having produced fewer children than they intended. American women born in 1960, for instance, desired an average of 2.3 children, but wound up producing 12 per cent fewer. In Europe, the gap between the numbers of children women of this generation wanted and the number they actually produced is even greater. Indeed, if European women now in their 40s had been able to produce their ideal number of children, the continent would be facing no prospect of population loss.

Continuing improvements in technology may so improve productivity that even the oldest nations may enjoy ample surpluses. Societies may spend a greater and greater percentage of their wealth on health care, but improving efficiency in the provision of everything else will make the burden easy to bear. Today, for example, a typical American must work 260 hours to earn enough money to secure his or her annual food supply. Yet as the economic historian Robert Fogel points out, 'If agriculture productivity grows at just two-thirds of its recent rates, then by 2040 a family's annual food supply may be purchased with about 160 hours of labour.'

---

7. Census of India, Vital Statistics, *http://www.censusindia.gov.in/vital_statistics/Vital_Rates/Vital_rates.aspx*

Meanwhile, a slowdown, or absolute decline in world population growth, combined with the disappearance of destabilising 'youth bulges' in different parts of the world, could lead to less competition for natural resources, a cleaner environment, and to a generally more peaceful and prosperous world. Some strategists believe that population ageing around the world will lead to a 'geriatric peace.' In a world of single-child families, popular resistance to military conscription will grow, as tolerance of military casualties will fall.

Baseline Scenario (20-50 years): If Europe's current fertility rate of around 1.5 births per woman persists until 2020, this will result in 88 million fewer Europeans by the end of the century. If European fertility rates remain unchanged, the only European countries that will avoid population loss by 2050, according to UN projections, will be France, the United Kingdom, Ireland and Luxembourg, and even these countries will face rapidly ageing populations. Without an increase in its fertility rate, France's working age population (aged 15-64) will decline by more than 9 per cent by 2050, while its elderly population will increase by 79 per cent.

By 2050, on present demographic trends, there will be 75 pensioners in Europe for every 100 workers; in Spain and Italy the ratio of pensioners to workers is projected to be 1:1. By mid-century, if current trends continue, Europe will be a society in which most adults have few biological relatives. In Italy, almost three-fifths of the nation's children will have no siblings, cousins, aunts or uncles—only parents, grandparents and perhaps great-grandparents. Even among immigrants, families with more than one child are becoming increasingly rare throughout Europe.

If the United States is able to maintain its current birth and immigration rates, it will vastly increase in size, and most likely in geopolitical power, relative to Europe and Japan. However, current trend lines suggest that the fertility rates in United States may well converge with those of other developed nations. Among major ethnic and racial groups, only Hispanics are reproducing above replacement levels, and that is primarily because of the comparatively high fertility of recent arrivals, who are themselves having decreasing numbers of children.

Meanwhile, it is unclear how long the US can sustain even current rates of immigration. One reason for this of course is the heightened security concern about terrorism. Another is the prospect of a cultural backlash against immigrants, the chances of which increase as native birth rates decline. A final reason is the prospect of a decreasing 'supply' of immigrants. Some Mexican demographers say, for example, that the country's fertility rate, which is officially measured at 2.5 children per woman, has already dropped below replacement levels. Puerto Rico, with a fertility rate well below replacement level and a median age of 31.8 years, no longer provides a net flow of immigrants to the mainland, despite an open border and a lower standard of living. Generally, fertility rates are dropping throughout Latin America and the West Indies, and are already below replacement levels in many major countries of the region, including Brazil, Chile and Cuba.

If current rates of economic growth continue, the output of the Chinese economy could rival that of the United States by 2020. Yet before China can emerge as a true economic powerhouse, it must contend with a demographic challenge that it so far shows few signs of addressing. Even after assuming a substantial increase in future fertility rates, the United Nations projects that by 2050, nearly one in four Chinese citizens will be elderly. Other estimates, based on the assumption that future fertility rates will increase less substantially, show that by 2050, there may be as few as two working age citizens available to support each retiree.

For the world as a whole, forecasts by the United Nations and others show that the world population growth could well turn negative during the lifetime of people now in their 40s and 50s, and is very likely to do so before today's children reach retirement age. A study by researchers at Austria's highly regarded International Institute for Applied Systems Analysis (IIASA), published in the prestigious journal *Nature*, predicts that world population will most likely peak before 2070 and then trail off rapidly. In such a scenario, most of the remaining growth of population would come from increases in the numbers of people over 60.

Worst Case Scenario (20 to 50 years): Some biologists now speculate that modern humans have created an environment in which the 'fittest,' or most successful individuals are precisely those who have few, if any, children. As more and more of the human race finds itself living under urban conditions in which children no longer provide any economic benefit to their individual parents, but are rather costly impediments to material success, people who are well adapted to this new environment will tend not to reproduce themselves. And many others who are not so successful will imitate them.

'The great range of conditions under which fertility has begun to fall all over the developing world,' notes Alaka Malwade Basu of the Harvard Center for Population and Development Studies, US 'and the most potent correlates of such decline—education, exposure to the mass media, exposure to the ideologies (rather than the material trappings) of modernisation—strongly suggest that the urge to control fertility and to have fewer children than one's parents comes largely from wanting to do what others do.'

So where will the children of the future come from? They may well come disproportionately from people who are at odds with the modern environment—from people who 'don't get' the new rules of the game that make large families an economic and social liability, or who, out of fundamentalist or chauvinistic conviction, reject the game altogether. If so, the future may well belong to fundamentalism.

References

Capretta, James C. (2007). *Sustainability of Public Pension Systems An Assessment of Reform Efforts in Twelve Developed Countries*. Washington, D.C.: Centre for Strategic & International Studies. January.

Census of India (2001). Fertility Tables: F-9, F-9 SC, F-9 ST AND F-10, Statement 3, Total Fertility Rates by Residence and Social Group-India. *http://censusindia.gov.in/Data_Products/Data_Highlights/Data_Highlights_link/data_highlights_F9_F10.pdf*

Howe, Neil and Richard Jackson (2008). *The Graying of the Great Powers: Demography and Geopolitics in the 21st Century*. Centre for Strategic and International Studies. May.

Siegel, Jeremy J. (2007). "Impact of an Aging Population on the Global Economy," *Conference Proceedings Quarterly* 24(3): 4. CFA Institute. September.

7

Population Movement and Diaspora

JUDITH M. BROWN

Introduction

The study of peoples has a long history but demography only really came into its own as an academic discipline in the later 19th century. At its heart is the statistical study of populations, particularly changes over time, and changes in spatial distribution. So it includes the study of changes in size, structure and distribution of populations, the effects of birth rates, death rates, youth and ageing, and of course migration. Professional historians have tended to leave demography to human geographers and social scientists of different kinds; but demographic issues in general, and migrations in particular, have been of crucial historical significance, and will continue to be so. We have only to think of some of the great movements of peoples in relatively modern times and their impact on history as we know it—for example the movement of 10 million people as slaves out of Africa, or the outmigrations of about 60 to 65 million people from Europe before 1914 into North America, and into the settler societies of South Africa, Australia and New Zealand.

Migration out of Asia has a long history, particularly movements of people from China and the Indian subcontinent. Both of these were multi-stranded flows from the original homeland, beginning with trading movements in Asia and beyond, developing into the movements of unskilled labour, and now culminating in the movements of skilled and professional people. It is impossible to be accurate about total figures but in the last decade of the 20th century it was estimated that about 31 million Chinese were living outside greater China, while there were over 9 million people of South Asian origin living overseas in every continent.[1] (As we shall see later, the communities created by outmigration go on growing, sustained partly by continuing migration but even more by natural increase.) Such staggering numbers have in recent times been enabled by the development of modern forms of travel—from the railway and the steamship in the 19th century, to the development of rapid and relatively cheap air travel in the later 20th century. The drivers behind such movements have been diverse—domestic population growth, economic and political disruption and the scarcity of resources, demand for labour abroad, and myths of fabulous wealth to be made overseas. People have felt both 'pushed' and 'pulled' from the homes of their forefathers. Moreover, the experience of movement, even within the homeland, or temporarily abroad, creates broader horizons and expectations, and a belief in the possibility of making oneself a better life. To take a particular example from India: Sikhs in the 19th century had experience of foreign travel often in the service of the British Indian army or in the colonial police forces within the British empire, and this, combined with the profound demographic disruption of 1947 in Punjab, has led to major movements of that particular community out of India. The result of such combined historical factors in and outside Asia has been the growth of significant global diasporas. This word has become popular in common parlance as well as in academic analysis.[2] Originating in the Greek and meaning 'to sow over', it now generally is used to describe a group of people living outside their homeland who are conscious of common ethnic, geographical and cultural bonds, who retain links with their original homeland, and for whom that homeland still plays a significant role in their sense of identity.

As we explore the dimensions and multi-faceted implications of population movement out of Asia and the formation of diasporas, I will first look at the demographic situation of Asia in global terms, and then turn to the case of the diaspora I have studied, namely that

1. Useful guides to populations flows out of Asia are: Pan (1999); Lal *et al.* (2006); Clarke *et al.* (1990); Cohen (1995). I have drawn on these works and also the research done for my own study, Brown (2006).

2. Cohen (1997).

from South Asia, to look at a number of issues which are likely to be of profound importance in the early 21st century.

Asia and the World: Demographic Trends

As the first decade of the 21st century ends we stand on the brink of a major global demographic shift which will alter profoundly the relations between the different parts of our global society, as well as economic, social and political relations within Asian countries themselves. This shift also alters markedly the context in which diasporas form and function. So let me start by trying to understand this.

In the 19th and early 20th centuries as industrialisation began to develop, fertility in western Europe and then America began to drop—quite slowly, from about 5 to 2.1 per woman or below. 2.1 is the replacement rate for the population and a critical point for the internal dynamics of a society. As one writer recently put it, the move to replacement fertility is 'one of the most dramatic social changes in history'.[3] As people acquired more wealth, and began to educate their children and, crucially, their womenfolk, the size of their families fell; and as they fell, the family grew richer. However, this combination of growing and diversifying economies, and a smaller population, provided the context in which labour was sucked into the more developed world. Workers of many kinds left Africa and then Asia, where rising populations combined with low levels of economic development produced poor societies, where opportunities were few, resources were thinly spread, and in which there were pockets of profound deprivation. It also coincided with the peak of the global influence of the British empire, which was essentially a global economic and political system, and as such enabled the flows of peoples within it in quite new ways and in far larger numbers. Understandably the peoples of the Indian subcontinent were caught up in this broad process even well after the formal ending of the British *raj*. So migrants left South Asia, for example, to work in other parts

3. The Economist, 31 October 2009.

The fertility rate is of course not the same as the birth rate which is the actual number of children born in a year in relation to every 1000 of the total population. The fertility rate is the number of children a woman is likely to have during her childbearing years (15-49).

of that empire as unskilled labour in conditions which have been called a new system of slavery,[4] as skilled imperial employees in East Africa and Southeast Asia, as traders in growing numbers as routes into new areas were opened by imperial intervention, and eventually after 1947 as semi-skilled and increasingly skilled and professional workers in Britain itself. The particular demographic balance of this historical period was the context for the creation of the great Asian diasporas.

However, this global demographic phase is now ending. Fertility is now declining globally, and it will probably only take another decade before the global average is below the global replacement rate. These trends are very clear throughout Asia. Of course the total population of Asia is still very large indeed, given that within it there are the two countries of the world with the largest populations, China and India. The 2009 estimate of China's population was 1.33 billion and India 1.16 billion.[5] But in most Asian countries the fertility rate has fallen and is now at or near replacement rate rather than high above it. The top 41 countries in the world as far as fertility rates are concerned are all in Africa. Of the South Asian countries Pakistan lies at 55 in the world order with a fertility rate of 3.6; Bangladesh at 82 with a rate of 2.74; India at 83 with a rate of 2.72. Indonesia lies at 109 with a fertility rate of 2.31 while China, not surprisingly given its long-standing and draconian policies of population control, lies at 158 with a rate of 1.79. Right at the bottom of the global list are Japan and South Korea with rates of 1.21 and even lower are the island states of Singapore (1.09), Hong Kong (1.02) and Macau (0.91). The growth rate of the Asian population tells the same story. Pakistan stands at 63 in the world list of growth rates with a percentage rate of 1.95. India comes in at 84 with a growth rate of 1.55 per cent. Bangladesh stands lower at 104 with a growth rate of 1.29 per cent. China stands at 146 with a growth rate of 0.66 per cent. Given that female education and fertility are so intimately linked it is worth noting also the expenditure on education as a percentage of GDP. India stands at

4. For a classic work on the system of indentured labour see Tinker (1974).

5. The figures in this paragraph are taken from the very useful online *CIA World Factbook*. Another useful source for comparative social, economic and demographic information online is the *Global Social Change Research Project*.

140 in the world order of national spenders on education, spending about 3.20 per cent of GDP on that area of social investment. Bangladesh is at 151, spending 2.70 per cent and Pakistan is at 155, spending 2.60 per cent of GDP on education. By contrast the UK stands at 47 spending 5.6 per cent in this area.

Given our interest in outmigration from South Asia particularly, the figures for migration are significant. The net migration rate is the difference between the number of persons entering and leaving a country during the year per 1,000 persons. India just falls into the category of countries from which there is a net outflow: it now 'exports' 0.05 persons per 1,000 of its population. Pakistan 'exports' 0.48; while Bangladesh is one of the largest exporting nations, given both its population size and the fact that it 'exports' 2.53 persons per 1,000 of the population.

This global shift in population, and the projected quickening of these trends, in Asia itself and in Asia's relations with the rest of the world, raises major questions about the global movements of people and the likely levels of migration out of South Asia in comparison with the past. Historians of course cannot predict the future, and can only suggest possible trends with an eye to the past. Clearly Europe and North America will need more skilled and semi-skilled workers, particularly as their populations age: where will they get them from? As Asian economies develop they will absorb more of their own potential workers, particularly skilled ones, while at the same time the growth rates of their own populations will decline. Not only will there be less incentive to leave the homeland in search of work or a better life; people in the diaspora may well return bringing both capital and skills.

Asian Diasporas: Contemporary Issues

Let us turn now from considering global demographic trends and their effects on Asia and its relations with the rest of the world, to look at South Asia's own diaspora as a particular case of Asian outmigration and the formation of a global diasporic community. We must first look in a little more detail at the making of the South Asian diaspora, particularly its dimensions and the diverse strands within it. By the end of the 20th century South Asians could be found living in every continent. The largest share of the diaspora was to be found in other Asian countries, particularly Malaysia, as a result of centuries of trading and more modern patterns of unskilled labour required to work on plantations. Europe was home to the next largest group, particularly the UK, a population which was primarily established after the Second World War. There are also significant numbers of South Asians in parts of Africa, particularly in East and South Africa, as well as in the Middle East, the Caribbean, North America and the Pacific. Their fortunes over time have varied. In some places the numbers have actually decreased as a result of political pressure, East Africa and Fiji being examples where long established communities began to haemorrhage at particular times of pressure in the late 20th century. In Australia and the USA numbers of primary migrants have risen as immigration rules have been relaxed and opportunities given in preference to skilled workers and professionals. In other places despite tighter immigration controls, family reunions, the import of spouses and natural increase have led to a significant growth in local South Asian populations. The United Kingdom is the primary example of this latter trend. In 1961 the UK's South Asian population stood at 106,300. By 1971 it had risen to 413, 155. In 1981 it had risen to 1.2 million. By 1991 to 1.4 million and in 2001 it was 2,083,759—which was 3.6 per cent of the total population. The current South Asian figures are not migration figures, of course. Over half the South Asian population in the UK is now UK born. This is in stark contrast to the social nature of the early South Asian migrants to Britain, who were mostly single male migrants living together in groups of kin or village neighbours. Family reunions and the bearing of new generations of boys and girls of South Asian ethnic descent in the UK transformed the diaspora population, making it permanent and self-sustaining. Although South Asian households tend to be larger than average households in the UK, the size of families is decreasing, for, as with migrants into economically developed societies everywhere, female fertility levels drop over time and as migrant groups rise up the socioeconomic ladder, just as they are doing in Asia itself.

If these are some of the dimensions of the global South Asian diaspora, how did it come into being? We touched on some of the bold demographic trends earlier, but we need to remember the great complexity of the South Asian diaspora as it has been built up over time. It has been made up of many interlocking strands, many different movements of people out of the subcontinent. The earliest people to leave India were traders, who fanned out east towards Southeast Asia, and west towards the eastern seaboard of Africa. Trading communities from southern India and Parsis were prominent in the eastward movement, while Gujaratis, Shia Muslims from western India and Parsis dominated the trade west to Africa. Gandhi's original one-year contract to South Africa in 1893 was of course with a Gujarati Muslim firm. Just 20 years earlier a British official had commented with amazement on the highly developed Indian presence in Zanzibar and on the East African coast. He found Indians 'monopolising whatever trade there might be, spending and keeping their accounts in Guzeratti, whether in small shops, or as large mercantile houses. Their silent occupation of this coast ... is one of the most curious things of the kind I know. It has been going on for forty years but I had no idea, till I came here, how complete their monopoly has become.'[6] Clearly the expanding presence of the British empire helped to make conditions conducive to peaceful trade for Indian commercial migrants. It also offered employment for many semi-skilled and trained people who went within the empire as clerks, technicians, engineers, policemen and civil servants. Such people contributed greatly to the formation of diaspora populations in Southeast Asia and East Africa. Contract workers became temporary members of Indian diaspora society as they helped in particular projects. The East African railways were built largely by Indians, many of them being from Punjab. Some stayed on after their contract ended, such as the Sikhs who were enumerated in the 1921 Kenyan census. However, on a much larger scale the global presence of the British empire enabled the movement of many thousands of unskilled indentured labourers to other parts of the empire outside Asia which needed workers, particularly in plantations where slaves had once worked. Such people were often desperately poor before they left India, had little idea where they were going, and certainly no understanding of the nature of a long sea voyage or the severe

6. Sir Bartle Frere (1873), quoted in Gregory (1971).

conditions which awaited them in their new homes. Although indentured labourers could return to India after their indentures expired, comparatively few did so: they had little to return to and had often lost all contact with their kin or neighbours in India. Those who stayed on as free men and women essentially founded the diaspora communities of today in such places as Natal, Fiji and the Caribbean.[7]

The ending of the British empire in the mid-20th century did not end the outmigration of people from South Asia. However, the migrants from independent India, Pakistan and the Bangladesh were in many respects different. Increasingly migration became a family movement rather than male movement alone which had characterised so much of the outward migration in the imperial years. This was to be of major consequence in the social establishment of permanent, self-perpetuating diaspora communities. Some migrants were unskilled or low-skilled workers who travelled mainly to the UK where their labour was needed in heavy industry as the UK rebuilt its economy after the war. Others were forced out of East Africa by 'Africanisation' policies from the late 1960s and went to a number of receiving countries but primarily to England, to join existing Indian communities there, particularly in the city of Leicester. Yet another labour destination of increasing importance from the 1970s was the Middle East, where newly rich countries with the profits of oil needed labour to build the infrastructure of booming economies. Increasingly South Asia provided more skilled and professional workers for this region: probably about half the Indian migrants to the Gulf region came from the state of Kerala alone. Finally there was a later 20th century wave of skilled migrants to countries which had formerly closed their borders to migrants of Asian ethnic background—Australia, New Zealand, Canada and of course supremely the USA.

The creation of a post-imperial diaspora, often building on earlier foundations, was in another way rather different. Before the mid-20th century South Asian overseas communities had been discreet groups, often with little contact with each other, not least because of difficulties in communications and the cost of travel, as well as the very specific origins of the different groups. By the end of the 20th

7. On indentured labour see Tinker (1974) and Northrup (1995).

century the South Asian diaspora was a truly global community, experienced as such by many of its members, rather than being just an analytical tool for scholars. For the reasons for this we have to look to modern communications and modes of travel—cheaper air travel, the telephone and the Internet. South Asians overseas keep in touch with the land of their familial origin by constant visits, phone calls and the Internet. Moreover they tend now to move onward from one destination to another, becoming 'twice and thrice migrants'. As their families have fanned out across several continents in extended marriage networks within the diaspora, so they quite literally feel part of a diaspora which reaches round the globe.

Given the size and diversity of the South Asian global diaspora, what issues does this raise in the present and for the future? We might first turn to issues arising from the diaspora's relations with its land of origin. I use the phrase 'land of origin' advisedly because in a sense it is not right to call the countries of South Asia the diaspora homeland as for so many overseas South Asians their homeland in the sense of their natal land is now outside South Asia. The interest of Indian governments of all political hues in its NRI populations from the beginning of the 21st century is a clear indication of the significance of diaspora populations in the view of India and the world. Other South Asian countries have not developed such sophisticated means of recognising diaspora populations and offering them new ways of reconnecting with their land of origin. In large part this is because Indians in the diaspora tend to be wealthier and more politically aware than Pakistanis or Bangladeshis, for example, and more capable of making their demands and interests felt. Nonetheless diaspora Pakistanis and Bangladeshis are of great significance to the countries from which they or their forebears came.

The first, most obvious and more easily measurable[8] aspect of this connection is financial—remittances of various kinds. These can range from presents in kind brought home on family trips, money sent back to build homes or other amenities to one's village, to regular financial

8. There are considerable difficulties in measuring all the flows of remittance, particularly the less formal modes of money transfer. See World Bank Development Reports 1978 to 2011, at *http://econ.worldbank.org/WBSITE/EXTERNAL/EXTDEC/EXTRESEARCH/EXTWDRS/0,,contentMDK:20227703~pagePK:478093~piPK:477627~theSitePK:477624,00.html*, about methodology and results.

remittances from workers abroad to their home region for family consumption, to formal investment by diaspora businessmen. Remittances to South Asia have been rising through the last four decades. In broad terms the poorer the home economy the greater the impact of such foreign monies will be. Various studies of Bangladesh, for example, have shown the immense significance at the end of the 20th century of foreign remittances by Bangladeshi migrants to the UK and the Middle East in particular. They play a crucial part in the macroeconomic viability of the country. At the micro level much of the total is invested in the rural economy, particularly in house building, land purchase, and the acquisition of machinery and other equipment including vehicles and consumer durables. Although the spending of remittances has often helped to boost the rural economy and improve its infrastructure, the availability of foreign money has important and unexpected socioeconomic effects—such as pushing up the price of land, increasing the size of a rentier landlord class, and altering marriage patterns. Not surprisingly migrants have become much sought-after marriage partners, and the cost of weddings, including dowry, has risen substantially. It was estimated that households with migrants spent nearly 9 per cent of the remittances on weddings![9] By 2008 remittances were a huge 11.4 per cent of GDP. In the mid-'80s remittances back to Pakistan were running at nearly six times those returning to Bangladesh—at well over $2,500 million. In 2008 remittances to Pakistan were 4.2 per cent of GDP. Remittances to India were initially somewhat lower and of course not nearly so significant in macroeconomic terms as a result of India's larger and more developed economy.[10] However by 2008 they were 4.2 per cent of GDP, a huge rise in absolute terms. By 2004 India had reached the top of the list of countries with significant remittance flows, receiving $23 billion, outstripping Mexico, the Philippines and even China. (In this year Pakistan stood 5th in the list with an inflow of $ 4.1 billion and Bangladesh 7th with an inflow of $3.4 billion.) In certain Indian regions foreign earned money is of immense importance, particularly Punjab and Kerala. Kerala's have grown dramatically since 1990 and

9. Islam (1995).
10. Knerr (1990).

in 2004 stood at Rs. 185 billion, one quarter of the state domestic product and 1.74 times the revenue receipts of the state. Significantly in Kerala these inflows have led to increased family expenditure on education and health in households with migrant members, as well as on the purchase of land and houses and consumer goods. It is not surprising that the Indian government began to take serious steps to attract NRI investment as part of the '90s liberalisation of economic policy.[11] It is a policy which, increasingly refined and expanded in recent years, is paying off dramatically. Although the current economic circumstances will slow down this rise in remittances, they remain a main aspect of the significance of the connection between diaspora Indians, and indeed all diaspora South Asians and their countries of origin.

Another aspect of the diaspora connection could loosely be called the cultural connection. At least in the case of the Indian diaspora overseas groups deliberately seek to intervene in society in the land of their origin with varied cultural agendas, some charitable and religious, and some more overtly political. Diaspora Sikhs for example are heavily involved in *seva* or service to the ancestral homeland of Punjab, either by personal work on return visits or by money donations to Punjab charities. The causes may include help for widows and orphans, medical, educational and welfare programmes, and the refurbishment of religious sites. Hindu cultural and religious organisations in the diaspora also act as a conduit for money aimed at the disadvantaged, often with a cultural agenda of 'uplift'. The Swaminarayan movement, for example, has an elaborate project of religious, cultural and social outreach, particularly among tribal peoples in Gujarat, which it proudly proclaims on its British website. Potentially more sinister is the evidence that Hindus in the diaspora are more prone to viewing India as a Hindu nation, divorced as they are from the realities of India as a 'plural' society. They have certainly been an important source of funding for parties such as the BJP who share this vision both of a clearly defined global 'Hinduism' and India as a Hindu nation.

---

11. For an interesting case study see Thandi (2004). On remittances in general and the impact on Kerala in particular see S.I. Rajan's contribution to Lal *et al.* (2006): 75-77.

Given the growing financial leverage of diaspora South Asians it is to be expected that they will make significant interventions in the cultural and political life of their countries of origin, even if they choose to remain citizens of their new homelands. How this will pan out in India, where a formal political status in India for NRIs is well established, is still unclear. There is already evidence that on some political issues diaspora groups have been seriously involved, even if they do not have formal citizens' rights in their land of origin sometimes with unwelcome results for the governments of South Asia. Britain has a very significant population of Pakistanis of Kashmiri origin, and they have been heavily committed to the cause of a united Kashmir, involving themselves in Kashmiri politics but also lobbying British, EU and US politicians on this issue. Younger members of the diaspora with no direct memories of living in pre-partition Kashmir are also involved in this movement, not just the older generation who actually moved away from the subcontinent. Sikhs in the diaspora have also been active participants in the politics of their Punjabi homeland, particularly during the troubled decade of the 1980s. For the Indian government this posed a profound problem—because the UK, for example, seemed to be a safe haven for people who were fermenting dissent in their Indian region of origin. Hindu nationalist groups such as the VHP and the RSS have also mushroomed amongst the diaspora, and in the USA the Federation of Hindu Associations (FHA) coordinates public action in the name of Hindu nationalism. No South Asian government can now forget the potential political influence of their diaspora. Nor can they blame their diasporas for becoming 'hostages to fortune'. Luckily most Indian diaspora groups are now well embedded in their new homes, are learning to participate in their political institutions, and are appreciated for their contribution to national culture and wealth. However, the pressure on Indians in Fiji in recent years, and the expulsion of Indians from Uganda by Idi Amin in 1972, are a reminder that we live increasingly in a global society, and that modern communications mean that Indian citizens at home very quickly hear and see on their television screens what is happening to their diaspora kin. Should anything like the East African crisis recur this would pose a major diplomatic problem for the governments of the subcontinent.

Finally we have to recognise the issues posed by the contemporary diaspora involvement in global politics. India had a foretaste of this potential problem with the Sikh diaspora's involvement in the politics of the Punjab in the '80s. By the start of the 21st century it was clear that radical Islamic movements had begun to attract younger members of the Muslim parts of the diaspora, particularly those originally from Pakistan. This was clear in the 2005 terrorist attacks on the London transport system. Three of the four bombers who died in these bomb attacks were young men from northern England whose families had originated in Pakistan. In Afghanistan today so-called 'foreign fighters' alongside the more local Taliban include people from among the diaspora. Typically those involved in the global politics of terror in the name of Islam tend to be young men with a significant level of education. These are the people to whom a radical international appeal for the violent defence of religion is made which appears to fulfill a need for identity, purpose and connection which is not available through the more routine practices of religion within their own diaspora communities, or in the roles offered to them in their new countries of residence. This is a hugely complex issue which is not the direct concern of this chapter. However it is a critical problem which needs the concerted and coordinated attention of both the countries of origin and of destination. For both sets of countries this is a problem both domestic and 'out there' which we all ignore at our peril.

Conclusion

Briefly to conclude as we look towards the 21st century. Because of the growing interconnection of the different parts of the world, and particularly because of mass migration forming major diasporas, being 'Asian' is now increasingly a global experience. It is no longer possible to consider oneself Chinese, Indian, Pakistani and so forth without acknowledging that the sense of national identity is modified and inflected by, the connection with major populations of Asian diaspora in all continents, to whom one is joined by ties of kinship. For Asian people in the diaspora this means holding in balance a sense of belonging to a land of origin while being citizens of the new homeland, and often having kin in yet other countries and continents.

Many Asians are truly 'transnational' people. I have focussed on the diaspora experience of South Asian countries and peoples, and I hope I have shown the scale of outmovement from the subcontinent and the diversity of the consequent diaspora communities. What is also clear is that no governments in Asia and particularly in South Asia can ignore this diaspora for its existence provides opportunities and also dangers!

References

Brown, Judith M. (2006). *Global South Asians. Introducing the Modern Diaspora.* Cambridge: CUP.

Clarke, C., C. Peach and S. Vertovec (eds.) (1990). *South Asians Overseas. Migration and Ethnicity.* Cambridge: CUP. More generally there is

Cohen, R. (ed.) (1995). *The Cambridge Survey of World Migration.* Cambridge: CUP.

Cohen, R. (1997). *Global Diasporas: An introduction.* London: UCL Press.

Gregory, R.G. (1971). *India And East Africa. A History of Race Relations within the British Empire.* Oxford: Clarendon Press. pp.40-41.

Islam, M. (1995). "Bangladeshi Migration: An Impact Study", in Cohen (ed.), *The Cambridge Survey of World Migration.* pp.360-66.

Knerr, B. (1990). "South Asian Countries as Competitors on the World Labour Market". Chapter 8 of C. Clarke, C. Peach and S. Vertovec (eds.), *South Asians Overseas: Migration and Ethnicity.* Cambridge: CUP.

Lal, B.V., P. Reeves and R. Rai (eds.) (2006). *The Encyclopedia of the Indian Diaspora.* Editions Didier Millet in association with the National Singapore: University of Singapore.

Northrup, D. (1995). *Indentured Labour in the Age of Imperialism, 1834-1922.* Cambridge: CUP.

Pan, L. (ed.) (1999). *The Encyclopedia of the Chinese Overseas.* Cambridge, Mass: Harvard University Press.

Thandi, S. (2004). "*Vilayati Pasia*: Some Reflections on the Potential of Diaspora Finance in the Socio-Economic Development of Indian Punjab", Chapter 11 of I. Talbot and S. Thandi (eds.) (2004). *People On the Move. Punjabi Colonial, and Post-Colonial Migration.* Karachi: OUP.

Tinker, H. (1974). "A New System of Slavery", *The Export of Indian Labour Overseas 1830-1920.* London: OUP.

8

Asia's Urban Futures and its Implications for Security

SARITA AZAD and NARENDRA S. SISODIA

Introduction

Researchers from North Carolina State University and the University of Georgia, while collaborating with United Nations population estimates, settled on May 23, 2009 as the date on which, for the first time in human history the global population became more urban than rural.[1] While this date is symbolic, it signifies a 'tipping point', a moment of transformation. According to the United Nations *World Population Prospects* report,[2] the global percentage of urban population grew from 13 per cent (220 million) in 1900 to 29 per cent (732 million) in 1950 and to 49 per cent (3.2 billion) in 2005. The world's total population is estimated to go up to 8.2 billion by 2030. If current trends continue, by 2030, 4.9 billion people constituting 60 per cent of the global population will be living in urban areas. According to UN-HABITAT[3] *homo sapiens* 'the wise human' will become the *homo sapiens urbanus* over the next 20 years. The current annual urban growth in South Asia is an estimated 2.53 per cent—faster than that of Asia (2.4 per cent) and the world (1.98 per cent).[4] Presently, more than half of the world's mega cities[5] are in Asia. The growth of these cities is unprecedented with their populations doubling every 15 to 20 years.[6] It is estimated that by 2030, 2.6 billion

1. Beall *et al.* (2010).
2. UN (2006).
3. UN-HABITAT (2010).
4. UNFPA (2007).
5. A metropolitan area with a total population in excess of 10 million people.
6. UN-HABITAT (2009).

people will live in Asian cities, representing 53 per cent of the world's urban population.[7]

Cities offer positive advantages of agglomeration, economies of scale, better infrastructure and economic and social opportunities; they serve as cultural melting pots; as centres of knowledge and innovation; as forums for political engagement and as sites of public investment.[8] Thus, they become magnets for people from less developed regions. But cities are also marked by congestion, slums, deprivation and poverty with large pockets of ungoverned or poorly governed spaces that are vulnerable to organised crime, violence and sometimes urban warfare.

In the coming decades, Asia will be a principal site of rapid urbanisation, with important consequences for human and national security. This chapter argues that if 'business-as-usual' continues in Asia's ongoing process of urbanisation, it will compound national and human security challenges, rendering pockets of dense growth particularly vulnerable. The chapter is divided into four parts: it first discusses the drivers and broad features of urbanisation followed by discussion on the consequent security challenges of this growth. Next, an attempt has been made to sketch the plausible security scenarios consequent to this growth and finally it summarises our conclusions.

Urbanisation: Drivers and Trends

Drivers

The most important driver of urban growth is natural growth. Globally, natural increase accounts for nearly 60 per cent of urban growth.[9] Asia accounts for more than two thirds of the annual increase in the global urban population. Southeast Asia and West Asia have annual population growth rates of about 3.6 per cent compared to the 3 per cent in East Asia (less if China is excluded). By around 2020-2025, urban growth rates in these sub-regions are expected to decline to 2.2, 2.0 and 1.6 per cent, respectively.

Migration is an important component of Asia's urbanisation.

7. IGES (2001).
8. Koonings and Kruijt (2009).
9. UNESCAP (forthcoming); UN (1993).

Between 20-30 per cent of urban population growth comes from rural-urban migration.[10]

Availability of employment and economic opportunities are the key factors that attract people from rural to urban areas. Today, around 65 per cent of the world's economically active population works in industry and services, mostly in urban areas.[11] Migrant youth play a key role in the shaping of cities and towns.

Agriculture is becoming less labour intensive because of mechanisation and employment opportunities are shifting to manufacturing and service sectors which flourish mostly in urban areas. Livelihood opportunities in rural areas are also shrinking due to declining viability of small holdings, and damage to arable lands due to environmental and other factors. Globalisation has increased economic opportunities in cities and urban agglomerations.

Another factor driving urban growth is instability and civil strife in parts of the global South coupled with weak governance. Cities in developing nations may be deficient in many ways, but they are perceived to be safer.

In Figure 8.1, we list the various pull and push factors driving urbanisation and show the negative and positive consequences of urbanisation. As indicated in Figure 8.1, factors like poor infrastructure, unemployment and deficient medical facilities drive people to migrate from rural to urban areas.

Trends and Features

The principal sites of urban transition in the coming decades will be Asia and Africa. The world's most developed regions, America and Europe, are already 70 per cent urban; by 2030 80 per cent of their population will be urban. At present, only 37 per cent of Asia's population is urban; over the next two decades it is expected to rise to 55 per cent (Figure 8.2).

---

10. Mathur (2006).
11. Thomas (2008).

Figure 8.1

Factors Driving Urban Growth in Asia

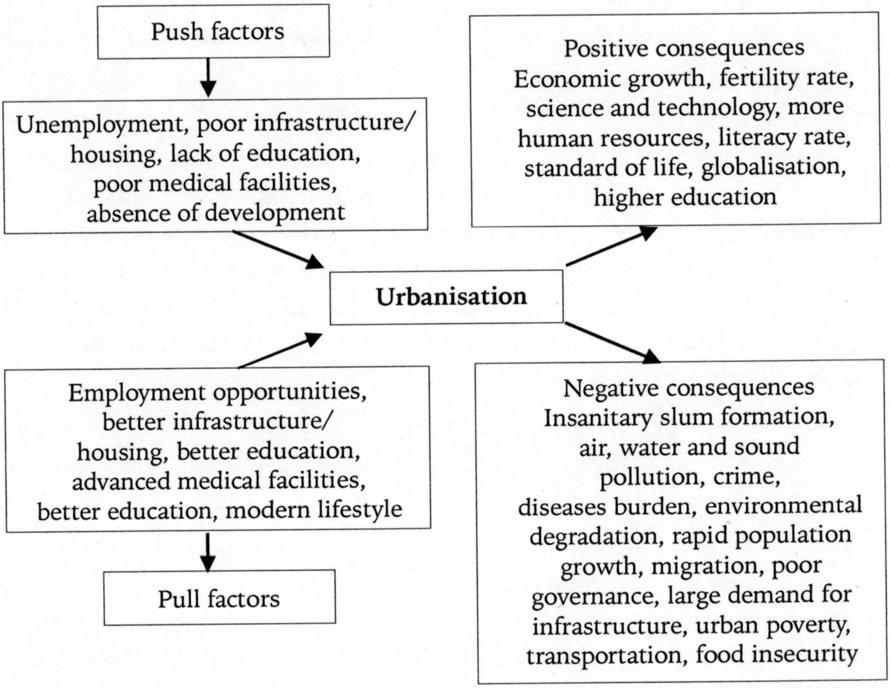

Some noteworthy features of this demographic change would be as follows:

1) The proportionate demographic weight of the developed countries will decline by nearly 25 per cent, thus transferring economic power to developing nations.
2) In the developed countries, labour will age and decline in numbers, thus depressing their economic growth and increasing demand for immigrant workers.
3) Most of the world's population growth will be concentrated in today's poorest, youngest and most heavily Muslim countries, lacking quality education, capital and employment opportunities.

Figure 8.2

Trends in Urbanisation by Region

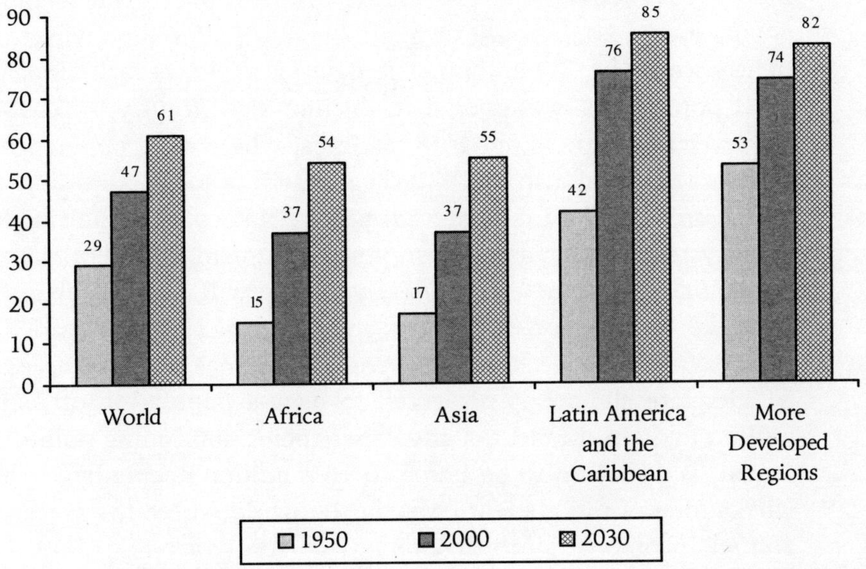

Source: "Trends in Urbanization, by Region", at *http://colli239.fts.educ.msu.edu/2006/12/31/ urbanization-trends-2004/*

4) For the first time in history, most of the world's population will be concentrated in cities, with the largest urban centres located in the world's poorest countries, where policing, sanitation, medical facilities are scanty.

5) Between now and 2050, according to the World Bank estimates, over 70 per cent of the world's population growth will take place in 24 countries classified by the Bank as low income or lower middle income with an average per capita income of less than $3855 in 2008.

6) An important feature of the ongoing urbanisation is the emergence of new mega cities. The two most populated countries of Asia; China and India, are experiencing the urbanisation process on a remarkable scale. From being 45 per cent urbanised today, China is expected to be 60 per cent urbanised by 2030 (Figure 8.3). India, which is 37 per cent urbanised at present is expected to be 41 per cent urbanised by

2030[12] (Figure 8.3). Together, China and India are projected to account for almost one-third of the world's urban dwellers by 2030.[13] Figure 8.3 shows that China's projected urban population by 2030 would be approximately 850 million whereas India's would be 500 million. The figure also shows that China's rural population is expected to decline significantly by 2030. However the same is not true for India, where rural population numbers may stabilise by 2030. The growth of mega cities in the Indian subcontinent is largely driven by rural poverty and high fertility rates rather than economic dynamism. Many of them have fairly stagnant economies, yet they will have to absorb massive population increases over the next few decades. Mumbai, where at least half the population does not have access to adequate shelter, is projected to have a population of 22.6 million in 2015. Karachi, a city experiencing continuing political unrest, is projected to be home to 16.2 million people by 2015. Dhaka, one of the poorest cities in the world where the average annual income of slum dwellers is currently around $150, is likely to have 17.9 million inhabitants. By 2015 there will be 21 mega cities worldwide of which 11 will be in Asia. In fact, four of these Asian cities will have over 20 million inhabitants.

7) Another major feature of rapid urban growth is the 'urban sprawl'[14]—scattered development with mixed land use in isolated locations on the fringes of a city—that breeds tension, undermines local resources and destroys open spaces.[15] In urban sprawls, typically, land is developed at a rate that is faster than the pace of population growth. In Kansas city, for instance, between 1990 and 1996, the population increased by 5 per cent whereas developed land went up by 70 per cent.[16] The World Bank[17] has noted that 2,000 cities with more than 100,000

12. Roberts and Kanaley (2006).
13. UN (2004).
14. Frumkin *et al.* (2004).
15. Burchell *et al.* (1998); Burchell (1999).
16. Brockerhoff (2000).
17. Angel *et al.* (2005).

Figure 8.3

Urbanisation Trends in China and India

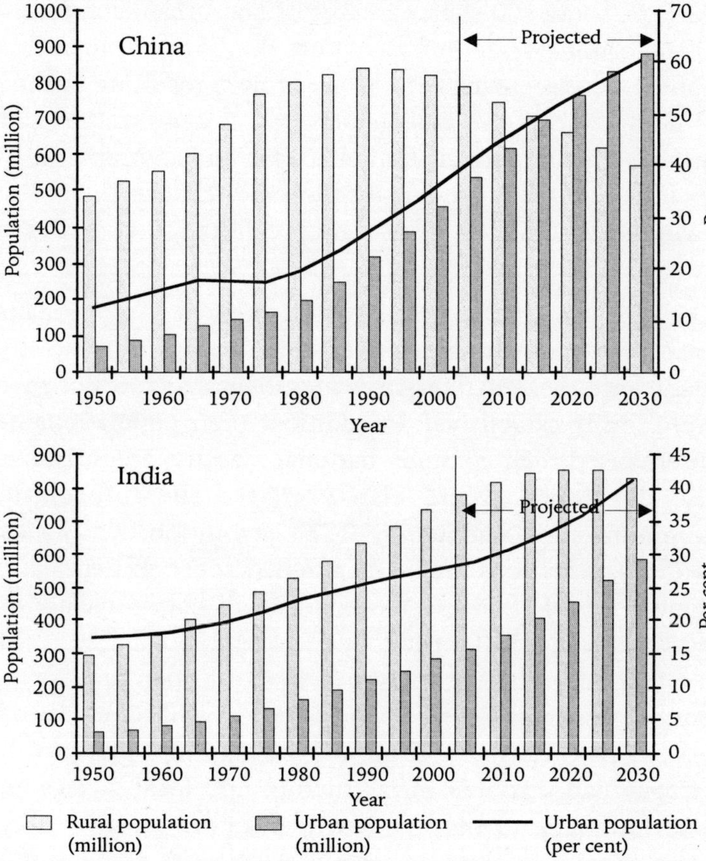

Source: Lamia *et al.* (2009) and Wendell (n.d.).

inhabitants had total built-up areas of the order of nearly 200,000 square kilometres—with average densities of some 8,000 persons per square kilometre.[18] If average densities continue to decline at the annual rate of 1.7 per cent—as was the case in the past decade—the built-up area of developing country cities will increase to more than 600,000 square

18. The weighted average built-up area density for developing country's cities with provisional sample of 90 in 2000 was found to be 8,049 persons per square kilometer. See Roberts and Kanaley (2006).

kilometres by 2030. Thus by 2030 these cities are projected to triple their land area, with every new resident converting, on average, some 160 square metres of non-urban land to urban use in the coming years. Infrastructure development in such areas is unlikely to keep pace with urban growth resulting in the growth of slums, lacking in basic amenities. Recent studies show that urban sprawls could also influence the Indian monsoons. Factors such as agricultural intensification and change in land use may have led to reduced monsoons precipitation over the last few years.[19]

8) The cities in the developed world grew at a more manageable pace than those in Asia's developing countries. Also, this took place once these nation-states and their structures of governance were firmly established. In addition, their populations had fully internalised their common national identity. The urbanisation of the developed world also predates the information and communication technology (ICT) revolution, which has led to rising expectations and a heightened sense of deprivation. The population of Dhaka, for example, will have virtually exploded by a staggering 5,400 per cent between 1950 and 2015. Karachi's population will have increased by 2,000 per cent in the same period. Conversely New York's populace will have grown by only 30 per cent between 1950 and 2015. But New York by 1950 already had a robust infrastructure and local government that was fully able to keep pace with its growth. If New York city were to grow at the same rate as Dhaka, its population in 2015 would be 604 million—two and a quarter times the current population of the US.[20]

Continuing urban dysfunction can only make extremist ideologies more appealing to the vast number of marginalised city dwellers, desperate for change. Among the consequences of Karachi's rapid growth were dramatic changes in the ethnic mix of its population and virtual collapse of law and order over much of the municipal landscape. As Karachi grows to become one of the five most populous

19. Niyogi *et al.* (2010).
20. UN-HABITAT (2009).

cities of the planet, the city's inability to control crime and terrorism will have dire consequences for Pakistan and its neighbours.

Urbanisation and its Implications for Security

This section will analyse the implications of urbanisation primarily from the perspective of human security. These consequences need not be inevitable, but are likely if business-as-usual continues in the domain of public policy and practice.

First, as pointed out elsewhere in this chapter, deprivation, poverty and social exclusion will become predominantly urban. Between 1993 and 2002, the number of poor people living on $1 a day declined by 150 million in rural areas, but increased by 50 million in urban areas.[21] Deprivation and disparities are particularly evident in slums and shanty towns, where inhabitants have no security and lack basic amenities like water. The poor in such habitations may have to pay 50 times more for clean water than those living in fully serviced colonies.

Second, in many urban spaces, particularly in poorer and marginal neighbourhoods, effective governance and public institutions are non-existent or are completely overwhelmed by the sheer magnitude of the governance challenge. This leads to situations where violence becomes 'the basis for alternative "parallel" forms of order, control, resource distribution, legitimacy and identity.'[22] In such pockets, the poor face the constant risk of low intensity urban warfare and live in a chronic state of insecurity.

Third, haphazard and rapid urbanisation leads to severe environmental degradation and the poorly served areas become at once the sources of disease and victims of epidemics. Cities are thus simultaneously environmental culprits and also prone to environmental disasters. The poor are highly vulnerable to devastation as a result of extreme weather events. Urban centres close to low-lying coastal zones are especially liable to flooding and economic loss.

Fourth, urban areas are marked by considerable social, cultural, religious, ethnic and linguistic diversity. These diversities accentuate

---

21. UN-HABITAT (2006 and 2007).
22. Haub and Sharma (2006).

tensions and conflicts arising from other factors, such as competition for limited opportunities and resources. Rapidly urbanising centres also witness a youth bulge, fosters violence in an environment of deprivation and denial.

Fifth, urban centres are increasingly becoming sources and targets of urban terror and warfare. They offer attractive opportunities for shock and publicity, greatly valued by terrorists. Recent terror strikes have targeted iconic symbols in cities like New York, Washington and Mumbai.

Sixth, another negative consequence of urban violence is the deterioration in inter-communal relations. As observed by Kruijt and Koonings, 'The fault lines of urban exclusion are drawn by class, caste, race, ethnicity and religion.'[23]

Finally as P.H. Liotta and James F. Miskel argue, '"ungoverned mega cities" create "an enduring culture of outrage" among large numbers of unemployed and underemployed.'[24] The declining capacities of public and economic institutions strain the relationship between the citizens and officials and populations blame each other for any disparities in their material conditions.

In spite of the many remarkable improvements made in Asian cities over the last 25 years, a third of Asia's urban population still lives in houses that lack sufficient living space. Table 8.1 shows that only 58 per cent of the urban population in India has access to proper sanitation, as compared to 92 per cent in Pakistan and 75 per cent in Bangladesh. China and Bangladesh rank the highest and the lowest on the Human Development Index (HDI) which is a measure of country's life expectancy, education and a standard of living. In general, countries with high GDP have better housing, water, sanitation services—but emit more $C0_2$.

The UN-HABITAT report notes that 63 per cent of south Asia's slum dwellers are Indian.[25] The largest number of slum dwellers in the country live in Mumbai (6.5 million)—more than the entire

23. Ooi and Phua (2008).

24. Godfrey and Julien (2005).

25. Leon (2008).

Table 8.1

Characteristics of Urbanisation in Asian Cities

	GDP Growth (Per cent) (2004)	*Sanitation, (Per cent of Urban Population with Access to Improved Sanitation) (2002)*	*Water (Per cent of Urban Population with Access to Improved Water Sources) (2002)*	*Slum Population (Per cent of Urban Population) (2001)*	*Poverty, (Per cent of Urban Population below National Poverty Line) (1998)*	*CO_2 Emissions (Metric Tonnes Per Capita) (2000)*
China	9.5	69	92	38	2.0	2.7
India	6.91	58	96	56	24.7	1.0
Bangladesh	5.52	75	82	85	36.6	0.2
Pakistan	6.38	92	95	74	24.2	0.7
Indonesia	5.13	71	89	23	N.A.	1.4

Sources: World Bank (2005). *World Development Indicators 2005*; World Resources Institute (2005). *World Resources Institute 2005: The Wealth of the Poor: Managing Ecosystems to Fight Poverty.*

population of Norway, Delhi (1.9 million), Kolkata (1.5 million) and Chennai (0.8 million). Over the next 20 years, cities will be the face of global poverty, with the growth rate of the urban poor being higher than their rural counterparts and consequently the risk of HIV/AIDS, tuberculosis, malaria and lifestyle diseases will increase substantially.

An important factor with potential to influence security in urban areas would be the ethnic and religious composition of the population.[26] Changes in the ethnic or religious composition of urban areas, coupled with other factors, create tensions and lead to violence. A case in point is India, where the Muslim minority is predominantly rural. However, its 35.7 per cent urbanised population is more than 27.8 per cent of its overall numbers and this trend is likely to continue. According to the Sachar Committee Report,[27] many Muslims have a perception of being discriminated against partly because they are under-represented in various walks of life. Rapid globalisation has further radicalised communities. Since poorer sections of society tend to live in ghettos these could further lead to the mushrooming of

26. Basant and Shariff (2010); Armstrong (2002).

27. GoI (2006).

minority dominated suburbs. Areas where large-scale migration is the norm as in the metropolitan area of Mumbai and Assam, ethnic or communal tensions can exacerbate. It should be noted that relatively larger numbers of the Muslims work as craftsmen, mechanics, electricians or are employed in the IT sector. These vocations are conducive to the formation of formidable networks. It is estimated that of the 48 countries with an annual population growth rate of 2 per cent or more, 28 are Muslim majority countries or countries with a Muslim minority in excess of 33 per cent. This trend needs to be viewed in the context that many Muslims live in poor communities that are vulnerable to radical appeals and many of them view the West with hostility.

Jack Goldstone of George Mason School of Public Policy, Virginia (US) believes that international terrorism may grow rapidly in developing countries. This could be facilitated by information technology, radical ideologies, concentration of vital targets and ample opportunities for hiring, sustaining and concealing terrorist networks.

Asia's Future Scenarios: 2030

Some scenarios that could emerge from these trends are as follows:

Scenario 1

If urban growth continues unchecked, one likely scenario is chronic urban chaos in several mega cities of Asia. The governance structures and public institutions in such cities are strained to the limit because of the continuous flow of migrants, poor housing, appalling sanitation, shortage of clean water, chronic power shortages and inadequate drainage. Vast tracts of urban spaces in slum areas no longer receive state protection. Law enforcement agencies rarely operate in such areas and they are often given over to gang lords and criminal networks who function with the connivance of the police. Hapless citizens have no option but to seek their protection but also have to pay extortion money to get it. The changing religious or ethnic composition in such urban centres creates acute competition for the limited resources and economic opportunities. Trafficking in humans, arms and drugs as well as violence and intra-gang warfare flourish in the absence of any law enforcement agencies.

Cities like Lagos in Nigeria and Karachi in Pakistan are already witnessing acute lawlessness, crime and violence. There is good evidence to show that the Mumbai terror attacks which resulted in the killing of 166 people in November 2008 was planned in Karachi. It was from here that the 10 gunmen set off in a small boat to Mumbai, finally boarding a larger boat owned by Lashkar-e-Taiba(LeT). The inability of the government to offer basic education and other services in Karachi has created a void which is partly filled by religious schools or *madrassas*. Some of these are funded by Jihadist organisations which target not only the West but Pakistan and its neighbourhood.

Pakistan is slowly descending into a state of chronic strife. And with its armed forces and law enforcement agencies so preoccupied, urban governance is unlikely to receive adequate attention. By 2025, the challenge of governing Karachi will be further compounded with Lahore becoming another mega city with a population of 10.5 million. Six other cities in Pakistan will have a population of two million or more including Peshawar, a flourishing weapons market which is already facing chaos.

While the cities in Pakistan today present a picture of chronic chaos and insecurity, other cities in Asia could also face a similar fate. Some cities in the '10-40' window (the area in Africa and Asia between longitude 10^0 and 40^0) are of particular concern because of their location, size, role in global economy and environmental vulnerability. Of eight such mega cities, Dhaka, Karachi, Lahore, Mumbai and Jakarta are located in this region. One reason for their vulnerability is their extremely rapid pace of growth as compared to the more manageable pace of growth of cities like Tokyo, London and New York.

Scenario 2

One of the principal security challenges faced by human kind in 21st century is likely to be the proliferation of weapons of mass destruction (WMD). Terrorist organisations are known to have made serious efforts to acquire nuclear materials. They have also attempted to seek biological and chemical weapons. The possibility that groups like the Al-Qaeda or LeT will at some stage succeed in acquiring tactical nuclear weapons or sufficient materials to produce such devices can not be entirely ruled out. The burgeoning cities of Asia would be tempting targets for such groups as they offer the opportunity for maximum damage with spectacular effects. Unlike rational nation states' deterrence does not apply to non-state actors who follow their own logic in making decisions. Hence, unless the agencies responsible for protection of major cities take adequate precautionary measures in the coming two decades, massive destruction by a nuclear device or by biological or chemical weapons is possible. The prospect is too horrible to contemplate but such an eventuality can come to pass.

Scenario 3

Most mega cities are located close to sea coasts in low-lying areas. Cities like Mumbai experienced extensive damage because the city's drainage system was not being able to cope with the floods caused by rain. Climate scientists forecast extreme weather events and disasters like the Asian tsunami of December 2004. Even for a developed country like the United States, the consequences of Hurricane Katrina proved to be deeply embarrassing for the federal government. Massive damage caused by natural events coupled with inadequate capacity to cope could destabilise city and national governments.

Climate change and the consequent rise in sea level is also likely to lead to migration from coastal areas to urban centres, further increasing the pressure on the mega cities.

Scenario 4

Recent history shows that deprivation, denial of rights, absence of effective judiciary and poor enforcement of the rule of law coupled with poverty and lack of development can lead to widespread alienation of people. Such alienation is exacerbated by globalisation and the ICT revolution.

Left wing extremism, which currently affects 162 districts in 14 states of India has been acknowledged as the gravest security challenge for India.[28] There is ample evidence to show that Naxal activists are also trying to mobilise support in urban areas. Similar

28. Bakshi (2009).

movement can arise in other countries located within the '10-40' window. Chronic neglect and exclusion make people particularly prone to embracing radical ideologies and even resorting to violence. Ungoverned spaces offer an excellent opportunity for radical ideologues and their adherents to pursue their goals even by resorting to brutal violence.

Conclusions

In this chapter an attempt has been made to highlight the range of security challenges and risks that rapid urbanisation is likely to pose to Asian countries in the coming decades. While the poor and slum dwellers will be particularly vulnerable, it also argues that poorly managed urbanisation can adversely impact even regional and international security. Strategy planners therefore need to view the phenomenon of urbanisation in a strategic perspective. The main objective of this study is to underscore the security challenges likely to be encountered so as to encourage in-depth research of the phenomenon. Policy interventions needed to effectively tackle the challenges may, *inter alia,* include sound planning for urban growth and effective implementation of such plans; due emphasis to environmental protection; vigorous efforts to provide basic amenities; slum improvement; inclusive growth and in general, pro-poor policies. It would also be necessary to take appropriate precautions to prevent disasters or to mitigate and manage them, if they cannot be prevented.

References

Angel, S., S.C. Sheppard and D.L. Civco (2005). *The Dynamics of Global Urban Expansion.* Washington DC: Transport and Urban Development Department, The World Bank.

Armstrong, Karen (2002). *Islam: A Short History.* New York: The Modern Library.

Bakshi, G.D. (2009). "Left Wing Extremism in India: Context, Implications, and Response Options", *Claws,* No 9.

Basant, Rakesh and Abusaleh Shariff (ed.) (2010). *Handbook of Muslims: Empirical and Policy Perspectives.* Oxford: Oxford University Press.

Beall, Jo, B.G Khasnobis and R. Kanbur (eds.) (2010). *Urbanisation and Development: Multidisciplinary Perspectives.* Oxford: Oxford University Press.

Brockerhoff, M.P. (2000). "An Urbanising World", *Population Bulletin* 55/3: 3-43.

Burchell, Robert W. *et al.* (1998). "The Costs of Sprawl Revisited," *Transit Cooperative Research Program Report* 39. Washington DC: Transportation Research Board, National Research Council.

Burchell, Robert W. (1999). "The State of the Cities and Sprawl", at *http://www.huduser.org/publications/pdf/soc99.pdf* (Accessed on December 9, 2009).

Frumkin, Howard, Lawrence D. Frank and Richard Jackson (2004). *Urban Sprawl and Public Health: Designing, Planning, and Building for Healthy Communities.* Washington DC: Island Press.

Godfrey, R. and M. Julien (2005). "Urbanisation and Health", *Clinical Medicine* 5: 137.

GoI (2006). *Social, Economic and Educational Status of the Muslim Community of India, A Report*, Prime Minister's High Level Committee, Cabinet Secretariat, November 2006 at *http://minorityaffairs.gov.in/newsite/sachar/sachar_comm.pdf* (Accessed on December 09, 2009).

Haub, C. and O.P. Sharma (2006). "India's Population Reality: Reconciling Change and Tradition", *Population Bulletin* 61/1: 3.

Institute for Global Environmental Strategies (2001). *Towards a Sustainable Asia and the Pacific, Report of ECO ASIA Long-term Perspective Project Phase II,* at *http://www.airies.or.jp/publication/jeq/jeq_v6n4/jeq6_4.html#0* (Accessed on January 11, 2010).

Koonings, Kees and Dirk Kruijt (ed.) (2009). *Mega Cities: The Politics of Urban Exclusion and Violence in the Global South.* London: Zed Books.

Lamia, Kamal-Chaoui *et al. (2009).* "Urban Trends and Policy in China" OECD Regional Development Working Paper, 2009/1, at *http://www.oecd.org/dataoecd/28/21/42607972.pdf*

Leon, A. (2008). "Cities, Urbanisation and Health", *International Journal Epidemiol.*

Mathur, Om Prakash (2006). "Youth in an Urbanizing World: Asian Perspectives", *Regional Expert Group Meeting on Development Challenges for Young People*, Bangkok, March, 28 at *http://www.un.org/esa/socdev/unyin/workshops/regm_asia_om_prakash_mathur_paper.pdf* (Accessed on January 7, 2010).

McGee, Terence and C.J. Griffiths (Forthcoming). *Global Urbanisation: Towards the Twenty-First Century.* New York: United Nations. "Population Distribution and Migration".

Niyogi, Dev, C. Kishtawal, S. Tripathi and R.S. Govindaraju (2010). "Observational Evidence that Agricultural Intensification and Land Use Change May be Reducing the Indian Summer Monsoon Rainfall, *Water Resources Research* at *http://www.landsurface.org/publications/J92.pdf* (Accessed on January 9, 2010).

Ooi, Giol ling and Kai hong Phua (2008). "Urbanisation and Slum Formation", World Health Organization, Thematic Paper 13, at *http://www.who.or.jp/publications/2008-2010/KNUS%20thematic_papers/KNUS_ThematicPaper13.pdf* (Accessed on January 06, 2010).

Roberts, Brain and Trevor Kanaley (eds.) (2006). *Urbanisation and Sustainability in Asia.* Philippines: Asian Development Bank.

Thomas, Susan (2008). "Urbanisation as a Driver of Change", *The Arup Journal* 1: 58-68.

UN (2006). *World Urbanisation Prospects: The 2005 Revision.* New York: UN Press.

———. (2004). *World Urbanisation Prospects: The 2003 Revision.* New York: UN Press at *http://www.un.org/esa/population/publications/wup2003/WUP2003Report.pdf* (Accessed on Dec. 23, 2010).

———. (1993). Proceedings of the United Nations Expert Group Meeting on Population Distribution and Migration, Santa Cruz, Bolivia, January 18-22, (ST/ESA/SER.R/133)at *http://www.un.org/esa/population/pubsarchive/catalogue/catint1.htm#1* (Accessed on January 25, 2010).

UNFPA (2007). *State of the World Population 2007*, at *http://www.unfpa.org/swp/2007/english/introduction.html* (Accessed on January 09, 2010).

UN-HABITAT (2010). *State of the World's Cities 2010/2011: Bridging the Urban Divide.* United Nations Human Setllement Programme. London: Earthscan. p.20, at *http://www.unesco.org/ulis/cgibin/ulis.pl?catno=188619&set=4C6B0941_0_ 26&gp=0&lin=1&ll=1* (Accessed on January 06, 2010).

———. (2009). *Urban World: Innovative Cities: Why Learning is the Key to Urban Development.* UN-HABITAT Report-2009.

———. (2009). "Urban World: Scaling New Heights New Ideas in Urban Planning at *http://www.unhabitat.org/pmss/listItemDetails.aspx?publicationID=2881* (Accessed on January 12, 2010).

———. (2006-07). *State of the World's Cities*, UN-HABITAT Report at *http://www.unhabitat.org/pmss/listItemDetails.aspx?publicationID=2101* (Accessed on December 09, 2009).

Wendell, Cox (n.d.). "The Asian Urban Ascendency", at *http://www.newgeography.com/content/001480-the-asian-urban-ascendancy*

9

Pandemics and its Consequences for the Future of Asia

ALI KARAMI

An epidemic is an abnormally high occurrence of a disease in a particular population or geographic area. On the other hand, a pandemic is a global epidemic that crosses international boundaries. Therefore, the outbreak of pandemics has destructive economical, political, social, psychological and security consequences, not only in the effected country but also in the region and the world.

The world is facing a growing threat from new diseases that are jumping the human-animal species barrier as a result of environmental disruption, global warming and the progressive urbanisation of the planet.

At least 45 diseases that have passed from animals to humans have been reported to UN agencies in the last two decades, with the number expected to escalate in the coming years.

Leading Causes of Death Worldwide

About 15 million (25 per cent) of 57 million annual deaths worldwide are the direct result of infectious diseases according to figures published by the World Health Organization (see Figure 9.1).

Worst Pandemics in History

The worst pandemics in history have been smallpox (430 BC–1979) which killed more than 300 million people worldwide in the 20th century alone, and most of the native inhabitants of the Americas. Another deadly pandemic has been the Spanish Flu (1918–1919) killing 50 to 100 million people worldwide in less than two years. Cholera (1817-till date) has also resulted in eight pandemics, with thousands killed worldwide. The worst pandemic that we could face in the 21st century is AIDS (1981–till date) which has so far killed 25 million people worldwide.

Figure 9.1

Leading Causes of Death Worldwide

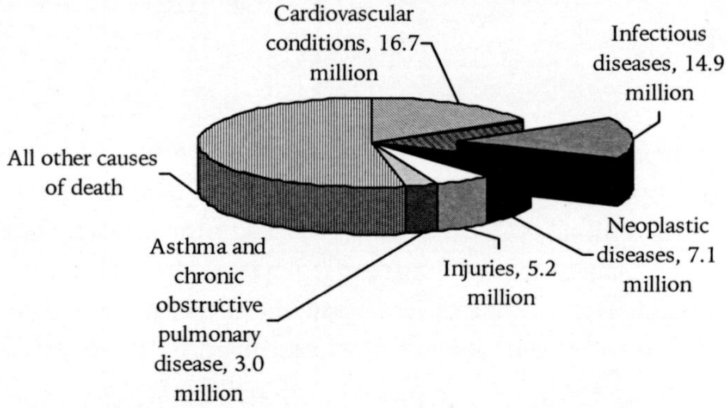

Infectious Diseases	*Annual Deaths (million)*
Respiratory infections	3.96
HIV/AIDS	2.77
Diarrhoeal diseases	1.80
Tuberculosis	1.56
Vaccine-preventable childhood diseases	1.12
Malaria	1.27
STDs (other than HIV)	0.18
Meningitis	0.17
Hepatitis B and C	0.16
Tropical parasitic diseases	0.13
Dengue	0.02
Other infectious diseases	1.76

Source: World Health Organization *(http://www.who.int/whr/en)*

Emerging Infectious Diseases

Pathogens with zoonotic origin have caused the majority of the emerging infectious disease events in the past six decades These diseases have the potential to cause significant morbidity and mortality in humans and animals, with resulting implications for international trade, travel, economies, and national security. Analysis of emerging infectious diseases from 1940 to the present demonstrates that the rate of emergence 'events' rose significantly over this period.

Figure 9.2

Global Examples of Emerging and Re-Emerging Infectious Diseases

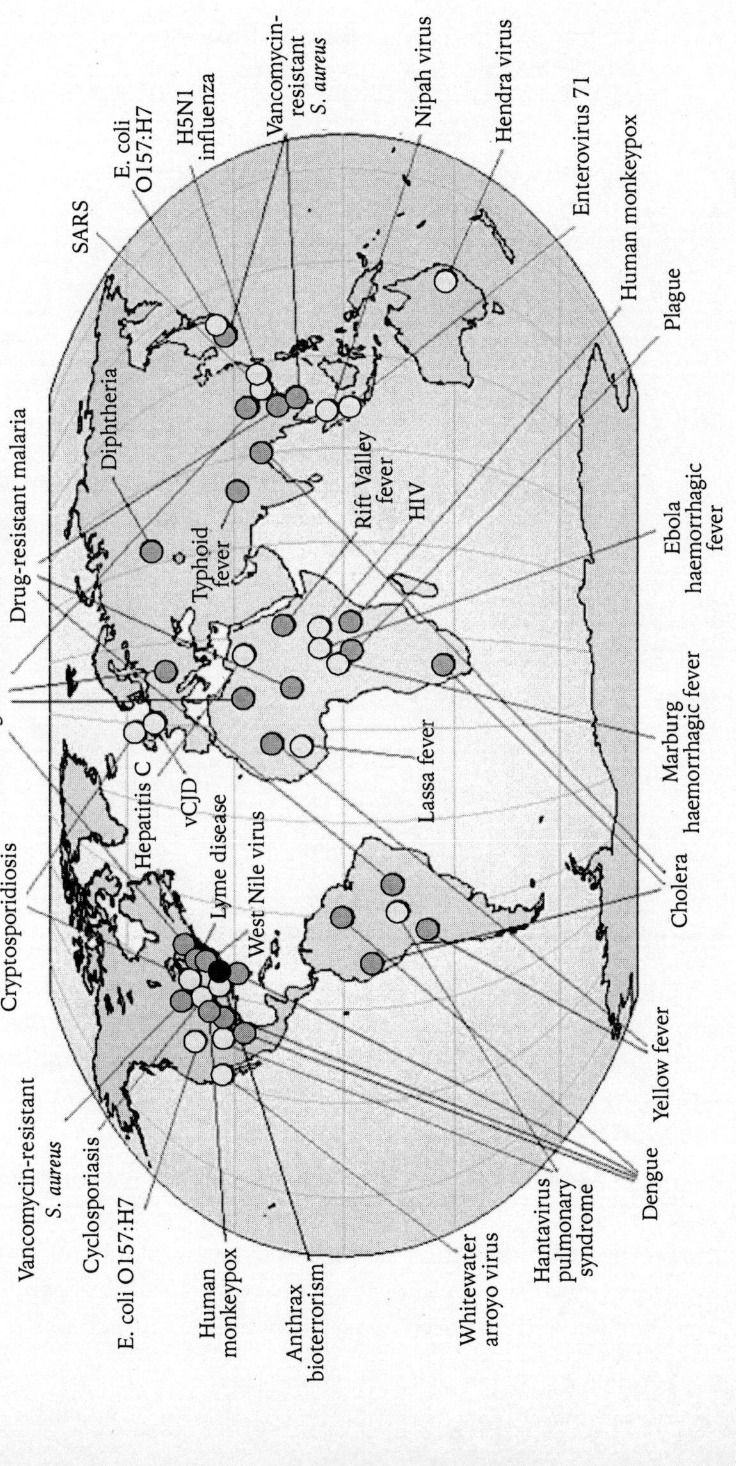

Figure 9.3

Overview of the Driver-Pathogen Interactions that contribute to the Emergence of Infectious Zoonotic Diseases

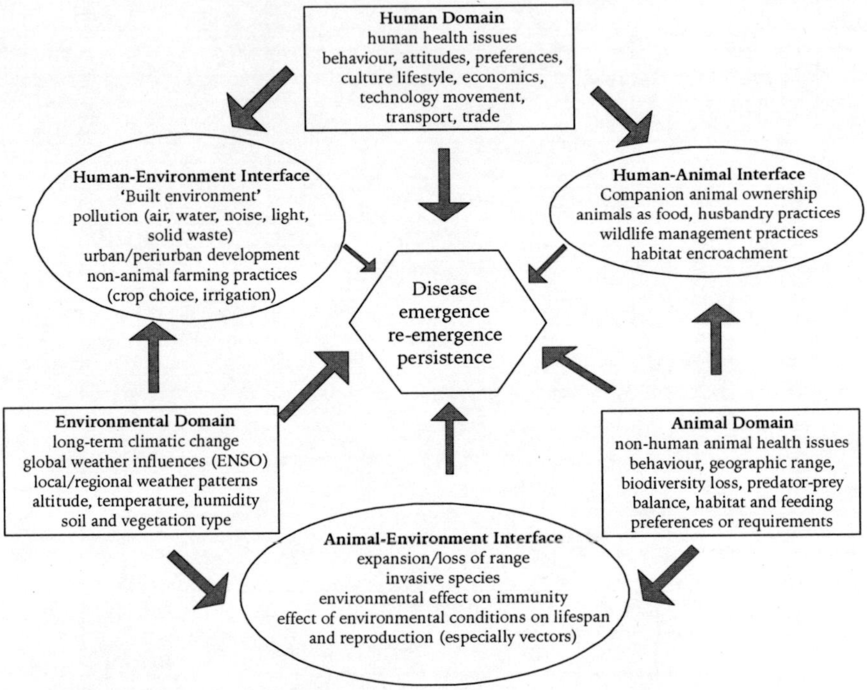

Source: Treadwell (2008).

Economic Impact of Pandemics in Asia

Asia is the world's largest and most populous continent, located in the eastern and northern hemispheres. It covers 8.6 per cent of the earth's total surface area (or 29.9 per cent of its land area) with 47 countries and approximately 4 billion people; it hosts 60 per cent of the world's current human population.

Asia today is an integral part of the global economy and is a major exporter and importer of goods and services. It provides a significant percentage of total world savings and receives a significant percentage of investment. In the short-term, even a localised pandemic in Asia would have a significant impact on the world economy.

Significantly, several pandemics have affected Asian continent during the last 50 years with great impact and consequences. In 2010, the world was in phase six of H1N1 Swine flu pandemic across the globe. Consequently, total losses emerging from infectious diseases over the past two decades have exceeded US $200 billion. In the course of the 1994 outbreak of plague in India, trade and travel restrictions were imposed internally and externally, which led to economic impacts that shocked the region's stock markets with losses of nearly US $2 billion.

The outbreak of Severe Acute Respiratory Syndrome (SARS) in 2003 showed that even a disease with a relatively small health impact can have a major economic effect. Globally, SARS is believed to have infected around 8,000 people, killing 800. The Asian Development Bank (ADB) estimated that the economic impact of SARS was around US $18 billion in East Asia, amounting to 0.6 per cent of the gross domestic product.

Total losses from emerging infectious diseases over the past two decades exceed US $200 billion.

Figure 9.4

Economic Impact of Influenza Pandemic by Percentage of GDP

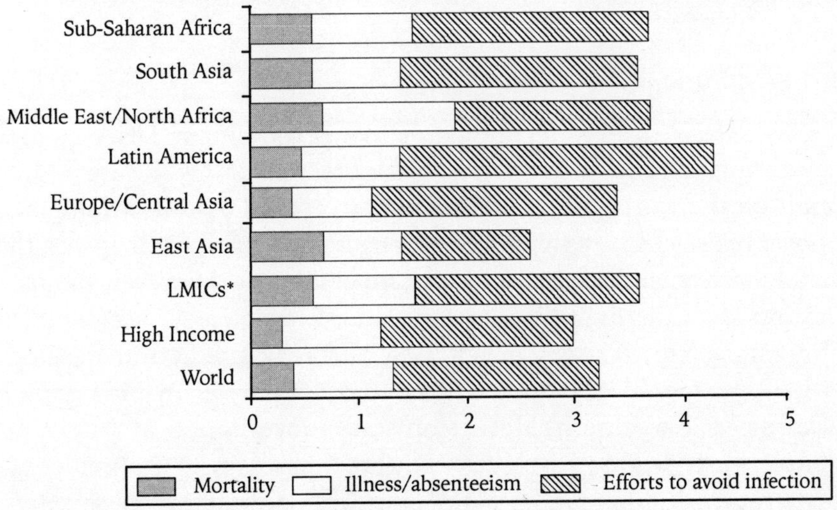

Note: * LMICS = Low and middle income countries.
Source: World Bank (2006).

Population

Asia is the most populated continent in the world. China and India will have the two largest population pools in the next 20 years and this will have a tremendous impact with regard to the emergences of new pathogens and outbreak of pandemics.

Figure 9.5

World Population Projections, Median Variant Forecasts

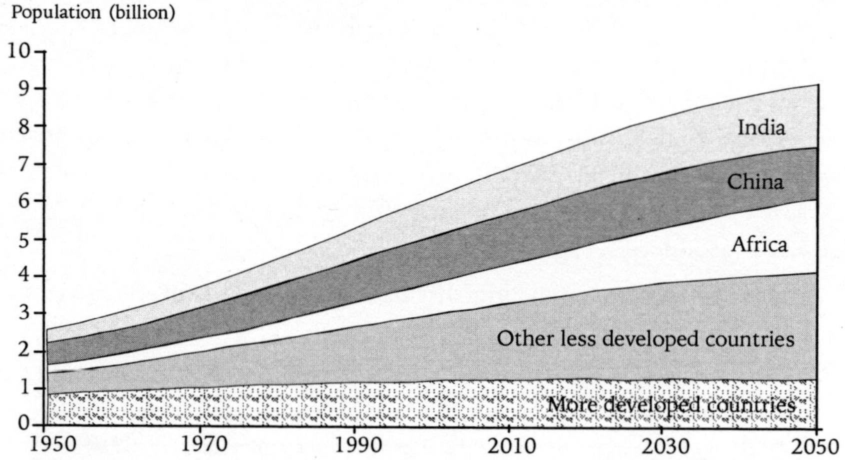

Source: United Nations (2007).

Threat of Weapons of Mass Destruction

Easy access to new technologies like recombinant DNA, genetic engineering, synthetic biology, and nanotechnology will have a great impact on the world if it results in bioterrorism. Possible development of novel bio-agents are much more dangerous than natural agents that could have tremendous impact in future epidemics. However, the main question is to distinguish between natural, suspicious, accidental or deliberate outbreaks and developing outbreak prediction methods. National, regional and international collaboration in bio-incident database, management, detection and surveillance of infectious diseases, early warning systems, bio-threat assessment to predict and prevent such epidemics or pandemics are some ways to counter a deliberate bioterrorism threat. An institutionalised Biological Weapons

Convention (BWC) is another way to increase the threat level from intentional use of infectious disease agent. We also need to enforce multilateral legally binding instruments to investigate any illegal activity without any political pressure. And we need to develop scientists and bio-researchers on bio-safety, bio-security, legal and ethical aspects of bio-research and dual use nature of some research to prevent the misuse of science in this subject.

It must also be noted that according to the BWC, it is the legitimate right of all governments to pursue their legal research on biodefence for protection, prevention, detection, diagnosis and treatment against biological warfare and bioterrorism and against any unconventional weapons of destruction and non-lethal weapons and emerging bio-threat. And it is the duty of all BWC members to dismantle all weapons of mass destruction (WMD) and prevent any research on development and production of any biological agents which could prove dangerous. According to the Article 10 of the BWC Convention, it is the duty of all member states to assist in full possible exchange of science and technology for peaceful purposes.

Box 9.1

Article 10 of the BWC Convention

(1) The States Parties to this Convention undertake to facilitate, and have the right to participate in the fullest possible exchange of equipment, materials and scientific and technological information for the use of bacteriological (biological) agents and toxins for peaceful purposes. Parties to the Convention in a position to do so shall also cooperate in contributing individually or together with other States or international organisations to the further development and application of scientific discoveries in the field of bacteriology (biology) for prevention of disease, or for other peaceful purposes.

(2) This Convention shall be implemented in a manner designed to avoid hampering the economic or technological development of States Parties to the Convention or international cooperation in the field of peaceful bacteriological (biological) activities, including the international exchange of bacteriological (biological) agents and toxins and equipment for the processing, use or production of bacteriological (biological) agents and toxins for peaceful purposes in accordance with the provisions of the Convention.

New Sciences, New Biological Agent's New Threats

Biotechnology, molecular biology and new life sciences like genomics offer us enormous potential in health, agriculture, industry, and environment. The flip side however is that technologies developed across multiple disciplines in the biological sciences will also have a profound global impact and concurrently have the potential to revolutionise biological warfare by facilitating an entirely new class of fully engineered agents referred to as advanced biological warfare (ABW) agents.

Emerging biotechnologies will likely lead to a paradigm shift in BW agent development; future biological agents could be rationally engineered to target specific human biological systems at the molecular level. This is a departure from the traditional model of BW agent development, which is focussed on the naturally occurring agent, not the target organism.

Biological science trends hold promise to change this, allowing BW agent developers to identify biochemical pathways critical for physiological processes and engineer specific ABW agents to exploit vulnerabilities. These future developments do not mitigate threats from traditional BW agents; as described earlier, advances in biology already hold promise to improve traditional agents.

The effect that biotechnology may have on biological warfare threats facing both military and civilian populations is presented in Figure 9.6.

The threat presented by traditional agents has been increasing since the early 20th century but eventually will level off because of two major factors:

(1) Development of targeted medical countermeasures probably will reduce threats posed by current biological warfare agents, and

(2) The number of natural pathogens and toxins that contain properties suitable for biological warfare is finite.

Like traditional agents, the threat posed by genetically modified traditional agents eventually will plateau partly because, ultimately, only a finite number of properties and genetic modifications can be used to enhance a traditional agent without altering it beyond recognition of the parental strain or serotype. Importantly, the large, yet finite, number of potential genetic modifications may well represent a multiplicative threat relative to that posed by the traditional agents; thus, the height of the threat bars are not fully to scale. Unlike threats posed by traditional and genetically modified traditional agents, the capability-based threat posed by ABW agents will continue to expand indefinitely in parallel with advances in biotechnology.

Figure 9.6

Timeline Describing Impact of Biotechnology on Biological Warfare Threat

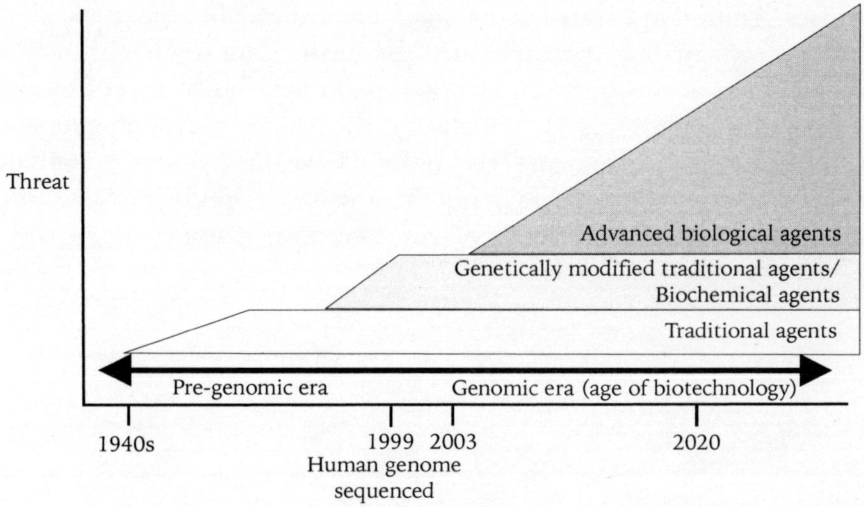

Note: This timeline depicts the relative threat level presented by traditional (e.g., naturally occurring bacterial, viral agents), genetically modified traditional (e.g., antibiotic-resistant bacteria), and advanced biological agents (novel BW agents created using biotechnological applications).

Killer Mousepox Experiment

This killer virus had been created via genetic manipulation. It was a purely scientific experiment. Australian researchers were interested in, of all things, mouse contraceptives.

They modified a mousepox virus to contain the gene for interleukin 4 (IL-4) as well as the mouse egg shell protein (ZP3). The egg shell protein was there to encourage a contraceptive response against the mouse's own eggs. The IL-4 gene was also present to increase the immune response against ZP3 protein, so as to make the contraceptive response more effective. The mousepox itself was a relatively benign virus, of little threat to the health of the mice themselves. The results were unexpected. When the genetically engineered mousepox was put into mice the mice simply died. The supposedly benign mousepox virus was discovered to become a killer in which 100 per cent of the mice died. The scientists thought they might learn something useful about mouse contraception, but instead they had learned how to create a universally fatal virus. After much debate, the results were published 18 months after the experiment.

Another interesting recent medical approach involves chimeric viruses. These are basically combinations of multiple organisms, thus ideally presenting the strengths of both. One such chimera a combination of the common cold and polio has shown great promise in brain cancer (curing it, not causing it). All these experiments and products clearly illustrate the paradox we face: basic scientific research, one of mankind's purest and most noble endeavours, increasingly reveals the seeds of our own destruction.

Figure 9.7

Patterns of Pathogen Discovery: Percentage of Novel Pathogen Species

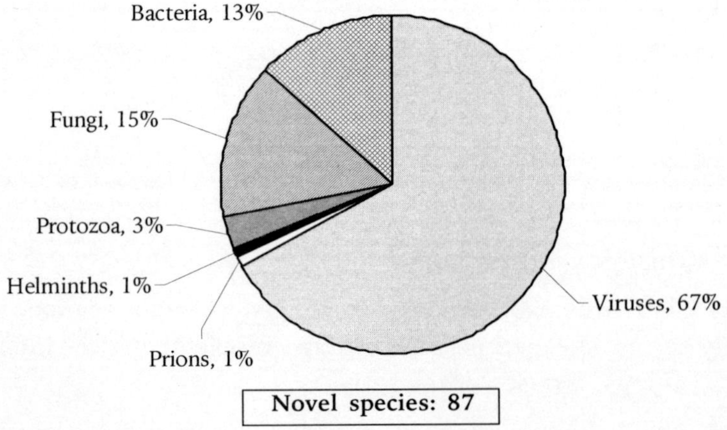

Source: "Infectious Disease Emergence: Past, Present and Future", at *http://www.ncbi.nlm.nih.gov/books/NBK45714/*

Future of Outbreaks in Asia

To better predict and prevent infectious disease outbreaks, scientific approaches are needed to gather and understand information about the nature of disease appearance and spread, and to understand genetic, population, social, political and ecological-level characteristics that enable pathogens to jump species and spread easily to humans. There are many factors effecting emergence of novel infectious diseases as national, regional and global bio-threat. These elements like geopolitical situation, socioeconomic, globalisation and trade in agriculture and animal, emerging market economies and international wildlife trade play an important role in future epidemics in Asia and other parts of the world.

Raising threat from biased bio-defence research and lack of organisation for BWC is another reason for an increase in the threat level from intentional use of infectious disease agent. Bio-research development and new tolls for manipulation of infectious disease agents and even developing new agents more dangerous than natural agents are becoming a reality. Hence, we urgently need regulations and legislations to prevent misuse of this science and technology against human health, food and animal health and national, regional and international security.

It is rather difficult to predict the future outbreak of pandemics in Asia for 2030. However, by studying the history of outbreaks, emergence and re-emergence of infectious diseases and considering factors affecting the emergence of possible outbreaks, we can postulate two scenarios:

Scenario One: Asia will face outbreaks of emerging infectious diseases of viral origin especially from family of flu viruses and other zoonotic viral diseases transmitted from animals to human during next two decades. Re-emerging of some viral, bacterial and parasitic disease is possible due to genetic and climate change and globalisation.

Scenario Two: Outbreak of novel agents delivered by malicious act by an inside or outside operator in Asia is a possibility. Bioterrorist attack by terrorist groups will cause economical, political and social damages and need to be carefully studied. Security measures like threat assessment, threat analysis, vulnerability assessment and analysis of major infrastructures is critical for prevention of future bioterrorist attack.

Preventive and defensive measures in civilian, defence and other forces should be taken into account to counter these kinds of irregular threats. Asian countries should work together in countermeasures against proliferation of WMDs specially the enforcement of BWC. Preparedness for rapid detection, diagnosis, treatment and bio-defence against these kinds of threats should be in the national and regional strategy of this very important region. International support is also critical in addressing this global issue.

To prevent future epidemics we need to evaluate and enhance Asian countries' surveillance system for human, animal and plant pathogens. For this purpose we need to collaborate for data collection and analysis. The prospects for successfully predicting emergence of events would be greatly enhanced by systematic data collection on the patterns of presence and prevalence of infectious agents in animal populations, which means developing and implementing a systematic, ongoing integrated disease surveillance programme that is global in scope.We need to enforce multilateral legally binding instrument to investigate any illegal activity without any political pressure. For predicting or preventing future outbreaks, Asian countries need to develop regional network for collecting and analysing information about infectious diseases, climate change, and any other factors effecting the creation of new outbreaks.

References

Asian Network of Major Cities 21 (ANMC 21) (2006). "Countermeasures to Combat Infectious Diseases in Asia", Taipei, August 22-24. At *www.infection-anmc21.org/index.html* (Accessed on January 27, 2010).

Centre for Non-Proliferation Studies (2009). *Convention of the Prohibition of the Development, Production, and Stockpiling of Bacteriological (Biological) and Toxin Weapons and their Destruction.* June 22. At *http://www.nti.org/e_research/official_docs/inventory/pdfs/btwc.pdf* (Accessed on November 08, 2009).

Fauci, Anthony S. (2006). "Emerging and Re-emerging Infectious Diseases: The Perpetual Challenge", *The Milbank Memorial Fund and the Association of American Medical Colleges*, January.

Garretson, Peter (2009). "Counter Bio-Terror", *CBW MAGAZINE* 2/1, September.

Indian Council of Medical Research (2004). "Emerging Infectious Diseases in South East Asia: Research Priorities", *ICMR Bulletin* 34(5-6): 30-35. At *http://icmr.nic.in/bulletin/2004/mayjun.pdf* (Accessed on November 04, 2009).

International Science & Technology Center (2008). *Biotechnology, Public Health, Agriculture Sustainable Nuclear Energy with Enhanced Safeguards, Safety and Security Environmental Remediation and Climate Change Mitigation Renewable and Environmentally Friendly Energy Technologies*. At *www.istc.ru/istc/istc.nsf/va.../Annual.../annual_report2008eng.pdf* (Accessed on December 05, 2009)

Institute of Medicine and National Research Council of the National Academies (2009). *Bio-Watch and Public Health Surveillance: Evaluating Systems for the Early Detection of Biological Threats*. Washington DC: National Academic Press.

Jackson, R.J. *et al*. (2001). "Expression of Mouse Interleukin-4 by a Recombinant Ectromelia Virus Suppresses Cytolytic lymphocyte Responses and Overcomes Genetic Resistance to Mousepox", *Journal of Virology* 75/3: 1205-10.

Jones, K., N.G. Patel, M.A. Levy, A. Storeygard, D. Balk, J.L. Gittleman and P. Daszak (2008). "Global Trends in Emerging Infectious Diseases", *Nature* 451(7181): 990–993.

Keush, G.T., M. Pappaioanou, M.C. Gonzalez, K.A. Scott and P. Tsai (eds.) (2009). *Sustaining Global Surveillance and Response to Emerging Zoonotic Diseases*. Washington DC: National Academic press.

Kilpatrick, A. Marm, A.A. Chmura, D.W. Gibbons, R.C. Fleischer, P.P. Marra and P. Daszak (2006). "Predicting the Global Spread of H5N1 Avian Influenza", *PNAS* 103: 19368-373.

McMichael, A.J. (2004). "Environmental and Social Influences on Emerging Infectious Diseases: Past, Present and Future", *Philosophical Transactions of the Royal Society B: Biological Sciences* 359(1447): 1049–58.

Okazaki, K. *et al*. (2000). "Precursor Genes of Future Pandemic Influenza Virusesare Perpetuated in Ducks Nesting in Siberia", *Arch Virol* 145: 885–893.

Parmentola, John A. (2004). "Army Transformation: Paradigm-Shifting Capabilities through Biotechnology", September at *http://www.nae.edu/* (Accessed on December 08, 2009).

Petro, James B., Theodore R. Plasse and Jack A. McNulty (2003). "Biotechnology: Impact on Biological Warfare and Biodefense—Advanced Biological Warfare (ABW) Agents", at *www.medscape.com/viewarticle/462541_3* (Accessed on December 05, 2009).

Relman, David A., and R. Eileen (2009). The *Domestic and International Impacts of the 2009-H1N1 Influenza A Pandemic: Global Challenges, Global Solutions*. Washington DC: National Academic Press.

Sandman, Peter M. (2007). "A Severe Pandemic is not Overdue: It's not when but if" *CIDRAP Business Source Weekly Briefing*, February 22.

Sleigh, Adrian C. (2006). *Population Dynamics and Infectious Diseases in Asia*. Hague: World Scientific.

Terrapinn Pvt. Ltd. (2010). *Asia Infectious Diseases Forum 2010*. At *www.terrapinn.com/2010/infectious/index.stm* (Accessed on January 09, 2010).

United States General Accounting Office (2004). *Emerging Infectious Diseases Asian SARS Outbreak Challenged International and National Responses*, April. At *http://www.gao.gov/new.items/d04564.pdf* (Accessed on November 5, 2009).

World Bank (2006). Global Development Finance 2006.

World Health Organization (2005). *International Health Regulations*, Second Edition. At *http://apps.who.int/bookorders/anglais/detart1.jsp?sesslan=1&codlan=5&codcol=15&codcch=725* (Accessed on Janaury 23, 2010).

Zkea.com (2004). "The Australian Experiment", at *www.zkea.com/archives/archive05002.html* (Accessed on December 9, 2009).

IV

Society, Identity, Religion and Governance

10

Hindu Nationalism, Diaspora Politics and Nation Building in India

CATARINA KINNVALL and TED SVENSSON

Introduction

In May 2009, for a second consecutive election, the Hindu Right—with the Bharatiya Janata Party (BJP) at its helm—suffered an unanticipated defeat. The Congress-dominated coalition United Progressive Alliance (UPA) secured an exceptional victory—with the Congress Party alone winning 206 seats, while the BJP managed to secure a mere 116 (Ramakrishnan, 2009).

Does the election result signal the end of the sway of Hindu nationalist conceptions of Indian society and the state or is it more accurate to perceive it as a temporary electoral setback? Should the results be interpreted as a shift away from a seeming inseparability between community, religion and politics in the context of Indian nation building? Will it impel the BJP to break the party's links with organisations emphatically promoting India as a primarily Hindu nation?

Answering the initial question in agreement with Puniyani (2009) we would contend that a general impression and sentiment of abatement has arisen, even if the BJP remains a well established governing party in a number of states. The party's top leadership has shown signs of dissension in the wake of 2009 elections, most noticeable in the decision of its Vice-President, Yashwant Sinha, to relinquish this position (Vyas, 2009a). Still, the party remains firmly associated with the Hindu nationalist movement and its core ideas. In a resolution adopted on 21 June 2009, for instance, it was stated that the underpinning ideology, *Hindutva*, 'is not to be understood or construed (as being) narrowly confined to religious practices or expressed in extreme forms. It is related to the culture and ethos of the people [...] a way of life [...] and, therefore, inclusive' (cited in Vyas, 2009b).

The religious nationalism emanating out of the activities of the Hindu Right is undoubtedly a core constituent of nation building in India. Does it, however, meet the conditions of being accommodative, of being a benign and favourable fundamental for nation building? We know of the tragic upheavals caused by its more violent manifestations as in, Mumbai in 1992-93, Gujarat in 2002 and Orissa in 2008. Still, it does, somewhat contradictorily, contribute to the demarcation and cohesion of being Indian. It does so by appealing to the mythical unity of the Hindu community, and by invoking an historical version of a glorious Hindu past and by providing an imagined Hindu national identity.

In this chapter we are attempting to study how Hindu nationalism has shaped or failed to shape the concept of a national identity in India. In particular, we are concerned with the role of religious nationalism as a facilitator or an obstacle to a state-anchored national identity as outlined in the introduction to this special issue. India is often conceived of as a deeply religious society, but one in which secularism has been allowed to frame the parameters of politics and state building. It is thus of interest to see how Hindu nationalism has affected Indian notions of secularism. In the following section we discuss some of the theoretical points of departure with regard to national identity and religious nationalism, followed by a general account of nation building in India and the emergence of the Hindu Right. We then proceed to discuss of how the concept of Hindutva has been used to construct religious boundaries around national identity at home and abroad. Of particular importance are the ways in which these constructions have been challenged in religious, secular and legalistic terms. We argue that religion can and has played a positive role in Indian nation building, but that Hindu nationalism has continuously adopted exclusionary practices against other religious communities and has hampered most forms of assimilatory processes beyond and within the so-called Hindu 'fold'.

Religious Nationalism and Nation Building in India

In the introduction to this special issue, Michael Barr indicates that one objective of our present engagement with religious nationalism is to grasp its success or failure in terms of particular national identity constructions. Hence, our engagement with religious nationalism should expound both its violent manifestations and its role in the re-/production of cohesive and stable societies. Rather than emphasising the divisive and potentially destructive functions of religious nationalism, we ought to note its tendencies towards 'hegemony' and 'assimilation'. It is a hegemony wherein—in Barr's terminology—elites are 'using, or trying to use, its political and social power to establish certain mores and values as the dominant and social force in the country', while 'trying to build a state-anchored national identity in essentially religious-nationalist terms'. An important aspect of the realisation of such a hegemony seems to be the assimilation—whether in the 'hegemonic group itself' or, as is often the case with minority groups, in a 'subordinate' position—into 'the broader state-anchored national community'. Of particular interest here is the extent to which the Hindu Right has interacted with other hegemonic interpretations of what constitutes Indian national identity and the extent to which such identity constructions have relied upon assimilatory or exclusionary practices with regards to non-Hindu minorities.

India became one of the first British colonies to attain independence and its political establishment was determined to make democracy work in a multi-religious, multi-lingual and multi-ethnic region that had not previously been united. India's 'independence' simultaneously meant a partitioning of British India according to the logic of the so-called two-nation theory as well as the integration of numerous Princely States that had previously been left outside of the colonial state's institutional arrangements. The partition of British India into two independent states—India and Pakistan—generated both large-scale communal violence and extensive migration in the immediate wake of independence. It also set the conditions for a long-standing antagonism between the two neighbouring states.

It was one of the great achievements of Indian independence in 1947 that, despite the partition and the horrendous acts that accompanied it (for a commendable analysis, see Pandey, 2001), secularism was accepted and enshrined as a basic value in the Constitution. Although the Constitution sought to enact and promote an inclusive nationalism, it departed from a number of Gandhian notions about what independent India should be(come). In the Gandhian vision of the future political system of India, the state and government were to be kept at minimal levels and power was to be decentralised to village *panchayats*. However it was the opposite that took place; centralisation and policing of unity and cohesion transpired as key concerns. A number of things advocated by Gandhi were never materialised, such as his call for dissolution of political parties, including the Congress (Austin, 2000: 27-32), as well as Gandhian notions and practices in the area of political mobilisation. B.R. Ambedkar—the most prominent political representative of Dalits in the late 1940s—proclaimed, for instance, in 1949 that, "[...] we must abandon the method of civil disobedience, non-cooperation and *satyagraha*" as "these methods" amounted to "nothing but the grammar of anarchy and the sooner they are abandoned, the better for us", (Constituent Assembly Debates, 1949). Hence, we witness a seeming departure from the Gandhian conception of 'India' in terms of power, legitimate political activity and sanctioned forms of statehood in the wake of independence.

Once the worst manifestations of the partition violence had abated, the Constitution had been promulgated and the first general elections had been successfully carried out in 1951-52, a period of seeming concord and harmonious co-existence emerged. Unfortunately, tension between different groups was on the increase already by the late 1950s, followed by a growing number of communal riots. Conflicts between Hindus and Muslims intensified in the 1980s and 1990s, and a number of secessionist tendencies emerged in various places, such as in the Punjab, Jammu and Kashmir, Nagaland, Assam, Tamil Nadu and Andhra Pradesh. There was also an increase in conflicts between 'higher' and 'lower' castes as political leaders adopted 'reservation' policies to gain electoral support from the (more numerous) 'lower' castes (for details, see Kohli, 1990; Brass, 2003; Dutt, 1998).

As political consciousness has risen among marginalised groups, religion and nationalism have become effective means of communication and protest as they divert attention away from class and caste adversaries and asymmetrical power relations. In this sense they have been instrumental in the search for a secure Hindu identity in the light of global change and modernity.

Constructing National Identity: India at Independence

Here it is worth contrasting the Hindu Right's recent rise to prominence and legitimacy with developments at the time of India's independence in August 1947. At this time the Rashtriya Swayamsevak Sangh (RSS)—the fountainhead of the Hindu nationalist movement—was deemed peripheral to any legitimate forms of political mobilisation and organisation. This was largely due to the involvement of some of its sympathisers in the murder of Mahatma Gandhi and its opposition to the emerging postcolonial state. Even if certain sections of the Congress were sympathetic to selected notions of Hindu supremacy, clear divergences between the mainstream of the anti-colonial movement and Hindu 'communalists', e.g., the RSS and Hindu Mahasabha, existed. As noted by Kumkum Sangari when discussing Gandhi's views on religion and nationality: '[i]n his constant reiteration that religion was "private" and an [sic!] "entirely a personal matter" Gandhi partly meant that religion comprised [...] an unmediated relation of each person to god, fell outside the purview of the state and was certainly not an entity that could determine nationality' (2002: 5; citations from *Harijan* 27 July 1947). At the same time, Gandhi realised the difficulties in disassociating religion from politics and argued in his autobiography that, 'I can say without the slightest hesitation, and yet in all humility, that those who say that religion has nothing to do with politics do not know what religion means' (Chandhoke, 1999: 44).

This statement still seems to ring true in South Asian politics. Some scholars even argue that, '[r]eligion has emerged as a key analytical category for interpreting South Asian politics' (Hirst and Zavoz, 2005: 3). In 1996, Mark Juergensmeyer wrote that, '[w]hat Hindutva is and how it is related to international patterns are not just academic questions. They are of practical, political importance, because in India religious nationalism is still a potent force' (1996: 129). The same is valid today. The influence of the Hindu Right does not only affect internal social and identity based boundary-drawing, but also India's relation to its neighbours, to institutions and practices of global governance and to the Indian diaspora. To exile it to the margins of international relations would thus be erroneous. In order to give religious nationalism in India its deserved attention, the core queries of the analysis are: why is religious nationalism time and again assuming a primary function? What are its exclusionary and potentially assimilatory and accommodating dynamics?

In the body of literature on the Hindu Right, an array of objectives has been ascribed to the movement. Sumit Sarkar, for example, has depicted its ambition as an attempt to mould 'Indian secular democracy into a "majoritarian" Hindu state which represses all religious and other dissent' (2005: 305)—an objective that its political wing, the BJP, occasionally, tries to free itself from. Although the Congress, in contrast to the BJP, represents continuity, stability and inclusiveness stemming from the legacy of the nationalist movement, it is a heritage that has been increasingly indicted for its corrugated 'secularism'—both by champions of a secular state and by advocates of religious nationalism. It is, on the one hand, asserted that the Gandhian strain of nationalist thought carried with it connotations drawn from practices and imageries integral to Hinduism. On the other hand, the tendency of the Congress since the 1980s to, at times, employ a language tinted by appeals to religious identities has raised questions about its commitment to secularism. It is analogously claimed that the Constituent Assembly, which functioned between December 1946 and January 1950, upheld a view of India and Indian citizenship as defined by its leaning on the 'majority' identity: one example being the decision to make the word Bharat part of the initial paragraph of the Constitution (Singh, 2005: 911), another the repeated articulation of a vague yet clearly delimited 'we' and a third the recurring references to the Hindu pantheon and mythology in the debates.

It is true that the Congress-dominated state tried to expunge communalism and the religious, if understood as equivalent to the traditional, in the wake of independence. It did so by stressing rationality, modernisation and industry-led development. However, even if the elite discourse ascribed no future 'place' for religion—

progress would 'free' India from the burden of the traditional and of inertia—the sacred remained a constitutive element of the secular. Even prior to the advent of the mounting political influence of the Hindu Right, the state played an active role in the production and reproduction of categorisations along religious lines.

Here it is worth drawing attention to the oscillation surrounding the issue of minorities and their position *vis-à-vis* the state, following independence. One such example involved the permit and passport system for persons crossing the Indo-Pakistan border—wherein a palpable distinction between Muslims and non-Muslims was eventually made (Zamindar, 2007). Another included the vacillation of the Constituent Assembly on the subject of political safeguards for religious minorities (Bajpai, 2000). Even though the Assembly had made such special considerations part of the draft introduced in 1948, the final version of the Constitution included no political safeguards for religious minorities. This exclusion of religious minorities from preferential treatment cannot be understood apart from the ways in which secularism as a principle has informed religious nationalism in post-independence India.

Religion and Secularism: Disowned Doubles?

India adopted secularism and guaranteed religious rights under the Constitution to overcome the faith-induced antagonisms of the pre-independence period and during the partition. However, the leaders of newly independent India opted for a type of secularism that implied continued state involvement in religious affairs. Rather than separating church and state, India opted for the principle of *sarva dharma samabhava*—'equal respect for all religions'. As a principle it has required government intervention in religious affairs and support of religious activities so that all Indians have an equal opportunity to practise their religions (Kolodner, 1995; Bhargava, 1996). Thus, Indian national leaders claim secular credentials by visiting places of worship of all religious denominations and the broadcast media allot time equally to the prayers of different religions.

At the time of independence, the leaders of the Congress did not see a contradiction in professing an Indian nation that rested on Hindu religious tradition, as this tradition was viewed as tolerant and based on indigeneous religious pluralism (Deol, 2000: 40). This choice of intertwining religion and politics was influenced by independence leaders such as Gandhi who often employed a discourse that resembled the Hindu notion of *dharmic* obligation. His continued reference to 'Mother India' invoked characteristics of Hindu religious worship and, despite the fact that he was a champion of Hindu–Muslim unity, his calls for religious tolerance and universalism were often based on Hindu beliefs and practices.

It was, in part, this 'inclusive' Hindu tolerance that alienated the Muslim League, and was at the heart of the two-nation theory professed by M.A. Jinnah. This theory, which culminated in the establishment of Pakistan, suggested that Muslims and Hindus were separate nations, offering Muslims and Hindus a nationality associated with a socioreligious community. The Indian concept of secularism can thus be viewed as an idealisation and romanticisation of Western 19th-century universalist ideas, integrated into an elite political culture. As argued by K.N. Panikkar (1997: 18–19), this is precisely the weakness of the Indian notion of secularism, as it keeps religion in play and enhances religiosity by preserving and projecting religious identities (see also Deol, 2000; Kolodner, 1995). This, it is argued, has increased the social distance between religious communities.

In a more contemporary reflection on the relation between communal belonging and secularism, Ashis Nandy questions the extent to which we should approach 'communalism and secularism as sworn enemies' or if it is more appropriate to consider them 'as the disowned doubles of each other' (1998: 283). In other words, the notion of a double, co-constitutive rejection is preferable to an understanding of the two terms as dichotomous. Hence, religion in India is a 'powerful, constitutive, and perhaps a definitive component of culture' (Chandhoke, 1999: 25). In this sense, modernity has not been able to destroy religious belief systems in India despite the expectations of some modernist theoreticians. If secularism is interpreted as the opposite of religion, it is only likely to benefit Hindu majoritarian nationalism. As Neera Chandhoke (Ibid: 94) has argued: 'if secularism can be interpreted in such a way that it serves to erase the "presence of religious or ethnic particularism from the domain of law and public life", and if it contributes to the construction of a homogenised citizenship, downgrading minority cultures in the process, there is urgent need to shift ground'. Hence, if we adhere to a purely legalistic definition of secularism as equality, we fail to see how some groups are able to reproduce inequalities in which weaker groups find it hard to use their constitutional rights.

The Emergence of the Hindu Right

The emergence of the Hindu Right must be viewed in this light. Hindu nationalism has consistently played into a hegemonic majority narrative in which Hindu values are said to be submerged into a 'false' equality as the state is constantly 'appeasing' the Muslim minority. As mentioned above, Hindu nationalism experienced an upsurge in the '80s and '90s, culminating in the BJP being asked to form a minority government in 1998 and another one (albeit stronger) in 1999. Hindu nationalism as a political project is not a new phenomenon, however. The present organisational framework assumed its initial shape when the RSS was established in 1925 (for analyses of the evolution of the RSS, see Jaffrelot, 1996; Blom Hansen, 1999; Bhatt and Mukta, 2000). The RSS later developed its political wing—the Jana Sangh—which in 1977 became part of the Janata Party that came to power after Indira Gandhi's emergency rule. In '80, the Jana Sangh left the Janata Party and formed the BJP as the political arm of the RSS. The BJP has close ties with Vishwa Hindu Parishad (VHP)—a non-governmental organisation that was formed in 1964 to spread 'Hindu ethical spiritual values' and to establish links with Hindus in other countries. VHP attained national notoriety in the early '80s when it organised an anti-Muslim campaign following the conversion of over 1,000 Dalits to Islam (see Kolodner, 1995; Patnaik and Chalam, 1998: 271). This organisation instigated the fear that other lower-caste citizens would follow suit, and that 'Gulf money' was being used to carry out these conversions and to undermine the Hindu nation (Kolodner, 1995). The 'family' of organisations created by the RSS is often referred to as the Sangh Parivar.

The exclusive nationalism involved in the creation of the RSS was influenced by Western examples. This is particularly apparent in the writings of V.D. Savarkar and M.S. Golwalkar. Savarkar's work *Hindutva: Who is a Hindu?*, published in 1923, is a core text for nationalist 'Hinduness', and rests on the assumption that the Aryans who settled in India constituted a nation now embodied in the Hindus (Jaffrelot, 1996). But it was Golwalkar who in 1939 gave the RSS the ideological authority it had previously lacked. In his book *We, or Our Nationhood Defined*, he claimed that Western countries had successfully fostered and nurtured a 'correct national consciousness'—different from the territorial nationalism guiding Indian nation building (Golwalkar, 1939: 62, in Jaffrelot, 1996: 52). In this, Golwalkar drew on a number of German writers who inspired him to look at Indian national identity in terms of geographical unity, race, religion, culture and language. The racial factor was by far the most important and the Muslim minority, he argued, posed the most severe threat by being a 'foreign body' lodged into the Hindu society, thus undermining the Hindu nation (Jaffrelot, 1996: 55; Chakravartty, 1994: 161-180; Patnaik and Chalam, 1998: 252-280; for detailed accounts of the rise of Hindu nationalism see also: Blom Hansen, 1999; Jaffrelot, 1998; van der Veer, 1996; Bidwai *et al.*, 1996; Bhatt, 2001).

As can be seen from this brief outline, Hindu nationalism possesses relatively deep roots. Over the last few decades, however, the movement has assumed increased significance. The mobilisation for the construction of a temple on the alleged birthplace of the Hindu god Ram in Ayodhya in Uttar Pradesh has been central to its rising influence. At first, the propelling of the matter onto the national stage revolved around the existence of a mosque, the Babri Masjid, on the Ayodhya site. The mosque was demolished by Hindu Right sympathisers in December 1992. Since then agitations on the subject have been linked to the construction of a temple (see Dutta and Sarkar, 1994; Chatterjee, 1993: Ludden, 1996; Desai, 2002). The demolition of the Babri Masjid had symbolic as well as material repercussions throughout India—most visibly in the communal violence that erupted in Mumbai between December 1992 and late January 1993 (see Shrikrishna Commission Report, 1998).

National Identity and the Construction of Religious Boundaries

During the last eight years, two entwined and co-constitutive global trends have been present in the Indian context. One is the unfolding tension of a 'war on terror', while the other refers to a more long-standing socioeconomic and political marginalisation of Muslims. The latter has been poignantly demonstrated in the Social, Economic and Educational Status of the Muslim Community in India: A Report—often referred to as the Sachar Committee Report, 2006. The report exposes the deplorable socioeconomic condition of a large number of Muslims and the increasing ghettoisation of Indian cities. It also discusses how violence against Muslims has increased the physical and psychological distance between Hindu and Muslim communities.

As we know, violence tends to mark out, reproduce and reify boundary-drawing. The use of violence is often connected to myths about the origin of the nation in which historical narratives play an important part. The (re)construction of historical narratives and myths is a contested process and concerns both a struggle for control over the cultural space as well as the articulation of political needs for a particular identity group in the present. Hence, a 'nostalgic' past based on collective memories, myths and traditions generates both legitimacy and possibilities for mobilisation. Even though these cultural attributes are constantly negotiated, contested and reconstructed over time, identity groups are inclined to adopt various myths of homogeneity and essentialism. As a result, this 'everyday primordialism' is framed as something you are born into and identity appears as a static and natural category (Fearon and Latin, 2000; Hutchinson, 1994).

The linkage and continuity between past and present is particularly important. Efforts are often made at the hands of hegemonic interpreters to trace the genealogy of an identity group back to a specific place, time and ancestor in order to derive an ideological lineage. Religion in particular serves as a powerful source. Religious revelations are turned into national shrines; religious miracles become national feasts and holy scriptures are reinterpreted as national epics (Smith, 2000: 80). In the case of India, Hindu nationalism has needed to demonstrate that the nation it wishes to create has always existed. This nationalist narrative is deeply rooted in religious discourse, which relates the present to a glorified past. As a consequence, the Hindu

Right has acted as a forceful catalyst in the elevation of religion into a primary (national) identity marker.

The Hindutva Movement in India: Establishing Religious Boundaries

It is in relation to such claims that Ashis Nandy has insisted on making a clear distinction between the *Hindutva* type of political ideology and Hinduism, where the latter is regarded as a 'faith and a way of life' that permeates Indian culture (quoted in Jaffrelot 1996: 133). *Hindutva*, in comparison, has become an attempt to close Hinduism off in, what Hent De Vries (2002: 1) would label, a 'conceptual totality', thereby relying on a violent manoeuvre to overcome the particular and to mask the discrepancy between its notions of 'Hinduness' (and Hindu 'culture') and Hinduism as a religion. The Hindu Right has attempted to make Hindus into a 'community' or 'fold' devoid of internal differentiations. The key imagery in such delimitation is the portrayal of Hindus as always-already belonging to and constituting a singular community. The Hinduism and the Hindu community projected by the Hindu Right are, thus, monolithic and unified, ancient and endless. Another crucial element of the disseminated narrative is that the expanse of Hinduism—and thus of Hindus—corresponds to the very ambit of Indian society (Oza, 2007: 153). The vast network of Hindu nationalist organisations is a vital component in the establishment and promotion of a sense of cohesion and immanence. The primary effect of this has been the cementing of primordial articulations of identity and the pitting of these against each other.

Such primordialisation has relied upon the projection of some common myths or themes onto the other, in this case the Muslims. For instance, in response to the Muslim League's insistence on a separate nation state, Muslims are depicted as responsible for the partition of the 'sacred' Hindu homeland in 1947. Although Muslims (today) constitute only 14 per cent of the population, India is the second largest Muslim country in the world—counting over 112 million people. This number has been hailed by Hindu nationalists as a threat to the Hindu majority as Muslims often tend to act as a vote bank (Kolodner, 1995; Oommen, 1994; Patnaik and Chalam, 1998). In the construction of the Muslim 'other,' Muslims are recurrently referred to as not truly Indian and as potential collaborators with neighbouring states and transnational Islamist groups. In addition, pointing to Indian Muslims' refusal to have a common civil code, Hindu nationalists argue that Muslims are creating a separate national identity that prevents them from integrating into Indian society.

This preoccupation with the Muslim 'other' has tended to define most interpretations of Hindu nationalism. However, Hindu nationalism has also been portrayed in more fundamentalist terms as a religious, conservative and traditional movement. In opposition to such depictions, Aparna Devare describes it as a 'modern phenomenon' since it displays a visible dependence on ideas conventionally considered integral to modernity, such as 'nation, state, science, rationality, notions of femininity/masculinity, and history' (2009: 157). This can be related to van der Veer's (1996) argument that the essentialisation of Hindus and Muslims must be understood in a larger historical context, where the discourse on 'Hindu spirituality' and 'Hindu tolerance' has a specific history. The ideal of religious tolerance in the West, he says, derives from a universalisation of religion that is part of a Western discourse of modernity and modern 'nation states'. This discourse has consequences for Muslim and Hindu populations incorporated into the modern world system. Being the old rivals of the Christian West, Muslims are labelled 'fanatic' and 'bigoted', while Hindus are seen in a more positive light as being 'tolerant'. Devare develops the argument to its logical extension while claiming that the Hindu Right version of Hinduism is most appropriately described as a strategic utilisation and a secularising of religion leaving 'little room for the sacral, spiritual, or transcendental' (2009: 159).

In this sense a number of authors have argued that Hindu nationalism is not a religious movement and that there are a number of factors that would impede any unified Hindu movement. Hindu religion, for instance, does not easily lend itself to organised movement in the way that Islam or Christianity may be able to do. As pointed out by Kolodner (1995) and others (see Panikkar, 1997; van der Veer, 1996), there is no recognised clergy, central church or dogma that all Hindus must follow. Neither is there any one single text that has been claimed to have divine authority, making Hindu fundamentalism a seeming contradiction as there are so few (as agreed upon) fundamentals. Second, it has been shown that the term 'Hindu' has not always permeated the identities of many Indians. Paradoxically, it means that what is probably the most fundamental aspect of traditional Hindu society—caste—may present the largest obstacle to the creation of a homogeneous Hindu nation (Kolodner, 1995). These obstacles have made it necessary to define the 'other' in essentialised terms as only then can a hegemonic national identity be created. Such tendencies go far beyond the Indian context and have affected Indians living abroad as well as foreign relations more generally.

Hindu Nationalism at Home and Abroad

Hindutva ideology and organisations have become increasingly visible in many diaspora South Asian communities since the early '90s (Bhatt, 2000; Brown, 2006; Rajagopal, 2000; Vertovec, 2000). The growing importance of diaspora politics can only be understood in regard to an increasingly globalised world where borders have grown more porous and fuzzy. Hence, diasporas challenge traditional conceptions of territoriality and ingrained ideas of what is inside and outside a state. As Sean Carter (2005: 60-61) notes: 'given the increased capacity for diasporas to "act at a distance" [...] we need to reconsider the ways that we think about the nation and *its* territorialities, as well as diaspora and *its* territorialities'. Most diaspora studies focus on the existence of a homeland and have predominantly been used to refer to 'classical' diaspora groups, such as the Jews, the Greeks and the Armenian exile communities (Brubaker, 2005). The Hindu diaspora fits this generalised picture due to its continued emphasis on India's sacred geography. India as a sacred space that abounded with sacred places has created a 'sentimental respect if not spiritual reverence for that place and its civilisational heritage remains exceptionally strong' (Vertovec, 2000: 4). However, the Hindu diaspora also challenges traditional accounts of 'long-distance nationalism' in Benedict Anderson's terminology. Hence, focus is not only on how diasporas attempt to change politics in the homeland, but also how nationalist organisations operating in the homeland attempt to mobilise Hindus abroad (Jaffrelot and Therwath, 2007).

The RSS, for instance, has established itself in some 150 countries, including 60 *shakhas* (branches) in the UK, while the VHP has become the central organisation claiming to represent the entire Hindu world and a *Hindutva* world view. The VHP has 12 branches in the UK, 25 chapters in the US, 2 in Canada, branches in six other European countries and numerous others in non-Western countries. Most of these are affiliated with Vishwa Hindu Parishad International (VHPI) (Bhatt, 2000; Brown, 2006; Mukta, 2000). The RSS's main concern has been the loss of Hindu identity as a result of Western materialism, immorality and corruption, while the overwhelming problem for the VHP has been the historical victimisation of the global Hindu community (Bhatt, 2000; Mukta, 2000). The RSS has especially pointed to the vulnerability of children and adolescents with regard to Western values, but also in relation to other minority communities in the West. Hence in the UK for instance, the religious boundaries between Hinduism and Islam have largely worked as class relations and have come to stand for differences in material wealth between the partial economic success of the East African Asian merchant communities and the rather impoverished Pakistani, Bangladeshi and Caribbean communities (Bhatt, 2000).

In the US, religious relations have functioned less as class relations than in the UK, which is related to the fact that the US Indian diaspora constitutes one of the highest paid minority communities (Rajagopal, 2000). However, there are many similarities in the way different minority groups have pressured the state for power. First, many Indian migrants have been engaged in a 'long-distance nationalism'. This has involved fund raising and charity for the benefit of the homeland, much of which has been collected by the Hindu Right—often without the donors' knowledge. Second, we see a re-invention of (Hindu) tradition and culture as a means to resist an 'ahistorical American culture' in which rebellion, sexual freedom and love marriages are encouraged. Both the Hindu Student Council (HSC) and the Vishwa Hindu Parishad of America (VHPA) take advantage of parental fears of Westernisation and encourage parents to send their youth to events organised by the Hindu Right. Third and finally, the racism experienced among many young South Asians has led to the search for secure identities in the reconstruction of one's dignity. Here the Hindu minority is frequently heralded as a 'model community' based on an ancient (and romanticised!) past (Mathew and Prashad, 2000; Brown, 2006; Rajagopal, 2000).

Despite differences between the US and the UK, the move among both diaspora communities is towards fixity and rigidity in the boundaries of Hindu identity (Raj, 2000; Brown, 2006). The global economy has affected Indian elites at home and abroad and has placed these people in important positions of power that can be (and have been) used to channel their material, cultural and political interests. In India, as argued earlier, these elites have repeatedly launched attacks on the 'appeasement' of religious minorities by political leaders (especially the Congress), using the language of 'victimisation' for the majority community. This feeling of victimisation has seemed to ring true for many Hindus in the West struggling with their minority status and discrimination (Mukta, 2000). In this sense the diaspora *Hindutva* movement is simultaneously concerned with 'minority Hindu rights' in the West and with 'majority rights of Hindus' in India (Bhatt and Mukta, 2000; Brown, 2006). In both cases this concern tends to be interpreted through a nationalist lens focussed on enhancing hegemonic interpretations of what constitutes Hindu national identity.

Here it is pertinent to consider the issue of foreign relations more generally since the impact of the Hindu Right has become of central concern to international relations and global stability *per se*. This has been particularly true in the wake of September 11, 2001 and the ensuing 'war on terror' during the Bush administration. India's relationship with Pakistan and Afghanistan is of imperative consequence to the developments in a volatile and conflict-ridden region. During its last episode in power, the BJP-led National Democratic Alliance (NDA) mobilised the Indian army along the border to Pakistan after the attack on the Indian Parliament in December 2001. In the preceding mandate period, it both initiated the ongoing nuclear arms race and fought a war with Pakistan in the district of Kargil. More recently, the BJP has been opposed to India's nuclear treaty with the United States, arguing that it endangers the 'independence' of India's nuclear policy (Bharatiya Janata Party, 2008). One of the main themes of Hindu Right rhetoric in recent years has, accordingly, focussed on the securing of territorial borders. The language has revolved around notions of security, belonging and differentiation coinciding with nation state frontiers and citizenship.

Hegemony and Assimilation: Challenges to Hindu Nationalism

It is clear from this brief overview of Hindu nationalism at home and abroad that the nationalism embodied and promulgated by the Hindu Right does not straightforwardly correspond to a religious nationalism. The religious is merely present in its instrumental deployment of symbols and practices inherent to Hindu traditions. Even if we would conclude that the conceptualisation of India advocated by the Hindu Right corresponds to the term religious nationalism, it would still be necessary to mark the exclusionary tendencies of its actions. Although Christophe Jaffrelot (2009: 8) maintains that the meaning ascribed to territory in Hindu nationalist discourse is primarily concerned with the deepening of 'national solidarity' and less with the unification of large parts of the subcontinent into an *Akhand Bharat* (Undivided India), it is a solidarity that is more symbolic (e.g. the rites and cartography of pilgrimage as discussed by Jaffrelot) than material. It is further a conceptualisation that adopts the silencing of internal divisions and the reinforcement of nation state borders as its focal points. At the same time, it is an understanding of space which tends to keep social stratifications and power asymmetries intact. Jaffrelot's argument that the 'desire to get beyond social divisions—especially beyond caste—is as old as Hindu nationalism itself' (Ibid.), is thus not unproblematic. With Sarkar it might, conversely, be noted that 'efforts to construct a more unified "Hinduism" had to confront a simultaneous development of multiple caste identities, while colonial (and postcolonial) modernisation strengthened both Brahmanical influence, and lower-caste and Dalit protests' (2005: 306). It is an observation that points at the impossibility, and the arbitrary endeavour to arrive at an unattainable totality and completion of the Hindu nationalist project.

To reconnect to the opening statement on the unexpected loss of the BJP in the last general elections, it ought to be noted that, while in power, the party failed to deliver in terms of integrative and inclusive measures—not only between, but also within religious communities. Hindu nationalism has not come to embody assimilatory practices—if understood in terms of Barr's conceptual framework—beyond the reach of the urban middle class. According to Nandy, its scope is restricted to spaces where citizens have undergone a process of 'massification' and have been 'made to speak only the language of the state' (1998: 295). It is, in other words, highly particularistic in its stances and its representations of the Indian population. As Kulkarni (2009), one of its key political advisors in the 2009 elections, wrote while analysing the poor performance of the BJP:

> [a]s far as taking the BJP closer to the minorities (Muslims and Christians) is concerned, both confusion and indifference within the party are of Himalayan magnitude. The mentality of a large section of the party is so dogmatic that any idea of promoting the welfare and development of Indian Muslims, or of addressing their legitimate concerns, is quickly brushed aside as 'appeasement'. In five long years after 2004, the BJP did not come up with a single worthwhile initiative which Muslims could welcome.

Where then should we look for a religious nationalism that represents a more tolerant, inclusive and accommodating approach? One possibility is, of course, to cohere with the so-called neo-Gandhians—a term used to refer to scholars like Ashis Nandy and T.N. Madan. As argued earlier, Nandy has insisted on making a clear distinction between the *Hindutva* type of political ideology and Hinduism as permeating Indian culture. In describing this culture, Nandy (1983: 84-85) emphasises how the colonial encounter was designed to hide the real self—the deepest social consciousness of the victims—from the outsider. Madan, similarly, has insisted that traditional culture could become the basis for a new Indian unity, while Chatterjee has argued in favour of a new historical nationalist project to 'fashion a "modern" national culture that is nevertheless not Western' (Chatterjee, 1993, quoted in Juergensmeyer 1996: 133). When Nandy and other neo-Gandhians oppose the oppressive and homogenising values and institutions of enlightenment, modernity and colonialism, they praise instead an authentic traditional Indianness which has survived both the impact of modernity and the depredation of Hindu nationalism. Here Nandy uses the language of 'critical traditionalism' as an emancipatory discourse for colonised (and re-colonised in the era of globalisation) societies.

Drawing on Juergensmeyer one could argue that the neo-Gandhians rightly bring to our attention how 'the Hindutva proponents have co-opted the authentic, inclusive Indian cultural tradition; [...] It is this authentic cultural core that provides an alternative to the Hindutva-secularism dichotomy, allowing for the cultural integrity of the former and the tolerance of the latter' (1996: 134). There is, however, an apparent problem in-built into such a claim, namely the longing or search for an 'authentic' cultural core. As Desai (2002: 78) points out, Nandy's 'critical traditionalism' has profound potential for authoritarianism: '[h]is conception of "tradition" or "culture" or "civilisation" (terms he uses interchangeably) is an elite and conservative, and a Brahminical, one'. Authentic tradition involves the search for a 'true' (religious) Hindu self that can resist the onslaught of modernity, secularism and the westernised middle classes of India.

To the vain search for authenticity might be added that any political project trying to unearth resonance in a representation of the Indian nation or of society as potentially complete or intact is destined to fail; or as Dipesh Chakrabarty formulates it: '[t]he assumption that there is a "whole" in India that always trumps all conflicts and diversity does not strike us today with any degree of obviousness beyond what the media or Bollywood can produce with cricket or the occasional war with Pakistan' (2008: 179). We thus propose that a more fruitful and constructive position is that offered by constructivist historians, such as van der Veer, Juergensmeyer and Oommen, who problematise the construction of knowledge and meaning and show how hegemonic interpretations of religion and nation are always constructed in relation to discourses of power. This means that those who produce the discourse also have the power to make it true, that is to enforce a particular reading of a threat according to which people and groups are defined (see Foucault, 1980: 201). This power to make a discourse seemingly true is particularly evident in cases where one group holds more privileges and resources and when it uses the language of difference as a way to legitimise its own dominance and to marginalise others (van Dijk, 1997: 144). Hence, throughout history there have been, as van der Veer (1992) notes, many competing versions of Hindu nationalism and these versions have had more or less political support at different points in time. In addition, it is important to move away from the concept of secularism as existing in opposition to religion and/or communalism and to recognise that secularism actually implies minority rights. As Chandhoke (1999: 293) argues, an understanding of minority rights within secularism can be incorporated only when appealing to the antecedent principle of equality between and within communities.

Conclusion

In this chapter we have evaluated the religious nationalism that the Hindu Right has come to represent and established that it is merely religious in name. It is principally exclusionary in its deployment of religion. For a more dynamic and open type of religious-based nationalism or identity formation, certain readings of the Gandhian legacy might offer a potential point of departure. Although these, as shown, suffer from deficiencies, they still contain the seeds of positive potentials as regards tolerance, inclusion and affirmation of belonging, particularly as these were developed in the Nehruvian visions of a secular society in which religion should exist in all its multiplicity. In order for a nationalism, or any attempt to mobilise a collective, to meet the requirements of being inclusive and tolerant, it needs to carry a tendency equivalent to the one which Sarkar—perhaps rather benignly—detects in 'Indian anti-colonialism', which 'at its best displayed an unusual capacity to criticise itself, an ability to both affirm and try to go beyond patriotic values' (2005: 307).

What the present form of Hindu nationalism lacks is such a self-reflexive, wavering, self-altering trait. It fails to recognise the constitutive emptiness and incompleteness of identity formation and of belonging. As such it is merely yet another example of a movement that vainly seeks to establish ontological security. It may be correct to argue that the 'religious nationalism' disseminated and enacted by the Hindu Right has a constitutive and central function; but the way it has been developed has merely served to strengthen exclusive, non-accommodating majoritarian forces that have often been destructive, corroding and subversive. It would hence be flawed to claim that Hindu nationalism does not manifest itself in, or simultaneously constitute, violence. Reinterpreting religious nationalism in a positive sense requires that we move away from hegemonic definitions of what constitutes a community and a nation towards a secularism that truly puts religious rights at the forefront by recognising the needs of the individual members of both majority and minority communities at home as well as abroad.

References

Austin, Granville (2000). *The Indian Constitution: Cornerstone of a Nation.* New Delhi: Oxford University Press.

Bajpai, Rochana (2000). "Constituent Assembly Debates and Minority Rights", *Economic and Political Weekly* 35 (21/22): 1837-45.

Barr, M.D. (2010). "Religious Nationalism and Nation-building in Asia: An Introduction", *Australian Journal of International Affairs* 64(3), 255-61.

Bharatiya Janata Party (2000). *Indo-US Nuclear Deal. Why Does BJP Oppose It?* at *http://www.bjp.org/images/other_publications/indo_us_deal_e.pdf*

Bhargava, Rajeev (1996). "How not to defend secularism", in Praful Bidwai *et al.* (eds.), *Religion, Religiosity and Communalism.* New Delhi: Manohar. pp.57-74.

Bhatt, Chetan (2000). "Dharmo Rakshati Rakshitah: Hindutva Movements in the UK", *Ethnic and Racial Studies* 23/3: 559-593.

———. (2001). *Hindu Nationalism: Origins, Ideologies, and Modern Myths.* Oxford: Berg.

Bhatt, Chetan and Parita Mukta (2000). "Hindutva in the West: Mapping the Antinomies of Diaspora Nationalism", *Ethnic and Racial Studies* 23/3: 407-41.

Bidwai, Praful, Harbans Mukhia and Achin Vanaik (eds.) (1996). *Religion, Religiosity and Communalism.* New Delhi: Manohar.

Blom Hansen, Thomas (1999). *The Saffron Wave.* Princeton: Princeton University Press.

Brass, Paul (2003). *The Production of Hindu-Muslim Violence in Contemporary India.* Seattle: Washington University Press.

Brown, Judith M. (2006). *Global South Asians: Introducing the Modern Diaspora.* Cambridge: Cambridge University Press.

Brubaker, Rogers (2005). "The 'diaspora' diaspora", *Ethnic and Racial Studies* 28/1: 1-19.

Carter, Sean (2005). "The Geopolitics of Diaspora", *Area* 37/1: 54-63.

Chakrabarty, Dipesh (2008). "The Public Life of History: An Argument Out of India", *Postcolonial Studies* 11/2: 169-90.

Chakrabarty, D. (1994). "Modernity and Ethnicity in India", *South Asia* 17: 140–52.

Chandhoke, Neera (1999). *Beyond Secularism: The Rights of Religious Minorities.* Delhi: Oxford University Press.

Chatterjee, Partha (1993). *The Nation and Its Fragments: Colonial and Postcolonial Histories.* Princeton: Princeton University Press.

Constituent Assembly Debates (1949). *Proceedings.* 25 November at *http://164.100.47.132/LssNew/constituent/Constituent.aspx*

Deol, Harnik (2000). *Religion and Nationalism in India: The Case of the Punjab.* London and New York: Routledge.

Desai, Radhika (2002). *Slouching towards Ayodhya.* New Delhi: Three Essays Press.

Devare, Aparna (2009). "Secularizing Religion: Hindu Extremism as a Modernist Discourse", *International Political Sociology* 3(2): 156-75.

De Vries, Hent (2006). *Religion and Violence: Philosophical Perspectives from Kant to Derrida.* Baltimore: The Johns Hopkins Press.

———. (2002). *Religion and Violence.* Baltimore: The Johns Hopkins University Press.

Dutta, P. and Sumit Sarkar (1994). "Manufacturing Hatred: The Image of the Ramjanmabhumi Movment", in M. Arslam and J. Rajan (eds.), *Communalism in India: Challenge and Response.* New Delhi: Manohar.

Dutt, Sagarika (1998). "Identities and the Indian State: An Overview", *Third World Quarterly* 19(3): 411–34.

Fearon, James and David Laitin (2000). "Violence and the Social Construction of Ethnic Identity", *International.Organization* (Autumn): 845-77.

Foucault, Michel (1980). *Power/Knowledge: Selective Interviews and Other Writings 1972-77,* in Colin Gordon (ed.), New York: Pantheon.

Hirst, Jacqueline and John Zavos (2005). "Riding a Tiger? South Asia and the Problem of 'Religion'", *Contemporary South Asia* 14(1): 3-20.

Hutchinson, John (1994). *Modern Nationalism.* London: Fontana Press.

Jaffrelot, Christophe(2009). "The Hindu Nationalist Reinterpretation of Pilgrimage in India: The Limits of *Yatra* Politics", *Nations and Nationalism* 15(1): 1-19.

———. (2002). "Is India Globalisable?", *Indian Horizons* 49(1): 135-40.

———. (ed.) (1998). *Hindu Nationalism: A Reader.* Princeton, New Jersey: Princeton University Press.

———. (1996). *The Hindu Nationalist. Movements and Indian Politics: 1925-1990s.* New Delhi: Penguin India.

Jaffrelot, Christophe and Ingrid Therwath (2007). "The Sangh Parivar and the Hindu Diaspora in the West: What Kind of 'Long-Distance Nationalism'?", *International Political Sociology* 1(3): 278–95.

Juergensmeyer, Mark (1996). "The Debate Over Hindutva", *Religion* 26(2): 129-36.

Kohli, Atul (1990). *Democracy and Discontent: India's Growing Crisis of Governability.* Cambridge: Cambridge University Press.

Kolodner, Eric (1995). "The Political Economy of the Rise and Fall(?) of Hindu Nationalism", *Journal of Contemporary Asia* 25(2): 233-253.

Kulkarni, Sudheendra (2009). "Hindu Divided Family", *Tehelka*, June 13, at *http://www.tehelka.com/story_main42.asp?filename= Ne130609hindu_divided.asp*

Luden, David (ed.) (1996). *Contesting the Nation Religion Community and the Politics of Democracy in India.* Pennsylvania: University of Pennslyvania Press.

Mathew, Biju and Vijaya Prasad (2000). "Satyagraha in America: The Political Culture of South Asians in the US", *Ameriasia Journal* 25/3: ix-xv.

Mukta, Parita (2000). "The Public Face of Hindu Nationalism", *Ethnic and Racial Studies* 23(3): 442-66.

Nandy, Ashis (1983). *The Intimate Enemy: Loss and Recovery of Self under Colonialism.* Delhi: Oxford University Press.

———. (1998). "The Twilight of Certitudes: Secularism, Hindu Nationalism and Other Masks of Deculturation", *Postcolonial Studies* 1(3): 283-98.

Oommen, T.K. (1994). "The Changing Trajectory of Constructing the Other: West Europe and South Asia", *Sociological Bulletin* 43(2).

———. (1997). *Citizenship, Nationality and Ethnicity.* Cambridge: Polity Press.

Oza, Rupal (2007). "The Geography of Hindu Right-wing Violence in India", in Derek Gregory and Allan Pred (eds.), *Violent Geographies: Fear, Terror, and Political Violence.* New York: Routledge. pp.153-73.

Pandey, Gyanendra (2001). *Remembering Partition: Violence, Nationalism, and History in India.* Cambridge: Cambridge University Press,.

Panikkar, K.N. (1997). *Communal Threat, Secular Challenge.* New Delhi: Earthworm Books.

Patnaik, Arun and K.S.R.V.S. Chalam (1998). "The Ideology and Politics of Hindutva", in T.V. Sathyamurthy (ed.), *Region, Religion, Caste, Gender and Culture in Contemporary India.* Delhi: Oxford University Press. pp.252-80.

Prime Minister's High Level Committee, Cabinet Secretariat (2006). *Social, Economic and Educational Status of the Muslim Community of India: A Report.* New Delhi: Government of India at *http:/ /minorityaffairs.gov.in/newsite/sachar/sachar_comm.pdf*

Puniyani, Ram (2009). "Elections 2009 Verdict: Whither Communalism", *Tehelka.* May 29, at *http:/ /www.tehelka.com/story_main42.asp?filename=Ws060609Ram_Puniyani.asp*

Raj, Dhooleka Sarhadi (2000). "Who the Hell Do You Think you are? Promoting Religious Identity Among Young Hindus in Britain", *Ethnic and Racial Studies* 23(3): 535-58.

Rajagopal, Arvind (2000). "Hindu Nationalism in the US: Changing Configurations of Political Practice", *Ethnic and Racial Studies* 23(3): 467-96.

Ramakrishnan, Venkitesh (2009). "Congress Resurgence", *Frontline*, 26/11, *at http://www.frontlineonnet.com/fl2611/stories/20090605261100400.htm*

Sangari, Kumkum (2002). "A Narrative of Restoration: Gandhi's Last Years and Nehruvian Secularism", *Social Scientist* 30(3-4): 3-33.

Sarkar, Sumit (2005). "Inclusive Democracy and Its Enemies", *Interventions* 7(3): 304-09.

Singh, Pritam (2005). "Hindu Bias in India's 'Secular' Constitution: Probing Flaws in the Instruments of Governance", *Third World Quarterly* 26(6): 909-26.

Smith, A. (2000). "The Sacred Dimensions of Nationalism", *Journal of International Studies* 29: 71-81.

Srikrishna Commission Report (1998). *Mumbai Riots, 1992-1993.* Mumbai: Sabrang Communications and Publishing, at *http://www.sabrang.com/srikrish/sri%20main.htm*

van der Veer, Peter (1992). "Ayodhya and Somnath: Eternal Shrines, Contested Histories", *Social Research* 59(1): 85-110.

———. (1996). *Religious Nationalism: Hindus and Muslims in India.* Delhi: Oxford University Press.

van Dijk, Teun (1997). "Political Discourse and Racism: Describing Others in Western Parliament", in Harold Riggins (ed.), *The Language and Politics of Exclusion: Others in Discourse.* London: Sage. pp.31-64.

Vertovec, Steven (2000). *The Hindu Diaspora: Comparative Patterns.* London and New York: Routledge.

Vyas, Neena (2009a). "Yashwant Sinha Resigns from Party Positions", *The Hindu*. June 14, at *http:/ /www.hindu.com/2009/06/14/stories/2009061457390100.htm*

———. (2009b). "A Setback, Not a Rout, says BJP", *The Hindu*. June 22, at *http://www.hindu.com/2009/06/22/stories/2009062257070100.htm*

———. (2009). "BJP to Do Introspection", *The Hindu*. June 9, at *http://www.hindu.com/2009/06/09/stories/2009060960631000.htm*

Zamindar, Vazira Fazila-Yacoobali (2007). *The Long Partition and the Making of Modern South Asia: Refugees, Boundaries, Histories.* New York: Columbia University Press.

11

Religious Trends and Extremism in Asia

BILVEER SINGH

Introduction

Although necessary, predicting the future, even the next 20 years, is fraught with immense uncertainty and a high degree of 'ifs', especially as far as security is concerned. This is all the more so with regard to religious trends, as this is one area that has seen tremendous and rapid changes and transformations that were unimaginable even a decade or two ago. While change is an inevitable certainty in world politics, the pace and the consequences of change have been unsettling. It has shaken the edifices of many societies, bringing about both welcome and unwelcome transformations, with the attendant instability often causing political and social tectonic shifts at great cost to all. The challenge posed by religious mobilisation, especially by extremist ideologies and religious agendas to the security and stability of West, Central, South, Southeast Asia and even parts of China has been well-documented. To that extent, the future is already here![1]

In the context of these changes, many factors are likely to influence the future. Technological and military modernisation, globalisation, economic growth, changing demographics, climate change, competition over strategic resources, nationalism and identity politics and rising militancy are often identified as the key drivers that are likely to shape the coming world. In this 'buffet', the importance of religion cannot be ignored, though for long, this was the case. Increasingly, religion can no longer be considered to be a part of an individual's private domain. The changing nature and characteristics

1. For example, see Alam (2006); Dhar (2006); Ahmed (2006); Hafez (2005); Mohanty (2006).

of religion have affected key aspects of national and international politics, sharpening fault lines, and often by intense domestic and international conflicts. While the end of the Cold War greatly diminished the role of ideology in politics, religion has emerged as the defining feature of identity. This in turn, fuels religious extremism and radicalism, as well as leads to the rise of dangerous terrorist organisations, especially in Asia, where they have used religion as mobilising and rationalising tool to further their political causes. As such, societies can no longer ignore the impact and influence of the developments in religion both in the national and geopolitical arenas.

Against this backdrop, this chapter attempts to analyse religious trends in Asia and their attendant consequences, especially as far as radicalism, militancy, extremism and even terrorism are concerned. It will also discuss how the political ideologies of various religions have influenced the political discourse in various parts of Asia, especially Southeast Asia, as well as the rise of religious extremism. The chapter will deal with the issue of whether terrorist groups will be able to displace civil religious organisations as the authentic representatives of religions in Asia. While all religions are undergoing change, because the rise of religiosity and revivalism is an almost universal phenomenon, the one religion that has come under focus and scrutiny, both fairly and unfairly, has been Islam. Even before the infamous September 11, 2001 terrorist attacks in New York and Washington D.C., many regions were already experiencing and even suffering from the wrath of Islamist extremism, although similar trends were evident among Christian, Buddhist, Sikh, Jewish and Hindu extremists. Yet, for a host of reasons, Islamist extremism and the violence associated with it, were already a major concern in South, Southeast, West and Central Asia. The '9/11 Incident' brought the situation into sharper focus following George Bush's launch of the 'global war on terrorism', with Islamist extremism as its single most important target. While discussing religious trends in Asia in general, the chapter will mainly spotlight the developments in Southeast Asia and their consequences for Asia and beyond.

Religious Trends in Asia

As one of the key centres of human civilisation, historically, religion has always played an important role in Asia. Over time, the worship of God by man took the form of organised religions. The Western world was mainly influenced by Christianity while Hinduism, Buddhism and Islam dominated most of Asia. Originating in the Indian subcontinent, Hinduism greatly influenced the psyche and attitude towards life of people residing in the subcontinent. Here, the theory of *karma*, where one's destiny in the next life was the product of one's actions in this life, greatly shaped the outlook of most Indians. Caste and deep social divisions are a byproduct of Hinduism and various belief systems that are prescribed in ancient texts. Islam is the second dominant religion that is widely practised in the Middle East, West and Central Asia as well as in South and Southeast Asia and even parts of China. Professing a highly regimented and rigid way of life, this largely male-dominated faith has greatly shaped the political and social outlook of its adherents. Buddhism, the third major religion to dominate Asia, was ostensibly the faith of peace and non-violence, taking the cue from Asoka's reform following the Kalinga War (265-264 BC). Buddhism quickly gained many adherents in East and Southeast Asia, and has remained a dominant social force in these societies. Due to the spread of these three religions in Asia, followed by the rise of Christianity and other minor faiths, the political-social fabric of Asian societies has been strongly divided by religious fault lines that have been superimposed by other divides based on race, language and culture, as well as different political systems and histories, not to mention conflicts between various groups in the region. All these have played an important role in dividing Asian communities.[2]

Religious trends in Asia are a reflection of the broader changes taking place in the world at large. These are also affected by a whole array of developments that have both direct and indirect implications for religions, their practice and the way in which adherents and non-adherents view their own and other religions. The 'Other' is often

---

2. For more information, see "Influence of Religion in Asia". Available at *http://www.bizymoms.com/vacationsandtravel/asia-pacific/influence-of-religion.html*

defined by differences based on religion and race. Some of the more noteworthy global trends include the following:

- Increasing democratisation.
- Globalisation creating an increasing divide between those who benefit and those that are discontented with its consequences.
- The 'economics-first' policies of governments and the attendant vulnerability to cyclical changes and negative fallouts of economic policies of major economies, mainly leading to impoverishment of the masses in many societies.
- Steady depreciation and weakening of state's sovereignty with the simultaneous rise of new non-state actors often compete with the state especially in the cyber age.
- Rising importance of governance, particularly involving issues of human security.
- Growing importance of non-traditional security issues, the increasing vulnerability of states and individuals to all kinds of threats, with many states unprepared and unable to combat them, and where extra-state efforts become necessary to manage and overcome them; and
- Increasing tendency to utilise soft power even though this does not necessarily negate the continued importance of hard power in inter-state relations.

What these developments augur is that there is a rapid change taking place at all levels in the international system, with the nature of issues becoming increasingly complex and often beyond the purview of a single state (even the great powers) to manage. States also have to deal with frequent political and economic 'shocks'. As was noted by the National Opinion Research Centre (NORC) of the University of Chicago, 'religious change around the world is a complex phenomenon. No simple description such as secularisation, religious revival or believing without belonging, captures the complexity of the process'.[3]

In the context of the wide ranging global changes, no state in Asia has been able to escape the influence and impact of religion in politics,

3. Seinfels (2009).

which is greatly affecting and shaping political discourse in Asia that is also in the process of economic development and claiming its place in international geopolitics. The impact of religion and religious ideology has, however, been varied in Asia.[4] Notwithstanding this, there has been an explicit tendency in the last 2 to 3 decades or so, strongly triggered by the 1979 Iranian Revolution, towards the rise of political religions in Asia, vying not just with existing civil religions but also other ideologies, often with the goal of replacing the more secular-oriented state-based ideologies. While civil religions usually tend to unify socially disparate communities, the process of religious politicisation can have major disruptive consequences, pitting one religious ideology against another, thereby destabilising states and the wider regional order.

Not many practitioners and thinkers would have imagined that the beginning of the 21st century would witness the centrality of religion in national politics. Many would have thought that modernisation, the rise of secularism and democratisation would have led religion to loosen its hold on Man. Yet, all the benefits and ills of globalisation, the explosion of information and communication technologies, migration and immigration, capital flows, the role of transnational corporations, transnational media organisations, non-governmental organisations and identity politics have resulted in furthering the proliferation of religion, religious beliefs, ideologies and practices.

As far as religious trends in Asia are concerned, an undeniable fact is its rise as a potent force in national and international politics. Religion has been used to legitimise the existing power structure and its wielders. Religion can and has been used to distract national discontent by focussing on other-worldly concerns. Many religious organisations have provided organisational and moral support to social movements, as is evident in the rise of liberation theology and its like in many parts of the developing world. Religion can also offer a concept of justice to mobilise masses into action for change or to safeguard a status quo and a regime. It is also mainly due to the character and role of religion in a political setting that a society is

4. Nathan (2007).

often labelled as being either secular or theocratic. The political-religious nexus has also been critical in playing either a conservative or progressive role, either by legitimising the existing political system and structure or supporting protests and resistance to bring about its downfall.[5]

An important impetus for the growing importance of religion in Asia was due the continent's encounter with modernity, mainly through colonialism and its attendant backlash. With the rise of Asian nationalism, often couched and spurred by local religions, secular-based economic and political systems often failed to deliver the 'promised future' with millions of masses uprooted from their traditional rural setting and joining unemployed and exploited hordes in various mega-cities. Where neoliberal economic policies succeeded, they were often accompanied by repression, rampant corruption, and uneven development where the gap between the rich and poor was savagely widened. All these developments provided the backdrop for rejection of modernity and the championing of the traditional alternative, with political and economic justice couched in religious terms. There were also important external factors that led to the rise of religious ideology, often as a protest against Western, usually American political, economic and even social-cultural domination. This was not helped by American and Western sponsorship of Islamist *jihadism* in Afghanistan from 1980 to 1990, aimed at containing and rolling-back Soviet occupation of the country. The net result of all these was the growing ascendancy of religion in national politics in many parts of Asia including in Southeast Asia.

There are a number of trends that are worth noting as these will have immense consequences for the political-strategic architecture over the next two decades or so. These include the following:

1. The rising religiosity of Asians despite professions of secularism.
2. The rising attraction of militant/radical Islam.
3. The growing number of Islam's adherents disproportionate to other religions.

---

5. Singh (forthcoming).

4. The growing importance of Christians in Asia.
5. The persistence of religious persecutions; and
6. The rise of denominations within mainstream religions.

The Southeast Asian Case Study: Islam in Indonesia

Presently, Southeast Asia is the hotbed of religion based conflicts. The violence in Muslim-dominated Southern Thailand and Southern Philippines has been ongoing for more than half a century. Indonesia, the largest Muslim country in the world, has witnessed Muslims *versus* Muslim and Muslim *versus* non-Muslim conflicts for many years. In Thailand, the Philippines and Indonesia, there are also a number of Islamist-based terrorist groups that are bent on either creating an autonomous Islamic, or totally independent Muslim state using violence to achieve this goal. However, most surprising of late has been the recent 'Allah' controversy in Malaysia that saw a number of churches and Sikh temples being attacked, presumably by Islamists who believe that the term 'Allah' was only reserved for use by Malaysian Muslims. The Malaysian case was merely a reminder of how tenuous interreligious relations are even in a country that is over all an economic success.

The Southeast Asian region is highly heterogeneous, with sharp fault lines in race, religion and language. The region hosts almost all the major religions of the world, with the majority of its people being either Islamic, Buddhists or Christians. All religions in the region are politically significant, having affected sociopolitical events at one time or another. Islam has been politically influential in Indonesia and Malaysia right from supporting the various anti-colonial struggles and since then, defining the state's character as is the case in Brunei. Christianity was extremely important in mobilising anti-American movements in the Philippines. It also played a critical role in the East Timorese struggle against Indonesia and it continues to be important in the Papuan struggle against Indonesia today. Buddhism played an important role in safeguarding the Thai monarchy as well as supporting anti-colonial struggles in Vietnam, Cambodia, Laos and Burma. However, as the dominant religious discourse in Southeast Asia in the last two decades has been associated with Islam, especially its role in the world's largest Muslim state, Indonesia, this will be dealt with in the following pages to study the trends and consequences for Southeast Asia and Asia in general.[6]

More specifically, in Islam religion as a political ideology is closely intertwined with what is known as the process of *Salafication*. This refers to the efforts by adherents, a minority though they may be, to jumpstart Islamic revival in a region, especially in countries with a significant Muslim presence. This has led to the rise of the purist Wahhabi-Salafi version of Islam gaining ground in Southeast Asia, evident from the propensity of Muslims to join aggressive extremist organisations, especially in Indonesia which has experienced much religious-oriented violence since 2000. Here, radical Islamic concepts associated with the creation of an Islamic state, the adoption of *Sharia* law, the propensity towards greater exclusivity and most important of all, the loose use and application of *jihad*, against Muslims and non-Muslims, have increasingly characterised the rise of Islam as a political ideology.

One of the most striking characteristics of post-Suharto Indonesia was the emergence of Islam as a pivotal political player.[7] Having been politically marginalised by the state for many years, first under Sukarno's 'guided democracy' and later, under Suharto's 'New Order', Islam has increasingly politically asserted itself following the lifting of political restraints in the aftermath of Suharto's downfall in May 1998.[8] More dramatically, a number of radical Islamic groups appeared and publicly promoted their Islamic political agenda.[9] While some argue that the emergence of Islamic radical groups in the aftermath of Suharto's downfall was partly engineered by some elements of the New Order regime and military to destabilise the country,[10] it is widely accepted that radical Islamic organisations have a long history in Indonesia.[11] The earliest of such movement in the modern era was

6. There are a number of major works on the subject. These include: Wahid (2009); Jurdi (2008); Rahmat (2008); Mubarak (2008); Nashir (2007); Taufik Adnan and Panggabean (2004); Turmundi *et al.* (2009) and Mulkhan (2009).

7. Schwartz (1999).

8. Fealy (2001).

9. Azra (2002); Hassan (2002).

10. Hefner (2001).

11. Bruinessen (2002).

that of the 'Padri' in West Sumatra. From 1780s, pilgrims returning from the Middle East set about 'reforming' local Islamic practices and applying Islamic law more strictly in the region. Islam was also a powerful element in other conflicts of the colonial period, including the Java War of 1825-1830, although its expression was more heterodox than severely orthodox as was the case in the Padri War (1821-1837). Thus, the assumption in some terrorism texts that Islamist radicalism is a new phenomenon in Indonesia is historically flawed.[12] The aspirations and attempts to build, peacefully or violently, a more formal Islamic state has been a major part of the country's political discourse and practice since its independence. Violence perpetrated by Muslim radicals is not a new phenomenon in Indonesia and many have argued that the Suharto regime's repression of political Islam contributed to the radicalisation of Muslim dissents.[13]

During the first two decades of the New Order, political Islam became the principal target of the state's exclusionary politics as well as the focus of ideological and political distrust. At least until the late 1980s, political Islam was effectively marginalised through an extensive public indoctrination campaign which stigmatised Islam as a political ideology dangerous for the unity and prosperity of the state. Political Islam was also undermined institutionally and ideologically with all Muslim political parties forced to merge into a single party and strictly controlled by the government. Also, all Islamic mass organisations had to accept the official state ideology, *Pancasila*, as the only legitimate ideology.[14] Despite, or for some, because of Suharto's repression, there has been a steady rise in Muslim consciousness and ritual formalism, since '80s, especially among the urban middle classes and student population. University campuses became fertile grounds for an Islamic awakening, with students being recruited into a diverse range of highly regulated cells. Some of these cells are inspired by the fundamentalist thought and organisational models of radical Islamic movements in the Middle East.[15]

---

12. Fealy and Bubalo (2005).
13. Mujani and Liddle (2004); Jones (2001).
14. Fealy and Bubalo (2005) *op. cit.*
15. Bruinessen (2002) *op. cit.*

The resurgence of political Islam, however, became more apparent after the fall of Suharto. The collapse of the New Order paved the way for an open contest for the control of public space among different elements of Indonesian society. Also, members of the newly liberated society suddenly got the freedom to express themselves. But many groups did not want actors with specific ideological leanings to dominate the dynamics of the changes taking place during the transition process. The emergence of a new liberated civil society permitted all kinds of ideas to surface and these also included ideas associated with political Islam and the role Islam was to play in Indonesia after being repressed for nearly half a century.[16] As a result, political Islam emerged as a major player in Indonesian politics. More dramatically, a number of radical Islamic groups appeared and publicly promoted ideological, symbolical and formal Islamic political goals.[17] It is difficult not to perceive the rise of political Islam during the post-Suharto period in the light of legalism and formalism. The intellectual transformation which occurred between the '70s and '90s seems to have lost its significance when ideological, symbolic and formal Islam began dominating the new discourse on Indonesia's political Islam. The use of Islam as the basis for a political party and the call for the implementation of *sharia* were clear indicators of the rising tide of political Islam.

In contemporary times, and especially after September 11, 2001, there is a tendency to see terrorism as largely being the consequence of the spread of a global ideology. As a result, Western views of both Middle Eastern and Indonesian Islam have become hardened and interaction between the two dramatically reduced. More than any other region of the Islamic world, the Middle East is now seen as the crucible of nihilistic *jihadism*. Indonesian Islam is still regarded as being primarily tolerant and pluralistic, but the emergence in recent years of local paramilitary *jihadist* and terrorist groups has created concerns about the perceived radicalisation and the eroding of the country's essentially 'moderate' Islamic character. One reason commonly advanced by Western observers for this 'extremist' minority

---

16. Schwartz (1999) *op. cit.*

17. Azra (2002) *op. cit.*

trend in Indonesia is the growing influence of Middle Eastern Islam. Globalisation and the increasing penetration of mass communication have contributed to this process, as also the generous Middle Eastern sponsorship of radical outreach programmes. Thus, the more Indonesian Islam is seen as having Middle Eastern qualities, the greater the threat it poses. Some have viewed this as the 'purification' of Indonesian Islam from 'Sufi' and Javanese influence.[18]

The reality, however, is far more complex than these stereotypes suggest. There is a wide variance in Islamist thinking and behaviour in the Middle East, from the innovative and the pragmatic, to virulent *jihadist-salafism*. To characterise all of Middle Eastern Islamism as dangerously radical is to overlook a large part of the complex and pluralistic Islamic political mosaic. Islamism has never been uniquely Middle Eastern, and today, it is even less so, underlined by neo-fundamentalism's growing detachment from the region. Indonesian Islam, while mainly moderate, has also had a long history of violent minority radicalism which owed little to external influences, whether from the Middle East or elsewhere.

Similarly, the relationship between Middle Eastern and Indonesian Muslims is far more variegated than is commonly assumed by many contemporary Western commentators. As the birthplace of Islam, the Middle East has been a powerful force in shaping the faith in Southeast Asia. Most of the major streams of thinking and practice in the Middle East have found their way to Southeast Asia. Rarely, however, have these processes entailed a direct transfer and unmediated application by Muslims in countries like Indonesia. More commonly, though not always, there has been an ongoing process of selection, modification and adjustments of various practices and ideas, combining them with pre-existing Islamic and non-Islamic features.[19]

Many factors have contributed to the rise of Islamist militancy and radical ideology being increasingly injected into the thought and practice of Indonesian Islam. Contemporary Indonesian radicalism is caused by a complex mix of local and international factors as well as religious, political and economic elements. Most radical Muslims have

---

18. Fealy and Bubalo (2005) *op. cit.*
19. Ibid.: 49.

long-standing political, social and economic grievances, and these provide the main motivating force for their radical religiosity. Politically, there is a sense of disillusionment with national politics and political processes. Most radical Muslims believe that Islam has been marginalised and oppressed in Indonesia, and that antagonistic domestic and international forces are determined to deny Islam its rightful place at the centre of national life. Muslims are portrayed as having failed to achieve most of their stated objectives. The refusal of religious minorities and 'less devout' Muslims to give constitutional recognition to the authority of *sharia* for the Islamic community (the Jakarta Charter in 1945) has been a constant source of grievance, with many radical writers asserting that Muslim were forced to make far greater sacrifices in the cause of national unity than other groups. They also point to the inability of Islamic parties to win a majority in any of the country's nine general elections as further evidence of failure. The state was also seen as fostering, if not tolerating, Christianisation and discriminating against devout Muslims in the bureaucracy and the military.

From the economic standpoint, there is disillusionment with economic programmes of various states, especially the exploitation of the poor by the rich. The unfair distribution of economic goods, in spite of the country being well endowed, has also provided ready recruits for the extremist cause.[20] Radicals also resent the economic sidelining of Muslims and refer repeatedly to the fact that Muslims own a disproportionately small share of the nation's wealth and had less opportunities for career and economic advancement.[21] It is the failure of 'nationalist projects' to deliver political, economic and social goods that has led to counteractions—namely, the adoption of the 'Islamic mode' of political, economic and social development (including the use of terrorism and violence), to redress, what is perceived as a national, regional and global injustice.[22]

Added to these domestic considerations are a whole array of international factors. Many Muslims are disillusioned with the

20. Singh (2007).

21. Fealy and Bubalo (2005) *op. cit.*

22. Singh (2007) *op. cit.*

international system, mainly dominated by the West, particularly the United States and their double standards. Though viewed as a democracy and supporting human rights, the United States' pro-Israel policies and sanction of Israeli repression of the Palestinians and Arabs, as well as its own largely anti-Islamic policies—evident in its almost non-action when Muslims were being butchered in Bosnia and elsewhere—have riled many into launching a *jihad* against the United States, Israel and their supporters. Also, international (Western) support for repression of Muslims by various secular governments is also a source of anger and motivation. The support given by the West to repressive policies of Egypt, Algeria, Pakistan and Suharto's Indonesia against their Islamic militants has led to the burgeoning of Islamic militancy and extremism in these countries.[23]

The rise of radical Islamic organisations in Indonesia also shows that various currents of Islamism and neo-fundamentalism have had an impact in Indonesia. Most often these ideas have been imported by Indonesian Islamists looking for new modes of thinking about the relationship between Islam, politics and society or indeed new models for activism. Various mechanisms have served as vectors for these ideas, from Indonesian students who travelled to the Middle East to the *jihadists* who went to Afghanistan in the 1980s and 1990s to the proliferating sources of Islamist information available through the Internet and satellite television.

Saudi support—financial and otherwise—has been critical to the emergence of *salafi* currents within the Indonesian Muslim community. Most *salafists* seem essentially concerned with questions of morality and religiosity—albeit of an intolerant kind—limiting their activities to preaching and education. Nonetheless, some *salafi* groups do indulge in acts of vigilantism and sectarian violence. Saudi propaganda has also served to promote—possibly unintentionally—the idea of a Muslim brotherhood. Indonesian Islamists seem, however, to have been selective in their appropriation of this notion. The gradualist approach of Hassan al-Banna has been more influential than the revolutionary thinking of Sayyid Qutb and his radical heirs. In this respect, there are parallels between the *Partai Keadilan Sejahtera*'s (PKS,

23. Ibid.

the Prosperous Justice Party) pragmatic adaptation of its ideology and the shift occurring among some Islamists in the Middle East (notably *Hizb al-Wasat*); although in Indonesia, the existence of a democratic polity means this process is more likely to achieve its full, moderating potential. Nonetheless, the darker side of the PKS also seem to have been influenced by anti-Western conspiracy theories subscribed to by some of its members.

Three organisations, in particular, have received significant Saudi support, both government and non-government: *Dewan Dakwah Islamiyah* Indonesia (DDII; Indonesian Islamic Propagation Council), *Jamiat Islam wal-Irsyad* (The Islamic Association for Enlightenment, usually known simply as *al-Irsyad*); and the *Persatuan Islam* (Persis; Islamic Association). The DDII was established in 1967 by leaders of the banned *Masyumi* Islamic party. Its focus has been propagation rather than practical political activity. DDII's chairman, Mohammad Natsir, was widely respected in Middle Eastern Wahhabi and Salafist circles, and he became the most important conduit for Saudi funds flowing into Indonesia during the '70s and '80s. *Al-Irsyad*, founded in 1913, is primarily devoted to Islamic education and propagation, and the Persis was established in 1924 as a modernist Muslim organisation. Both *al-Irsyad* and Persis have Islamic schools that have played a prominent role in the education of Indonesian Islamists. The role of religious schools, locally known as *madrasahs* or *pesantrens*, is particularly important in spreading radical Islamist thought. The efforts to exercise control over such religious schools by reforming the Indonesian education system have largely been in vain.

Together with *Lembaga Ilmu Pengetahuan Islam dan Arab* (the Indonesian Institute for Islamic and Arabic Sciences or LIPIA), a branch of Al-Imam Muhammad Ibn Saud University in Riyadh, DDII played a critical role in the growth of *salafism* in the '70s and early '80s. DDII, as the main disburser of Saudi money in Indonesia during these decades, provided scholarships for young Indonesian Muslims to study at Middle Eastern institutions, including several of the leading centres of salafist learning such as the Al-Imam University in Riyadh. However, Saudi support did not orient the DDII specifically toward Wahhabism or Salafism. DDII also played a key role in popularising the Muslim brotherhood concept by translating a number of seminal

Muslim brotherhood texts in the late '70s and '80s, the most popular of which was Sayyid Qutb's '*Signposts*'.

The 1979 Iranian Revolution had also a galvanising effect on younger Indonesians, who viewed it as proof that Muslims could overthrow powerful and repressive Western-backed regimes, and replace them with an Islamic political and economic system. The most important development was the internationalisation of *jihad* from the late '70s, culminating in the anti-Soviet *Mujahidin*-led war in Afghanistan during '80s. This was critical to the rise of extremism and terrorism in Southeast Asia. More than 500 Indonesian—and possibly as many as 1000—went through foreign *mujahidin* training camps from the early '80s until the mid-'90s. Their reasons for attending these camps were complex. Some responded to the active recruitment efforts of Islamic organisations, notably the Saudi-based Muslim World League. For others, like the many Arab Islamists who travelled to Afghanistan, more practical motives also seem to have been at play; in particular, the opportunity Afghanistan provided for gaining military training that could be used in their home countries. It was there that they gained experience in arduous battlefield conditions, learned terrorism-related skills such as bomb making and running clandestine operations, and were indoctrinated with pan-Islamic virulent anti-Western ideologies.[24]

Indonesian *mujahidins* had a varied exposure to their Arab counterparts. On arrival in Pakistan, many went through Abdullah Azzam's *Maktab al-Khidmat*, before going on to the training camp of Abdul Rasul Sayyaf, the Afghan commander who had the closest links with Saudi Arabia and Osama bin Laden. A small number of Indonesian *mujahidins* trained at the camps of other Afghan leaders such as Gulbuddin Hekmatyar and Jamil-ur-Rahman. The experience of Indonesian volunteers greatly intensified their sense of global Islamic solidarity in support of the *Ummah*. Importantly, they were able to establish links with Muslim radicals from across the Islamic world. These contacts would later prove invaluable in gaining financial assistance, access to technical know-how and connectivity into the global terrorist network. The practical effect of the '*mujahidisation*' of

---

24. Fealy and Bubalo (2005) *op. cit.*

Indonesian radical groups has been a great increase in their capacity to wreak havoc and destruction—critical elements in a terror campaign. Money, explosives, technical expertise and covert operational methods were available to experienced and resourceful Afghanistan veterans and their associates.[25]

In addition to the *mujahidin* factor, increasing numbers of Southeast Asian Muslims received their education in the Middle East, where they were exposed to the more puritanical and radical expressions of the faith from Saudi Arabia, Egypt, Pakistan and Palestine. In terms of human movement, students have been perhaps the most important contemporary conduits of Islamist ideas from the Middle East to Indonesia. They went to the Middle East, especially Egypt and Saudi Arabia, in large numbers to study with prestigious Islamic scholars and immerse themselves in 'authentic' Islamic culture. In recent years, the number of Indonesians in the Middle East has risen dramatically, due not only to the increase in Indonesian government scholarships but also additional financial assistance from Middle Eastern governments and private donors. While these students did not typically study Islamist ideas and thoughts, the time spent in the Middle East provided opportunities to interact with Islamist groups and exposed students to their radical ideas. In Egypt, for instance, Indonesian students often assembled in Muslim Brotherhood circles, thereby radicalising them.[26]

Another conduit for Islamist ideas has been education and *da'wa* supported by government and non-government organisations and individuals from the Middle East. Saudi-sponsored educational and *da'wa* activities in Indonesia expanded dramatically in the '80s, probably as part of Saudi Arabia's broader ideological conflict at that time with Iranian Islamism. It would be wrong, however, to view Saudi activism in Indonesia as reflective of a coherent strategy or aim. Saudi religious propagation and educational activities often seemed to manifest different motives and at times competing interests. Saudi sponsorship has undoubtedly been provided to those groups whose

25. Ibid.
26. Ibid.

religious inclinations are closest to Wahhabism, notably Indonesian Salafi groups.

Globalisation, particularly as it relates to the transmission of information, has also a significant effect. Cyber technology and satellite television stations such as *al-Jazeera* and *al-Arabiya* have greatly increased the speed and volume of information flows to radical groups in Southeast Asia from other parts of the Islamic world.[27] In the pre-globalised world, it was at least possible to believe the myth that Islam is not only a religion but also a complete way of life. In Islamic discourse this is the 'one religion one culture' paradigm. Globalisation has shattered this myth. The communication links are now worldwide, rapid and increasingly dense. People, customs, societies and civilisations previously more or less isolated from one another are in regular and almost unavoidable contact. This has two consequences for the Muslim communities. First, it allows others to experience the reality of different Islamic cultures. This experience can demonstrate not only what is common to the Muslim *ummah* but also what is 'different'. Second, the experience of this difference can be unsettling if it is viewed as a deviation from 'the Islamic way'.[28]

While the first consequence makes one conscious of the social and cultural diversity of the Muslim *ummah*, the second consequence produces a reaction of rejection of this cultural and social 'hybridity', and a desire to replace it with the authentic 'Islamic way'. The struggle between 'hybridity' and 'authenticity' perhaps constitutes the most important challenge of globalisation for the Muslim *ummah* and is one of the underlying causes of the emergence of Islamic fundamentalist and extremist movements. Islamic fundamentalism refers to a strategy by which Islamic 'purists' attempt to reassert their construction of religious identity and social order as the exclusive basis for a re-created political and social order. They feel this identity is at risk and being eroded by cultural and religious 'hybridity'. They try to fortify their interpretation of religious ways through selective retrieval of doctrines, beliefs and practices from a sacred past.[29]

---

27. Fealy and Bubalo (2005) *op. cit.*
28. Hassan (2002) *op. cit.*
29. Ibid.

Religious fundamentalism is thus a problem produced by the encounter between modernity and a religious community in all its diversity and cultural 'hybridity'. In the context of Indonesia, Azra observed that Islamic radicalism was predicated on the perception that indigeneous Islam was syncretic and hybrid, and needed to be purified and transformed into 'authentic' Islam through the application of the radicals' interpretation. This is the root of the radical Islamic fundamentalism in Indonesia. Azra also suggested that the Islamic radicalism and most of the radical Islamic organisations are led by Indonesians of Arabic descent who reject indigeneous Indonesian Islam which tend to be *Sufi* and Javanese-influenced in favour of their '*salafi*' 'authentic' Islam which is closer to the Arabic Islam.[30]

While there is a propensity towards Islamist radicalism in general, at the same time, there is the paradoxical development of Islamic parties being unable to garner popular support at the polls in Indonesia.[31] Thus, despite nearly 90 per cent of Indonesians being Muslims, Islamic-based parties have always lost out to nationalist ones. There are a number of reasons for this—the Islamic parties are: (i) narrow-based, largely ideological and have been discredited in the past; (ii) the highly divided and competitive nature of the Islamic parties; (iii) the fact that given the exclusive nature of Islamic parties they have not been able to represent Indonesia's multi-racial and multi-religious character; and (iv) probably most importantly, the lack of a national figure that is able to rally Indonesians to the cause of Islamic parties. Thus, despite a general trend towards Islamisation, politically, this has not yet borne fruit yet, even though this failure may spur on the Islamists in future. For this they will rely on the conspiracy theories that Islamic parties are failing in largely Islamic Indonesia mainly due to the efforts of the enemies of Islam, both within and without, to deny them power because Indonesia's enemies will only be able to subjugate and exploit Indonesia as long as Indonesian Islamists are marginalised.

From the discourse of the role of religion as a political ideology in Indonesia, it is clearly evident that this is indeed a very powerful force

30. Azra (2002) *op. cit.*

31. Fealy (2009).

today. While secular ideologies, especially socialism, have been peddled in the region, it is the new vigour and potency of Islam as a political force that has dramatically impacted the politics and security of Southeast Asia. While Indonesia has borne the brunt of the Salafists, it is not alone. Malaysia, Thailand, the Philippines, Singapore, Myanmar and even Brunei are experiencing the impact of Salafism. This in turn is forcing these states to undertake counter-measures to manage, what can be regarded, as the surfacing of a new political force that is the antithesis of the existing status quo. This is likely to remain for sometimes to come and how it is managed will indicate extent of the rising role of religion as a political ideology in Southeast Asia.

Religious Trends in Asia and Extremism

Do the religious trends augur well or badly for Asia? One thing is certain—religious extremism is not something new and has been in existence for a long time. More important, there are a host of factors that have fuelled religious extremism, both internal and external, and as long as these factors remain embedded in societies, religious extremism is here to stay. In hindsight, while the United States discovered the realities and danger of religious extremism and terrorism following the September 11, 2001 attacks, societies in West, Central, South and Southeast Asia have been living with the scourge for many decades prior to September 2001 and hence, have had a longer lead time in understanding the phenomenon of religious extremism and the violence associated with it.

Broadly speaking, there are two main schools of thought as far as religious trends and extremism are concerned. The first argues that the threat will continue over the next 2 or 3 decades, in a continuation of past and present phenomenon, as the causes are very deep-rooted. This is all the more so as religious extremism is not only viewed as a weapon of the weak, especially the resort to violence, but many religious-oriented elites often mobilise this 'resource' as their key source of empowerment. Hence, rationally speaking, religious extremism is here to stay.

The second school argues that religious extremism is suffering from economies of scale, and as the opportunity costs are going up, this ceases to remain an attractive option. As more and more people and elites become cognisant of the phenomenon and more importantly, of the tremendous political, economic and social costs associated with it, the law of diminishing returns is coming into play with religious extremism no longer viewed logically as a viable option. Many have argued that though in the post 9/11 era, the dangers posed by religious extremism, especially as seen in wars, conflicts and violence in Asia, Africa and even Europe were seen as immediate but this is not likely to be the future trend. This is partly evident from the rejection of 'Bushism' by the new administration of President Barack Obama and the latter's more even-handed approach to world politics.

As far as the nexus between religion and extremism is concerned, religion can act both as a 'stopper' and 'facilitator' of extremism. While all religions have demonstrated a propensity for violence, the spotlight has been on Islam and extremism. As far as Southeast Asia is concerned, while Islam was traditionally known and celebrated for its moderation and its capacity to co-exist with other religions as well as absorb pre-Islamic practices and traditions into its *weltanschauung*, mainly due to the influence of Sufism, of late, there has been increasing tension within Islam and between Islam and other religions in the region. The ongoing conflicts in Southern Thailand and Southern Philippines are evidence of this. Similarly, Indonesia has been under siege from Islamist radicals for many decades even though the secularists had on the whole held the upper hand. Still, since the fall of President Suharto in May 1998, the Islamists have been aggressively pursuing their Islamisation agenda, partly facilitated by the space provided by political democratisation. The same is true of Malaysia, where there have been tensions within the Islamic community and contest for political pre-eminence especially between the United Malays National Organisation, UMNO (the leader of the ruling coalition since 1957) and *Parti Se-Islam Malaysia* (PAS), largely confined to the northern state of Kelantan, acting mainly as the opposition party. The current ongoing violence spurred by the use of the term Allah is further evidence of how tenuous interreligious relations can be in Malaysia and how easily these can become a cause of violence.

De rigueur, it has come to be accepted that in societies divided by sharp racial and religious fault lines, a serious failure in governance can, among other reasons, fuel extremism. This is especially so with regard to issues of political, economic and social justice. As long as governments are perceived to be even-handed and devoid of religious discrimination and oppression, the rise of extremism can be somewhat stalled and managed. The converse is also true. In this regard, successful governance can help in reducing the appeal of religious extremism and the terrorism associated with it, as well as marginalise radicalism and extremism. Effective governance and related nation building policies can strengthen the state as well as inter-ethnic and interreligious harmony, thereby delegitimising and reducing the potential numbers of recruits to extremist causes. The converse is also true. While individuals can confront various crises, including identity-related ones, by becoming increasingly religious and even spiritual, this does not necessarily imply a support for extremism and terrorism. However, when misgovernance prevails and this is accompanied by overt discrimination and repression, then, one of the many consequences can be resort to religious extremism and even violence, as it evident in many parts of Asia today.

Possible Religious Trends in 2030 and their Implications

From the Indonesian case study and understanding of broader global trends affecting religions in Asia as a whole, a number of conclusions are possible.

Political Islam will Grow in Strength and Importance

While it is true that no religion has been dominant forever and each religion has flourished when a particular political and cultural group was in power, Asia-based religions are likely to assert themselves in the next 2 to 3 decades. While Christianity has been globally significant since the 17th century, in line with the dominance of the West, there is a steady shift of geopolitical power to Asia with the rise of China, India, Japan and possibly Indonesia, in turn, leading to the greater global importance of Hinduism, Buddhism and Islam. Not only will the number of adherents of these religious increase in numbers, (especially Islam), the ideology associated with these religions will also become more influential. In this regard, the growing importance of political Islam that commenced in the late '70s, and its subsequent radicalisation since the '90s, is likely to continue, thereby impacting the broader geopolitical architecture. In Asia, especially in West, Central, South and Southeast Asia, Islam will increasingly shape political events, in turn, having ripple effects in the wider Asia-Pacific region. Whether the rise of political Islam will necessarily create a more unstable world and lead to what Samuel P. Huntington called 'civilisational wars' remains to be seen. The truth of the matter is that while all religions profess to be peaceful, yet in reality, much violence has been carried out in the name of all religions. History is littered with religions being used and abused to start conflicts even though, more often than not, there are important social, economic, political and strategic underpinnings to such conflicts. Thus, political Islam *per se* cannot be accused as being the source and cause of conflict even though, without doubt, the last two decades have witnessed much violence perpetrated by *jihadists* all over the world in the name of Islam.

Political Secularism will Retreat in the Face of Rising Charismatic Religious Assertiveness

Even though the language and grammar of secularism have been attractive, it has failed in many societies to deliver on the 'promised future'. While many will continue to adhere to secularism in general, the concerted rise of religiosity and religious ideology will slowly force political secularism to retreat. In the past, secular regimes were able to tame and contain the rise of religion through suppression or co-option but this will be increasingly difficult as the secular states become weakened because of various failures and religion-based groups, especially of charismatic persuasions, become effective in mobilising popular support. While religious practices vary from country to country, in the face of the general disillusionment with secular politics and policies, there will be a greater tendency to fuse religion with politics so that embedded religions play an increasing role in national politics and where national morality and justice will be increasingly based on the dominant religions while providing space for the recognised minorities. Whether this will prove to be a basis for domestic stability or instability remains to be seen, as the praxis of this new reality will largely determine its outcome.

Whatever the final outcome, what cannot be denied is that by 2030, we would be witnessing a regional and global order where the expectations of the theorists of modernisation, of progressive secularisation and Westernisation would have been effectively challenged by the resurgence of all religions, especially in Asia. More important, it will be the political and politicised religions that will increasingly limit the space of political secularism, leading in actuality to a process of 'desecularisation' with widespread implications for Asian societies and beyond. Increasingly, the prophets of secularism will be marginalised and probably displaced by religious revivalists and religious nationalists. The likely success of the religious revivalists will be based on their ability to ameliorate national problems as well as their ability to create a more authentic religion-based society. Thus, while the notion of church-state separation will continue to be pursued as an ideal, there are likely to emerge powerful forces that will greatly strengthen the role and power of the 'church' *vis-à-vis* the 'state', and secularism will suffer as a result.

Rise of Religious Denominations and Conflicts within Mainstream Religions

While there is a greater tendency towards giving prominence to religions, at the same time, there is also growing disillusionment with the manner in which mainstream religions have been performing especially in the political, economic and even social spheres. The net result of this has been the rise of breakaway sects and denominations within all mainstream religions, best evident in Islam. Not only will this weaken mainstream Islam as a united and cohesive force but it can also potentially lead to increased internecine conflicts within the religion, as has been signposted in various Islamic states such as Pakistan, Indonesia and even Malaysia. The agitation and persecution of the Ahmadiyya sect in Indonesia is a clear case in point. In the Indonesian case, contradictory moves can be observed: on the one hand, the *Majlis Ulama Indonesia* (MUI), the Indonesia's Ulama Council, the national body that oversees religion, has been trying to 'homogenise' Islam through nationwide *fatwas*, for persecuting deviant sects for example, yet, at the same time, due to the loss of legitimacy of mainstream religions, breakaway denominations are also becoming a fact. While Indonesian Islam is unlikely to emerge as a national homogeneous force, at the same time, time-honoured religious pluralism is likely to continue. To that extent, political secularists will also, to retain power and dominance, be inclined to fuel such internecine conflicts, with domestic stability becoming a major casualty.

Continuity of Securitisation of Religion at the National, Regional and International Levels

With increasing threats posed by religious extremists, especially from various Islamist groups in different parts of Asia, often in collusion with like-minded groups in the Middle East, governments, for a whole hosts of reasons, including for regime and national security, are likely to continue securitising religion, employing extreme measures to deal with extremism as it poses a existential threat to the state.

Continuity with Self-Radicalisation and Deradicalisation Measures

With extremist groups being targeted by national and international security agencies, self-radicalisation will increase with more and more extremists operating either as 'lone wolves' or being indirectly radicalised through the cyberspace. At the same time, in an effort to stamp out the threat posed by religious extremism, governments are likely to abandon their hands-off attitude towards religion and adopt à more interventionist attitude towards religious education (especially in the *madrasahs*) and religious discourses in order to curb the propagation of religious extremism. This would be viewed as part of the middle to long-term strategy to overcome the threat posed by religious extremism, something that is already clearly evident from the Southeast Asian experience.

Emphasis on Inter-Faith Dialogue Amidst Rising Religious Diversity

While various Asian religions will attempt to claim the special and unique place in the national consciousness of its adherents, an important and direct response to the rise of religious assertiveness has been the emphasis on inter-faith dialogues. This is true not only in Asia but also in Europe and North America. The *raison d'etre* of this is to dilute and tame the growing ferocity of religious assertiveness as well as to ensure social and religious peace in all societies that are characterised by racial and religious pluralism and heterogeneity. While there has been a tendency towards hate and vilification of the 'other', at the same time, in view of the reality of religious pluralism, with religious mosaic rather than uniformity being the actual reality, peace through understanding has also been emerging as an important response for dealing with the situation.

Conclusion

Modernisation, globalisation and democratisation are unlikely to erode the importance of religion in Asian societies. If anything, religion will become increasingly significant as political and religious elites have been able to 'sell' it as a useful 'commodity' that benefits the society and nation. Thus, the importance of religion will be on the ascendant with significant political and sociocultural consequences. At the same time, whether religious extremism will rise or subside will largely depend on the effectiveness of governance. Extremist religious ideology will be more easily peddled in an environment where secular policies and politics have failed, with followers of extremism more prepared to give the religion-based alternative a chance. In short, the rise of religious extremism is usually a result of failure of governance, especially where secular approaches and models are in vogue and where they have not fulfilled the aspirations of the majority of the masses. To that extent, understanding religious trends in Asia is important as this will signpost the type and nature of the threats that can emanate from religious extremism.

References

Ahmed, Imtiaz (ed.) (2006). *Understanding Terrorism in South Asia—Beyond Statist Discourse*. New Delhi: Manohar Publishers.

Alam, Imtiaz (ed.) (2006). *Religious Revivalism in South Asia*. Lahore: South Asian Policy Analysis Network.

Azra, Azyumardy (2002). "Globalisation of Indonesian Muslim Discourse: Contemporary Religio-Intellectual Connection Between Indonesia and the Middle East", in Johan Meuleman (ed.), *Islam in the Era of Globalisation*. London: Routledge-Curzon.

Bruinessen, Martin Van (2002). "Genealogies of Islamic Radicalism in Post-Soeharto Indonesia", *Southeast Asian Research* 10(2): 117-54.

Dhar, Maloy Krishna (2006). *Fulcrum of Evil: ISI-CIA-Al Qaeda Nexus*. New Delhi: Manas Publications.

Fealy, Greg (2009). "Indonesia's Islamic Parties in Decline", *Inside*, May 11, at *http://inside.org.au/indonesia%E2%80%99s-islamic-parties-in-decline; "Islamic parties fading in Indonesia's voting"*, UPI, April 25, 2000 at *http://www.upi.com/Top_News/2009/04/25/Islamic-parties-fading-in-Indonesia-voting/UPI*.

———. (2001). "Islamic Politics: A Rising or Declining Force?", in Damien Kingsbury and Arief Budiman (eds.), *Indonesia: Uncertain Transition*. Adelaide: Crawford House Publishing.

Fealy, Greg and Anthony Bubalo (2005). *Joining the Caravan: The Middle East, Islamism and Indonesia*. Sydney: Lowy Institute.

Hafez, Mohammed M. (2005). *Why Muslims Rebel—Repression and Resistance in the Islamic World*. New Dehli: Viva Books.

Hassan, Norhaidi (2002). "Faith and Politics: The Rise of the Laskar Jihad in the Era of Transition in Indonesia", *Indonesia* 73: 353-375. April.

Hefner, Robert W. (2001). "Secularisation and Citizenship in Muslim Indonesia", in Paul Heelas (ed.), *Religion, Modernity and Post-Modernity*. Oxford: Blackwell Publishers.

Jones, Sidney (2001). "Indonesia: Violence and Radical Muslims", *Indonesian Briefing*, (Brussels/Jakarta; International Crisis Group) 10 October.

Jurdi, Syarifuddin (2008). *Pemikiran Politik Islam Indonesia: Pertautan Negara, Khilafah, Masyarakat Madani dan Demokrasi*. Yogjakarta: Pustaka Pelajar.

Mohanty, Jatin Kumar (2006). *Terrorism and Militancy in Central Asia*. New Delhi: Kalpaz Publications.

Mubarak, M. Zaki (2008). *Genealogi Islam Radikal Di Indonesia: Gerakan, Pemikiran dan Prospek Demokrasi*. Jakarta: Pustaka LPEES Indonesia.

Mujani, Saiful and R.W. Liddle (2004). "Politics, Islam and Public Opinion: Indonesia's Approaching Elections", *Journal of Democracy* 15(1): 109-23.

Mulkhan, Abdul Munir (2009). *Politik Santri: Cara Menang Merebut Hati Rakyat*. Yogjakarta: Kanisius.

Nathan, K.S. (ed.) (2007). *Religious Pluralism in Democratic Societies: Challenges and Prospects for Southeast Asia, Europe and the United States in the New Millennium*. Singapore/Kuala Lumpur: Konrad Adenauer Stiftung/Malaysian Association for American Studies. pp.1-60.

Nashir, Haedar (2007). *Gerakan Islam Syariat: Reproduksi Salafiyah Ideologis di Indonesia*. Jakarta: Pusat Studi Agama dan Peradaban Muhammadiyah.

Rahmat, M. Imadadun (2008). *Ideologi Politik PKS: Dari Masjid Kampus ke Gedung Parlemen*. Yogjakarta: LKIS Yogjakarta.

Schwartz, Adam (1999). *A Nation in Waiting: Indonesia's Search for Stability*. Sydney: Allen and Unwin.

Seinfels, Peter (2009). "Globally, Religion Defies Easily Identified Patterns", *The New York Times*, October 23, at *http://www.nytimes.com/2009/10/24/us/24beliefs.html?_r=1*

Singh, Bilveer (2007). *The Talibanization of Southeast Asia: Losing the War on Terror to Islamist Extremists*. Westport, Conn: Praeger Security International.

———. (forthcoming). "Religion as a Political Ideology in Southeast Asia", in Isthiaq Ahmed (ed.), *The Politics of Religion in South and Southeast Asia*.

Taufik Adnan, Amal and Samsu Rizal Panggabean (2004). *Politik Syariat Islam Dari Indonesia Hinga Nigeria*. Jakarta: Pustaka Alvabet.

Turmundi, Endang and Riza Sihbudi (eds.) (2009). *Islam dan Radikalisme di Indonesia*. Jakarta: LIPI Press.

Wahid, Abdurrahman (2009). *Ilusi Negara Islam: Expansi Gerakan Islam Transnasional di Indonesia*. Jakarta: The Wahid Institute, Gerakan Bhinneka Tunggal Eka and Maarif Institute.

V

Transformational Technologies and their Impact on Society

12

Cyber Security Challenges for Asia in a 2030 Time Frame

ROLAND HEICKERÖ

Introduction

In order to provide a roadmap of where Asia is heading in the future, the 12th Asian Security Conference (ASC) by Institute for Defence Studies and Analyses (IDSA) focusses on exploring certain alternative scenarios on Asia's future in 2030. One of the topics to be discussed during the conference is how the development of information and communications technology (ICT) affects cyber security and what challenges could be foreseen for the region that would impact on security policy. The objective is to describe cyber security and cyber threats in a 2030 time frame.

The chapter describes initially driving forces, megatrends and changing factors of the ICT and some of the technologies, products and services that could be expected on the market in the future. The next part discusses a growing concern of different types of cyber threats foreseen regarding actor and adversaries and the development of new types of information weapons. A short reflection is made concerning future challenges for the Asian ICT-sector. Based on the information from the previous part a scenario has been drafted describing a potential case that might evolve over time and their impact and consequences for security policy in the region. Finally, the chapter ends with a short discussion on describing the need for regulative bodies to get engaged for improved cyber security.

The methodology is based on information retrieval and discussion with senior R&D experts from the ICT-sector as well as security policy analysts mainly from the Swedish Defence Research Agency, FOI, with specific knowledge of the Asia region.

Predicting how the future might evolve is both easy and difficult. Scenarios and forecasts are very potent methods and should be used not in order to define the future but to prepare for a future that might come. It is a way to present ideas, thoughts and opinions of various kinds to be analysed and discussed interdisciplinary. On the basis of the scenarios strategies can be worked out on how to act towards the changes that could appear over time.

In some cases the predictions vary from being quite negative and dystrophic to bright and shiny and utopian. In other cases, technology is seen as the vicious driver or as the salvatory that will solve all of today's problems. Nevertheless, depending on perspective, technological development is the key driver for the change towards the future. Especially ICT will have a great impact on a forthcoming society. In a 2030 perspective much of today's visions, ideas and R&D efforts in research labs are realised in the market. But, the conceptualising will not be in the way as we think and believe today. The future will take unexpected directions.

Industrial and Technological Drivers and Trends in the ICT Sector

Drivers for Technological Changes

From an industrial-political point of view there are a number of factors acting as drivers for technological change.

One important factor is the convergence within and between technologies and systems. For instance within ICT fixed telecommunication converges[1] with wireless communication and mobile telephony overtakes many of the fixed services. Another type of convergence is between telecom, computer, and the media industry creating a new industrial form sometime mentioned as Infocom. Nanotechnology and biotechnology will be important and integrated parts of future ICT. A third type of convergence is based on the usage of internet-protocol (IP) for all types of fixed and wireless communication, with the implication that telecommunication networks transform into computer networks. Over time the switches are exchanged to routers.

1. Fixed-mobile convergence (FMC).

Interoperability is a factor that has been identified as an important driver. Standardisation of system and components creates new possibilities to connect products from different companies and sectors, such as the Telcos[2] and the computer branches, to well functioned units.

Improved connectivity is another factor meaning that all mobile devices and computer like mobile phones connects to internet and starts to use new services and applications.

A fourth factor is the development of internet by itself that not only changes the possibility to communicate and interact but also develops new business models and logics of behaviours. It will have a direct impact on efficiency and productivity in all sectors and on all levels. Ideas and thoughts can be spread to a large number of people worldwide more or less immediately. Content could be exchanged widely. A free flow of information, can bridge the gap between cultures and organisations. An overall improved communication also leads to cultural and social challenges to deal with. For some parties the development is encouraging for others can be seen as a threat. Internet will probably be divided into one open and 'free' internet and one closed and regulated ditto in parallel with the open network. The Internet 2 for instance is an initiative[3] to connect universities and research institutions.

Except all the above mentioned factors there are also a number of institutional changes that acts as technology drivers such as:

a) the creation of global production networks;

b) the formation of global innovation networks and clusters; and

c) the development of global standardisation organisations.

Technology Trends

From an information and communication technology stand point several trends have been identified and divided into hardware and software areas as well as networks and services.

---

2. Telcos: telecommunication operators and vendors.
3. *http://www.internet2.edu/*

Hardware and Software

Hardware such as computers, components and elements will develop in a rapid pace in the future. The predicted introduction of quantum computing could put the logic of Moore's law aside. Instead of doubling processing power every 18 months, the growth in computing power could move in an almost vertical direction over time. The development of neurological computers and networks will also increase capacity hundredfold. Future computers will have a lot in common with the human brain both regarding logic and structure as well as how information is processed and used.

Nanotechnologies[4] will shrink components and chips but also lead to new type of devices such as microscopic radio antennas built into fabric of clothes. The material becomes intelligent. The positive outcome of miniaturisation is that more functionality could be added on the circuits per unit area as well as improved energy efficiency. The battery length time will be improved drastically. Carbon as basic component for circuits is replaced by coal based materials.

Instead of carrying around gadgets, functionality such as radio chips connected to the internet could be implanted under the skin streaming information to the brain. Embedded devices are a consequence of the biotech convergence with the ICT.

Regarding software development, with modularisation and autonomous programming the speed to develop software is much improved. The second hand market for computer programmes flourishes. Large parts of already written programmes are recycled and used in new forms and adapted to other situations and applications than they were originally written for. But the major shift will be the transformation of hardware functionalities into software such as the software radio. Hardware will just be a box that physically encloses the software.

Networks and Services

From a network point of view major changes are foreseen in a 2030 perspective. Broader bandwidths combined with new algorithms for traffic surveillance will improve the network transmission capability.

4. Nanotechnology deals with structures of the size 100 nanometres or smaller.

With dynamic resource allocation, it will be possible to give priority to services and traffic between network and users, to create alternative routing ways and conduct graceful degradation of services if needed. The transmission capacity will increase drastically over the years. The influx of new users and more capacity demanding services puts pressure on massively investment in network built up, service development and a continuously upgrading of systems.

It will be possible to access internet in many different ways depending on actual situation and status. The allocation of needed resources could be handled either case by case or connection by connection. Ad hoc networks that open up and close down after an operation is performed will be a significant characteristic. Another characteristic is nomadic computing that allows access to the internet regardless of type of network, place or time; 'always connected'. The convergence will create networks highly collaborative, personalised, intuitive and self-reflective. Every individual has its own network connected to other networks.

Technologies such as laser and radar act as complementary bearers to radio communication for receiving and transmitting data wireless. By 2030 internet goes into space and communication and positioning satellites become vital part of the global-orbital network.

The future internet should be seen as a place to store information in new ways.[5] Information is the most important part not the storage place and access form. Internet is a pipe for delivery of content, ideas and thoughts. It gives totally new possibilities to collect information on what is ongoing in an instant and immediately way. Service interaction is the next phase. From passive to active interaction, from e-mail to instant communication, from short sequences of low quality to always connected and high quality sessions on a large scale. Personalised services could be provided to individuals anywhere in the world.

Ultra intelligent electronic agents are used to seek information adapted to the individual user needs and demands. The agent will be a tool to help sorting out and refine the enormous amount of information available.

---

5. Interview with Vint Cerf, *Svenska Dagbladet,* November 2, 2009.

To improve accessibility of services and network for users from all countries, user-friendly interfaces are implemented including for instance translation and interpretation programmes in a real time mode. Artificial intelligence and virtual reality will be commodities. Holographic moving pictures in 3D could be projected from small devices.

Telematics, telemedicine and intelligent machine-machine interaction will play a major part in future internet communication. Cameras, thermometers and sensors of different kind are connected directly to the Internet as well as all major electric power systems. For instance, it will be possible through the net remotely to manage and steer energy consumptions. A huge number of devises, tens of billions will be connected worldwide. Machines communicate with other machines autonomously and without human interaction.

Network Security

The internet[6] and wireless communication[7] has developed in four phases since the early stages in the '60s and '70s. The first was the technology definition phase, second the network builtup and capacity phase. The third is the implementation and interaction phase of useful services and applications on a broad scale. Content is the 'killer application'. The fourth will be the network and information security phase. It should be noted that all phases to some extent are developed in parallel as new technologies and services continuously are implemented and used.

Regarding security issues especially two main aspects have to be addressed and solved in a future perspective; overall information security and personal integrity. The latter issue will be dealt with differently in democratic and open societies *versus* more closed regimes. There is a risk that the technological evolution with increased capability to supervise and control information flow and individuals, leads to a non-desired direction.

---

6. The first concept of internet, the ARPANET (Advanced Research Projects Agency Network), was developed by (DARPA) Defence Advanced Research Project Agency during the '60s.

7. Nordic Mobile Telecommunication system—NMT, the first public wireless system was launched in 1981. Basic research was made in late '60s and during the '70s by the Nordic PTT's.

Information security could be divided into personal security as well as system, network and service security. In the forthcoming years a lot of effort will be put into better and more secure web servers, new identifications and authentication processes using for instance biometrical and DNA techniques. Identity management will be a crucial area to develop. As more and more devices and users are connected, there is a need for more and securer IP-addresses such as the IP version 6(IPv6).

Improved encryption such as quantum ciphering technology is under development and might be realised on the market in a 2030 perspective. By using quantum ciphering methods it is very difficult for an antagonist to crack a system. But utterly important is that when transmitting and receiving high bit data wireless, it will be possible for an operator to see if a third party tries to interfere and monitor the traffic between users. Any attempt to intercept calls will change position of the quantum data and by that give the operator instant information that a third party tries to manipulate an ongoing session!

Network security is also a matter of network architecture and topology. By using small tactical networks with low effects, redundancy, networks in parallel, large amounts of nodes, links and sensors etc., improved security can be achieved. It should be possible to separate network and network elements from each other when necessary. Other methods to avoid interception and manipulation of information is to use short distance communication technologies and mobile nodes ad hoc, embedded systems, stealth techniques and frequency hopping for wireless transmission.

To improve surveillance capability by the operator's hardware and software sensors is implanted in the networks. They act as active warning system to indicate and control any possible malicious activities. If any threats is revealed the system activates functionalities for autonomous counteractions.

Cyber Threats in a Future Perspective

Background

Within a 2030 perspective there will be cyber threats of different kinds. Some of them extrapolated from today's situation while others will be completely new and unknown. To a large extent the ominous pictures emanates from the actual status in a specific region and area. Conflicts could have historical backgrounds and roots transferred into a future context.

Generally speaking the formidable explosion of ICTs and accessibility of information started in early '90s will see to that the cyber space becomes the main area for future conflicts. The ongoing trend to connect more or less all networks and devices into gigantic net of networks that open up for a number of vulnerabilities.

The barriers against antagonistic operations are likely to decrease over time due to continuing price reductions in combination with easier access to information on techniques and procedures. Knowledge of how to conduct information attacks is being disseminated to a large number of people by the computer networks, at the same time the expanding computer networks are making the society increasingly vulnerable to such attacks. The resulting situation is characterised by a growing asymmetry in costs: it is increasingly cheap to carry out a destructive cyber attack, while it is increasingly expensive to defend against one.

A directed and qualified cyber attack against critical information systems could have great effects on society and be lethal depending on what system is being attacked. With small means it is possible to affect critical infrastructure on a large scale, if the motives and willingness are right. Moreover, the internet makes it possible to act anonymously provided that the cyber antagonists have proper skills and knowledge of how to avoid digital tracing and computer forensics.

Information *per se* is viewed from a wide range of aspects as a valuable asset of great importance to use and protect in peace time and war time. It creates both new dimensions to conflicts and arenas for fighting war with an inbuilt psychological impact. The cyber space has emerged as a dimension to attack enemy centres of gravities and critical vulnerabilities and break its will to resist. With information warfare (IW) it is possible to achieve decisive military as well as political defeat of an enemy at a low cost without necessarily occupying the territory of an enemy. In 2030 the shift towards what some military analysts describes as the sixth generation warfare could be realised.[8]

Actors and Adversaries

Actors and adversaries cover from states with large resources to cyber criminals and terrorist organisations down to single individuals such as insiders acting malicious on the networks.

In 2030 the vast majority of developed countries have implemented military concepts built on theories of network centric warfare[9] (NCW) and future combat systems[10] (FCS) of course with specific distinguishing characteristics. Most countries will have military IW units capable of conducting offensive and defensive actions in order to protect its cyber sovereignty.

The future concepts involve a number of factors such as network enabled capability by using network, sensors and information more efficient in order to coordinate and allocate resources, units and tasks. Other parts are self-synchronisation and improved situational awareness. One goal is to influence the opponent's decision process and by that to control his actions. By influencing and controlling an adversary's possibility to access information, information dominance and superiority could be achieved.

System thinking is a key factor in the NCW concept in the sense that an opponent is viewed as a system with centres of gravity and critical vulnerabilities. By attacking these systems such as telecommunication, banking and financial systems, power grids etc., with different means both traditional weapons and IW ditto, a system crackdown could be achieved in a very short period of time and by that; victory. A defeat in the first cyber battle between contracting parties may be the defining condition for victory.

---

8. There is an ongoing discussion on how to define the transformation of warfare. The fourth generation of warfare is sometimes viewed as today's modern warfare characterised as blurred lines between war and politics, soldier and civilian, conflict and peace as well as battlefield and safety. The sixth generation will be part of the Revolution in Military Affairs, RMA, with cyber warfare and autonomous units as basic parameters.
9. See for instance Alberts *et al.* (2000).
10. *http://www.globalsecurity.org/military/systems/ground/fcs.htm*

Cyber criminals, terrorists on the internet as well as disgruntled persons of different kind will have some common characteristics when acting on the net though their motives, resources etc., but differ regarding what type of effect they would like to achieve. It is a trade-off between resources, motives, effects and consequences. Social networks are the marketplace for providing ideas, to recruit, to coordinate and to provide malwares to potential aggressors.

The logic of cyber criminality is money. The future 'all-connected network' will be a formidable working space for conducting frauds, thefts, virtual robbery and blackmailing attempts etc., on massive scale directed against individuals, organisations and financial and banking institutions. Even single country could be targeted. It is truly a global movement and an international phenomena not restricted by geographical borders, national heritage or laws. The cyber mafia acts as large conglomerates with enormous resources always looking for lucrative options.

More or less all types of terrorists regardless of situation, geographical position, motives and cause will use the internet for seeking information, to coordinate resources and to conduct operations on the net of various kinds. The advantages for cyber antagonists are the fact that modern society is heavily dependent on computer networks. The inbuilt vulnerabilities in the systems will be grateful targets to attack.

Disgruntled individuals and small groups of computer skilled people will probably be a growing menaces in the years to come. They can be part of a criminal organisation or a terrorist group. They can also act solely by themselves as a one-man army using autonomously and self-copying malwares dispatched on a massive scale against specific target objects.

In the future, cyber operations will be conducted by proxies. Cadres of cyber mercenaries are willing to enlist for money and or by political-national-religious reasons to act as deputy incharge for large scale cyber operations. The logic behind using third parties is that both the originator and the intentions could be concealed. Any traces that points out a specific part as being the aggressor will be hidden in the cyber mist. Single countries could stand behind such operations as well as organisations or even individuals that would like to get an advantage over its competitors.

Development of New Type of Information Weapons

There is an ongoing development of new types of information related means and weapons that could be used for malicious activities in the electromagnetic spectrum[11] and on the internet. This includes both hardware and software techniques as well as methods of acting.

The future IW toolbox will include means such as radio frequency weapons to disturb human brains and nervous systems and electromagnetic energy weapons (EMP) with the purpose to knock out electronics and components.

One area of specific characters is micro-organism cultures directed to eat electronic components. Another area is 'psychotropic' or 'psychical' weapons. The purpose with the latter ones is to affect human physiology and brain by using neurolinguistic influences and audio-visual effects through computer programming. The research area is fenced with a strong security and there is very little open information on this type of mind control weapons. If they exist, they could to some extent be compared to the development of non-lethal weapons to reduce human physical and psychological abilities by using electromagnetic pulse waves for crowd control and thermal and voice energy.

Offensive components such as malware and malfunctions are implemented on all levels of a command chain in order to corrupt or compromise an adversary's computer and network system (not necessary limited to military command and control systems but also civilian ditto). New types of intelligent, self-copying and autonomous stealth-driven viruses are foreseen that could be implanted in systems and programmes hiding for years and being activated when needed. This type of intelligent and adaptable viruses have the capability both to transform and to reproduce itself if necessary. Other type of malwares have the ability to 'sniff' the net autonomously searching after vulnerabilities and backdoor openings. They act as loose cyber

11. The electromagnetic spectrum involves electronic warfare (EW) including techniques such as radar, radio, laser, infra-red etc.

dogs either stealing information, manipulating or distorting it. They could also be used for overtaking computers and networks.

Regarding defensive and protecting parts there is a concern for hostile actions in form of 'algorithm bombs' and 'software bombs'. This type of malware can distort a section of an algorithm and limit the functionality which creates unreliable behaviours. Logical bombs could either be syntactical or semanticall. The purpose with syntactical bombs is to destroy the logic of information system by delaying information and/or by developing unpredictable behaviours through malwares such as viruses and trojans. With semantical bombs the goal is to manipulate information in order to destroy the trust of the system by changing and deceit information that may be harmful for the decision-making process.

Other type of weapons is distance virus weapons. For instance viruses introduced through radio channels and laser lines communication beamed directly onto computers and user terminals.

To summarise; future IW weapons involves a number of methods including both psychological and technical aspects directed against enemy critical information systems and command and control functions both military and civilian ditto. One important goal is to change human perception capability and to influence the decision process. The objective is to achieve syntactical and semantically effects by manipulating, intercepting, delaying, distorting or destroying vital and critical information and information systems.

The reduced entry barriers to cyber warfare are allowing an increasingly wide range of actors, including vindictive insiders, financially motivated criminals, ethno-nationalists, ideological militants, nation states, and other assorted cyber terrorists, to use information warfare tools to achieve their goals. The weapons will be cheap and easily accessible and used on a massive scale.

Some ICT Challenges for Asia

The Asia region is foreseen to play a major role in the world economy by 2030 together with South America. To some extent they have overtaken US and Europe's role as drivers for the technological-industrial development. The booming economies of India, China,

Indonesia, South Korea, Taiwan and Japan as well as other countries in the area are predicted to continue over the next 20 years period of time. But with growing economies new challenges will occur that has to be dealt with. Especially China and India with their high growth rates respectively, will act as centres of gravity in the regions and on the world stage that other countries have to relate to.

One of the key drivers for the economy boost is the ICT-sector. All major Asian countries are aspiring to play important parts in the development of future internet. They are strong in different areas and segments. For instance Japan in automation, robotics, telemedicine and multimedia services, South Korea on mobile devices and computer games, Taiwan in semiconductor developments. China is today a major player in computer hardware and telecommunication. Within a few years they will have several leading companies in telecommunication branch such as Huawei, ZTE and others. India is one of the top nations in the world regarding software development and programming with companies such as TATA, Infosys and Wipro. Asian companies compete heavily and successfully on the world market in all aspects of the ICT-sector.

The technological convergence will even sharpen competition over time. The integration between telecom and computing, the transformation of hardware into software as well as an all connected and integrated network will lead to a change of business logics. China wants to become a major software supplier and develop their own programming capability and operative systems. By that, they will directly challenge India's role. India has an advantage due to its large, skilled, well educated and English spoken population. But over time the situation may change as the competitors try to catch up. As a way not to be too dependent on foreign communication technology India and other countries probably will define and build their own integrated computer-telecommunication networks. It is a strategy to reduce the risks for built-in backdoor functionalities and to gain control of critical equipments and information systems.

One of the greatest concerns that create a lot of friction and frustration that might have an impact on the ICT development in the region is the Chinese regime's reluctance to respect patents and property rights. China has been accused several times for failing to interfere against false copying of products and software. There are indications of espionage on a large scale that emanates from that country, both virtual such as the GhostNet[12,13] and physical ditto. It is important to point out that this is not necessary sanctioned by the regime.

Within a short period of time many Western companies and their governments respectively, might start to act against what they feel is an unfair and unjust way of behaviour. Demand for trade barriers and boycotts of Chinese products could be raised. This in turn could lead to a slow down of technology transfer from the West to China that also have an impact on other countries in the Asian region.

Another growing concern is China and other countries in the region's willingness to control the internet by filtering information and closing down web servers to prevent what is seen as information critical of the regime. How this will evolve in the future is an area that has to be followed thoroughly.

A possible scenario, but not necessary a likely ditto, is the trend to outsource industrial capacity and software development from Western companies to Asia decreases over time. A tendency is that some companies backsource their engagement due to lack of efficiency and a fear to lose control over product development. On the other hand Asia with its booming economies might outsource some of their capacity to the West over time.

Scenario

The cyber space is foreseen to be a prime arena for conflicts fuelled by political, economic, religious and national manifestations, a tendency that increases over time. The level and intensity of the activities are governed both by recent incidents and historical ditto whereas conflicts are spreading from the physical sphere into cyber space. Symbols of different kinds are often used as tools for escalating conflicts. In a short period of time an unpleasant situation could occur

12. Markoff (2009).
13. Roy (2009).

that is hard to control or manage. A cyber conflict could diffuse rapidly over borders and lead to consequences concerning security policy.

Future cyber antagonism of different kinds will be a growing menace that is going to affect more or less all nations and regions connected to the internet, directly or indirectly. Countries depending on advanced information and communication technologies from industrial, commercial and social aspects are especially vulnerable to cyber attacks. India and other rapidly developing Asian nations that invest heavily in ICT are no exceptions with a number of built-in technological system dependencies and critical vulnerabilities. In 2030 new areas of tension, domestically or internationally originated, will appear. Some of them are unknown today but others could to some extent be foreseen.

A fictive scenario is viewed to highlight possible future challenges in the cyber space to deal with. It covers a situation where tensions between two major countries in the Asia Pacific are spread into the cyber sphere and played by proxy using cyber mercenaries and nationalist driven hacktivists.

Cyber War by Proxy

By 2030 the power has shifted from an American-European centric world order to an Asia-focussed ditto. The ties between South America and Asia are much stronger than they were 20 years before. Several countries have continued and even increased their rapid economical and technological development that started in the early '90s and 2000s. But with economic growth new tensions develop.

US is still a premium super power from a military point of view but lacks the political will as well as public support to conduct expensive expeditionary operations outside its region. The US administration has withdrawn from many conflict arenas but look after its interest with different means and methods. Also the Europeans lack the will to engage themselves outside its borders for many reasons. The changes in security policy open up for a power vacuum to be filled by new competitors in the world arena.

A growing economy in the booming regions has led to an increased military spending. Especially the cyber space has been identified as a prime arena to declare sovereignty. The most advanced countries develop capabilities for information warfare such as IW units and cyber militias.

The globalisation has slowed down and refocussed towards trades mainly within and between the regions. Africa tries to find its role in the world arena by engaging in alliances. Since a period of time some leading African countries have been trying hard to connect to both the Asian region and to the South Americas. Especially one Asian country acts aggressively to get foothold. Some analyst says that the engagement in Africa by some regimes is the same old colonialism but shaped in a new way and by new actors.

Since a period of time the tensions in the Asian region have increased fuelled by two of the leading countries. Industrial-political frictions have already occurred. In the UN General Assembly both countries accuse each other of acting aggressively. There is a much concern from the international community due to the fact that both countries have nuclear weapons. In order to cool down the hot feelings diplomatic attempts have been initiated. The smaller economies in the neighbourhood are either forced to choose side or try to keep as low profile as possible to avoid any attention.

Over time the conflict escalates to minor border struggles. In national news magazines and other media, nationalists are spreading propaganda such as that it is everybody's right to punish the aggressor. Internet is boiling with rumours. Instant messages are continuously shoved into mobile devices with spiteful information. Hordes of people around the globe declare their willingness to act against what they see as the opponents from both sides. In order to take advantage of the situation the secret service in one of the countries decides to launch an operation limited in time and size called the Cyber Blast. They would like to teach the opponent a lesson but not to start a full scale war. It is too dangerous especially regarding the nuclear issue. It must be a covert operation.

On Darknet II contacts are made with a special group of hardcore cyber mercenaries to enrol in the struggle. The contractors are willing to fight against an opponent if they get the right payment of course! Some of them have a background as specialists in information security from some of the world's leading ICT companies. Others have military experience from different IW units. The unified factor for all members is money. They are eager to help the best they can. They have done this type of operations before. In their business proposal they take care of the total operation from preparing to launch an attack as well as to sweep away any traces. It is a good deal for all involved parties.

The first step of the mission is to identify potential backdoor openings in the critical ICT system of the opposite party, in this case the root servers. By attacking the servers the communication will break down. To avoid traces the mercenaries contacts a criminal organisation distributed in several countries. They have on their hand enlisted different loosely connected hacker groups spread out around the globe. The hackers will play the main role in the campaign. But they do not know who is behind the operation and the purpose of it. They do not care because it is all about money! The interaction between the parties is made anonymously, encrypted and with fake names on the Darknet II.

By attacking the root servers the opposite side's preparedness and readiness could be mapped and their information security strategies be disseminated. The hackers is going to use several methods such as large distributed denial-of-service attacks (DDoS) to saturate networks and servers with information, to conduct defacement operations and change information in hostile computers and hack devices on a major scale. Thousands of networks and millions of subscribers, is estimated, directly or indirectly to be influenced by the operation not only in the attacked country but all over the world. Tens of million of automated devices connected to the internet has been overtaken for that purpose and could be used as huge zombie networks for DDoS if necessary. Any eventual attempts to counteract the operation by the attacked party and by its allies will be supervised (blocked!) by the mercenaries.

As a physiological additional service, propaganda and virulent information is going to be pushed out constantly by the hackers with messages to prominent individuals in a wide range of countries to stop the provocation. Heart breaking films in 3D with manipulated stories will be spread over the net showing the evilness of the hostile country. It will have a great effect on swooning hearts and minds.

Depending on how the operation proceeds, the mercenaries have another trump card to be used if necessary. If needed, they can loose their cyber dogs to crawl around autonomous on the network to seek and destroy the opponent cyber system causing a system collapse. But doing that the risk for escalation increases and this is something they want to avoid as far as possible.

In addition but without knowledge of the work done by the cyber mercenaries and the hacker groups, a nationalist-driven youth organisation have decided to give their helping hand to fuel the conflict. They want to encourage exaggerated individuals worldwide to engage. Social forums on the internet are used by the nationalist-driven antagonists for recruitment, to dispatch malwares and to help hacktivists of different kind with lists of IP numbers of target to attack. Especially target objects with symbolic value are preferred. In a couple of cases electromagnetic pulse energy weapons were used by overhaste nationalists to knock out electronics used by the opponent embassies and consulates.

Just within some days the operation is over. The attacked country tried to counteract the hostile manoeuvres by moving important information on servers to friendly nations and to increase the cyber protection of valuable systems and networks but failed. They also tried to dissemble their cyber dogs but the effects were invisible due to the effective blockade by the mercenaries. Before a dangerous escalation occurred, the premier superpower decided to interfere together with the international diplomatic community in order to stop the hostilities. It succeeded to some extent. The current situation could be defined as a cyber stalemate.

The attacking country won a political victory at least in their eyes all in line with the theories of the sixth generation warfare. They achieved their goals to teach the opposite side a lesson. In reality there was no winner at all except for the cyber mercenaries and the criminal groups. They got their shares and they are heading towards new goals. They can add one more successful operation to the curriculum. In the aftermath of the crisis IT-forensic could not find out whom or what parties lay behind the operation. The traces point out computers and networks from all over the world but no responsible persons or organisation have declared their participation in the cyber attack. Some of the nationalists were brought to justice for agitations as well as being responsible for the antagonistic electromagnetic pulse attack against the ambassador and his staff. The penalty was low due to their age.

Discussion

The ICT development will play a crucial part for how cyber security will evolve over time. It covers the whole span from network and service protection to the overall security of the state, and organisations down to the individual citizen including questions regarding personal integrity.

For countries under development, the technological evolution offers some positive and advantageous parts compared to more developed countries. When investing and building new types of networks and infrastructures mistakes can be avoided made by forerunners. Accurate and modern security measures and authentication systems could be implemented. By using good network topology, built-in vulnerabilities and interdependencies could be identified and by that be limited. To some extent it is difficult to build away all types of vulnerability due to system dependencies, especially for the SCADA-system.[14] But with enhanced network planning the overall system security could be improved.

Regarding antagonistic cyber operations conducted by a wide range of antagonists the development could in a short period of time lead to an unpleasant direction that is hard to control or manage. An escalation could appear, more or less unintentionally. In reference to the cyber attacks against Estonia in 2007 and Georgia a year later, there is a growing concern that activists of different kinds will carry out large and coordinated cyber operations towards critical objects.

---

14. SCADA—supervisory control and data acquisition, e.g. command & control system in critical networks such as energy sector, air traffic controls etc.

Such operations could lead to security policy consequences and spread to other areas. A snowball effect occurs with national security implications and diffuses rapidly over borders. At the same time it is very difficult to identify the originator of a cyber attack as well as the purpose and motives. There is an obvious risk that wrong perpetrator is pointed out and the responses to an attack are inversely proportional.

When discussing the cyber security today and for the future for Asia and other regions some questions could be raised; is a potential cyber operation a task for intervention by the law enforcement authorities or a matter for the military or by any other organisation to deal with? Should it be carried out and solved on national level or internationally? How should phenomena such as cyber terrorism, cyber crimes and cyber espionage be handled? One tricky area is how to deal with non-state hackers engaging in every aspect of cyber aggression while providing host governments' plausible deniability. For instance, the activities made by 'black hat' hackers is not limited to only one specific area but covers a wide range on the whole scale of malicious behaviours from cyber crime to cyber warfare.

There is an urgent need for common criteria's and agreements between all major nations on how to behave in cyberspace and the level of response if being attacked. There is a need for regulations and operating procedures on how to act in order to limit consequences. The problem is how and what should be regulated and in what form it should be done.

Regardless of possible explanations or reasons to engage or not in regulative bodies but also in the UNIDIR[15] for cyber arms control as well as cyber crimes, cyber terrorism and cyber espionage. It is important to pursue international cooperation to hinder or reduce negative effects of antagonistic cyber operations. It must be solved on a broad scale involving all major parties, nations and law enforcement agencies. Conventions have to be rewritten due to the fact that cyber war blurs principles as proportionality, neutrality and distinction. Cyber rules of engagements need to be discussed.

15. UNIDIR—United Nations Institute for Disarmament Research.

There are a lot of areas to be addressed and solved. Agreement in cyberspace has to deal with issues like censorship of the Internet, sovereignty and how to handle rogue actors who might not be subject to a treaty. It must also includes all forms of networked and digital activities not limited to the internet and the cyberspace such as electromagnetic pulse weapons but also covering the development of new type of information means.

Cyber security for Asia as well as for other regions is a challenging topic that will increase in importance over time.

References

Alberts, D.S., J.J. Gartska and F.P. Stein (2000). *Network Centric Warfare: Developing and Leveraging Information Superiority*. CCRP Publication. 2nd Edition (Revised). August 1999. Second Print. February.

Burrus, D. (1994). *Technotrends: How to Use Technology to Go Beyond Your Competition*. Collins.

Canton, J. (2006). *The Extreme Future: The Top Trends That Will Reshape the World for the Next 5, 10, and 20 Years*. Dutton Adult.

Heickerö, R., D. Larsson (2008). *Terror Online. Cyberhot och informationskrigföring*. Conopsis Förlag.

Negroponte, N. (1995). *Being Digital*. Vintage Books.

References on the Internet

Arora, A., V.S. Arunachalam, J. Asundi and R. Fernandes, *The Indian Software Industry*. Heinz School. Carnegie Mellon University, Pittsburg USA. *http://docs.google.com/viewer?a=v&q=cache:7SR2yaB-JpAJ:www.heinz.cmu.edu/project/india/pubs/rndmgmt.pdf+indian+it+industry&hl=sv&gl=se&sig= AHIEtbQBr9ni_jqNsBx9CMJROTY8gpsj0Q*

Burch, J. (n.d.). *Nanofuture 2030. A Trip Through the Time... . http://www.nanofuture2030.com/*

Chief of Force Development. National Defence Canada (2009). 27 January. *http://www.cfd-cdf.forces.gc.ca/documents/publications/Signed_Eng_FSE_10Jul09_eng.pdf*

Future Combat Systems (n.d.). *http://www.globalsecurity.org/military/systems/ground/fcs.htm*

Future Technology in Japan 2030. http://memebox.com/futurescanner/show/619-future-technology-in-japan-2030

Internet 2. http://www.internet2.edu/

Markoff, J. (2009). *Vast Spy System Loots Computers in 103 Countries*. New York Times. March 28 *http://www.nytimes.com/2009/03/29/technology/29spy.html? pagewanted=2&_r=2&partner=rss&emc=rss*

Roy, B. (2009). "China´s Silent Warfare", *Paper No*. 3147. 13 April *http://www.southasiananalysis. org*

The ForEx Hotpsot (2009). *Indian IT in 2009: A flashback. http://www.theforexhotspot.com/indian-it-in-2009-a-flashback*

The Future Security Environment 2008-2030.

US Soldier Natick. Soldier R&D Center (2009). *Future Soldier 2030 Iniative. http://www.wired.com/images_blogs/dangerroom/2009/05/dplus2009_11641-1.pdf*

Zarli, A., A. Kazi, M. Hannus, M. Bourdaeu, E-Ekholm and R. Andersson (2007). *Strat-CON: A Strategic Vision for Future R&D and Innovation in ICT-enhanced Construction*. Centre Scientifique et Technique du Baitment. Sophia Antipolis cedex, France., VTT-Technical Research Centre Espoo, Finland. *http://www.ice-proceedings.org/projects/408/ICE%202007/Concurrent% 20Innovation %20(Approaches%20from%20the%20construction%20industry)/9-065_Zarli_final.pdf*

13

Future of Asian Space Powers

AJEY LELE

Background

The first satellite was sent into the outer space in October 1957. The space (also referred to as outer space) was dominated for the initial three to four decades by a small number of Western powers like the US, UK, France and the erstwhile USSR (subsequently Russia). However, since the '80s, some Asian states have made considerable progress in this field. This is very heartening because in many parts of Asia, the overall growth of technology as such, was very limited between the '60s and the '80s. This chapter attempts to look at the future of the space programmes of a few important Asian states. It also examines the major drivers in the growth of space programme and develops futuristic scenarios.

New Geography

The economic and technological growth of Asian states is characterised by significant discontinuities *vis-à-vis* their geographical positions for example some prosperous/rapidly developing countries are surrounded by poor and failing economies. Such economically developed 'islands' are making investments in various advanced technologies and space is one of them. However, economic prosperity is not seen as the only reason for investing in space technologies. It could also be attributed to various other reasons such as social development to education to strategic compulsions. In certain cases, the political leadership driven by ambition is also instrumental in promoting investment in space programmes since the domain delivers a 'power' signal.

More than 50 countries in the world (approximately 52) have launched their satellites in the space either indigeneously or with the help of other countries. About one-third of these states are from Asia. There are nine states that possess the independent capability to place satellites in orbit, including production of the necessary launch vehicles.[1] Within Asia, Japan, China, India and Iran have demonstrated their capability to undertake independent satellite launches. North Korea has made claims regarding orbital launches but these are still unconfirmed. Therefore, with only a limited number of countries possessing such capabilities a kind of 'artificial geography' of space faring nations can be seen in outer space.

Past cataclysms have repeatedly rearranged the earth's geography over billions of years. But outer space could be said to have remained pristine and untouched in all these years. Only over the last half a century have human beings started putting satellites into the space. Asia is a vast landmass, home to many countries, but it has a limited footprint in the outer space. Many countries in the region do not have full potential to undertake independent space programmes. These states have understood that in a post Cold War world, it is not essential to possess the entire configuration of launch capability-tracking capability and satellite manufacture capability to possess assets in space. Thus, they are engaging with powers both within and outside the region to enter into the space arena. Space faring nations are also keen on such cooperation for various reasons, from economics to geopolitics.

During the last few years Asian states like China and India have made noteworthy progress in the space arena. China's progress has been most noteworthy with their three successful human spaceflights. On the other hand, China caused a 'space tsunami' by successfully carrying out an anti-satellite test. This test has culminated in raising a major debate on issues relating to space security. Japan, China and India have successfully completed their first moon missions during 2008-09. All these are indicative that in the 21st century a new

1. Information on this available at *http://en.wikipedia.org/wiki/Satellite#Launch-capable_countries*, accessed on December 10, 2009.

geography is emerging in space.[2] Few other nations like South Korea and Malaysia are keen to enhance their space capabilities. North Korea is also desperately trying to enter the club of space-faring nations. Given this backdrop, forecasting the future trajectory of these states raises many questions. What are the interests of Asian states in space? What are their evolving capabilities? From military to market—what are their core areas of interest? Will their space programmes add more credibility to their power status?

For the purpose of this analysis countries in Asia are broadly put into four groupings. One, Japan-China-India: these are states with comprehensive end to end space capabilities with considerable investments and independent launch capabilities. Two, states like South Korea and Malaysia who are demonstrating potential for the future. Three, states such as Indonesia, the Philippines, Vietnam and Pakistan who have considerable requirements for satellite derived products but face technological and financial limitations. In the fourth group are Iran and North Korea—the states which probably use space launches as technology demonstrators to implicitly inform the world about their ballistic missile capability.

Space Powers in Asia

Japan, China and India: Their space programmes started roughly at the same time during '70s. However, subsequently Japan took the lead and was followed by China and then by India. Today, all these three states could be categorised as emerging space powers with credible space programmes. They have demonstrated their capability in the arena of Deep Space Missions[3] by reaching close to the moon with the success of their respective moon missions. Their space programmes are basically dedicated to their national strategic considerations, though their objectives, policies and programmes diverge considerably.

---

2. The concept of space geography is discussed at *http://cisac.stanford.edu/events/asias_rising_space_powers_emerging_capabilities_and_possible_us_responses/*, accessed on November 12, 2009.
3. Missions in which the spacecraft travels a distance of more than 100,000 km are normally called Deep Space Missions. To reach in the vicinity of moon spacecrafts have to travel an approximate distance of 400,000 km.

These countries share the following broad characteristics:[4]

- Independent access to space—they have their own launch vehicles and also develop their own satellites and sensors.
- Primary focus is socioeconomic development.
- Space assets have a role in national security policy.
- Their space programmes have international recognition. These states have bi/multilateral cooperation with leading space powers.

In addition China has developed an independent manned space programme and has also undertaken a spacewalk. Japan's focus is more towards achieving advancements in aerospace technologies and scientific pursuits and it is an active member of International Space Station (ISS).

South Korea and Malaysia: Both these states have the promise of becoming significant entities in the space exploration industry. They have limited technical and scientific capability but a significant political desire to excel. Malaysia's entry into space domain was in 1996 via private route with the launch of Measat, the first Malaysian privately owned satellite. Presently, these three geostationary satellite networks provide television broadcasting, as well as general communications services over a very wide area covering almost 70 per cent of the world's population. In 2009 they launched a LEO (Low Earth Orbit) satellite with the help of South Korea. Malaysian space activities caught the attention of the world when with Russia's help the first Malaysian astronaut reached ISS on October 10, 2007.[5] But, subsequently Malaysia has not been able to keep the momentum going because of lack of funds.[6]

South Korea has unveiled very ambitious plans for space development. A decade ago the South Korean President Kim Dae-Jung had initiated a five-year programme to design, build and launch a

4. Sundarajan (2006).
5. Interestingly, the visit happened as a part of offset agreement through the purchase of Sukhoi SU-30MKM fighter jets for the Royal Malaysian Air Force.
6. Various details about the space programme are available at the official website of Malaysian National Space Agency, *http://www.angkasa.gov.my/index.php?option=com_frontpage& Itemid=1*, accessed on November 16, 2009.

commercial space cargo rocket, and to use the rocket to create a commercial launch business in South Korea.[7] However, the reality has been a bit different. So far, South Korea has relied on foreign assistance to send more than 10 satellites into orbit. Their Korea Space Launch Vehicle-1 (KSLV-1) was not able to deliver a satellite into the orbit during 2009 and now they are working on KSLV-2. In 2008, a Russian Soyuz spacecraft carried South Korea's first astronaut (woman) to the space station at an approximate cost of $28 million.[8] The country has major space ambitions and proposes to develop a large-sized rocket capable of carrying 300 tonnes of freight into space by 2017, and intends to begin construction of a space shuttle launching system in 2020 and intends to land a probe on the moon's surface by 2025.[9]

Iran and North Korea: The attempts by both these states to undertake satellite launches using indigeneously developed rockets are being viewed by many as an attempt to hide their testing of ballistic missile systems under the cover of a satellite launch. North Korea first attempted to place a small satellite into the earth's orbit on August 31, 1998 but failed. Its subsequent attempts (latest in April 2009) have also failed to put a satellite into the orbit. The state has officially declared the 2009 attempt a success but no independent tracking facility was able to locate the satellite. On the other hand, Iran's ambitions should not be solely viewed as an attempt to use a civil space programme for the clandestine manufacture of longer-range missiles. Iranian efforts to exploit space began under the Shah who tried to improve his country's scientific standing. In 1959, Tehran became a founding member of the United Nations' Committee on the Peaceful Uses of Outer Space (UNCOPUOS).[10] After few initial failures, Iran launched its domestically built Omid (Hope) satellite on the Safir-2 rocket in February 2009. This was the first time that Iran placed an indigeneously made satellite into orbit, joining the ranks of

---

7. Sientzen (2000).
8. *http://en.wikipedia.org/wiki/Korean_Astronaut_Program*, accessed on November 12, 2009.
9. "S.Korea Outlines Space Programme", November 20, 2007, *http://www.physorg.com/news114789828.html*, accessed on Dec18, 2009.
10. Kass (2006).

eight other nations that successfully orbited domestically built objects. They propose to launch seven more satellites mostly in LEO. In August 2008, Iran's space agency announced its plans to send an astronaut into space within 10 years.[11]

South and Southeast Asian States: South Asian states like Pakistan and Sri Lanka also have an interest in the space arena. Sri Lanka could be said to be a beginner. Pakistan is interested in earth imaging and upper atmospheric research but their space programme continues to remain at a nascent stage. Southeast Asian states like the Philippines, Singapore, Thailand, Indonesia and Vietnam are also keenly investing in space technologies. Their interests are in the field of communications, control of resources and education. Varying degrees of investments are being made by these states. Some of them are just in the process of starting their space programmes. The Indonesian space programme has a long history but without much progress for want of technology and finances. All these states are not keen to reinvent the wheel and are depending on space faring nations to make quick progress.

Drivers of Space Programmes

Various drivers have influenced the growth of space programmes in Asian countries. These drivers can vary from state to state. Broadly, they can be analysed at structural and domestic levels. At the structural level, it is important to keep in mind the changing global balance of power and growing competition as well as cooperation among space faring nations. While at the domestic level the internal political dynamics, the economic factors as well as the technological developments need to be examined. A few of these drivers are as follows:

Power Dynamics

Space technology is critical for progress and space systems are strategic assets for a state. Over the last 50 years, this technology has been effectively used for socioeconomic development by its possessors. It still remains more of an exclusivist technology and due to its dual

11. Shin (2009).

use nature the possessor of this technology views it as a symbol of national power. The concept of power has different connotations for different states depending on the circumstances. Quantification of national power and finding its correlation with regard to the success achieved by that particular state in the space arena could be a labourious but a worthwhile exercise.[12]

The four commonly accepted instruments of national power: i) political, ii) economic, iii) informational, and iv) military can be used for the purpose of macroanalysis. The political instrument of national power allows the execution of a nation's foreign policy through diplomatic means. The economic instrument is the leveraging of a nation's wealth to influence the behaviour of others. The informational aspect allows a nation to disseminate (or withhold) information collected with the help of space assets. The military instrument essentially shows the capability of a state to influence the outcome of any war.

For the grouping of Japan-China-India these four instruments of national power have varying shades of importance. In context of India, the economic instrument may not be of a major significance at present because its space industry is still in its formative years. A country like Japan has made significant investments in its space programme both at the commercial level as well as at the state level. Japan is in a position to influence the fate of major global projects like the international space station (ISS) because of its scientific and financial commitments to this project.[13] The Indian space programme suffered considerably in the past because of the sanctions that followed its nuclear test. In 1992, there was a serious deterioration in US-India space relations because Washington objected to an agreement between the Russian space agency Glavkosmos and Indian Space Research Organisation (ISRO) for sale of cryogenic rocket engines to India. However, the recent success stories of Indo-US nuclear deal and

12. RAND has published a report authored by Tellis *et al.* (2000). Such methods of quantification could be used for measuring national power.

13. It is difficult to indicate the exact financial commitment made by Japan for this project. However, it is estimated that the overall project cost could be $100 billion and Japan could be a major contributor. The Japanese experiment module-Kibo is the largest science module of the ISS.

participation of states like the US and Russia in India's moon mission clearly demonstrate the emergence of a strong international collaboration and cooperation.

The satellite services of these three states play an important role in communications, broadcasting, tele-education and tele-medicine services and weather forecasting services. They are sharing this information with other states as well depending on their individual arrangements. This real time information accessibility demonstrates the potency of the informational superiority these states possess. The innate dual-use nature of space technology and particularly the availability of remote sensing satellites with sub-metre resolution capability, clearly demonstrates their relevance for the militaries of these states. China has already conducted a successful ASAT (anti-satellite) test and is reported to have developed satellite jamming technologies. This is a direct indication of their military potential.

These three states have already published their vision documents detailing their plans for next two decades.[14] These plans show, that for them, space has assumed much greater significance than being mere tool for socioeconomic development. Economics and security are the main pillars of their future space architecture. They view space technology as a symbol of national power.

Among these three states China appears to be more focussed towards identifying its space programme with nationalism. It has already succeeded in sending a human being into the space—becoming only the third country in the world to do so and their *taikonauts* (Chinese for astronauts) have successfully undertaken space walks while wearing 'made in China' spacesuits. India also has a human space flight programme but it will take more than a decade for it to fulfill this dream.

China proposes to set up an independent space station constituting a core module, two experimental modules, a manned spaceship and a cargo spaceship. Within the next couple of years they will be testing the space docking technology. Subsequently, they will develop a space laboratory and will establish cargo services to manage logistics in

14. They are available in form of roadmaps for coming two decades like vision documents, policy statements etc.

space.[15] There is a strong possibility that the first human to put its foot on moon in the 21st century could be a Chinese.[16] If China succeeds in doing this before the US then it could be perceived as a significant expression of its power. The states in the other three Asian groupings, mentioned above, are still in the process of developing their space technology and hence are unlikely to showcase their space accomplishments as symbols of national power in coming two to three decades. This is not to argue that their space achievements would not have any correlation with any of the above stated commonly accepted instruments of national power. But, in the overall analysis they are likely to remain as Tier-three or Tier-four space powers.[17]

International Cooperation

International collaboration has been the key in the initial success of the space programmes of Asian states and even today it plays an important role. During the initial period, Japan was helped by the US while China was helped by the USSR/Russia in the development of their respective space programmes. For India help came from different quarters—France, the US and the erstwhile USSR. Other countries in the region are being helped by countries within and outside the region. Presently all major space players in Asia have collaborations with Russia, the US and the EU.

Presently, significant cooperation could be seen between China and the EU. On May 24, 2007 both sides signed the 'China-EU Space Cooperation Actuality and Cooperative Plan Protocol', which stipulates distinctly the fields and direction of cooperation. They have established four work groups, i.e.: i) science and exploration work group, ii) microgravity work group, iii) education work group, and iv) earth observation work group. They have many other plans too.[18] China's collaboration with the EU's global navigational project Galileo is well-known and the first 'China–Europe Galileo Cooperation Conference' was held in Beijing in June 2006. With the success of

15. *www.chinadaily.com.cn/china/2009.../content_7528607.htm*, accessed on Dec 6, 2009.
16. The Economist (2009).
17. Literature normally refers United States, Russia and European Space Agency (ESA) as tier one and Japan, China and India as tier two space powers.
18. *http://www.cnsa.gov.cn/n615709/n620682/n639462/102448.html*, accessed on December 6, 2009.

Indo-US nuclear deal, collaborations between India and US are expected to increase multifold in the space arena. Human space flights, deep space missions and asteroid studies are expected to be the future areas of collaboration.

Russia is already collaborating with India and China for the Moon and Mars missions. Success of these missions and the importance of information gathered could determine the nature of further collaborations. A case in point is the success of the Indian Chandrayaan-1 mission in finding water on the moon's surface in collaboration with National Aeronautics and Space Administration (NASA). Initially, NASA was not interested in India's second moon mission but now they are keen to cooperate to further their research in this area.

States from other three categories are looking for support both within and outside the region. Iran has tacit support from China and Russia. Pakistan is relatively a weak player in the space arena and is dependent on support mainly from China. In Southeast Asia, aggressive investments are being made by the US and China in space technology. As per industry estimates, by 2011-12 over US $2 billion worth of new satellites may be launched over the Asian region. Southeast Asia is expected to be major player in this space industry. The US has already launched satellites for Vietnam and has sealed deals with Malaysia, Thailand, Indonesia and the Philippines backed by loan guarantees. China has promised to build and launch a communications satellite for Laos. In 2009 it signed an agreement with Pakistan, granting a $200 million loan for satellite construction. It will also be establishing ground control segments for them at Lahore and Karachi.[19]

Over the years many states in the region—with the exception of Japan and India—were toying with the idea of forming a Asia-Pacific Space Cooperation Organization (APSCO). Sixteen years after the idea was mooted it started operations in Beijing in December 2008. It has seven member states, China, Bangladesh, Iran, Mongolia, Pakistan, Peru and Thailand. Indonesia and Turkey have also signed the APSCO convention. Representatives from Argentina, Malaysia, the Philippines,

19. Indian Express (2009).

Russia and Sri Lanka also attended the founding ceremony. The organisation aims to promote multilateral cooperation in space science and technology. Its members will work together for development and research, space technology application and training of space experts.[20] Such a multilateral cooperation could help the members from the Southeast Asian region in getting greater access to technology allowing them to exploit natural resources and help in disaster reduction. Such a grouping has the potential to develop into a major pressure group. States like India and Japan have a few collaborative projects with states in the region but are still far from using satellite technology as a tool for increasing their regional influence. Sri Lanka has asked a private company in the UK to design and build its first satellite. This agreement was signed in November 2009.[21] The current trend indicates that the US and China could play a major role in the region at least for the next few decades.

On the other hand, the development of space technology in Asia from the '70s to '90s remained restricted because of the policies of the US. It used the economic and technological backwardness of Asian states to its advantage. As mentioned earlier, states like India faced a technological apartheid because of the sanctions regime. Japan was also exploited by the US.[22] Japan's dream of an indigeneous satellite development programme did not materialise initially because of the US policies. There was a dispute between the US administration and Japan regarding the so called unfair trade practices followed by Japan which were making it difficult for US industry to penetrate the Japanese market.[23]

However, it is now unlikely that major space powers would hold themselves back from cooperating with Asian countries in years to come. There could be various reasons for this. First, in view of the financial constraints, even NASA or European Space Agency (ESA), may not find it to be possible to fund major independent space projects so they would like to collaborate with countries like India and

20. People's Daily (2008).
21. Taverna (2009).
22. Shastri (1986).
23. Oros (2007).

Japan. In fact, given the current status of US space shuttle programme and its future it has been suggested that they should think of taking the help of China in the future for space visits of their astronauts.[24] Second, access to key global natural resources and commodities on other planets is likely to be one of the important space agendas of the future. Apart from having the requisite 'hardware' in place to do so there would also be a need to raise global consciences on this issue and having 'dependent' space powers could become an advantage. Third, for economic reasons, Asian market offers good business opportunities. The uncertainties in these projections could emerge in scenarios where a few states within the region conduct nuclear tests.

Tool for Socioeconomic Development

The major focus of countries in all four groupings is to have space programme for the purposes of socioeconomic development. Their main priorities have been in areas of meteorology, communication, disaster management and remote sensing. Space technology becomes a powerful tool for resources management, food security, fisheries, rural development, health care and education. Countries of the first group have achieved much success in all these fields and are expected to further improve their existing platforms and sensors. They are likely to possess enhanced imaging capabilities in the near future. With issues related to climate change taking centre stage, future satellites would be launched for continuous observation of global warming and climate change. In 2009 Japan launched a satellite (Ibuki) for monitoring greenhouse gases around the world. China and India which have become global 'punching bags' on the subject of climate change would need to have their own systems in space for monitoring climate change. This may also allow them to challenge any false claims made against them by the western world.

The states from other three groupings in Asia are presently at varying levels of proficiency regarding the use of space for broadcasting, communications, meteorology and mapping, using either their homebuilt or other satellites in conjunction with their own

---

24. Cheng (2009).

ground stations.[25] In future, these states would mostly depend on powers like the US, Russia, EU and China for their requirements. On the whole, satellite technology is expected to continue to play an important role as a tool for socioeconomic development in all Asian countries. The role of technology is expected to increase significantly for data monitoring of climate change and for the purposes of disaster management.

Ballistic Missile Capability

Missiles and space launch vehicles belong to the family of basic rocket technologies. In yesteryears, the US space launchers were developed from missiles. The basic difference between these two different genres of missiles is that of placing a nuclear weapons payload in a ballistic (i.e., re-entering) trajectory, *versus* placing a satellite payload in orbit. Launch trajectory, size and number of stages all have a role in distinguishing the two different uses.[26] The capability to launch a satellite indirectly demonstrates the potential of a state to develop a missile. Countries that are under the international scanner due to their defiance of certain global non-proliferation/arms control norms find it difficult to conduct missile tests to prove their prowess and hence follow the 'satellite launching' route.

Today, almost half of the global nuclear weapon powers (within and outside NPT) are from Asia. A suitable delivery platform is a prerequisite for the establishment of any nuclear force. An intercontinental ballistic missile (ICBM) is an important component of any nuclear weapon architecture. In Asia, nuclear capable countries like China, India and Pakistan already have a reasonably well developed missile infrastructure. Amongst them China has proven ICBM capability (Dongfeng). There have been unconfirmed reports that India plans to develop the 8,000 km range ICBM called Surya/ Agni-V. In 2006, North Korea unsuccessfully test fired a missile called Taepodong-2 having a range of around 4 to 4,500 km. States like Japan have an active commercial space launch programme and hence have the technology which could provide the basis for a long-range ballistic missile programme.

---

25. Aerospace America (2009).

26. Samson (2009).

Currently, Iran and North Korea are being viewed as states using satellite programme as a front for their missile ambitions. North Korea has already conducted nuclear tests and states like US are convinced that Iran also has nuclear ambitions. Hence, the space programmes of these states are being viewed with suspicion. However, it would be inaccurate to dismiss their space programme only as a front for missile testing.

In 1959, Tehran became a founding member of the UNCOPUOS. Initially the Iranian political leadership viewed space technology as tool to improve their political, social and economic standing. Leaders like Rafsanjani and Khatami wanted to modernise the country. Khatami undertook various reforms to modernise the country to enable the nation to become more active in space. He gave the country the vision of becoming a space power as a vehicle for modernity.[27] Its space programme began in 1998[28] with the stated aim of using this technology for socioeconomic development. In February 2009, Iran successfully launched its first domestically produced satellite using an indigeneously built rocket launcher. North Korea did the same in April 2009. However, in spite of their claims to success there is not much evidence available to corroborate their proposition. Indonesia is also interested in launching its own satellite with its own launcher. Its space agency Lapan, set up in 1964, is collaborating with the military to develop more efficient rockets. A few years ago Indonesia inked a formal technology transfer agreement with China (2005) for the development of missiles.[29] Space programmes of these states are being viewed with some suspicion.

The intentions of Iran and North Korea are also being doubted because undertaking an unimpeded space launch is possible only if a state's geography offers it that luxury and that is not the case with these two. Geography places major compulsions on Iran to undertake any launches because the countries both on its western and eastern borders are unlikely to grant over flight permissions for its launches. Even with more friendly states in the north, Iran cannot evade the issues of liability and public and environmental safety. The only

27. Kass (2006).
28. Bharath and Pant (2008).
29. Aerospace America (2009).

possibility of making safe launches (not 100 per cent) could be from a region close to Chah Bahar.[30] If this is the case then why is Iran interested in developing launch vehicle technology? Is this to support their nuclear ambitions? With regard to space, the best option for Iran and North Korea is to have cordial relations with other states that can provide them launching facilities. For example South Korea and Japan can provide facilities for North Korean satellite launches.

Iran and North Korea need to 'fake' satellite launches to develop their missile programmes. On the other hand, both the states understand that apart from its military utility satellite technology in itself is also important for socioeconomic development. Hence, these states are likely to continue investing both in satellite manufacturing as well as launcher technologies with a greater bias towards missile specific technology. The uncertainties will persist if the six-party talks succeed and North Korea becomes an 'acceptable' state. In this scenario China and Russia could help North Korea to satisfy its genuine requirement of having access to space. A regime change in Iran could bring about the possibility of third party interlocutors—in which case India could play a role in helping Iran to launch its satellites (presently India is avoiding such requests from Iran!).

Deep Space Missions

Only three Asian countries have so far attempted deep space missions. Japan, China and India successfully completed their first moon missions during 2007-2009. All these states have a definitive roadmap regarding their future moon missions. They are preparing themselves for robotic and human landings on moon. They are also looking for exploration on Mars very seriously. Tier-1 space powers like US and Russia are associating themselves with the deep space mission programmes of these states in some form or the other. However, the present approach of these states indicates that they are likely to pursue an independent path as far as their moon missions are concerned but would be willing to collaborate for Mars missions.

The interests of these states regarding the moon missions range from scientific research, and exploration of resources to establishment

30. Sheldon (2006).

of human colonies. Moon missions offer them opportunities to test the various technologies which could have strategic, technological and commercial relevance. Any significant success in deep space could even play some role (in whatever limited form it may be) in changing the present unipolar world into one with multiple power centres.

South Korea also has plans to land a probe on the moon by 2025. However, the present status of its space programme does not give much confidence. By 2030, China is likely to succeed in putting a man on the moon. Japan has plans of developing a moon base for further planetary exploration missions. Any mission failure during next two decades in the development and testing phase of various technologies could cause a significant technological setback to the space programmes of these states.

Economics

The overall gamut of space technology can be placed into two categories: one, communication or imaging technologies, and two, technologies required for space experimentation, planetary research etc. The technology output is visible and quantifiable for first category but as far as the second category is concerned the research becomes an ongoing process and achievements are hard to sell to politicians and common people. This category demands sustained monetary investments over many years. It becomes difficult for many states to continue making such investments.

For China and India budgetary constraints has not been an issue for the last couple of years. The success of the Chinese space programme in various fields during last two decades clearly demonstrates the availability of state support. China's space budget remains relatively opaque. Various estimates put China's spending at around $2 billion to $3 billion. Of this a significant amount is spent on the manned space programme, lunar missions and space stations. It is the reverse in the case of India. The spending is more on projects of socioeconomic relevance. Today, the value of ISRO's overall assets is approximately $25 billion.[31] Over the last 10 years ISRO's budget has shown a steady increase and has almost doubled between 1999

31. Kasturirangan (2009).

and 2009. But, ISRO continues to spend more than 85 per cent of its $1 billion budget on development-related missions, and only 10-15 per cent on advanced research and development, and on missions such as Chandrayaan.

Japan's space programme did not function under any unified body when it commenced. For almost three decades many of the organisations responsible for developing space technology were reporting to different ministries in the Japanese government. Naturally, this was detrimental for overall growth of the programme. A series of failures between 1996-2003 caused a major setback to Japan's space programme. This had an adverse impact on budgetary allotments as well.

Now, after the establishment of a unified body the Japan Aerospace Exploration Agency (JAXA) in October 2003, Japan's space programme has stabilised. Presently, Japan spends around $2.5 billion in pursuit of its space ambitions. Its investments in ISS are also significant. South Korea spends around $250 million, Iran around $100 million per year and Pakistan spends nearly $10 million. As most of the other Asian states are beginners in this field, no authentic information about their budgetary provision is available.

The overall trend indicates that states would continue to provide the necessary economic support for their space programmes and these investments are only going to increase in the coming years. Particularly Group one states are likely to have significant investments. They have a very clear-cut roadmap for next two decades and no extravagant budgetary requirements are being envisaged. Their space agencies have already started earning revenue and their space industry is expected to grow in years to come. Malaysian and South Korean ambitions are not being matched on ground with respect to their technological expertise. Therefore, political leadership in these states may not provide the requisite support for highly ambitious and long-term projects. Apart from its nuclear and missile ambitions, Iran wants to grow as a technologically advanced country and hence it will continue supporting its space programme. Uncertainties can take form of significant unmanageable economic crises. Under such circumstances, states would mainly cap funding of ambitious programmes like colonisation of moon and human space flights but other programmes of socioeconomic importance will continue.

Strategic Factors

Group one states are seen as being more ambitious in defining their priorities in space than ever before. Their space policies are in response not only to their own aspirations of emerging as major global players but also to the space efforts of other powers.[32] They have seen the advantages gained by US forces from their military space assets. Even a country like Japan passed a law during 2008/09 to allow military use of space and it proposes to strengthen its national security through the development of space.

In particular, post the 1991 Gulf War, the militarisation of space is not being viewed as a taboo by the global community. Japan has launched spy satellites in response to the North Korean threat and India and China have dual use remote sensing satellites. India proposes to launch communication satellites for its armed forces in the near future. India and China have planned independent regional/ global navigational systems. Smaller states within the region like Pakistan, Indonesia and Iran may get Chinese support to develop their own military related space assets. The future emphasis could be towards development of small satellites which are cheap, relatively easy to launch and offer almost the same value as normal satellites.

China appears to be viewing war in space as an integral part of future military operations. Chinese test of its ASAT weapon in 2007 has reinforced China's status as a true military space power; equal to the US and Russia. Now key US space systems are at a clear risk in any future conflict with China.[33] In March 2009, China announced its plans to launch a military space laboratory, the Tiangong-1. The project is being led by General Armaments Department of People's Liberation Army (PLA).[34] It is also known that China has developed satellite jamming capabilities as well. Naturally, this puts the satellite systems of not only the US but also that of other states within the

32. IDSA and Indian Pugwash Society (2009).
33. Tellis (2007).
34. Abas (2009).

region at risk. Many Western analysts feel that there is 'suggestiveness' in Chinese actions regarding the weaponisation of space. General Xu Qiliang, commander of the PLA Air Force was interviewed on November 1, 2009 by China's PLA Daily where he articulated the importance of space for the military. According to him, military competition has shifted towards space and it is a historical inevitability.[35] At the beginning of 2010, a senior US defence official argued that, 'the Chinese have stated that they oppose the weaponisation of space but their actions seem to indicate the contrary intention.'[36] India has also announced its plan to develop anti-satellite technologies (not test!). Countries in the region which do not have indigeneous satellite manufacturing and launch capabilities can still possess anti-satellite capabilities with reasonable knowledge of missile technology or even expertise in developing satellite jamming capabilities.

Future Chinese actions would largely depend on how far the international community (read the US) succeeds in establishing a globally acceptable space regime. The US has already withdrawn from the anti-ballistic missile (ABM) treaty with Russia. It is strongly pushing its missile defence programme by trying to overcome technological limitations. The US approach in all these years indicates that it has no intentions of getting trapped under any treaty mechanism that could harm its interests in space. In view of this, it is unlikely that any globally acceptable space treaty mechanism will emerge in the coming decades.

Other Important Drivers

Race for Resources

China's 'Lunar Probe Project' has found that there is about 1 million tonnes of Helium-3 on the moon's surface which would be enough to meet mankind's energy needs (only a little more than 10 tonnes of Helium-3 is available on the earth). Meeting China's power demand would need only 8 tonnes of Helium-3, equivalent to 220

35. Brown (2009).

36. Space Daily (2010a).

million tonnes of oil or about 1 billion tonnes of coal.[37] The moon programmes of Group one states are biased towards resources mining including Helium-3. It may even take another three to four decades to transport such resources from moon to earth. However, an 'invisible' race for resources amongst China, Japan and India appears to have already begun.

Space Tourism

The commercial space market is in existence since 1970. At present, the world market for satellite-based services—telecommunications, television, global positioning systems, and earth observation (weather, environmental, search and rescue etc.)—is valued at nearly $90 billion. The problem with the commercial space market is that it has not been large enough to attract private investment in the technologies needed to lower the cost of access to space. Space tourism holds great promise as an economic 'driver' for more frequent flights, leading to competition for lower launch costs, which could in turn attract other customers to the space market.[38]

All these years, sending a human to the space has remained a costly affair—$25 million-$30 million per trip. Countries in the region such as Malaysia and South Korea have depended on US and Russia to send their astronauts into the space. India also has signed a deal with Russia in this regard and as a commercial activity, two Indian space travellers will be flying in the non-reusable 'Soyuz-TMA' ship to be piloted by a Russian cosmonaut.[39] However, all these efforts need to be viewed from the point of view of using space travel as a tool to enhance the country's international image, popularise space science and generate nationalistic pride in its population. Couple of years ago, China succeeded in sending men to the space in its own spacecraft.

However, the coming years may witness a significant change in the attitude to space travel in form of a shift from state sponsored to private activity. Burt Rutan's SpaceShipOne, the winner of the Ansari X-Prize, is helping open a new frontier of economic development. In

37. Space Daily (2010b).
38. National Space Society (2010).
39. Business Standard (2009).

cooperation with Richard Branson and other entrepreneurs, a new space market is likely to emerge. Few Japanese companies and individuals are keen to invest in this industry and have already made business plans to that effect.[40] Various new ideas are being discussed and even businessmen from states like Singapore are working towards possessing next generation space vehicles which could offer a five minute trip to fly 100 km above the earth surface. The Space Tourism Society in Malaysia feels that building a space tourism vehicle would be more expensive and third world countries should enter this business as administrative supporters for space tourism activities and organisations. They may also invest in programmes like training astronauts and so on.[41]

Asia may not take the lead in space tourism in the next couple of decades but a few private entities from Asia may join the global bandwagon. The major uncertainty in this field could be the approach of governments. Different governments would try to regulate the industry based on their perceptions about the passenger safety standards offered by private companies and the overall impact of private spacecrafts on national security.

Innovative Experiments

Asian states are working on various areas of technology from space satellites to heavy lift launchers, to space food and space clothing (for moon travel) and asteroid mining. Any significant developments in areas like 'smart' materials, robotics, communication systems and power and energy devices are expected to bring about a revolution in various aspects of space research. Japan is working on ambitious projects like space solar power which involves collecting solar power in space and zapping it down to earth, using laser beams or microwaves. It is expected to achieve this within next two decades but it will require strong economic and technological support. Japanese scientists are working on innovative concepts like the space elevator

40. Ms. Misuzu Onuki has published probably the first Japanese language book about new space in Japan. This 203-page book, titled *I Will Go to Space Next Week* (2009), is a comprehensive round-up of commercial space activities being undertaken around the world. Topics include sub-orbital and orbital vacation options, marketing and branding opportunities, and commercial projects such as zero gravity manufacturing and commercial lunar development.

41. Zakaria *et al.* (2007).

as well. Significant breakthroughs in carbon nano technology are expected to boost this project. India has a major interest in reusable launch technologies. During next two decades, Group one states are expected to enhance their expertise in these fields by taking a 'step by step' approach.

Scenarios

As the above discussion indiactes, there are various drivers which could determine the future of the space programmes of Asian countries. Each driver will influence the trajectory of an individual state's space programme. Based on the above drivers, one can decipher the following two scenarios by 2030.

Scenario I: Space Power as Soft Power

In 2030, Asia will continue to exhibit a rapid growth in the field of space. Japan, China and India will continue to be the leading Asian space powers. They would remain Tier two space powers at the global level. However, China would succeed in putting a man on moon before the US does. China and Japan would overtake India in Mars missions.

China and India would have their own global/regional navigational systems operational. Group one countries would have improvised remote sensing systems with state-of-the-art sensors giving day/night and all weather and all terrain imageries with resolutions of a few centimetres. Their space and environmental satellites would be fully operational. India would have fully developed the capability to put 6-8 tonne satellites in the space and will have a fully matured cryogenic technology. Iran and North Korea would continue to use satellite launches to demonstrate their missile capabilities but with limited success.

Many rich Asians would visit space. Japan/Singapore/South Korea would have major stakes in the global space tourism business while India would be a major player in transponders. Indian satellite launching facilities would offer best of the economical options but would face competition from China. South Korea would be a beginner in this field.

China's military space station would have lived out its life and based on this experience they would have launched another such station. China's international space station would be constructed with participation from APSCO members as junior partners. Indian and Japanese satellites would face temporary blackouts because of jamming from unknown sources (*a la* 2009-10 cyber attacks).

Non-nuclear Iran would make a slow but steady progress in space technology and would have its own satellites mainly in LEO. South Korea and Indonesia would have independent launch facilities. Many of the Southeast Asian states would remain dependent on regional and global powers for support for their space ambitions and would have numerically more satellites in space. Many Asian states would have more (mini/micro/nano/pico) satellites. Space would play a prominent role in enhancing the soft power status of Japan, China and India.

Scenario II: Moon still not in reach...

The space programmes of Japan, China and India would continue to evolve in all fields but for deep space missions, Japan and India will overtake China. They both will develop a healthy collaboration with US and their robotic missions will successfully bring samples of Helium-3 and other minerals back to the earth. In the deep space arena, China experiences technical setbacks. A man on the moon still remains elusive for all! China and Russia start helping Iran to take its space programme to greater heights. At international forums US starts using every opportunity to create a furore about Chinese military space stations and claims that the entire Chinese space programme has a strong military bias. A globally acceptable space regime is still no where in sight.

Wild Card: Star Wars

Iran goes nuclear. A few other states in the region start showing signs of nuclear intentions. India successfully develops a missile defence shield. Nuclear weapons lose their shine as weapons of deterrence. China claims that the ultimate high ground is space and the best deterrence is space weapons. It initiates a programme for space based weapons. Space becomes a vital factor in the global military power balance.

Conclusion

This chapter has made a short appraisal about a few of the important drivers that will determine the future of space technology among the countries in Asia. For these nations space has become a vital element for progress. Some parts of Asia have already witnessed the impact of space technology on society. They have experienced its utility in various facets of life from weather forecasting to education to navigation to intelligence gathering. Both space 'haves and have-nots' in the region consider this technology as an instrument of change. For them this technology also has a major military relevance.

However, even after two decades many Asian states are predicted to remain earthbound. They would try to get maximum benefits of space technology by engaging with space faring nations. Given the steady growth of various existing and emerging space programmes in the region, it is expected that the coming years would witness the profound impact of this technology on Asia's culture and commerce on the one hand and society and security on the other.

References

Abas, M. (2009). "Space Warfare: From Fiction to Reality", *ADJ*, September, p.15.

Aerospace America (2009). "Southeast Asia Reaches Towards Space", *Aerospace America*. p.8, October.

Bharath, G. and Harsh Pant (2008). "The Strategic Dimensions of Iran's Leap into Space", *Journal of Defence Studies* 2(1): 122. Summer.

Brown, Peter J. (2009). "Space is Suddenly on the Agenda", *Asia Times*, Novomber 12.

Business Standard (2009). "ISRO Seeks Russian Spaceship for Manned Flight", *Business Standard*, October 05.

Cheng, Dean (2009). "US-China Space Cooperation: More Costs Than Benefits", *Web Memo* No.2670, October 30, The Heritage Foundation.

IDSA and Indian Pugwash Society (2009). *Space Security: Need for a Proactive Approach*. IDSA-Pugwash Working Group Report. New Delhi: Academic Foundation.

Indian Express (2009). "Ready for Lift-off", *Indian Express*. Oct 30. *http://english.peopledaily.com.cn/90001/90776/90883/6554845.html*, accessed on Dec 18, 2009.

Kass, Lee (2006). "Iran's Space Programme: The Next Genie in the Bottle?", *Middle East Review of International Affairs* 10(3): 16. September.

Kasturirangan, K. (2009). "The Emerging World Space Order", in Ajey Lele and Gunjan Singh (eds.), *Space Security and Global Cooperation*. New Delhi: Academic Foundation. p.33.

National Space Society (2010). "Space Tourism: Opening the Space Economy", *NSS Position Paper on Space Tourism, 2008, http://www.nss.org/tourism/position.html*, accessed on January 2, 2010.

Oros, Andrew L. (2007). "Explaining Japan's Tortured Course to Surveillance Satellites", *Research Review of Policy* 24(1): 29-48. January.

People's Daily (2008). "Asia-Pacific Space Cooperation Organisation Starts Operation", December 17. *http://english.peopledaily.com.cn/90001/90776/90883/6554845.html,* accessed on Dec 18, 2009.

Samson, Victoria (2009). "North Korea's launch", April 13, *http://www.secureworldfoundation.org/blog/2009/04/north-koreas-recent-launch.html,* accessed on December 16.

Shastri, Ravi (1986). "Japan's Space Porgramme", *Strategic Analysis:* 1107.

Sheldon, J.B. (2006). "Iranian Space Ambitions and U.S. Engagement", *Astropolitics* 14: 239.

Shin, Jenny (2009). "A Chronology of Iran's Space Activities", *Centre for Defence Information.*

Sientzen, Frank (2000). "A New Asian Space Race Emerges", 25 January, *http://www.fas.org/news/skorea/2000/korea_space_000124.htm,* accessed on December 30, 2009.

Space Daily (2010a). "US Official Questions China Space Intentions", *Space Daily,* January 13.

———. (2010b). "Change-2 Satellite's Camera Resolution Reaches One Meter", *Space Daily,* January 14.

Sundarajan, Venkatesan (2006). "Emerging Space Powers—A Comparative Study of National Policy and Economic Analysis for Asian Space Programs (Japan, China and India)", *American Institute of Aeronautics and Astronautics,Space.* p.1.

Taverna, Michael A. (2009). "Snowing Smallsats", *Aviation Week & Space Technologies,* November 30.

Tellis, Ashley J., Christopher Layne and Melissa McPherson (2000). *Measuring National Power in Post-Industrial Age.* CA, US: RAND.

The Economist (2009). "A Wary Respect", *The Economist,* October 22.

Tellis, Ashley (2007). "Punching the U. S. Military's 'Soft Ribs': China's Anti-satellite Weapon Test in Strategic Perspective", *Carnegie Endowment, Policy Brief No.* 51, June.

Zakaria, N.R., R.Z. Dato, A.A.A. Majid and J. Othman *(2007).* "The Symbiotic Relationship between Astronaut Program and Space Tourism Development—A Third World Perspective", Paper presented at second *IAASS Conference,* Chicago. May 14.

14

Pro-Poor Renewable Technology and its Impact on Society

Decentralised Renewable Energy Technologies

DAVID E. FUENTE[1]

Introduction

Increased international attention to climate change, greenhouse gas (GHG) emissions, and geopolitical energy security has placed renewable energy technologies at the centre of mainstream public media as well as national and international policy discourse. As home to two of the globe's most populous countries and rapidly growing economies, Asia currently consumes more total energy than the Americas or Europe. And, this trend is likely to continue. According to the International Energy Agency (IEA) (2009c), energy demand in the ASEAN nations alone will increase by 73 per cent by 2030, much faster than any other region in the world.

In parallel with their increasing energy consumption, Asian countries are quickly moving to become global leaders in clean technology manufacturing and renewable power generation. With respect to manufacturing, in 2009 China became the largest manufacturer of wind turbines and solar panels, surpassing Denmark, Germany, and the US (Bradsher, 2010). Additionally, Asia's commitment to becoming a global leader in renewable power generation is reflected in the aggressive renewable energy targets and policies adopted by India and China as well as strong private investment in clean technology across Asia. As part of its ambitious

---

1. David E. Fuente serves as Programme Head, Infrastructure and Governance at the Centre for Development Finance at Institute for Financial Management and Research (IFMR). While the author is grateful to the Centre for Development Finance (CDF) and IFMR for their institutional support, the views presented in this chapter are solely the author's and should not be attributed to CDF or IFMR.

National Action Plan on Climate Change (NAPCC)[2] announced in 2008. India plans to increase its grid connected solar capacity from 3 megawatts (MW) to 3 gigawatts (GW) by 2017. Including the ambitious targets for off-grid solar energy India seeks to have 20 GW of installed solar capacity by 2022. Similarly, China has set a target for renewable energy to constitute 15 per cent of its overall energy portfolio and seeks to have 40 GW of installed wind capacity, 1.8 GW of solar capacity, and 30 GW of installed biomass capacity by 2020 (NDRC, 2007).

Asian countries are also becoming the primary target for clean energy investment. Amidst the largest global recession since the Great Depression, clean energy investment in Asia rose, for the first time surpassing clean energy investment in the Americas. In 2009, the Asia-Pacific region attracted 37.3 billion USD in renewable energy investment, nearly 25 per cent of the global investment in renewable energy technologies. This increase of nearly 25 per cent stands in stark contrast to a global decrease of 6.5 per cent in clean energy investment (Romano, 2010).

Overall, advancements in thin film solar, energy storage, smart grid technology, and demand-side management will likely drive innovation in, and ultimately the impact of, renewable energy technologies in the next two decades. These and other advancements in renewable energy technologies will shape climate related diplomacy across Asia and have significant implications for the environmental quality, industrial competitiveness, and economic growth of Asian nations. While these dimensions of the renewable energy opportunity are both interesting and important, this study examines an oft overlooked dimension of renewable energy: technologies designed for, and targeted towards, Asia's poorest citizens.

Despite its impressive economic growth and strong commitment to renewable energy, Asia is home to over 800 million people who lack access to electricity services, which represents approximately 50 per cent of the world's unelectrified population. Perhaps more astounding, approximately 75 per cent of the world's population who rely on

---

2. Information on India's NAPCC can be found here: *http://pmindia.nic.in/Pg01-52.pdf*

biomass fuels to meet their cooking needs—nearly 1.8 billion people—reside in Asia. Thus, despite Asia's impressive economic growth many of the region's poorest citizens are yet to enjoy the economic, social and health benefits that accompany access to reliable energy services.

Across the globe there is an upsurge in activity in developing new renewable energy technologies, products, and services to meet the energy needs of the poor. Under the banner of market based approaches to development, excitement about this 'new' market segment—commonly referred to as the base of the pyramid (BoP)[3]—has spawned the interest of multinational corporations, multilateral development donor organisations, foundations, and social venture investors alike. This is evidenced by Shell Foundation's investment of 25 million dollars[4] to develop commercially viable improved cook stoves as well as Acumen Fund's investment of over 2.5 million dollars[5] in companies that provide lighting and electricity services to Asia's poorest citizen.

While the amount of money dedicated to the pro-poor renewable energy space is small in comparison to investments made by governments and mainstream venture capital and private equity investors, renewable energy technologies for the BoP may have significant economic, health and livelihood implications for Asia's poorest. In an attempt to highlight an important, though oft overlooked, segment of renewable energy technologies, it introduces the reader to a range of pro-poor renewable energy technologies and examines the magnitude of the challenge, opportunity, and potential impact of these technologies on Asia's rural poor. Due to the fact that India has served as the vanguard testing ground for these renewable energy technologies, products and services this chapter primarily focusses on the Indian experience with these technologies to date.

---

3. Readers interested in learning more about the BoP should refer to Prahalad and Hart (2002) and Hammond *et al.* (2007).
4. *http://www.shellfoundation.org/*
5. *http://www.acumenfund.org/investments/portfolios/energy-portfolio.html*

Decentralised Renewable Energy Technologies

Over the past decade scientists and entrepreneurs have made impressive strides in improving the reliability, and reducing the cost, of a number of decentralised renewable energy technologies, including biomass gasification, small scale photovoltaic, micro wind, small scale hydro power. While a complete exploration of each of these technologies is beyond the scope of this study, this section provides an overview of the current state of electrification across Asia, introduces the reader to three decentralised renewable energy technologies (biomass gasification, small scale hydro power, and solar home systems), and explores the potential impact of these technologies on society.

Current Scenario

According to the IEA (2009a), 1.5 billion people across the globe lack access to electricity,[6] 55 per cent of whom live in Asia. Not surprisingly, there are striking differences in electrification rates between China/East Asia and the South Asia regions (see Table 14.1). In fact, of the approximately 800 million people who lack access to electricity across Asia, 76 per cent reside in South Asia. While regional and sub-regional electrification rates help place Asia in a global comparative perspective, they mask the uneven progress across Asian nations. (Table 14.2 provides an overview of electrification rates in countries that make up the China/East Asia and South Asia regions.) In South Asia, for example, Sri Lanka boasts a 77 per cent electrification rate while Afghanistan's electrification rate is a mere 14 per cent. Perhaps even more striking, in the China/East Asia region nearly 100 per cent of China, Malaysia, Singapore and Thailand's citizens have access to electricity. This stands in stark contrast to electrification rates of Cambodia and Myanmar, which are 13 and 24 per cent, respectively (IEA, 2009a).

6. It is important to note that official government statistics about electrification often do not reflect whether citizens receive regular or adequate electricity supplies. In India, for example, villages are considered electrified if 10 per cent of the households are connected to the grid. Similarly, 'electrified' households often receive electricity at irregular intervals for very limited periods—e.g. every other day for one to three hours. Thus, while electrification rates may appear quite promising in many Asian countries, the estimates presented here likely underestimate the need for regular, consistent electricity in rural households across Asia.

Figure 14.1

Global Electrification: Regional Aggregates

	Population without Electricity (Million)	*Total Electrification Rate (%)*	*Urban Electrification Rate (%)*	*Rural Electrification Rate (%)*
Africa	589	40	66.8	22.7
North Africa	2	98.9	99.6	98.2
Sub-Saharan Africa	587	28.5	57.5	11.9
Developing Asia	809	77.2	93.5	67.2
China and East Asia	195	90.2	96.2	85.5
South Asia	614	60.2	88.4	48.4
Latin America	34	92.7	98.7	70.2
Middle East	21	89.1	98.5	70.6
Developing Countries	1,453	72	90	58.4
Transition Economies and OECD	3	99.8	100	99.5
World	**1,456**	**78.2**	**93.4**	**63.2**

Source: IEA, 2009a.

Similarly, national statics mask the stark divide between rural and urban electrification across Asia. In aggregate nearly 94 per cent of Asia's urban residents enjoy access to electricity while the electrification rate for rural communities across Asia stands at a mere 67.2 per cent. This trend stands in greater relief at the country level. For example, while India boasts a 93.5 per cent urban electrification rate, only approximately 53 per cent of its rural residents have access to electricity. Not surprisingly, an examination of state level lighting trends reveals even more diversity in the progress of electrification. For example, only 11 per cent of the residents of the Indian state of Bihar report using electricity as their primary lighting source, while 95 per cent of their counterparts in the state of Punjab report doing so (NSSO, 2007).

As can be seen above, there is vast diversity in Asian citizens' access to electricity. The region as a whole, which houses two of the world's most rapidly growing economies, has made impressive progress over the past two decades with respect to economic growth. Despite this progress, however, the data presented above indicate that

Table 14.2

Asian Electrification: China, East Asia and South Asia

	Population without Electricity (Million)	Electrification Rate (%)		
		Total	Urban	Rural
China and East Asia	195.1	90.2	96.2	85.5
China	8	99.4	100	99
Brunei	0	99.7	100	98.6
Cambodia	11.2	24	66	12.5
Chinese Taipei	0.2	99	100	98
DPR Korea	17.7	26	36	10
East Timor	0.9	22	52	10.5
Indonesia	81.1	64.5	94	32
Malaysia	0.2	99.4	100	98
Mongolia	0.9	67	90	36
Myanmar	42.8	13	19	10
PDR Laos	2.7	55	84	42
Philippines	12.5	86	97	65
Singapore	0	100	100	100
Thailand	0.4	99.3	100	99
Vietnam	9.5	89	99.6	85
Other Asia	7.1	83.4	96	80
South Asia	613.9	60.2	88.4	48.4
Afghanistan	23.3	14.4	22	12
Bangladesh	94.9	41	76	28
India	404.5	64.5	93.1	52.5
Nepal	16.1	43.6	89.7	34
Pakistan	70.4	57.6	78	46
Sri Lanka	4.7	76.6	85.8	75
Developing Asia	**809**	**77.2**	**93.5**	**67.2**

Source: IEA, 2009a.

many of Asia's poorest citizens, who often reside in rural areas, do not have access to basic infrastructure and services such as electricity. Extending access to reliable, grid-based electricity services to Asia's rural citizens would require investments to expand and upgrade many nations' grid infrastructure and substantial increases in electricity production capacity. In fact, to achieve universal electricity access 'globally' the IEA (2009c) estimates that 35 billion USD (in 2008 dollars) of investment is required annually through 2030. Faced with a large, yet geographically dispersed, consumer base with small individual energy demands, governments have struggled to provide reliable grid based access to the rural poor which has been both slow and insufficient. As Asian countries continue to make progress in extending reliable electricity supply to their citizens, decentralised renewable energy technologies offer a potential means of accelerating the process of providing electricity to Asia's rural poor.[7]

The Scope of Decentralised Renewable Energy Technologies

Decentralised renewable energy technologies have the ability to leverage local feedstocks, employ local labour and have the potential to provide power for household, commercial and agricultural activities in rural areas. Despite the fact that decentralised renewable energy technologies have been available for well over three decades (Rao, 1982), they have seen limited application in many countries across Asia to date. Over the last two decades, however, considerable progress has been made in reducing the cost, and improving the operational reliability, of a suite of decentralised renewable energy technologies. This, combined with increased interest in promoting social entrepreneurship through market-based approaches to poverty reduction, has led to the recent development of decentralised renewable energy technologies and business models to serve the rural poor that show promise of commercial viability. While interesting advances have been made in the areas of community scale photovoltaic power generation and micro wind power, this section introduces three decentralised renewable energy technologies currently operating in India: (i) biomass gasification, (ii) small hydropower, and (iii) solar home systems.

Small scale biomass gasification plants typically have a generating capacity of 25 to 100 kilowatt (kW) and are well suited for villages having 800 to 1,200 households (Bairiganjan *et al.*, forthcoming). With respect to technology, gasification plants consist of a reactor that

7. Please note, rather than advocating that decentralised renewable energy technologies replace traditional electricity supply, this study advocates a convergent approach to electricity supply wherein decentralised renewable energy technologies supplement traditional approaches.

receives air and solid fuel (e.g. wood chips or crop residue), converts them into gas via partial proposes, and removes impurities by cooling and washing. The clean combustible gas, referred to as producer gas, is sent to either a diesel generator with the capacity to operate in dual fuel mode or a gas engine generator capable of running on producer gas. In India, small scale biomass based power plants generate power for approximately 8 to 13 INR (0.17-0.28 USD[8]) per kilowatt hour (kWh) (Bairiganjan *et al.*, forthcoming).

The feedstock for biomass gasification plants can range from processed wood pellets to agricultural residue and commercially available fuel wood. While biomass gasification companies could develop and maintain plantations to ensure a reliable supply of feedstock for the power plant, this approach has often not proved financially feasible or desirable given the relatively high cost associated with serving the rural, low income consumers. In India, the two leading companies in the small scale, rural biomass gasification space—Husk Power Systems[9] and DESI Power[10]—source feedstock (e.g. agricultural waste or wasteland vegetation) directly from farmers or purchase fuel wood from the local market. Due to their relative versatility with respect to feedstock, biomass gasification plants are amenable to a wide range of geographic locations.

In theory, the electricity produced from biomass gasification plants can be sold to an existing power grid, provided energy regulation permits independent power producers to sell to the grid, or distributed directly to local consumers.[11] At present, most Asian countries have implemented market reforms that enable independent power producers to sell power to the grid (Haanyika, 2006). In India, Husk Power and DESI Power target consumers who are currently not connected to the grid and distribute electricity directly to local consumers using a company built, owned and operated distribution system, or microgrid. Due to transmission losses associated with the

8. This study uses an exchange rate of 46.6 INR to the dollar.
9. *http://www.huskpowersystems.com/*
10. *http://www.desipower.com/*
11. In India, and many developing countries, biomass gasification technology is employed primarily for captive power production. Despite the viability of the technology, relatively few companies have attempted to use this technology to meet the energy needs of rural communities.

microgrid and the high marginal distribution costs associated with serving low consumption customers, the catchment area for small scale biomass gasification plants falls within a two to three kilometre radius of the power plant.

Small scale hydro power plants generate electricity using small, high efficiency turbines. Unlike medium and large scale hydro power, which necessitates the construction of a dam and can entail human displacement, small scale hydro power plants generate electricity via run of the river or partial flow diversion (Sharma, 2009). In addition to lowering the capital costs associated with plant construction, and ultimately the cost of power production, small scale hydro power plants subvert many of the negative social and environmental consequences of large hydro power projects. Unlike biomass based gasification plants, which are amenable to any location with a robust supply of biomass feedstock, small scale hydro power plants have limited geographical scope and require a perennial water supply to generate power. (See Table 14.3 for a comparative assessment of biomass gasification and small scale hydro power.)

Table 14.3

Biomass based Independent Power Plants and Small Hydro Plants

	Biomass Plants	*Small Hydro Plants*
Generation capacity (general)	25 kW to 150 kW	100 kW to 1000 kW
Raw material	Crop residue, woody biomass, fuel wood	Run of the river generation
Distribution model	Directly supplies to end-user or small entrepreneurs distributing to end users through a company owned and operated grid	Leverages grid infrastructure to supply electricity to grid, usually does not directly supplies to end user
Cost of production	Rs. 8 -13/kWh	Rs. 2-2.5/kWh
Range of distribution	2-3 km radius of plant	Dependant on local grid infrastructure
Cost of fuel	Dependent on fuel type	No fuel cost

Source: Bairiganjan *et al.*, forthcoming.

Small scale hydro power typically operates at larger capacities than biomass based power generation. SBA Hydro and Renewable Energy (SHREY), a small hydropower company based in the Himalayan region of India, operates plants that range from 800 kW to 1 MW. Thus, unlike current small scale biomass gasification power companies operating in India, which serve one to two villages, SHREY's small scale hydro power plants serve approximately 25 villages. In addition to the larger capacity of their plants, SHREY is able to serve a greater number of villages due to the fact that they sell and distribute power through the existing grid network. By securing access to the grid[12] from the state government and negotiating a preferential feed in tariff, SHREY has a guaranteed buyer for all of the power it generates and is able to rely upon the local utility to execute the billing and collection functions. Thus, SHREY is able to both meet the electricity demands of consumers in its target consumer villages and provide supplemental power to the grid for other users' consumption.

In contrast to both small scale biomass gasification and small scale hydro power, solar home systems (SHS) are designed to meet the electricity needs of individual households or enterprises. This technology, used by companies such as the Solar Electric Light Company (SELCO)[13] in India, is composed of stand alone components that are sourced from domestic and international suppliers and assembled onsite at the user's homes (Bairiganjan *et al.*, forthcoming). SHS generate electricity via a photovoltaic panel placed on the roof of the house, or enterprise, and store electricity in a locally available motor cycle batteries, which can store power for relatively long durations. The systems employed by SELCO can generate approximately 10 to 35 watts of electricity, which is sufficient to power 4 to 10, 7 watt compact fluorescent lamp (CFL) bulbs, a fan, and select small appliances (Hande, 2009). Here it is important to note that while SHS have the potential to meet household energy requirements they are not designed to meet communities' agricultural energy requirements.

12. As a technical matter it is important to note that accessing the grid requires both an enabling policy framework that is favourable to small scale, independent renewable energy companies as well as additional capital investment to step up the power generated to a grid-compatible voltage.

13. *http://www.selco-india.com/*

Unlike biomass gasification and small scale hydro power, which allow users to pay per quantum of electricity used or hours of service, SHS require individual consumers to invest capital upfront to install the systems. At a price point of approximately 7,000 to 18,000 INR (150 to 386 USD), SHS are largely out of reach of the lowest income consumers in rural India. Recognising this SELCO, which has installed over 100,000 SHS to date in rural India, has partnered with rural banking institutions to obtain end-user financing for their SHS systems.

The three decentralised renewable energy technologies outlined above represent three distinct models of electricity provision. First, the operating model employed by SHREY represents a decentralised energy production model that leverages existing grid infrastructure. As noted above, this model has the potential to reach users that are connected to grid infrastructure but receive irregular or insufficient electricity supply. Interestingly, this population of users is not represented in the statistics presented in Table 14.2 and likely represents a significant number of consumers in Asia's less prosperous countries. Second, the operating models employed by both DESI Power and Husk Power represent off-grid solutions to electricity provision. This model has the potential to serve the 800 million people in Asia currently not connected to existing grid infrastructure. Interestingly, however, this operating model also has the potential to connect to, and supplement, the grid if and when the grid reaches these communities. Finally, the SHS model employed by SELCO offers a stand along energy solution to households. Although this model offers an energy solution for households who are not connected to the grid infrastructure, it offers limited to no potential to leverage, or be integrated into, the grid if it reaches these communities. As a result, SHS may be best suited to remote communities across Asia who are unlikely to benefit from large scale grid infrastructure.

Potential Impact of Decentralised Renewable Energy Technologies

Across many countries in Asia governments have struggled to extend reliable electricity services to rural citizens. As noted above, nearly 800 million Asian citizens lack access to electricity. Extending grid access to these citizens, who overwhelmingly represent the rural poor, has proven difficult due to the high costs associated with serving a geographically dispersed consumer base with relatively low individual energy requirements (Haanyika, 2006; Zomers, 2001). In addition to those without access to electricity services, Asian countries are likely home to hundreds of millions of citizens who cope with irregular and insufficient electricity supply. The fact that rural consumers have shown a willingness and ability to pay for high quality services combined with the fact that decentralised renewable energy technologies can leverage local resources, have relatively low distribution costs, and can be sized to meet local demand suggest that decentralised renewable energy offers one potential means of meeting the energy requirements of these consumer segments across Asia. Unfortunately, while there is a robust literature on energy consumption across the globe the empirical literature on the energy-development nexus is quite thin. That said, in addition to well publicised environmental and climate related benefits of meeting increasing electricity demand with renewable energy resources, decentralised renewable energy has the potential to contribute to improving economic livelihoods,[14] enhancing economic integration, and promoting national energy security for Asia's developing nations.

Economic Development

For decades the development community has recognised the important link between access to modern energy sources, poverty alleviation, and sustainable development. In fact, rural energy development is closely associated with numerous development objectives including job creation, environmental protection, wealth distribution and public health (Gan and Yu, 2008). This is perhaps best reflected by the centrality of energy access in the Millennium Development Goals (MDGs), which have driven the global development agenda for the past eight years. According to the statement released at the Summit, '[t]o meet the goal accepted by the international community to halve the proportion of people living on less than US$1 per day by 2015, access to affordable energy services

14. For a discussion on the link between energy and economic development see (Toman and Jemelkova, 2003).

is a prerequisite' (UN, 2001). The connection between access to electricity services and economic wellbeing is further highlighted by Ranganathan and Ramanayya (1998) surveyed 5,000 households in the Indian states of Uttar Pradesh and Madhya Pradesh which indicated that households with access to electricity reported nearly twice the income of their non-electrified counterparts.[15] Additionally, a study by the UN Millennium project estimates that the access to electricity for rural households in the Philippines could yield a return of 81-151 USD per month due to improved returns on education and wage income (Modi *et al.*, 2006). While this may seem promising, it is important to recall that there may be a significant time lag between when rural communities gain access to electricity services and when they reap significant benefits from electrification.[16]

Although access to energy services is an important driver of economic development, it is not a panacea for poverty alleviation. Development professionals and scholars are now well aware that access to energy services is a necessary but not sufficient driver of economic and social development (Barnes and Binswanger, 1986; Pachauri *et al.*, 2004). When coupled with access to other enabling infrastructure such as roads, water supply, and health services, decentralised renewable energy has the potential to contribute to increased economic livelihood through both direct and indirect means (WEC, 1999). With respect to agriculture, reliable energy services can facilitate access to irrigation[17] via electrical pump sets, which can have considerable impact on farmer incomes. In fact Barnes *et al.* (2002) suggest that access to pump irrigation can increase farmer income by 50 per cent (Toman and Jemelkova, 2003). Additionally, according to Barnes and Binswanger (1986) access to electricity services is correlated with increased incidences of multiple cropping.

---

15. It is important to note that Ranganathana and Ramanayya (1998) do not claim attribution between energy access and increased incomes.

16. Ranganathan and Ramanayya (1998) suggest there is a five-year time lag for the rural poor to reap significant benefits from electrification.

17. According to Barnes *et al.* (2002), rural electrification was concurrent with increased investments in electrical irrigation pumps. It is important to note that increased irrigation without appropriate incentives for the judicious use of water may have a detrimental impact on groundwater sustainability. This phenomenon was widely observed after the proliferation of irrigated agriculture in India after the Green Revolution.

Decentralised renewable energy services also have the potential to enable value added post-harvest agricultural processing (Barnes and Binswanger, 1986)and can enable the development of cold chains for dairy and agricultural produce, which when combined with road connectivity and market linkages can deliver substantial increases in rural income.

Decentralised renewable energy can also improve the health and wellbeing of the rural poor, which has indirect effects on households' economic activity. Cooking and lighting are the primary domestic uses of energy among rural households. Thus, when households gain access to electricity, they typically shift from kerosene to electricity to meet their lighting needs (IEA, 2007). A recent study by Pokhrel *et al.* (2009) suggests that the indoor use of kerosene lamps is positively correlated with increased incidences of tuberculosis, particularly in women. Similarly, improved lighting provides additional opportunities for children to study safely in the evenings.

Interestingly, decentralised renewable energy also has the potential to shift the role of rural communities and rural consumers in energy services delivery. Even when rural communities are connected to the grid, their electricity needs are often subordinated to those of industry and urban areas. As a result, they are forced to cope with irregular and insufficient electricity supply. Decentralised renewable energy offers a potential means to reverse this urban-rural dynamic by placing rural locales at the centre of energy production. As evidenced by the experience of SHREY in the Indian Himalayas, decentralised renewable energy can meet the electricity demands of rural consumers while providing supplemental power to the existing grid infrastructure. Although a full examination of the potential impact of this on rural communities is beyond the scope of this chapter, this may have interesting implications for the role of rural communities and rural locales in national energy security and development.

Energy Security

In addition to climate change and increasing international attention to curb GHG emissions, interest in promoting renewable energy technologies across Asia has been buoyed by a desire to lower energy imports and promote national energy security and energy independence (Han *et al.*, 2008; Gan and Yu, 2008). According to the IEA, by 2030, 90 per cent of the incremental energy demand will come from non-OECD countries with India and China accounting for over 53 per cent of this increase (IEA, 2009b). Similarly, by 2025 China is projected to overtake the US with respect to oil and natural gas imports and India is projected to surpass Japan as the third largest importer of these energy sources. The recent 60 billion USD deal signed between Australia and China for the supply of 30 million tonnes of coal every year for the next 20 years also signals that China's appetite for imported energy sources goes beyond oil and natural gas (Krishnan, 2010). In the context of increasing economic development in developing Asia and the rising economic prominence of ASEAN countries, renewable energy technologies—including decentralised renewable energy technologies—have a clear role to play in promoting energy security.[18]

Given current government priorities, decentralised renewable energy technologies will likely constitute a small proportion of renewable energy development in many Asian countries. Thus, while decentralised renewable energy technologies can, and likely will, contribute to national energy independence, their potential value for energy security lies in the distributed nature of their power production.[19] As noted numerous times throughout this chapter, distributed renewable energy technologies have the potential to meet the needs of local consumers while providing supplemental power to the electricity grid. In an age of increasing threats of international and domestic terrorism, more severe weather events, ageing centralised infrastructure, and distributed energy production technologies can contribute to the development of a grid that is more resilient than large scale centralised approaches to electricity supply alone.

---

18. According to Hausmann and Wagner (2009: 14), '...countries are also revealing some bias towards domestic energy production as a means of protecting Balance of Payments which may be very relevant in episodes of high oil price volatility. For example, Weidenmier *et al.* (2008) show how internal energy production protected Brazil's macro economic conditions during the oil price spike in 2007-08'.

19. It is important to note that realising the potential of distributed energy technologies would require the development and application of a new generation of smart grid technology to improve load balance efficiency and power distribution.

Summary and Conclusions

Over the past decade Asia has become the world's largest consumer of energy, adopted aggressive renewable energy targets, and is emerging as a leader in renewable energy technology manufacturing. However, despite its strong economic performance, many of Asia's least prosperous citizens lack access to modern energy services. According to the IEA (2009c), without significant investment to extending services approximately 1.3 billion of the world's poorest citizens, many of whom live in Asia, will still lack access to electricity and modern cooking fuels by 2030. As discussed in this chapter, decentralised renewable energy technologies have the potential to provide electricity services to Asia's poor, supplement the existing power supply, add resiliency to the power grid, and alter the role of rural locales in national energy development. Additionally, the economic benefits of providing electricity supply may significantly contribute to poverty reduction and help transform rural locales into more robust centres of economic activity. This has the potential to reduce urban rural migration, thereby reducing pressure on Asia's megacities, as well as improve security via the well documented poverty-security nexus. In order for decentralised renewable energy technologies to become an economically viable and significant component of the Asian energy story, however, significant advancements are required in energy policy as well as the development of micro-metering, remote read technologies, thin-film solar, and energy storage. The challenge of providing modern energy services to poor is not new. As stated by Rao (1982: 615), '[v]iable—although small-scale—commercial technology for harnessing new and renewable energy resources is available for application in rural areas, but the wider application and acceptance of this technology will require the development of effective "software" [sic] for the promotion of alternative energy resources. It appears that the real issue of energy supply is an institutional problem, not a technological one.'

References

Bairiganjan, S., R. Cheung, E. Delio, D. Fuente, S. Lall and S. Singh (forthcoming). *Power to the People: Investing in Clean Energy for the Base of the Pyramid in India.* Washington, D.C: World Resources Institute.

Barnes, D.F. *et al.* (2002). "The Benefits of Rural Electrification in India: Implications for Education, Household Lighting, and Irrigation", *Background Study for India Rural Energy Access Strategy.* Washington D.C.: SASEI, World Bank

Barnes, D.F., K. Openshaw, K.R. Smith and R. van der Plas (1993). "The Design and Diffusion of Improved Cooking Stoves", *The World Bank Research Observer* 8(2): 119-41, at *http://www.jstor.org/stable/3986529* on 2 February 2010.

Barnes, D.F. and H.P. Binswanger (1986). "Impact of Rural Electrification and Infrastructure on Agricultural Changes, 1966-1980", *Economic and Political Weekly* 21(1): 26-34.

Bradsher, K. (2010). "China is Leading the Race to Make Renewable Energy", *The New York Times,* January 30, at *http://www.nytimes.com/2010/01/31/business/energy-and environment/31renew.html?scp=1&sq=china%20renewable&st=cse* (accessed on January 31, 2010).

Gan, L. and J. Yu (2008). "Bioenergy Transition in Rural China: Policy Options and Co-benefits", *Energy Policy* 36: 533-40.

Haanyika, C.M. (2006). "Rural Electrification Policy and Institutional Linkages", *Energy Policy* 34: 2977-993.

Hammond, A.L., W.J. Kramer, R.S. Katz, J.T. Tran and C. Walker (2007). *The Next 4 Billion: Market Size and Business Strategy at the Base of the Pyramid.*

Han, J., A.P. Mol, Y. Lu, and L. Zhang (2008). "Small-Scale Bioenergy Projects in Rural China: Lessons to be Learnt", *Energy Policy* 36: 2154-162.

Hande, H. (2009). "CEO of SELCO", *Personal Communication,* March.

Hausmann, R. and Rodrigo Wagner (2009). "Certification Strategies, Industrial Development and a Global Market for Biofuels", *Belfer Center Discussion paper* 2009-15, October. Cambridge, MA: Harvard University at *http://belfercenter.ksg.harvard.edu/publication/19856/certification_strategies_industrial_development_and_a_global_market_for_biofuels.html* (accessed on January 4, 2010).

International Energy Agency (IEA) (2007). "India's Energy Prospects—Chapter 20 Focus on Poverty", *World Energy Outlook 2007.* Paris, France: International Energy Agency at *http://www.worldenergyoutlook.org/database_electricity/WEO2007-Chapter%2020.pdf* (accessed on January 12, 2010).

———. (2009a). *The Electricity Access Database.* Paris, France: International Energy Agency. At *http://www.worldenergyoutlook.org/database_electricity/electricity_access_ database.htm* accessed on January 3, 2010.

———. (2009b). *World Energy Outlook 2009: Fact Sheet.* Paris, France: International Energy Agency. At *http://www.iea.org/weo/docs/weo2009/fact_sheets_WEO_2009.pdf* accessed on January 3, *2010.*

———. (2009c). *World Energy Outlook 2009: Executive Summary.* Paris, France: International Energy Agency (IEA) at: *http://www.worldenergyoutlook.org/docs/weo2009/WEO2009_es_english.pdf* (accessed on January 3, 2010).

Krishnan, A. (2010). "Australia, China Sign $60 billion Coal Deal", *The Hindu,* February. At *http://beta.thehindu.com/news/international/article102174.ece* (accessed on February 7).

Modi, V., S. McDade, D. Lallement and J. Saghir (2006). *Energy and the Millennium Development Goals.* New York: Energy Sector Management Assistance Programme, United Nations Development Programme, UN Millennium Project and World Bank.

NDRC 2007). *Medium and Long-Term Development Plan for Renewable Energy in China.* Abbreviated Version. English Draft. National Development and Reform Commission (NDRC). People's Republic of China. At *http://www.chinaenvironmentallaw.com/wp-content/uploads/2008/04/medium-and-long-term-development-plan-for-renewable-energy.pdf* (accessed January 3, 2010).

NSSO (2007). "Household Consumer Expenditure", *National Sample Survey 63rd Round (July 2006-June 2007).* New Delhi: Government of India Ministry of Statistics and Programme Implementation.

Pachauri, S., A. Mueller, A. Kemmler and D. Spreng (2004). "On Measuring Energy Poverty in Indian Households", *World Development* 32(12): 2083-104.

Pokhrel, A.K., M.N. Bates, S.C. Verma, H.S. Joshi, C.T. Sreeramareddy and K.R. Smith (2009). "Tuberculosis and Indoor Biomass and Kerosene Use in Nepal: A Case-Control Study. Environ Health Perspect", doi:10.1289/ehp.0901032 at *http://ehsehplp03. niehs.nih.gov/article/fetchArticle.action?articleURI=info:doi/10.1289/ehp.0901032* (accessed on January 10, 2010).

Prahalad, C.K. and S.L. Hart (2002). *The Fortune at the Bottom of the Pyramid: Eradicating Poverty Through Profits.*

Ranganathan, V. and T.V. Ramanayya (1998). "Long-Term Impact of Rural Electrification: A Study in UP and MP", *Economic and Political Weekly* 33(50): 3181-184.

Rao, G.L. (1982). "Rural Energy and Rural Habitat", *Habitat International* 6(5-6): 599-619.

Romano, B. (2010). "Asia Tops All for Clean Energy Investment Growth. Recharge", *The Global Source for Renewable Energy News*, January 7, at *http://www.rechargenews.com/business_area/finance/article202919.ece* (accessed on January 10).

Sharma, S.K. (2009). "CEO of SBA Hydro", *Personal Communication*, August 25.

Toman, M. and B. Jemelkova (2003). "Energy and Economic Development: An Assessment of the State of Knowledge", *Discussion Paper* 03-13. Washington, DC: Resources for the Future at *http://www.rff.org/documents/RFF-DP-03-13.pdf* (accessed on February 10).

United Nations (2001). Commission on Sustainable Development: Ninth Session". Agenda Item 4, Decision, Energy for Sustainable Development, Section 6.22. New York: United Nations.

WEC (1999). *The Challenge of Rural Energy Poverty in Developing Countries*. London, UK: World Energy Council, WEC.

Weidenmier, Marc. D *et al.* (2008). "Is Sugar Sweeter at the Pump? The Microeconomic Impact of Brazil's Alternative Energy Programme", *National Bureau of Economic Research Working Paper* 14362.

Zomers, A.N. (2009). *Rural Electrification Utilities Chafe of Challenge*. The Netherlands: Twente University Press, Enschede.

———. (2001). *Rural Electrification Utilities' Chafe of Challenge*. Enschede, The Netherlands: Twente University Press.

VI

WMD and International Security

15

The Relevance (or Otherwise) of Nuclear Weapons in the 21st Century

PERVEZ HOODBHOY

By 2030, the strategic world will be very different from what it is today. The United States, the sole hegemonic power of the early 21st century, will still be the most powerful among nations. But it shall only be one player among several. Science and technology—the creators of wealth and power—are rapidly diffusing across the globe, aided by globalisation and the Internet. They are creating powerful rival nation states which no longer bend to American wishes. Nuclear monopolies belong to history; breakout countries like North Korea and Iran have put yet another nail in the coffin. Interestingly, the winds of change are driving countries along very different nuclear trajectories—both towards and away from weapons.

Profound changes are already visible in the US. Although it was the first country to invent and use nuclear weapons, its enthusiasm started waning after the end of the Cold War. A realisation slowly dawned that every warhead added to its arsenal of 30,000 certainly increased maintenance and security costs but brought little benefit. Arch-conservative 'cold warrior', and an inner member of the US nuclear policy establishment, Paul Nitze, was years ahead of his colleagues when he wrote in 1999: 'I see no compelling reason why we should not unilaterally get rid of our nuclear weapons...To maintain them is costly and adds nothing to our security...we can achieve our objectives with conventional weapons. There is nothing to be gained through the use of our nuclear arsenal.'[1]

1. Nitze (1999).

More recently, in the now famous articles published in the *Wall Street Journal* (WSJ) in 2007 and 2008, the four famous horsemen—George Shultz, William Perry, Henry Kissinger, and Sam Nunn—called for nuclear global elimination.[2] Coming from the hawkish Kissinger particularly, this was a bombshell of sorts and left Republican conservatives in a state of shock. But strangely, the Pentagon concurred, and there is little doubt that a serious reassessment of the worth of nuclear weapons to the US is in the works. The election of Barack Obama as president gave an additional impetus towards decreasing the salience of nuclear weapons in US strategic thinking. Reaffirmation of Strategic Arms Reduction Treaty (START), as agreed upon by presidents Obama and Medvedev in 2009, certainly points in that direction.

One needs to be clear about motives. America's apparent change of heart comes primarily for pragmatic reasons, not high moral principles!

The first is nuclear terrorism. Nuclear weapons have utility in determining power relations between nation states. But they are worse than useless in dealing with holy warriors, for whom reward lies in the hereafter. By engineering a nuclear catastrophe in some Western city, Osama bin Laden and his disciples dream of provoking a nuclear response from the US against Muslim holy sites and populations—Mecca, Cairo, Tehran, and Islamabad. This, in their minds, would hasten the advent of the *dajjal*, a mythological one-eyed creature who will hasten the day of ultimate victory. Together with other non-state actors, religious extremists stand greater chances of success in a world awash in nuclear bombs and fissile materials. Hence a non-nuclear world is safer for the US.

The second reason for the changed US mood is that nuclear weapons are unnecessary for remaining the top dog in today's world.[3] The US has an enormous advantage in conventional weaponry. Twenty-first century warfare does not belong to dumb nukes. Instead,

---

2. Shultz *et al.* (2007; 2008).
3. *http://newwars.wordpress.com/2009/11/23/revisin-the-american-way-of-war-pt-1/ http://newwars.wordpress.com/2009/11/24/revising-the-american-way-of-war-pt-2/*

laser weapons, drones, hi-tech ships, aircraft, and space based assets are the actual war-fighting instruments rather than static instruments of deterrence. All fighting forces want smart, precision-guided weapons with inbuilt microprocessor chips and computers. Fuel-air explosives—the rich man's mini-nukes—carry enormous destructive power, zero radiation effects, and can also be delivered with great precision by giant bombers.

Add to this the fact that nuclear weapons have lost most of their scare power. US nuclear weapons have not been used for 65 years—and the enormity of consequences if they are actually used—means that they are viewed as distant and abstract threats. From the American point of view, an adversary's newly acquired nuclear weapons are a highly unwelcome equaliser. Indeed, if Saddam Hussein had succeeded in his plans, the course of Iraq's history might have been quite different. It has finally dawned on US strategists that, in the long run, other nations can be prevented from going nuclear only if there is some semblance of uniformity—non-proliferation norms carry meaning only when they apply to all actors, both 'good' and 'bad'.

There is nothing surprising about America's new realisation. What is surprising, however, is that it was so long in coming. The bellicosity of the George W. Bush regime, and the attack of September 11, 2001, slowed the path to this eventuality. Of course, I do not mean to suggest that an anti-nuclear consensus has finally emerged in the US. So, for example, even as the 'Four Horsemen' argue in their latest WSJ op-ed[4] page that the US must 'work to realise the vision of a world without nuclear weapons', they want significant investments 'to undo the adverse consequences of deep reductions over the past five years in the laboratories' budgets for the science, technology and engineering programmes that support and underwrite the nation's nuclear deterrent.' This is nothing but an excuse to maintain a potent nuclear arsenal that can be periodically upgraded. Clearly, US national interest rather than broad universalism guides their analyses.

4. Shultz *et al.* (2010).

Still, as mentioned earlier, on balance, the good news is that there are encouraging trends in the US towards making deep cuts in its nuclear arsenal, and this has already inspired a positive reaction in Russia. A real test of US intentions—and Obama's strength—will be to bring on line the Comprehensive Nuclear-Test-Ban Treaty (CTBT). This treaty, signed in 1996, would prohibit any testing of nuclear weapons or devices. Countries that still need to come on board, apart from the US, are China, North Korea, India, Israel, Iran, Indonesia, Pakistan, Egypt and Columbia. India and Pakistan have committed not to test, albeit politically and not formally. Optimistically, Obama will be able to muster sufficient support for his country's ratification against the Republican opposition. The next few months will tell.

South Asia's Nuclear Future

Let us now transport the two main issues discussed above—nuclear terrorism and reduced utility of nuclear weapons—into the South Asian context.

In 1974, India's demonstration of nuclear capability triggered Pakistan's own 'Manhattan Project' that culminated in the Chagai-1 tests of 1998. Today, with 70-100 fission weapons spread across Pakistan and fissile materials produced or processed at numerous locations, the threat from religious extremists—both outsiders and establishment insiders—is real but unquantifiable.

There is little doubt that the Pakistan army takes the safety of its nuclear weapons seriously and has taken a wide variety of protective measures. But in spite of the apparent professionalism of the Strategic Plans Division, which has nuclear custodial responsibility, procedures and technical fixes for securing nuclear weapons are only as good as the men who operate them. This lies at the very heart of the safety issue. For more than 25 years, the Pakistan army had nurtured Islamist radicals as proxy warriors for covert operations on Pakistan's borders in Kashmir and Afghanistan. This fostered extremism inside parts of the military and intelligence. Today, some parts are at war with other parts, as is evident from the dozens of suicide attacks on the military and intelligence establishment. Some attacks were so intricately planned that they obviously had to have essential help from the inside.

One does not know if radical Pakistani Islamists can eventually hijack a weapon, or acquire the technical expertise and the highly enriched uranium needed for a crude *in-situ* nuclear device. But it is quite certain that, having gone to the trouble of getting it, they will use it if they can. One should not assume that London or New York will be the preferred targets because Islamabad and Delhi may be just as good—and certainly much easier. If a retaliatory nuclear response from India on Pakistan's cities is triggered, this would be the fulfillment of a dream to ignite the ultimate conflict that would destroy both *kafirs* (unbelievers) and *munafiqs* (Muslim hypocrites). In the twisted logic of the fanatics, those who follow Islam imperfectly and those who oppose it are equally bad. The numerous suicide bombings of mosques, and of Pakistan's public places, have now established the Talibanic theorem: *munafiq* = *kafir*. Thus it is not just the United States but also India—and perhaps Pakistan still more—that need to fear nuclear terrorism.

There is a second interesting parallel with the US situation: powerful India has unwittingly reduced its huge strategic advantage over weaker Pakistan to near nil by going nuclear. Only at the risk of starting a nuclear war could India have responded to the Kargil invasion (1999), the attack on the Indian parliament (2001), or the Mumbai massacre (2008). Of course, India may freely construct any number of 'Cold Start' type strategies over the next few decades, and of a two-front war under a 'nuclear over-hang' (by itself an interesting newly invented phrase), articulated by the Indian General Deepak Kapoor in January 2010. But these are highly risky games, and Pakistan may react out of all proportion to the degree of Indian success. While mutual terror induces a quasi-peace, the downside is that Indian and Pakistani nuclear trajectories can never be too far from the brink. Although this fact does not seem to bother either country unduly, it is dangerous for precisely this reason.

A prediction: notwithstanding the complication induced by the China factor, I think it is only a matter of time before the Indian establishment matures into producing its own Nitzes and Kissingers.

Towards Global Zero?

At the beginning of 2010, the Bulletin of the Atomic Scientists (BAS) at the University of Chicago decided to move its famous Doomsday Clock from five minutes to midnight backwards by one minute.[5] This reflects cautious optimism that, on balance, the world is safer today than in previous years. Created in 1947, the Doomsday Clock has been adjusted only 18 times prior to today, most recently in January 2007 and February 2002 after the events of 9/11.

The BAS statement explains:

> This hopeful state of world affairs leads the boards of the Bulletin of the Atomic Scientists—which include 19 Nobel laureates—to move the minute hand of the Doomsday Clock back from five to six minutes to midnight. By shifting the hand back from midnight by only one additional minute, we emphasise how much needs to be accomplished, while at the same time recognising signs of collaboration among the United States, Russia, the European Union, India, China, Brazil and others on nuclear security and on climate stabilisation.[6]

The statement continues:

> ...A key to the new era of cooperation is a change in the US government's orientation toward international affairs brought about in part by the election of Obama. With a more pragmatic, problem-solving approach, not only has Obama initiated new arms reduction talks with Russia, he has started negotiations with Iran to close its nuclear enrichment programme, and directed the US government to lead a global effort to secure loose fissile material in four years. He also presided over the UN Security Council last September where he supported a fissile material cut-off treaty and encouraged all countries to live up to their disarmament and non-proliferation obligations under the Nuclear Non-proliferation Treaty...[7]

One might continue this note of optimism: populations in the West now openly question the need for nuclear weapons instead of buying into the rhetoric of indispensability. The absurdity of maintaining

5. *http://www.thebulletin.org/content/media-center/announcements/2010/01/14/doomsday-clock-moves-one-minute-away-midnight*
6. Ibid.
7. Ibid.

nukes in post-Cold War Europe is apparent. Where is the enemy? Why put your own people at needless risk of accident and sabotage? Antagonise neighbours with whom you no longer have much of a quarrel?

I am not proposing Osama bin Laden for the Nobel Prize. But he and his followers must be credited with enhancing awareness about nuclear dangers. Even more, their maniacal actions have shown the futility of deterrence.

That was all the good news.

The bad news is that proliferation risks will rise in proportion to the number of nuclear power plants in non-nuclear states, and that the demand for such plants will increase in proportion to fossil fuel depletion and climate change severity. Learning to separate plutonium and uranium from reactor wastes puts a country high on the learning curve towards nuclear weapons. In fact, even purely peaceful nuclear programmes aimed at generating power can be rapidly redirected towards weapons production if a country so decides. It is, after all, all about learning the art of managing neutrons: they can be used to release fission energy slowly for power purposes, or rapidly to create an explosion. (The same is not true for fusion energy!)

Then, there is the imponderable: what will happen if there is an actual use of nuclear weapons over the next 20 years? The shock wave—amplified by the instant communications of modern times—would impact differently in different parts of the world. Where strong anti-nuclear movements exist, the sheer horror would force a move towards abolition. But, depending upon whether the perpetrator is another country or an non-state actor, one can imagine that other countries may want to rush towards acquiring these weapons lest they too become victims.

Sixty-five years after they were first tested and then used, nuclear weapons continue to be a menace to the human race. What might it take to bring about global nuclear disarmament?

A fissile material cut-off is key. Production of the basic stuff that goes into bombs—highly enriched uranium and weapons-grade plutonium—will have to cease. This underlines the need for an international agreement based upon some painstakingly worked out technical document that allows uranium enrichment for power generation but firmly closes any loopholes for weapons, and that involves minimally intrusive verification procedures. Disposition of existing fissile stocks by some relatively proliferation-proof means must be part of the package. The resistance to ceasing fissile material production will not come from the five nuclear weapon states—they already have more material than they want. But India and Pakistan are in a full-fledged nuclear arms race, a race that is only partially in response to the other. Today, they are the world's only countries that are openly increasing their fissile material stocks. Swimming against the tide of global nuclear arms reductions, they fear possible international agreements. Before the inevitable happens, they want to push their nuclear programmes forward as hard as possible. China, pointing at the small size of its arsenal relative to those of the US and Russia, has also resisted being drawn into an agreement.

Notwithstanding the one minute of Doomsday Time recently added to our safety, life on the planet remains deeply imperilled. Immediate threats to human security will come increasingly more from economic collapse, groups bent on terrorising civilians, or from resource scarcity exacerbated by climate change and exploding populations, rather than from conflict between nuclear armed countries. Against these new dangers, nuclear weapons are a liability. Their possession by a few countries stimulates desire in other countries and complicates things immensely. The sooner South Asia realises this fact the better.

References

Nitze, Paul (1999). "A Threat Mostly to Ourselves", *The New York Times*. October 28.

Shultz, George P., William J. Perry, Henry A. Kissinger and Sam A. Nunn (2007). "A World Free of Nuclear Weapons," *Wall Street Journal*. January 4.

———. (2008). "Toward a Nuclear-Free World", *Wall Street Journal*. January 15.

———. (2010). "How to Protect Our Nuclear Deterrent—Maintaining Confidence in our Nuclear Arsenal is Necessary as the Number of Weapons goes down", *Wall Street Journal*. January 19.

16

Asian Security, Chinese and Indian Power, and Nuclear Non-Proliferation

SUMIT GANGULY and DAVID P. FIDLER

Introduction

The future of the Nuclear Non-Proliferation Treaty (NPT)[1] will receive much attention in 2010 because of the NPT review conference in May. The Obama administration's push for a world free of nuclear weapons will further intensify the spotlight on the NPT and other agreements and instruments that make up the nuclear non-proliferation regime, including the Comprehensive Nuclear-Test-Ban Treaty (CTBT),[2] the Fissile Material Cut-Off Treaty (FMCT),[3] and United Nations (UN) Security Council Resolutions 1540[4] and 1887.[5] With China's and India's emergence as increasingly important geopolitical players, the national, regional and global security interests of these countries will loom larger in the nuclear non-proliferation context than they have in the past. Thus, the relationship between Asian security concerns and Chinese and Indian interests will become more important over the next two decades with respect to the NPT and associated agreements and instruments. This chapter explores how these concerns and interests are likely to shape the nuclear non-proliferation regime over the next 20 years.

We make two central arguments. First, we argue that the health of the NPT and its related agreements and instruments will not

1. UN (1968).
2. UN (1996). For information on CTBT, see McGrath (2009).
3. At present, states have not concluded negotiations on a FMCT in the UN Conference on Disarmament. For background on the FMCT, see Reif and Foley (2009).
4. UN (2004).
5. UN (2009).

constitute the most pressing issue for Asian security generally or China or India individually. This argument holds even on the assumption that efforts to roll back North Korea's proliferation and to prevent Iran from going nuclear do not succeed in the coming years.

Second, we argue that Chinese and Indian interests in the nuclear non-proliferation regime are, for different and similar reasons, likely to reflect a conservative approach to nuclear non-proliferation issues. Both China and India will face greater expectations in this realm as their geopolitical importance grows, but their political and geopolitical interests concerning nuclear weapons will not tend towards major substantive changes in the NPT, strong support for the CTBT, or swift conclusion of the FMCT. Thus, China and India will act to shore up their status as emerging great powers possessing nuclear weapons, but will do so in ways that protect their national, regional and global security interests in nuclear weapons and nuclear deterrence.

Our arguments suggest that both the general context of Asian security and the power and interests of China and India mean that the hopes for dramatic breakthroughs on the NPT, CTBT and FMCT and for significant progress towards a nuclear-free world will be belied. However, the nuclear non-proliferation regime will not collapse or fall apart because of the security situation in Asia or Chinese or Indian behaviour. The regime will continue but will not change dramatically because this outcome will best serve both Chinese and Indian security interests over the course of the next 20 years.

The Nuclear Non-Proliferation Regime: Overview

Getting to a World without Nuclear Weapons: Advancing a Complex Regime Complex

President Obama's resurrection of the vision of a world free of nuclear weapons[6] has placed the existing and proposed instruments supporting nuclear non-proliferation under heightened scrutiny. The ambition behind the idea of a nuclear-free world helps illuminate the extent and intricacy of the 'regime complex' that supports the goal of

6. President Obama committed his administration to the pursuit of a world without nuclear weapons in a speech in Prague in April 2009. See White House (2009).

nuclear non-proliferation. At the heart of this complex is the NPT, which, despite grave concerns about its effectiveness in the past 10-15 years (see below), remains, in the words of the UN Security Council, 'the cornerstone of the nuclear non-proliferation regime and the essential foundation for the pursuit of nuclear disarmament and for the peaceful uses of nuclear energy.'[7] Supporting the NPT's objectives are two proposed treaties that have not yet come into force or been finalised—the CTBT and the FMCT. Growing fears about the potential for nuclear terrorism—a different but sinister type of proliferation—have prompted a number of policy responses, including the International Convention on the Suppression of Acts of Nuclear Terrorism[8] and UN Security Council Resolution 1540, which obligates UN members to take all necessary actions to prevent nuclear, chemical and biological materials from falling into the hands of terrorists.

President Obama's strategy for a nuclear-free world reflects the complex reality of the non-proliferation regime. His strategy calls for strengthening the NPT, enacting the CTBT (which will require US ratification), finalisation of the FMCT, and stringent measures to secure nuclear materials from terrorists.[9] The United States is negotiating with Russia to implement steep cuts in their nuclear arsenals, as part of their NPT obligation to work towards nuclear disarmament which will also serve to strengthen the treaty.

NPT Troubles

However, the vision of a nuclear-free world and the breadth of President Obama's ambitions for nuclear diplomacy should not obscure the serious problems that the nuclear non-proliferation regime faces now and in the foreseeable future. The centre piece of this regime, the NPT, is subject to multiple concerns that affect the rules on non-proliferation, disarmament and peaceful uses of nuclear energy. Over the past few decades, a number of NPT non-nuclear weapons states—Iraq, Libya, Syria, North Korea and Iran—have either violated or are suspected of violating their obligations of not to acquire nuclear

7. *supra* note 5, at Preamble, p. 6.
8. UN (2005).
9. *supra* note 6.

weapons capabilities.[10] These repeated actual or purported 'breakout' challenges to the NPT have shaken confidence in the treaty's effectiveness against states determined to acquire nuclear weapons or the capability to develop them quickly. Nor were the NPT and its processes the mechanism through which states addressed the actual or suspected Iraqi, Libyan and Syrian proliferation.

North Korea's development of nuclear weapons, and its controversial withdrawal from the NPT, has also damaged the credibility of the NPT as the central non-proliferation agreement. North Korea's actions have sidelined the NPT and produced a *sui generis* negotiating process, the 'six party talks', through which the United States, Russia, China, South Korea and Japan are trying to persuade North Korea to give up its nuclear weapons capabilities. To date, this process has not been successful in its professed objective, which has enhanced the leverage North Korea has gained by becoming a nuclear-armed state—precisely the opposite of what according to the NPT states should have emerged from this unfortunate episode. Even more worrying is what some experts suspect; that North Korea's success in defying the NPT and its supporters might tempt Japan and South Korea to hedge their bets by moving, secretly, towards acquiring the capability to deploy a nuclear deterrent.

Although there is as yet no evidence that Iran has developed nuclear weapons, it has repeatedly been found in violation of its obligations under the NPT with respect to the development of its uranium enrichment activities. Indeed, the mounting violations forced the International Atomic Energy Agency (IAEA) to refer Iran's behaviour to the UN Security Council,[11] which has adopted resolutions ordering Iran to stop its enrichment programmes.[12] Iran has defied the Security Council in the same manner in which it has defied the IAEA and rejected efforts by Western countries to negotiate a solution to the impasse. Many experts believe that continuation of Iran along this trajectory will prompt Egypt and Saudi Arabia to begin to develop their

10. Allison (2010).

11. IAEA (2008).

12. UN (2006; 2007 and 2008).

capabilities to field a nuclear deterrent against a nuclear-capable Iran.[13] There are also concerns that Israel might try to attack Iranian nuclear facilities to forestall Iran's nuclear ambitions, just as they did against Iraq in 1981 and Syria in 2007.[14] Such a move by Israel could ignite a very dangerous regional conflict pitting the Israel and the United States against Muslim countries, parastatal groups (e.g., Hezbollah, Hamas), and terrorist organisations (e.g. the Al-Qaeda).

The disarmament pillar of the NPT has also been under stress because non-nuclear weapons states within the NPT have grown increasingly frustrated at the lack of progress towards nuclear disarmament by the NPT's nuclear-weapons states (NWS), especially the United States and Russia. Debates over what the disarmament provisions in the NPT actually mean and whether the NWS have fulfilled their obligations[15] have had little impact on them, because they have been more concerned with other problems in the post-Cold War period. Incantations of allegiance to the goal of general disarmament have become NWS rituals, but, in the eyes of many non-nuclear weapons states, the NWS have not been serious about this aspect of the NPT.

The third pillar of the NPT—the assurance that states can access and use civilian nuclear energy technologies—has also come under pressure. The fact that Iraq could develop its nuclear weapons programme while being subject to IAEA safeguard inspections demonstrated that the NPT's safeguard regime was not sufficiently robust to deter and detect proliferation activities.[16] The development of the additional protocol of safeguards was intended to plug any loopholes,[17] but its adoption remains voluntary, which perhaps explains why, to date, a number of key NPT states, including Iran and India, have not accepted it as part of their safeguard practices.[18] This reluctance to make access to nuclear energy technologies more difficult

13. Beeston (2006).

14. The Economist (2010).

15. Joyner (2009) and Preez (2006).

16. Dolley and Leventhal (2001).

17. IAEA (1997).

18. IAEA (2009). Proponents of a nuclear-free world often call for the universal adoption of the Additional Protocol. See George and Action (2008).

is expected to increase because globally nuclear energy is being increasingly seen as one of the few readily available non-carbon based energy sources.[19] The building of more nuclear power facilities will, however, raise concerns among NPT states about nuclear terrorism,[20] and it might lead them to push for greater restrictions on technologies needed for nuclear energy development. The NPT's third pillar will, therefore, continue to be under stress.

CTBT and FMCT Problems

Strengthening the NPT involves not only addressing the weaknesses within the treaty but also advancing nuclear non-proliferation by achieving a comprehensive global ban on testing nuclear weapons through the CTBT and on producing fissile material for nuclear weapons through the FMCT. President Obama has recognised the CTBT's importance for attaining non-proliferation and disarmament goals because he has pledged to work for the US ratification of it.[21] US acceptance of the CTBT would, experts believe, be a 'game changer' for bringing this treaty into force because pressure would mount on other CTBT holdouts, such as China and India, to join as well. But, whether the US senate will ratify the CTBT remains uncertain and controversial,[22] especially in light of growing US concerns about Chinese military power, including its more sophisticated ballistic missile defence capabilities.[23]

Negotiations on a FMCT have, to date, not been successful, and the prospects for such a treaty have not markedly improved since the proposal for a ban on production of fissile materials for nuclear explosives was made. Problems have ranged from China insisting that any FMCT has to be linked with significant progress on nuclear disarmament and prevention of an arms race in outer space to the US rejection of comprehensive verification during the Bush administration.[24] In short, 'the prospects of ... states agreeing to a cut

19. Echávarri (2010).
20. On the links between nuclear energy and terrorism, see Cravens (2002).
21. Remarks by President Barack Obama, *supra note* 6.
22. On the US politics on CTBT ratification, see Dunlop and Preez (2009).
23. Global Security Newswire (2010).
24. Reif and Foley (2009).

off in the near term are slim, and the agreement does not appear to have the level of political support from the major powers that would be needed to break the current deadlock, make the necessary difficult compromises, and reach an agreement in the near term.'[25]

Missile Defences and Conventional Military Forces

The future of the nuclear non-proliferation regime is complicated by two other policy considerations—missile defence systems and the balance of conventional military forces. Controversies surrounding the deployment of missile defence systems in Europe by the United States during the Bush administration[26] and concerns expressed in the United States and Asia about Chinese advances in missile defence capabilities highlight the complex politics missile defences create.[27] As is well known, sophisticated missile defences create anxieties in the nuclear realm because such defences are perceived to weaken the stability of deterrence between potential nuclear-armed adversaries.[28] The likely response to such a situation is the strengthening of offensive capabilities, either by acquiring more nuclear weapons or improved delivery technologies. This pattern of defensive-offensive actions threatens the disarmament aspect of the nuclear non-proliferation regime by perpetuating the incentives for states to maintain nuclear arsenals and make them more robust. Addressing the potential instability that development of missile defences can create among nuclear-armed states, forms part of the policy agenda of the non-proliferation regime, even more so given its vision for a nuclear-free world.

Proponents of this vision also acknowledge that the balance of conventional military forces also forms part of the calculus.[29] Countries that face opponents with superior conventional forces have tended to favour the deployment of nuclear weapons to deter conventional aggression. The United States resorted to this strategy during the Cold War when faced with the purported conventional

25. Nuclear Threat Initiative (2006).

26. Fidler (2008).

27. Jacobs and Ansfield (2010).

28. Nuclear Threat Initiative (2009).

29. Harvey (2003).

military superiority of the Soviet Union in the European theatre. Many experts believe that North Korean and Iranian nuclear proliferation moves towards gaining a nuclear weapons capability flow from their desire to deter the overwhelming conventional military power of the United States. Similarly, Pakistan relies on its nuclear weapons to deter what it perceives to be the existential threat posed by India's superiority in conventional military forces. Thus, making progress in strengthening the nuclear non-proliferation regime also must involve addressing security concerns created by the imbalances in conventional military forces.[30]

Nuclear Terrorism

Experts disagree on whether nuclear terrorism poses a significant threat, but the United States, with the support of like-minded countries, has targeted nuclear terrorism for serious collective action in support of the nuclear non-proliferation regime.[31] Although a strong, well-functioning NPT would contribute towards preventing nuclear terrorism, much of the policy activity against this threat takes place outside the NPT, which remains, fundamentally, a state-centric instrument. Moving more aggressively to prevent non-state actors from obtaining either nuclear weapons or, more likely, fissile material has involved new treaties (Convention on the Suppression of Acts of Nuclear Terrorism, 2005), UN Security Council resolutions (Resolution 1540), and new informal, partnership mechanisms (Global Initiative to Combat Nuclear Terrorism[32]). The intensified focus on nuclear terrorism has, in the eyes of some experts, diverted attention from the lack of progress on disarmament and addressing weaknesses in the non-proliferation regime as revealed in the case of Iraq, North Korea and Iran. Nevertheless, as evidenced by President Obama's emphasis on the need to combat nuclear terrorism, this issue has become a fixture in the non-proliferation regime for the foreseeable future.

30. Centre on American and Global Security (2009).

31. For example, President Obama hosted in April 2010 a global summit on nuclear security as part of the effort against the threat of nuclear terrorism. See Riedy (2010).

32. US Department of State (n.d.). *The Global Initiative to Combat Nuclear Terrorism*, at *http://www.state.gov/t/isn/c18406.htm*

Nuclear Non-Proliferation and Multipolarity

It is becoming a conventional wisdom on international issues to highlight the difficulties presented by the emerging multipolarity for collective action among states. With respect to the challenge of multipolarity, '[t]he nuclear order,' Perkovich argues, 'is no different.'[33] However, the conjunction of multipolarity and the contemporary nuclear non-proliferation regime should be analysed carefully.

Geopolitical Multipolarity not the Cause of the Regime's Troubles

Most of the hand wringing about the non-proliferation regime results from developments that occurred before commentators began speaking of the dawn of a multipolar world. Actual or alleged proliferation efforts by Iraq, Libya, Syria, North Korea and Iran were exposed or occurred after the end of the Cold War in the period of US predominance, which implies that geopolitical multipolarity was not the cause of these efforts. Similarly, the failure to put the CTBT into effect, the lack of progress on the FMCT, the re-emergence of concern about missile defences, the glaring superiority of US conventional military power, and rising fears about nuclear terrorism all occurred during the American 'hegemonic' moment during the post-Cold War period. In short, the problems facing the nuclear non-proliferation regime do not stem from the multipolarity which say experts is now affecting the dynamics of international politics.

The Impact of 'Embedded Multipolarity'

This conclusion does not mean that US political, economic and military dominance in the post-Cold War period is to be blamed for all the problems faced by the nuclear non-proliferation regime today. This regime has multipolarity embedded in its structure and dynamics by virtue of: (1) the participation of multiple nuclear-armed powers; and (2) the underlying, interdependent bargaining between these powers and the non-nuclear weapons states.[34] This embedded multi-

33. Perkovich (2008).

34. Embedded multipolarity is not unique to the NPT. It appears in other treaties, such as the World Trade Organization (WTO). However, in the trade and other areas, states have found ways to by-pass the effects of multipolarity by negotiating in different forums to achieve their objectives. Thus, in trade, states have negotiated regional and bilateral agreements as multilateral negotiations in the WTO have stalled. However, in the context of nuclear non-proliferation, such 'forum shifting' behaviour has proved difficult because of the NPT's perceived centrality and the pervasive importance of the interests of the nuclear-armed states.

polarity has added to the difficulty faced in addressing problems relating to non-proliferation, disarmament, and access to peaceful nuclear technologies. Although parties to the NPT agreed, albeit with some difficulty, to extend the treaty indefinitely at the 1995 Review Conference, all the other developments in the NPT regime have only come in the form of non-binding, voluntary commitments (e.g., the 13 practical steps to implement Article VI of the NPT adopted at the 2000 Review Conference[35]) or instruments (e.g. the IAEA Additional Protocol), adherence to which has been poor or controversial. Other proposals to strengthen the NPT, such as making withdrawal from the NPT more difficult,[36] have also had little impact because the negotiating environment is not conducive to major changes in the treaty.

The embedded multipolarity of the NPT also appears in the politics of the CTBT. Here, the nuclear-armed powers, including those not party to the NPT, control the destiny of the CTBT because, as of August 2009, six of the nine Annexe 2 countries that must ratify the CTBT before it can be implemented are nuclear-armed states (China, India, Israel, North Korea, Pakistan and the United States).[37] Just a glance at this list is enough indication of the difficulties in getting them all to agree to a comprehensive ban on all nuclear testing. Similarly, the FMCT negotiations have long been stalled because of the inability of the key participating states, especially the nuclear powers, to agree. As the *Nuclear Threat Initiative* stated, 'After ... years of inactivity, it is time to question whether the consensus-based Conference on Disarmament is capable of moving forward and negotiating a fissile cut off.'[38]

---

35. *NPT Review Conference 2000: 13 Practical Steps*. At *http://www.vmpeace.org/pages/npt_13_steps.htm*

36. See, e.g., Note Verbale dated 20 May 2005 from the Permanent Mission of Germany addressed to the Secretary-General of the Conference, 2005 Review Conference of the Parties to the Treaty on the Non-Proliferation of Nuclear Weapons, NPT/CONF.2005/WP.56, May 23, 2005. At *http://www.un.org/events/npt2005/npt-conf2005-wp56e.pdf*

37. Preparatory Commission for the Comprehensive Nuclear-Test-Ban Treaty Organisation, Status of Signature and Ratification, at *http://www.ctbto.org/the-treaty/status-of-signature-and-ratification/?states=4&region=63&submit.x=20&submit.y=4&submit=submit&no_cache=1*

38. Nuclear Threat Initiative, Fissile Material Cutoff Treaty, at *http://nti.org/e_research/cnwm/ending/fmct.asp*

Double Jeopardy: Embedded and Geopolitical Multipolarity

Into the difficult environment of embedded multipolarity comes the larger geopolitical multipolarity that is increasingly affecting every major international issue, whether the context is the WTO's Doha Development Round talks, for addressing the global financial and economic crisis (e.g. the move from the G8 to the G20 as the main forum for addressing global economic issues), or climate change negotiations. Many commentators argue that the emerging geopolitical multipolarity makes collective action among states more difficult, as illustrated by the US National Intelligence Council's prediction that the next 20-25 years in world affairs will see 'multi-polarity without multilateralism.'[39] Strengthening the nuclear non-proliferation regime, therefore, involves a double burden—overcoming the problems associated with embedded multipolarity in the non-proliferation area while navigating the shoals of geopolitical multipolarity, where nuclear non-proliferation is only one of many areas of strategic contestation among the great powers.

Shoring up and deepening the non-proliferation regime during this convergence of embedded and geopolitical multipolarity entails two central tasks. First, to overcome the long-standing problems that have plagued the NPT and supporting instruments, such as the CTBT. Second, to address these problems in a way that answers to the needs of the great powers in the context of geopolitical multipolarity. For example, how the United States and India view the specific problems within the non-proliferation regime will be affected by how these states view Chinese power, broadly defined. Thus, China may make no changes in its nuclear arsenal or doctrine but, because of its rising material power and influence, it will still make the United States and India less interested in making major changes in their nuclear deterrent capabilities (e.g., reluctance to ratify the CTBT and conclude a FMCT).

How the double burden of embedded and geopolitical multi-polarity affects efforts to strengthen the nuclear non-proliferation regime is difficult to predict. This burden does not preclude major breakthroughs, such as the United States ratifying the CTBT or Iran

39. USNIC (2008).

agreeing to back away from acquiring a nuclear weapons capability. The remainder of this chapter focusses on the roles and positions that India and China will have and take in the contemporary context of embedded and geopolitical multipolarity with respect to nuclear non-proliferation. This approach is worthwhile because both China and India have been important nuclear powers for decades and are the two countries most responsible for the emergence of geopolitical multi-polarity in world affairs.

Nuclear Non-Proliferation and Asian Security

President Obama has made nuclear non-proliferation issues central to his administration's conception of US national security for the foreseeable future, especially because of concerns about potential Iranian proliferation, the threat of nuclear terrorism, and Obama's desire to see a nuclear-free world. Whether China, India and other Asian countries accord the same level of security importance to nuclear non-proliferation is doubtful. In short, neither India nor China consider nuclear proliferation to be a critical threat to their power and influence or believe that nuclear disarmament is in their strategic interests. Differences between the United States and the Asian giants reflect the expected divergence of interests one would anticipate in the context of geopolitical multipolarity. Exploring this divergence will however, help delineate how geopolitical multipolarity might affect plans for strengthening the nuclear non-proliferation regime over the next two decades.

The Threat of Nuclear Proliferation and Asian Security Interests

Although, at present, neither China nor India favour any further proliferation of nuclear weapons in the international arena, historically they have both evinced a higher security and political tolerance for such proliferation than the United States. In terms of North Korea, India and China did not contemplate waging war on that country in the mid-1990s to prevent North Korean proliferation as the United States did under the Clinton administration. Nor, going farther back, did China seek to pre-empt militarily, India's development of nuclear weapons or punish India for doing so (as the United States and Western countries did by imposing sanctions), nor did India attempt the forceful prevention of Pakistan's acquisition of nuclear weapons or refuse to try to improve relations with Islamabad because of Pakistani nuclearisation. Although increasingly more willing to express their concerns, India and China have not been leaders in the effort to convince Iran not to develop a nuclear weapons capability.[40]

Many reasons go into explaining China's and India's past and present security approaches to nuclear proliferation. We should remember that China did not accede to the NPT until 1992, and India still has not joined this treaty. Thus, for most of the period following the NPT's adoption, India and China expressed vocal opposition to a treaty they believed was discriminatory in principle and harmful to their national security interests in deterring potential threats. When not a NPT party state, China even helped Pakistan develop its nuclear weapons programme and thus directly aided proliferation.[41] This historical background suggests that China's and India's relationship with the NPT today is coloured by a different historical experience than that of the United States or other keen NPT supporters.

Another reason why Indian and Chinese security interests do not necessarily give pride of place to nuclear non-proliferation as an objective is the perception that further nuclear proliferation in the wake of North Korean and Iranian efforts does not constitute a serious threat to their security and political interests. Although North Korean proliferation has raised concerns that Japan and South Korea might become more interested in developing nuclear weapons, most experts agree that such proliferation will not occur unless US security commitments to these countries, including continued extension of the US nuclear umbrella, precipitously weaken. Any Japanese or South Korean moves towards developing nuclear weapons will also create additional difficulties in the domestic politics of both countries.

The six-party talks with North Korea involve China, Japan and South Korea, and these talks form the locus of diplomatic activity on this problem, which makes the efforts to strengthen the NPT quite irrelevant for solving the impasse with North Korea. Walking North

---

40. On China's equivocation The Economist (2009), see Subrahmanya and Kumar (2009a). On India, see Subrahmanya and Kumar (2009b).

41. Smith and Warrick (2009).

Korea back into the NPT seems, at best, a very long-term project, and China's predominant role in the six-party talks is primarily to contain North Korea's proliferation aftershocks rather than roll back what Pyongyang has done. Thus, from China's perspective, it is a limited problem than one that threatens a domino-effect proliferation in Asia or beyond.

Beyond the improbable likelihood of Japan[42] and South Korea[43] developing nuclear weapons in response to North Korea's proliferation, it is unlikely that Asia will see other countries in the region trying to enter the nuclear club. Thus, China and India, as the emerging Asian giants, are unlikely to have to address proliferation threats in their respective Asian neighbourhoods, which makes nuclear proliferation less of an immediate regional and national security interest for these countries.

In terms of fears about Iranian nuclear proliferation, neither India nor China want to see a nuclear-armed Iran, but both countries have not shown much willingness to play leadership roles, with the United States and its European allies, in getting Tehran to toe the non-proliferation line. This lack of leadership is more acute with respect to China because it is, like Iran, a member of the NPT and is committed to the treaty's objective and purpose, which is potentially threatened by Iran's behaviour. However, both India and China view their relations with Iran through more than the non-proliferation lens because, for example, of their mutual need for Iranian oil as an energy resource.[44] Thus, larger geopolitical concerns influence India's and China's thinking about Iran, concerns that geopolitical multipolarity makes even more relevant to how these emerging powers calculate their strategic interests.

Nor do China or India have any strategic interest in aligning themselves openly and strongly with the hostility the United States and Israel express towards Iran over its purported moves to gain nuclear weapons capabilities. Neither seem willing to contemplate

42. For one important, if idiosyncratic view, see Katzenstein (1998).

43. Choi and Park (2008).

44. See e.g., Dorraj and Currier (2008) and Kronstadt and Katzman (2006).

using force against Iran or supporting Israeli or American pre-emptive strikes against Iranian nuclear facilities. Fears that Iranian proliferation will cause Saudi Arabia and Egypt to go nuclear do not appear to worry China and India enough for them to escalate their efforts to dissuade Iran from the path it appears to be taking. These observations support the idea that neither India nor China consider nuclear proliferation regionally and beyond to be a critical threat to their strategic and security interests now and in the foreseeable future.

China, India and Nuclear Disarmament

Another key aspect of the non-proliferation regime is the commitment in the NPT for NWS to engage in meaningful nuclear disarmament. As stated earlier, non-nuclear weapons states within the NPT have long been dissatisfied with the disarmament efforts made by the NWS, especially the United States and the Soviet Union/ Russia. President Obama's push for a nuclear-free world requires him, for many reasons, to have an agreement with Russia on serious cuts in their respective nuclear arsenals.[45] The disarmament objectives however appear different from the Chinese and Indian perspectives. Both India and China have small nuclear arsenals intended only for deterrence, and, thus, they have not been in the eye of the storm over nuclear disarmament within and beyond the NPT.[46] Indeed, China and India have leveraged the perceived lack of disarmament by the United States, Soviet Union/Russia, and other nuclear powers in negotiations on the CTBT and FMCT, effectively linking progress on these new instruments to more serious disarmament action by the countries with large stockpiles of nuclear weapons.

Thus, neither India nor China have the geopolitical and non-proliferation challenges with respect to disarmament that the United States and Russia confront. At present, and for the foreseeable future barring any radical arms control breakthroughs by the United States and Russia, China and India do not face first-order disarmament pressures that would channel their actions within geopolitical multi-polarity. The likelihood of any such radical disarmament development

45. Levy and Baker (2009).

46. On the Indian and Chinese nuclear arsenal, see Norris and Kristensen (2008a and 2008b).

in US-Russia relations is slim given the continuing problems between the United States and Russia on a host of issues.[47] Modest arms control progress between Moscow and Washington D.C. will likely occur,[48] but probably not at the level that will trigger significant demands for China and India to reduce their small deterrent capabilities and, thus, transform how these two countries think strategically about their nuclear arsenals.

Even if those demands are made on India and China, their interests within the emerging geopolitical multipolarity will continue to support the preservation of their existing nuclear capabilities. China will want to maintain a credible deterrent *vis-à-vis* the United States, and India will protect its nuclear capability as a hedge against nuclear-armed China. With India remaining nuclear, Pakistan will not countenance talk of disarmament. North Korea has learned the value of having nuclear weapons, and is unlikely to give them up easily through the diplomacy of the six-party talks. Nor would North Korea disarmament have the positive spillover effect of causing any other nuclear power to move towards disarmament. Israel will not disarm, especially if Iran continues to its quest for nuclear weapons. In essence, we are likely to see the continuation of the status quo and the geopolitical strategic reasoning behind it, which stands in the way of widespread disarmament actions as contemplated by the NPT and as would be necessary for a nuclear-free world.

India, China and Nuclear Terrorism

One area where convergence of great power interests is apparent in the nuclear realm is with respect to nuclear terrorism. None of the existing great powers in the emerging multipolar system has any interest in fostering nuclear terrorism. At the same time, at least from the perspective of China and India, these countries have taken steps to ensure the security of their nuclear facilities and are not expected to be the source of potential 'loose nukes' or easily purloined fissile material. There are greater concerns regarding the safety of Pakistan's nuclear weapons and fissile material,[49] but, given Pakistan's suspicions

47. Applebaum (2009).

48. Kralev (2009).

49. Corera (2006).

of Indian power, India has little policy space in which to contribute seriously to nuclear security in Pakistan. Given China's continued assistance to Pakistan for its civilian nuclear programmes, and the possibility of a Sino-Pakistan accord modelled on the US-India civilian nuclear deal, China can play a more effective role in helping Pakistan ensure that terrorist do not get access to its nuclear materials. Overall, Chinese and Indian cooperation to strengthen the security of nuclear materials is 'low hanging' fruit technically and politically, and thus Indian and Chinese participation in such efforts do not constitute a threat, or any tremendous benefit to, their respective strategic interests.

Chinese and Indian Power and Embedded Multipolarity in the Nuclear Non-Proliferation Regime

As noted earlier, the nuclear non-proliferation regime operates in the context of an embedded multipolarity, a context necessitated by the need to get both nuclear and non-nuclear states to cooperate on a diverse range of issues. The problems this regime currently faces, and the fears experts have expressed about its future efficacy, stem in large part from the diplomatic difficulties of getting the nuclear-armed states to agree with each other and with non-nuclear weapons states. This embedded multipolarity functioned during the Cold War and the post-Cold War period, and will continue to be a feature of nuclear diplomacy in the emerging geopolitical multipolarity created by the rise of new great powers, particularly China and India. Increased Indian and Chinese power will exacerbate the problems experienced with embedded multipolarity, making progress on solving specific problems with the non-proliferation regime harder rather than easier. However, we do not believe that this environment will cause the regime to collapse; rather, Chinese and Indian power will ensure that the regime's evolution follows a conservative rather than a radical trajectory.

China

As a party to the NPT, China has no interest in being a revisionist nuclear power and wrecking the NPT, as perhaps some of its pre-accession proliferating behaviour indicated it was ready to do. China is working hard to ensure that its emergence as a great power is accompanied by a sense that China is a 'responsible power.'[50] Thus, China will continue to support calls for strengthening the NPT, accelerating nuclear disarmament, and working for a nuclear-free world, as it did in supporting UN Security Council Resolution 1887 in September 2009.

Beneath the supportive rhetoric, China will pursue its national and strategic interests strongly, which means that its position will continue to cause difficulties in the various parts of the non-proliferation regime. China will have a cautious approach to the CTBT with the condition that the United States must ratify the CTBT before China accepts it. Chinese insistence that the United States and Russia engage in more serious arms control buys it time to upgrade, modernise and potentially expand its nuclear arsenal,[51] especially because of China's concerns about the US development of stronger missile defence capabilities.[52] China has also sent strong signals that it, too, is ready to develop better missile defence systems,[53] which, in all likelihood, will make the United States, Russia and India nervous. In other words, Chinese policy within the non-proliferation regime will remain firmly committed to preserving China's nuclear deterrent capabilities. Thus, China will manoeuvre to ensure that neither the CTBT nor the FMCT materially interferes with its maintaining a robust nuclear deterrent. This approach would simply replicate Chinese behaviour since its accession to the NPT, but, today, what China wants and does matters more because of the growth in its power and influence regionally and globally. Here, we see the embedded multipolarity of the non-proliferation regime and geopolitical multipolarity converging to strengthen China's already strong hand in nuclear diplomacy.

India

Although India is not a party to the NPT, it has no interest in seeing the NPT collapse and fail. Indeed, during his state visit to the United States in November 2009, Prime Minister Manmohan Singh

---

50. Kang (2009).
51. Cirincione (2010).
52. Nuclear Threat Initiative (n.d.).
53. Jacobs and Ansfield (2010).

made it clear that India would like to join the NPT as a NWS.[54] Singh's statement was the first public expression by India's highest ranking official that India would like to join the NPT as a NWS. In addition to offering Indian support for the NPT, this statement has the potential to create new dimensions and controversies to nuclear diplomacy in the near future.

By expressing its desire to join the NPT as a NWS, India forces the non-proliferation community to confront India's long-standing criticisms of the treaty, which overlap with existing worries about the NPT's weaknesses as described earlier.[55] By all accounts, India has been a responsible nuclear power. Its continued exclusion from the NPT would be only because of an arbitrary date in the treaty that lays down which countries can be NWS rather than being decided on the basis of conduct.[56] India has not fostered proliferation, unlike China and Pakistan. It has a small nuclear arsenal for deterrence, unlike some recognised NWS that have large stockpiles despite NPT obligations to disarm. Through the Indo-US nuclear accord, India has accepted the IAEA oversight of its civilian nuclear facilities, and India's record is better in this regard than that of Libya, Iran, Iraq, North Korea and Syria, which joined the treaty as non-nuclear weapon states but violated, or are suspected of violating, the NPT.

In short, the non-proliferation regime is not in trouble because of India but because the NPT is flawed and has been abused by the very countries that agreed to abide by its rules. India is now willing to join the NPT and bring its legitimacy as a democratic nuclear power and its growing geopolitical influence to bear on shoring up the NPT's objectives. All that is required is an amendment of the treaty's cut-off date for recognition as a NWS. Existing NPT members can accept India's cooperation to help strengthen the NPT, or they can reject India's interest, which does not improve the NPT's prospects. Which way will existing NPT members go?

---

54. Fidler and Ganguly (2009).
55. Ghose (2009).
56. Under Article IX.3 of the NPT, 'a nuclear-weapon State is one which has manufactured and exploded a nuclear weapon or other nuclear explosive device prior to 1 January 1967.'

If NPT members follow the UN Security Council, they will reject India's overtures. As part of President Obama's effort to advance the cause of a nuclear-free world, the Security Council unanimously adopted Resolution 1887 in September 2009, which '[c]alls upon all States that are not Parties to the NPT to accede... as non-nuclear-weapon States...'[57] NPT members could hide behind this resolution and avoid addressing India's new position. However, such a response simply avoids a policy question that deserves attention on its merits.

The key states will be the NPT's existing NWS, especially China, Russia and the US because all NWS must approve the amendment needed to permit India to join as a NWS. Neither China nor Russia faces additional strategic risks by allowing India to join the NPT as a NWS because India is already a nuclear-armed power, and supporting Indian accession to the NPT could be a way to improve relations with India as its regional and global influence grows with little to no negative fallout.

The United States is caught between recognising India as a democratic, responsible nuclear power (e.g., the US-India nuclear accord) and the Obama administration's policy that non-parties to the NPT should join only as non-nuclear weapons states (Resolution 1887). Given India's NPT shift, the United States cannot reconcile these positions, meaning it must make a choice that has no room for 'triangulation.' The US choice will likely determine how European nations and Japan respond, as happened in the case of the US-India nuclear accord.[58]

Opposing India's desire to join the NPT as a NWS on the basis of Resolution 1887 or narrow national interests will do nothing to strengthen the NPT—the troubled centrepiece of the global non-proliferation effort. If a more robust NPT is vital for shoring up the non-proliferation regime and making progress towards a nuclear-free world, then bringing India into the treaty, especially when it is emerging as a great power, makes more sense than believing that India will disarm unilaterally simply to join the NPT. Indian participation in

---

57. *supra* note 5, p.1.

58. Ganguly and Mistry (2006).

the NPT will not, by itself, eliminate the problems the NPT now confronts, especially those caused by North Korea, Iran, and the potential of nuclear terrorism. But, with India supporting the NPT, the world would have all nuclear-armed great powers committed to the same rules—an unprecedented circumstance in the history of nuclear diplomacy.

India's NPT move shrewdly promotes Indian interests, influence, and ideas in nuclear diplomacy, but this move does not mean that India's national interests will support any effort to strengthen the nuclear non-proliferation regime. India inside the NPT will have strategic concerns and needs identical to India outside the NPT, and, thus, Indian approaches to the CTBT and the FMCT are unlikely to change in the absence of a transformative development elsewhere in the regime (e.g. the United States and China ratifying the CTBT). Barring some scientific or technological breakthrough that increases India's nuclear weapons establishment's confidence in the reliability of India's nuclear arsenal and adequacy of its stockpile of fissile material, India will continue to be unwilling to join the CTBT and FMCT. India's nuclear weapons programme has a long-standing and deeply rooted support in the political elite, nuclear scientific community, and the politically active public, which will make it difficult for an Indian government to do anything that potentially threatens the credibility of its deterrent capability.[59] This commitment to India's deterrent is unlikely to decrease as it perceives China's political, economic and military (conventional and nuclear) power and influence increasing.

As with China, now and in the foreseeable future, what India wants and does carries extra weight in most diplomatic contexts, including in nuclear diplomacy. Making progress on strengthening the nuclear non-proliferation regime has to contend with not only India's tradition of stubbornness on nuclear matters but also its emerging importance as a nuclear-armed great power. Like China, India will not wish to be perceived as a revisionist challenger to the general international order or the nuclear non-proliferation regime. It too will take a conservative approach to changes in this regime, and it will act strongly to ensure that the changes reflect its strategic interests.

---

59. The best discussion remains Tellis (2001).

Indian and Chinese nuclear conservatism will act as a heavy counterweight to the visionary aspirations of a world free of nuclear weapons. In the context of the embedded multipolarity within the non-proliferation regime, India and China, although rivals, will continue to play very significant roles in the regime's functioning and evolution.

Conclusion

Predictions about the future of nuclear diplomacy are fraught with dangers. Our sense of the trajectory of the nuclear non-proliferation regime over the course of the next two decades sides with neither the doomsayers who fear a nightmarish nuclear disorder nor the visionaries who believe in the possibility of a world without nuclear weapons. We argue that Indian and Chinese strategies will help imbue nuclear diplomacy with a sense of conservatism that keeps the regime from collapsing and from being revolutionised. Our conclusion flows from the combined impact of the limitations within the non-proliferation regime created by its embedded multipolarity and the constraints created by the emergence of geopolitical multipolarity.

To be clear, we are not claiming that the conservatism likely to characterise nuclear diplomacy is the best outcome in all scenarios. Serious dangers lurk, especially with the possible cascading effects in the Middle East of Iranian nuclear proliferation. However, from what can be gleaned from Chinese and Indian behaviour on the Iranian question, neither country is willing to act vigorously to stop Iran's move towards a nuclear weapons capability or to oppose efforts to talk Iran back from the weaponisation brink.

Embedded multipolarity has always made China and India important in the development of the nuclear non-proliferation regime. India's and China's growing significance as great powers in the context of geopolitical multipolarity will increase their importance in this regime over the next few decades. Given this reality, a conservative approach to the non-proliferation regime will not protect China and India from bearing responsibility for the regime's demise if foreseeable or unexpected changes crack the pillars of non-proliferation, disarmament, and safeguarded access to peaceful nuclear energy. Given that their rivalry and wariness of each other drives their conservatism in nuclear diplomacy and strategy, India and China have lot of work to do in order to be in a position to ensure that their bilateral problems do not prevent what limited progress on nuclear non-proliferation, arms control, and nuclear security can be made in the years ahead.

References

Allison, Graham (2010). "Nuclear Disorder", *Foreign Affairs:* 74-85, January/February.

Applebaum, Anne (2009). "For Russia, More than a 'Reset'", *Washington Post*, March 24. At *http://www.washingtonpost.com/wp-dyn/content/article/2009/03/23/AR2009032302138. html*

Beeston, Richard (2006). "Six Arab States Join Rush to Go Nuclear", *The Times*, November 4. At *http://www.timesonline.co.uk/tol/news/world/middle_east/article624855.ece*

Centre on American and Global Security (2009). *The Future of Nuclear Weapons*. November, at *http://www.indiana.edu/~cags/docs/FutureNuclearWeaponsFINAL.pdf*, p. 8.

Choi, Kang and Joon-Sung Park (2008). "South Korea", in Muthiah Alagappa (ed.), *The Long Shadow: Nuclear Weapons and Security in 21st Century Asia.* Palo Alto: Stanford University Press.

Cirincione, Joseph (2010). "China's Nuclear Modernisation", *Carnegie Proliferation Brief* 2(8). At *http://www.carnegieendowment.org/publications/index.cfm?fa=view&id=93*

Corera, Gordon (2006). *Shopping for Bombs: Nuclear Proliferation, Global Insecurity and the Rise and Fall of the A.Q. Khan Network*. New York: Oxford University Press.

Cravens, Gwyneth (2002). *Terrorism and Nuclear Energy: Understanding the Risks*. Brookings Institution. Spring. At *http://www.brookings.edu/articles/2002/spring_weapons_cravens.aspx*

Dolley, Steven and Paul Leventhal (2001). *Overview of IAEA Nuclear Inspections in Iraq*. Nuclear Control Institute. June 14. At *http://www.nci.org/new/iraq-ib.htm*

Dorraj, Manochehr and Carrie L. Currier (2008). "Lubricated with Oil: Iran-China Relations in a Changing World", *Middle East Policy* 15(2): 66-80.

Dunlop, Sean and Jean du Preez (2009). *The United States and the CTBT: Renewed Hope or Politics as Usual?*. Nuclear Threat Initiative. February. At *http://www.nti.org/e_research/e3_ctbt_united_states.html*

Echávarri, Luis (2010). "Climate Change: The Case for Nuclear Energy", *OECD Observer*. At *http://www.oecdobserver.org/news/fullstory.php/aid/3125/Climate_change:_The_case_for_ nuclear_energy_.html*

Fidler, David P. (2008). "Introductory Note to the Agreement between the Republic of Poland and the United States of America Concerning the Deployment of Ground-Based Ballistic Missile Defence Interceptors in the Territory of the Republic of Poland", *International Legal Materials* 47: 1042-43.

Fidler, David P. and Sumit Ganguly (2009). "Singh's Shrewd Move", *Newsweek*. December 14. At *http://www.newsweek.com/id/225533*.

Ganguly, Sumit and Dinshaw Mistry (2006). "The Case for the US-India Nuclear Agreement", *World Policy Journal* 23(2): 11-19.

Ghose, Arundhati (2009). "Who's Afraid of the NPT?", *The Indian Express*. September 30. At *http://www.indianexpress.com/news/whos-afraid-of-the-npt/522972/*

Global Security Newswire (2010). "Pentagon Received No Warning of Chinese Missile Defense Test". January 12. At *http://www.globalsecuritynewswire.org/gsn/nw_20100112_1311.php*

Harvey, Frank P. (2003). "The Future of Strategic Stability and Nuclear Deterrence", *International Journal* 58(2) 321-46.

IAEA (2009). *Strengthened Safeguards System: Status of Additional Protocols* (as of December 15). At *http://www.iaea.org/OurWork/SV/Safeguards/sg_protocol.html*

———. (1997). *Model Protocol Additional to the Agreement(s) between States and the International Atomic Energy Agency for the Application of Safeguards*. INFCIRC/540 (Corrected). At *http://www.iaea.org/Publications/Documents/Infcircs/1997/infcirc540c.pdf*

IAEA Board of Governors (2008). *Implementation of the NPT Safeguards Agreement and Relevant Provisions of Security Council Resolutions 1737 (2006) and 1747 (2007) in the Islamic Republic of Iran*. GOV/2008/4. February 22. At *http://www.globalpolicy.org/images/pdfs/0225iaeareport.pdf*

Jacobs, Andrew and Jonathan Ansfield (2010). "With Defense Test, China Shows Displeasure of U.S", *New York Times*. January 10. At *http://www.nytimes.com/2010/01/13/world/asia/13china.html*

Joyner, Daniel H. (2009). *International Law and the Proliferation of Weapons of Mass Destruction*: Oxford: Oxford University Press. pp.3-76.

Kang, David C. (2009). *China Rising: Peace, Power and Order in East Asia*. New York: Columbia University Press.

Katzenstein, Peter J. (1998). *Cultural Norms and National Security: Police and Military in Postwar Japan*. Ithaca: Cornell University Press.

Kralev, Nicolas (2009). "U.S.-Russia Arms Control Treaty Expires", *Washington Times*. December 5. At *http://www.washingtontimes.com/news/2009/dec/05/arms-control-treaty-expires/*

Kronstadt, K. Alan and Kenneth Katzman (2006). "India-Iran Relations and U.S. Interests", CRS Report to Congress. August 2. At *http://italy.usembassy.gov/pdf/other/RS22486.pdf*

Levy, Clifford J. and Peter Baker (2009). "U.S.-Russia Nuclear Agreement is First Step in Broad Effort", *New York Times*. July 6. At *http://www.nytimes.com/2009/07/07/world/europe/07prexy. html*

McGrath, Kaegan (2009). *In Focus: The Comprehensive Nuclear-Test-Ban Treaty (CTBT)*, Nuclear Threat Initiative. October 9. At *http://www.nti.org/e_research/e3_special_ctbt.html*

Norris, Robert S. and Hans M. Kristensen (2008a). "Indian Nuclear Forces, 2008", *Bulletin of the Atomic Scientists* 64(5): 38-40.

———. (2008b). "Chinese Nuclear Forces", *Bulletin of the Atomic Scientists* 64(3): 42-44.

Nuclear Threat Initiative (2009). *Ballistic Missile Defense (BMD)*. October. at *http://www.nti.org/f_WMD411/f2d.html*

———. (2006). *Fissile Material Cutoff Treaty*. August. At *http://www.nti.org/e_research/cnwm/ending/fmct.asp*

———. (n.d.). *China's Opposition to US Missile Defense Programs*, at *http://www.nti.org/db/china/mdpos.htm*

Preez, Jean du (2006). "Half Full or Half Empty? Realising the Promise of the Nuclear Nonproliferation Treaty", *Arms Control Today*. December. At *http://www.armscontrol.org/act/2006_12/DuPreez*

Perkovich, George and James Action (2008). "Abolishing Nuclear Weapons", *Adelphi Paper No.* 396. London: International Institute for Strategic Studies.

Perkovich, George (2008). "Principles for Reforming the Nuclear Order", *Institut Francais des Relations Internationales Proliferation Paper*: 17, Fall.

Reif, Kingston and Madeleine Foley (2009). *Factsheet on the Fissile Material Cutoff Treaty (FMCT)*. Centre for Arms Control and Non-Proliferation. July 15. At *http://www.armscontrolcenter.org/policy/nuclearweapons/articles/071509_factsheet_fmct/*

Riedy, Andrew (2010). *Global Nuclear Security Summit, Centre for Arms Control and Nonproliferation*. December 9, 2009. At *http://www.armscontrolcenter.org/policy/nonproliferation/articles/120909_global_nuclear_security_ summit/*

Smith, R. Jeffrey and Joby Warrick (2009). "A Nuclear Power's Act of Proliferation", *Washington Post*, November 13. At *http://www.washingtonpost.com/wp-dyn/content/article/2009/11/12/AR2009111211060.html*

Subrahmanya, K. and Shantha Kumar (2009a). "An Iranian Nuclear Bomb, or the Bombing of Iran?", *The Economist*, December 3.

———. (2009b). "India Votes Against Iran's Nuclear Plan", *The Deccan Herald*, November 28. At *http://www.deccanherald.com/content/38273/india-votes-against-irans-nuclear.html.*

Tellis, Ashley J. (2001). *India's Emerging Nuclear Posture: Between Recessed Deterrent and Ready Arsenal.* Santa Monica: The Rand Corporation.

The Economist (2010). "Israel and Iran: The Gathering Storm", *The Economist,* January 9, at 28-29.

———. (2009). "An Iranian Nuclear Bomb, or the Bombing of Iran?". December 3.

UN (2009). *UN Security Council Resolution 1887*, S/RES/1887 (2009), September 24. At *http://daccess-dds-ny.un.org/doc/UNDOC/GEN/N09/523/74/PDF/N0952374.pdf?OpenElement*.

———. (2008). *UN Security Council Resolutions 1803* (March 3).

———. (2007). *UN Security Council Resolutions 1747* (March 24).

———. (2006). *UN Security Council Resolutions 1737* (December 23).

———. (2005). "International Convention on the Suppression of Acts of Nuclear Terrorism", *UN General Assembly Resolution 59/290, A/RES/59/290,* April 15. At *http://www.un.org/ga/search/view_doc.asp?symbol=A/Res/59/290*

———. (2004). *UN Security Council Resolution 1540, S/RES/1540 (2004)*, April 28. At *http://daccess-dds-ny.un.org/doc/UNDOC/GEN/N04/328/43/PDF/N0432843.pdf?OpenElement*

———. (1996). *Comprehensive Nuclear-Test-Ban Treaty.* Opened for signature September 24, 1996 [not in force]. At *http://disarmament.un.org/treatystatus.nsf/44e6eeabc9436b78852568770078d9c0/0655d51a30692632852568770079dda2?OpenDocument*

———. (1968). *Treaty on the Non-Proliferation of Nuclear Weapons.* Opened for signature. July 1, 729 U.N.T.S. 161.

US Department of State (n.d.). *The Global Initiative to Combat Nuclear Terrorism.* At *http://www.state.gov/t/isn/c18406.htm*

US National Intelligence Council (2008). *Global Trends 2025: A Transformed World.* November. p.81.

White House (2009). *Remarks by President Barack Obama.* Prague, Czech Republic, April 5. At *http://www.whitehouse.gov/the_press_office/Remarks-By-President-Barack-Obama-In-Prague-As-Delivered/*

17

Biological and Chemical Terrorism

Assessing the Threat in Asia

ANGELA WOODWARD

Introduction

The global threat of biological and chemical terrorism is undoubtedly real,[1] although the problem of how to accurately assess this threat and extrapolate it over time has vexed analysts and policymakers for decades. Many are agreed on the independent elements that ought to be considered—for example, motivations for selecting biological or chemical means of attack, access to pathogens and chemical agents, and the capability to effectively weaponise them—but without a structured framework for considering their respective importance, certain factors are overemphasised, and resulting assessments are unbalanced and speculative. This hampers collective efforts to develop appropriate policy solutions to the current and future problem of chemical and biological terrorism. As there have, thankfully, been relatively few terrorist incidents involving biological or chemical weapons to date, attempts to develop predictive models from precedent has proven difficult.

In this chapter considers the prospects of biological and chemical terrorism, particularly in the Asian region, looking ahead to 2030. Yet biological and chemical terrorism is not strictly a problem impacting only a handful of states, or a particular region. Any terrorist event involving biological weapons (BW) or chemical weapons (CW) would evidence a failure in one or more state's counter-proliferation and

1. Global Security Newswire (2009).

counter-terrorism policies and in the global 'web of prevention'[2] and could have serious repercussions for many other countries. As a lawyer who works with states around the world to strengthen their domestic regulatory framework in order to prohibit and prevent these weapons, I know the challenges that many states encounter in trying to shore up this 'web'.

Few could have foreseen how the rapid advances in biology and chemistry even over the last 10, or even 5, years could impact on the terrorist threat, with 'dual-use' materials, equipment and technologies now more readily accessible. Attempts to extrapolate what the situation might be like in 30 years time are extremely difficult.

The chapter seeks to explain the nature of biological and chemical ('bio-chem') terrorism; propose a methodology for bio-chem terrorism threat assessment; highlight certain trends impacting on this threat in the Asian region; and endeavour to make some policy recommendations in order to reduce these threats in the years ahead.

Biological and Chemical Terrorism

So what is biological and chemical terrorism? Definitions of these terms differ, in terms of precision and scope. Generally speaking, biological terrorism involves the use of pathogens and toxins by non-state actors to inflict harm against humans, animals and plants (agro-terrorism). Such harm can include attempts to cause mass death or illness among human or animal populations, either directly or through contaminated food supply, and efforts to destroy crops and sabotage agricultural production. Importantly, it also includes the psychological and economic harm to populations through the panic associated with deliberate (overt) or even covert biological attacks.[3] For example, the 2001 anthrax letters attack in the United States led to a disproportionate economic and psychological harm compared with the actual number of deaths.[4] It must be remembered that biological terrorism is at the far end of the spectrum of biological risks (natural

2. The 'web of prevention' in the BW policy field refers to overlapping policies and measures to reduce the threat of BW, including laws, regulations, codes of conduct for scientists, physical security measures for laboratories and pathogen collections, law enforcement training etc. See Rappert and McLeish (2007).

3. Although it can prove difficult to determine if terrorism caused a particular disease outbreak.

4. Five people died and 17 people were sickened, but survived.

disease outbreak, unintended consequences, accidents, negligence, vandalism/sabotage and the deliberate use of BW) and that risk assessment across the spectrum is prudent, given that many of these other risks pose a more immediate problem to states.[5] Chemical terrorism similarly seeks to inflict such harm, but through the use of chemical agents or toxins.

Assessing the Threat of Biological and Chemical Terrorism

Analysts at the Center for Nonproliferation Studies at the Monterey Institute of International Studies, US, developed a helpful methodology for conducting bioterrorism risk assessment for consideration by the Weapons of Mass Destruction Commission (WMDC) (Blix Commission) in 2004 (Ackerman and Moran, 2004).[6] While they consider that bioterrorism is a 'distinct' issue from chemical, nuclear and radiological terrorism, with its own highly specialised problems deserving of bio-focussed responses, arguably the similarities in the problems of biological weapons (BW) and chemical weapons (CW) control (especially when compared with nuclear or radiological weapons) as well as the growing convergence between the two fields of science and their respective treaty regimes[7] supports the application of this methodology to chemical terrorism threat assessment.

The Ackerman/Moran model postulates that bioterrorist threat assessment is based on the interaction between the consequences and the likelihood of an attack. When chemical terrorism threat assessment is included, the model specifies that:

Biological or chemical terrorist threat = consequences of attack * likelihood of attack.

Ackerman and Moran break this down into sub-elements as follows:

Consequences of an attack = value of asset being defended * hazard posed by [biological or chemical] agent(s) * vulnerability of asset being defended;

Likelihood of attack = motivation * capability of attacker(s).

5. Trevan (2009).

6. Ackerman and Moran (2004).

7. The 1972 Biological Weapons Convention (BWC) and 1993 Chemical Weapons Convention (CWC).

This structured threat assessment, they argue, requires the examination of factors traditionally excluded from bioterrorism threat assessment (for example, non-physical effects of a biological attack) and makes the process more objective (taking the terrorists' subjective interpretation into account). They also point out that there is a tendency to infer terrorists' intention from a potential or actual capability, and vice-versa, which is misguided.[8] For example, while Islamic extremist groups Jemaah Islamiyah and Abu Sayyaf are known to possess manuals on the production of biological and chemical weapons, this alone does not mean they had the intent or even the capability to successfully do so.

Consequences of an Attack

Applying the Ackerman/Moran model, the following factors are relevant to a threat assessment of the consequences of a biological (and chemical) attack.

The Value of the Asset to the Defender

The 'assets' that may be targeted by terrorists include human lives, and animal and crop production (economic assets): it is the terrorists' perception of their value to the defender that should guide assessment of this element. While policymakers should always seek to protect human life, they inevitably have to make choices about resource allocation and will likely need to carry out a 'cost-benefit' analysis to determine the monetary value of economic assets and how much they are willing to spend to prevent their harm, *versus* replacement value.

The Harm Potential of the Biological or Chemical Agent

There are infinite permutations and combinations of the harm potential of these agents, so it is necessary to carry out assessments of each biological (or chemical) agent that might realistically be employed by terrorists.[9] The factors that terrorists will take into account in selecting a biological agent for a terrorist attack form the basis for this

8. Ackerman and Moran (2004): 6.

9. However, some states' biodefence programmes seek to develop countermeasures for even implausible scenarios, which may lead to the imagined threat becoming real (for example, increasing the pathogenicity of a particular agent in order to develop a medical prophylaxis, thereby creating the problem they are attempting to solve).

threat assessment: for example, how likely it is to kill its intended victim (pathogenicity); the degree to which it is contagious or infectious; its resistance to protective or prophylactic countermeasures; and the degree of risk to the terrorist in handling it.

The biological agents often cited as being of potential interest to terrorists include: bacterial organisms (e.g., anthrax and plague); viruses (e.g., ebola, haemorrhagic fevers and even smallpox[10]); toxins (e.g., botulinum toxin, ricin and saxitoxin); and certain rickettsiae and funghi.[11] The trade in certain precursor chemical agents is also subject to national controls to help prevent their diversion to chemical weapons programmes or their access by terrorist actors,[12] although the developing world views these counter-proliferation measures as restricting their peaceful development.

Vulnerability to Biological or Chemical Weapons

Certain factors make populations around the world more susceptible to the deliberate spread of disease through bioterrorism, or reduce its ability to respond with protective and prophylactic measures after a biological or chemical weapons attack. The globalised economy has increased the routes and speed of disease transmission: for example, the severe acute respiratory syndrome (SARS) outbreak in 2002-03 was spread from mainland China to Hong Kong, Canada and beyond by infected air travellers within hours. Global public health programmes have eradicated certain diseases (in the case of smallpox) and significantly reduced the incidence of other naturally occurring diseases, but this has indirectly facilitated a reduced natural immunity around the world to certain diseases, or in specific countries to diseases that are endemic in others. Having a high standard of

10. The terrorist use of smallpox would be particularly dangerous as the World Health Organisation deemed that it was eradicated through a worldwide vaccination programme and destroyed all but two stocks of the virus held in the US and Russia (although the Russian stocks are widely deemed to have been insecure and subject to potential 'leakage').

11. Ackerman and Moran (2004) and Kellman (2004).

12. For example, UN Security Council Resolution 1540 requires all states to adopt and enforce measures to prevent nuclear, biological and chemical weapons proliferation to non-state actors, including transfer controls. Although it does not specify a list of agents for control. In addition, states participating in the Australia Group agree to coordinate their export controls for precursor chemical agents, *inter alia*, to help prevent CBW proliferation, with a proviso that such controls should not hamper legitimate trade for peaceful purposes. See the Australia Group website *http://www.australiagroup.net/en/index.html*

public health globally is therefore vital in reducing populations' vulnerability to disease, including deliberate disease through bioterrorism. The ability of health systems to respond to medical emergencies is also a factor in chemical terrorism, where large numbers of victims will need simultaneous treatment.[13] It must be remembered that certain countries or regions may be more vulnerable to particular diseases, or may have limited capacity to respond to bio-chem attacks, thereby increasing their vulnerability.

Likelihood of an Attack

Ackerman and Moran also highlight the relevance of terrorists' capability and motivations in conducting a biological attack when carrying out a threat assessment: both capability and motivation must be present to determine a significant risk of terrorist attack. These factors are also examined in great detail by other analysts. This section will outline some of the relevant issues and examine their relevance to the prospect of bio-chem terrorism to the Asian region.

Terrorists' Capability to Conduct a Biological or Chemical Attack

a) State Sponsorship

Despite the complete prohibition on biological and chemical weapons in international law,[14] some states are still believed to harbour ambitions, fanciful or realised, of possessing a CBW capability. Should these states have CBW capability, perhaps hiding it within a permissible BW or CW defence programme, and the desire to support CBW proliferation to terrorists through financial, logistical, technical or other assistance, then this significantly shortcuts a terrorist groups lead time to otherwise acquire this capability. Countries providing a 'safe haven' for terrorists (through negligence, ineffectual law

13. For example, Russian special forces deployed a chemical agent, which they revealed much later to be fentanyl, into a theatre packed with Chechen rebels and their civilian hostages as part of a rescue attempt, but delayed medical treatment and secrecy about the agent used led to over 100 civilian deaths.

14. The use of biological and chemical weapons is prohibited under the 1925 Geneva protocol, which has now achieved customary international law status binding upon all states; the development production and stockpiling of biological weapons (as well as use, in the case of chemical weapons) are banned under the 1972 BWC and 1993 CWC; and states must take prescriptive measures to prohibit and prevent the proliferation of biological, chemical and nuclear weapons to non-state actors, particularly terrorists, under UN Security Council Resolution 1540 (2004).

enforcement or because they lack complete control of their territory), also provide crucial support for any bio-chem terrorism objectives the terrorists may harbour.

An Organised Group, with Financial and Logistical Resources

A terrorist group motivated to acquire a CBW capability does require certain attributes, whether or not is has garnered state-sponsorship. To maintain the discipline and secrecy necessary to harbour such an activity, the group would need to be 'vertically organised, highly integrated and ideologically uniform.'[15] Without state sponsorship, terrorist groups would also need fairly substantial capital to fund an organised, large-scale attack involving a weaponised agent.

Acquisition of Materials and Equipment

It is a relatively inexpensive process to purchase or steal terrorism-relevant biological agents, acquire samples from the natural environment or infected animals or crops,[16] or create pathogens through synthetic biology techniques. Many chemical agents of interest to terrorists may be purchased in alarmingly large quantities off-the-shelf, such as fertilisers or chlorine. Studies have also shown that dual-use equipment for the production and weaponisation of biological and chemical agents is available for sale on the internet. Alarmingly, state surpluses have also been offered for sale in this way.

Acquisition of Knowledge/Skill (Especially for Weaponisation)

Possessing the raw materials for a biological or chemical weapon is one thing, but delivering it to a target population effectively is another. Terrorists may try to develop the necessary knowledge and skills 'in-house', or they may bring in outside expertise.[17] It is widely considered that the logistical and technical hurdles in developing a BW

15. Zanders (2004).

16. For example, Aum Shinrikyo cult members travelled to Zaire during an ebola outbreak to collect samples from victims which they intended to cultivate back in Japan; see Kellman (2004): 425.

17. The risk posed by former Soviet bioweaponeers assisting terrorist activities after the collapse of the Soviet Union led to the creation of a large 'threat reduction programme' aimed at redirecting these scientists to peaceful applications of their scientific and engineering knowledge.

programme capable of producing a viable weapon and dissemination device capable of inflicting mass casualties still appears to be beyond most terrorist groups. The Aum Shinrikyo cult in Japan, which released sarin gas into the Tokyo subway on 20 March 1995 killing 12 people and seriously injuring at least 50 more, had previously made many unsuccessful attempts to weaponise biological agents. Its vast wealth was insufficient to guarantee success.

Terrorists' Motivations for Conducting Biological or Chemical Terrorism

The likelihood of a terrorist attack involving biological and chemical weapons requires capability and motivation. There are particular reasons why terrorist groups might choose to employ these weapons over others that are more accessible and more likely to achieve significant casualties, psychological harm, societal chaos and economic disruption (e.g., conventional explosives or even firearms). However, terrorists may infer certain advantages to employing these weapons over others, as described in following paragraphs.

Desire to Inflict Significant Casualties and/or Mass Panic

There are different methods for predicting the casualty rates for biological and chemical terrorism scenarios, although the variability of certain factors (particularly relating to effective delivery) makes it extremely difficult to calculate with accuracy. There is certainly the potential for a bioterrorism event to result in thousands of casualties. A terrorist's cost-benefit analysis could show that bioterrorism results in more deaths than conventional weapons and at less cost than efforts to acquire a radiological weapon capability, for example. At the very least, a suspected biological attack, a hoax, or even an attack with relatively few deaths can result in mass panic.

Willingness to Break the Global Taboo against CBW Use to Achieve their Goals

The taboo against the use of biological and chemical weapons by state or non-state actors remains extremely strong, but there have been exceptions. The Aum Shinrikyo cult worked on sarin, VX gas, anthrax, botulinum toxin, ebola and hydrogen cyanide with clear evidence of their intention to use these on human populations. The perpetrator of the 2001 anthrax mailings also showed a total disregard for human life, using the postal system as a delivery mechanism, thereby contaminating mail intended for millions of recipients.

Relatively Easy to Carry Out and Difficult to Detect

A biological or chemical terrorism attack involving the successful delivery of a large quantity of material and resulting in significant casualty rates may be relatively difficult to achieve. However analysts have recently been determining the ease with which terrorists might execute attacks by contaminating food supplies, or by manipulating life science technologies for harm. The issue of food contamination is particularly worrisome, as food production processes might actually facilitate the delivery of tainted products to the consumer, by which time it is extremely difficult to determine when and where the deliberate contamination occurred, or by whom. Meanwhile, a disease outbreak might not even be traced to a covert bioterrorism attack. All this points to the need for effective public health surveillance and response in order to mitigate the effects of such an attack, but the issue of the public health sector's involvement in law enforcement to identify the location and cause of an attack, let alone the perpetrator, once a deliberate attack is suspected, is fraught with sensitivities.

Prospects for Bio-chem Terrorism: Trends in the Asian Region

States in Asia face terrorist threats involving terrorists located and operating within Asia; located in Asia and operating outside the region; and from terrorists located elsewhere and targeting Asia. The burgeoning biotech industry across Asia has significantly increased the region's vulnerabilities to bioterrorism and has focussed global attention on Asian efforts to mitigate these risks while also pursuing its right to peaceful development.

I do not purport to be an expert in terrorism in general, nor in the particular groups that are located or operate in the Asian region. But what I am familiar with is the extent to which states around the world have prohibited biological and chemical terrorist activity in their territory and have taken steps to prevent the proliferation of CBW, including to terrorists and other non-state actors. Most examples are drawn from the BW area, as Verification Technology Information Centre's (VERTIC) legislative assistance programme, which cooperates and shares information with states to develop new laws to prohibit and prevent nuclear, biological and chemical weapons, heavily focusses on BW-related legislative support. By sharing my thoughts on the status of prohibition and prevention in the Asian region, I aim to identify some trends in Asian states' vulnerability to bio-chem terrorist attacks and ability to prevent such attacks occurring within their territory or in other states.

Across Asia, the status of states' legislative preparedness to prevent and respond to bio-chem terrorism is patchy although some states, such as India, have tackled this task comprehensively. It must be said, however, that no state in the world has a 'gold standard' regulatory framework in this area.

South Asia

India and Pakistan have relatively comprehensive national legislation in this area (with Pakistan currently finalising a new BWC Act), while the other states (Bangladesh, Bhutan, Maldives, Nepal and Sri Lanka) have very few relevant legislative measures in force and do not appear to be making attempts to improve the situation. These states are at an increased risk of being 'safe havens' for terrorist activities involving biological and chemical weapons, without the means to effectively investigate and prosecute those engaging in such activities.

Critically, these states lack:

- Legislative provisions punishing activities involving biological weapons (development, production, acquisition, stockpiling or use, attempts, financing, etc.) despite being members of the relevant treaties (to facilitate the detection and punishment of attempted or actual use of BW).
- Control lists for biological agents and toxins, dual-use equipment and technology (to license imports and exports, regulate domestic transfers, and license facilities and personnel to handle controlled agents).
- Preventive measures to account for, secure and physically protect dangerous biological agents and toxins (to prevent terrorist access to CBW materials stored in facilities or in transit).

- Preventative measures to control transfers of dangerous biological agents and toxins (to reduce vulnerability through theft or loss of terrorist relevant materials); and
- National biosecurity oversight mechanisms (to implement biosecurity laws; monitor their effectiveness and issue updated subsidiary regulations; report to Parliament on biosecurity effectiveness; and liaise with other states and intergovernmental bodies on this issue).

Central Asia

Certain states in this region formerly housed Soviet 'anti-plague' stations and other elements of the large Soviet offensive biological weapons programme, and so have a history of legislative measures to protect their personnel and the environment. While certain states have comprehensive legislation in some areas, particularly those explicitly required under WMD treaties or the UN Counter-Terrorism Conventions, they lack specific regulation required under United Nations Security Council Resolution (UNSCR) 1540 (such as preventive measures to account for, secure and physically protect dangerous biological agents and toxins). Other states have prohibited BW and CW at law, yet lack effective preventive measures. Encouragingly, many states are progressively strengthening their regulatory frameworks to prohibit bio-chem terrorism, alongside activities to enhance physical security of terrorist-relevant materials.

East Asia

Perhaps unsurprisingly, China, Japan and South Korea lead the field in this region. Japan was in the unfortunate position of having to develop legislation reactively, in light of their experience prosecuting Aum Shinrikyo cult leader Shoko Asahara for the sarin gas attack (the case took eight years to conclude).

Southeast Asia

Worryingly, certain states in this region which have a growing biotechnology industry and harbour radical Islamic terrorist groups lack even the most basic measures prohibiting biological weapons and comprehensive regulations preventing terrorist acquisition (for example, they lack control lists and preventive measures to account for, secure and physically protect dangerous biological agents and toxins). There is some evidence that they are attempting to ameliorate these deficiencies, with new legislative bills under preparation. Inter-regional cooperation will be crucial to effective enforcement of these laws.

West Asia

Certain states in this region are widely considered to harbour active offensive biological and chemical weapons programmes or, in the case of Iraq, used to possess such programmes. Combined with the presence of radical Islamic terrorist groups in the region, the potential for state sponsorship of biological and chemical terrorism in this region deserves more attention by the international security community. While there is some movement in certain states towards a more robust biosecurity regulatory environment (principally certain states in North Africa and the Gulf Cooperation Council), the progress is slow and uneven. Regional geopolitics also mean many states in this region remain outside the BWC and CWC regimes and lack sensitivity to CBW proliferation issues.

Policy Recommendations

Analysts and policymakers around the world need to pay more attention to the chemical, but particularly biological, terrorist threat. The respective treaty regimes should be strengthened, particularly compliance monitoring and enforcement of the 1972 Biological Weapons Convention, starting with the existing confidence-building measure arrangements. Intra- and inter-regional cooperation on biosecurity and (bioterrorism prevention) and chemical security (chemical terrorism prevention) is absolutely essential to developing a more effective web of prevention, as terrorist activities transcend borders. All states face common challenges in this area and aside from facilitating helpful communication, such cooperation could develop regional initiatives in tackling them.

References

Ackerman, Gary A. and Kevin S. Moran (2004). "Bioterrorism and threat assessment", The Weapons of Mass Destruction Commission, *Paper No. 22*, November, *www.wmdcommission.org*. pp. 3-4.

Global Security Newswire (2009). "WMD Terrorism Threat Persists, Report Says", *Global Security Newswire*, May 1. *http://gsn.nti.org/gsn/nw_20090501_3145.php*

Kellman, Barry (2004). "Biological Terrorism: Legal Measures for Preventing Catastrophe", *Harvard Journal of Law & Public Policy* 24(2): 417-88 and 430-36.

Rappert, Brian and Caitriona McLeish (eds.) (2007). *A Web of Prevention: Biological Weapons, Life Sciences and the Governance of Research*. London: Earthscan. October.

Trevan, Tim (2009). "Improving National Biological Risk Assessment Methodology and Encouraging International Coordination of Biological Risk Assessment, Management and Mitigation", International Council for the Life Sciences presentation to the Stanley Foundation workshop *Resolution 1540: At the Crossroads*, October 1, 2009, New York, US (a contribution to the official Comprehensive Review of the Status of Implementation on Resolution 1540 conducted by the 1540 Committee, September 30–October 2, 2009) at *http://www.stanleyfoundation.org/1540/ICLSBioRiskStanleyFoundation2.pdf*

Zanders, Jean Pascal (2004). "Assessing the Risk of Chemical and Biological Weapons Proliferation to Terrorists", *The Nonproliferation Review* 6(4): 30. Fall 1999. Cited in Ackerman and Moran (2004): 9.

VII

Asian Militaries and the Future of War

18

Changing Security Threats

Future Asian Armies in 2030

YONG-SUP HAN

Introduction

There are two big missions for armies in the year 2030 in Asia. One is dealing with conventional conflicts i.e., North Korea's all-out military attack on South Korea if the Kim family regime and its bellicosity remain until 2030. Another small though unlikely example could be border clashes along the Chinese border. The other big mission originates from growing non-traditional security threats such as terrorist attacks, natural disasters, and pandemic disease. The latter threat will require multilateral security cooperation because one nation state alone cannot deal with transnational terrorism which is likely to continue to 2030.

On the issue of conventional combat operations, South Korea and the United States will maintain their security alliance together with the US-Japan alliance in northeast Asia. On the possibility of border clashes, China, India and Pakistan will retain their armies at approximately current strengths up to 2030 with some downsizing of military personnel because of high-tech military modernisation to gain a qualitative edge over the neighbouring countries. Similarly, South Korea (Repubic of Korea) will continue to build up its army *vis-à-vis* North Korea (because North Korea is not likely to reduce its military) while strengthening asymmetric military capabilities *vis-à-vis* South Korea-US allied military forces. Because of the size of the North Korean forces, the South Korea forces need to be prepared to confront and defeat North Korea's conventional forces in case of attack. These requirements could increase if North Korea decided to use a nuclear weapon against the South Korea and US forces in a future war. The United States and Japan alliance will also retain their armies at similar levels after taking account of future hybrid warfare.

Future armies will focus on building a combined armed forces structure capable of executing traditional and irregular warfare. For irregular warfare, countries in Asia will foster multilateral cooperation with other countries. Weapon systems will become advanced enough to utilise the enhanced battle space awareness through networking and integrating all the weapon systems on ground and in the air. Unmanned ground and aerial systems including robot technology will be employed. Unless a wiser conflict prevention mechanism can be developed through a political and historical analysis of root causes of conflicts, these state-of-the-art military weapons are more likely to compound the problems rather than solving them.

The ending of the Cold War resulted in the emergence of a number of non-state actors over the last two decades who have continuously defied the modern sovereign states. As a result, state-centric inter-state security had to give way to intra-state cultural, psychological or economic, violent conflicts initiated by non-state actors. The future prospects of security therefore appear uncertain to the extent that the nation states are unable to control prevent or manage new security issues on their own. Since the changes that have been observed in the post-Cold War era are still unfolding, the future course of wars and the shape of militaries remain valid subjects of study. This requires an in-depth analysis of the future security environment and new force planning.

This chapter seeks to analyse the nature of conflicts in the next two decades, whether conventional or non-conventional, especially in east Asia and will also examine what Asian militaries will look like in 2030. What might be the inter-state balances among major powers, especially in Asia? How will North Korean challenges unfold in the context of northeast Asia? And how will Asian armies prepare themselves to handle these future challenges.

Emerging Security Threats in Asia in 2030

Growing Non-Traditional Threats in Asia

The 2006 US *Quadrennial Defense Review* (QDR) defined four military challenges that the countries are likely to face in the 21st century. These as shown in Figure 18.1 are:

1. Traditional threats (invasions like North Korea might carry out).
2. Irregular threats (terrorism and insurgencies as in Iraq and Afghanistan).
3. Catastrophic threats (employing weapons of mass destruction (WMD), and particularly attacks aimed at friendly cities and civilians), and
4. Disruptive threats (technologically advanced attacks that a near-peer might make in the future).

Figure 18.1

US Security Assessment

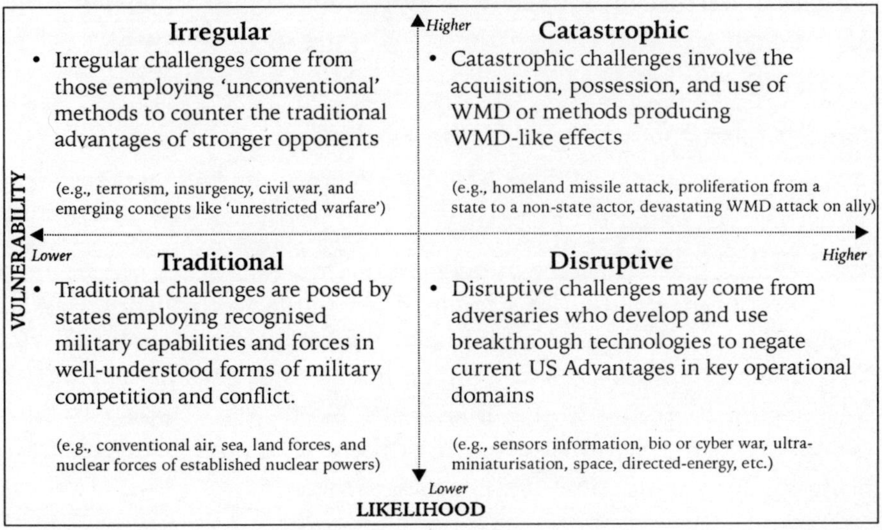

Source: The US Department of Defence, *The Quadrennial Defense Review*, June 2006.

Although the United States and its NATO allies are engaged in anti-terrorism warfare in Afghanistan and Iraq, these wars are not likely to end soon. The size and frequency of terrorist wars is expected to grow as we near 2030. There is diverging assessment as to what kind of terrorist groups will prevail in the long run. In particular regard to Asia, perhaps the possibility of some ethnic wars aided by terrorist networks cannot be excluded if China and India are unable to handle social instabilities arising from growing gaps of income and social opportunities inside their countries and if these two countries fail to keep social unrest under control within their territories.

The US Secretary of Defence Robert Gates has argued in the January/February 2009 issue of *Foreign Affairs* that there is the need to balance US strategy between irregular and more traditional challenges, referring to the US response to new threats in terms of 'hybrid warfare'.[1] In reality, the categories of warfare will be so blurred that it would be difficult to differentiate irregular wars from traditional wars.[2] Nevertheless, a combination of irregular and traditional wars is likely to increase over time in Asia.

Moreover, some terrorist wars will continue in the Philippines and Indonesia. Terrorism is likely to flourish after the US pull-out from Afghanistan and Iraq though the actual time of withdrawal is yet to be determined.

Threats Stemming from Weapons of Mass Destruction

The countries of northeast Asia have historically had some interest in WMDs. An initial estimate of WMDs in northeast Asia for 2030 is given in Table 18.1.

In accordance with the Chemical Weapons Convention (CWC, 1997) and the Biological and Toxin Weapons Convention (BTWC, 1975), many states will no longer have chemical and biological weapons by 2030. But China, Russia and North Korea appear to have retained these capabilities and are likely to do so through 2030, probably even with some new developments.

1. Gates (2009).
2. Hoffman (2009).

Table 18.1

Estimated Northeast Asian Weapons of Mass Destruction in 2030

Country	*Chemical Weapons*	*Biological Weapons*	*Nuclear Weapons*	*Theatre Ballistic Missiles*
China	Some?	Some?	500-1,000	>1,000
Japan	—	—	—	—
Mongolia	—	—	—	—
North Korea	Some	Some?	10-40?	>1,000
Russia	Some?	Some?	1,000s	100s in Asia
South Korea	—	—	—	Some?
Taiwan	?	?	—	Some?
United States	—	—	1,000s	100s in Asia

Note: This table is modified to include the year 2030.
Source: Bennett (2008).

It is difficult to estimate the quantities that are available even now, let alone in 2030, and thus the chemical and biological entries in Table 18.1 are left uncertain. Nevertheless, any conflict that develops in northeast Asia could involve at least some chemical and biological weapon use.

Indeed, if North Korea remains an independent state in 2030, the atrophy of its conventional forces over time will likely force it into evermore reliance on chemical and biological weapons, as well as nuclear weapons.

Table 18.1 also shows the projected number of nuclear weapons by 2030. It is reported that China today has only a few hundred nuclear weapons, but its inventories could grow to 500 to 1,000 nuclear weapons in 2030, especially if it puts multiple re-entry vehicles on its missiles. If China does not respond positively to the US president Obama's call for elimination of nuclear weapons, China will keep its nuclear arsenal at more than the current holdings. Russia and the United States each have declared arsenals of thousands of nuclear weapons, though these numbers are supposed to decline by 2030. Given the uncertainties and the prospects of North Korean efforts to acquire fissile materials beyond the facilities that it has closed, it seems reasonable to assume that North Korea could still have 10 to 40 nuclear weapons in 2030, if the current regime remains.

It is assumed in Table 18.1 that both South Korea and Japan will abide by their denuclearisation policy till 2030. Still, in both countries, there is an implicit debate on whether or not they should do so in a context where North Korea would not abandon or eliminate its nuclear holdings. If Seoul and Tokyo, for some reason, decide to go nuclear, there are significant chances of a regional nuclear weapons arms race, since China would want to maintain its superiority over Japan and Korea. In addition, if the South Korea and Japan develop nuclear weapons, Taiwan might also do so. The United States will not allow South Korea and Japan to go nuclear because it could lead to a nuclear nightmare! This is why five parties of the six-party talks emphasised North Korea's complete and verifiable denuclearisation.

In 2030, China, North Korea and Russia will also have large numbers of theatre ballistic missiles. Meanwhile, Japan and the United States are moving towards a regional missile defence system, while South Korea keeps pursuing local missile defence capabilities within the peninsula context.

Traditional Threats Emanating from North Korea

The North Korean regime is in jeopardy. Its economy has largely failed, harvests are of less than subsistence level, creating conditions of unemployment and famine. While North Korea has had an aid-based economy for many years, it has not obtained the level of aid in 2009 and 2010 that it had got in previous years. As a result, even the military may be suffering from food shortage. Moreover, North Korea's foreign currency revenues have gone down because of the sanctions imposed by the United Nations Security Council since June 2009 on arms exports to other countries. If North Korea does not eliminate its nuclear weapons and materials, the sanctions will continue which will aggravate North Korean economic stringencies further. Either out of North Korea's desperation fearing Kim Jong-Il's abrupt demise or lack of any progress in its nuclear negotiations with the United States or the six-party talks, North Korea is using force more frequently than before. This is worrisome because earlier North Korea used to exercise blackmail or coercion *vis-à-vis* South Korea.

Thus in looking forward to 2030, North Korea could evolve in one of the following three ways:

First, North Korea's government could fail and the country will break up. The various areas could be controlled by warriors. This condition would almost certainly be unstable and eventually lead to civil war or anarchy at least in parts of North Korea. The situation could eventually force South Korea and Chinese intervention, leading to some degree of unification.

Second, the Kim family could continue to rule North Korea under Kim Jong-Il's son, Kim Jung-eun. However, it is uncertain whether the North Korean elites will accord him with the same amount of loyalty that they give Kim Jong-Il.

Third, the Kim family regime could fail and a military coup could occur. A military regime in the North Korea would still face all of the problems, though its leadership would show more flexibility than Kim Jong-Il.

If any government failure occurs in North Korea, the North Korean regime could also take revenge. This could lead to internal turmoil and finally perhaps to collapse. Thus, it would be more difficult to deal with North Korea after the collapse or implosion unless countries in northeast Asia succeed in establishing a certain regional cooperation mechanism to prevent this.

Armies of Major Countries in Asia in 2030

The United States

The United States economy is likely to recover from its current problems before 2030 and has an increasing GDP. In the aftermath of the conflicts in Iraq and Afghanistan, the United States will possibly downsize its military, as in the post-Vietnam war era, to less than 1.4 million personnel and constrain the growth of its military budget. The United States is expected to retain 500,000 to 600,000 army personnel in the year 2030.

In 2030, the United States security goal for Asia will be to maintain peace and regional stability and to sustain US influence in the continent. The United States will particularly want to avoid a regional nuclear arms race. The United States will also want to retain its alliances with the South Korea and Japan, especially in the light of the growing Chinese influence. But in view of the growing national wealth of Korea and Japan the United States will not only be cautious in offering military assistance but will also want the two countries to contribute more towards the defence budget of the alliance. Indeed, if the US military finds itself overcommitted in the Middle East over the next several decades, it will be constrained to pull out its forces from Korea and Japan to meet its defence needs in other places. This trend was seen in the global posture review process that was undertaken during the Bush administration. As explained earlier in the chapter, the United States will be preparing for irregular and traditional warfare, so its defence expenditure is not likely to come down at least in the foreseeable future.

China

By 2030, China will be an ascendant regional power, trying to establish itself as a major regional military power. China's economy is likely to continue to grow to be among the top two world economies. Its military is expected to continue to grow both in economic and technology terms.

China's primary national security objectives would include preventing a refugee inflow from North Korea into China, preventing attacks from any power, controlling its territorial borders as well as surrounding land, sea and air spaces, and preventing internal ethnic conflicts. China will seek to influence its neighbours and the United States through economic and political relations where possible, but also through military coercion if required.

China's military expenditure has been growing rapidly in recent years. Though the total exact figures are difficult to ascertain because the released information runs short of transparency, China is expected to allocate between $200 to $300 billion for its military budget in the year 2030. Chinese army's manpower is expected to be the highest in the world. Because of demands of border security and domestic stability China's army in 2030 will remain at almost its current strength of one and quarter million.

Japan

By 2030, Japan's economy may well be revitalised, and it will be a major world economic power with a GDP that is 30 to 40 per cent of the US GDP. Still, it will most likely have a small military, about the same size as today, with a military budget that is less than one per cent of its GDP. Japan will continue with the 120,000 manpower it has now. Given Japanese's strategic location as maritime power, the size of Japan's army would not affect the Asian strategic equation too much.

Japan's security objective is to prevent North Korean and other attacks on Japan, to protect its lanes of communication at sea and its air spaces, and sustain its alliance with the United States, while contributing to peace in Asia and in the world. For the foreseeable future, Japan views the Chinese and the North Koreans as threats.

Japan would also be concerned about the evolution of the regional balance, including the growing Chinese naval presence in the East China Sea and the overall growth of Chinese military strength.

South Korea

It seems likely that by 2030, the South Korean economy will be revitalised and able to sustain a real annual growth of 3 to 5 per cent in GDP. South Korea will maintain about 500,000 active duty personnel, consistent with its demographics though the military budget is likely to grow to about $50 to $60 billion in 2030. The South Korean army will retain some 350,000 military personnel. The numerical imbalance between the North and the South will be supplemented by the South's huge investment in military modernisation in order to gain qualitative advantage over the North.

In terms of regional security, the South Korea will seek to prevent a North Korean invasion or other attacks, and in the case of partial or full unification, to prevent a Chinese invasion or other attacks. The South Korea will want to prevent other regional threats and to control its surrounding sea and air spaces. The South Korea will also want to sustain its alliance with the United States.

If North Korea's collapse has already resulted in Korean unification, or China intervenes on behalf of North Korea, then the South Korea's main concern will be how to prevent Chinese intervention. If unification takes place, then Korea's concern will again be how to prevent or deal with the threat posed by China. This will necessitate a stronger alliance with the United States unless Korea and China can establish a more cooperative relationship during or after the unification process.

Russia

In the years until 2030, the Russian economy will probably be strengthened by its oil and natural gas wealth. The broader Russian economy will continue to grow by 2030, but will still have many difficulties. By 2030, the Russian leadership will feel strengthened and anxious to re-establish Russia as a major power. Russia is expected to keep about 300,000 army personnel in the year 2030 with defence expenditures of $100 billion.

Thus in 2030, Russia's security objectives will include confirming its position as a major power, preventing invasions or other external threats, and extending its influence beyond Russian borders. But the central Russian government is likely to be more focussed on the European region, giving the Far East much less attention or resources.

India and Indonesia

India is expected to keep its military strength commensurate with its economic strength. India has a shared border with Pakistan which is the main security concern not only for India but also for the rest of the world because of the terrorist threats emanating from that country. Since India also shares a border with China, so it is compelled to strengthen its army and air force. Therefore, by 2030 India is likely to have an army of 900,000 to one million with increasing emphasis on mechanisation and high-tech army capabilities.

Indonesia will also feel the need for a stronger army because of increasing number of terror threats. It is expected that Indonesia will retain its current army manpower of 200,000 in the year 2030.

Changing Army Missions, Strategies and Capabilities

As identified earlier, one of the major missions of Asian armies in 2030 would be to deal with a belligerent North Korea. The other could be to handle border issues with China. On the issue of transnational threats including growing terrorism threats, countries in Asia will strengthen multilateral military cooperation through sharing information and taking joint counter-measures. Once terrorist attacks occur, stabilisation, peacekeeping operations (PKO), and humanitarian aid in the affected area will become more relevant and urgent. As the international community increases its PKO operations and capabilities, countries in Asia will also be expected to expand their respective PKO units. At the same time, countries in Asia will restructure their armies to strengthen their special purpose operation capabilities against terrorism and insurgencies.

Future armies in Asia will adapt their concept of traditional warfare by combining it with irregular warfare. As shown earlier in the chapter, the future will see more of hybrid warfare. Future armies will place emphasis on upgrading their battle space awareness ability by taking advantage of information technology and computers and sensors. This trend began in the United States and is labelled as network-centric warfare.

Another trend will be to restructure the army for more speedy, agile, and light brigade size forces. However, increasing insurgencies and suicide bombing attacks in Iraq and Afghanistan have caused the US army to reconsider the effectiveness of this trend. As a result, traditional emphasis on heavy armoured units for some reason has become more relevant. Therefore, there will be a mix of light brigades and heavy brigades in the concept force of the future.

Weapons in the future battleground will be integrated to demonstrate synchronised and joint capabilities with the help of high-tech weapons and networked battle space awareness and precision guided munitions. For example, Dragon Assault Ships, Scorpion Gunships, the Aerospatiale SA-2 Samson, the Amplified Mobility Platform armed with huge automatic machine guns which were seen in the movie *Avatar* will be introduced into future battles because of technological development. Aerospatiale SA-2 Samson with helicopters will also enable the air to ground combined warfare.

The mobility and speed of weapons will be strengthened to be able to execute rapid deployment operations. To avoid casualties and ensure manoeuvrability for surveillance and reconnaissance and actual battle engagement, unmanned aerial vehicles, unmanned ground vehicles, unattended ground sensors, armed robot vehicles and robots will be developed and deployed in the battlefields of the future.

References

Bennett, Bruce (2008). *Future ROK Army Development* (Santa Monica, CA: RAND, 2008).

Gates, Robert M. (2009). "A Balanced Strategy: Reprogramming the Pentagon for a New Age," *Foreign Affairs*, Jan/Feb.

Hoffman, Frank G. (2009). "The Changing Character of War", The US National Defence University Institute for National Strategic Studies, *Global Strategic Assessment 2009: America's Security Role in a Changing World.* Washington D.C: NDU Press.

19

Asian Air Power in 2030

Capabilities and Technologies Required for Potential Future Scenarios

JOHN P. GEIS

Introduction

Preparing for the future is as much an art as it is a science.[1] It is partially art, in that science cannot discern all that is to come. It is partially science, as many of the events which are to come, are knowable and inevitable. They need not be surprises.[2]

This chapter builds on an effort that was commissioned by the Chief of Staff of the United States Air Force in 2007. The results in this chapter are derived, in part, from these study efforts. These study efforts, called Blue Horizons, are an ongoing effort to provide 'a new look at the future.' They were also designed to 'confirm Air University as [the Air Force's] in-house think tank' and to improve the relevance of Air Force education to the decision-making processes in Washington.[3]

Using data gathered in the 2008 iteration of the Blue Horizons study, this chapter specifically explores the nature of the air power capabilities for the Asian region in the year 2030.[4] Specifically, it will argue that the types of capabilities that Asian and global powers will

1. Enbelbrecht *et al.* (1996).
2. Schwartz (2003).
3. Memorandum of Agreement entitled 'Strategic Studies (Blue Horizons) Special Interest Item,' signed by General John D.W. Corley, Vice Chief of Staff of the United States Air Force on 17 May 2006.
4. The 2008 study used an alternate futures methodology that is equally applicable to all parts of the world. While this chapter focusses on the Asian implications, many conclusions found in this apply to the United States, Europe and Oceana as well.

require in 2030 will largely be invariant across the types of warfare that could be fought. Secondly, it will demonstrate that the types of new research and investment needed to field these capabilities are essentially the same, regardless of conflict type. In the end, it shows that future air forces, in Asia and elsewhere, will need to be designed so as to speed up the decision-making cycle, to have reasonably long-range capabilities, and to span a diverse mission set. Lastly, unmanned platforms will continue to play an increasing role in future operations.

In making this argument, Section II will discuss the methodology that underpins the Blue Horizons study. Section III will briefly discuss the four alternative futures that corroborates with the original study. While not only three of the four scenarios are specific to Asia, the location of a particular scenario is less important than the challenges it presents for air power planners. These scenarios were chosen based on the diversity of these challenges, and as such, they have planning validity for air forces on the Asian continent and elsewhere.[5] Section IV presents a brief summary of an operations analysis of 58 capabilities and 172 key underlying technologies that were evaluated against the alternative futures. Finally, it summarises those conclusions that seem pertinent to India and her fellow nations of Asia.

Methodology

The study began by creating a set of alternative future scenarios, as is discussed in Section III below. While these were independent of the other research in this volume, striking similarities exist between the futures of this study and others presented here.

In building these scenarios, the study participants engaged in extensive background research on culture, economy, military and political systems; conducted interviews and actual site visits at the locations in question; interviewed senior members of the Department of State, the national intelligence agencies,[6] and the Department of

5. Schwartz (1991) argues that choosing scenarios that deliberately stress an organisation in disparate ways is one of the valid methods of scenario planning.
6. There is nothing in this work, nor any source used to compile this work which is or draws upon classified material.

Defense; and discussed their findings with senior leaders of the governments in the affected states and regions.[7]

These researchers—22 senior military leaders—then engaged in modified Delphi method[8] of generating conclusions about both the present as well as each alternative future scenario. These conclusions were then revetted against a series of experts to adjust hypotheses and then re-engage in additional research and interviews. In these follow-on sessions, a formal Delphi method[9] was used.

Members of the Headquarters, United States Air Force's Strategic Planning Directorate (HQ USAF/A8), Air University students, and researchers from a variety of agencies developed a list of future concepts or systems representing key capabilities that could be designed, engineered, and produced before the target year of 2030.[10] These future concepts were vetted by scientists in the relevant disciplines to ensure scientific and technological feasibility.

The final aspect of this analysis involved using a value-focussed-thinking quantitative model to formally evaluate the potential future concepts for utility across the range of alternative futures.[11] This model was developed and run under the direction of the US Air Force Center for Strategy & Technology, with the assistance of Innovative Decisions, Inc., whose members include some of those cited in the seminal works on this method in the endnotes.

---

7. The researchers included 19 students and faculty at Air University schools in the 2007 academic year.
8. Dalkey and Helmer (1963) discuss the method in depth, as well as its origins in RAND's Project DELPHI.
9. Ibid.
10. The term 'concept' has a specific meaning in some parts of the budgetary community, which is not intended here. In this study, 'concept' refers to a notional future system that technologically can be built to meet the challenges of the world of 2030. Fifty-eight such concepts or systems are embedded in this study.
11. The methodology is described in Geis (2009a) and Geis and Parnell (2009). This methodology parallels that used in the Air Force 2025 Study. For details on the Air Force 2025 model itself, see: Jackson *et al.* (1997). For more on value-focussed thinking methodology in general, the reader is referred to the following works: Keeney and Raiffa (1976); Keeney (1992); Kirkwood (1997); Parnell *et al.* (1998).

Alternative Futures

The gold standard of future planning remains the development of alternative future scenarios.[12] Schwartz describes two separate means of deriving these alternative futures. One deals with the definition of various drivers of change, and using these to create a strategic planning space.[13] The other method Schwartz cites is to use a prescriptive planning document to derive disparate challenges for the organisation being examined.

The Blue Horizons effort made use of the United States National Security Strategy which describes four key challenges that will confront the international community in the decades to come.[14] These are: the rise of a peer China, a resurgent Russia, failed states, and extremist ideologies that manifest themselves as insurgencies.[15] Using these four different conditions, the researchers built four alternative futures which would stress air force capabilities across Asia in four very different directions.

The following are brief descriptions of the four alternative future scenarios. It is important to realise that these scenarios are not necessarily predictions of what will be, but rather are plausible descriptions of environments that could exist, and that if they were to occur, would present disparate challenges for which air forces in Asia and elsewhere must be prepared. These scenarios were used to evaluate the concepts and technologies that follow.[16]

---

12. Englebrecht *et al.* (1996): 9-17; Schwartz (1991).
13. Ibid. Schwartz' book describes this procedure in great detail. For an abbreviated description that captures the essence of Schwartz' argument, see Englebrecht *et al.* (1996): 1-17.
14. Although unstated in the National Security Strategy of the United States of America, there are, in fact, two drivers which generate these four scenarios. The first is the type of actor which will present the most serious future challenges, with the poles of this driver being state and non-state. The second driver is the predominant type of military operations (conventional or unconventional. These two sets of drivers and poles can generate the four futures found in the National Security Strategy. As Schwartz points out, however, to choose scenarios directly from a policy document which stresses the organisation in disparate ways, is an acceptable methodology.
15. Strategic Studies Institute (2006).
16. Schwartz suggests that it is crucial to examine the future scenarios from the perspective of a person standing in the future and looking back towards the present. The evaluation of the concepts was done via the Delphi method and through wargaming exercises specifically looking from the perspective of the world in 2030.

Peer China[17]

In this world, China rises to peer status with the United States by the year 2030. Its culture remains fairly constant; its political system will be under the control of its sixth post-Mao generation leadership; its economy will likely be the largest on Earth, though per capita income will still lag behind the EU and the US; and its military spending, while likely greater than the United States, will have produced a military almost equal to the United States.

China has long viewed itself as the 'Middle Kingdom' or the centre of civilisation. With the largest population in the world and a fast-growing economy, China is well positioned to reinvent itself. In 2007, China's economic growth was more than 11 per cent. Even amidst the Great Recession, China's economy grew by 8.7 per cent in 2009, and is expected to grow by 9.5 per cent in 2010.[18] This economic growth is critical to China's internal harmony; it also provides the means for China to acquire the resources and build the means to project its power beyond the region.

China is expected to continue to follow President Hu Jintao's vision of the 'harmonious society' (*xié shè huì*). Hu describes 'harmonious society' as a scientific development concept,[19] shifting China's primary focus from a pure economic growth model to a more balanced, Confucian-style approach aimed at maintaining growth while addressing social issues such as the gap between rich and poor, environmental degradation, and government and corporate corruption.[20] In this future, China, remains authoritarian, but continues to build on policies

---

17. This section is compiled in part from Geis *et al.* (forthcoming). This monograph traces the drivers behind China's rise in the areas of economics, culture, politics, and military strength.
18. Hansson (2010).
19. Jintao (2006). President Jintao's definition is found in these quotes: 'China will pursue a scientific outlook on development that makes economic and social development people-oriented, comprehensive, balanced and sustainable; We will work to strike a proper balance between urban and rural development, development among regions, economic and social development, development of man and nature, and domestic development and opening wider to the outside world; It is also rooted in the cultural heritages of the Chinese nation'.
20. Waley (1938). Note: 'Confucian-style' in this context refers to the long standing positive cultural orientation towards authority as benevolent. Authoritarianism, paternalism, and subordination of individual needs to that of the governed, which are found throughout Confucian analects. As Caine points out in chapter 2, the population will defer to the authorities unless the legitimacy of the regime is called into question. See also Berling (2007) and Gamer (2003).

promoting openness and integration with the international community. The fundamental precept of this opening is China's '24 Character Strategy' first articulated by Deng Xiaoping. The '24 Character Strategy' refers to 24 Chinese characters which translated to: 'observe calmly; secure our position; cope with affairs calmly; hide our capacities and bide our time; be good at maintaining a low profile; and never claim leadership.'[21] It complements Hu's call to 'hide brightness, nourish obscurity.' These ideas will likely continue to guide China's leaders as they chart China's course towards growth while avoiding conflict among global actors.

Goldman Sachs' report, *BRICs and Beyond* (2007), discusses a range of predictions for China's economy in 2030 ranging from a low of $11,000 per capita GDP ($16 trillion total) to as much as $22,000 per capita (GDP of $32 trillion). The report states that at any level above the low end of this forecast range, China's economy will surpass the United States in overall economic size sometime in the 2020s.[22]

While China espouses a 'harmonious world' philosophy, China does appear to be taking all the necessary steps to emerge as a major global power. History suggests that major powers are involved in conflict more frequently than are lesser powers.[23] As such, China's military modernisation and conduct is worthy of monitoring by all nations in the Asian region.

China has developed and will continue to develop significant capabilities for future leadership roles, which will enable power projection, anti-access, and area denial. China will have anti-access capabilities, including 'assassin's mace'[24] weapons, to deter or counter

21. Office of the Secretary of Defense (2007): 6.
22. With a population estimated to be around 350 million, the United States GDP in this timeframe would therefore be approximately $21.35 trillion. Goldman Sachs Report (2007). It should be noted that the Chinese economy in 2006 and 2007 grew at a rate more than three per cent faster each year than the Goldman Sachs upper estimate.
23. Correlations with increased power and conflict onset have been found by Reiter and Stam (2002). Further, Russett and ONeal (2001) find that Sinic cultures are more war-prone than any others.
24. The Chinese word for 'assassin's mace' here is pronounced '*shashoujian*,' which translates to 'the inferior defeats the superior.' Using an indirect strategy discussed by Sun Tzu, China seeks to counter advanced technology with weapons designed to 'leapfrog' current systems and prevent adversary access to the China region.

any potential adversary near Chinese territory. Specific aims of the anti-access strategy will be to slow down the deployment of adversary forces and compel these forces to operate from distances further than desired.[25] To achieve these aims, Chinese doctrinal writings propose a combination of conventional and asymmetric weapons. These include the use of medium-range ballistic and cruise missiles,[26] modern 'fourth and fifth generation' aircraft,[27] advanced surface to air missiles,[28] and expanding its regional covert operations capabilities. These same weapons, along with electronic jamming, anti-satellite weapons, electro-magnetic pulse (EMP)[29] weapons, and systems for computer network attack are being designed to enable degradation of adversary's command and control and early-warning capabilities. Finally, China seeks to develop a robust naval capability sufficient to make it difficult for adversaries to approach her coastline.[30] This will likely involve the building and deployment of an amphibious landing capability[31] and up to three aircraft carriers. [32]

By 2030, China is expected to have a very modern military. Its navy will have at least a few, and possibly several carrier battle groups, and China will have all the elements necessary to deploy a carrier strike group well before 2030. In addition, China is on track to field state-of-the-art ballistic missile submarines, probably much sooner than 2030.[33]

25. Cliff *et al.* (2007).

26. Wall (2003).

27. Chengdu Aircraft is developing the J-10A. Chinese engineers have designed this canard aircraft to be larger than the J-12 but with many of the same features including plasma-stealth technology to provide stealth characteristics without significantly altering the fourth-generation fighter shape of the J-10. Fisher (2004).

28. China's aviation and defence industry is quickly advancing as well. Modern SA-10/20 surface to air missiles, from both land and ships, provide coverage across the entire Taiwan Strait today. The Russian variants of the SA-20 missiles are sometimes designated the SA-300. Follow-on systems with ranges of beyond 300 km are likely in this time frame. See Office of the Secretary of Defense (2007): 31.

29. An electro-magnetic pulse is a burst of electronic energy that propagates through space (or the atmosphere) that can damage computer equipment and electronic circuitry. These pulses can be generated by upper atmospheric nuclear weapons bursts, or via high-powered microwave (HPM) pulse emitters. This latter form of the phenomena is often referred to as HPM. For a primer on the effects of these weapons, see Geis (2003).

30. Ibid: 111.

31. Office of the Secretary of Defense (2007: 23).

32. Hsiao (2008).

33. Office of the Secretary of Defense (2007: 23).

In addition to the conventional capabilities above, China is also developing emerging, unconventional forms of military power including space and counter-space systems, directed-energy (DE) weapons, and information operations. In the eyes of Chinese analysts, modern states' dependence on space represents a strategic weakness.[34] To that end, China is developing anti-satellite options including ground attack, co-orbital 'killer' satellites, directed energy (DE) weapons, and electronic attack.[35] China's goal is 'information supremacy,' thereby increasing battlefield transparency for Chinese commanders while creating 'fog' for their enemy.[36] By 2030, China will use asymmetric forces to confuse, weaken, and slow their adversaries. After decades of sustained growth and modernisation, China will be a military peer of the United States, at least regionally, and will be a rising superpower with limited blue-water naval capabilities.

For Asian air force thinkers, there are two sets of challenges a rising China may present. First, Chinese leaders face several largely internal stressors that could threaten goal of achieving a 'harmonious society' in a 'harmonious world.' These challenges include the possibility of a sharp economic downturn, loss of domestic food production, or an inability to meet domestic energy needs. Any one of these three could foment internal instability, or cause the Chinese government to find itself with vital interests that clash with those of its neighbours on matters such as water rights or access to resources.[37] Second, as China emerges as one of the world's great powers, it is unlikely that China will be able to avoid assuming the mantle of leadership in world crises or affairs. At least a minor change to the '24-Character Strategy' would seem to lie ahead, as budgetary strains in the Western states will likely lead to increased pressure on China to assume its fair share of global peace-keeping and

---

34. Wang (2000)
35. Tellis (2007). For reasons both for and against a Chinese Military Strategy in Space, see Ajey Lele's chapter on the "Future of Asian Space Powers" in this book.
36. Ibid.
37. With regard to food production, there is early evidence of some of this friction with China's neighbours. Press reports from 2007-2010 have indicated that China may be harbouring plans to divert the Brahmaputra River for both hydroelectric power and agricultural reasons. This would affect the flow of a river which is a principle lifeline for hundreds of millions of people in India and Bangladesh. The unintended consequences of such a diversion could be severe. See Samanta (2009). See also The Daily Mail (2009).

humanitarian relief responsibilities. This would have significant implications for Chinese airpower structures. For the rest of Asia, air forces will simultaneously need to be able to counter a potentially aggressive China, should internal stability fail; or work with a 'harmonious' China in regional humanitarian operations should China's peaceful rise continue.

Resurgent Russia[38]

Developed prior to the Russia's invasion of Abkhazia and South Ossetia, this alternative future scenario poses a conflict of interests between a modernised and stronger Russia, and the United States and nations in Southwest Asia. This scenario is made more plausible by recent changes in Russian governance, which appears to be on a path toward greater centralised control.[39] This combined with Russia's historic paranoia and belief that it needs a buffer along its perimeter —a concept incompatible with the idea of self-determination of governance in the international community—create the tensions found in this scenario. Russia, the world's largest and most mineral-rich nation may present a formidable challenge in the future as it taps its vast oil, natural gas, and mineral resources.[40]

Russia has had a turbulent history as it moved from its Tsarist past, through the Soviet interregnum, to its brief flirtation with democracy. This history and its associated cultural pressures have instilled in the Russian psyche a desire for stability and strong leadership.[41] Furthermore, Russia tends to value stability and strong leadership even when these traits conflict with post-Renaissance democratic ideals.[42] After each change in governance, Russia has always returned to an authoritarian style government that seeks to lead Russia back on

38. The Resurgent Russia scenario comes largely from Hailes *et al.* (2009).

39. Discussion by Tkachenko (2010). Dr. Tkachenko indicated that Russia's experiment with democracy had 'failed' and that the state was looking to a one-party model with a liberal economy, similar to that of Singapore.

40. Russia's energy reserves rank 1st in the world in natural gas, 9th in oil and 2nd in coal. See CIA (2009).

41. Goldman (2007).

42. For example, the Russian people prefer internal stability to freedom of their media. See Grigoryev (2004).

to the world stage. Their history explains why Russia often displays the mentality of a paranoid nation.[43] As such, a resurgent Russia[44] may become a challenge for the international community.

Russia is already reasserting itself as a world power in terms of its geography, politics, nationalism, and religion.[45] Prime Minister (formerly President) Vladimir Putin is working to restore a sense of nationalism in the Russian people. Among the recent efforts to restore this Russian pride include the claiming of the North Pole[46] and reviving the Russian space programme to be the first country to send a manned mission to Mars.[47] This 'flexing' of international muscle and technological prowess is an effort to show Russian citizens that they are part of a strong and resurgent Russia. In pursuit of security Russia is spending more of its GDP on its military, and is using its economic clout generated by oil and gas to wield power over her neighbours.[48]

Three major factors appear to drive Russia's future. Her paranoia and need for security along her borders, is the first. The prospect for significant economic growth, enabled by Russia's mineral wealth, is the second. Lastly, significant demographic changes including a decline in its overall population. These population changes are exacerbated by the concomitant increase in the Muslim population in Russia's border regions, especially near the Middle East and South Asia.

The economic forces at work, principally the revenue and power generated by its oil and gas sales, will enable Russia's resurgence. Russia's mineral, coal, oil, and natural gas resources are the largest on Earth.[49] In addition, Russia has vast reserves of iron, platinum, uranium, nickel, cobalt, and a host of other key minerals needed for

43. Ibid.
44. Anderson (2003).
45. Ibid.
46. Zarakhovich (2007).
47. Space Daily (2007). It reports that Russia is not only investing billions of additional dollars into its space programme, but that it intends to put a man on Mars not later than 2025.
48. Weir (2007). Since Weir's commentary, Russia has again used its status as the principal natural gas supplier to Europe to demonstrate its international clout. Russia cut off gas supplies to Europe in order to negotiate not only higher prices for gas supplied to Ukraine, but to suggest to Ukraine that Russia would 'have to respond' if Ukraine joined NATO. See: Russian News and Information Agency (2008).
49. Energy Information Administration (n.d.).

modern manufacturing. Many of these lie in areas of Siberia that have only recently become accessible, and are now being tapped.[50]

Meanwhile, Russia's population is declining. Its population peaked in the early 1990s at around 148.5 million, and has since dropped to only 140.7 million.[51] Although there are many social factors contributing to this decline, the nation's dismal health care system is arguably the most direct cause. Russia has a 40 per cent preventable mortality rate as a result of poor preventive medicine, sub-standard medical facilities, and limited health care accessibility.[52] Meanwhile, Russia's Muslim population along its southern borders continues to increase. Thus, ethnic Slavic population in Russia is declining while the Muslim population is increasing, fusing a potential population time bomb for the future.

This simultaneous exploitation of her mineral wealth with a declining population will produce a situation where per capita income is likely to rise. At the same time Russia will not have the population for manpower-intensive military operations. This will force Russia to modernise its military, using advanced technology to compensate for smaller forces.[53]

Russia's vital interests will extend, at a minimum, to its border states. Russia will field a modern military defense of her homeland, and secure a buffer around the Russian state. While focussed on their immediate region, Russia will possess asymmetric capabilities. Russia has already made forays into advanced technologies like nanotechnology in order to improve its capabilities. These investments

---

50. Internal Russian sources estimate their mineral wealth to be much greater than the value of their fuel reserves, possibly in excess of 30 trillion US dollars. See: Russia the Great (2009). The title of the website here may strike some readers as comical, but it is evidence of the intense national pride which ingrained in the Russian psyche. It is this pride which makes security and prominence in world affairs so vitally important to the Russian people and their culture.

51. 1990s population data is taken from Ward (1997). For current population data see CIA (2009).

52. Gitelman *et al.* (2005). Russia has a very high infant mortality rate, a high suicide rate, and a working-age population death rate that is 350 per cent of the European average. For more information see CIA (2009) and the World Health Organization, "Mental Health", *http://www.who.int/mental_health/prevention/suicide/suiciderates/en/* (accessed January 29, 2009).

53. This is in marked contrast to the Soviet military model of building large quantities of unsophisticated equipment, because it had a surplus of manpower.

could lead to miniaturised inexpensive unmanned aerial vehicles (UAVs) capable of delivering bio-engineered weapons. Recent Russian cyber attacks against Estonia and Georgia demonstrate that the Kremlin is interested in and will pursue non-traditional approaches to warfare.[54] Putin himself has discussed 'new spirals' in an arms race that could include nuclear weapons based in space, and will maintain global power projection capabilities.[55] In short, 'Russia is back, and it no longer accepts its decline into obscurity.'[56] If vital interests conflict, states in Russia's near abroad should be prepared to contend with a smaller but more modern and professional Russian military.

In sum, the resurgent Russia of this alternative future is a major supplier of global energy resources aligned with neither the West nor the East. As a result, it will be particularly concerned with defending its natural resources and its supporting infrastructure. Its military will be smaller than during the Cold War, but more capable with professional soldiers and technologically advanced systems. They will have the ability to project the nation's full combat power into their 'near abroad' including Eastern Europe, the Caucuses, and Central Asia, but will have limited ability to deploy conventional forces beyond this region. In part to make up for the limitations in its conventional forces, Russia will develop significant strategic reach through its nuclear forces and development of advanced strategic technologies of all the Air Force warfighting domains, including air, space, and cyberspace.

For the militaries of Asia, Russia's modernisation may pose two challenges: First, Russia's xenophobia has resulted in multiple operations into areas of South Asia including Chechnya, South Ossetia and Abkhazia. Further military operations by Russia to secure her perimeter or protect her interests appear likely. Second, as many of the areas in which Russia has historically intervened are in or border the oil-rich Middle East, managing the consequences of disrupted energy flows may be among the challenges Asian nations may face from a resurgent Russia in the future.

---

54. The Economist (2007).
55. Tirpak (2006).
56. Geopolitical Diary (2008).

Failed State: Nigeria[57]

While not a specifically Asian case study, this failed state scenario embodies the challenges typical of failed states and ungoverned spaces. Such situations require various combinations of humanitarian relief operations, peace-keeping, peace-making, and efforts designed to restore the ungoverned space to independent functionality. The roles and missions that appeared in this failed state scenario would, in great part, apply to any situation where a major disaster resulted in the government becoming unable to affectively function.[58] In Asia, such circumstances have been or can be caused by cyclones or typhoons, tsunamis, or extremely large earthquakes. They can also be caused by governmental collapse.[59] Nigeria is used here merely as an illustration of these challenges.

Nigeria has been called the best example of the 'paradox of plenty,' where tremendous natural resources create great wealth, which in turn creates 'extravagant corruption, deep poverty, polarised income distributions, and poor economic performance.'[60] While the US Department of State views Nigeria as relatively stable, increasing conflict is occurring along a religious fault line that bifurcates the nation. The 2009 Failed State Index ranks Nigeria as the 15th country most likely to fail out of the 177 states they analysed,[61] where failure implies that the state cannot govern itself nor can it provide for internal security and the basic needs of its people. Further, when states fail it is usually a long-term problem. A World Bank study shows that states listed as failed in 1980 are generally still failed today, and they estimate that the average failed state will require 56 years to recover.[62]

57. The text in this section is derived from Kinnan *et al.* (2010).

58. This lack of functionality need not apply to an entire state. For example, the Indonesian Tsunami of December 26, 2004, left much of Aceh as an ungoverned space with over 100,000 dead and nearly 500,000 displaced. The result was an area of Indonesia which for a time being was left ungoverned and in need of rapid delivery of aid and other societal stabilisation services, even though the government in Jakarta was still functioning.

59. As of 2009, the Fund for Peace ranked seven Asian states as being among the 20 states most likely to fail. Among these were: Iraq, Afghanistan, Pakistan, Burma (Myanmar), North Korea, Bangladesh and East Timor. See Foreign Policy (2010).

60. Lubeck *et al.* (2007).

61. Foreign Policy (2010).

62. Wyler (2007).

Few states have the potential to be as disruptive to the global economy as a failed Nigeria. Nigeria is a one of the world's 20 largest economies and one of the world's largest suppliers of light 'sweet' crude oil, exporting over 2.4 million barrels a day.[63] By 2030, roughly a quarter of United States' oil imports will likely be supplied by Nigeria.[64]

Nigeria's infrastructure investments have been spotty. Reliable electricity exists for the cities and the road network is best developed in oil-rich areas. The challenge is the top one per cent of the wealthiest families in Nigeria control over 80 per cent of the oil profits, and they have been directing investments in areas that improve their personal portfolios—much of this overseas.[65] Should oil revenue not be used to improve national infrastructure, this would increase animosity between regions, and create issues of governmental illegitimacy.

Nigeria has the largest population in Africa, and it is growing. Expected to surpass 225 million people before 2030, Nigeria could become the fifth most populous nation on Earth.[66] Despite being a former British colony with English as its official language, Nigeria is diverse, with over 350 separate ethnic groups.[67] Four main groups make up over three quarters of this population: Hausa and Fulani (29 per cent), Yoruba (21 per cent) and Igbo (18 per cent), the remainder are made up of eight other significant population groups with their own languages that define them politically and culturally.[68]

These disparities and the trappings of Nigeria's colonial past have created tensions that make establishing an integrated, coherent, and

63. CIA (2009).

64. Lubeck *et al.* (2007), report that by 2015, 25 per cent of United States oil imports could come from Nigeria. Given that Nigeria's wells are not expected to run dry, this level of supply is expected throughout this timeline.

65. Thompson (2007).

66. United Nations Population database project Nigeria's population to reach 226,855,000 by 2030. UN (2005; 2006). The United Nations calculates that Nigeria's population will double in 32 years based on the following formula: $\log(2)/\log(1 + r)$, where r = population growth rate.

67. Levinson (1998). As a note, the CIA (2009) lists the number of ethnic groups in Nigeria being slightly smaller, at only around 250. However, whether Nigeria has 250 or 350 different ethnic groups is not crucial to the central point that Nigeria is an exceptionally diverse nation, and that this diversity is challenging to manage.

68. Foreign Policy (2008).

legitimate government difficult.[69] By 2030, Nigerians will have an average age of 16.7 years and a life expectancy of 54—it will likely have many disaffected and underemployed.[70] It already has the sixth largest Muslim population in the world,[71] and has a nearly equal balance of Muslims and Christians. This balance is approaching a tipping point because of the faster population growth in the Islamic north, which is ruled under Sharia Law, unlike the Christian provinces in the south.[72] By 2030, Nigeria will have a Muslim majority, which will fundamentally change Nigeria's domestic political situation.[73]

With limited industrial development and with oil production consigned mainly to the Christian south, 90 per cent of funding to the states and localities is provided by the federal government, largely

---

69. Library of Congress (2006).
70. See Goings (2007). According to the CIA (2009), the youth population (under age 16) accounts for 41.7 per cent of the total population. Given the average fertility rate of 5.6 children, the relatively low life expectancy of Nigerian men and women (less than 54 years of age), the percentage of young people will likely continue to increase.
71. Ibid. shows Nigeria to have approximately 146,255,000 people, of which half, or 73 million are Muslim. This places Nigeria at between fourth and sixth place in terms of states with Muslim population—very nearly tied with Egypt and Turkey. For more information, see: *https://www.cia.gov/library/publications/the-world-factbook/geos/ni.html#People* as of January 23, 2009.
72. Paden (2007).
73. This percentage is a collogue synthesised from research reports from the United Nations Development Programme, the United Nations Population Programme, and the World Bank; a briefing by Goings (2007); and statistical information found in the CIA (2009). These sources generally agree that Nigeria's population is currently more than 50 per cent Muslim, although some Islamic publications claim higher figures. The last official recorded census taken in Nigeria was in 1991. In 2006, Nigeria's National Population Commission attempted a new census, but the results of this effort are widely dismissed because of flawed collection and calculation methodologies and a failure to collect information about controversial demographics like religion. Charges of political corruption in the census process levied at President Obasanjo and his political party further tainted the results. As a result, the 2006 census was rejected by the 36 governors who are required to approve the results, under Nigeria's constitution, as state population statistics directly affect the proportional representation in the National Assembly and the federal allocation of funds to each state. Previous census attempts have led to conflict between the 12 Islamic states and the 24 non-Islamic states. The unofficial 2006 population statistics did show a 63 per cent increase in the number of people over the 1991 census. The United Nations, World Bank, and the CIA population projections generally agree that the overall population growth rate is approximately 2.025 per cent annually. CIA (2009) states as of 2008, the voting age population accounts for 55.3 per cent of the Nigerian population. Population growth rates are higher in the 12 northern Muslim provinces, potentially because under the Sharia law practiced there, men are allowed to marry up to four women, while the Christian provinces ban polygamy. Based on these data, it is expected that by 2030, the voting age population of the 12 northern states will make up the majority of voters within the country.

from oil export revenues.[74] State governors budget and distribute this money, with much of the oil wealth flowing to the predominant political party.[75] While revenue sharing provides much needed government funding for the non-lucrative agrarian north, it also intensifies ethnic tension between the north and the oil producing south, where politicians frequently 'skim off' some of the earnings. This has resulted in unrest and military *coup d'états* in 1966, 1975, 1983, 1985 and 1993.[76]

As the Islamic population in the north grows, Nigeria will face a transfer of power. In this scenario, the ruling and corrupt Christian government loses the elections to a well-organised and united slate of Islamic candidates and parties. The conflict between the two religious factions intensifies as the ruling party refuses to cede control of the oil wealth and its trappings, and refuses to hand off power to the newly-elected Islamic government, which declares Nigeria an Islamic Republic. This situation triggers a national crisis and the failure of the Nigerian state. Nigeria splits into lawless areas and criminal fiefdoms. With hundreds of ethnicities, Nigeria is ripe for fragmentation into a myriad of pieces. With no central authority, legitimate economic activity rapidly declines, and is replaced by criminality. Oil workers flee the violence, abandoning their facilities in search of safety, which effectively halts oil production throughout the Niger Delta region and the Gulf of Guinea. The resultant global oil shock is painful. All major economies are threatened, and the population of Nigeria—roughly one-quarter of a billion strong, is faced with imminent pestilence, famine, and civil war. The resultant humanitarian crisis would be 130 times larger than Darfur.

With Nigeria on the brink of civil war, the global community, will be faced with the difficult choices of whether, how, and when to intervene. Easing global oil prices would require stabilisation of the nation in a peace enforcement operation.[77] Simultaneously with protecting the oil fields and economic infrastructure to help the country re-build post-

74. Paden (2007).
75. Ibid.
76. Maier (2000).
77. Department of Defense Dictionary of Military and Associated Terms, s.v., *http://www.dtic.mil/doctrine/jel/doddict/index.html* (accessed 12 May 2008).

crisis; operations to relieve human suffering throughout the country, and transition to a legitimate indigeneous government will be necessary. Accomplishing these missions quickly is essential.

Whether in Nigeria, or after a state failure or natural disaster in Asia, airpower must be able to do several things to mitigate human suffering i.e., stop the spread of disease, and restore order. The key initial airpower capability will be airlift. To ensure against the spread of disease, clean water and medicines, airpower will need to reach the affected population quickly. Many disasters will also require security and medical personnel to be transported to the region quickly. In saving lives, minutes matter; and sea lift, while able to carry more, will not be fast enough for an initial response. Secondly, the ability to swiftly coordinate relief operations across a myriad of international governmental and non-governmental organisations will be critical, as a failure to succeed in this endeavour could result widespread unnecessary suffering. While leadership is not inherently an airpower capability, airlift will play such a major role early in the crisis, that leadership familiar with airpower capabilities will be crucial. To fully understand the scope of the crisis, surveillance and reconnaissance will be required, which is best accomplished by air and space assets.

Asian air forces, therefore, need to prepare to carry out missions of humanitarian aid, transport of first-responder personnel, conduct surveillance and reconnaissance missions to determine where aid is most critically needed, and accept the initial leadership responsibilities to manage the initial response when the local government becomes incapacitated. Further, given that major disasters like the Indonesian Tsunami required the coordination of many nations to address, air forces across Asia need to develop working relationships that enable them to coordinate these efforts to best aid people who find themselves in a disaster region or failed state.

Jihadist Insurgency

The last alternative future scenario examines the possible challenges posed by a well-resourced and well-financed insurgency emanating from the heart of the Middle East. As was seen with the Taliban and Al Qaeda, some insurgent groups can be sufficiently well-financed to destabilise or control territory or even nations. They also seek to export extremism, seeking greater influence. This has recently been true especially in the regions of the Middle East, Africa and Southwest Asia.[78]

Given the economic and geostrategic importance of many of these areas, successful insurgencies can cause significant global economic disruptions and challenge the security of established members of the community of nations. Any economic disruption resulting from a successful insurgent takeover of a country in the Middle East or Southwest Asia would threaten the vital interests of many nations and require a response.

Throughout the Middle East and Southwest Asia, several cultural factors create an environment in which insurgent warfare can flourish. There are conflicts within the region over religion, to include schisms within the Muslim world; tribal loyalties often superseding national identity; and widespread poverty. All of these create conditions conducive to terrorist activities.

Religion is the single-most pervasive aspect of Middle Eastern society, with at least three distinct Islamic sects: Sunnism, Shiism and Wahhabism/Salafism—all competing for dominance.[79] Sunnism recognises the Quran and the Sunnah[80] as the sources of faith, and the majority of Muslims in the world are Sunnis.[81] The rift between the Sunnis and Shiites is rooted in a conflict over who should have taken the reigns as the leader of Islamic people, or the 'caliph,' which ensued after the religion's founder, the Prophet Muhammad, died. This difference in succession has implications for traditions central to

---

78. Al Qaeda has used the theological construct that all Muslims are part of the *Ummah* (community of believers). This implies that an attack on any part of the community is an attack upon all. So-called 'Islamic' insurgents have used this argument to suggest that the West's creation of the Israeli state in 1948 is an on-going attack on Islam, requiring a response by all faithful Muslims. With this rationale, Jihadist insurgents are attempting to spread their version of Islam, and their desire to attack the West to increasingly large segments of the *Ummah* or community of believers. See Mackinlay and Al-baddiway (2007).
79. Tensions between the Sunnis and Shiites, especially in Iraq have been written about widely. See Haas (2006) and Stannard (2006).
80. The Sunnah translates into English as 'trodden path' and essentially refers to the way the prophet Muhammad lived his life.
81. Vassiliev (1998).

the faith.[82] Wahhabism and Salafism are religious-political movements within Islam whose ideological bases lie in an attempt to recapture a pure, undistorted Islam.[83] Wahhabism is often traced to Muhammad ibn Abd al-Wahhab (1703-1792) who taught on the Saudi Peninsula, while Salafism is a stream of Islamic fundamentalism similar to Wahhabism that originates from outside the Arabian Peninsula. Both Wahhabist and Salifist movements reject all changes in Islam after its early period, often referring to Islamic variants accommodating modern culture as heresy.

After religion, the most significant source of cultural identity for most Middle Eastern people is their family or tribal membership. Two concepts of the tribal system, kinship and nobility, affect relationships and behaviour in the region.[84] In this feudal system, the dominant tribes essentially run businesses and extort money and resources in exchange for protection from outside invaders. Tribes generally do not trust each other, thus arranged marriages to gain influence with rival tribal Sheikhs are still used to dampen the likelihood of conflict. This 'mafia' type of social arrangement is a normal method of business payment between them.

The population in most Middle Eastern and Southwest Asian nations is growing rapidly, is increasingly urban, and young. Today, urban dwellers comprise over 75 per cent of the population and increasing.[85] Providing education for the resulting number of urbanised youth is challenging, with the combined literacy rate among Middle Eastern nations at 52 per cent and declining, with only a little

82. Shiites believe that the legitimate successor to the Prophet Muhammad was his son-in-law and closest confidant, Ali. Sunnis regard the first caliph was Abu Bakr. The differences between these faiths is based in part on the way the Prophet lived his life, much of which was handed down by either word of mouth and general practice (the *Sunnah*) or via collections of the prophetic tradition (the *Hadith*). Even the Sunnis came to recognise Ali as the fourth caliph, but by that time, a divergence in the interpretations of some of the Prophet's actions had occurred across the two sects. This divergence in practices and beliefs persists till today. This disparity impacts the more fundamentalist beliefs of Salafism and Wahhabism, as these sects believe that the proper practice of Islam was defined by the first three caliphs. The Wahhabi and Salafist followers ascribe to the puranitical form of Sunni Islam regarding succession. In the end, this pits the Wahhabi and Saflist followers against the Sunnis, in that they believe in only a strict and ancient interpretation of traditions, and pits them against the Shiites by virtue of their disparate beliefs in early succession.

83. Schwartz (2003).

84. Helms (1981).

85. Wilson and Graham (1994).

more than half of all children in the Middle East attending secondary schools. This poor quality of public education is responsible for a 'low level of knowledge attainment and poor and deteriorating analytical and innovative capacity' among Arab children.[86] In the long-term, this will create unemployment and underemployment of poorly educated young men, potentially fuelling unrest. Many who do get an education get it through the *madrassa* system dedicated to Islamic studies.

The influx of petro-dollars throughout the Middle East has helped ease tensions between the various groups and factions. Standards of living have risen, and in terms of per capita income, some nations of the region are now among the wealthiest on earth.[87] Over time, however, the picture becomes bleaker. Peak oil production has likely passed, and by 2030, will be markedly less than today.[88] The rapidly rising population of the region means these decreasing revenues will be divided among an increasingly larger number of people, causing per capita income to decline and poverty to increase. This will place a significant strain on the social safety nets of most Middle Eastern nations.

Within this alternative future, conflicts between Islamic factions combined with increasing poverty destabilise a region in the heart of the Middle East where a Wahhabi sect steps in to provide social services, and exercises *de facto* control over population and territory. From this base, this sect initiates an insurgency from the heart of the Middle East.[89]

Should such a scenario unfold, the insurgents would likely have access to the resident military and civilian infrastructure of the region. Indigeneous military capabilities of many Middle Eastern nations are a mix of weapons from all over the world including Russia, the United States, France and China. If extremist elements were able to gain control of national resources, specifically the military, this would present a significant threat to international interests. Further, as advanced technologies proliferate, an insurgent group will eventually

86. United Nations Human Development Programme (2002).

87. The per capita income in Qatar, for instance, is over $100,000 per year, ranking it 2nd in the world, just after the principality of Liechtenstein. Kuwait is 6th. For comparison, the United States is 10th with a per capita income of around $48,000 per year. See: CIA (2009).

88. United States Department of Energy (2004).

89. Refer to Footnote number 82 for the conflict within Muslim factions. See Haas (2006) and Stannard (2006).

be able to access weapons capabilities previously held only by nation states.

Therefore, this alternative future creates a stressing scenario. It posits that the monarchies that make up the majority of governments in the oil-rich Middle East will be directly or indirectly attacked by this insurgency, threatening global access to the region's oil and natural gas supplies. Further, the extremist beliefs of these insurgents will drive them to use the resources at their disposal, and the wealth those resources confer, to launch a sustained, high-tech, and well-financed terrorist campaign against the nations of the Arabian Peninsula, and against countries like the United States who would seek to defend the status quo.

In such a scenario, the community of nations would need to band together to defeat this insurgency, as disruptions to global energy supplies would threaten growth not only in North America and Europe, but throughout the developing world, especially India and China, as well.

To assist in such a global effort, Asian air forces would need the capacity to work closely in international coalitions. The proximity of Asian air forces and basing structure to this scenario will be important, as placing 'non-believers' on the ground in the Middle East could exacerbate this insurgency. Thus, an Asian air basing infrastructure capable and willing to host coalition forces from other parts of the world would be an important contribution. This aversion to non-believers in Islamic territory may also increase the value of some robotic or unmanned systems. The capacity to do reconnaissance and precision strike against insurgent leaders, and conduct lift of supplies to the threatened Arab states will be important airpower capabilities. Communications technologies that enable a coalition of nations from disparate parts of the world to work in concert with each other will be crucial for success. As the insurgents will likely have access to some advanced defensive systems due to arms and technology proliferation, Asian and coalition air forces will need to have robust defensive capabilities aboard their aircraft.

Operations Analysis Results

As mentioned above, the researchers developed a quantitative model[90] to evaluate 58 separate notional future systems for their potential utility across these four alternative futures. Each future scenario had its own separate model with its own internal weighting factors specific to that future. The expectation was that the types of systems required in each scenario would be distinct. One of the major findings in this study is that the types of systems needed for major state-on-state conflict cover, as a lesser included case, the types of systems and capabilities required for insurgent warfare and failed state scenarios. This can be graphically seen in Figure 19.1. Notice that the four lines depicting the ratings of the 58 systems are nearly parallel across all four models, showing that little variation occurs in required capabilities regardless of the type of warfare encountered.[91]

As these capabilities were explored further, there was only one core air force capability that showed substantively or statistically significant variation across the four futures. This variation was in the area of space. The study does show that space-based capabilities are less relevant to insurgent and failed state scenarios than they are in state-on-state warfare. This is highlighted further in Figure 19.2, where this same capability list was plotted in a state-on-state *versus* a non-state actor scenario. All of the major spikes in the figure are systems that contain a significant space component. Again, other than these spikes, the parallelism in the rank-ordering of these future systems between types of warfare is striking.

These 58 future systems were mapped to a mutually exclusive and comprehensively exhaustive list of 172 key enabling technologies. A quantitative model was then used to evaluate the utility of each enabling technology based on the value of the systems to which it applied. Even more so than with the systems evaluated, the key

---

90. A full discussion on the model design can be found in Geis *et al.* (2009a).

91. Had the systems for irregular warfare been fundamentally different from those needed for conventional conflict, this graphical plot would have approximated the letter 'X,' with the plot lines for the different types of conflict intersecting on the chart, and having very different slopes.

Figure 19.1

Scoring of All 58 Systems across All Alternative Futures

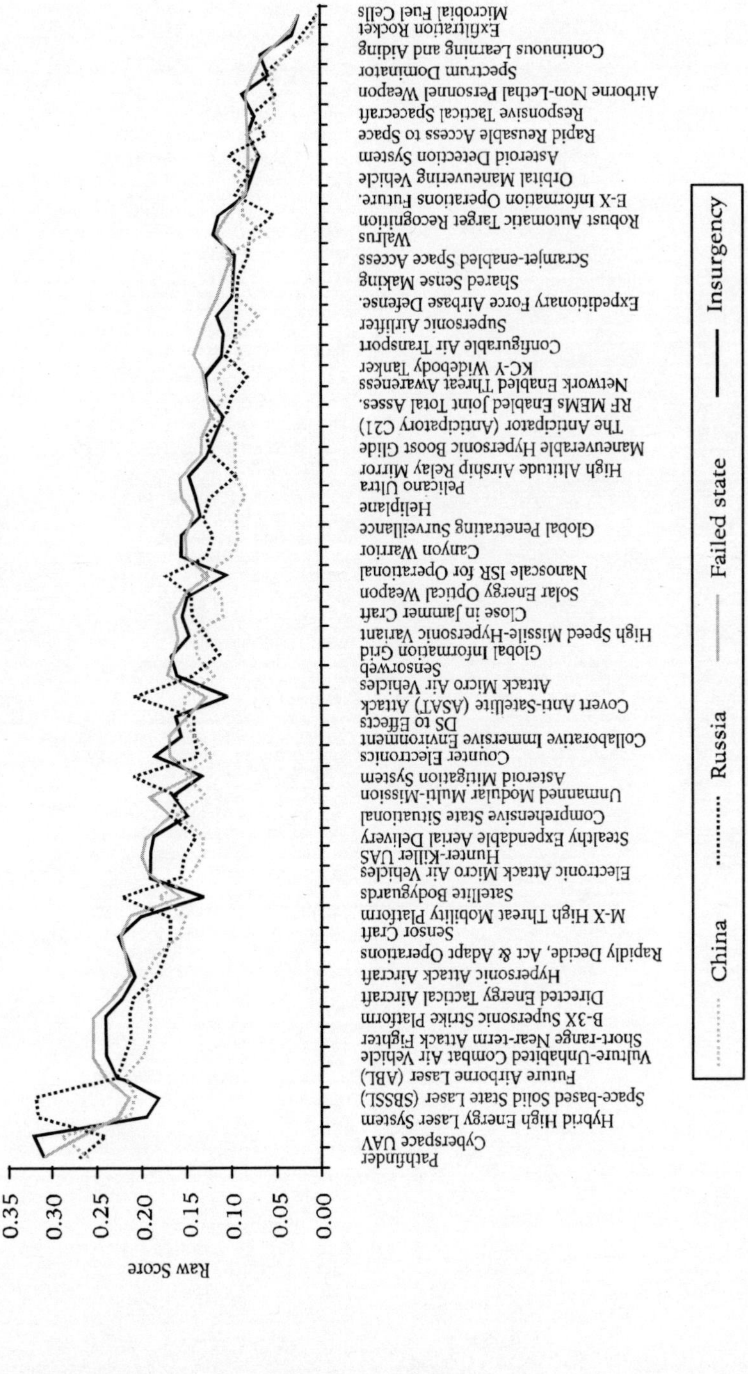

Source: Geis *et al.* (2009b).

Figure 19.2

Scoring of the 58 Systems in State-on-State versus Non-State Warfare

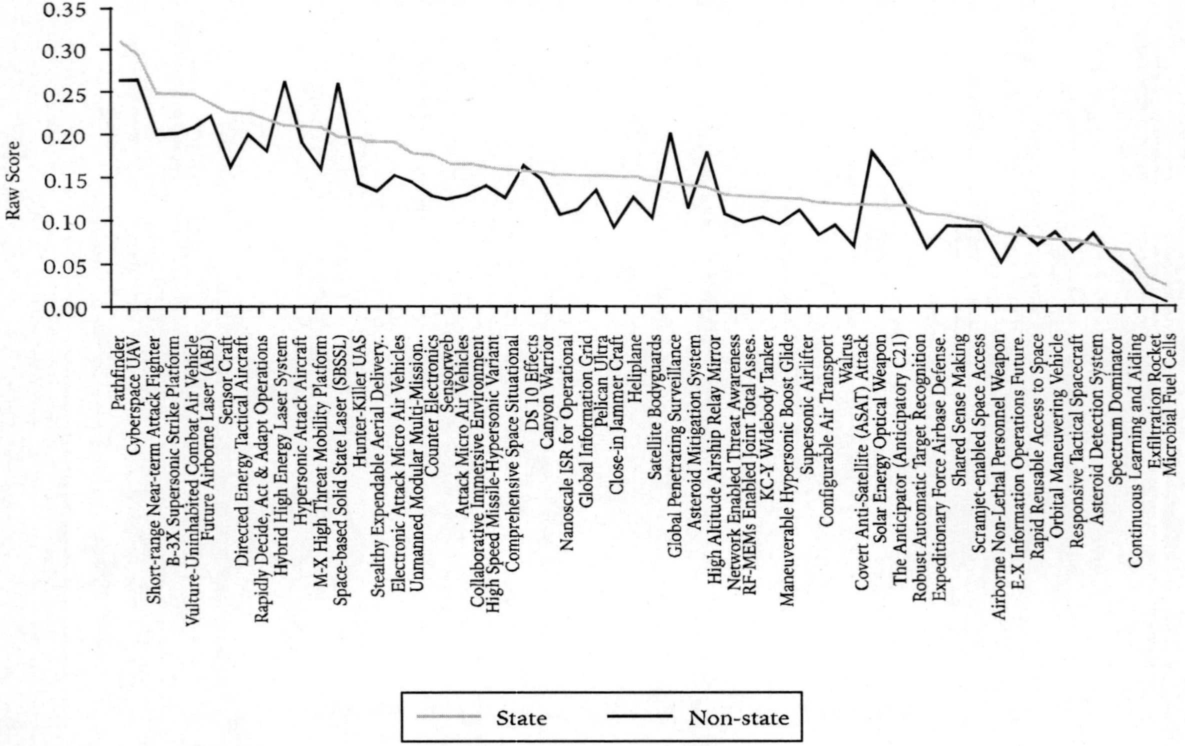

Source: Geis *et al.* (2009b): 21.

underlying technologies did not vary from scenario to scenario. In fact, the four technology scoring curves are even more closely clustered than they were in scoring the 58 conceptual systems.

In the end, the analysis showed that all but one of the future systems required key enabling technologies that ranked below 100th in score, with even the highest rated concepts having several technology enablers in or near the tail of the technology ranking curve. Detailed analysis shows that disinvestment in the bottom 20 per cent of technologies results in the inability to field some systems that placed in the top 25 per cent, and will foreclose nearly one-half of the future options. The fundamental implication for all air forces in 2030 is that any budgetary strategy that disinvests in science and technology research is a very high-risk strategy, both economically, and militarily.

Conclusions and Recommendations

As stated above, the strategic environment in 2030 presents difficult challenges stemming from accelerating technology interacting with a shifting strategic landscape that will produce massive, dynamic change. This change acts as a catalyst creating disturbing and disruptive threats and is a serious challenge to air forces in Asia.

For Asia and elsewhere, future enemies, like those of the past, will continue to be motivated by resources, fear, and hate.[92] What is changing is that to a level never before seen, these enemies will be empowered through education, technology and globalisation to directly challenge states and attack places that heretofore would never have been able to reach. As already seen in Iraq, Afghanistan, New York, London and Mumbai, future enemies will be more difficult to find, harder to hit, more widely distributed, and potentially more dangerous.

---

92. These motivations for conflict have remained unchanged for as long as the history of warfare has been recorded. Thucydides, in his *History of the Peloponnesian War* (431 BCE), argued that it was resources, fear and hatred that frequently were at the root of conflict between Athens and her nearby fellow city-states.

Historically, as depicted in Figure 19.3, the types of conflicts that were rare, such as the World Wars, were the conflicts of greatest impact. As we move towards 2030, single actors or small groups will have the capacity to create high impact events, making future warfare more dangerous.

Also as a result of technological advances, the speed with which warfare occurs will increase. The observe-orient-decide-act cycle, often called the 'OODA-loop' will shrink toward an 'OODA-point.' Increasingly, warfare decisions will be executed at machine speeds by machines pre-programmed with commander's intent. The airman will no longer be in the loop, but rather on the loop—able to stop the execution of the machine code as necessary, but unable to execute a decision cycle fast enough to remain ahead of a technologically savvy adversary.

Figure 19.3

Spectrum of Conflict versus Impact

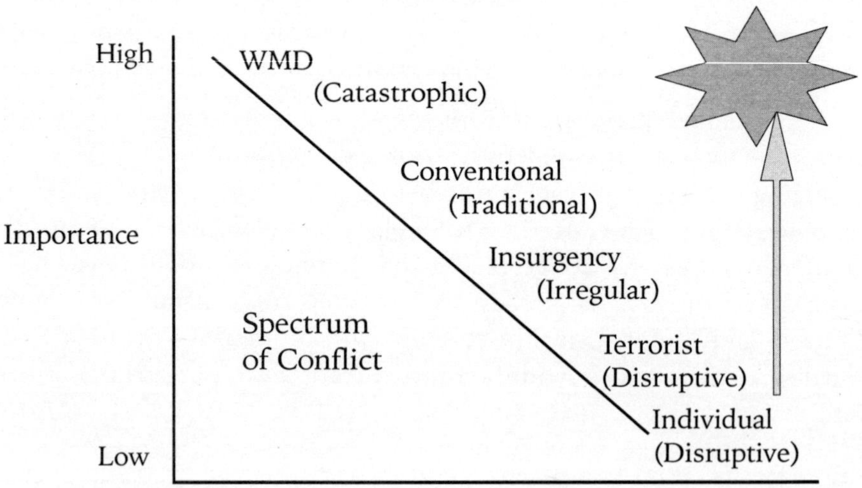

Source: Moseley (2008).

Figure 19.4

The Observe-Orient-Decide-Act Cycle or OODA-Loop

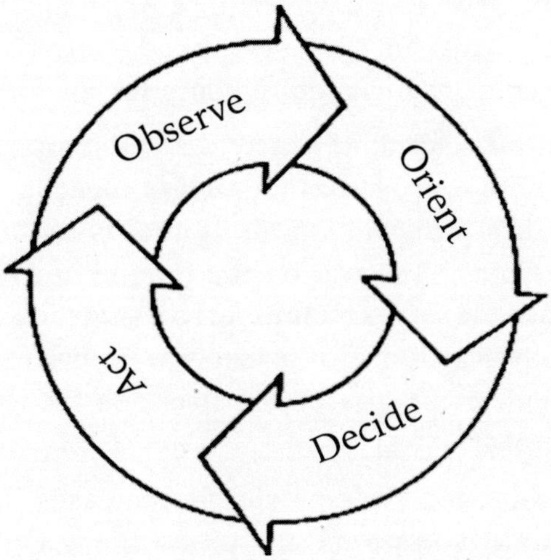

This very form of warfare is already taking place today. In the domain of cyberspace, most computers are armed with programmes designed to execute their owner's intent of keeping the hard drive free of viruses and malware. Anti-virus software is installed on computer systems, because the speed with which a virus can intrude into the computer is faster than the speed with which a human can react. This same dynamic will spread over time to other fields of warfare. Unmanned vehicles and missiles will be equipped with the ability to seek and destroy adversary targets, and defense systems will need to react at machine speeds to keep air bases and population centres safe from attack.

In 2030, targets will be more mobile, distributed, fleeting, deeply buried, often located in highly urbanised areas, and/or close to sites protected under international law. As a result, air forces will need systems and technologies to quickly locate and identify targets, attribute attacks, and respond to threats. Future weapons will need to be precise. Technologically advanced nations, including Russia and China, may well be employing directed energy weapons in this time frame. These will allow engagements to take place with forensic precision and at the speed of light, so that only the target is harmed with no collateral damage.

Dealing with this new reality will require Asian air forces to adapt. There are commonalities in the top-ranked systems that suggest fundamental changes in future requirements for air forces will occur.

Cyberspace continues to rapidly increase in importance, both as an area for gathering data, but also as an environment in which conflict will reside. Al Qaeda's principle recruiting tool is the Internet, and it has been for some time.[93] The war on the ground in Afghanistan, and the efforts to rid Asia of extreme terrorist groups is largely a manifestation in physical space of a lost war in cyberspace. Thus, a new domain is opening in warfare, and it is one for which Asian air forces need to be ready.

The role for unmanned systems clearly increases in the future—half of the top-ranked systems are unmanned. Dull, dirty, and dangerous missions are often considered for the principal use of unmanned or remotely-piloted systems. The future will place increased importance on monitoring vast stretches of territory.[94] This can be done more easily via robotics and computers than by manned platforms. Unmanned systems may also confer an advantage in survivability. Surface-based defenses are improving rapidly, and future aircraft will be increasingly vulnerable. Inexpensive unmanned disposable drones may be a more cost-effective strategy to overwhelm and destroy high-tech modern defensive positions than attacking with, and losing, expensive manned aircraft.

Asian governments will need to shorten their acquisition cycles. As technology moves forward at an increasing rate of speed, new systems will become obsolete more quickly than in the past. Adequate solutions to current airpower issues that are available quickly will be more valuable than 'perfect' solutions that take years to acquire.

---

93. Lia (2008).

94. Constant monitoring of difficult terrain is something better performed when swapping out the crew members every couple of hours is possible to remain fresh in the reconnaissance mission. This is easier with remotely-piloted aircraft (RPA) than a manned platform. With an RPA, the aircraft can continue to monitor and record a particular site, often for 24-36 hours at a time, while the pilots can be swapped out and be given rest breaks to ensure their ability to fully concentrate on the mission.

In a continent as vast as Asia, range and persistence become highly valued airpower capabilities. Most of the high-ranking systems in the study were both of longer range and greater persistence than those which scored poorly. Short-range aircraft require either support from a tanker infrastructure, or increased numbers to compensate for reduced endurance. Either makes short-range and short-endurance systems to be of diminished utility.

As DE weapons reach the battlefield in the 2020s, Asian air forces will need to have effective countermeasures in place. High-powered microwave weapons are likely to be fielded by at least two Asian powers, and will be capable of disrupting, degrading or destroying computer-based command and control systems. Hardening of these systems, both on the ground and in the air, will be an increasingly important consideration as the year 2030 approaches.

Terrorism and piracy will likely remain challenges for Asian nations throughout this time period. This study suggests that greater transparency will be a key element in disrupting or degrading these networks. Intelligence, surveillance and reconnaissance capabilities will be important, as will be the ability to constantly monitor some positions. It is here that unmanned or remotely-piloted systems will have some of their greatest value. It is important to note that these two issues can be related, as terrorist groups can be funded by hijacking assets on the high seas. This has already occurred off the coast of Africa. Yet, the Indian Ocean and Straits of Malacca are among the most important waterways on earth. Asian air forces must play a role in monitoring these areas.

Finally, what is evident across the four scenarios, and is evident in an analysis of the rankings of the underlying technologies, is the importance of communications capabilities enabling forces from different states to work together. Whether in major conventional operations, combating terrorism and piracy, or the conduct of humanitarian relief; the sheer scope of future challenges combined with budgetary constraints means that it is unlikely that major operations will be undertaken by a single nation alone. Instead, close cooperation will be required. Asian air forces need to invest in communications technologies that enable coordination and cooperation with prospective partners so as to operate as an integrated team when the mission dictates. Synergistic command and control capabilities are important in the world of 2030.

In short, Asian air forces in 2030 will need to be versatile. All of the classic mission types will remain, and new ones will arise. States slow to adapt, or those mired in extensive bureaucracy may not succeed, as future military operations will likely involve shortened time scales and compressed decision cycles. Scientific research and development programmes to stay ahead of these compressed decision cycles are essential. The world of the next 20 years is one of exponential change. Asia's air forces will need to be prepared to adapt to this change.

References

Anderson, John (2003). *Religious Liberty in Transitional Societies: The Politics of Religion.* New York: Cambridge University Press. p.118.

Berling, Judith A. (2007). *Confucianism.* Ask Asia.org. *http://www.askasia.org/teachers/essays/essay.php?no=38*

CIA (2009). *The 2008 World Factbook.* See: *https://www.cia.gov/library/publications/the-world-factbook/* as of January 29.

Cliff, Roger, M. Burles, M.S. Chase, D. Eaton, K.L. Pollpeter (2007). *Entering the Dragon's Lair, Chinese Antiaccess Strategies and their Implications for the United States.* Santa Monica, CA: RAND Corp. p.11.

Dalkey, Norman and Olaf Helmer (1963). "An Experimental Application of the DELPHI Method to the Use of Experts", *Management Science* 9(3): 458-67.

Enbelbrecht (Jr.), Joseph A. Robert L. Bivins, Patrick M. Condray, Merrily D. Fecteau, John P. Geis II, and Kevin C. Smith (1996). *Alternate Futures for 2025.* Maxwell AFB, AL: Air University Press. p.1.

Energy Information Administration (n.d.). *Official Energy Statistics of the United States Government: Russia. http://www.eia.doe.gov/emeu/cabs/russia_pipelines.html* (accessed March 31, 2009).

Fisher, R.D. (2004). *Impact of Foreign Weapons & Technology on Modernization of China's People Liberation Army.* Centre for Security Policy. January.

Foreign Policy (2010). "The Failed States Index 2009", *Foreign Policy*, April. Available on-line at: *http://www.foreignpolicy.com/articles/2009/06/22/the_2009_failed_states_index* Accessed April 20, 2010.

Foreign Policy (2008). *Failed States Index 2007.*

Gamer, Robert E. (ed.) (2003). *Understanding Contemporary China.* Boulder, CO: Lynne Rienner Publishers Inc..

Geis, John (2009a). "Toward Blue Horizons: Air Force Requirements in 2030", Paper presented at the annual meeting of the ISA's 50th Annual Convention *Exploring the Past, Anticipating the Future.* New York City, NY: Marriott Marquis. February 15.

Geis, John and Greg Parnell (2009). "Towards Blue Horizons", Paper presented at the *Institute for Operations Research and Management Sciences (INFORMS) Annual Convention.* San Diego, CA. October 12.

Geis, John P. II (2003). "Directed Energy Weapons on the Battlefield: A New Vision for 2025", *Center for Strategy and Technology Occasional Paper* 32. Maxwell Air Force Base, AL: Air University. April. *http://www.au.af.mil/au/awc/awcgate/cst/csat32.pdf* (accessed February 10, 2009).

Geis, John P. II, Gregory S. Parnell, Harry Newton, and Terry Bresnick (2009a). "Toward Blue Horizons", *INFORMS Annual Meeting.* San Diego, CA. October 12.

Geis, John P. II, Christopher J. Kinnan, Ted Hailes, Harry A. Foster, and David Blanks (2009b). *Blue Horizons II: Future Capabilities and Technologies for the Air Force in 2030.* Maxwell AFB, AL: Air University Press. July. p.20.

Geis, John P. II, Blaine Holt, Scott Caine, Ed Donaldson, and Ralph Sandfry (forthcoming). *Discord or Harmonious Society: China in 2030.* Air University Press.

Geopolitical Diary (2008). "Putin's Most Recent Surprise Move", *http://www.stratfor.com/geopolitical_diary_putins_most_recent_surprise_move* (accessed January 29, 2009).

Gitelman, Zvi, Stephen White and Richard Sakwa (2005). *Developments in Russian Politics.* Durham: Duke University Press. p.216.

Goings, Stella A.J. (2007). *Nigeria: Socio-Economic Factors 2007.* Washington D.C.: United States Agency for International Development. September 18.

Goldman Sachs Report (2007). BRICs and Beyond, Goldman Sachs Report, November, *http://www2.goldmansachs.com/ideas/brics/BRICs-and-Beyond.html* (accessed March 5, 2008).

Goldman, Stuart D. (2007). *Russian Political, Economic, and Security Issues and United States Interests.* Congressional Research Service.

Grigoryev (2004). "Russia: The Media and Unfreedom of the Press", *International Communications: A Media Literacy Approach.* Armonk, NY: M.E. Sharpe.

Hailes, Theodore C., Ronald Buckley, David Blanks, Mark Butler, Phillip Preen and Michael Tarlton (2009). *Resurgent Russia in 2030: Challenge for the USAF.* Maxwell Air Force Base, AL: Air University Press. September.

Hansson, Ardo (2010). "China Quarterly Update, March 2010". Forecast made by the World Bank. Available on-line at *http://web.worldbank.org/WBSITE/EXTERNAL/COUNTRIES/EASTASIAPACIFICEXT/CHINAEXTN/0,,contentMDK:22502137~pagePK:1497618~piPK:217854~theSitePK:318950,00.html* accessed April 12, 2010.

Haas, Richard N. (2006). "The New Middle East", *Foreign Affairs* 85(6). November-December.

Helms, Christine Moss (1981). *The Cohesion of Saudi Arabia.* Baltimore, Maryland: Johns Hopkins University Press. p.53.

Hsiao, Russell (2008). "China Navy Floats Three Carrier Plan", *Asia Times*, January 8. *http://www.atimes.com/atimes/China/JA08Ad01.html* (accessed January 21, 2009).

Jackson, J.A., G.S. Parnell, B.L. Jones, L.J. Lehmkuhl, H. Conley, and J. Andrew (1997). "Air Force 2025 Operational Analysis", *Military Operations Research* 3(4): 5-21.

Jintao, Hu (2006). *Scientific Outlook Development.* Lecture. New Haven, CT: Yale University. April 24.

Keeney, R.L. (1992). *Value-Focused Thinking: A Path to Creative Decisionmaking.* Cambridge, MA: Harvard University Press.

Keeney, R.L. and H. Raiffa (1976). *Decision Making with Multiple Objectives and Value Tradeoffs.* New York: Wiley Press.

Kinnan, Christopher J., Daniel B. Gordon, Mark D. DeLong, Douglas W. Jaquish, and Robert S. McCallum (2010). *Failed State 2030: Nigeria—A Case Study.* Maxwell AFB, AL: Air University Press.

Kirkwood, C.W. (1997). *Strategic Decision Making: Multiobjective Decision Analysis with Spreadsheets.* Belmont, CA: Duxbury Press.

Levinson, David (1998). *Ethnic Groups Worldwide: A Ready Reference Handbook.* Phoenix, AZ: Oryx Press. pp.156-57.

Lia, Brynjar (2008). "Al Qaeda's Appeal: Understanding its Unique Selling Points", Lecture at the *Treating Terrorism Conference*. Dubai, United Arab Emirates. March 17.

Library of Congress (2006). *Country Profile: Nigeria*. Federal Research Division. June. p.1.

Lubeck, Paul M., Michael J. Watts and Ronnie Lipschutz (2007). *Convergent Interests: United States Energy Security and the "Securing" of Nigerian Democracy*. Washington D.C.: Center for International Policy. February. p.2.

Mackinlay, John and Alison Al-baddiway (2007). "Rethinking Counterinsurgency", *RAND Counterinsurgency Study* 5. Santa Monica, CA: RAND Corporation. p.22.

Maier, Karl (2000). *This House has Fallen: Midnight in Nigeria*. Public Affairs. p.59.

Moseley, T. Michael (2008). *Blue Horizons 2007: Horizons 21 Project Report*. Maxwell AFB, AL: Air University Press.

Office of the Secretary of Defense (2007). *Annual Report to Congress: Military Power of the People's Republic of China, 2007*. United States Congress. p.6.

Paden, John (2007). *Brief to the National Intelligence Council's Seminar on Nigeria*. September 19.

Parnell, G.H. Conley, J. Jackson, L. Lemkuhl, and J. Andrew (1998). "Foundations 2025: A Framework for Evaluating Future Air and Space Forces", *Management Science* 44/10: 1336-50.

Retier, Dan and Allan C. Stam (2002). *Democracies at War*. Princeton, NJ: Princeton University Press.

Russett, Bruce and John ONeal (2001). *Triangulating Peace: Democracy, Interdependence and International Organisations*. New York: W. W. Norton and Company. p.258.

Russia the Great (2009). "Mineral Resources", *http://russia.rin.ru/guides_e/4319.html* (accessed January 24, 2009).

Russian News and Information Agency (2008). *Wrap: Russia, Ukraine Agree on Gas; Discuss NATO*. December 2. *http://en.rian.ru/world/20080212/99058682.html* (accessed January 24, 2009).

Samanta, Pranab Dahl (2009). "China Begins Building a Dam on its Side of the Brahaputra", October 15. Available at *http://www.indianexpress.com/news/china-begins-building-dam-on-its-side-of-the-brahmaputra/529244/0* accessed January 10, 2010.

Schwartz, Peter (2003). *Inevitable Surprises: Thinking Ahead in a Time of Turbulence*. New York: Gotham Books.

———. (1991). *The Art of the Long View*. New York: Doubleday.

Schwartz, Stephen (2003). *The Two Faces of Islam: Saudi Fundamentalism and Its Role in Terrorism*. New York: Anchor Books. pp.138-40.

Space Daily (2007). "50 Years after Sputnik, Russia Revives Space Ambitions", *Space Daily*. September 30. *http://www.spacedaily.com/reports/50_years_after_Sputnik_Russia_revives_space_ambitions_999.html* (accessed January 23, 2009).

Stannard, Matthew B. (2006). "Analysis: Sunni-Shiite Rivalry is a Constant Undercurrent of Tension", *San Francisco Chronicle*, August 13. *http://www.globalsecurity.org/org/news/2006/060813-islam-rivalry.htm* (accessed January 25, 2009).

Strategic Studies Institute (2006). *The National Security Strategy of the United States of America*. White House: Washington, DC. Available online at: *http://www.strategicstudiesinstitute.army. mil/pdffiles/nss.pdf* as of December 7, 2009.

Tellis, Ashley J. (2007). "China's Military Space Strategy", *Survival* 49(3): 46, Autumn.

The Daily Mail (2009). "China, India Lock Horns over Dam", *The Daily Mail*, Islamabad, Pakistan, October 17. p.1, available at: *http://www.indianexpress.com/news/china-begins-building-dam-on-its-side-of-the-brahmaputra/529244/0* accessed January 11, 2010.

The Economist (2007). "A. Cyber-Riot", *The Economist* 383, Issue 85/28: 55, May 12.

Thompson, Bill (2007). "Give Me Rice, But Give Me a Laptop Too", *BBC News online*. December 11.

Tirpak, J.A. (2006). "Washington Watch: Now, A Russian Buildup?; Keep an Eye on China; Services to Lose Power", *Air Force Magazine* 89(7): 12-29.

Tkachenko, Stanislav Leonidovich (2010). "Discussion during session on 'Geo-Politics in Asia: Country Perspectives'", at the *12th Asian Security Conference 2010*. New Dehli, India: Institute for Defence Studies and Analyses. February 13.

UN (2006). *World Population Prospects: The 2006 Revision*. Population Division of the Department of Economic and Social Affairs of the United Nations Secretariat.

———. (2005). *World Urbanisation Prospects: The 2005 Revision, http://esa.un.org/unpp* (accessed January 23, 2009).

United Nations Human Development Programme (2002). *The Arab Human Development Report 2002*. New York: United Nations Human Development Programme Regional Bureau for Arab States. p.35.

United States Department of Energy (2004). *Strategic Significance of America's Oil Shale Resource*. Report. Washington D.C. March. *http://www.fossil.energy.gov/programs/reserves/npr/publications/npr_strategic_significancev1.pdf* (accessed January 29, 2009), p.2.

Vassiliev, Alexei (1998). *The History of Saudi Arabia*. London: Saqi Books. p.563.

Waley, Arthur (ed.) (1938). *Analects of Confucius*. London, UK: George Allen & Unwin Ltd.

Wall, Robert (2003). "Growing Threat Countries Increase Focus on Land-Attack Cruise Missiles", *Aviation Week & Space Technology* 159(8): 38, August 25.

Wang, Hucheng (2000). "The US Military's 'Soft Ribs' and Strategic Weaknesses", *Liaowang* 27. Reprinted in Xinhua Hong Kong Service, July 5, in FBIS-CHI-2000-0705, July 25, 2000.

Ward, Kinkade (1997). *International Brief: Population Trends—Russia*. United States Census Bureau, Washington D.C., February.

Weir, Fred (2007). "Russia Intensifies Efforts to Rebuild its Military Machine", *Christian Science Monitor*, February 12. *http://www.csmonitor.com/2007/0212/p04s01-woeu.html* (accessed January 23, 2009).

Wilson, Peter and Douglas F. Graham (1994). *Saudi Arabia: The Coming Storm*. Armonk, NY: M. E. Sharpe. p.234.

Wyler, Liana S. (2007). "Weak and Failing States: Evolving Security Threats and United States Policy", *CRS Report* RL34253, November 15. p.8

Zarakhovich, Yuri (2007). "Russia Claims the North Pole", *Time*, July 12. *http://www.time.com/time/world/article/0,8599,1642905,00.html* (accessed January 23, 2009).

20

Asian Navies: Trends Towards 2030

VIJAY SAKHUJA

This chapter provides an overview of Asian naval trends in 2030. It is divided into five sections. The first section studies the rationale for the emergent trends in the growth of Asian naval power. The second section presents the broad trends in Asian naval spending over the next two decades. The next two sections offer an assessment of the trends in 'platform' and 'techno-operational' centric developments in Asia towards 2030. The fifth section offers a brief perspective on climate change induced developments in naval technology that Asian countries would have to integrate into their naval construction plans and force planning. Finally, it attempts to tabulate the macro naval trends in Asia that could evolve over the next two decades.

In the 21st century, Asian countries are exuding a sense of confidence which is reflected in burgeoning trade, a promising civil-military science and technology base, proficient human resources, and a desire to build robust maritime capabilities. There are at least 11 discernable reasons which resonate in the Asian naval thinking. First, the Asian countries have set strategic goals that envisage building capabilities to preclude intrusive dominance of the littorals by any external power reminiscent of the colonial-imperial supremacy that came 'from the sea', 'to the littorals' and 'into the heartland'.

Second, the threat of a nuclear intervention impacts on Asian strategic thinking particularly in China and India and necessitates an appropriate response from the sea. Also, of interest are the post Cold War international trends in the deployments of nuclear deterrents; the US, Russia, France and Britain have moved significant numbers of their nuclear arsenals to submarines.

Third, the evolving maritime military industrial complex and an abundant skilled human resource aims at self-reliance to avoid over dependence on external sources of military hardware. In the past, several Asian states have been subjected to economic and military sanctions with severe constraints on military technology transfers and severing of spare part supply chains that resulted in low levels of operational readiness. But on the flipside, the sanctions also provided the necessary impetus for some countries to develop an indigeneous science and technology base and a sophisticated military industrial complex.

Fourth, naval planners are now confronted with the challenges posed by asymmetric threats ranging from terrorism and piracy that can potentially disrupt Asian maritime supply chains. The operational strategies of Asian navies are primed for energy and trade transportation security and protecting sea lanes of communication. These are significant drivers for Asian naval growth.

Fifth, the Asian navies gain salience because of the imperatives of globalisation and economic growth. The coastal regions are home to an intricate network of maritime infrastructure (ports, harbours, oil and gas terminals and rail/road systems) connecting the littoral with the hinterland. The Asian naval power is derived from the strategic necessity of protecting economic hubs in the coastal region that are the engines of economic development.

Sixth, the Asian countries must contend with the 'ripple effects' of the ongoing modernisation of naval forces among regional countries that are investing significant resources to build maritime capability for power projection, sea control, 'out of area' operations and regional influence.

Seventh, the navies are required to exercise jurisdiction in their respective exclusive economic zones (EES) and maintain maritime order. This responsibility has seen a major shift in the patterns of growth of naval forces and rise of coast guards and marine enforcement agencies.

Eighth, the Asian countries also see their navies as tools for Humanitarian Assistance and Disaster Relief (HADR) missions thus facilitating speedy operations by relief agencies. These roles assist in the projection of 'soft power' through disaster diplomacy as witnessed during the 2004 Indian Ocean tsunami that devastated a number of countries in Asia.

Ninth, some of the platforms of the Asian navies are over two decades old and require a replacement that would naturally be equipped with enhanced capabilities corresponding with the innovations currently sweeping global navies.

Tenth, the critical necessity to develop naval interoperability among forces is visible. In that context, joint exercises, interoperable missions and maritime multilateralism are shaping the current wave of naval transformation among Asian navies who have established a variety of naval cooperation mechanisms with advanced navies involving training, joint exercises and crew exchanges.

Finally, access and basing arrangements among friendly navies help states consolidate alliances, coalitions and partnerships that are considered important for regional security. Several Asian countries have bilateral arrangements with regional and extra-regional countries and are developing, either individually or jointly, naval bases and maritime infrastructure to allow access and basing for naval forces of alliance partners and friends.

Trends in Naval Spending

The current economic downturn has resulted in the slowing down of the global GDP growth rate that increased by only 2 per cent in 2008 compared to 3.7 per cent in 2007.[1] Notwithstanding the current financial crisis, according to market analysts Frost & Sullivan, Asia's overall defence spending continues to grow and could account for 32 per cent or $480 billion of global military spending by 2016, up from 24 per cent in 2007 unlike the US, the biggest spender in 2007 with 39 per cent of the world arms market which would account for 29 per cent or $435 billion.[2] Further, Asian military spending will be led by China (from $120 billion in 2007 to $255 billion by 2016) and India (about $100 billion for procurement in the next five years).

1. UNCTAD (2009).
2. Bangkok Post (2009); Asian Defence Industry Monitor (2009).

Likewise, the market analyst, AMI International, has predicted a boom time for naval ship building industry. New naval construction programmes over the next two decades are expected to be worth $640 billion.[3] It is also noted that the Asia Pacific region would lead in global naval acquisitions with China, India, Japan and South Korea expected to invest nearly $60 billion over the next five years. This figure is projected to reach $108 billion over the next decade and $173 billion by 2030.[4]

It is also observed that: 'Looking at the global market by regions, the Asia-Pacific area is strong, and we expect it to move past NATO countries to become the second largest source of future naval spending,'[5] after the United States. Further, several Asian navies are moving towards the 'third-generation status' built around a three-dimensional balanced naval force capable of operating in a complex battlefield environment. According to Frost & Sullivan, 'Asia will account for nearly one-third of global military spending (over the next decade), up from about a quarter in 2007'. The *Jane's Defence Systems Forecast* has predicted that over the next 10 years, 80 to 100 submarines could be added to the Asian naval inventory.[6]

The above naval defence spending figures appear to be quite conservative; for instance, Australia recently announced plans to acquire 12 diesel-electric submarines and an Australian Strategic Policy Institute (ASPI) assessment has pegged the cost of these vessels at $32.6 billion.[7] Vietnam has signed an agreement with Russia in 2009 for six kilo submarines for $2 billion.[8] The Republic of Korea has plans to build three 3,500 tonne next-generation submarines code-named 'KSS-III' by 2020 and these are estimated to cost $3.7 billion.[9]

Similar trends are seen for Indian aircraft carrier ambitions. The two Indian aircraft carriers Vikramaditya (Gorshkov) and Vikrant

3. Karniol (2009).
4. Ibid.
5. Wendell (2009a; 2009b).
6. Ibid.
7. Nicholson (2009).
8. Torode and Chan (2009).
9. *Korea.net* (2004).

(Project 71 indigenous aircraft carrier-IAC) is estimated to cost nearly $3 billion excluding the aircraft and weapons systems for the carriers. India plans to acquire as many as 40 aircraft for the carriers. As far as other major platform acquisitions are concerned, Project 17A stealth frigates are estimated to cost $7,600 million and Project 75 Scorpene submarines $3,500 million.[10]

The F-35 joint strike fighter (JSF), being developed by the US, UK and Australia[11] is likely to cost around $80 to $90 million.[12] As far as Australia is concerned, these aircraft are to be on board the Canberra class LHD 01 being built at the Navantia ship building yard, in Ferrol, Spain.[13] Taiwan is procuring 32, UGM-84L sub-launched Harpoon Block II missiles for two Sea dragon class submarines from the Boeing subsidiary McDonnell Douglas, and these units are expected to cost $200 million.[14]

The cost of naval platforms in China cannot be ascertained due to lack of information; however some estimates can still be made. For instance, the Chinese built F22P frigates for the Pakistan navy at a cost of about $200 million[15] and a destroyer would cost about $300-400 million depending on the weapon and sensor fit.[16] The Type 051B Luhai-class destroyer consists of No. 167 Shenzhen that participated in operations off Somalia costs $300 million.[17]

---

10. "Executive Analysis of the Indian Defence Industry", available at *http://www.researchandmarkets.com/reports/612555/executive_analysis_of_the_indian_defence.htm* accessed on December 30, 2009.
11. "Joint Strike Fighter F-35 Lightning II", available at *http://www.raaf.gov.au/aircraft/jsf.aspx* accessed on January 2010.
12. Jung Sung-Ki (2010). "S. Korea Eyes F-35B Fighterjets for Landing Ship", available at *http://theasiandefence.blogspot.com/2009/03/s-korea-eyes-f-35b-fighter-jet-for.html* accessed on January 2.
13. Bitsinger (2008).
14. "Taiwan's (Un?) Stalled Force Modernisation", available at *http://www.defenseindustrydaily.com/date/2009/12/page/2/* accessed on January 2, 2010.
15. The procurement contract for the four 2,250 tonne frigates includes six S-9EC helicopters and is worth an estimated $750 million. For a detailed discussion on the F22 P programme, see *http://www.defence.pk/forums/naval-forces/42058-pakistan-gets-second-f22-p-frigate-pns-shamsheer-3.html* accessed on January 2, 2010.
16. Author's estimates.
17. "Type 051B Luhai-class Destroyer", available at *http://chinadefense.xinjunshi.com/ChinaDefense/PLANavyEquipment/34.html* accessed on January 2, 2010.

A not so conservative figure pegs Asian naval spending for aircraft carrier programmes at, '$100 billion in this decade, while infrastructure to support the ships over the next 50 years will cost another $100 billion. The acquisition of armaments, aircraft, helicopters and associated systems will cost more than $100 billion over the next five decades.'[18]

Future Platform Centric Development

Given these trends in Asian naval spending, the future acquisitions programmes for Asian navies are likely to focus on building aircraft carriers, hybrid platforms capable of fighter aircraft operations, expeditionary vessels for long distance sustained operations as also for HADR excercises, underwater platforms (conventional and nuclear), cruise missiles (anti-ship and land attack), missile defence systems, multirole jet fighters, manned and unmanned platforms with attack capabilities, and space-based assets for C4ISR (command, control, computers, communications, intelligence and reconnaissance support services).

Aircraft carriers: Currently nine countries across the globe operate 21 aircraft carriers and of these 12 are nuclear powered. There is a strong desire among some Asian navies to possess aircraft carriers to serve them in a number of activities that range from littoral warfare, sea control, support operations on land, naval diplomacy, and also in fulfilling humanitarian roles. These aspirations are clearly visible in white papers, naval strategies and published doctrines. Among the Asian countries, only India has an operational aircraft carrier (INS Viraat acquired in 1986). Thailand has classified its carrier (HTMS Chakri Naruebet commissioned in 1997) as an offshore patrol helicopter carrier. China is in the process of retrofitting Shi Lang (the 67,000 tonne Soviet carrier Varyag purchased as scrap in 1996), while Japan and South Korea operate large platforms that are capable of launching VTOL (vertical take-off and landing) aircraft but currently do not host fighter jets.

India is currently building a 37,500 tonne carrier, also known as IAC Project 71, christened INS Vikrant, the delivery for which is slated for 2014-15.[19] There are some uncorroborated reports that IAC IIIS is

18. Sethi (2009).

19. Times of India (2009).

likely to be nuclear powered and could be a 60,000 tonne vessel. In December 2009, India issued a request for information (RFI) for state-of-the-art, multirole, new generation carrier-based fighter aircraft.[20] These include Sweden's SAAB Sea Gripen, European Aeronautic Defence and Space Company (EADS) Eurofighter Typhoon, Boeing Integrated Defence System F/A-18 EIF Super Hornet and the French company Dassault's Rafale.

The Japanese navy is building a 13,500 tonne, Hyuga class helicopter carrying destroyer (DDH). It is comparable to an aircraft carrier and can host the VTOL version of aircraft.[21] In the initial stages, Japan may not like to arm the vessel with such an air complement because of regional concerns, but it may consider training Japanese personnel for F-35s with foreign navies so as to be in a position to upgrade the vessel to a light carrier at a later date when the need arises. Likewise, the Republic of Korea's navy acquired the Dokdo class landing platform helicopter.[22] A special urethane coating on the deck has been given to prevent damage to the deck by the 'jet flux' generated from the engine exhaust to enable operation of VTOL aircraft such as the F-35B.[23]

As far as China is concerned, there have been reports that China is building an aircraft carrier that could be of 60,000 dead weight tonnage (DWT) and host the Shenyang Aircraft Corporation's modified J-11 or the new Shenyang fighter sometimes called J-13 (smaller than the Su-33 but has stealth features) or the carrier version of the Chengdu Aircraft Corporation's J-10 fighter.[24] However, it is not known when China would commence the construction of the indigenous carrier and at which shipyard.

Submarines: Submarines are not new to Asia. Australia, China, Japan, India, Indonesia, South and North Korea, Pakistan, Singapore and now

20. "Indian Navy Issues RFI for Carrier-based Fighter Aircraft", available at *http://www.domain-b.com/defence/sea/indian_navy/20091229_fighter_aircraft.html* accessed on January 2, 2010.

21. "Japan Launches Carrier Sorta", available at *http://defensetech.org/2007/08/28/japan-launches-carrier-sorta/* accessed on December 5, 2009.

22. "LP-X Dokdo (Landing Platform Experimental) Amphibious Ship", available at *http://www.globalsecurity.org/military/world/rok/lp-x.htm* accessed on March 10, 2009.

23. For detailed discussion see Sakhuja (2009a).

24. Fisher (2009).

Malaysia have operational experience in these platforms. Thailand, Vietnam and potentially Taiwan would soon join the list of navies operating submarines. Further, to make submarines more lethal, these platforms are equipped with missiles, torpedoes, and advanced electronic warfare suites. Above all, the air independent propulsion (AIP) makes these vessels a formidable platform. As noted earlier, 80 to 100 submarines could be added to the Asian naval inventory.

There are several reasons that prompt Asian navies to develop a submarine arm. It is generally agreed that battleships dominated World War I, aircraft carriers during World War II, and submarines will be the leading platform in future wars. The exploits of submarines during World War II, the sinking of the Indian anti-submarine frigate during the 1971 India Pakistan war, HMS Conqueror sinking the Argentinean navy flagship General Belgrano have clearly illustrated the relative supremacy of submarines. In recent times, the 1994 USS Kitty Hawk-PLAN Han incident and the 2006 incident involving a Chinese Song class diesel submarine surfacing within weapons range of the USS Kitty Hawk have corroborated the potential and stealth nature of these platforms. The latter incidents have showcased to medium power navies that submarines are a cheaper deterrence option. Further, the growing submarine force of China and India is worrisome to the Southeast Asian countries that see these as destabilising the regional security environment. Also, the Chinese and Indian quest for a credible sea-based deterrent has resulted in two nuclear submarines bases—the Sanya naval base in China and the upcoming Rambilli naval base in India in the Bay of Bengal which have attracted Asian attention.

Expeditionary platforms: Expeditionary vessels serve as excellent platforms for command stations for fleet operations, power projection, induction of forces in distant lands, logistic support and for disaster response operations involving on shore supply of relief materials like food, water and shelter. Besides, these vessels can provide emergency electrical power and potable water by mooring in the vicinity of the disaster site. Their capability is unique when seaports and airports are damaged and unusable. In such conditions, these platforms serve as logistical bases. Asian navies realised the importance of expeditionary platforms during the 2004 Indian Ocean tsunami that hit several Asian shores. Australia, China, India, Japan, Republic of Korea and Singapore plan to augment their expeditionary capability by building/acquiring new platforms.

As mentioned earlier, in the case of the Japanese and South Korean navy such platforms serve as 'pseudo aircraft carriers'. In 2006, the PLA navy launched the 20,000 tonne Type 071 LPD (landing platform dock) expeditionary vessel that[25] is highly versatile and can perform a variety of mission roles including its classic role as an amphibious assault vessel. It can function as a platform for humanitarian aid during disaster relief operations and for casualty and refugee evacuation from conflict zones. In the Indian context, in 2007 the Indian navy acquired the INS Jalashwa, the US Trenton class LPD(H). There are plans to build four such LPDs in the coming years.[26]

Unmanned aviation: Worldwide trends suggest an improved funding picture and favourable performance reviews for the UAVs. For instance, the spend on UAVs in the US military rose from $360 million in 2001 to more than $2 billion in 2006 and by the end of the decade, the annual UAV spend is expected to reach $3 billion, equal to the total amount spent on these aircraft during the 1990s.[27] UAV operations are expanding in missions involving airborne intelligence, surveillance and reconnaissance to attacking targets. An increasing number of Asian navies (India, Japan, Republic of Korea and Singapore) are using UAVs to patrol territorial waters and for maritime security missions such as countering human trafficking, drug smuggling and illegal fishing. UAVs are also valuable force multipliers and provide a real or near-real time tactical picture at sea and with some sensors they can detect irregular maritime activity and even attack select targets. Some Asian navies like India, Japan and Singapore have integrated UAVs into their tactical doctrines.

Future Technological-Operation Centric Development

In 2030, the naval battle space would be significantly driven by the information age and rapid technological advances in weapons and sensors. These developments have a direct impact on the way future wars will be conducted. What is important is that emerging military technologies when combined with operational doctrines and organisational structures would undergo major changes in future naval

25. Scott (2007).
26. Indian Express (2009).
27. Sherman (2005).

operations. These would involve: (a) fleet engagements on the high seas supported by satellites; (b) operations against enemy forces involving stealth surface platforms, subsurface launched cruise missiles and unmanned combat air systems (UCAV) as well as launched precision guided munitions; (c) space-based communications for command and control across the combat spectrum. These developments point to the fact that naval operations would cover the sea-space-shore continuum.

At the operational level, force formulations would include a large number of networked, geographically dispersed platforms and off-board systems that complement the power projection achieved through multi-mission assets. This force should be able to efficiently conduct a wide spectrum of low-end missions involving asymmetric threats to engaging a sophisticated enemy with a full suite of weapons and sensors. Highly manoeuvrable platforms designed to conduct over-the-horizon, ship-to-shore tactical operations with high speed ability as also to easily transit the sea-space-shore interface are ideal for tactical surprise and swift introduction of forces.

Anti-Ship Ballistic Missiles (ASBM)

The current discourse on ASAT in Asia, particularly China's shooting down of the satellite in 2007 has been gathering momentum. Also, in recent times, the Chinese ability to attack US aircraft carriers has raised several issues among Asian naval powers particularly India and Japan. Of particular concern is the Chinese plan to modify the DF-21 ASBM (Mach 10, it can cover 1,200 miles in less than 12 minutes and is capable of hitting moving targets at 2,000 km) to attack and cripple large sea targets such as the aircraft carriers, expeditionary platforms and fleet formations. China is also able to equip the DF-21 with an electromagnetic pulse (EMP) bomb that can render the 'neurological networks' of an aircraft carrier's C4ISR systems non-functional.[28]

Ballistic Missile Defence (BMD) at Sea

Ballistic missile defence (BMD) at sea has also caught the attention of Asian naval powers. The need for a ship-based BMD system gains

28. Sakhuja (2009b).

salience and criticality in the context that ballistic missiles that can be launched from shore batteries and also from submarines. In the Chinese context, the Type 094 Jin class SSBN is fitted with 12 X JL-2 ballistic missiles (8,000 km range) with multiple independently targeted re-entry vehicle (MIRV) capability of smaller yield is a well acknowledged threat.

Japan, Korea and Australia are engaged in fitting out the Aegis BMD system onboard their naval vessels. Under a $33 million contract, Lockheed Martin is fitting out four Japanese destroyers with the Aegis BMD weapon system.[29] Likewise, the first Aegis weapon system for the Royal Australian Navy's air warfare destroyer (AWD-1) programme was completed in 2009[30] and these are to be fitted onboard the Hobart class Australian air warfare destroyer or the SEA 4000 (three ships) that are scheduled to join the fleet from 2013. As far as the Korean navy is concerned, in May 2007, Hyundai Heavy Industries launched the 7,600 tonne Sejong the Great to be fitted with the Aegis system and there are plans to launch the second Aegis destroyer in 2010 and a third in 2012.[31] The Indian navy was given a presentation on the Aegis BMD system for ships in 2009.[32] In 2006, Lockheed Martin and Hyundai Heavy Industries of South Korea signed a MoU to build and export 4,000 to 6,000 tonne warships fitted with Aegis weapons systems.

Air Independent Propulsion (AIP)

The air independent propulsion (AIP) is the most sought after system in modern diesel-electric submarines and can be a game changer. It can substantially enhance the underwater operation time and avoid frequent surfacing to charge the batteries. In fact, for some, the AIP is the 'poor man's nuke' that has the capability to overcome the performance difference between nuclear powered submarines and AIP fitted vessels. In essence, AIP submarines are a formidable platform particularly when operating in shallow waters, narrow choke

29. Sieff (2007).
30. Lockheed Martin (2009).
31. Parry (2009).
32. India Defence Online (2009).

points or maritime gateways. Rear Admiral Malcolm Fages, a US navy submariner has observed,

> The marriage of air independent, non-nuclear submarines with over-the-horizon, fire and forget anti-ship cruise missiles and high endurance, wake homing torpedoes...[means that] traditional ASW approaches, employing radar flooding and speed, are not likely to be successful against this threat.[33]

Directed-Energy Weapon (DEW)

At another level, directed-energy weapons could shape the future Asian sea-based battle space and therefore merit attention. According to Rear Admiral Nevin P. Carr, head of the US office of naval research, 'We're going to need to fight at the speed of light, and by 2030, I think the technology will support direct-energy weapons.'[34] That is how the US naval planners envisage future weapons; however, the big question is: would such weapons find their way into Asian naval inventories. Laser beams, handheld laser guns and laser designated weapons onboard sea-based platforms could be fielded by some Asian naval powers. Technological advancements are underway in the domain of laser technology in Asia, particularly in LASIK surgery, to correct vision problems. In the military domain, special warfare troops may undergo surgery to improve their night vision.

Stealth Design, Propulsion and Chemicals for Warships and Submarines

There will also be significant developments in the field of stealth technology making naval surface, underwater and air platforms more difficult to detect by radar (air defence systems), sonar (underwater signatures: acoustic and hydrodynamic), infrared sensors, electro-magnetic field sensors, and even satellites.

At the structural level, hull shape, material properties, propulsion and auxiliary machinery, noise dampening systems, active signature-compensation systems would drive future construction programmes. New technology could include new paints and special coatings for underwater platforms, and aviation assets. At another level, non-magnetic plastic/carbon-fibre composite hull, surfaces and edges of

---

33. Benedict (2005).
34. Tilghman (2010).

stealth technology, water jet propulsion instead of propellers are some of the technologies that would be fielded by Asian navies in the future.

Climate Change-Induced Technological Developments

In a study titled 'National Security and Threat of Climate Change', constituted by the US Centre for Naval Analysis, Vice Admiral Richard Truly US Navy (retd.) has observed that, '...the stresses that climate change will put on our national security, will be different than any we've dealt with in the past...for one thing, unlike the challenges that we are used to dealing with, these will come upon us extremely slowly, but come they will, and they will be grinding and inexorable.'[35] Climate change is inextricably linked to naval construction programmes.

While the navies engage in technological-operational transformation, they will have to contend with the phenomenon of greenhouse gases (GHG). The shipping industry is a significant contributor of GHG and has invited international concern. The ship building industry has begun to take measures to reduce emissions and is incorporating the necessary technology to counter climate change. The issues relate to identification of the GHG emitting substance inventory on board ships such as ozone depletion substances (ODS) used on board for refrigeration and fire fighting systems and their phase-out plans as well as identifying halon alternatives, and fuel-efficient machinery for propulsion. Naval vessels, though very small in number when compared to the global shipping fleet, would have to address the problem of climate change by taking proactive measures.

Macro Trends

It will be useful to point out that it is rare for a navy to be equally adept at surface, underwater, air, and space warfare. Thus the force structures in the future i.e., by the year 2030, would be in accordance with past experience, expertise gained over the years, technological advancements, indigeneous military-industrial complex, and advantages and the disadvantages of newer capabilities.

Further, naval construction has long lead-times. Beginning with staff requirements, design, tendering, construction, series production

35. The CNA Corporation (2007).

and finally acceptance involve, on an average, more than 10 years. During this period, technology advancements are moving at a fast pace, sometimes outdating naval platforms by the time they are put into service. In fact obsolescence is rapid and uncontrolled particularly in the current age of high technology and information systems. It is generally accepted that navies will continue to chase technologies as warfare becomes more complex and driven by innovation and uncertainly with regard to actors.

Force Structuring

Asian navies will be faced with establishing requirements, defining priorities, taking decisions and finally allocating resources for an optimal and potent military force. A judicious mix can result in a well-balanced force capable of undertaking a variety of missions across a wide spectrum encompassing conflict-peace and OOTW (operations other than war). Oddly enough, the problem of force structuring is aggravated by the flexibility of many modern military systems that can be deployed across a wide spectrum of threats from the asymmetric to conventional. For instance, even in the US, about 10 per cent of the defence budget was allocated to counter-insurgency assets and 50 per cent to 'conventional warfare,' while the remaining 40 per cent was considered 'dual use'.[36]

Quest for Three-Dimensional Navy

There is a quest among Asian navies to develop a three- dimensional navy. In this context, submarines are significant constituent of the emerging Asian naval order of battle primarily because of their anti-access capabilities. Also the 'ripple effect' of the ongoing focus on submarines among other countries is acting as a catalyst.

Build or Buy Debate

Asian countries would continue to be confronted with the 'build or buy' dilemma. Barring China, India, Japan, Republic of Korea and Singapore, the indigeneous high-end naval ship building capability is still evolving and Asian countries continue to scout for foreign building

36. "US Seeks Force Transformation with Dramatic Shift in Defence Priorities" available at *http://defencedebates.wordpress.com/2009/04/13/us-seeks-force-transformation-with-dramatic-shift-in-budget-priorities/*accessed on January 9, 2010.

yards for their needs. Also the ability to develop sophisticated weapons systems is still limited to a few Asian countries. But it would be pertinent to mention that Asian countries remain apprehensive of Western vendors who impose preconditions such as human rights, accountability, not to mention licensing and end-user certifications. For instance, President S.B. Yudhoyono was blunt about Indonesia's reasons for opting for Russian hardware, stating that, 'Russia does not attach any conditions whatsoever. Russia is all business and does not attach any political conditions and that is the way we like it, and that is why we took up the offer.' Be that as it may, the current trends in naval acquisition by Asian navies offer opportunities for the Western military industry.

Export of Naval Hardware

There is some naval export potential among Asian countries particularly China, Republic of Korea and India. However, Japan is constrained by its constitutional requirements to export military hardware. Among the Asian countries, China leads naval hardware sales having exported ships, aircraft and submarines to other countries. It recently sold F-22 frigates to Pakistan.

Is There an Arms Race in Asia?

The current acquisition trends do not reflect an arms race and thwart the conventional argument that acquisition of offensive platforms would lead to escalation during crisis. However, as the naval capabilities of China and India grow, they are bound to expand their nautical horizons from closer shores to 'out of area operations'. The two sides are likely to develop their respective naval technological edge in the next two decades. Likewise, Japan and Republic of Korea too would build up substantive naval capability in response to China's naval nuclear and conventional capability. The other Asian countries would follow trends and keep pace with regional modernisation efforts.

Concluding Remarks

Although the process of modernisation of Asian navies commenced in the '90s, yet the slow rate of acquisition created a mismatch between their numbers and the expanding roles of the navies. Further, the indigeneous warship building effort has not been able to keep pace with the platform requirements of the navies leading to import substitution.

In terms of profiles and capabilities of the players of the region, the Chinese, Japanese and the Indian navies are clearly the leading players with sustained and dominant roles in power projection, carrier-based naval aviation, expeditionary deployments, maritime reconnaissance and surveillance, proficiency in prosecuting net-centric information warfare and sea-based missile defences. These navies would transform to ensure continued monopoly and dominance. As far as the Asian sea-based nuclear deterrence is concerned, it would remain the forte of the Chinese and Indian navies in the coming future.

In the next two decades, the Chinese threat could be regarded as unitary threat affecting India, Japan, South East Asia, the Philippines, Vietnam and South Korea. Its nuclear and naval arsenal and the vision of expanding operations into the second and third island chain of maritime defences, could affect the whole of Asia. The regional security would be further complicated by the naval presence and intervening dynamics of extra-regional naval powers particularly the US. In the Indian Ocean, the competitive maritime dynamics among US, China, India and Japan would be shaped by the justification of sea lines of communication (SLOC) security and the preservation of maritime trade and commerce.

There is likely to be a higher fiscal allocation for naval growth partly driven by regional trends as also due to the imperative of ensuring the safety of sea-based commerce. The strategic vision of the Asian navies would evolve to build a credible naval posture based on a robust technological base.

References

Asian Defence Industry Monitor (2009). "Asia Set for Defence Spending Spree", March 6.

Bitsinger, Richard A. (2008). "Making a Comeback? Aircraft Carriers in the Asia Pacific", *IDSS Commentary* 68/2008. Available at *http://www3.ntu.edu.sg/rsis/publications/Perspective/RSIS0682008.pdf* accessed on January 2, 2010.

Bangkok Post (2009). "Asia to Take Lead in Arms Spending", *Bangkok Post*, March 5.

Benedict, John R. (2005). "The Unravelling and Revitalisation of U.S. Navy Antisubmarine Warfare", *Naval War College Review:* 102. Spring.

Devindra Sethi (2009). "Asia Bent on Acquiring Aircraft Carriers", *Maritime India*. November. Available at *http://www.upiasia.com/Security/2009/11/02/asia_bent_on_acquiring_aircraft_carriers/2837/* accessed on January 5, 2010.

India Defence Online (2009). "India and United States to Cooperate on Missile Defence", *Indian Defence News and Strategic Intelligence*, January. Available at *http://indiadefenceonline.com/276/india-and-united-states-to-cooperate-on-missile-defence/* accessed on January 5, 2010.

Indian Express (2009). "Navy to Build Four Amphibious Warships", *Indian Express* December 13.

Korea.net (2004). "3,500-ton Class Submarines to Debut by 2022". Available at *http://www.korea.net/news/news/newsView.asp?serial_no=20060105018* accessed on January 2, 2010.

Karniol, Robert (2009). "Boom Time Ahead For Asia-Pacific Navies", *Straits Times*. November 9.

Minnick, Wendell (2009a). "Asian Naval Programs Confident Despite Economy", *Defence News*, May 11.

———. (2009b). "Asia Forking Out on Defence Despite Slowdown", *AFP*, April 6.

Lockheed Martin (2009). "First Aegis Weapon System Completed for Royal Australian Navy", December. Available at *http://www.lockheedmartin.com/news/press_releases/2009/120109_LM_Aegis_Australia.html* accessed on January 5, 2010.

Mc Parry (2009). "South Korea, US Team up on Aegis Warships", *World Military Forum*. July. Available at *http://www.armybase.us/2009/07/south-korea-us-team-up-on-aegis-warships/#printpreview* accessed on January 5, 2010.

Nicholson, Brendan (2009). "New Submarine Fleet to Cost '$36 Billion'", *The Age (Australia)*. October 30.

Sakhuja, Vijay (2009a). "Aircraft Carriers in Asia Pacific Region: Developments in China, Japan and South Korea", *South Asian Defence and Strategic Review*. December, available at *http://www.defstrat.com/exec/frmArticleDetails.aspx?DID=217*, accessed on January 3, 2010.

———. (2009b). "Missile Defence: Protecting Aircraft Carriers", *Society for Study of Peace and Conflict* 164. May 14.

Scott, Richard (2007). "China Launches Type 071 LPD", *Jane's Navy International* 112(2). March.

Sherman, Jason (2005). "Wave of the Future?", *Sea Power*. US: Navy League of the United States. available at *http://www.navyleague.org/sea_power/jul_05_18.php*

Sieff, Martin (2007). "Japan Buys Another Aegis System", Missile Defence. August. Available at *http://www.spacewar.com/reports/Japan_Buys_Another_Aegis_System_999.html* accessed on January 5, 2010.

Tilghman, Andrew (2010). "Navy of 2030 Could Bring Sci-fi to Reality", *Navy Times*. January 6.

Times of India (2009). "Hunt on for Fighters for Aircraft Carriers", *Times of India*. November 9.

The CNA Corporation (2007). "National Security and the Threat of Climate Change", CNA Corporation Report. The Military Advisory Board. p.14

Torode, Greg and Minnie Chan (2009). "Vietnam Buys Submarines to Counter China", *South China Morning Post*. December 17.

UNCTAD (2009). *Review of Maritime Transport 2009*. Geneva: United Nations Conference on Trade and Development. pp.xiv-xv.

21

Defence R&D in Asia

Achievements and Future Directions

NABANITA R. KRISHNAN

> We are living in an age where developments in science and technology have become a major determinant of what happens with the income and wealth of nations.
>
> —Dr. Manmohan Singh, *Prime Minister of India*, January 2007

It has been proved beyond doubt that technology is a critical input for sustained economic growth and hence the science and technology policy should be an important component of the economic policy of nations. The bedrock of a nation's progress are the efforts put in by the government for Research & Development (R&D) in key areas. One such area is defence R&D. The countries which lead in defence R&D are also the nations that wield substantial technological and political clout.

This chapter studies the defence R&D scenario in Asia, assesses the technology levels and achievements of the last 20 years, and attempts to gauge its future directions. It is important to do so, because, as noted by Arnett (1997), military technologies are usually capital intensive, not labour intensive. Hence they become a major decision point for developing countries with access to cheap labour but limited capital. This chapter looks at seven major countries of Asia—India, China, Pakistan, Japan, South Korea, North Korea and Iran. The countries have been selected keeping in view the importance of their activities in today's geopolitical scenario as also the level of technological superiority they have been able to establish at least in certain key areas.

Defence Budget: The military budget is a key parameter which determines the focus of governments and the importance they place on acquiring capability. According to the *Asian Defence Monitor,* Asia is expected to outstrip the rest of the world in defence spending within seven years, as China and India upgrade their armed forces. Asia's overall defence budget will account for 32 per cent of global military spending by 2016, up from 24 per cent in 2007, a year in which the US was the biggest spender with 39 per cent of the world arms market. Figure 21.1 below shows the defence outlays of key Asian countries.

Figure 21.1

Regional Military Spending, 2008

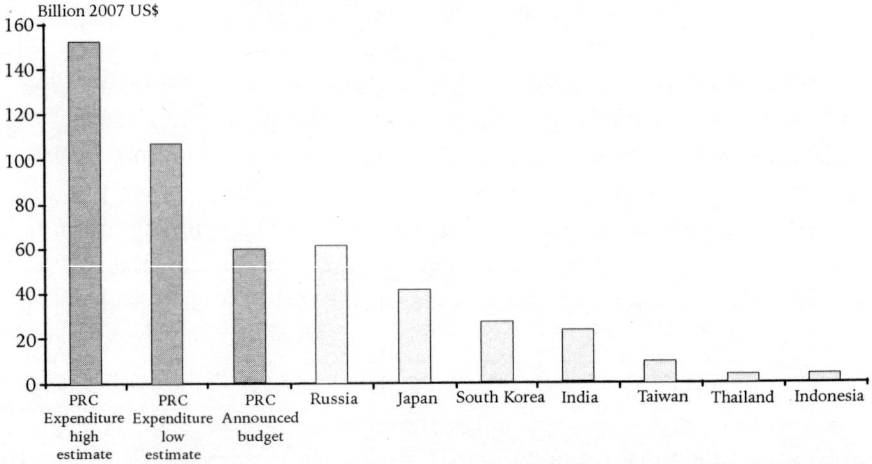

Note: This figure compares China official and DoD-estimated military expenditures with that of other regional militaries. Military expenditures are derived from government sources. Of note, Russia's budget data grew significantly over the period of review between the 2008 and 2009 editions of this report. All figures are in 2007 US dollars.

As per the figure Russia and China are the highest spenders followed closely by Japan, South Korea and India. Despite the hike, India's defence spending is still at about 2 per cent of the GDP, compared to China's 7 per cent and Pakistan's 5 per cent.

Comparative data on the R&D budget for defence, given in Table 21.1, shows China as a frontrunner, at par if not ahead of the world's leading nations. This forms the basis for the discussion on technological capabilities that follows.

Table 21.1

Comparative Data on the R&D Budget for Defence

Country	*R&D Budget as % of Defence Budget*
India	6
China	20
USA	15
France	13
Israel	9
S. Korea	5.4
Germany	5
Japan	3.8

Following paragraphs take an individual look at each of the Asian countries listed above.

Japan

In the '70s, the national mission in Japan was to bootstrap domestic industries to world standards, an example of which was the highly successful VLSI (very large scale integration) project funded by the Ministry of International Trade and Industry (MITI)—which helped propel the Japanese electronics industry, well past the US semiconductor industry in devices and consumer electronics. This was in reality 'applied R&D'. Its technology basis came from abroad and hence the catch-up policy was found to be very expensive. A policy change in the '80s shifted the focus to basic research as Japan realised that an indigeneous science base was needed to prepare for subsequent technology life cycles. Japanese R&D policy allows tax credit for R&D expenditure with additional benefits to small and medium enterprises (SMEs)—which have helped to build a healthy technology environment for Japan's industry.

Science & Technology: Japan's technological skills has gained world-wide respect. In the 20 years since World War II, its technical human resource figures rose sharply and by 1995 had overtaken those of the US with over 80 people per 10,000 labour force, compared to 70 for US. This has gone a long way towards re-establishing Japan as one of the world leaders in technological capability. In fact relative to its labour force size, Japan has more engineers than any leading industrial nation, except Sweden (NSF, 1996). These are concentrated in the fields of electronics, electrical engineering and in computer science with over 70 per cent employed in industry, 13 per cent in education and about 6 per cent in government.

Defence R&D in Japan has been driven by World War II and its after-effects, like so many of its other institutions. As a result, Japan is constrained to fulfill certain international conditions for possessing minimum defence capabilities necessary for a sovereign country and in view of the security treaty between Japan and the USA of 1951, together with a perceived potential nuclear threat from North Korea, Japan has been dependent on the US for building up its post-World War II defence structure. Its premier defence R&D agency is the Technical Research & Development Institute (TRDI) under Japan's Ministry of Defence (MoD). While being largely dependent on American imports of defence technology, the TRDI has over time succeeded in building up a modern defence industry customised to Japan's specific requirements. It has an approximate budget of $1.5 billion which is roughly 3.8 per cent of its defence budget. Over 70 per cent of this budget is devoted to development of engineering prototypes, about 20 per cent to in-house research and test and evaluation, while 5 per cent of the budget is reserved for personnel and miscellaneous. The organisation has just over 1,100 personnel, of which 75 per cent are civilians and the rest are service cadre. Over 45 per cent of the total civilian personnel are research engineers and about 28 per cent provide administration support—a considerable figure which is a tacit indication perhaps of administrative/ bureaucratic procedures to be followed, akin to India.

TRDI's current focus in aeronautics is on—high by-pass turbofan engines for patrol and transport aircraft and a fifth generation combat aircraft demonstrator—its most challenging venture. Not being part of the US led F-22 and F-35 deal, the Japanese MoD has sanctioned the next stage development of Shinshin—intended to be a eight tonne combat aircraft with two indigeneously developed turbofan engines, indigeneous stealth capability, radar and fly-by-light control technologies. While avoiding US participation it has been built with French assistance and is now in the test & evaluation phase. The final model is intended to have a super cruise (without afterburners) and axis symmetric thrust vectoring nozzle which when ready, will mark Japan's success in combat aircraft technology. An active phased array radar manufactured by Mitsubishi Electronics, which claims spectrum agility between C- and Ku-bands, provides protection against jamming while jamming other radars. It also combines search and track features. This together with electronic sensory measures (ESM) and electronic counter measures(ECM) measures, which when ready will put it on par with the best being developed. Transmit/receive (TR) modules developed indigeneously will be at the heart of the phased array radar which will also include high-powered microwave (HPM) attack as one of its capabilities. Given its acknowledged strength in electronics, this is definitely within Japanese indigeneous capability. The TRDI is also working on jet powered UAVs with a nose mounted optics package to be used as target drones or for high speed surveillance and has tested its autonomous control technologies, which could eventually lead to a unmanned combat air vehicle (UCAV) development. A possible interest in high-altitude long-endurance (HALE) development could be forthcoming with new advanced optical sensors being developed for missile defence missions.

Japan's collaboration with US on missile defence has led to the development of the SM-3 interceptor missile which seeks to use advanced Japanese laser technologies. Japan's recent achievement was the successful test of the innovative clamshell nosecone designed in collaboration with the US as part of the missile defence shield. Japan has also with its precision manufacturing capability, the Raytheon air defence missiles and associated radars.

On the naval front, the TRDI is also working on a high speed stealthy trimaran, capable of both high and low speeds while using radar and special materials for stealth. A new air independent propulsion (AIP) powered submarine and helicopter carrying destroyer are under development. There is no obvious intention to build aircraft carriers—indicating Japan's modest ambitions for the defence of Japanese territory and its larger exclusive economic zone (EEZ) but not beyond, which is in stark contrast to China's ambitions. However, Japan does intend to stay abreast of cutting edge transformational defence technologies and its capability to achieve this, must not be taken lightly.

Future Trends: An April 2007 report released by TRDI, talks of the medium to long-term defence technology plans of Japan. The focus will be on ballistic and cruise missile defence, network-centric warfare including command, control and intelligence, defence against off-shore attacks, defence against cyber attacks and terrorism. Potential technologies include energy storage, power MEMS (micro-electro-mechanical systems) and carbon nano tube technology for reducing size and weight of power sources. Nuclear, biological and chemical (NBC) protection, detection and countermeasure technology will be another area of focus which will use terahertz imaging technology and bio-sensors. Precision guided weapon technology will include semi-active mm wave seekers, passive radio seekers and low vulnerability propellants. Ammunition with intelligence, guidance and terminal control together with high power laser and microwave technology are key areas which will keep Japan at the cutting edge of defence technology. Equipments to counter electronic and electromagnetic attacks, digital water marking and quantum cryptography technology to enhance security of information sharing are other areas of future research.

Considerable work has already been done in the field of NBC systems as also information security and secure communication systems in which evaluation and perhaps top-up is expected to be completed in the next 2 to 3 years. Over the next 10 years Japan expects to achieve considerable expertise in unmanned systems and their attendant technologies *viz.*, autonomous control and navigation, networked robotic systems for land application, multi-function intelligent ammunition technology and countermeasures for electronic attacks. As is evident the underlying technology can be traced back to electronic systems and miniaturised components. The foundation in VLSI technology laid in the '70s stands even today as the secret of their mastery over controls and automation. In 10-15 years time frame, Japan will work towards achieving expertise in stealth and supersonic cruise technology—an area fairly new but which they believe to be of strategic importance.

The Japanese government appears to have played a major role in determining the areas on which the defence R&D should concentrate. Utilising complementary skills in partnership with USA, they have decided to focus maximum attention on electronic systems and ballistic missile defence and leave defence of the seas beyond its escrowed encryption standard (EES) to the superior US forces. At the same time it has realised the importance of broadening its technical base in aeronautic systems, without having to rely on US support—a fine mix of indigeneous and imported technology which should stand them in good stead in the current geopolitical climate.

Pakistan

Pakistan's military has always played a decisive role in the politics of the country. With over 650,000 personnel on active duty, it is reported to be the world's seventh largest armed force. Pakistan began its military production capability almost from scratch in 1951 when it established the Pakistan Ordnance Factories (POF) at Wah cantonment, near Rawalpindi, to produce small arms, ammunition and explosives. In the initial years of nationhood it received substantial assistance from the US, hence very limited attention was given to domestic production, but after the sanctions in 1965 and 1971, Pakistan relied on China to expand its facilities and infrastructure. The Ministry of Defence Production (MoDP) was created in September 1991 to coordinate the military production facilities. The ministry also includes seven other specialised organisations devoted to R&D, production and administration.

Science & Technology Index of Pakistan: Pakistan's focus on S&T achieved a 6.25 fold jump from 1965 to 1995 in terms of the numbers of scientists and technologists in the workforce. About 47 universities and 237 R&D institutes are engaged in S&T. An important R&D unit is the National Engineering and Scientific Commission (NESCOM) which reportedly is a civilian controlled scientific and research organisation carrying out research in many engineering and scientific areas, with focus on the design and production of the defence systems. NESCOM is one of the largest and well known research organisations in Pakistan with more than 80,000 scientists and engineers, majority of whom are PhDs from reputed foreign universities.

The Defence Science & Technology Organisation (DESTO) is Pakistan's official defence research organisation established in 1963 to undertake basic research and reverse engineering. It conducts R&D on weapon systems and renders technical advice on weapons related issues to the government. It works on a wide spectrum of technologies including aerodynamics, propulsion, armaments, explosives as well as biological and chemical defence. Not many details about this organisation are available in the public domain. Pakistan's defence budget was about $7.8 billion—about 4.5 per cent of GDP in 2006. Exact figures of its R&D budget are not easily available but they are estimated to be at least at 8 per cent of the defence budget. While headquartered at Chaklala garrison, DESTO has R&D units in a number of places including Chattar, Karachi and Rawalpindi. Pakistan has over the years collaborated extensively with China and North Korea on a number of weapon system developments. Hence the exact degree of indigeneous capability is a little difficult to assess. However its capability to produce a spectrum of weapon systems ranging from the Al-Khalid MBT (main battle tank) to JF-17 fighter aircrafts, to the Hatf, Ghaznavi and Ghauri and Babur is fairly well documented. Let us however attempt to profile the development activity at its various facilities across the country.

The Armaments Research and Development Establishment (ARDE), since its inception in 1974 has been working on the development and production of arms and ammunition in collaboration with the public and private sectors. The Institute of Optronics at Chaklala has established production and testing facilities for night vision devices and is progressively attempting to indigenise night vision components. Another agency, Margalla Electronics created in 1984 as a self-reliance project aims at providing repair and rebuild of imported electronic equipment, whose mandate has been extended to include upgrades and thereafter original design and production. A Military Vehicles R&D Establishment (MVRDE) established in 1972 is focussed on military vehicles—both armoured and wheeled as well as engineering equipment. The country's most widely known defence establishments are the National Development Complex (NDC) and the Pakistan Aeronautical Complex (PAC). The PAC was set up in the '70s for repair and overhaul of imported aircrafts and systems. Its mandate was extended in later years to include upgrade programmes and joint ventures—chief of which have been the K-8 jet trainer programme and the JF-17 combat aircraft project with China. However there seems to be no visible indication of any in-house technology contribution and indigeneous contribution to the two aircraft projects seems to be limited and restricted to manufacturing under China's technical guidance. The PAC is today involved in some system upgrades and manufacturing avionics systems in partnership with foreign agencies. Like India, Pakistan too has a massive Ordnance Factory setup under MoD consisting of 14 factories and 8 subsidiaries with a workforce of over 30,000 strong engaged mainly in production of licensed hardware in addition to their own low-tech arms and ammunition.

According to the *Business Monitor*, Pakistan's defence industry consists of over 20 major public sector undertakings (PSUs) and over 100 private companies—the PSUs are into production and assemblies while the private firms supply parts, components etc. The public sector includes the PAC and the NDC. Pakistan also has a thriving private industry working in certain areas of strategic interest. One such company is the Al-Technique Corporation of Pakistan (ATCOP) engaged in the R&D and production of lasers and electro-optic systems as well as in (ultra high-very high) VHF/UHF communication. Nearly 30 per cent of its turnover is spent on R&D. A number of public and private companies are engaged in R&D and manufacturing of unmanned aircraft and specialises in airframes, launch mechanisms and command and control systems. Private companies are developing micro and mini UAVs for tactical reconnaissance, surveillance and in the area of Signals Intelligence (SIGINT).

The NDC is of course the most important of Pakistan's defence establishments. It consists of a cluster of R&D and manufacturing units under the Pakistan Atomic Energy Commission (PAEC), with the mandate to develop weapon systems most famous of which are ballistic missiles. Turnkey facilities were set up for M9, M11 missile by China. The facilities were completed in the late 90s and were used to produce the Hatf III/ Ghaznavi/M11 and possibly Hatf IV/Shaheen/ M9 solid fuel ballistic missiles. Missile parts are believed to have been sourced from within Pakistan but the country remains dependent on China and other sources for missile guidance and special steels for rocket motors. The cooperation with China continues on Shaheen II. Pakistan has succeeded in building with Chinese assistance, extensive manufacturing and testing facilities for missile sub-systems. A similar story is that of Al-Khalid based on Norinco's T90-II. Pakistan has also taken assistance from Turkish firms for establishing C4I networks for its strategic delivery systems. Turkey has also offered to assist Pakistan in developing its own design capability in this area. Some degree of design and analysis is being undertaken at its aerodynamics and structural analysis centre with fairly modern computer numerically controlled (CNC) facilities for machining and heat treatment.

Naval Systems: Pakistan's experience in naval system development seems to be limited, but with some success in towed sonar development and simulators for sensor and weapon system operation. This is one area in which India has an obvious technological edge, due in part to the fact that India has a longer coastline to defend.

Future Trends: Pakistan is focussing on enhancing its indigeneous capability in electro-optics. Its future area of work has been identified as thermal imager techniques for night vision devices. On the missile systems front, Pakistan has tacitly acknowledged its aim of developing expertise in extended range cruise missiles—a follow up on Babur with possible capability for launch from submarines and also with an extended range upto 1,000 km. Shaheen and Ghauri will also be upgraded to enhance their range and perhaps manoeuvrability with greater focus also on attendant propulsion and guidance technologies. There is however no visible output/development activity in the material sciences which might be a critical factor if Pakistan wants to build up its indigeneous capability across all technology domains.

The wholesale import of Chinese/Russian technology may have helped to jumpstart Pakistan's fledgling missile/aeronautics capability but it remains to be seen how much original capability has been developed over the last two decades of technical cooperation with China. Has the technological capability of Pakistani scientists and engineers really improved dramatically or are they a nation content to utilise proven and readymade systems, in their bid to attain faster technological superiority over India. This is a question which needs greater analysis.

China

Although military modernisation figured as the last of the four pillars in modernisation priorities, China has realised that technology is the cutting edge of modern combat and has embarked on an ambitious programme to revamp its technological capabilities. Over the last two decades, the People's Liberation Army's (PLA) ability to purchase, co-produce and absorb foreign weapons and military technology is reflected itself in its growing strength.

China's national security and economic competitiveness has been guided by four main principles: (i) acquisition of foreign systems by technology transfer through joint ventures, (ii) licensing and co-production arrangements, promotion of commercial initiatives in scientific labs, (iii) creation of a venture capital industry to promote innovative technology startups, and (iv) ensure a greater role for industry in R&D. As a result its industrial growth has taken off almost simultaneously with technological growth. Its vast defence infrastructure has transformed itself into a strategic enterprise in close and active cooperation with research institutes and universities.

Science & Technology in China: China has understood the importance of S&T for a rapid economic growth. It launched in quick succession several major programmes which would be the backbone of its technological growth. These were:

- National High-Tech R&D Programme (863 Programme), which aims at promoting applied research and accelerating high-tech development, in line with demands of important national strategies. It covers 19 research fields in 6 high-tech priority areas, including IT, biotechnology, advanced agricultural technology, advanced materials technology, advanced manufacturing and automation technology, energy technology as well as resource and environment technology. Started in 1986, the programme had received totally US $5.8 billion for the first 15 years. Its budget in 2004 allocated approximately US $3.8 billion for 3,888 projects.
- National Basic Research Programme of China (973 Programme), for the development of comprehensive and multidisciplinary basic research and also involves important cutting edge basic research and fostering the creativity of outstanding scientists. The programme is implemented by National Science Foundation and other bodies.

- National Key Technologies R&D Programme which works to provide technical support for industrial restructuring, the sustainable development of society, and the enhancement of living standards by achieving breakthroughs in key technologies, introducing technical innovations, and the application of new high-tech technologies.
- Programme 211 which aimed at establishing about 100 higher education institutions as a national priority for improving quality of teaching, level of scientific research and administrative efficiency of higher education institutions. The funding of Project 211 comes from the Central government, ministries, local government and higher education institutions. These programmes laid the foundation of what is today a thriving S&T structure which is paying rich dividends in all major spheres—most importantly defence.

Figure 21.2 which shows at a glance China's strategic focus on developing technology organisations. Diffusion of knowledge takes place as and when required between various arms of the S&T structure, guided brilliantly by state directives.

Defence Budget: China's defence expenditure comprises salaries, allowances and pensions, investment in the development of advanced weaponry and purchase of equipment. In 2005, China's budget was reportedly $35 billion. The official defence budgets have remained relatively small in terms of their shares of GDP (1.6 per cent in 2002) and total government expenditure (8.5 per cent in 2002). In 2008 this figure has officially gone up to $60 billion while US estimates put it at over $100 billion. The published PLA budget excludes several important categories of spending, including R&D, cost of weapons procurement etc. A realistic estimate of Chinese defence spending would be two to three times higher than the official figure, putting it almost at par with Russia and Japan. The official figure has steadily increased from about $10 billion in 1996 to about $60 billion in 2008, while realistic figures indicate a growth from $40 to $110 billion. The breakup of the defence budget is as follows: 19 per cent for the army, about 24 per cent each for the navy, and air force, while 5 per cent is exclusively devoted to ballistic missile systems and 28 per cent to R&D. Since 1995, China's overall R&D expenditure has been growing at more than 20 per cent

Figure 21.2

Public Governance of S&T and Innovation in China: The Institutional Profile

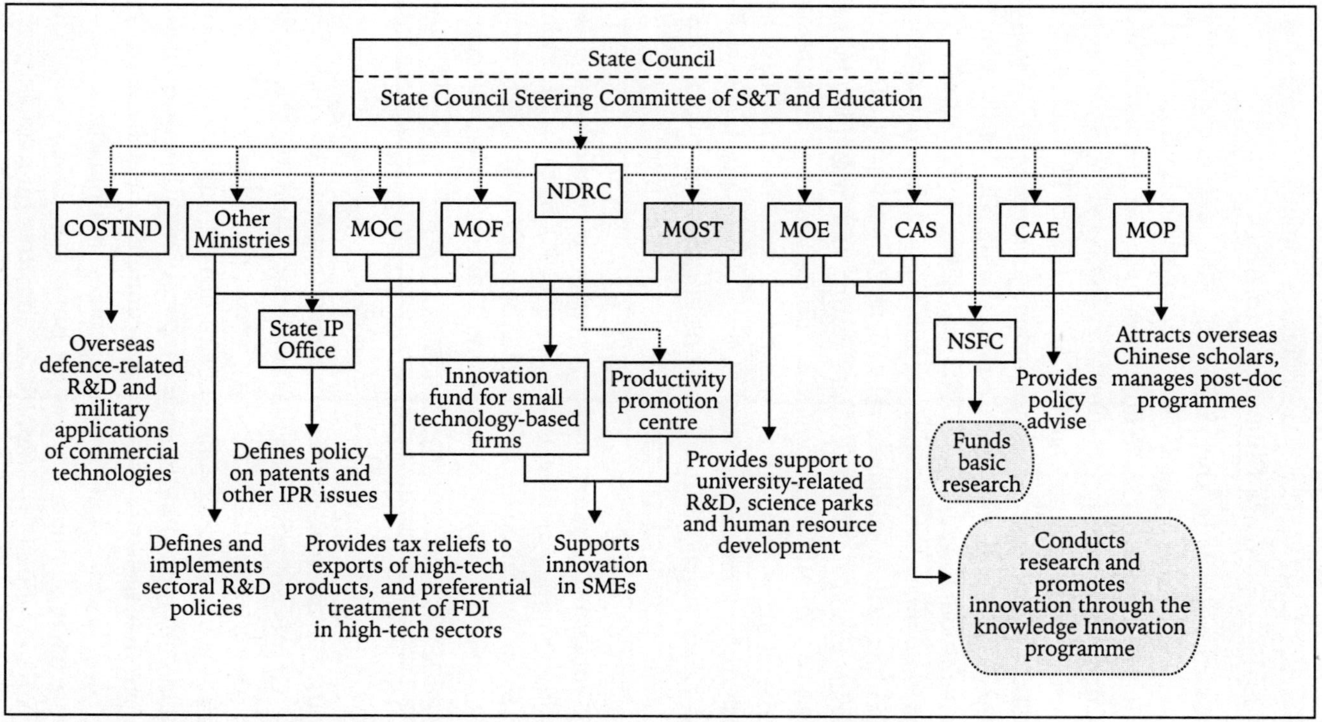

Source: *OECD Reviews of Innovation Policy China*, Synthesis Report 2007.

per year, surpassing the 6 per cent rise in the US and 5 per cent in Japan and Europe. The budget figures indicated above speak volumes about the importance China gives to R&D.

Defence R&D: In the '80s and '90s, defence R&D was mainly controlled by the Commission of Science, Technology and Industry for National Defence (COSTIND), whose place in the overall S&T structure of China is indicated in Figure 21.2. COSTIND was established in 1982 by the merger of the Defence Science and Technology Commission (DSTC), the National Defence Industry Office (NDIO) and the Science Technology and Equipment Commission (STEC) of the Central Military Commission (CMC). COSTIND was given responsibility for research, development, production of certain high technology weapons and for providing policy guidance related to military production. It also had overall responsibility for China's testing and evaluation bases. In March 1998 COSTIND underwent a substantial transformation and its responsibilities changed significantly. It became a ministry level agency under the control of the State Council. It was put under civilian control and all its strictly military responsibilities were taken away and given to a new PLA department under the CMC called the General Armaments Department (GAD). In 2007, the State Council approved a new investment system under government regulation and control, with positive military-civilian interaction. In 2008, the State Administration for Science, Technology and Industry for National Defence (SASTIND) under the Ministry of Industry and Information Technology (MIIT) was established.

The new SASTIND, in spite of a significant reduction in status, does however continue to exercise control over R&D within the industrial enterprises that are contracted with the PLA-GAD, such as the Chinese National Nuclear Corporation (CNNC). SASTIND is mainly responsible for military R&D and military production and has broad authority over China's 10 military industrial corporations. Its duties among others include preparation of policy guidelines related to the management of science, technology and industry for national defence, organisation and management of all international cooperation and exchanges, and it plays an important role in regulating China's exports (and possibly imports) of sensitive military exports—including missile-related and nuclear exports.

Defence Technology Developments

Land Systems: The PLA has extensively leveraged access to foreign technology for modernisation. With Russian assistance it has developed a series of new tanks—the heavy Type 99 which uses the reflex gun-launched anti-tank missile, the medium weight Type 96 which uses a 125 mm main gun and is derived from Russian and Ukrainian technology, the new Type 63A amphibious tank for the PLA marines and the new assault wheeled light tank which is a copy of the 105 mm Russian bastion anti-tank guided missile (ATGM), with a range of 5 km which out-ranges the 105 mm gun used by Taiwanese tanks. The PLA is now producing an Infantry Fighting Vehicle (IFV) armed with a 30 mm and 100 mm gun combination, used by Russian BMP-3A IFV.

Type 98 which evoked much interest in the West has removable cheeks for advanced armour. The main weapon is an adaptation of the Russian 125 mm smooth bore, stabilised with fire on the move capability and is armed with the Russian reflex gun-launched laser guided missile of 5 km range. A special feature is the laser based countermeasure to detect and blind the enemy's optics and automatically direct counterfire. Few T-98s have however been produced due to its high production cost. China is also developing technology for deep penetration warheads, with Israeli assistance and thermobaric warheads developed with Russian technology in the mid-'90s, when it began co-producing Shmel shoulder-fired thermobaric rockets.

For its army aviation forces, its domestically produced helicopters S8, S9, S11 are heavily dependent on European design and engine technology. Eurocopter is co-developing with China a five tonne transport helicopter EC-175, which will have production lines in both China and France by 2011. The S10 development has a consulting collaboration with Eurocopter and Italy's Agusta Aerospace, and has unique design features like a V-shaped fuselage to better deflect blasts.

The Chinese electronics and aviation industry has also produced satellite and microwave communication systems, optical fibre links, surveillance equipment etc., of fairly advanced design. China's has laid special emphasis on strengthening its network control and utilisation expertise, which includes computer network attack, defence and exploitation. Although there is no formal doctrine on this, the PLA have coined the term 'integrated network electronic warfare' to cover the integrated use of electronic warfare, computer network operations (CNO) and limited kinetic strikes against control nodes to disrupt battlefield network information systems. The PLA has established information warfare units to develop viruses to attack enemy units and measures to protect friendly units. Despite a late start China has shown phenomenal growth with the development of an information warfare (IW) doctrine, involving think tanks and academicians, after studying the 1991 Gulf War. It has ensured adequate Internet literacy and penetration among the people and is investing heavily in cyber education and in training hackers. The state however maintains a tight grip on Internet usage by its citizens through a state-of-art monitoring mechanism.

Missile Systems: Chinese mastery in related missile technologies has grown together with their programmes for development of DF-3, DF-4, DF-21 and DF-31. The early versions of DF-3/DF-4 using liquid propellant technology gave way to the solid propellant used in the DF-21 and DF-31/41. Today they have achieved notable success in the area of high energy solid propellants, re-entry thermal protection materials, strap-on boosters, guidance systems for post-boost phase vehicles, control surface actuators, advanced high energy fuels, digital navigation and control and separating warheads—as confirmed by Foreign Technology Assessment (FTA) in the Military Critical Technologies List of the late '90s. This capability development to a great extent has been derived from the massive import of dual use technologies adopted as part of their industrialisation efforts. The Chinese have systematically utilised their purchasing power to acquire a number of technologies specifically in the area of navigation, avionics, composites etc. Russian and Israeli assistance played a considerable role in the advancement of Chinese military technology.

Chinese capability in the field of submarine launched ballistic missiles (SLBMs) has been demonstrated with the development of the JL-1 and JL-2 and JL-3 stage solid propellant missiles respectively. The JL-2 uses inertial guidance, has a range of 8,000 km, will carry at least 3-4 multiple independent re-entry vehicles (MIRVs) and reportedly has a circular error probability (CEP) of 500 m and may carry penetration aids to deflect air and missile defences (AMDs). China has also established expertise in the development of land attack cruise missiles (LACMs) by making parallel technology acquisitions from Russia/ Ukraine and dual use technology from the West. Their indigeneous development (HN-2/DH-10) is expected to have a range of 1,500 km with Global Positioning System (GPS)/Global Navigation Satellite System (GLONASS) guidance supplemented later by terrain contour matching (TERCOM), likely to be equipped with high explosives (HE) and then modified to carry electromagnetic pulse (EMP). Both air and sea launched versions are being developed. The relatively successful experience in small turbofan engine technology used for its anti-ship cruise missiles (YJ-82, HY-4 and Mach 2 supersonic) will aid them in developing turbofan engines for large cruise missiles.

The Chinese have also attempted to build anti-missile systems. In addition to indigeneous development they have purchased off-the-shelf missile defence systems from Russia including the S300 system for deployment around Beijing. It has built considerable expertise in radar systems for tracking and terminal guidance systems. The most important development however was that of FT-2000 anti-radiation missile, designed to neutralise and counter airborne jamming devices—in order to eliminate China's vulnerability to medium and long range surface to air missile (SAM) jamming. The system is available in two versions, a mobile transporter launcher on a 8X8 chassis and also a fixed variant. The FT-2000 also has advanced capability against tactical ballistic missiles and airborne warning and control system (AWACS).

Other developments include the KS-1 designed to engage aircraft and helicopters at altitudes ranging from 500 m to 25 km. This is a single chamber dual thrust solid fuel missile with a maximum speed of 1200m/s. The improved KS-1A has an advanced 3D C-band mono-pulse planar phased array radar operating in a 300 Mhz bandwidth with a detection range of 120 km and tracking range of 90 km. It can track 100 airborne targets and simultaneously engage 50 targets. The HQ-9, an important innovation, is a long range all weather SAM used against aircrafts and cruise missiles. A shipborne version is being developed on the air defence missile destroyer. It uses a track via missile terminal guidance system and its development owes much to the import of S-300 systems from Russia. It has a slant range of 200 km up to an altitude of 30 km. The proximity fuse on the warhead has a maximum effective range of 35 m and becomes active at 5 m. The HQ-9 like the S-300 and the FT-2000 is cold-launched.

China's indigeneous efforts at ballistic missile defence (BMD) have been a minor success but they are reportedly not as sophisticated as the ones made in India. Their intercept capability is limited to an altitude of 30 km. The recent tests of exo-atmospheric missile interception conducted on January 10 2010 have not revealed data on the exact interception altitude but point to China's determination to master this critical technology.

Maritime Systems: Over the last two decades Chinese leadership have realised the importance of maritime power. The mainstay of maritime modernisation has been its material modernisation programme which included larger ships, aircrafts, more sophisticated systems and long range delivery vessels with force multipliers. One major problem, however, is its dependence on foreign sources for propulsion, navigation and weapon sub-systems. Its military strategy changed from static coastal defence to active off-shore defence in the mid-'80s. China's first and second generation warships were mainly of Soviet design with many design and construction flaws. However, since the late '90s there has been a quantum improvement in its third generation vessels which are equipped with features like high weapon density, endurance and even stealth. China has never been able to develop advanced sonars indigeneously and has always relied on foreign acquisitions, mainly French and Russian. China's overall anti-submarine warfare (ASW) capability remains weak because of the limitations of its sensors.

Submarine Capability: China took up the development of nuclear submarines in 1958 with Soviet assistance. The building of a new generation Type 093 SSN (nuclear attack submarine) and a Type 092 SSBN (nuclear ballistic missile submarine) was taken up in the 1990s, followed later by the Type 094 SSBN armed with JL-1 and JL- 2 SLBMs (submarine-launched ballistic missile). Equipped with two pressurised water nuclear reactors, the Type 094 was launched in July 2005, faced sea trials from 2006 and is expected to be commissioned by 2010-2012. A new version Type 096 with greater propulsive power (additional water jetstream turbines) and lower noise level (< 100 db), greater operating depth and displacement and with 16 vertical launch missile tubes is reportedly under development. China is also reported to have succeeded in developing a high-temperature gas-cooled reactor (HTGR)—a new generation revolutionary breakthrough still under development elsewhere. The HTGR was part of the 863 high-tech plan of China and if successful, promises to give People's Liberation Army's Navy (PLAN) submarines unprecedented speed, low-noise level, reactor safety and a technology edge in the field.

Chinese Airpower Systems: China's aerospace capability is progressing rapidly. This has been achieved by a judicious mix of indigeneous skill sets and imported foreign technology through outright purchase of major platforms. Considerable technological assistance has been obtained via joint ventures with European countries including France, Italy, UK and Israel. Series production of J-10, JF-17, FBC-1 and Y-8 is underway as also that of short-range ballistic missile (SRBM), ground/air launched cruise missiles, UAVs and UCAVs.

The Chinese quest for indigeneous development began when they impounded some new MIG-21s sent from Russia to North Vietnam. This was the beginning of a comprehensive reverse engineering programme, through which the aircraft was converted into a top class interceptor, with enhanced serviceability and reliability. China also managed to persuade Russia to sell the RD-93 and AL-31FN turbofan engines for its two aircraft programmes. By purchasing about 200 refurbished Rolls-Royce Spey 202 engines it acquired access to European technology, and also began developing its own WS-10 turbofan—a 13,500 kg thrust vectoring engine expected to fly in J-10 and which has reportedly been certified for production. It has a collaboration agreement with the Ukraine for transporting aircraft manufacture and has begun processing with France a variety of helicopters while simultaneously developing its own designs with active support of European majors like Eurocopter, Aérospatiale and European Aeronautic Defense and Space Company (EADs).

China has also embarked on an ambitious programme for development of the J-XX a fifth generation fighter plane expected to enter service around 2015. A twin engine multirole fighter with enhanced stealth and manoeuvrability capability, it is considered superior to the Rafale and EF-2000 but is inferior to the F-22. With an internal weapons bay to reduce radar cross-section (RCS) it would be powered by two RD-33 or AL-31 F-41 engines. Interestingly, Chinese aircraft designers will actually accomplish a 'generation leap' if the J-12 goes into service with People's Liberation Army Air Force (PLAAF). All aircraft produced in China before this (apart from the licensed Su-27) have been third generation aircrafts. China will have to take western/ Israeli/Russian help to make the J-12 a truly fifth generation machine.

UAV/UCAV Development: Chinese efforts towards unmanned systems, was demonstrated on the occasion of the 60th anniversary celebration of the PRC, where about 10 tactical UAVs were on display. Futuristic concepts, such as the 'Dark Sword' or the 'Xianglong',—a UCAV with high manouverability at supersonic speeds are under development—but China is reportedly yet to master the technology for more secure control and communication links for the operation of UAVs.

Use of Space for Air Surveillance: To leapfrog its modernisation process, China has identified space as the next important area to be controlled and has given a major boost to its space industry with emphasis on space launch and space-based systems for C4ISR operations. It has launched its own Beidou navigation system in response to the GPS and is simultaneously participating in the European Galileo programme. The Chinese Beidou system is a regional system covering the country and neighbouring areas and will provide communication, navigation and positioning features exclusively to Chinese users.

China's Directed Energy Weapons Capability

China's foray into DEW began as part of programme 863 in the late '80s and helped evolve cutting edge technology in many areas most specially in optoelectronics and laser technology. Today Beijing's laser technology industry consists of 3,000 engineers in 300 scientific organisations with nearly 40 per cent of the R&D devoted to military applications. Recognising its potential China has invested heavily in DEW development over the last two decades. Russia continues to be a source of military laser technology for China, with a number of its design bureaus working in this field. The September 2006 test proved that China has enough capability in high power laser technology to build low earth orbit (LEO) satellites. China had reportedly developed by 1999 a laser based, anti-missile, anti-satellite system and had conducted tests of this new technology, which helped them to test miniature nuclear weapons and helped PLAN in locating hard-to-find US nuclear submarines. Chinese efforts are also on for the development of free electron laser weapons with added advantages of adjustable wavelength and bandwidth and a potential range of 5,000 km. An anti cruise missile laser weapon incorporating the most mature high energy laser technology with deuterium fluoride(DF) chemical laser has also reportedly been developed. China has developed the concept of correcting waveform distortion using adaptive optics, utilising continuous faceplate deformable mirrors made of silicon dioxide, with PST actuators providing wave front compensation. The Shanghai Institute of Optics and Fine Mechanics (SIOM) has developed a sophisticated multifunctional and high energy laser beam system, and laser fusion technology which is a good indicator of China's basic strength in high energy laser technology. China considers itself a world leader in adaptive optics next only to US and Germany. It is also actively developing large scale laser-range finders, lidar, excimer lasers and researching atmospheric effects on laser transmission. The Beijing Aeronautical Manufacturing Technology Research Institute (BAMTRI) has established a centre of excellence in photoelectronic technologies in technical and financial collaboration with western firms. Guangzhou has been assisted by Lucent Technologies and others to establish itself as the 'photon valley' of China.

Not much is published about China's strength in other DEW systems *viz.*, EMP and HPM. However, reports indicate that China, Cuba and Iran are jointly developing an HPM weapon called 'E bomb'. Chinese designers are also working on countermeasures for reducing HPM interference and damage, and are designing transmitters and receivers which are less sensitive to known HPM wavebands and their duty ratios. China is known to be working on radio frequency (RF) and microwave energy beam weapons and research is underway to produce controlled EMP.

Future Trends: According to the US report on *China's Military Power 2009*, China is preparing to transform itself into an 'innovation oriented' society by 2020 and has outlined a plan which defines its S&T focus in terms of—basic research, leading edge technologies, key fields and priority subjects and major special items.

It's basic research portfolio would focus on material design, aeronautics and astronautic mechanics, information technology and nanotech. China has recorded outstanding progress in nanotech starting virtually from scratch in 2002, to being a close second to the USA today.

In the leading edge technology development, China will focus on new materials, research smart materials and structures, high temperature super conducting and high efficient energy materials. Advanced energy technology priority will include hydrogen energy and fuel cell technology, alternative fuels and advanced vehicle technology. Laser and aerospace technologies will be another key thrust area. China's defence industry will concentrate on advanced manufacturing and information technology with focus on radar, counterspace capabilities, secure C4ISR, smart materials and low observable technologies.

Perhaps the most important of the Asian countries in today's context, China has in the last two decades exhibited to the world what is achievable in terms of technological capability, when there is a clear vision, well directed state control and focus on economic and technological progress.

India

India became independent in August 1947, hence while being an ancient civilisation, it is at 60 still a young nation. The British laid the foundations of the defence industry before independence, because of which most Indian establishments continue to follow the British style of functioning and organisational structures.

Science & Technology: A global research report on science and engineering research in India indicates that government spending on science research, is currently 0.9 per cent of GDP which is expected to go up to 1.2 per cent in 2012. However, the availability of qualified researchers has not kept pace with intended enhanced spending. In spite of an 80 per cent growth in scientific publications in the past seven years India contributes only 3 per cent of the world output—far below that of Japan. China which had slumbered through the '80s/ '90s, has shown a dramatic growth after 2003.

The R&D arm of the Indian Ministry of Defence is the Defence Research & Development Organisation (DRDO). Started in 1958, DRDO has grown from a modest beginning of 10 units to its present 50 laboratories engaged in a wide variety of activities. It operates with a financial outlay of about 6 per cent of India's defence budget, which is very modest in comparison with the R&D expenditure of world leaders with the USA at 15 per cent , China at 20 per cent and Israel at about 9 per cent. About one-third of this budget is allocated for project and technology development, another third is earmarked for strategic systems development and the remaining third is utilised for manpower, training and infrastructure development. DRDO's technology spectrum encompasses the entire gamut of defence requirements ranging from aeronautic and naval systems to materials and life sciences as also from soldier selection and protection to sophisticated ballistic missile defence and strategic systems. It could arguably be one of the few organisations of the world which encompasses such a wide gamut of technology disciplines under a single umbrella.

The aeronautics stream consists of a number of laboratories each of which focusses on key areas *viz.*, development of combat aircraft, UAVs, lighter-than-air systems, aero-engines, AWACS and avionics systems. Progress in this important sphere have led to the development of critical technologies including—fly-by-wire digital flight control systems, control laws for unstable configuration, open architecture mission computers and composite structures etc.

DRDO has developed a slew of missiles ranging from the strategic Prithvi and Agni to tactical SAMs like the low-level quick reaction Trishul, the medium range air defence Akash and the top-attack anti-tank guided missile—Nag. A wide range of technologies including re-entry vehicle structure, twin-engine liquid propulsion, solid propulsion, stabilisation and launch from moving platform, autonomous navigation, pre-fragmented and submunition warheads, have been indigeneously developed as a result of these projects.

DRDO has developed a number of electronic systems including a family of radars ranging from the man-portable battlefield surveillance radar to the sophisticated target acquisition and tracking radar which can cover an area ranging from one to 300 km. DRDO has built a family of electronic warfare(EW) systems including land-based and naval EW systems, command, control and communication systems, This has resulted in an indigeneous technology base encompassing high accuracy direction finding systems, jamming technologies, electronics support and countermeasures, travelling wave tubes and TR modules.

DRDO also has a number of labs working exclusively for naval applications in the field of underwater sensors and weapons, special materials and fleet support systems and critical oceanographic studies undertaken in the Indian Ocean region. The major technologies developed by DRDO include transducer arrays and state-of-art signal processing techniques for sonars and propulsion batteries, homing systems and on-board fire control computers for torpedoes, naval paints and protective agents, in addition to mechanical support systems.

In the field of armaments and combat vehicles, DRDO's flagship product is the MBT Arjun. India is one of the few countries in the world to have developed its own MBT (main battle tank). Some other notable innovations include the multi-barrel rocket launcher system Pinaka, engineering and bridging systems which have fostered a number of variants and spawned key technologies such as composite armour, hydro-gas suspension, flow formed rocket motors, mobile launchers and composite propellant technology.

DRDO also has a number of labs working in the Life Science cluster in support of the man behind the machine. The areas of interface cover almost the entire gamut of soldier requirements right from selection and training to performance evaluation, protection, clothing and nutrition in hazardous environments.

Advances in the field of material sciences have been made specifically in conventional metallic alloys, metal ceramics, polymer matrix composites, intermetallics etc. Progress continues apace in the area of smart materials, fullerenes and stealth materials.

Future directions: In the near and mid-term, Indian R&D will focus on the following:

Missile Systems: Focus will be on hypersonic air breathing propulsion together with dual mode ramjet-scramjets for extended air defence. A natural off-shoot of the Brahmos programme will look at developing longer range cruise missiles. Sensor development will focus on inertial and navigation sensors and radar seekers including infrared and laser radar seekers.

Electronics system development will push the envelope to include synthetic aperture radars (SARs) and ground moving target indicator (GMTI), solid state lasers and long range electro-optic systems for UAVs/aerostats and high speed data links. Future developments are expected to look into requirements for the futuristic soldier encapsulating his protection, sensing and combat capability. Unmanned land and naval systems and their attendant technologies have also been identified, including robotics and UAVs with collaborative intelligence network-centric operations. On the naval front super-cavitating technology, air independent propulsion and high energy thermal engines have been identified for future development. Encompassing all these fields will be the proposed development in material sciences with stealth, nanotechnology and multi-spectral camouflage technology taking a leading role.

Aeronautics of the future will focus on the next generation of combat aircraft featuring super-cruise and stealth with thrust vector control. Extended altitude and endurance envelope of UAVs in the MALE/HALE class as also AEW&C with SAR and 360° coverage will be other focus areas in the future.

Over the years a number of DRDO systems have been produced and inducted into service. However the Indian armed forces continue to rely heavily on imported systems and the fact remains that India is among the leading arms importing countries of the world. This can be attributed to two reasons. Firstly, indigeneous systems have taken a long time to develop, mainly because they were first time *ab initio* efforts as in the case of the MBT LCA and the missile family. In addition a manufacturing and industrial base had to be created to ensure production capability. Defence production in India is further hampered by a lethargic public sector led by the ordinance and defence PSUs. The second contributing factor was the technology denial regimes which came into force after the 1998 nuclear test, through which supply of critical components and parts was withheld, leading to major delays in project completion. This actually turned out to be a blessing in disguise because India was then forced to develop some of the critical components which it had been denied. However as on date there is no government policy which specifies the quantum of indigeneous defence acquisition and hence the armed forces have preferred to procure proven systems from abroad. This has had a cascading effect on indigeneous development as lack of opportunities to field these systems has blocked the path for improvements and upgrades.

South Korea

Following the withdrawal of the US forces at the end of the Korean War and the collapse of South Vietnam in the early '70s, the Republic of Korea initiated a well thought out plan to develop the defence industry. In the '80s most R&D programmes were government driven and focussed on improvement of conventional weapons but R&D on certain key technologies resulted in laying the foundation for particular capabilities. In the '90s industry-driven R&D projects became more common and more and more facilities were granted to private industry and even licensed production was encouraged.

The government's efforts meanwhile were reserved for developing core technologies and components for high-tech precision weaponry.

Science & Technology: In 2007 South Korea was about 6th or 7th in world rankings for scientific and technological competitiveness according to the International Institute of Management Development. Today it has risen to fifth position in science competitiveness while falling to 14th place in technology competitiveness. To boost capability South Korea has looked to outsourcing and technology integration to boost its R&D capability. The gross R&D investment of South Korea is 3.2 per cent of GDP which is slated to be enhanced to 5 per cent by 2012. South Korea envisages energy scarcity as the greatest challenge in the coming decades and as it imports 98 per cent of its energy requirements, the development of weapon systems based on low carbon green energy is top priority for South Korea's science establishment. Hence development of hybrid engines, hybrid fuel cells, hydrogen engines, high density synthetic fuels, hydrogen and solar cells have become a focus area.

South Korea is following a multi-pronged strategy to meet its national goals. This includes the convergence of S&T with defence R&D, creating a close synergy between defence, private industry and the IT sector and forging an alliance between industry, academia R&D institutes and the Agency for Defence Development (ADD).

The ADD was established in 1970 for dedicated R&D and promoting domestic production of basic weapons with technical assistance from the US. However R&D was not given much priority until the '90s, when indigeneous technology was suddenly given priority and research institutes of the ADD started working in co-ordination with academia and industry. The academia conducts the basic research, government funded institutes carry out applied research and development of core technologies, while the defence industry focusses on commercialisation and production—a structure typical of most developed countries of the world. The ADD is today the premier R&D arm of the Ministry of Defence. It operates with a budget amounting to about 5.4 per cent of the defence budget which in 2006 was about $26 billion. This is expected to go up to 7 per cent in 2012. ADD utilises about 61 per cent of the R&D budget, with 24 per cent of the amount allocated to industries and 14 per cent by other institutions. ADD's mission is the research, development, test and evaluation of weapon systems and related technologies to achieve self-reliance. The organisation is controlled by a board of trustees with the president as the executive head. It has about 2,500 employees in seven institutes and one defence test centre. It deals with a wide range of disciplines such as PGMs, C4I2SR for ground, naval and aircraft systems.

The seven institutes under ADD are the:

- Precision Guided Munition Institute.
- C4I2SR Institute.
- Neo Technology and Energy Institute.
- Ground Systems.
- Naval Systems.
- Aircraft Systems Institute.
- The Systems Test Centre.

Some of the major achievements of the South Korean defence R&D and industry are:

KT-1: a single engine turbo-prop basic training aircraft, the first indigeneous aircraft jointly developed by Korean Aerospace Industries (KAI), Daewoo and ADD. Launched in 1988, its first flight was in November 1991. It was introduced into service in 2000 and is today exported to Indonesia, Central America and Southeast Asia. An armed advanced trainer with light attack capabilities has also been developed. The KT1 has a max speed of 648 kmph and a range of 1,700 km with a service ceiling of 11.5 km.

The Hyunmoo cruise missiles, are long range (500-1,500 km) subsonic cruise missiles capable of carrying a 500 kg conventional/500 KT thermonuclear warhead. Developed by ADD, the missiles are similar to the US Tomahawk with inertial guidance systems aided with GPS. They are designed to be used on destroyers and submarines with vertical launch systems. Barred by Missile Technology Control Regime (MTCR) regulations, South Korea focussed on developing long range cruise missiles, without restrictions on payload and range and also created the missile command to manage these missiles.

The K2 Main Battle Tank, is another indigeneous product of South Korea. It has a 1500 hp engine, advanced suspension, kinetic energy penetrator munition and composite armour. This MBT which was declared production-ready in 2006, following 11 years in development and a research budget expenditure of approximately $230 million. More than 90 per cent of the tank is reportedly indigeneous which points to a high sufficient level of technological maturity.

The K11 dual barrel airburst weapon, the K21 Infantry Fighting Vehicle, the K9 Thunder—a 155 mm self-propelled howitzer and the Chiron, Haesung, Blue Shark and satellite communication systems are some of the other indigeneous products from the ADD stable.

Specialised research centres include the Korean Advanced institute of Science & Technology for electro-optics and electronics; the Seoul National University for automatic control and marine sonics and the Advanced Institute of Military Science &Technology for system concepts and analysis. In 1998 the government initiated the five-year science and technology renovation plan which focussed on dual use technologies which were of considerable use to defence projects.

South Korean defence production has been primarily carried out by its three major manufacturers—Samsung, Daewoo Hyundai and their subsidiaries. While Samsung focusses on artillery, electronics, military vehicles and aerospace, Daewoo manufactures small arms and ordnance and Hyundai builds military vehicles and ships. Today these three companies are among the Top 100 world arms producers—a testament to the fact that the private sector forms the backbone of South Korean defence production and this is on the increase.

South Korea will in the future concentrate on developing extended range cruise missiles, and perhaps next generation technologies for combat aircraft and land systems. However their main thrust seems to veering towards developing green technologies for their systems including fuel cells, hybrid engines etc.

Like some other countries of Southeast Asia, South Korea has also built up considerable expertise in electronics and basic control systems. However they have not attempted to deviate much from their niche areas, because US support and protection will be available to them in any military conflict in the future and hence precious financial resources do not need to be squandered on expensive defence R&D.

Iran

In the past, Iran had lacked the indigeneous capability to produce arms and ammunition but in the aftermath of the Iranian revolution in 1979, military sanctions imposed by the West forced Iran to pursue a path of self-sufficiency by gradually building up its own military-industrial complex. Today Iran produces vast quantities of military equipment which is exported to over 30 countries around the world including seven European countries. Iran's defence apparatus operates in close collaboration with Russia, North Korea and China.

In November 1982, the Islamic Revolutionary guards Corps (IRGC) was expanded to include a Ministry of IRGC (IRGCM), which set up arms factories of its own. The IRGCM was put in charge of military procurement and large amounts of money were allocated to munitions and weapons programmes. The other Iranian defence industries were under control of the Ministry of Defence and Armed Forces Logistics, which by 1982 were centralised under the Defence Industries Organisation (DIO).

Science & Technology in Iran: Under the Second Five-Year Plan(1995-2000), science and technology were declared as top national goals with stress on infrastructure, research and education. The emphasis of R&D centres was on three fundamental areas—metallurgy, electronics and aerospace. The aim of state funded centres was to develop a scientific and professional technical community within the country. At the same time support for S&T education was given a major boost with expansion of Iranian academia. All of this combined to give a major boost to S&T in Iran.

Defence Budget: Iran's 2007 defence budget was estimated to be $7.31 billion by the International Institute for Strategic Studies. At $102 per capita, this was lower than that of other Persian Gulf nations and lower as a percentage of gross national product than that of all other Persian Gulf states (2.6 per cent of GDP in 2007). Iran's ranks 25th in the world in defence expenditure. Its budget for defence R&D has never been tacitly detailed/accepted and its expenditure is spread over different domains and units.

Defence R&D: Iran's defence R&D is conducted by the Defence Technology and Science Research Centre (DTSRC), a subsidiary under DIO—a unit whose existence is shrouded in secrecy, and appears mainly in the entity list of western governments. DTSRC's main facility is located in Karaj, near Tehran. DTSRC develops guidance systems, propellants, and solid- and liquid-fuel engines, and also conducts aerodynamics and wind-tunnel studies. However defence product development is carried out by a number of other agencies also, mostly under the DIO umbrella.

Aeronautics: Iran set up the Aviation Industries Organisation of the Armed Forces (AIOAF) to oversee the task of indigenisng aerospace technologies and focussed on three goals: providing and expanding basic aeronautics, with emphasis on the integrated design of aerospace; 'smart weaponry' and 'globalisation' concepts; and creating a concentrated and modern management structure for the new technologies. They carry out design and manufacture of aircraft in addition to life extension programmes. Currently there are 19 state-owned centres around the country involved in aerospace and related activities, which employ over 100,000 technicians and engineers.

Iran has undertaken many joint development contracts and projects with Russia following the break up of the Soviet Union. Project Integral (also known as Shafagh), was one such joint project between Iran's Aviation Research Centre (now part of the Malek Ashtar University) and the Russian Eurasia/Mukhamedov OKB to develop a jet trainer aircraft. However, these did not progress well and the Iranians are now keen to pursue some of these projects alone.

According to *Military Balance 2008*, Iranian national aerospace policy suffers from a lack of long-term planning, although it has succeeded in getting rid of its reliance on foreign sources in many major fields. Since the Iran-Iraq war, Iran has concentrated on the indigeneous design and production of UAVs. The main organisation in charge of developing UAVs in Iran is the Qods Aviation Industries. It was established in 1985 to design and produce a variety of cost-effective UAVs from composite materials designed for missions such as battlefield reconnaissance, surveillance, attack, electronic warfare, communications relay, traffic and border control, cartography, training, decoy, and aerial targeting. The organisation functioned under the ministry of IRGC, which was later merged with the DIO in 1992. Iran also reported that it had successfully tested a 'stealth' UAV during naval exercises in the northern Persian Gulf. In February 2007 it claimed to have started mass production of a stealth drone of 700 km range which was to be used for surveillance and was due to its shape and material reportedly undetectable by radar. Qods also develops its own navigation and guidance systems.

The more established IAMI has also developed several UAVs which are now been in service and the IAMI has offered the system to other countries, including Malaysia. The Ababil UAV is another Iranian project. With a canard configuration and accurate aerodynamic design the Ababil is equipped with a pneumatic launcher, which can be also launched by using a rocket launch system and from a ship deck. The Ababil is equipped with the Shahid Noroosi guidance and control system designed and manufactured in Iran. Configured for a 30 km range extendable to 120 km the Ababil is Iran's first complete system foray into UAV development. Currently IAMI is designing a new generation jet-powered UAV, named Ababil-Jet, equipped with an indigeneous jet engine, developed from a French design, at IACI.

Missile Systems: Iran's missile capabilities have increased vastly since the first Shahab-3 test in 1998. In addition to obtaining Scud-B missiles from Libya, Syria and North Korea, Iran also initiated its own surface-to-surface missile project, run by the DIO and IRGCM. The DIO built the solid-propellant Oghab (Eagle) artillery rocket with a 40 km range, which is an unguided 230 mm artillery rocket with a range of 34-45 km. It is spin-stabilised in flight but has a proven circular error probably in excess of 500 m, making it a highly inaccurate weapon. It carries a 70 kg (150 lb) high explosive fragmentation warhead, though it may also be able to carry chemical warheads. According to US sources, a modified version has been developed that can be carried and fired from Iranian Air Force F-14 Tomcat and F-4 Phantom II aircraft. The missile was developed from the Chinese Type-83 artillery rocket during the Iran-Iraq war, with the assistance of the People's Republic of China.

The Aerospace Industries Organisation (AIO) is a relatively newly established division created by the integration of all the scientific centres working on missile R&D and production projects, with the idea of pooling all the available resources throughout the missile industries, whether under the control of the DIO, or the IRGC. It has over 13 large factories, employing more than 10,000 personnel. The Karaj Missile Development Complex controlled by the DTSRC, houses the missile design and testing facility, which worked with Chinese and Russian assistance on the Shahab-3 programme.

The AIO carries out missile related research, offers technical engineering consultancy and carries out R&D on sensors, gyroscopes and accelerometers. Its major product line includes a number of systems, the most prominent being the medium range Zelzal artillery rockets incorporating Chinese solid propellant technology, Fateh-110 surface-to-surface missile, and finally the Shahab family of liquid and solid-fuel SSMs. The range of these rockets and missiles varies from 45 to 75 km for Fajrs, 100 to 150 km for Naze'ats, 200 to 250 km for Zelzals, and 300 to 2,000 km for Shahab missiles. SRBMs with a range of 200-700 km have been developed which are possibly indigeneously modified adaptations of the Chinese M9 and M11 missiles. The majority of the R&D for Zelzal (Zelzal-3 has a CEP of 4 km)was conducted at DTSRC and also supported by a computer research centre in the Lavizan military district north of Tehran and by a missile test facility in the suburbs of Semnan. Chinese experts have been assisting in the development of guidance systems and solid-fuel technology for the Zelzal-3, while Russian experts are believed to be providing design assistance for the Zelzal. Russian experts are also conducting theoretical classes on composites at DTSRC, Sharif University, Amirkabir University, and the Science and Industry University.

The Shahab-I is basically the same as Scud-B, with some small improvements. Shahab-2 is a copy of Scud-C, and Shahab-3 with a range of about 1,500 km, is an enlarged version of the generic Scud, being the Iranian version of the North Korean NoDong-1 missile (itself a derivative of the Scud-B), also incorporating technologies derived from Russia and China, plus numerous indigeneous improvements. The latest improvements are the addition of a new manoeuvrable warhead and solid propellant which has increased its shelf life, stability and accuracy at reduced cost, and has much in common with missiles of the Shahab family. Iran has an active relationship with North Korea in ballistic missile field, and receives missile parts and sub-systems in exchange for test data. Iranian experts are now trying to optimise Shahab-3's flight characteristics to make it harder to intercept by anti-missile missiles, such as Arrow and PAC-3. The Shahab-4 and 5 programmes reportedly started in the '90s with the aim of targeting Israel and Europe, are dependent on Russian technology specially with regard to guidance, engine sub-systems and specialised metals. The Shahab-4 has a range of 2,000 km with a warhead of 1,000 kg and both 4 and 5 are liquid fuelled. Reports have also suggested a strong connection between Shahab-5 and DPRK's Taepodong-2 missile, which in turn is largely derived from Chinese technology.

According to a CRS report, although Iran continues to declare it has no plans to develop an ICBM programme, there is strong speculation that the Shahab-6 could be an active or abandoned Iranian ICBM or even space-launch programme. Iran launched its first commercial satellite on a Russian rocket in 2005 and announced that it had allocated $500 million for its space programme over the next five years. In February 2008, Iran reportedly launched a low-orbit research rocket in preparation for a later satellite launch, which it claimed to have done in August 2008, followed in early February 2009, by the successful launch of its Omid (Hope) satellite on a Safir-2 (or Ambassador-2) rocket.

Electronics Systems: Iran also has a comprehensive defence electronics industry, mainly concentrated near Shiraz. Iran Electronics Industries (IEI) supplies the Iranian armed forces with communications and precision measurement equipment; radars and sonar, night vision goggles and thermal imaging equipment; naval and air navigation systems; ECM and ECCM equipment, encrypting and decrypting equipment, simulators and software. IEI collaborates with numerous domestic and foreign companies, many of which are in Europe. IEI has over 700 qualified and trained engineers and has developed a high potential in R&D which today forms the technological backbone of its output. Shiraz Electronics owned and controlled by Iran's MODAFL is an important subsidiary of IEI. It works on radars, microwave electronics, naval and avionics systems. It also maintains a Shiraz Electronics Research centre for R&D on new products.

By obtaining design capability, Iran is now capable of manufacturing systems adapted to its specific requirements and environmental conditions.

Maritime Industries: The new Iranian doctrine includes manufacturing completely autonomous mobile shore-based missile batteries and missile boat teams which offer as little detectable signature as possible. For Iran, 'stealth' means being small, mobile and built of composite materials, without relying on radar-homing guidance, with the purpose of defeating radar detection or electromagnetic jamming. Various projects of significance include several catamaran projects, Zuljenah, Zolghadr, Falagh-2, Azarakhsh, and Ashura torpedo and missile boats, Unes-22 hovercraft, and two ground-effect flying boats.

Land Systems: Iran's major military industrialisation plans also include the designing and fielding of a main battle tank called

Zolfaghar, which in its latest version—Zolfaghar-3 is almost identical (externally) to the American M-1 Abrams tank. However, despite the fact that the original design phase began in 1991, and the first prototype of the 40-tonne tank was ready in three years, the Zolfaghar has yet to complete its test programme and enter series production.

Besides the Zolfaghar, Iran's major ground forces projects include the Boragh and Cobra tracked APCs; tactical vehicles; and a T-72 licensed production line, complete with reactive armour and laser designation warning system. Iran appears to focus less on this sector, because obviously it is less threatened on the ground than on the sea.

In addition to defence industries, individual services of the Iranian armed forces have developed their own production and overhaul capabilities under the title of 'self-sufficiency jihads' (or Task Forces). Since the '80s, the 'self-sufficiency *jihad*' directorates have frequently sought the assistance of Iranian industrial universities—including Sharif, Amirkabir, Shiraz and Esfahan universities—wherein students work on projects under the supervision of their professors, an example of which, is the Shariff Industrial University which has been working on no less than 60 military projects, as well as holding training courses for the military technical personnel.

Future Trends: According to *Military Balance 2008*, Iran will increasingly focus on stealth technology, by introducing radar-absorbing coatings, smart systems and precision guided munitions, as force multipliers. Iran will also field as many R&D projects as budgetary constraints allow. More funding may be allocated to aviation, which will result in collaborative design and development of advanced fighter aircraft and transport planes. Despite efforts to rectify existing problems, this sector is perhaps the least developed in the Iranian defence industry, suffering mainly from management problems. Iran's advanced laser programme, which is progressing fast, aims at creating a lethal capability by the end of the decade.

Iran is also expected to develop a large launch vehicle based on ex-Soviet ICBM technologies. This capability will give Tehran the option of launching heavier payloads to higher orbits, or larger warheads at greater range.

Iran has made considerable progress in the field of micro-electronics, and has shown its capability to produce 'smart' systems, such as munitions capable of precision targeting. It intends to incorporate these force-multiplier capabilities in aerospace, armour, naval missile and vehicle military industrial sectors, and to supply its large Basij (mobilised volunteer) forces with as many hi-tech capabilities as possible. Iran is also expected to invest heavily in the coming years in command, control, communications, computers, information (C4I) and information management/distribution capabilities, as well in information and psychological warfare techniques.

Close cooperation with China and North Korea and their common political stands and foreign policy inclinations will ensure that Iran continues to receive technical cooperation from these countries in the foreseeable future and hence the importance of having its own indigeneous capability in every technology domain will not be a issue of concern for Iran. One point however is that Iran has developed considerable in-house expertise in missile systems, has succeeded in learning from its mistakes and is also possibly not sharing all its knowledge with its partner countries. It is also clear that in comparison to North Korea whose primary focus is on missile systems, Iran has been able to develop indigeneous capability in a number of additional areas specially defence electronics, electro-optics etc., which will play a critical role in the future development of their land, naval and aeronautic systems.

North Korea

North Korea operates under a highly inflexible Soviet-style military philosophy where decisions are made at the top, while discouraging operational flexibility and initiative at lower levels of command. The Ministry of People's Armed Forces(MPAF) in peacetime has responsibility for procurement of weapons, defence R&D, intelligence-gathering and military training.

According to SIPRI the country's military spending in 2002 was $5 billion, which went up to $6.6 billion in 2007. In 2008, the North Korea's GDP stood at $26 billion. Its military investments are primarily in the field of nuclear, biological, chemical systems and missile programmes.

Science & Technology: S&T policy in North Korea is subject to high degree of government direction and control and S&T development emerged as a distinct national strategy only over the last decade. In 2000, science and technology along with ideology and arms were projected as the three pillars for building a powerful nation. S&T became a important focus of the 2002 reforms which articulated a strong desire to became an S&T nation by 2022.

In the early '80s, the emphasis was on emerging computer technology with pilot plants for IC fabrication and joint ventures and technology cooperation agreements which allowed advanced study in European countries by the Korean elite. A second phase began in the early '90s when computer science colleges were established and an electronics industry was established. A number of research institutes are responsible for S&T research including Academy of Sciences and the Kim Chaek University. Priority is on three core technologies—information technology, nanotechnology and bio-engineering. The defence ministry receives the major share of resources and products. The focus is on electronic warfare and special programmes for computer hackers and electronic intelligence have been established.

Missile Development: North Korea's interest in developing ballistic missile capability is primarily aimed at establishing a strong military force against South Korea, Japan and the US. Accordingly the reach of its ballistic missile programme has been extended from short range to intermediate range and finally ICBMs. Its missile programme is based primarily on Soviet Scud missile technology and it has developed infrastructure for R&D, testing and production. The indigeneous infrastructure has been supplemented by imports of specialised materials and components.

Its missile development programme has been neatly phased over the decades. Its foray into ballistic missiles started with the reverse engineering of Soviet FROG rockets. This solid propellant, ballistic artillery with a range of 50-60 km and a 400 kg high explosive chemical warhead was successfully developed in the mid-'70s. In 1975 North Korea entered into a collaboration with China for producing a short range missile, designated the Dong Feng-61 which was a single stage mobile missile with a range of 600 km and a one-tonne payload. The project was suspended in 1978 but North Korea's technical involvement in the project helped to build its own copy of the Scud missile. At almost the same time a strategic partnership with Egypt also helped in the reverse engineering process of Scud. The Scud B finally developed by North Korea is a single stage liquid fuelled ballistic missile with a range of 300 km and 1,000 kg payload—an improvement over the range and payload of the FROG, but with a relatively unsophisticated on-board guidance system. Based on this effort, North Korea launched an indigeneous version of Scud-B, named Hwasong-5, for which they must have built new facilities or converted existing facilities for production of subsystems such as engines and guidance systems. Key facilities include the Sanum-dong R&D facility, the Musudan flight test facility and the Sungni Automobile factory for mobile launchers.

The Hwasong-5 tests yielded an equal number of successes and failures, which did not stop serial production nor delivery to Iran for use in their war against Iraq. This gave valuable feedback on the operational use of the missile leading to an improved version-Hwasong-6 with a longer range, reduced payload and a slightly modified engine for longer burn time. The CEP was probably less accurate at 1-2 km compared to the Hwasong-5. A number of tests were conducted between 1990 to 1993. However the production of Hwasong-6 was phased out in mid-'90s as North Korea started work on the No-dong missile. North Korea reportedly produced several hundreds of Hwasong-5 and 6 missiles from mid-'80s to mid-'90s and their apparent capability to reverse engineer and upgrade the Scud missiles in a very short time frame is an impressive technical feat which might have been achieved with substantial help from China. Another point to be noted is that while there have been imports of raw material and components for the programme, no major sub-system were found to be manufactured abroad, indicating their considerable expertise in missile production. However, sophisticated delivery system capability might be difficult with the Hwasong having too small a diameter to deliver a nuclear warhead.

The development of Hwasong 5/6 made North Korea more ambitious to upgrade its technical capability with a new missile design capable of targeting Japan and in early '90s the No-dong programme was well underway with a range of 1,200 km and a payload of 1,000 kg, the missile was essentially a scaled up Scud with a similar liquid propellant and larger engine, a single stage with about 50 per cent larger length and diameter (16 tonnes weight, 15 m length and 1.2 m dia). North Korea could have had Soviet assistance in the development process and in 1993 the first successful test was reportedly conducted. Lack of sufficient evidence of tests make it difficult to assess the efficacy of the No-dong though both Iran and Pakistan have also conducted tests on it. A CEP of 3-5 km is expected. Most of the production capacity is indigeneous with the exception of imported electronic components from Japan and special steels alloys from China.

With the development phase of No-dong completed, North Korea with the idea of targeting on US cities, moved up the scale to its most ambitious venture—the Taepodong missile. In the early '90s it initiated the development of two ballistic missiles Taepodong 1 and 2. The TD-1 was estimated to be a two stage missile with a modified No-dong as first stage and Scud-C as second stage, resulting in a range of 2,000 km, a mass of about 20 tonnes with a payload of about 1,000 kg, while TD-2 was expected to have a range of 4,000-8,000 km with similar payload. In 1998 the TD-1 was launched and surprisingly included a third stage designed to launch a satellite with the second stage engine modified for a long burn time at relatively low thrust, allowing the third stage which was solid fuel rocket motor, (carrying a satellite)to reach a high altitude before attempting to put satellite into orbit. This solid fuel engine might have been developed with Chinese assistance. Unlike No-dong, the TD-1 was not mobile launched but could have been silo based. The test launch of TD-1 created enough uproar internationally and temporarily signalled a halt to North Korea's long range missile tests. While capable of delivering small payloads to greater distances including continental USA, the TD-1 with a small third stage would not be able to handle nuclear warheads. Its accuracy is also reportedly less impressive and hence it could be a technology demonstrator and a possible space launch vehicle. The next version the Taepodong 2 an ICBM capable of hitting continental US with nuclear sized payload is believed to be under development. This would require a larger first stage with a cluster of four No-dong engines operating in concert—a potential cause of failure. The second stage could be shorter and larger in diameter thus reducing mass and allowing it to attain higher speeds to reach longer ranges. A solid rocket third stage and re-entry heat shield could be major challenges. An NIE assessment claimed that North Korea does not have the technological capability to build ICBMs of 4,000 to 6,000 km with nuclear payloads. However there are other reports claiming that this could be achieved, with a missile body of lighter materials such as aluminium, magnesium and an improved engine. North Korean scientists are also reportedly working on improved guidance and controls with re-entry technology maybe as the single largest challenge. Another challenge could be the missile's capability for countermeasures against BMD such as decoys etc. In the final analysis the TD-2 has not yet been flight tested successfully—after the two unsuccessful tests of 2006 and 2009—hence its capability is unverified.

Yet another new development seems to be based on the SS-N-6, a single stage liquid fuelled submarine launched Soviet missile of the '60s era. It is shorter and fatter than the No-dong—its development is pure guesswork with no concrete evidence. North Korea has reportedly integrated the Golf-II missile stabilisation and launch technology into the new class of ballistic missile submarines.

North Korea has enjoyed solid technical support from Russia and China which gave the required thrust to its missile development programmes basically by incorporating proven designs obviating the need for protracted testing, helped to jumpstart its status as a missile power. This combined with its known record of missile proliferation to countries like Iran, Pakistan, Libya and Middle East has made North Korea a favourite target for strategic analysts. But in terms of indigeneous technological capability it remains far behind its more illustrious Asian neighbours.

Conclusion

While China and India have both established expertise in design, manufacturing, test & evaluation facilities in almost every technology domain of defence systems, China has the comparative edge in scientific publications, papers and patents. The design and manufacturing capability of Iran has also increased over the last decade and it has understood the importance of investing human resources and finances in research and development to aid its long-term capability buildup. Pakistan and North Korea however continue to be heavily dependent on China and Russia for their present and next generation weapon systems both in terms of assistance in design and infrastructure buildup. India too has been the beneficiary of Soviet assistance but because its defence R&D setup has been kept separate from its defence production—the benefits of Soviet technology transfer have not passed onto R&D. This turned out to be an advantage in the long run, as coupled with the sanctions of technology regimes, India had perforce to build indigeneous capability in key technology areas *viz.*, missiles, aeronautics, secure communication systems etc. However the same lack of state control which did not ensure technology flow between its production and R&D setup, also did not ensure that indigeneous systems got their rightful place in the country's military arsenal—a mistake that China took painstaking care not to commit.

Defence R&D like many other institutions, has been influenced by the emergence of Asia as an important player on the global stage. Of the Asian countries, China emerges as the strongest technological leader, followed by India and Iran. South Korea and Japan while being technologically strong in certain key areas, remain on a different plane as they operate under the umbrella of US protection and support. North Korea with its concentrated focus on nuclear and missile systems, while being of interest to strategic policy analysts, cannot be viewed through the same technological prism as the other nations.

However there are many lessons for developing countries in the emergence of China as a technology leader. First of all is the clear and farsighted vision of Chinese leaders and their well-conceived strategy to ensure technology leadership. The multi-directional attention to all spheres of science and technology—starting from promoting excellence in academic institutions and universities, to incentives for industry, understanding and exploiting the benefits of international collaboration and ensuring its flow to Chinese industry, promoting and incentivising excellence in technical HR, showcasing indigeneous products in its military exercises—all smack of well coordinated, well directed, long-term strategic planning, which are yielding rich dividends today. It is this clear-sighted, long-term planning which will ensure China's top position in the global technology stakes in the near-term and long-term future. India and other nations must learn that if they wish to be a leading force in Asia, a holistic government directed approach with focus on indigenisation, will be essential for long-term benefits compared to reliance on the vagaries of quick import with attendant short-term gains.

References

Adams, Jonathan *et al.* (2009). "Global Research Report China", *Thomas Reuters*, November. At *http://researchanalytics.thomsonreuters.com/m/pdfs/grr-china-nov09.pdf*

Arnett, Eric (1997). *Military Capacity and the Risk of War China, India, Pakistan and Iran.* SIPRI Military Research and Development. At *http://books.sipri.org/product_info?c_product_id=159*

————. (1996). *Military Research & Development.* SIPRI Military Research and Development

Bokhari, E.A.S. (1999). South Korean R&D and Defence Production. *www.defencejournal.com/may99/southkorea.htm*

"China Nuclear Facilities Role of COSTIND". Updated January 2011. *At http://www.nti.org/db/china/costind.htm*

Congressional Research Service Reports (CRS) (2003). *Iran: Arms and Weapons of Mass Destruction Suppliers Updated.* January 3. At *http://www.fas.org/sgp/crs/nuke/index.html*

Council of Foreign Relations (2009). *Annual Report to Congress: Military Power of the Peoples' Republic of China.* March. At *http://www.cfr.org/china/annual-report-congress-military-power-peoples-republic-china-2009/p18943*

Fisher, Richard (2007). *Japanese Military Technology Advances.* December 6. At *www.strategycenter.net*

Gen Yamamoto (n.d.). "Japan: Government and Defence Industry", RUSI. At *http://www.rusi.org/downloads/assets/6yamamoto.pdf*

Globalsecurity.org (2009). *Iran's rapidly Developing Solid Propellant Ballistic Missile & Potential Space Booster Program 2008.* March 25-July 17. At *http://www.globalsecurity.org/wmd/world/iran/solid-prop.htm*

Govt. and Defence Industry (2004). *Rusi Defence Systems.* Autumn. Japan

Hildreth, Steven (2009). *CRS Report Iran's Ballistic Missile Programs: An Overview*, February 04. At *http://www.fas.org/sgp/crs/nuke/RS22758.pdf*

IDSA (2007). *Modernisation of China's Maritime Forces and Land Systems.* IDSA Study.

International Institute for Strategic Studies (2008). "The Military Balance". At *http://www.iiss.org/publications/military-balance/the-military-balance-2008/*

Kobayashi, Sadao (2007). *Research and Development Efforts for the Future.* April. *www.mod.go.jp/trdi/*

Malik, Amitav (2009). *China's DEW Capability.* IDSA (In house) study.

Military Balance 2008.

Military Power of the People's Republic of China. December 26, 2009.

Mustafa, Malik Qasim (2008). "Pakistan's Defence Production". At *www.issi.org.pk/journal/2004_files/*

National Program for Science and Technology. http://china.org.cn

NIST (2005). *A Study of Defence Technical R&D, Comparison of US and Japanese European R&D Policies.* March. *www.depo.org.pk*

NSD Bio Group LLC (2009). *Research Report on Chinese High Tech Industries.* January. At *http://www.uscc.gov/researchpapers/2009/NSD%20BioGroup%20Final%20Report%20'Sunrise'%20Report%2002June2009.pdf*

Porter *et al.* (2008). *High Tech Indicators Technology Based Competitiveness of 33 Nations 2007 Report*. Georgia Institute of Technology. At *http://www.au.af.mil/au/awc/awcgate/nsf/nsf_hi_tech_indicators_33_nations.pdf*

Paek, Jae (2009). "Defence Budget Layout for Successful Promotion of Defense Reform", Centre for Resource & Manpower Development, Korea. Institute for Defense Analyses. November 2. At *http://www.kida.re.kr/eng/pcrm/data/data20091102.pdf*

Pinkston, Daniel A. (2008). *The North Korean Ballistic Missile Program*. February. At *www.strategicstudiesinstitute.army.mil/pdffiles/pub842.pdf*

Research and Development Efforts for the Future. April 2007. *www.mod.go.jp/trdi/*

Scobell, Andrew John M. (2007). "North Korea's Military Threat", At *www.strategicstudiesinstitute.army.mil/pdffiles/pub771.pdf*

South Korean Defence R&D. Conference on Managing Defence R&D. New Delhi, December, 2008.

22

War in 2030

MARTIN VAN CREVELD

To quote that great expert on defence and closet poet, Donald Rumsfeld:

> as we know, there are known knowns. There are things we know we know. We also know there are known unknowns. That is to say we know there are some things we do not know. But there are also unknown unknowns, the ones we don't know we don't know.[1]

Clearly anybody who claims he (or she) knows what the world of 2030 will be like is a charlatan; furthermore, whatever does happen until then will not happen in the same way, and at the same pace, in various places around the world. With these qualifications in mind, I am prepared to add a fifth category to Rumsfeld's four and say something about the things I think I know.

I

First, driven by strategic, economic and technological factors, ownership of nuclear weapons will continue to spread to additional countries. Such ownership is determined by two factors, capability and will. As of 2010 even North Korea, an isolated country whose citizens are said to be literally starving, has been able to join the nuclear club; hence it seems that capability has ceased to be a serious constraint on proliferation. As of writing this study, there are nine nuclear countries. Had it been a question of capability alone, the number could easily have increased to 50 or 60. Only in parts of Africa, Central Asia and Latin America are there still countries whose economic or industrial or technical or scientific infrastructure is too backward for them to build nuclear weapons within a reasonable time—say, 10 years—should they want to.

---

1. See *http://state.msn.com/id2081042.*

This does not mean that, 15 years hence, there will be 50 or 60 countries armed with nuclear weapons and their delivery vehicles. Many European countries and several Latin American ones are capable of building nuclear weapons. However, presumably they will do so only if they feel that their vital interests, indeed their very existence, is being threatened by Russia or the US, respectively. Unless and until this happens, the most likely region in which proliferation may take place is Asia. From Turkey through Iran and Indonesia, Malaysia, South Korea, Taiwan and Japan, Asia contains many countries that have what it takes to build nuclear weapons or will acquire that capability in the foreseeable future. Some also have the will; in particular, Iran (which may be followed by Turkey, which may be followed by Saudi Arabia, which may be followed by Syria, which may be followed by Egypt).[2] In East Asia and Australasia, the factor most likely to trigger off a nuclear arms race is a US withdrawal from those regions. In that case, since China and North Korea have already gone nuclear, South Korea, Taiwan, Japan, Indonesia and Malaysia are likely to follow.[3]

Ongoing efforts at nuclear disarmament notwithstanding,[4] it is therefore necessary to postulate a world with 15, 20, perhaps even 25, nuclear countries of which 6 to 8 may be located in South, Southeast and East Asia. Given the enormous differences between their economies, technical capabilities, and strategic aims, obviously these countries' arsenals will vary very much in size. Some will have many warheads—though none is likely to acquire nearly as many as did the superpowers during the Cold War—others just a few. Some will go on to build tactical nuclear weapons, some would not. Some of these countries may purchase next generation combat aircraft should they become available for sale. One or two of them may acquire ICBMs, as Iran is currently accused of planning to do; however, the vast majority will no doubt content themselves with short, medium, and intermediate range missiles as well as cruise missiles. All will be able to inflict 'unacceptable' damage on their neighbours, meaning that

2. See, for Egypt, Sydney Morning Herald (2007).
3. On the way proliferation may proceed see Braun and Chyba (2004).
4. Fletcher and Pan (2009).

they will have what it takes to turn much of them into radioactive deserts. What will such a world look like, militarily speaking? That is the next question we have to consider.

II

One assumption we can safely make is that an effective, one hundred per cent reliable system to intercept ballistic missiles with nuclear warheads will not be found in the next two decades (if ever). Especially if the missiles are multiple independently targetable re-entry vehicled (MIRVed), as some undoubtedly will be; and especially if they are provided with various modern penetration aids.

Attempts to build a defence against nuclear-tipped missiles are now approximately 50 years old. Focussing on the US as the most technologically-advanced country of all, in the late 50s there was a missile named Nike Zeus which, however, was never deployed. The Nike was followed by the Sprint, which was followed by the Spartan, which was followed by the Sentinel. None of these missiles was nearly accurate enough to intercept incoming ballistic missiles by means of a direct hit. Hence they relied on nuclear warheads to destroy their targets; a hair-raising proposition which, fortunately for everybody on earth, was never put to the test, let alone turned into an operational reality. The Sprint and the Spartan and the Sentinel having been made obsolete by the Soviet introduction of MIRV, they were followed by the Strategic Defense Initiative, which was followed by the National Missile Defense. Still anti-ballistic missiles were but part of the story. Space-based lasers (which were to drive the energy needed to activate them from exploding hydrogen bombs), ground-based lasers, and other, even less credible, systems have all been proposed and rejected. Counting all systems, the sums spent on ballistic missile defence have easily exceeded $100 billion. All of which have gone straight down the drain.

Like the US, the USSR in the '60s worked on an anti-ballistic missile system known to NATO as the Galosh. Similar to the Nike Zeus, it too relied on a high-yield nuclear warhead and it too was, thankfully, never tested against a real life ICBM (though a battery of Galoshes was deployed around Moscow). Being small, other countries are more likely to take an interest in smaller missiles. Here, too, we have some experience that may be extrapolated into the future. During the First Gulf War much attention was focussed on the American Patriot missiles. They were, however, a total failure; the war over, it turned out that not a single incoming Scud had been downed. Though the Patriot was later upgraded, the new version proved almost as dangerous to friendly aircraft as to the enemy.[5] In any case it has never been tested in action against anything more dangerous than Saddam Hussein's Al-Samoud short range missiles. Even so, the results appear to have been mixed. A few Samouds, fired at Kuwait during the Second Gulf War, may have been downed but others got through. Clearly, no system which cannot do much better than that is even nearly good enough.

Israel's Arrow missile is a very great technological achievement but a military stillbirth. Like the Patriot, in theory the Arrow is 'operational' and one battery has been deployed to cover central Israel.[6] However, earlier versions of the missile have a long history of failed tests. Needless to say, each time this happens lessons are drawn and improvements introduced. Nevertheless, nobody can guarantee how it will perform the next time it is launched; hence it cannot guarantee the survival of anybody or anything. To be really useful—to permit a country to use war as an instrument of politics against another nuclear country without running the risk of national suicide—a defence against nuclear missiles would require not 100 per cent reliability but 10,000. At a guess, no system capable of coming even close to meeting that requirement is likely to emerge during the next 20 years or so.

What applies to the US and its *protégé*, Israel, is even more applicable to the rest. Some members of the European Union have now been talking about developing anti-missile defences for a decade or more, but so far not even a prototype has been produced. One reason for this is that the EU cannot agree who the enemy is; is the threat likely to come from the east, as during the Cold War, or is it the south that demands attention? In view of political disunity and

5. Rose (2003).
6. See for details "Missile Defense and Israel's Deterrence against a Nuclear Iran", n.d., at *http://www.inss.org.il/upload/(FILE)1216205936.pdf*

financial constraints, no European system is likely to be produced in the foreseeable future. Most other countries do not have either the technological infrastructure or the necessary financial means. Russia, China, India, Pakistan and Iran are unlikely to succeed where the US has failed. Twenty years hence, these and other countries will almost certainly be as defenceless against nuclear bombardment as they are now. Since, in the meantime, delivery vehicles will undoubtedly multiply, in all probability they will become more so.

The failure to build a reliable defence against nuclear missiles has far-reaching implications. Back in the early 60s, US defence planners came up with something known as Mutual Assured Destruction, or MAD. Though that doctrine was later discarded, and though the US has since devised many other fanciful doctrines, in practice MAD continued to prevail and does so today. Various other countries have also devised nuclear doctrines of their own. Some are better known, others less. Some required certain kinds of weapons and delivery vehicles, others different ones. Doctrine may have driven technology or the other way around. In the end, none of it mattered.

As a doctrine, MAD could be ignored, or discarded, or replaced, or even ridiculed. As a matter of practical reality, fear of escalation has caused it to remain in force not only in the US but wherever proliferation took place. Over a period of some 50 years, it has very largely kept the peace among all nuclear countries without exception. This situation is especially evident if one compares what big powers have done, or not done, to each other since 1945 to what they did during the three centuries before that. Nor is it likely to change over the next 20 years.

III

Let us assume, then, that nuclear proliferation continues apace, MAD prevails, and no nuclear war breaks out. In that case, what can we expect to happen to other forms of armed conflict? Over the last 60 years, the answer to this question has become evident. First the superpowers, then other nuclear countries have ceased to fight each other in earnest and on any scale. A very good illustration of the way things work is provided by South Asia. The largest regional powers,

India and Pakistan, hate each other as much as any two countries in history could have. During the 24 years between 1947 and 1971 they waged no fewer than three bloody wars against each other; once India had demonstrated its nuclear capability by means of its so-called PNE (Peaceful Nuclear Explosion), though, they did not do so even once. Even the so-called Kargil War of 1999 was really a skirmish, not a war. India and Pakistan have agreed to notify each other of manoeuvers held close to each other's borders. Later they also agreed to give advance notice of ballistic missile tests—a measure meant to prevent false alarms and accidental war—and establish a hot line between their capitals.[7]

Of course that does not mean that there will be no conventional armed conflicts left in 2030, let alone that nuclear weapons will inevitably turn old enemies into turtledoves. What it does mean is that, since nuclear proliferation is now well within the capacity even of third-world countries, such conflicts are almost certain to be waged between, or against, smaller and smaller, less and less important, ones. As a look at any of the available international handbooks will show, the size of conventional forces, as well as the armed conflicts that they have fought against each other, has been shrinking for decades. I for one fully expect the decline to continue.

Some people believe that the shrinkage of conventional forces is compensated for, perhaps even created, by the advent of modern weapons including, above all, precision-guided munitions; in other words that the growth of military power, instead of depending above all on quantitative factors as in the past, has become almost exclusively qualitative.[8] I disagree. That modern munitions and weapons are much more effective, and only require far smaller number to hit a similar number of targets,[9] than their predecessors is beyond question. What I dispute is the claim that they are more effective in relation to each other. Pitted against a modern warship, a modern warship is no more effective than its 1945 predecessor was against its

---

7. AP, "India, Pakistan Agree on Nuclear Safety", July 8, 2005, available at *http://news.ninemsn.com.au/article.aspx?id=57188*
8. See for example Kober (2005).
9. For some calculations pertaining to this subject see Kuehl (1995); Israel (2003).

enemy. Pitted against an F-15, a MiG-29 is no more effective than a World War German Messerschmitt-109 was against a British Spitfire or an American Mustang of the same period. While there may be short-time fluctuations, there is no reason to believe that, in the race between airpower and its nemesis, anti-aircraft defences, one side or another is capable of gaining the upper hand—the more so because the electronic gadgets on both sides are quite similar. Thus those who simply compare modern weapons with older ones, commit the most elementary error of all: that of pretending there is no enemy.

Since modern weapon systems are as capable as they are, in case they are employed against each other the outcome will be heavy attrition—as heavy, for example, as was the case during the 1973 Arab-Israeli War and at some points during the Iran-Iraq War. Since the outcome will be heavy attrition, logically if war is to be waged in earnest such systems should be built in greater, not smaller, numbers than their predecessors. This, of course, is not happening. The reason is not because of financial constraints, as most people believe. Rather, it is because the proliferation of nuclear weapons and the prevalence, even if unacknowledged and undeclared, of MAD prevents a growing number of countries from using their conventional weapons against each other to any great extent. Certainly it would be too much to expect that these factors will make all countries give up conventional war, and the forces earmarked for waging it, in the next 20 years. On the other hand, to the extent that countries still continue to wage such wars, those wars will almost certainly be smaller and more localised than those of the past.

IV

Apart from noting the decrease in size and numbers, what else can be said about the forces that will wage conventional wars in 2030 and the weapons they will use? Perhaps the first thing to say is that, the constant talk about 'integration' to the contrary, the basic distinctions will not be obliterated. By this I mean that, in 2030 as today, armed conflicts will still have to distinguish between operations conducted on land, in the air, and at sea as well as the forces designated to fight in these different environments.

To start our survey on land, perhaps the most important development will consist of the decapitation of the forces. The process has been under way for a long time. Not so long ago, the most powerful belligerents such as Russia (the former USSR), Germany, the US, France, Britain and Japan used to mobilise and deploy millions of troops. Those troops were organised in armies, even army groups. Their commanders were generals with so many stars that there was barely enough room on the epaulets. Today the stars are still there. However, the forces have shrunk almost as rapidly as did Alice in Wonderland after she ate the mushroom; which, incidentally, makes nonsense of any talk about 'flattening' the military organisations.[10] In view of the anticipated decline in the scope of conventional war, 20 years hence the largest remaining unit will almost certainly be the division. More likely, it will be the brigade.

To talk of self-contained, independent brigades is one thing, to build them is another. Decade by decade, inventories are swelled as new and often unprecedented types of equipment are introduced; weapon systems, munitions, many kinds of electronic gear, transport, etc. Also, operating and maintaining that equipment is becoming more complex. Complexity in turn means that a more sophisticated command and control system is required to link everything with everything else. The concept of small, highly mobile forces carrying immense firepower while waging 'netwar' or 'swarming' is attractive on paper;[11] however, the truth of the matter is that brigades are too small to contain all the necessary personnel and equipment and still have enough men left to carry fire to the enemy. For this reason, much have to be left to the rear services, service providers, second echelons, or whatever the formations responsible for logistics, maintenance, and administration are called. All around the world, armed forces will be lucky if they can prevent these services from swelling. More likely they will continue to expand, making nonsense of any talk about increasing the fighting 'teeth' at the expense of the 'tail'.

Some of the heaviest weapon systems appear to be on their way out. This applies above all to tanks (I could tell a story of how the Swedish

10. Fukuyama and Shulsky (2000).

11. Arquilla and Ronfeldt (2000).

Army, against my advice, spent a billion dollars buying German Leopard IIs, only to have them rusting somewhere in the snow). The same applies to tube artillery. Invented around 1350, tube artillery is now almost seven centuries old. Throughout this period, guns were always becoming, if not larger and heavier, certainly more powerful than their predecessors had been. Often they stood as symbols of military might as in salutes and the like. However, coming a decade after Israel decided not to go ahead with its new 'drawing' gun, Rumsfeld's decision to cancel the Crusader artillery system[12] was the writing on the wall. Currently few, if any, countries are still producing any tanks and guns. As a result, usually those lost to enemy action or wear and tear cannot be replaced.

In their absence, infantry will be the queen. At a time when large systems have become too vulnerable to precision-guided munitions (PGMs), infantry's great virtue consists of its ability to disperse and hide—especially in urban terrain, where much future combat is likely to take place. Infantry, of course, has always fought mainly on foot. Hitherto all attempts to design a vehicle that will provide troops with protection against fire and still permit them to observe the enemy and fight have failed; hence it will continue to do so in the future, too. On the other hand, infantry will still require transport as well as fire support. To this end various kinds of vehicles up to armoured personnel carrier (APCs) inclusive will remain in use.

Wheeled or tracked, the vehicles in question will carry all kinds of PGMs, including new generations of missiles as well as mortars and the like. Some of the infantry will be carried in helicopters, which given the latter's maintenance requirements means that rear services will grow larger still. It will have at its immediate disposal a variety of small unmanned aerial vehicles (UAVs) useful for surveillance, reconnaissance, target acquisition, and the like. All these will be held together by sophisticated networks of portable computers and radios, permitting the last private in his or her foxhole (or, presumably, sleeping bag!) to locate, and communicate with everybody else.[13] Other things equal, the best troops will be those who grew up with

12. USA Today (2002).

13. See, for a short account of what is being done, Buxbaum (2005); also, Weiner (2004).

these devices and can operate them as if they were a part of their own bodies.

In the air, the larger and more expensive any type of combat aircraft the less of a future it has. Heavy conventional bombers such as the B-52 and B-1, are Cold War relics and will have no successors. No doubt attempts to extend their lifetime will continue; until, like the dinosaurs, they die out one by one as attrition takes its toll. More modern, unconventional aircraft such as the F-117 and B-2 are useful only against countries that do not have nuclear weapons. Not having nuclear weapons, the countries in question are not likely to have terribly sophisticated anti-aircraft defence either; which in turn means that the aircraft are merely white elephants. The Eurofighter, Joint Strike Fighter, F-22, F-35 and F-40 will only be built, if at all, in very small numbers, and then more by way of keeping air forces' *raison d'etre* than to serve in real life war.

The place of all these aircraft will be taken by various kinds of ballistic missiles, cruise missiles, and UAVs. In particular UAVs, which are equally useful for certain kinds of police work, represent a growth industry. Along with PGMs, which will increasingly be mounted on them, they will make the life of any large, heavy, ground-based weapon systems very difficult if not impossible. Cruise missiles, which are relatively simple and cheap to build, will be produced by many additional countries and used against stationary targets. Some will also be made to carry nuclear warheads.

Compared to ballistic missiles cruise missiles are slow. On the other hand, they are easy to transport from one firing position to another and their flight trajectories are very low. These two qualities together make them almost as hard to intercept as their faster cousins, with the result that they can contribute as much to MAD as ballistic missiles do. A number of additional countries will launch earth-circling satellites. Given the expense, however, few if any of them will acquire the full array of space-based communications, navigation, surveillance, reconnaissance, target acquisition, and damage assessment capabilities that the US alone currently possesses.

As manned combat aircraft largely disappear, helicopters and air transport will retain their importance. It is, however, likely that, in many countries, these units will be organised in a different way. Instead of being concentrated in the hands of air forces, as most of them are at present, helicopters and short-range transport may be handed over to the ground forces and navies so as to simplify command and control and shorten OODA (observe, orient, decide and act) loops. Some experts have suggested that, to the contrary, air forces should set up specialised anti-terrorist and anti-guerrilla units complete with their own organic ground combat units; so far, though, the military of no country seems to have taken up that proposal. Everything considered, of the three services the one whose future appears most in doubt is the air force.[14] In the end it may well be left with nuclear-tipped missiles as well as space assets. The former will be useful for nuclear deterrence, the latter for assisting the other two services. That, however, will be all.

At sea, there is now only one country that still maintains an ocean-going navy with global capabilities (including, crucially, the air component without which navies are more or less blind and only have a very limited striking range). Whether or not they admit it, the rest have been reduced to playing the role of coast guards. Whether, 20 years hence, the US will still be willing and able to maintain its vastly expensive navy is out of the purview of this chapter. Suffice it to say that, in case the answer is negative, no other country is likely to take its place in this respect. This explicitly includes China. Having swallowed Hong Kong as a boa constrictor swallows its prey, China's next target is Taiwan. Hence Beijing's navy is likely to grow. It will add submarines and, perhaps, even a small carrier (as to large carriers, so long are the necessary lead-times that China almost certainly will not be able to have one in operation by 2030 even if it started working on one tomorrow).[15] On the other hand, unlike the US, China neither is a global island nor has a highly developed naval tradition. Nor, again unlike the US, does it have any particular desire to export its ideals.

Capital intensive as it is, perhaps even more than land combat naval combat is likely to become smaller and more localised. As has

---

14. Farley (2007).

15. See, on China's ambitions in this regard, "Chinese Navy Working towards Aircraft Carrier Capabilities", *Marport*, May 15, 2009, at *http://blog.marport.com/2009/05/15/875/*

been the case since 1945, fear of escalation will prevent powerful countries capable of building powerful navies from engaging in battles of the Atlantic, let alone of the Pacific. Instead what naval combat, if it takes place, will be waged near the coast and around choke points. Prime candidates for the role are the Straits of Hormuz, the Straits of Malacca, and the Straits of Taiwan. Another probable place is the Straits of Korea—Tsushima, for those who have forgotten!

V

Whereas conventional war is on its way down, becoming smaller and more localised, sub-conventional, low intensity, non-trinitarian, fourth-generation, or whatever it may be called is clearly on the way up.[16] During the '90s, those who saw things developing in this direction were often dismissed out of hand. Now that London, Madrid, and of course New York and Washington D.C. have all been targeted by the new kind of war, this is happening much less often. As was to be expected, nuclear weapons and MAD have not done away with the root causes of war. All they have done is to create a situation where, when it comes to fighting, sovereign entities with territories and borders (states) are increasingly being joined by entities which have neither borders nor territories and are not sovereign. The number of such entities now runs into the hundreds, perhaps more; day by day they are born, merge, separate, and die, often without any kind of formal announcement. Like it or not, terrorism, guerrilla, insurgency and of course the attempts to counter them are here to stay and represent the future. And this, there is every reason to believe, not just in developing countries, where such struggles have long been endemic, but in many developed ones as well.

If there is one lesson to be derived from the history of the last 60 years, surely it is that modern armed forces are ill-suited for such wars. Ruthless though they were, the Germans in 1941-1945 had the greatest difficulty in keeping down some of the territories they had occupied. Later the British lost the struggles in Palestine, Malaysia, Kenya, Cyprus and Aden, after which they gave up the rest of their

16. The most important works on these kinds of war are Creveld (1991); Kaldor (1999); Hammes (2004).

empire more or less without a struggle. The French lost in Indochina and Algeria, the Americans, in Vietnam and in Somalia. The Portuguese were defeated in Angola and Mozambique, the South Africans in Namibia, the North Vietnamese in Cambodia, Soviets in Afghanistan, the Indians in Sri Lanka, the Indonesians in East Timor, etc. The list is practically endless. After decades of struggle, the Israelis have been driven from the Gaza Strip. Their 2006 performance in Southern Lebanon, too, was nothing to boast of.

As current events in Afghanistan illustrate very well, when confronted with this kind of struggle the richest, most powerful, most modern, best equipped, armed forces that ever existed almost invariably flounder. Nor does the willingness to go to almost any length in inflicting death and destruction—the Indonesians in East Timor may have killed as many as half a million people—make much of a difference. This is not the place to analyse why so many insurgencies have succeeded whereas so many attempts to contain or defeat them have failed. Suffice it to say that, as of the early decades of the 21st century, no country however homogeneous, however rich, and however wallowing in its content appears to be safe any longer against the new forms of war. Suffice it to say, too, that something has gone very, very wrong indeed. If there is one task that future armed forces face, it is to analyse the reasons for the failure and make sure they can cope if called upon. Should they fail in this task, then in many cases their existence, and that of the societies they serve, may well be in doubt.

As armed forces adapt themselves to the new world, many of the trends mentioned in Section IV of this chapter will be reinforced. Tanks, artillery and other heavy weapons may be useful when it comes to conquering a country, but their role in policing it is necessarily limited. Countries may be smashed from the air, as Serbia in 1999 was. However, it is impossible to govern them from there; the heavier and more capable the aircraft, the less useful it is in the kind of struggle under consideration. *A fortiori* space-based assets, being very far away, will probably never play more than a marginal role in counterinsurgency.[17] In the past, many insurgents have made use of

---

17. On some space weapons currently under consideration see Deblois *et al.* (2004).

the sea, especially for re-supply. However, fighting them is best done by means of relatively small, relatively agile vessels rather than the behemoth that used to rule the waves during the Cold War; as is also proved by the fact that, no sooner did a couple of Katyusha rockets land in Aqaba (near Jordon), the US warships lifted their anchor and went to sea.[18]

Intelligence agencies, especially those that rely on eavesdropping and can provide HUMINT (Human intelligence), are on their way up.[19] So are Special Forces and, on the other end of the scale, constabularies capable of keeping an eye on things on a day to day basis. Also on their way up are electronic fences, surveillance cameras, devices capable of reliably identifying people, night vision equipment, devices capable of looking inside bags, suitcases and containers, small vehicle portable UAVs, and the like. Everything else is more or less useless and is, or should be, on its way down.

VI

Concerning the general principles of military organisation, the following may perhaps be said. First, by 2030 presumably even the few advanced countries that still retain conscription, such as Norway, will have done away with it. One reason for this is because modern weapon systems are so expensive, hence so few in number, as to be altogether swamped by the number of personnel that conscription could make available; another, because those weapon systems require so much training and so much expert maintenance as to turn short-time conscript service into a dubious proposition.

So far, the armed forces of advanced countries. However, it is a cardinal proposition of the present study that many, perhaps most, armed conflicts will not be fought by advanced armies but by the rag-tag forces of developing countries engaging in low intensity warfare, counterinsurgency, civil war, or whatever. The lack of an appropriate

18. CBC, "Rockets Fired at U.S Navy's Ships in Aqaba", August 12, 2005, available at *http://www.cbc.ca/story/world/national/2005/08/19/missiles_from_jordan050819.html*

19. On the importance of HUMINT (and the Americans' failure to get it in Iraq) see Peters (2005).

economic and technological infrastructure means that the forces in question will not have many advanced weapons but be forced to rely on leftovers. Under such conditions conscription, albeit carried out haphazardly, will retain a role. So will semi-regular forces loyal not to the state but to individual warlords and the like.

A type of personnel whose importance is likely to grow over the next 20 years is the mercenary.[20] Mercenaries have a long and, in many cases, dishonorable history going back to ancient Greece if not before. Most of the time they served as auxiliaries and specialists as, for example, the Genoese crossbowmen serving the French at Crecy in 1346 did. However, there were also times and places when they formed the bulk of the forces; think, in particular, of the 15th, 16th and 17th centuries. Only during the 19th century did European countries make an attempt to dispense with them and outlaw them, a move motivated partly by the desire to strengthen state control and partly by the idea that mercenaries were uncivilised.

In the years since the end of the Cold War, mercenaries have made a comeback. In part, this is because forces fighting each other in less developed countries often lack the skills that mercenaries possess and are prepared to pay for them. In part it is because too many developed countries, citing various reasons, have sent forces to wage war in (to misuse Neville Chamberlain's famous description of Czechoslovakia) 'faraway countries about which we know nothing'. Since experience shows that public opinion will not support such wars for very long, it is best to use mercenaries. Mercenaries are people who have enlisted to fight for gain in a specific war at a specific time and place. Having done so, in case they are killed they will only have themselves to blame.

Over the last three decades or so, few issues have occupied as much of the attention of decision-makers and the public alike as that of women in the military.[21] Without going into detail, I would like to express my opinion that this development has peaked. Almost four decades after armed forces started taking in more women during the

---

20. Lanning (2005); Scahill (2008).

21. See, for a comprehensive discussion Creveld (2001).

late '60s, in all regular armed forces without exception women's role remains marginal—as is evident from the fact that, in Iraq, just two per cent of US casualties are female.[22] The corresponding Israeli figure in Southern Lebanon in 2006 was smaller still. Nor is there any question of them taking over future armed forces in the sense of greatly increasing their presence, or entering combat in any numbers, or occupying many senior positions. There is, however, a caveat. As has been the case at least since Judith killed Holofernes after having sex with him, women will continue to take a relatively important part in terrorism, guerrilla, and insurgencies of every kind. Including, without doubt, of the kind which requires that they blow themselves up.

VII

Obviously the above developments, as well as many others which could not be discussed here, will only come about if people make them happen. On the other hand, people's actions are themselves driven by social, economic, and technological factors over which they have little or no control. Since this chapter has focussed on such factors and not on individuals, I do expect that most of the developments outlined will, in fact, come about. Acting and interacting—they will not impact every part of the world in the same way, and at the same speed. Much will depend on geography, national strategy, etc.

Whether or not a country becomes involved in warfare against its neighbours (or against that universal policeman, the US) will depend on its location, the neighbours it has, the resources it commands, and the policies that it, and other countries, adopts. Whether it is torn by non-trinitarian, or fourth-generation war, or by insurgency, or guerrilla, or terrorism, will depend on whole legions of economic, social, and cultural factors. A list of threats that face Finland will not be applicable to Algeria, nor a list of things that Japan needs to do in order to defend itself against Israel.

What I have tried to do is to take as global a view as possible and provide a large-scale map of the future. Precisely where India finds

22. See the tally at *http://search.yahoo.com/search?p=american+casualties+iraq&sm=Yahoo%21+Search&fr=FP-tab-web-t&toggle=1&cop=&ei=UTF-8* (23.8.2005)

itself on this map, and what it should do to find its way on it—those are questions best left to Indians to ponder.

References

Arquilla, J. and D. Ronfeldt (eds.) (2000). *Swarming and the Future of Conflict*. St. Moncia, CA: RAND. pp. 237-60.

Braun and C.F. Chyba (2004). "Proliferation Rings: New Challenges to the Nuclear Nonproliferation Regime", *International Security* 29(2): 5-49. Fall.

Buxbaum, P.A. (2005). "Making C2 Work as One", *Armed Forces Journal: 36-38*. August.

Creveld, M. Van (2001). *Men, Women and War*. London: Cassell.

———. (1991). *The Transformation of War*. New York: Free Press.

Deblois, B.M., R.L. Garwin, R. Scott Kemp and J.C. Marwell (2004). "Space Weapons", *International Security* 29(2): 5-84. Fall.

Farley, R. (2007). "Abolish the Air Force", American Prospect, November. At *http://www.prospect.org/cs/articles?article=abolish_the_air_force. Conclusions: Going Down, 1945-?*

Fletcher, M.A. and Ph. P. Pan (2009). "US and Russia to Reduce Arsenals", *Washington Post*, July 7. At *http://www.washingtonpost.com/wp-dyn/content/article/2009/07/06/AR2009070600784.html*

Fukuyama, F. and A.N. Shulsky (2000). "Military Organisation in the Information Age; Lessons from the World of Business", in J. Arquilla and D. Ronfeldt (eds.), *Swarming and the Future of Conflict*. St. Moncia, CA: RAND. pp.237-60.

Hammes, Th. X. (2004). *The Sling and the Stone: On War in the 21st Century*. St. Paul, MN: Zenith.

Israel, I. Ben (2003). "The Revolution in Military Affairs and the Operation in Iraq", in S. Feldman (ed.), *After the War in Iraq; Defining the New Strategic Balance*. Brighton: Sussex Academic Press. p.69: Table 6.5.

J. Scahill, Blackwater (2008). *The Rise of the World's Most Powerful Mercenary Army*. New York: Nation.

Kaldor, M. (1999). *New and Old Wars; Organised Violence in a Global Environment*. Stanford, CA: Stanford University Press.

Kober, A. (2005). "Does the Iraq War Reflect a Phase Change in Warfare?", *Defense and Security Analysis* 21(2): 121-42. June.

Kuehl, D.T. (1995). "Airpower vs. Electricity: Electric Power as a Target for Strategic Air Operations", *Journal of Strategic Studies* 18(1): 250-60. March

Lanning, M.L.C (2005). *Mercenaries: Soldiers of Fortune, from Ancient Greece to Today's Private Military Companies*. Navato, CA: Presidio.

Peters, R. (2005). "The Case for Human Intelligence", *Armed Forces Journal 24-26*. July.

Rose, D. (2003). "Patriot Downed Jet", *New York Daily News*. April 15.

Sydney Morning Herald (2007). "Egypt Launches Nuclear Power Program", *Sydney Morning Herald*, July 29. At *http://www.smh.com.au/articles/2007/10/29/1193618803345.html*

USA Today (2002). "Rumsfeld Kills Crusader Artillery Program", *USA Today*, May 8.

Weiner, T. (2004). "Pentagon Envisioning a Costly Internet for War", *New York Times*. November 13.

VIII

Geopolitics in Asia: Country Perspectives

23

The Geopolitics of Asia in 2030

An American Perspective

AARON L. FRIEDBERG

Alternative Structures of Power

Despite changes in technology, patterns of economic exchange, the role of non-state actors, and the increasing prominence of international rules and institutions, the stability and character of relations in any system of states is still largely determined by the distribution of power among them. Moreover, despite the increasing attention paid in recent years to 'soft power,' 'smart power,' and other similar concepts, 'hard power'—measured roughly by the size and sophistication of a nation's economic, scientific and industrial base, and the quality and quantity of its armed forces—remains the essential currency of politics among nations. Finally, despite the globalisation of the international economy and the growing interconnectedness of all parts of the planet, in the strategic realm, where geography, topography and distance remain critical, it still makes sense to analyse regional systems (or sub-systems) and power balances.

The distribution of power in any system can be described as either balanced or unbalanced. In the latter case, one state is so powerful that it can outmatch any conceivable grouping of lesser states. Unipolar systems have historically been quite rare, at least at the global level. Indeed, it is possible that the post-Cold War preponderance of the United States is the only situation that comes close to answering to this description. Conditions approximating unipolarity have, however, existed at various times in different parts of the world. Imperial Rome's domination of the Mediterranean, southern Europe and northern Africa, and China's preponderance in East Asia prior to the intrusion of the Western powers are two examples.

Systems in which power is balanced, or distributed somewhat more equally among a number of states, are the historical norm. Balanced systems can be further sub-divided into two types: bipolar, in which two states are so much more capable than the rest that even shifts in alignment of lesser states from one side to the other cannot alter the essential balance between the two 'poles;' and multipolar, in which three or more states possess roughly equivalent capabilities.

Theorists of international relations have devoted much energy to debating the merits of these different systems, with particular attention to the question of their relative stability, usually defined as susceptibility to major wars. At the start of the Cold War many analysts expressed concern that a system with only two global 'superpowers' would prove to be even more prone to devastating conflict than the multipolar systems that had preceded it. By the time the Soviet Union collapsed the consensus view, at least among American political scientists, was that bipolarity had proven to be highly stable, as suggested by the fact that the Cold War ultimately ended with a whimper rather than a bang! (Although whether this had more to do with the number of poles, or the size of their respective arsenals of nuclear weapons is a topic of continuing discussion.) The prospect of a return to multipolarity was greeted with anxiety in many quarters, a condition alleviated by the increasingly widespread belief by the turn of the 21st century that the United States was actually the sole remaining superpower. Whatever could be said for bipolarity, unipolarity clearly had its attractions, at least for those at the pinnacle of the global power pyramid.

The purpose of this chapter is not to rejoin the debate over whether the 'unipolar moment' is, in fact, over, but rather to speculate on a somewhat more limited question. Looking ahead 20 years to 2030, what is likely to be the distribution of power within the Asian international sub-system (or regional system)? This area will be defined here to include the entire Eastern Eurasian landmass from South and Southeast Asia to Siberia, the major off-shore islands of the Western Pacific and Oceania, and, depending on its disposition, the United States. While it is a Pacific power by virtue of its geography, unlike all of the other players, America is an Asian power by choice and by invitation.

Following the scheme suggested above, I will examine a range of possibilities from unbalanced/unipolar to balanced/bipolar to balanced/multipolar. Rather than attempt to examine every possible scenario, I have chosen to focus only on those that appear at this time to have some reasonable chance of occurring. In each case I will discuss the factors that might cause a particular distribution to emerge, assessing their plausibility and offering some speculation about each system might function.

Unipolar Asia

American Hegemony

In the immediate aftermath of the Cold War the United States enjoyed a huge advantage in both economic and military capabilities over any other nation in Asia, or anywhere else in the world for that matter. Today, in relation to China and, to a lesser extent, India, the margins are somewhat smaller, though still substantial. While the narrowing of the 'GDP gap' between the US and China has received the most attention, the latter's ongoing military build-up is beginning to reach the point where it could produce a noticeable shift in the regional balance of power. Whereas, 20 years ago, US air and naval forces could operate with impunity right up to the edge of China's coastal waters and airspace, the PRC's acquisition of layered anti-access capabilities will soon make this a more complex and risky task. China's deployment of larger, more secure intercontinental range nuclear forces will also begin to raise questions about the ability of the United States to extend deterrence to some of its friends and allies in the region. In this respect, as in the economic and diplomatic domains, China is beginning to have the capabilities necessary to match or offset American power in Asia, if not yet on a global scale. As regards the remaining major players in the region: Russia clings to its nuclear weapons and natural resources but appears otherwise to be a nation in steep decline; Japan has lost much of its economic dynamism, faces a sharply negative demographic shift and does not seem able to generate the resolve or the resources necessary to transform itself into a major military power; only India is growing rapidly in both military and economic terms, *albeit* at a slower pace, and from a lower base, than China.

If present trends continue then, over the next 20 years, China will pose an increasing challenge to American preponderance. But, of course, these trends may *not* continue and, in particular, China may not manage to keep growing at anything resembling the rates it has attained over the past three decades. The burdens imposed by environmental, demographic, and resources constraints, official corruption, increasingly dysfunctional development policies, foreign protectionism, energy price shocks, and social unrest could combine to knock China off its current steep trajectory. If that happens (if, for example, China grows at an average of 5 to 7 per cent annually over the next two decades rather than somewhere between 8 and 10 per cent) and if, at the same time, the United States is able to rejuvenate its own economy while sustaining its current military advantages, then the era of unipolarity may be extended for some time into the future.

Even if this is the case, however, the US is unlikely to regain its previous position of overwhelming advantage over all comers. Unless it experiences a wrenching systemic crisis, China's wealth and power will continue to grow, *albeit* at a markedly slower pace, and India too will be becoming stronger and more influential, certainly in South and Southeast Asia and perhaps beyond.

Chinese Hegemony

The extension of American preponderance in Asia would come as a surprise to many people. The emergence of China as the dominant power, in East Asia at least, would not. A recent Pew Foundation poll of public opinion in Japan, South Korea, Indonesia, Vietnam found, for example, that large majorities of those questioned expect Beijing to become 'the leader in Asia,' though what this means and when it is anticipated is not clear from the survey data.

In order for China to displace the United States as the 'pole' around which Asia is organised, several things would have to happen. First, and most obviously, Beijing would have to find a way to sidestep all of the various obstacles just identified and continue on its path of rapid economic and military expansion. Second, the United States would either have to choose or be compelled against its will to withdraw substantially from the region, pulling back its forward-based forces and allowing its alliances and quasi-alliance relationships to be dissolved or drained of any real strategic significance. Third, Beijing would have to find ways to prevent the other regional actors from trying to join together to form a countervailing coalition capable of balancing its power and challenging its influence.

While it might seem implausible that all of these conditions could be achieved simultaneously, in fact they could turn out to be linked in ways that would make them mutually reinforcing. Suppose that China is able to sustain its rapid growth while the United States struggles economically in the wake of the recent financial crisis and remains bogged down in costly counter-terror and counterinsurgency operations in Southwest Asia, the Middle East and Africa. Under these conditions at some point policymakers in Washington might conclude that Chinese regional preponderance was inevitable and the best option for the United States was to accept reality and adapt to it. Realising (or perhaps anticipating) that they could no longer count on American help, one or more of the local powers might decide that its best option was to follow suit. The loss of potential balancing partners could have a cascading effect, as one nation after another tried to hop on China's bandwagon.

The end result of such a process would be a new kind of 'hub and spokes' arrangement, only this time with China at the centre and the other regional players (including Japan, South Korea, India, Australia and Russia) maintaining amicable, but strategically detached relationships with one another. In such circumstances Beijing might not be able to exert positive control over its neighbours, but it would have considerable influence over all, and perhaps an effective veto over the policy choices of some.

Bipolar Asia

A Sino-Indian Divide

Depending on India's disposition and capabilities in 20 years time, it might choose to contend with China for power and influence in Asia, broadly defined, and it will almost certainly seek to do so in parts of South, Southeast and Central Asia. If, as in the previous scenario, we postulate that the PRC has continued to rise while the United States has declined and/or largely withdrawn from East Asia,

India is likely to be the only state remaining with anything approaching China's capabilities and potential.

It is conceivable that the two dynamic continental Asian powers might be able to achieve some sort of *modus vivendi*, perhaps reflected in a tacit spheres of influence arrangement in which China would be preponderant in East Asia and India would dominate South Asia. There are several reasons to be sceptical for that such an amicable and mutually agreeable balance will actually emerge. First, again on current trends, Beijing is unlikely to regard India as an equal in 20 years time. Especially if China has by then managed to head off or contain potential threats from its eastern coast, it will have more resources to devote to the south, making the distribution of effective power with India even more lopsided than it would otherwise be. Beijing may therefore feel under no pressure to give Delhi what it wants. Following a more accommodating course would also involve a major reversal in long standing Chinese strategy and the abandonment of some substantial commitments and investments. Leaving South Asia to India would presumably involve easing back on support to Pakistan and Myanmar and accepting a settlement of outstanding border disputes that would be seen by many in Beijing as leaving China dangerously exposed to Indian meddling in Tibet. Moreover, it is not at all clear what China would gain in return for such concessions. Commitments from Delhi to limit its involvement in East Asia and to forego actions that might threaten China's use of vital sea lanes across the Indian Ocean could easily be reversed at some point in the future. By contrast, if it were to abandon the positions that presently give it leverage against India in South Asia, Beijing would have a very difficult time in recreating them. China's growing reliance on energy imports from the Persian Gulf and Africa make an expansion of its activities in the Indian Ocean region seem far more plausible than a willing contraction. For its part, an ever more powerful India will probably be less inclined to tolerate what it regards as Chinese intrusions into 'its' region and more willing, and better able, to oppose them in various ways.

Given all of this, a Sino-Indian relationship with an increasing element of competition seems more probable than one that is purely cooperative and congenial. At least in the near-term, however, India is unlikely to have the resources necessary to compete with China on an equal footing. Indian strategists might not be averse to the idea of a bipolar Asia, with their country as one of the poles. But in 20 years time they are unlikely to be able to balance Chinese power alone, even in their own backyard.

Sino-American 'Bi-Gemony'

If China continues to grow, and the United States remains vigorous and engaged, in 20 years time the two nations may have arrived at a position of broad equivalence, at least in terms of their influence in Asia. While it is possible to imagine circumstances under which the two Pacific powers would agree to some kind of spheres of influence agreement, or cooperate with one another over the heads of the other regional players, such scenarios do seem unlikely.

A tacit division (such as the one that a Chinese admiral recently suggested, presumably in jest, to his American counterpart) in which China would dominate everything out to the 'second island chain' and the US would pull back to the mid-Pacific, would not appeal to Washington. Aside from the fact that it would leave America's allies on their own, such a division would not guarantee US access to, or transit through, the most economically and strategically important region in the world. It is true that Great Britain eventually gave way in the western hemisphere to a fast-rising America. But, by the end of the 19th century, those two countries saw themselves as drawn together by their shared commitment to popular government (as well as a common language and cultural heritage). Unless and until China makes the transition to something more closely resembling liberal democracy, no American president is going to be able to make similarly sweeping strategic concessions to Beijing. For its part, the Chinese regime as presently constituted will continue to see an ideologically driven America as posing an enduring challenge to its legitimacy and long-term survival. It is therefore unlikely simply to accept with comfort the indefinite presence of US bases, forces, and allies around its periphery.

Despite the continuing search for areas of potential mutual gain that would encourage them to put aside their ideological differences and geopolitical mistrust and share regional (and global) leadership, on a broad range of issues—from North Korea and Iran, to Taiwan, counterterrorism, the delineation of exclusive economic zones (EEZs), climate change and, increasingly, trade—US and Chinese interests appear to diverge at least as often as they converge. While it is possible that this could change with the passage of time, for the moment the basis for a true 'G2' simply does not exist.

Multipolar Asia

A US-China-India Triangle

Triangular systems containing three roughly equal 'poles' have a strong tendency towards instability. The fact that if one power aligns with another the third will be overmatched lends an element of tension, uncertainty and mistrust to all three sets of bilateral relationships. One party will generally try to put itself in the position of pivot, extracting concessions from its two 'suitors' while holding out the promise of alignment to both. (The Soviet Union attempted to do this with Nazi Germany and the Anglo-French alliance before the outbreak of the Second World War, and the United States tried a similar gambit for a brief period in the late '60s and early '70s with the Soviet Union and China.) But this is a game that cannot be played indefinitely. Triangles have a tendency to collapse into simpler, two-sided structures.

In the situation now emerging in Asia, India might be tempted to pursue a policy of 'equidistance,' avoiding overly close alignment with either the United States or China. While there seems little real prospect of a true Sino-Indian *entente*, Delhi could hold out the prospect of maintaining its traditional posture of non-alignment in order to win concessions from Beijing, while at the same time dangling the promise of closer strategic cooperation with Washington.

The problem for India is that such a policy would probably not win it the kind of concessions it wants from China (regarding Pakistan, for example) but could very well limit the kinds of cooperation (on technology and intelligence sharing) it could achieve with the United States. Aside from Indian concerns over the continuing growth of Chinese power, other more positive factors are already inclining it to 'lean' towards the United States (or, rather, are causing the two to lean towards one another). Among these are growing economic, educational, and familial links between the two societies, and the somewhat belated recognition of the depth of the two nations' shared commitment to democratic values. While a triangular Asian system is possible, over the next 20 years the United States and India are more likely to be closer to one another than either will be to China.

A Continental-Maritime Divide

One final possibility would combine elements of multipolarity and bipolarity. Assuming a continuation of both Chinese growth and American engagement, relations between the two powers may become increasingly competitive and contentious rather than more cooperative. Instead of being dominated by a Sino-American condominium, Asia could effectively be divided into two camps. On the one hand would be a grouping of continental nations physically contiguous to, and strategically centred on, China. Most of these would be economically dependent and comparatively weak in relation to the PRC and all would have some form of authoritarian government. Included in this coalition would be North Korea, Russia, Kazakhstan, Kyrgyzstan, Tajikistan, Pakistan, Myanmar, Laos and possibly Vietnam. On the other side would be a group consisting primarily of liberal democracies, aligned with the United States, physically separated from China by oceans, mountains or intervening territory, and with a largely maritime orientation. Among these would be Japan, South Korea, the Philippines, Indonesia, Australia, Singapore, Thailand, India, and possibly Mongolia.

The outlines of such a structure can already be seen in the interactions among these states. Depending on how events unfold (and depending, in particular, on the course of Sino-American relations), the degree of polarisation between the two groups and the extent to which their members coalesce may vary over time. At one extreme, the situation could come to resemble a new Cold War, with the United States and China sharply at odds with one another, and each trying to bind its friends into a more tightly integrated coalition. At the other, relations within and between the two groupings could remain highly fluid, even to the point that the distinction between them might seem to disappear.

Assuming a continuing, and perhaps mounting, measure of tension and rivalry between them, Washington and Beijing will both try to weaken each others' nascent coalitions, by neutralising or prizing away one or more of its members. China seems already to be attempting this in its relations with South Korea, Thailand, Australia, India, and now Japan. The United States may eventually respond by wooing Vietnam and, if Moscow's anxieties about Chinese expansionism continue to grow, then Russia as well. The interactions that would result from such gambits could eventually come to resemble the complex diplomacy of multipolar Europe in the 19th and early 20th centuries.

24

China and India

Geopolitical Centre of Asia in 2030

LI LI

The first decade of the 21st century has been characterised by the simultaneous rise of China and India. As many agencies like the World Bank, the International Monetary Fund, and the US National Intelligence Council predicted that China and India would continue to rise in the next 20-40 years in spite of some uncertainties, the two countries have become major determinants of the future of Asia and the world. This chapter deals with the possible geopolitics in Asia of 2030 by foreseeing that the gravity of Asia will shift westward, from the western Pacific rim (Japan, South Korea, China and Southeast Asia) to China and India. It also explores the drivers of this change and its implications for Asia and the world.

China and India in 2030

When we talk about China and India in coming 20 years, there are basically four alternative scenarios: (i) a simultaneous rise of China and India; (ii) a rising China and a lagging India; (iii) a rising India and a lagging China; and (iv) a simultaneous slowdown of China and India. This chapter will only examine the first scenario: a simultaneous rise of China and India. The reasons are threefold: first, it is an existing geopolitical phenomenon of Asia which has started years back. Second, the author believes that this trend will continue in the next 20 years. Third, among the above four scenarios, no one has more impact on the geopolitics of Asia and the world than the first one.

For decades after revolution or independence, the significance of China and India to Asia and the world mainly derived from the demographic element. With one-third of the world's population, they

Table 24.1

China and India in 2030: Four Scenarios

Scenarios	*Probability*	*Impact on Asia*
A simultaneous rise of China and India	High	Great
A rising China and a lagging India	Low-Medium	Modest
A rising India and a lagging China	Low	Modest-Great
A simultaneous slowdown of China and India	Low-Medium	Modest-Great

have been the two largest developing countries. In the recent past, they have also become well-known for their rapid economic growth, with India at a pace of 7 per cent plus and China almost at double digit rate of growth. If they can sustain the rapid growth in the next 20 years (even if at a little bit slower pace, and India may outpace China's growth rate sooner or later), by 2030, the two Asian giants will multiply their respective national power by combining the economic might with the demographic strength.

As indicated by Table 24.2, in 2030, China and India will have one-third of the world population, with India overtaking China to be the largest country in terms of population.

Table 24.2

*Population**

	2004		*2008*		*2030*	
	Population	*Share*	*Population*	*Share*	*Population*	*Share*
China	1,315	20.3	1,327	19.8	1,346	16.4
India	1,103	17	1,140	17	1,449	17.7
China+India	2,418	37.3	2,467	36.8	2,795	34.1
World	6,480	100	6,692	100	8,200	100

Note: * Population in million and share of world population in percentage.

Source: World Bank, "Population Growth Rate" at *http://www.worldbank.org/depweb/english/modules/social/pgr/*; Free World Academy "Global Trends 2030" at *http://www.freeworldacademy.com/globalleader/trends.htm*

Table 24.3 implies that, by 2030, China might be the second largest economy in real US dollar terms, only surpassed by the United States. India's share of world economy will also be almost tripled to 5.4 per cent. If China and India are combined in economic strength, they will account for one fourth of world economy, surpassing the United States.

Table 24.3

*Economic Trend in Real Dollar Terms**

	2005			*2008*			*2030*		
	GDP	*Share*	*Per Capita GDP*	*GDP*	*Share*	*Per Capita GDP*	*GDP*	*Share*	*Per Capita GDP*
China	1893	5.2	1.451	4326	7.1	2.94	16509	20.3	11.29
India	644	1.8	0.588	1218	2.0	1.07	4436	5.4	3.2
Japan	4978	13.6	38.96	4909	8.1	38.21	6184	7.6	53.58
USA	10996	30.1	37.1	14204	23.4	47.58	19309	23.7	51.36
China+ India	2537	7.0	1.049	5544	9.1	2.247	20945	25.7	7.493
World	36487	100	5.672	60587	100	8.613	81508	100	9.905

Note : * GDP in billion US$, share of world GDP in per cent, and per capita GDP in thousand US$.

Source: Glenn, Jerome C. *et al.*, "International Futures Model 2010: State of the Future", at *http://millennium-project.org/millennium/2010SOF.html;* World Bank, "Economic Policy and External Debt", at *http://data.worldbank.org/topic/economic-policy-and-external-debt*

Table 24.4 indicates that, in terms of purchasing power parity (PPP), China and India will respectively be the first and third largest economies. Like the size of their population, their share of world economy will reach one-third from the current one-sixth.

Although India's economy will be only one-fourth of China by 2030 in real US dollar terms, it matters due to its potential and considerable share in PPP terms. As Figure 24.1 indicates, China and India will remain the powerhouses in the next 20 years. The International Futures Model predicts that by 2020 India will overtake China to be the most rapid economy, while the Carnegie Endowment for International Peace foresees that by 2050 India will become the third largest economy in real US dollar terms, and its PPP-GDP will be 97 per cent as large as that of the United States.[1]

1. Dadush and Stancil (2009).

Table 24.4

*Economic Trend in PPP Terms**

	2005			2008			2030		
	GDP	Share	Per Capita GDP	GDP	Share	Per Capita GDP	GDP	Share	Per Capita GDP
China	4732	9.5	3.627	7984	11.5	6.02	23616	22.1	16.14
India	2158	4.4	1.971	3375	4.9	2.96	8752	8.2	6.314
Japan	3434	6.9	26.87	4498	6.5	35.22	4764	4.5	41.28
USA	10996	22.2	37.1	14204	20.5	46.97	19309	18.1	51.36
China+ India	6890	13.9	2.849	11359	16.4	4.604	32368	30.3	11.58
World	49616	100	7.713	69309	100	10.357	106902	100	12.99

Note :* PPP-GDP in billion US$, share of world PPP-GDP in per cent, and per capita PPP-GDP in thousand US$.

Source: Glenn, Jerome C. *et al.*, "International Futures Model 2010: State of the Future", at *http://millennium-project.org/millennium/2010SOF.html;* World Bank, "Economic Policy and External Debt", at *http://data.worldbank.org/topic/economic-policy-and-external-debt*

Figure 24.1

Average Growth Rate 2005-2030 (%)

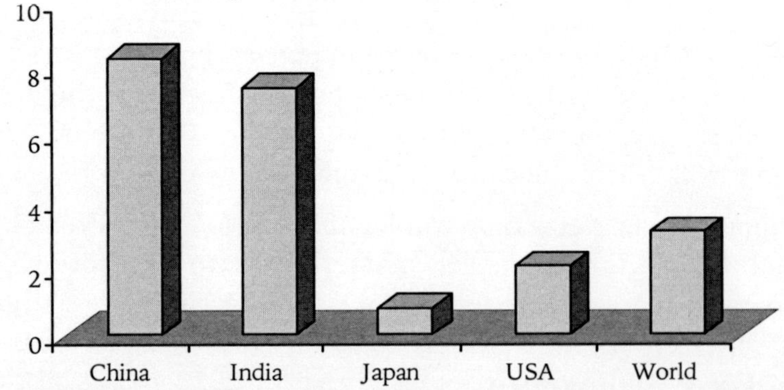

Source: Glenn, Jerome C. *et al.*, "International Futures Model 2010: State of the Future", at *http://millennium-project.org/millennium/2010SOF.html*

Drivers of the Simultaneous Rise

As growing economies, China and India enjoy a lot of commonality in terms of driving forces of their rapid growth. Energetic labour force, fast-growing middle class, pragmatic national strategy, and peaceful international environment are the major drivers among others.

Energetic Labour Force

Labour force will contribute a lot to the big gap of growth rates between the two growing economies and the advanced economies. In the case of Japan, the economy has already suffered from the shrinking work force. Unlike the United States, Japan is reluctant to accept foreign labour migrants. As the Carnegie's report pointed out, even if 'large and sustained increases in the fertility rate' can begin now, it 'would not reverse the aging trend for decades in Europe and Japan.'[2] It means that the advanced economies will only be able to move at a snail's pace in the next 20-40 years. According to some models, 'by the 2030s, Japan's GDP growth is projected to drop to near zero.'[3]

On the contrary, China and India are affluent in working-age population. Some scholars predict that by 2030 India will have the youngest labour force in the world, 'with half the population under the age of 25,' and its working-age population is expected to grow continuously till 2050.[4] Although it might create some pressure on employment, it will ensure meeting the growing labour force demands by the rapid economic growth. As far as China is concerned, while some scholars presume that China's population is ageing, the absolute size and quality of its labour force will still be a valuable asset for China's economic future. By 2030, the number of 15-24 year olds entering the labour force will be around 178 million,[5] much more than the whole Japanese population (115 million). Thanks to the three-decade social development, the quality of China's labour force has been greatly upgraded. As the Free World Academy (2005) described, 'these people are well educated, enthusiastic about business entrepreneurship, eager to work as much as they can.'[6]

---

2. Ibid.
3. NIC (2008): 21
4. "India will be Third Largest Economy by 2030, says a Research Report", June 6, 2005, *http://news.indiamart.com/news-analysis/ii-india-will-be-thi-9670.html*
5. Dobson (2009).
6. "The Future of China and North Asia: From Here to 2030", *http://www.freeworldacademy.com/globalleader/china.htm*

Fast-Growing Middle Class

Due to the economic growth, China and India's middle class has rapidly expanded in recent years, with China from 1 per cent of the population in 1990 to the current 35 per cent and India from 1 per cent to 5 per cent.[7] In the next 20 years, the numbers will continue to increase sharply. According to the World Bank, in 2000, only 13.5 per cent of the global middle class were from China and no Indians belonged to this group. By 2030, citizens from China and India may together account for 44 per cent of the global middle class, 'with the great majority (38 per cent) being Chinese, in fact half of the total 740 million new entrants into the global middle class will be Chinese nationals.'[8] This will mean a consumption explosion and will boost their respective growth as well as the world economy.

Figure 24.2

Chinese and Indian Weight in the Global Middle Class

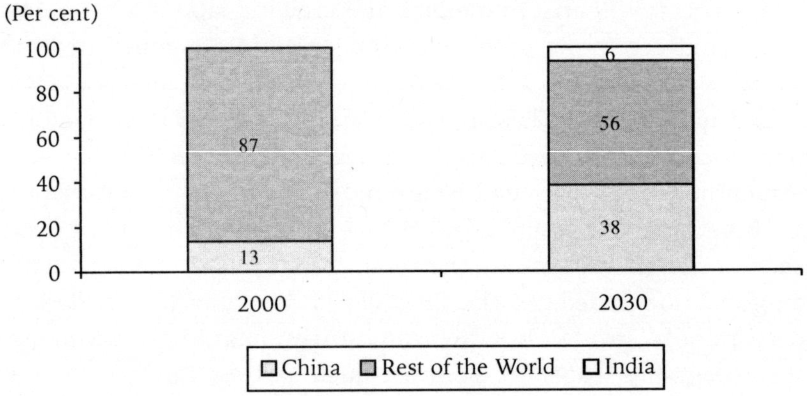

Source: World Bank (2007).

Pragmatic National Strategy

Since the '80s and the late '90s, China and India have respectively put their national strategic focus on economic development, with a belief that, 'the strength of a nation flows primarily from the strength

7. "India to Be Middle Class Growth Driver by 2020", July 9, 2008, *http://www.rediff.com/money/2008/jul/09gs.htm*

8. World Bank (2007).

of its economy.'[9] To pursue an economic emergence, they have internally invested more on well-beings and set forth a number of pro-market reforms, and externally adopted a modest and flexible foreign policy to ensure a peaceful and benign external environment.[10] This economy-oriented national strategy has yielded fruit. The economic miracles have upgraded their respective positions on the world stage. The current achievements have convinced leaders from China and India to continue this pragmatic national strategy, although the two countries have divergent models.

More important is that this pragmatic national strategy will ensure peace between China and India, which is actually a precondition for their simultaneous rise. To a considerable extent, the improvement of China-India relations should be attributed to their similar strategic focus. Although the two countries still do not trust each other (especially between the medias), and tensions may rise now and then due to their disputed border, there is a consensus on the political level that they should work for their common development, and that 'there is enough space for them to grow together.'[11] In other words, the prospect of a severe hit to the rapid growth may prevent the two rising powers from a conflict. Moreover, as their economic interaction continues to increase sharply, a stronger lobbying group for good relationship is expected to emerge on each side.

Peaceful International Environment

Thanks to globalisation, the interdependence among nations is getting deeper and deeper. The cost to wage a war is so high that big powers are poised to avoid fighting against each other. At the same time, many global challenges like financial crisis, terrorism, energy security, and climate change require countries especially big powers to work together and find a global solution. Apart from peace between China and India, in the next 20 years, the probability is very low for China or India to get involved into a major conflict with any other power. As far as the Sino-US relations are concerned, their respective

9. Vajpayee (1998).

10. For detailed discussion, see Li (2009).

11. Joint Declaration by the Republic of India and the People's Republic of China. November 21, 2006, available at *http://www.meaindia.nic.in/*

pragmatism will overcome their ideological dispute, and more common interests will emerge as their economic gap becomes smaller. As the 2008-09 global financial crisis and the 2009 Copenhagen Conference on Climate Change indicate, the coexistence of cooperation and competition may continue to characterise the Sino-US relations in the years to come, which means that there will be neither a conflict nor a cold war between them.

Geopolitical Implications

The simultaneous rise of China and India will transform the landscape of Asia as well as the world. By 2030, an 'Asian century' might sail, with China and India being the engine; and the trend toward a multipolar world will be strengthened as China and India become bigger players on the global stage.

Rise of Asia

While some people are debating whether the 21st century is an 'Indian century' or a 'Chinese century', the simultaneous rise of the two giants means that it is an 'Asian century'. The late Chinese leader Deng Xiaoping said in 1988, 'unless those two countries (China and India) are developed, there will be no Asian century.'[12] By 2030, if China and India account for a fourth of world economy or a third in PPP terms, a 'genuine Asian century' is certain to come.

Regional Integration

Simultaneous rise of China and India and the peace between them will make sub-regional cooperation more vibrant and efficient. The existing sub-regional institutions like East Asia Summit (EAS), South Asian Association for Regional Cooperation (SAARC) and Shanghai Cooperation Organisation (SCO) could be more powerful as it is more difficult for them to be exclusive to China or India. To adapt to the transforming landscape, some new sub-regional institutions might also come into being. Moreover, as a bridge between West Asia and East Asia, the rise of India will make a genuine Asian integration possible for the first time.

---

12. Xiaoping (1993).

A Multipolarised World

As implied by Table 24.3, by 2030, the United States will remain the number one global power especially in terms of per capita GDP and military strength. However, with China and India catching up, the United States will become 'less dominant.'[13] As the recent global financial crisis and the Copenhagen Conference on Climate Change have indicated, the United States will have to consult China and India more often in dealing with global challenges, instead of just making unilateral decisions and then asking others to follow. The simultaneous rise of China and India will also challenge some existing multilateral institutions which are dominated by western norms. How well adapting to the emerging landscape will determine the relevance and efficiency of these institutions. The Carnegie's report points out that the relevance of G20 has already surpassed that of the G8.[14]

Technological Innovation

As mentioned above, by 2030, the middle class will increase sharply in China and India. If half the combined population joins the group, it equals to almost four United States in terms of population. If only a third become middle class, it is still 2.6 times more than that of the United States. Although the Chinese and Indian populations have the right to live as happy and comfortable as the US citizens, we cannot deny the fact that the improvement of well-beings in China and India will put pressure on energy, food, water resources, and environment. When many scholars predict that resource competition between India, China and other great powers could result in conflict in the future, the author would like to regard the simultaneous rise of the two giants as a stimulus to stronger international cooperation on technological innovation, because war will never be a solution to these problems.

Challenges Ahead

Since the probability of wars among big powers is low in the next 20 years, this author predict that the major blocks which may derail the rise of China or India will come from within respectively.

13. NIC (2008): xi.

14. Dadush and Stancil (2009).

First is related to the success of their critical economic reforms. After years and decades of economic miracles, the two giants (especially China) have respectively entered a new critical stage of economic transition, with China from an export-oriented and investment-driven economy to one based on domestic consumption. In this regard, the Indian economy has also become more open. Only a soft landing of these transitions can ensure a sustained rapid growth of China or India.

Second is related to the dealing with growing gap between the poor and the rich. Due to the Chinese pious belief in egalitarianism and the existence of corruption, the growing gap between the poor and the rich has become a major factor for social resentment and internal instability. Although the Chinese government has achieved a lot in reducing poverty, it is required to do more to diminish such a gap in a short-term. Although this issue seems less urgent for India due to its unique social structure and political democracy, the recent revival of the Maoist movement may raise an alarm.

Third is related to the simmering nationalism resulting from their respective rise. As a rising power, the government is expected by its citizens to be firmer in safeguarding national interests. China and India have collided in this regard. The recent tension arising due to their border issue implies that, the stronger they are, the more difficult for the two countries to make any territorial concession. How to keep such nationalism from breaking the peace on their border will be a great challenge for political leaders on both sides.

Conclusion

As China and India will respectively continue to focus on economic development and be able to keep aloof from a major war due to globalisation making wars too costly to produce a winner, it is very probable that the two emerging economies will continue to grow rapidly in the next 20 years. Their simultaneous rise will promote the transformation of the landscape of Asia and the world. It may activate an 'Asian century' and accelerate regional integration. A bigger share of the world economy will also enable them to play a significant role in world affairs, and the contour of a multipolar world will be much clearer therefore. Nevertheless, they must be cautious about some internal challenges. They have to work hard to ensure a more fair society and a successful economic transition. Moreover, the two governments must work together to prevent their bilateral relations from being held hostage by nationalism, because confrontation will hurt both and cooperation is a guarantee for their simultaneous rise.

References

Dadush, Uri and Bennett Stancil (2009). "The G20 in 2050", *International Economic Bulletin*. November, at *http://www.carnegieendowment.org/publications/index.cfm?fa=view&id=24195*

Dobson, Wendy (2009). "Gravity Shift: Thinking about China and India in 2030", *Canada-Asia Agenda* (5): 2. November 30, at *http://www.asiapacific.ca/sites/default/files/CAA5ChiIndia.pdf*

Li, Li (2009). *Security Perception and China-India Relations.* New Delhi: KW Publishers.

Nation Intelligence Council (2008). "Global Trends 2025: A Transformed World", *NIC 2008-003*, p. 21. At *http://www.acus.org/files/publication_pdfs/3/Global-Trends-2025.pdf*

Vajpayee, Atal Bihari (1998). "Address by Prime Minister Atal Bihari Vajpayee at the India Economic Summit-1998", November 29. At *http://www.indianembassy.org/special/cabinet/Primeminister/pm(indiaeconomicsummit).htm*

World Bank (2007). "Global Growth and Distribution: Are China and India Reshaping the World?", *The World Bank, Policy Research Working Paper* 4392. November. Development Economics Prospects Group. At *http://www-wds.worldbank.org/external/default/WDSContentServer/IW3P/IB/2007/11/12/000158349_20071112111936/Rendered/PDF/wps4392.pdf*

Xiaoping, Deng (1993). "A New International Order should be Established with the Five Principles of Peaceful Coexistence as Norms", *Deng Xiaoping wenxuan* (Selected Works of Deng Xiaoping), Volume III. Beijing: Renmin Chubanshe. p.282.

25

Japan and American Factor in Asia

MAKOTO IOKIBE

A nation's military strength cannot be sustained without economic and financial backup. Security and economy are two sides of a coin and cannot exist alone. It does not mean, however, that the connection between security and economy is a direct one. National strategy plays the important role of an intermediary between the two. It is up to a government to decide the extent to which a country allocates its various resources for its security build-up.

For example, there is a glaring difference in Japanese military priorities before and after World War II. Japan opened itself to the world under the pressure from Western powers in the mid-19th century, which was the era of imperialism when non-western countries were colonised by Western powers.

The Meiji government adopted the 'rich country and strong army' as its slogan to survive this imperialist onslaught. Japan's fast paced modernisation both in the industry and military sectors made it possible for it to gain victory over Russia in 1905, i.e., 51 years after the opening up of the country in 1854. This however came at a high cost: the proportion of military expenditure in the total national budget was above 30 per cent even in peace time (preparing for next wars), and more than 50 per cent in the time of war. Thus, the military not only became strongest sector in pre-war Japan, but also extended its control over the political process and political life of the people, to the extent of waging wars through much of the '30s—and eventually lost the country in 1945.

Learning lessons from its pre-war experiences, post-war Japan became a successful economy but without strong army. It only maintained a modest defensive capability. Japan relied for its deterrence capability upon its alliance with the USA. At first, this was inevitable because in 1951, for Japan had one of two super powers, Soviet Russia as a threatening neighbour, whom Japan, weakened by its defeat in WW II, could not overcome by its own military efforts. What was surprising was that even after achieving the rapid economic growth in the '60s, Japan continued to keep its military expenditure below one per cent of its GDP and refrained from acquiring any nuclear weapons, aircraft carriers, nuclear submarines, offensive missiles and bomber aircraft. On the other hand, Japan tried to establish friendly and cooperative relations with as many countries as possible, and to extend economic aid to developing countries in Asia and the world, believing that economic development would in the long run lead to social and political stability and thus help to build peaceful world.

Such a way of life as civilian power or soft power is not unique among middle or small powers, but quite exceptional among big powers. India as well as China in 2030, no doubt great economic powers far stronger than Japan, would not follow the Japanese model, rather they would probably be both big economic and military powers, because each of the two giants would be surrounded by uneasy neighbours and face external and internal strife. Of course, the two giants, with strong national pride and spirit of independence would not be willing to rely for their security upon other superpower. Their national psychology and strategy would prompt them to be powerful economic states with strong military capabilities.

The world in 2030 would be an era of mutual dependence amid rapid globalisation, whereby necessary goods, can be acquired through peaceful trade. The arrival of nuclear weapons has made countries much more cautious about going to war. Wars of aggression are widely condemned internationally as is per the United Nations Charter. No respectable country would opt for war to expand its territory or obtain natural resources.

But a few do try to do so with threats of military attack. After the end of the Cold War, Saddam Hussein's Iraq invaded Kuwait. Also there is a certain Asian neighbour who boasts about having Japan within range of its missile and nuclear weapons. Generally speaking, rapidly emerging powers tend to challenge the status quo, sometimes even resorting to force, like Japan and Germany in the crisis of the '30s. Now China and India are the emerging powers. No one can tell whether they would be cooperating with each other in 2030 or not but I would be optimistic that India will be smart and mature enough to avoid a fatal destructive war and to build a relationship based on long lasting mutual interest and common good.

The US presence in Asia, in my view, would continue to play an important role in 2030. Because, although economically, the US might be surpassed by China and India, yet military, the US would remain the predominant superpower. Second, America has a strong will to be a leading pacific nation as was expressed by President Obama in his speech in Tokyo November (2009). We should not underestimate American resilience and its capacity to recover its economic power on the back of freedom and diversity of the civil society. Third, Asia which has many disputes within the region needs the American presence as stabilising force. For instance, Japan and South Korea do not have deterrence power *vis-à-vis* the North Korean nuclear threat. What is more desirable for Asia, to have Japan and South Korea as nuclear powers, or to use the power of US deterrence for Asian Security? Each option has both positives and negatives, but if US factor is taken out, Asian countries will be forced to struggle even more for their security.

Fourth and last, Japan has been hosting US presence in Japan not only for its own security but also for the stability of Asia Pacific region as a whole. Japan's security strategy is to combine two factors: to utilise US security power and to strengthen Japan's own military capability. In the two decades since the end of the Cold War, Japan has dispatched missions to ensure international peace and security. Japanese forces have been working mainly for humanitarian and reconstruction purpose in various parts of the world, including Cambodia, East Timor, Golan Heights, Nepal, Rwanda, Iraq, Indian Ocean (Arabian Sea), Gulf of Aden and Haiti. Although the Hatoyama government was somewhat seeking to change its security policy, it was not at the cost of the Japan-US alliance, which was established after the bloody war in the Pacific and now is entering into an age of maturity stage after muddling through the period of Japan-US economic disputes between 1971 and 1995.

North Korea would face the hardest time in the coming 5 to 10 years, but in 2030 the North Korean crisis would be over. China, on the other hand, would attain its peak around 2030.

If China adopts a hawkish foreign policy backed by its ever expanding military build-up, it would be difficult for Japan to keep its military expenditure at the modest level of below one per cent of its GDP. To cope with the military rise of China would be the most vexed issue in Asia by 2030.

26

Russia's Asia Policy in 2030

KONSTANTIN KHUDOLEY and STANISLAV TKACHENKO

Introduction: Scenarios

When examining the contemporary international processes and the role of globalisation in the changing balance of power in the world, Asian countries always become the centrepiece of the analysis. However, the Asian approach to globalisation differs significantly from the European or North American ones. The Asian nations do not call for 'superseding the state' or creating supranational structures to manage the economy or handle security issues. On the contrary, they pursue their interests by strengthening the system of the sovereign state to guard against the devastating effects of globalisation and the increasing international competition. The reaction of the Asian states to the international financial and economic crisis of 1997-98, as well as to the current crisis that began for Asia in the mid-2008, showed that it was the state and its institutions, namely the government, as well as state-owned companies and banks, that are the last line of defence of the national economy against external shocks. As of now, in the field of politics and military security the superiority of state over the other actors of Asian politics is beyond doubt. On this basis we would like to suggest four possible scenarios of how Asia might evolve in the future up to the year 2030. We would also like to speculate as to how Russia might adjust its strategy in the region *vis-à-vis* a long-term Asian development.

Scenario One: Multipolarity

Initially the idea of multipolarity was proposed by Russia as an attempt to forestall the deterioration of its political and economic standing which it inherited from the Soviet Union and which it had seen fall steadily year after year ever since. Russia's share in the global economy had dropped (from approximately 10 per cent to 1.2 per cent), its influence in Europe and the post-Soviet space was also in decline. Russia's public diplomacy efforts proved to be ineffective even in the countries whose elites and populations were generally well disposed to maintain a special relationship with Moscow.

The concept of multipolarity, which has been reflected in almost all the doctrines and policy documents governing the military-political aspects in Russia, looks better in theory than in practical application. From the Russian perspective the world's leading nations should re-establish what following the Vienna Congress (1815) came to be called the 'Concert of Europe'. One should recall that it was founded on a common aspiration of the leading nations of the period (the UK, Russia, France, Austria and Prussia) to avoid turmoil in European politics and to maintain the status quo in the aftermath of decades of wars and upheavals caused by the Great French Revolution and the reign of Napoleon. Although it survived in the original form for only about a quarter of a century, the 'Concert of Europe' was able to create mechanisms of deterrence granting Europe almost a 100 years of peace (1815-1914).

Russia appeals to overcome unilateralism in contemporary world politics, dominated by the United States and NATO, receive verbal support from virtually all the leading Asian states. However, thus far there is no clear concept as to which states should participate and in what way such multipolarity could be established. The periodic summits and meetings of foreign ministers of India, China and Russia, joined by their Brazilian counterpart in the summer of 2009 at the summit in Yekaterinburg, suggest that the idea of multipolarity as one of the options for the development of Asian politics is still alive. From Russia's perspective such three-pole architecture of security and balance of power in the mainland of Asia is optimal. It was exactly what Prime Minister of Russia Yevgeny Primakov spoke about in the autumn of 1998, putting forward the idea of a 'triangle' comprising the three countries. However, now, a decade later, it has become obvious that the idea of a strategic partnership and joint management of Asian security is unworkable. The long-term national interests of the three states are quite different. Their views on their future roles in world politics also diverge.

For example, Russia seeks to restore its influence in the post-Soviet space and does not dream of the more distant regions where it used to play a key role.

China is progressing gradually to the status of the world's leading economic power (hoping to reach it by the middle of this century), and its main interest is to peacefully bring its political influence in the world in line with its increased economic and military power.

India aspires to increase its role in international affairs which may result in obtaining the status of a permanent member of the UN Security Council, as well as in establishing a fully integrated union under its leadership in South Asia.

In the future, up to 2030 Russia will continue its efforts to create an Asian multilateral security system based on the balance of regional powers. It will try to delay the reform of the UN and the Security Council. It will not oppose the extrusion of the US presence from post-Soviet states and will attempt to replace it in Central Asia.

This scenario for Asian security is quite plausible given that by 2030 there are no major crises (conflicts with the use of nuclear weapons, a large-scale military conflict between states in the region, disintegration of large states, etc.) that could unravel the evolvement of the Asian security system realising a nightmare scenario that would be impossible to predict.

Scenario Two: Leadership of China

By 2030, the Chinese economy will equal that of the US and the stock market in Shanghai will be the largest in the world, far ahead of the NYSE (New York Stock Exchange), Tokyo's Nikkei and London's Stock Exchange. In 2010 already, the Chinese economy has become the second largest in the world, enabling it to acquire a qualitatively different status. From now on, China will be able to determine the direction of global economic processes, and its opinion will not be disregarded even by such giants as the United States, European Union, or Japan. In the autumn of 2009, some Russian economists acknowledged the reorientation of the Russian economy towards the Chinese market and the inclusion of the country in the global division of labour as a supplier of raw materials or semi-finished products as a major success of Russia's economy during the global crisis of 2008-09. Indeed, by maintaining high GDP growth rates and boosting the consumption capacity of its national market, China is increasing its attractiveness as a centre of magnetism for the world economic processes. Thus, the current Chinese leaders are planning to turn the regional leadership of China into the global one.

Nevertheless, the scenario of 'leadership of China' seems unlikely for several reasons associated with acute and intractable problems of modern China:

1. A total lack of political reforms and failed attempts to reconcile the ideas (rhetoric) of socialism with the market economy.
2. The preservation of a huge and inefficient public sector in the form of large industrial enterprises in the mainland provinces of the country, whose maintenance is becoming increasingly burdensome for the country's budget.
3. A growing divide between China's affluent coastal area and the poor central and western parts, which could heighten social tensions and political instability.
4. The economic slowdown due to the global crisis and as part of a long-term global trend which started in the OECD countries in the middle of the previous decade.
5. Growing unemployment and dissatisfaction with the policy of moderate reforms of the Communist party and the military elite.
6. Uncertain impact of China's accession to the WTO on the country's economy and its export-oriented industries.
7. Increasing complexity of the political and economic relations between China and the United States, Taiwan, Japan and several other neighbouring states.

China will undoubtedly be the most notable actor of Asian politics by 2030, but its influence will be counterbalanced by other states or their alliances. Russia will make great efforts to develop economic ties with China, but security cooperation within the SCO framework, or the Russia-India-China triangle, or the BRIC countries will be minimal.

Scenario Three: US Leadership

The US's actual defeat in Iraq and the perceived difficulties inherent in the completion of operations in Afghanistan and the withdrawal of American troops have already led to an apparent decrease in the US capacity to project its military and economic power in the Asian region. It is no coincidence that during his visit to China in November 2009 Barack Obama cautiously raised the question of establishing the G2—an alliance between the largest power of the previous century (USA) and the largest power of this century (China). It is significant that the Chinese did not show interest in such a prospect. In other words, Beijing does not believe that Washington will be able to restore its influence in the world, undermined by consequences of the neo-conservative rule, or to restore its ability to exert decisive influence on the events in Asia.

Nevertheless, the ability of the US to act independently in protecting its own interests in Asia as well as in alliance with other states such as Japan, South Korea, and in the future, possibly, India, gives us good reason to consider a scenario in which Washington would be able to preserve its key position in the region as fairly realistic in the long run. Virtually all Asian countries are interested in the US to remain a potent regional power for various reasons. China vitally needs access for its products to the US market. India is interested in increasing cooperation with the United States in the areas of information technology and high-tech. Japan, South Korea and Taiwan view Washington as the chief guarantor of their security and territorial integrity. Therefore, in 2030, just like now, the US influence in Asia will be significant, while in addressing the most pressing military and political issues—absolutely crucial.

Russia is quite happy with a moderate US meddling in the affairs of Asia since it counterbalances the positions of some major regional players (China, Japan, India, etc.). Therefore, Moscow will not oppose the US anywhere in the Asian region except in Central Asia. The litmus test of Russia's reaction to the US policy in Asia is the Russo-

Iranian relations and Moscow's readiness to support tougher sanctions against Iran over its nuclear programme. Since non-nuclear Iran serves the long-term interests of Russia, Moscow will try to promote the goals of US policy towards this state, while avoiding a complete rupture of Russo-Iranian relations. This is an extremely difficult task for the Russian diplomacy, and there is no guarantee that it will be able to handle it successfully in the next few years.

Scenario Four: Chaos

This scenario seems unlikely for the entire of Asia since the forces that promote order and stability in the region are considerably stronger than the forces and processes of destruction.

On the one hand, some parts of Asia, among which we tend to consider Afghanistan and the neighbouring areas of Pakistan, Central Asia around the Fergana valley, and some areas of possible conflict on the Korean peninsula, the lack of effective governance in some countries of Asia, as well as the desire of some outside extra-systemic players to destabilise the situation, could lead to chaos and armed conflicts.

On the other hand, we are convinced that as of now there is no state in the Asian region that is interested in turmoil of revolutionary proportion or that is betting on a large-scale conflict instead of diplomacy and the search for compromises in an attempt to enhance its status in the regional system of security and economy.

Russia will try to prevent the realisation of this scenario in every way possible, as the chaos on its southern borders could become a threat not only to its national security, but in the long run, its territorial integrity as well. The acquisition of nuclear weapons by new states of Asia in the long run could lower the threshold of their use to dangerously low levels. A nuclear conflict in the most populous part of the world would lead to global shocks of unprecedented scale. Consequently, Russia's policy will be aimed at the preservation of controllability of Asian security and the maintenance of regional stability.

IX

Alternative Scenarios

27

The Geopolitics of Asia in 2030 from China's Perspective and Interest

CHIEN-PENG (C.P.) CHUNG

Although a view from China on the geopolitics of Asia in 2030 has to take into account the priorities and preferences of neighbouring states and those further afield whose actions have impacts on Asian countries, it must necessarily proceed from China's perspective of its own development, and will naturally reflect its national interest, or at least that of its governing elite.

Crucial yet Credible Assumptions

It is important to make some crucial yet credible assumptions as to how the world would appear or remain in 2030, in the absence of which there may be nothing fruitful to work on or talk about. Two major assumptions could be held. One is that countries, particularly major ones, adapt to environmental changes, particularly global warming leading to decreases in food and water resources, without collapsing into chaos. The other is that no hegemonic or world war will occur from now until 2030.

China's Domestic Developments

Geopolitical developments in Asia in 2030 will in many ways be the results of, or responses to, China's domestic developments. These developments should therefore be taken into account first and foremost in our prognosis. From now till 2030, political, not economic, modernisation will be the central challenge facing China. This means that the two basic contradictions inherent in the Chinese political system, of market capitalism based on the rule of law *versus* a political plutocracy that operates on secrecy and arbitrariness, will have to be somehow reconciled, in order for the country not to experience large-scale and crippling social turbulence.

An essentially technocratic approach to governance can be expected to prevail. This will entail minimal reform of the political system, combined with a continued focus on strengthening the legal structure, and building capacity and skills within the public administration as substitutes to democratisation.[1] The fear of large inequalities across China and popular airings of dissatisfactions and grievances leading to social unrests will cause the elite to resist introducing direct elections to levels above the township.

Economics-oriented national elite born in the mid-'60s to mid-'70s, many members of whom are educated overseas, some with PhDs, and backed by the military, will exercise power. They will do so by appealing to the preservation of social stability and national sovereignty to forestall chaotic fragmentation and a repeat of imperialistic humiliation, with occasional well-publicised financial concessions to the economically-disadvantaged and ethnic minorities. Nationalism, of the type that is explicitly state-patriotic but implicitly Han-Chinese, will provide a minimal social glue to give the regime some degree of support or at least acquiescence; leaders will turn a blind eye to corruption practices unless they are publicly exposed; society will become more pluralised with more self-organised citizens and workers' groups, *albeit* still under the purview of the authorities; and individual liberties and choices other than political ones will continue to increase.

With rising wages, direct investment in economically backward areas, and fiscal incentives first put in place by the authorities to buffer the 2008-09 global recession, a 'new economic model' has evolved. This model prioritises the promotion of domestic demand,[2] which will make it become nearly as important as exports in constituting the economic growth engine of China by 2030.

China's Gross Domestic Product and Per Capita Disposable Income

China will overtake the United States economically in purchasing power parity (PPP) terms between 2025 and 2030 and become the

1. Gobbicchi (2007).
2. Yong (2008); ESRI (2005).

largest economy by 2030, accounting for about 16 per cent of the world's gross domestic product (GDP).[3] The chief economist of the World Bank, Justin Yifu Lin, expected in 2008 that China's economic growth can be maintained at about 8 per cent until 2030.[4] More likely, China's economy will sustain an average growth rate of 6.5 per cent from now till the late 2020s, but as it matures, it may decline to between 4-4.5 per cent by 2030.

China's annual per capita disposable income (PCDI) will grow at an average of 4.6 per cent between 2010 and 2020, and 3.7 per cent from 2020 and 2030, estimating slightly conservatively.[5] At this rate of growth, by 2030, the Chinese will have a PCDI of around $13,500 in PPP terms, increasing from 19 per cent in 2009 to 42 per cent in 2030 of the current average level in high-income countries.[6] As China's middle class grows and income levels climb, its consumption share of GDP will increase to at least 50 per cent by 2030, which is the average for developed economies in the first decade of the 21st century.

Challenges and Opportunities China Presents to the World in 2030

By 2030, China would have been perceived as the strongest Asian power and the world's second largest comprehensive power.[7] The United States and China would have formed an informal but crucial 'G2' ('Chimerica') relationship in the world, whereby most of regional problems in Asia and the Pacific will be managed jointly by both states after mutual consultations in regular meetings. With the acquiescence of the US, international rules and the voting weights and leadership compositions of international institutions will be revamped to reflect China's expanding role and clout in world affairs, particularly those relating to economic matters. At the same time, notions long-held by Americans of the universality of human rights standards and general

3. Anonymous (2005).
4. Tony (2008).
5. Angus (2007).
6. Zhu (2008).
7. Xinhua News Agency (2008).

application of democratic choice to all human societies will come under more persistent and voluminous criticisms from Chinese championing cultural relativism.

With Taiwan's economic enmeshment with mainland China ('Chaiwan') and consequent decline of the island's fixation with formal independence and sub-ethnic mobilisation, China reached a political agreement with Taiwan under the principle of 'two parts, one China, no attack.' This move greatly undercut justification by US authorities to its people for maintaining US forces in the Pacific at the level of 2010.

Militarily, China would have a couple of aircraft carriers, more than a rudimentary blue-water navy, contingents of warships making regular and extensive port calls to naval bases of countries in Asia and beyond, and an effective coast guard to keep foreign navies off its proclaimed maritime exclusive economic zones (EEZs). However, even with the 'Finlandisation' of Taiwan, as China's strategic intentions and defence budgeting have not been clear, this has prompted arms acquisition and military force modernisation programmes in its regional neighbourhood, particularly in Southeast Asia, India and Australia. China will be prepared to station troops abroad for peace-keeping purposes upon invitation by the governments of the host countries.

Economically, with capital liberalisation, the Yuan/Reminbi has become a key currency in the monetary baskets of many Asia-Pacific nations, and Shanghai the financial capital of Asia and the Pacific to rival London and New York. During the 2008-09 global recession, about half of China's foreign exchange reserves have been invested in the US, mostly in US government debt.[8] By 2030, with efforts by Chinese authorities to diversify foreign debt holdings and encourage domestic consumption, the figure has decreased to less than 40 per cent. At the same time, the balance of trade will have shifted much more than at present towards favouring the US, as China's economy matures and demand increases for high value-added goods and services.

8. Wines (2009).

Product imitation will be replaced by technological innovation as the driving force of the Chinese economy. Investments in various stages of production processes will be performed in different locations in China (and India) and tied together seamlessly by a complex logistical chain extending across both countries. China, together with India, ('Chindia') will dominate world exports of middle to high technology goods and services, but with rising wages, will at the same time create new opportunities for exports to their markets.

By 2030, the total primary energy demand by China may reach 3,800 Mtoe (million tonnes of oil equivalent), about the total consumption of the US, Canada and Japan in 2006;[9] with net imports of oil and natural gas reaching 720 Mtoe and 157 billion cubic metres respectively.[10] Expansion in China's overseas investments will take the form of mergers and acquisitions to acquire control and ownership of mineral resources, which will lead to steady but sharp rises in the price of oil and natural gas.

Regional Integration

By 2030, countries of the Association of Southeast Asian Nations (ASEAN) and China, Korea and Japan (10+3) would have cultivated a sense of identity as members of an East Asian community. Levels of interaction in East Asian countries will involve not only inter-governmental exchanges, but also those of the private sectors such as education, media, culture and non-governmental organisations. Pursuing these relationships will result in the thickening, deepening and livening of many more overlapping areas of interest than present, in terms of trade, investment, tourism, non-traditional security, economic assistance and sharing development experiences.

By 2020, an ASEAN economic community (AEC) to advance the free flow of trade, investment, capital and skilled labour within ASEAN would have been established by its member governments, in order to create a single market and industrial production base in Southeast Asia and lower the cost of doing business there to compete with

9. IEA (2007).
10. Zhidong (2007).

manufacturing networks in India and China.[11] The AEC subsequently became a part of the 10+3 free trade area. Intra-regional transactions within the 10+3+India, Australia and New Zealand will have by then made up more than 60 per cent of each country's trade value. The region will have well-functioning local currency swap arrangements and bond markets, with the Asian currency unit (ACU) already a key regional currency accounting unit, thus setting the stage for a future monetary union among these countries, if and when deemed desirable by their governments. By 2030, the 10+3+Australia and New Zealand will have a GDP of $30 trillion, followed by North America at about $26 trillion and Europe at close to $19 trillion.[12]

Differences involving disputes over maritime territories and disagreements within regional security arrangements among countries will remain. However, they will not be allowed by regional governments to obstruct mutually beneficial cooperation. As legacies of the past, the status quo or lines of actual control of land borders will not be contested as actual boundaries.

Doubting the will and ability of the US to provide a secure and permanent security umbrella in the Middle East, and facing nuclear-armed Iran and Israel, Gulf Cooperation Council (GCC) governments have decided to extend mutual cooperation from economics to the military. A lively rice-for-hydrocarbon trade would have developed between South/Southeast Asia and GCC countries.

United States

In 2030, the US will remain the pre-eminent world military power and central pillar of an open international trade framework that the rest of the world has benefited from.[13] The European Union does not possess America's power projection capabilities in Asia, although it already surpasses the US in population, GDP and industrial output, and continues to merge politics and military. However, the US will be forced by circumstances of the multiple increases in the power

11. Plummer (2008 and 2009).
12. ExxonMobil, "GDP by region–2030", *http://www.exxonmobil.com/Corporate/energy_o_eco_gdp.aspx* (accessed November 30, 2009).
13. Glaser and Morris (2008).

leverages of China and India within Asia's geopolitical landscape to take into account the priorities and preferences of the rising Asian powers, and tread carefully in crafting and executing its own policies toward Asia.

US troop strength and arsenal in Japan and South Korea will be reduced by more than half, as part of burden sharing by allied countries and to deploy US soldiers as far away as possible from potential enemy lines of fire. Concomitantly, a greater number of advanced fighter planes, 'invisible' bombers, transporters, advance-warning aircrafts and nuclear-armed submarines will be based in Guam, which is at present around three hours by flight and two to three days of sailing time to the Taiwan Straits and five hours by flight to the de-militarised zone (DMZ).[14]

Due to the reluctance of Southeast Asian and Central Asian countries, Russia and South Korea to support attempts to contain China, and the drastic lowering of US military expenditure since the end of its adventures in Iraq, Afghanistan and Yemen, the US military role in Asia in 2030 will be that of a 'near balancer'. In line with this role, US joint exercises and deployments conducted with regional militaries will be of a voluntary and temporary coalition type, stressing confidence-building, law-and-order maintenance, search and rescue, and humanitarian and disaster relief.

India and the Subcontinent

India will account for 5 per cent of the world's GDP by 2030,[15] and emerge as the crucial swing constituency in the Asian balance of power. With the Indian Ocean assuming a larger and growing role in the military thinking, defence planning and operational functions of the expanding forces of China in particular, but also Japan and Russia, in the protection of their sea lanes of communication, India's principle security objective is to ensure an enduring and peaceful balance of power in Asia. As such, although it may draw closer to the US, Japan and Australia in facing up to a formidable Chinese military with regional power projection capabilities, India will not sacrifice its

14. Guang (2009).

15. Anonymous (2005).

freedom of foreign policy action in favour of bilateral military alliances that might constrain its options.

The leaders of India and China will respect each other as rising powers and work hard at mutual accommodation. India and China will be more cooperative in the area of wealth production. Since India and China are both facing rising demand for imported energy and insufficient domestic reserves, and knowing that competition for fossil fuel will drive up energy costs for both countries, they would have formed oil and natural gas importers' cartels, and engaged in joint explorations for hydrocarbon in third countries. Since the Kathmandu-Lhasa railway came into operation, Nepal's trade and investment posture has become more oriented toward China.

In security relations, both the Indian and Chinese People's Liberation Army (PLA) navies would have conducted joint exercises in the South China Sea and Indian Ocean, and India and China will tread very carefully to make sure that neither side will trigger any military confrontation. Although Pakistan and China remains close friends, China has permanently given up the idea of using Pakistan to check India strategically, as Pakistan has become an unstable, heavily-Islamicised and decentralised confederation of Punjab, Sindh, Baluchistan and Pashtunistan that has for years ceased to possess the desire to be a rival to India.

Japan

Japan's GDP per capita will decrease steadily between 2010 and 2030, as a result of shrinking population and labour force, and deep reluctance to permit large-scale immigration. Yet, Japan is likely to remain the world's most technologically advanced nation after the US. It is also likely to remain one of the largest dispensers of official development aid to the poorer countries of Asia and the Pacific, although the absolute amount has been decreasing steadily for the two decades before 2030. China will be close behind Japan in both these aspects of technological advancement and aid dispensation.

While engaging in occasional joint military exercises with regional Asian and Pacific countries, Japan will not find common cause with China or any other country in jointly balancing US power on the world stage. The Japan-US alliance by 2030 will be an equal compact but one with far less importance than what it was 25 years before, with China beyond containing, and the Japanese government having declined to get entangled in certain US conflicts that it deemed were not in Japan's national interest to do so.

Korea

Following the collapse of North Korea's economy and replacement of its Kim dynasty with a civilian-military Junta, a confederation between North Korea and South Korea was established with China's blessing. To obtain China's consent for the reunification of Korea and satisfy its demands for the neutralisation of the Korean peninsula, South Korea negotiates with the US on the complete withdrawal of its military forces from the Korean peninsula and with China on the dismantling of the nuclear arsenal of the former North Korea.

Southeast Asia

Southeast Asian countries will recognise and accept that China exerts the most political, economic and soft power in the region among external powers. To lessen the chances of terrorist attacks on, or attempted blockades of, Chinese oil tankers in the Straits of Malacca, the Chinese authorities have invested heavily in a pipeline for oil and another one for gas running strategically from the western Burmese port of Sittwe to Kunming, capital of China's southwestern province of Yunnan.

There is greater awareness of Islam's political identity and influence in Southeast Asia. Although home-grown groups advocating violence have developed under the influence of pan-Islamic ideology, moderate Islam is much more widely supported than radical/fundamentalist Islam politically. The electorates in Malaysia, Brunei and Indonesia are prepared to vote for secular governments oriented towards economic growth within a capitalist economy which have seen results, although parliamentary opposition blocs of moderate Islamic parties are also sizable. Indonesia has resource and industrial potential, but political divisiveness and regional differences are likely to hamper its economic development and strategic weight as the largest country by territory and population in Southeast Asia.

Russia

Russia will emerge as the single most important country source of energy supply to the three leading Asian consumers—China, Japan and India—and hence is positioned to play a major role in affecting Asian security. The share of Russian oil going to Asia will increase from 6 per cent today to about one-quarter by 2030, and the share of Russian natural gas shipments flowing to China, Korea and Japan will rise from a couple of percentages now to around 20 per cent by 2030.[16]

Production under licence and reverse engineering has greatly reduced China's need to purchase Russian military hardware and technology for the 20 years since 2010. However, mineral resources and primary processed products (e.g., crude oil, unprocessed wood, fish and seafood, iron ore, petrochemicals and potassium fertilisers, etc.) in Russia's exports to China has remained between 80-90 per cent. This in effect turns Russia into a valuable raw material feeder to China's economic machinery.[17] Russia will be an independent actor in world affairs, but friendlier to China than to the US, in an implicit balance with China of two authoritarian regimes against a 'hegemonic' US.

Australia

Australia prefers to avoid having to choose between China and the US, and willing to see the US share power with China in the Asia-Pacific if that will keep the peace.[18] Building up strategic capacity—particularly the air force and navy—will allow Australia to do more to support US military activities, or to defend themselves.[19] This is a position that China understands although it is not one that it welcomes.

Even in 2030, Australia has yet some ways to go to be able to relate comfortably and collaboratively with its Asian neighbours, in shedding their perceptions that it is still strategically bonded to the US in always having to seek Washington's endorsement of its strategic

16. Reuters (2009).
17. Weitz (2007).
18. White (2009).
19. Ibid.

directions. Encouraging a faster rate of immigration from Asian countries to Australia and appointing more Australians of Asian descent to ministerial positions in federal and state governments would change the colour of this perception somewhat.

United Nations: Bilateral Alliances

The United Nations (UN) Security Council will be reformed with new permanent members and strengthened to make it a more effective global collective security institution. Due to greater financial affordability and larger economic interests on the part of China and other Asian countries, UN peace-keeping operations will see more of their active participation worldwide. With the economic and military ascendance of major third-world countries, Cold War military alliances, if not already dismantled, will be rendered moribund.

The Regional and World Order in 2030

With China having surpassed Japan in every way except per capita income, memories on both sides, whether they are about past humiliation or glory, will become truly history, and common cultural and historical heritage will be greatly emphasised in bilateral interactions. As to Sino-Indian relations, Buddhism, particularly of the Mahayana and Dhyana/Chan/Zen variants, could be a central axis, developed within an Asian civilisational context. Although mutual trust at strategic levels between Beijing and Washington is still lacking because of different social systems and national interests, both China and the US see themselves as the largest and most responsible stakeholders in hedging against regional and global turbulence,[20] and are indeed locked in as such, being held accountable by other countries for the conduct of their foreign diplomatic, economic and military policies as the two state actors whose actions have the biggest impact on the rest of the world.

Strategic weight ultimately depends on economic power, and strategic concerns ultimately depend on economic interests. Long-term trends are working against maintenance of US primacy *vis-à-vis* the

---

20. Jisi (2007).

rising powers, especially in Asia, although as a political unit and foreign policy actor, the US will still maintain a plurality in both hard and soft power measures. The flow of economic influence from West to East will be inexorable, cultural attraction of India, China, Korea and Japan to the West will be at least on par with that of the US and Europe to these Asian nations, and a true multipolar security world order would have emerged.

The rise or re-emergence of China and India, and Asia's growing economic clout, were perceived in the first two decades of the 21st century by some people in the West as a threat to Western control, and more fundamentally, to their sense of superiority toward Asia and Asians. By 2030, there will be no doubts in anyone's mind that occidentals and orientals are co-equal partners in the making of a new world order.

References

Anonymous (2005). "Asia in 2030", *Business Asia* 37(19): 1. October 17.

ESRI (2005). "Minutes of Forum 'The Chinese Economy and the Japan-Asian Relationship in 2030'", Workshop, *ESRI Economic Policy Forum: Vision of Japan in the 21st Century Series*, ESRI. Secretariat, Economic and Social Research Institute, Cabinet Office, Government of Japan, Tokyo, Japan. January 31), *http://www.esri.go.jp/en/forum1/minute/minute21st_4-e.html* (December 20, 2009).

Glaser, Bonnie S. and Lyle Morris (2008). "Chinese Perceptions of U.S. Decline and Power", *China Brief* 9(14). July 9. *http://www.jamestown.org/programs/chinabrief/single/?tx_ttnews%5Btt_news%5D=35241&cHash=db9748f805* (accessed November 30, 2009).

Gobbicchi, Alessandro (2007). "The World in 2030: Regional Trends", The Military Centre for Strategic Studies-Rome. *http://www.difesa.it/backoffice/upload/allegati/2007/%7B702FD6D4-EAC9-47C2-A805-9E8DB5C01D13%7D.pdf* (accessed November 29, 2009).

International Energy Agency (IEA) (2007). *World Energy Outlook*. Paris: Organisation of Economic Cooperation and Development. p. 119.

Jisi, Wang (2007). "America in Asia: How much does China Care?", *Global Asia* 2(2): 28. (Fall).

Maddison, Angus (2007). "Six Transformations in China 960-2030AD", Lecture. Asian Development Bank Institute, Tokyo, Japan. September 23.

Pengzhan, Zhu (2008). "A Glimpse of a Prosperous 2030 and What can Foster It", *Media Economics*. May 27. *http://www.chinavalue.net/Group/Topic/5727/* (accessed November 30, 2009).

Plummer, Michael G. (2008). "Integration Strategies for ASEAN: Alone, Together, or Together with Neighbors?", Seminar, Asian Development Bank Institute, Tokyo, Japan. March 19.

Plummer, Michael G. (2009). "Assessing the Economics of the ASEAN Economic Community", Seminar, East-West Center, Honolulu, HI. November 4.

Qilin, Guang (2009). "Meijun yinxing zhanji zhengzhu Guandao, sishi zhendui Zhongguo" ("America's invisible warplanes increasingly deployed on Guam, as if targeting China"), *China Central Television News broadcast*. May 6, 5.44 pm.

Reuters (2009). "Russia Unveils $2 Trln Energy Growth Plan to 2030", November 26, *http://uk.reuters.com/article/idUKGEE5AP25J20091126* (December 20, 2009).

Sagami, Tony (2008). "China GDP to be 2.5 times the size of US by 2030", *Asian Market*, Stock Market in China. May 3. *http://blogs.moneyandmarkets.com/china-and-asia-stock-alert/china-gdp-to-be-25-times-the-size-of-us-by-2030/* (accessed November 30, 2009).

Weitz, Richard (2007). "China and Russia Hand in Hand: Will it Work?" Global Asia 2(3). (Winter), under "Feature Essays", *http://www.globalasia.org/Back_Issues/Volume_2_Number_3_Winter_2007/China_and_Russia_Hand_in_Hand__Will_it_Work.html* (accessed December 3, 2009).

White, Hugh (2009). "Australia's Strategic Future After the White Paper", Entry posted June 19, *http://www.eastasiaforum.org/2009/06/19/australias-strategic-future-after-the-white-paper/#more-5008* (accessed November 30, 2009).

Wines, Michael (2009). "China's Leader Says He Is 'Worried' Over U.S. Treasuries", *New York Times*. March 13.

Xinhua News Agency (2008). "Thinktank: China Expected to Become Second in Objective National Strength by 2030", *People's Daily Online*. January 29. *http://english.peopledaily.com.cn/90001/90776/6347378.html* (December 20, 2009).

Yong, Wang (2008), "Domestic Demand and Continued Reform: China's Search for a New Model", *Global Asia* 3(4) (Winter), under "*That Sinking Feeling: Asia Hangs on as the Crisis Deepens," http://www.globalasia.org/Back_Issues/Volume_3_Number_4_Winter_2008/Domestic_Demand_and_Continued_Reform_Chinas_Search_for_a_New_Model.html* (accessed December 4, 2009)

Zhidong, Li (2007). "China's Long-Term Energy Outlook and the Implications for Global Governance", *Asia-Pacific Review* 14(1): 22. May.

28

Hegemony or Balance of Power?

Regional Order and Conflict in a Transforming Asia

G. JOHN IKENBERRY

Introduction

Asia is a regional order in the midst of a grand transformation. It is one of the great dramas of the 21st century. For some observers it is like witnessing the final end of the American era and the gradual transition from a Western-oriented world order to one increasingly dominated by Asia. Historian Niall Ferguson argues that, 'the bloody twentieth century is in fact a story of the "descent of the West," a "reorientation of the world" in which the Atlantic powers ceded their mastery of the world to the East. To be sure, the "old order" in Asia is giving way to something new, but the contours of the "new order" still remain faint and uncertain.'[1]

The sources of this geopolitical change in Asia are many—economic, political, social, technological, demographic and military. But at its core, the transformation is driven by a steady shift in the distribution of power, led by the rise of China and India. This is a double transformation. Asia as a region is shifting and evolving in the wake of the growth of its leading states. Asia is expanding as a region and fast growing states are rising up to dominate it. But the global system is also shifting and evolving as Asia steadily grows in power and importance relative to the rest of the world. Asia is growing in size and power relative to the West. In the background is the old security and economic order in East Asia, dominated by the United

1. This study draws on a series of articles and book chapters that I have written in recent years on the rise of China, American grand strategy in East Asia, and the future of regional order. See Ikenberry (2008a); Ikenberry (2008b); Ikenberry (2008c); Ikenberry (2006); Ikenberry (2009); and Ikenberry and Moon (2008).

States. For half a century, East Asia and much of the wider global system has been organised around American hegemonic leadership. This leadership has been anchored in an array of bilateral security partnerships and trade ties that connect the United States to countries along the crescent of East Asia.

In today's drama, the most potent driver of change is the rise of China—a potential challenger of American hegemonic leadership. But other developments in the region are also undermining the old order and threatening to generate instability. One is the 'normalisation' of Japan. Reflected in the political agenda of its new Democratic Party of Japan (DPJ) government, Japan is seeking to establish a more mature sense of national identity and statehood—and it is seeking to reclaim for itself the traditional rights of sovereignty and self-defence that come with normalcy. It is doing so even as its relative power position in the region is declining. At the same time, the flourishing of democracy and populist politics in South Korea has made it easier for its leaders to question the country's client status and alliance dependence on the United States. The growth and integration of the East Asian regional economy has also diminished the centrality of American markets and investment and refocussed commercial relations on China. Meanwhile, the rise of India and the return of Russia have expanded the geopolitical 'space' of Asia and brought the Eurasian great power politics into it. Finally, America's own changing global security priorities and alliance thinking—driven by its war on terror—has created new uncertainties and controversies in the region about Washington's long-term security ties and commitments to the region.

How will this power transition in Asia and the global system work itself out? What sort of regional order—and global order—is likely to emerge from this? What are the sources of continuity and stability that will help shape the flow of change? What are the sources of conflict and instability? Will China and the United States find themselves increasingly in a grand conflict, competing for allies, influence, and leadership? To what extent will American hegemonic leadership and its long-standing system of alliances and regional partnerships remain critical to the shape and stability of Asia? What can the United States and other countries do to shape and direct the way India and China rise up in the global system?

These moments of 'power transition' are an old and recurring problem in international relations—and they are fraught with danger. The logic is simple. As scholars such as Paul Kennedy and Robert Gilpin have it, world politics is marked by a succession of powerful—or hegemonic—states that rise up to organise the international system. They create and enforce the rules and institutions of order that ensure a stable system in which to pursue their interests and security. But nothing lasts forever. Steady and long-term shifts in the distribution of power among states give rise to new challenger states which eventually engage in geopolitical struggles over the terms of order. Rising states want to translate their newly acquired power into greater authority and control over the global system, to reshape the rules and institutions in accord with their interests. Meanwhile, declining states fear the loss of authority and control and worry about the security implications of their weakened positions.

The danger posed by power transitions is captured most dramatically in the case of late-19th century Germany. Germany's ascent began with its unification under Bismarck in 1870 and the rapid growth of its economy. By the 1880s and 1890s it was acquiring overseas territories and building a modern navy. In 1870, Britain had a three to one advantage in economic power over Germany but by 1903 Germany had pulled ahead of Britain in overall economic and military power. The rise of German power triggered the classic dynamics of a power transition: as Germany unified and grew, so too did its dissatisfactions, demands, and ambitions; and as it grew more powerful, a security competition emerged and Germany increasingly appeared as a threat to other great powers in Europe. In the strategic realignments that followed, Britain, France and Russia—all former enemies—banded together to confront an emerging and ambitious Germany. The result, of course, was a European war.

But not all power transitions generate war or overturn the old order. Britain ceded power to a rapidly growing America in the early decades of the 20th century without any great conflict or a rupture in relations. Japan grew from 5 per cent of the American GNP in the late '40s to over 60 per cent of its size in the early '90s without challenging the existing international order. Clearly there are different types of power ascents and transitions. Some states have grown rapidly in economic and geopolitical power and, in the end, accommodated themselves to the existing order—such as post-war Japan.

No one knows what sort of order is emerging in Asia. But we can envisage alternative futures. A great deal depends on whether the American-led alliance system continues to play a dominant role as a framework for security cooperation in the region. Will that alliance system be extended, updated, and integrated with other trans-regional security groupings, or will it gradually erode and give way to a more traditional great power system? If the region is to become defined in terms of great power relations including—China, India, Japan, Russia, and the United States—will it evolve into a cooperative concert of powers or be marked by the traditional patterns of competition and rivalry?

I see four possible futures: one possibility is the emergence of a multipolar balance of power system. This is a future where a great power order emerges. China, India, Russia, Japan and the United States become both more equal and more independent as geopolitical players. A second possibility is the rise of an autocratic-democratic divide. Here the United States builds a coalition of democracies and China and Russia lead a rival coalition that divides Asia. Third, there is the possibility of a Chinese-American co-hegemony. Here the United States and China share leadership in the region and build a stable working system. Finally, there is the possibility of the continuation of the American security hegemony and alliance cooperation. This is a future in which the changes in the region are mediated and accommodated within the old regional framework. India integrates into this order and China accommodates itself to it. In each of these possibilities there are both more or less conflict-prone variations. A grand transition from an order built on hegemony to an order based on the balance of power can involve the movement from one equilibrium point to another. Or it can lead to a breakdown of the norms and understandings of great power cooperation, ushering in rivalry, arms competition, and instability.

In this chapter, I argue that there are aspects of all four of these potential 'futures' unfolding in the region. But I am sceptical that the region will take on the classic patterns of a power transition. To be sure, the region is evolving towards a more decentralised and shifting great power system. China, India, Japan, and other middle-powers in the region will increasingly become regional players in their own right. But this order will also retain traces of the logic and character of the American-led global system. Security competition and conflict associated with the ongoing power transitions is not inevitable. This is because of three reasons. First, the old American-led order—at the regional and global level—is still a formidable presence. China is still dwarfed by the scale and scope of the American security order and the liberal capitalist system. Rising states in Asia still have reasons to engage and integrate into this order. Second, the old order has both realist-oriented and liberal-oriented institutions and practices that make it possible for great powers to operate in more cooperative ways than in the dangerous old days of great power balancing and security competition. Third, possibilities for great power cooperation are also reinforced by the unusually large array of strategic interests that these states share, including the United States and China. Fourth, the countries in the region do not want a Cold War-style struggle between democracies and authoritarian states.

Overall, my argument is that power shifts and full-blown power transitions do not necessarily lead to the collapse and transformation of regional and international order. In the past, regional and international orders have risen and fallen in the wake of great power wars. This prospect does not exist today, even if only because of nuclear deterrence and the primacy of the liberal democracies and the world capitalist system. So there will be an evolution in the order and not sharp discontinuities. This is good for stability and peace.

This chapter will do three things. First, I will explore the logic of the old order that has provided the basis for stability in East Asia and trans-Pacific ties between the United States and the region. Second, I will lay out a set of possible 'future orders' in Asia that I have sketched above. Third, I will look at the sources of continuity and stability that exist both within the region and within the wider American-led global system. At the end, I will return to my general argument about the evolving logic and character of Asian regional security and international order.

The Old Order in East Asia

The debate about power transitions and the future of China and East Asian regionalism is taking place in the context of an existing American-led security and economic order. This order has been remarkably durable and legitimate, producing a stable world order for almost half a century. But forces of change, including the rise of China, are creating pressures for a reorganisation of the regional system.

Despite its success as an order, there is a widespread view that the post-war East Asian system of economics, politics, and security is not well organised. The contrast with Europe is striking. Europe engineered a stable post-war peace, built around a Franco-German accord and layers of regional institutions—NATO, the EU, OSCE (Organization for Security and Co-operation in Europe), the Council of Europe, and others. In contrast, East Asia has no region-wide system of cooperative security, while it does have unresolved historical antagonisms, conflicting economic systems, divided and disputed territories, and rapidly shifting power relations.

Yet partly by accident and partly by design, a relatively stable and peaceful order did emerge in East Asia over the last half a century. It is an order organised around 'hard' bilateralism and 'soft' multilateralism. At its core is the US-Japan alliance and the wider system of bilateral alliances that connect the United States to Korea, Taiwan, and other Asian countries. Supplementing this security system is a variety of soft regional dialogues, including APEC, ASEAN regional forum, ASEAN plus three, and the Asian Summit.[2]

2. As Gill and Green (2009) note: 'Over the past sixty years, Asia's stability has rested on the foundations of bilateral alliances between the United States and Japan, Australia, and South Korea principally, but also the Philippines and Thailand. However, in recent years the regional architecture has been reinforced with the long-standing Association of Southeast Asian Nations (ASEAN) and a more mature ASEAN Regional Forum (ARF), as well as with other multilateral mechanisms such as the Asia-Pacific Economic Cooperation (APEC) forum, the ASEAN Plus Three (APT) process, the Shanghai Cooperation Organisation (SCO), the Six-Party Talks on Korean Peninsula stability, and the newly formed East Asia Summit (EAS). Reflective of the region itself, this new architecture is highly fluid and engenders both cooperation and competition among the region's powers. What is more, the future direction and success of these arrangements and the implications for global and regional security and prosperity remain unclear even as the elements of this dynamic regional architecture expand and become more complex.'

In essence, post-war order in East Asia has been built in accordance with an American-style hegemonic logic. The United States has exported security and imported goods. It is an order where the US-Japan alliance—together with the wider 'hub and spoke' system of bilateral security ties—provides the hidden support beams for the wider region. It is an order based on a set of grand political bargains. The United States provides security, open markets, and working political relations with its partners, and in return these countries agree to affiliate with the United States, providing it with logistical, economic, and diplomatic support as the United States leads the wider system.

From the outset, this bilateral security order has been intertwined with the evolution of regional economic relations. The United States facilitated Japanese economic reconstruction after the war and created markets for Japanese exports. The American security guarantee to its partners in East Asia provided a national security rationale for Japan to open its markets. Free trade helped cement the alliance, and in turn the alliance helped settle economic disputes. The export-oriented development strategies of Japan and the other Asian 'tigers' depended on America's willingness to accept imports and huge trade deficits, which alliance ties made politically tolerable.

Over the decades, this American-led alliance system has been quite functional for both the United States and its partners. This is true in at least four respects. First, the 'hub and spoke' alliance system provides the political and geographical foundation for the projection of American influence into the region. With forward bases and security commitments across the region, the United States established itself as the leading power in East Asia. Second, the bilateral alliances bind the United States to the region, establishing fixed commitments and mechanisms that increase certainty and predictability about the exercise of American power. Worry is reduced in the region about American comings and goings. Third, the alliance ties create channels of access for Japan and other security partners to Washington. In effect, the alliances provide institutionalised 'voice opportunities' for these countries. Finally, the US-Japan alliance has played a more specific and crucial role—namely, it has allowed Japan to be secure without the necessity of becoming a traditional military power. Japan could be defended while remaining a 'civilian power' and this meant that Japan could rebuild and re-enter the region without triggering dangerous security dilemmas.

In these ways, the US-Japan alliance and the bilateral alliance system have been more than defence arrangements—they have also served as political architecture for the wider system. Through this system, American power has been linked and rendered more predictable, while Japan has been able to reassure its neighbours, integrate into the region, and pioneer a civilian pathway to growth and influence. In effect, in the post-war era, if Japan was the Germany of East Asia, the United States played the role of France. Just as the Franco-German partnership was the linchpin for the reintegration of Germany into Europe, the US-Japan alliance was the linchpin for Japan's re-entry into Asia. Importantly, China's unspoken support for the US-Japan alliance over the decades reflects the fact that these stabilising and reassurance functions of the alliance were widely appreciated in the region.

Even today, as change erodes aspects of this order, this old logic of order still has its virtues. Indeed, it is hard to envisage a wholly new logic of order for East Asia that is equally functional. It is difficult to imagine a peaceful and workable regional system without these bilateral security underpinnings and a continuing hegemonic presence of the United States. Looking into the future, the challenge will be to adapt to this regional order to accommodate the rise of China and the 'normalisation' of Japan—but do so in ways that retain the virtues of the old order.

Four Possible Futures

The great transformation of Asia is being driven by a long-term power transition. This entails the rise of China and India and the reworking of the economic, political, and security relations that follow in its wake. At the heart of this power transition is China. China is quickly on its way to becoming a formidable regional and global power. The size of its economy has quadrupled since the launch of its market reforms in the late-'70s and by some estimates it will double again in the next decade. It has become one of largest bases for industrial manufacturing in the world, and it consumes roughly a third of the world's iron, steel and coal. It has accumulated massive foreign reserves, topping $1 trillion at the end of 2006. Chinese military spending has increased at an inflation-adjusted rate of over 18 per cent a year, giving it capacities to project force with greater reach, sophistication, and fire power. The growth of Chinese power has also been matched by active diplomacy, and its influence is growing not just in Asia but also in the Middle East, Africa, and Latin America. Indeed, while the Soviet Union rivalled the United States as a military power, China is emerging as both a military and economic rival, heralding a potentially more profound shift in the distribution of global power.

In the context of these power shifts, there are four possible pathways away from the old order. These pathways lead to various sorts of regional orders, built around either a reorganised hegemonic system or a balance of power among regional great powers. We can look at these various configurations of power and order and speculate on the consequences for peace and stability.[3]

The Return to Multipolarity

One possible future in Asia is a return to a multipolar system of order. Multipolarity is a description of the distribution of power and the relations among states. Three or more major states would occupy roughly equal power positions in the region. China, India, Japan, the United States and Russia would be the major players, with South Korea, Indonesia and Australia also involved in the multipolar mix. How such a system would operate is less clear. The centralised security environment could generate competition and arms races that could destabilise the region. But the balance-oriented organisation of power could also provide countervailing pressures on China and create a more open and cooperative concert of powers.

The shift toward multipolarity would involve two sorts of movements. First, there would be a decentralisation of power. It would entail a diffusion of power away from the United States. China too would rise but its power would be matched by other great powers, including India. Second, there would be a rise on new 'poles'. That is, there would be several power centres, each with its own allies and

---

3. Other efforts to develop scenarios for the future include: Overhot (2008).

clients. Each of the great powers would be a pole in a multipolar system in which smaller and secondary states would be connected. A pole is a state that organises and assists several smaller and secondary states. It is a pole to the extent that other states connect to and depend on that state for various benefits and services, including stability and protection. They are geopolitical 'hubs' around which less powerful states affiliate.[4]

The movement toward multipolar order in Asia would be encouraged and reinforced by the return to multipolarity at the global level. This is a development widely anticipated by scholars and political pundits. This is a vision of a world order organised around one dominant power transforming into a system in which several powers exist and compete. The system loses its core. The United States loses its centrality in the operation of the wider global order.[5] Hegemony gives way to shifting security ties and competing geopolitical centres of gravity. The American alliance system loses its coherence and other states and regional powers—China, India, Russia, the EU, and so forth—gain positions of power and leadership within various regional spheres.

What would be the consequences of multipolarity—globally and within Asia—for patterns of conflict and cooperation? The American hegemonic order could simply yield to an international system where several leading states or centres of power establish their own economic and security spheres. The global order would become a less unified and coherent system of rules and institutions, while regional orders emerge as relatively distinct, divided, and competitive geopolitical spheres.[6]

This fragmented order might devolve into several competing subsystems, each connected to its own leading state. These could be

---

4. For a survey of the literature on polarity, see Buzan (2004).

5. The National Intelligence Council's (2008) recent survey of global change sees the '"return to multipolarity" as the master trend of the coming decades.' As the report argues: '"[B]y 2025 the international system will be a global multipolar one." "Power will be more dispersed with the newer players bringing new rules of the game while risks will increase that the traditional Western alliances will weaken."' See National Intelligence Council (2008). For a discussion of the logic and implications of a 'return to multipolarity', see Posen (2009).

6. For essays exploring a wide array of post-American hegemonic orders, see Fry and O'Hagan (2000).

regional blocs or they could be non-geographical coalitions of states that trade and affiliate together. The borders of these groupings could be more or less exclusive and preferential. The breakdown of the American-led liberal international order might be relatively mild in which preferential barriers between groups of states are low but still consequential. The global system could fragment into rival political-economic strategic networks. States—and the groups and firms within them—are able to operate both within and across these networks. But over time, political and economic affairs become increasingly routed through these rival coalitions. The global system is not closed or devoid of multilateral rules, but it is fragmented into sub-systems of networked relationships.

Within Asia, a multipolar order could either be dangerous or conflict-prone or not. The great powers in the region would be more or less independent geopolitical actors. The danger and instability would come if the regional powers felt insecure and ignited an arms race. Alliances and America's extended deterrent would give way to states seeking their own security. This might even involve an insecurity that drives Japan to acquire nuclear weapons. It is not heartening to note that the European great powers found themselves over several centuries engaged in security competition and war until they found ways to build a stable balance of power system. East Asia could be entering this process without a long regional history of great power balancing.

On the other hand, a multipolar system of great powers in Asia could produce a stable balance that keeps the peace. The distribution of power would be sufficiently diffused among several states that no one state—such as China—would be able to reach for regional dominance. Coalitions of states would form and reform in ways that prevent the rise of a regional hegemon. Likewise, the fact that most of the major powers in Asia have nuclear weapons—China, India, Russia, and the United States—could mute the threat of war. In Europe, the great powers developed norms of restraint and accommodation that facilitated stable relations.[7] An Asia with four or

7. See Kissinger (1954). It accounts of great power balancing and the evolution of its practices and principles. Craig and George (1981); Schroeder (1994).

five major powers could develop the same norms of mutual respect and forbearance.

But there are some doubts about the likelihood that Asia will move towards a full-scale balance of power system. China and the United States remain substantially more powerful than the other states, and these imbalances will continue to grow as China's economy and military capabilities grow. Japan is not likely to play a truly independent great power role in the next few decades. At the same time, the American alliance system shows no dramatic signs of eroding. The rise of China has had the effect of providing more than a few states in the region with a rationale for holding onto the American security partnership. There are affinities between the democracies that reinforce these alliance patterns. As a result, an old-style balance of power system based on a multipolar distribution of power is not likely.

Democratic-Autocratic Divide

A second possible future in Asia is one where a grand divide opens up between the liberal democracies and authoritarian great powers. The United States and its democratic allies will increasingly find themselves organising to counter illiberal adversaries, and Asia will be split down from the middle. This development foreshadows rising competition and conflict and imposes severe upper limits on the potential for regional and global cooperation.

In this view, the world is not marching towards a universal liberal democracy and the 'end of history.' Rather it is polarising into camps and is on the threshold of a new rivalry between the old Western liberal states and repressive and dangerous autocracies, most notably Russia and China. Unlike the autocracies that failed so spectacularly in the 20th century, the new autocracies are said to be not only compatible with capitalist success but perhaps even to be the rival alternative forms of capitalism. Unlike their predecessors, the new autocracies show new forms of adaptability and resilience as market economies. But like their predecessors, these autocracies are said to be intrinsically hostile to democratic states and liberal internationalism and harbour far-reaching revisionist ambitions.[8]

8. See Deudney and Ikenberry (2009).

Several recent developments seem to support this emerging view. Democratic transitions have stalled and reversed. In China, the communist party dictatorship has weathered domestic challenges while presiding over decades of rapid economic growth and capitalist modernisation. Rising oil prices have empowered authoritarian regimes. In Russia, the Putin government has rolled back democratic gains and appears increasingly autocratic. At the same time, relations between Russia and the West have deteriorated from the near amity of the early post-Cold War era. Relations between China and the West remain contentious with divisions over Taiwan, human rights, and oil access. And much less powerful autocratic states, such as Venezuela and Iran, are destabilising revisionists in their regions. There even appear to be signs that these autocratic states may increasingly make common cause against the hegemonic Western states with nascent alliances such as the Shanghai Cooperation Organisation. This newly conflict-prone international setting has returned the United Nations—particularly the Security Council—back to its Cold War paralysis. In this view, the liberal West confronts a bleak future in which its values and interests are fundamentally contested.

Various leaders and experts have offered visions of a coalition of democracies. Former Prime Minister Taro Aso, in his position as foreign minister, articulated a notion of an Asian 'arc of freedom and prosperity' that would bring the region and global democracies closer together. This was a 'values' strategy aimed at strengthening Japanese cooperation with Europe and NATO and putting Japan in a position to exert more leadership in the region. As Aso put it: 'I firmly believe that Japan must make its ties even firmer with friendly nations that share the common views and interests, namely of course the United States as well as Australia, India, and the member states of the EU and NATO, and work towards expansion of this "arc of freedom and prosperity."'[9] American experts have also sketched an agenda for a stronger strategic collaboration among the democracies in Asia.[10]

Important foreign policy implications follow from this view of a coming democratic-autocratic divide. One of the most prominent

9. Foreign Minister Taro Aso's speech before the Japanese Institute for International Affairs, 30 November 2006.

10. See, for example, Green (2006).

proponents of this view, Robert Kagan, insists that it is time for the United States and the other liberal democracies to abandon their optimistic expectations, hopes, and programmes for global convergence, engagement, and cooperation as an illusion. Instead, the liberal democracies should strengthen ties among themselves, perhaps even through a formal League of Democracies. And they should gird themselves for increasing rivalry and conflict with the resurgent autocracies.[11] Containment not engagement, military rivalry not arms control, balance of power not concert of power—these are the guideposts for an American foreign policy appropriate to this coming geopolitical divide.

The spectacular rates of capitalist growth in autocratic China and the reassertion of an authoritarian central state in Russia combined with economic growth, has reopened the great debate about the trajectory of modern societies. These developments suggest that there are multiple paths to capitalist modernity and that authoritarian states are quite compatible with capitalism. This implies that there is no inevitable connection between the economic liberalisation associated with capitalism and economic globalisation, on the one hand, and political liberalisation associated with liberal democracy and limited government constitutionalism, on the other. Within the two century sweep of the debate over industrial modernity, the autocratic revival thesis represents a broadening from the 'end of history' position but—importantly—accepts that it is capitalism not socialism that is the solely viable economic system.

The autocratic return has also triggered a reassessment of the reasons for the failure of earlier autocratic states. Historian Azar Gat has argued that the earlier failure of authoritarian capitalist states was due to contingent factors rather than some deep misfit between industrial capitalism and closed authoritarian political systems. He argues that the failure of Nazi Germany and Imperial Japan—both of which were capitalist states—resulted from their insufficient territorial size and industrial base rather than some deeper flaw in their logic.[12] Conversely, the Anglo-American victory derived not from the

11. Kagan (2008).

12. Gat (2007).

advantages of liberal democratic political institutions but rather from their greater territory, population, and economic output. In short, the 'selection out' of these earlier authoritarian capitalist states was inappropriately attributed by the liberal narrative to intrinsic weaknesses rather than contingent circumstance.

The implication of this view is that Asia will break into competing ideological camps. The liberal democracies will be allied, perhaps led by the United States. China will provide the leadership and geopolitical heft for the rival camp. Both China and the United States will offer alternative models of modernity and development. There will be a Washington model and a Beijing model. China will develop its own allies as states within Asia and outside the region would move toward illiberal and authoritarian styles of development. The result could be a new Cold War conflict: a long-term struggle between two visions of modernity.

It is however doubtful that China—as the leading authoritarian capitalist state—really can offer a fundamental non-liberal vision of the future. Of course, some analysts think that China is developing such a global hegemonic vision. Journalist Martin Jacques argues that, 'China is adopting the trappings of Western capitalism but it is pioneering a very different form of hegemony—illiberal, hierarchical, and culture-based—that amounts to a sharp movement away from the Western logic of liberal modernisation. China will rule the world and do so on very different terms.'[13] But China has already made moves to integrate within the world capitalist system. The result is that China is already increasingly working within rather than outside of this liberal international order. It is seeking to increase its status and authority within the existing system rather than laying the foundation for exerting leadership in an alternative world order.[14]

---

13. Jacques (2009). See also Leonard (2008); Paus *et al.* (2009).

14. This is the view of Yong Deng, who argues that Chinese foreign policy is fundamentally oriented toward gaining greater status and recognition in the international system but not seeking a radical reorganisation of its underlying organisational principles. The aim is to gain position and respect within the existing system and work with American hegemonic leadership. As Deng suggests, since the late-1990s, the Chinese government has been more concerned 'over how the U.S. hegemony is managed than over the power configuration itself. ...' See Deng (2008).

More generally, looking at the overall situation in China and Russia, there is little evidence for the emergence of a stable equilibrium between capitalism and autocracy that can be dignified as a new model or pathway of modernity. Compared to where these countries were several decades ago, they have made remarkably great progress in throwing off centuries of accumulated economic and political backwardness, and by the yardstick of world historical change they have moved and are moving in directions consistent with the liberal modernisation narrative. Russia and China are not liberal democracies but they are much more liberal and democratic than they have ever been, and many of the crucial foundations for sustainable liberal democracy are emerging. To be sure, for Russia, the cushion of plentiful oil and gas is retarding political liberalisation; high energy prices and exports help subsidise bad government. But China has no such luxury as it faces an array of developmental restraints, most notably over population, environmental decay, and energy dependence. In the final analysis, autocracy's deep intrinsic flaws are an impediment to the realisation of the full modern development sought by the people of these countries.

American and Chinese Co-Hegemony

A third vision of Asia's future offers the opposite scenario. In this view, China and the United States are being thrown together because of common problems and aligned interests. The recent financial crisis has revealed the extent to which the two major states are tied together. Over the next decade, China and the United States could engage each other, strike bargains, and develop a strategic relationship that effectively constitutes a joint hegemonic leadership of the region.

This possible future begins with the extraordinary interdependence that the United States and China have developed. It is clearer today than ever before that each needs the other's cooperation—grudging or otherwise—to realise its own goals. China needs the American domestic market and Washington's continued commitment to uphold an open world trading system. It needs investment and a stable regional and international environment—which the United States, more than any other state, can make possible. The United States relies heavily on Chinese willingness to hold its debt and work within existing Western-oriented rules and institutions. Chinese cooperation is essential for America's efforts to combat the spread of nuclear, chemical, and biological weapons.

The sudden rise of this mutual dependence is striking. The United States has become China's great trade partner, which is essential to China's trade-driven strategy of development. American consumption is tied to China's cheap exports. The United States borrows and consumes. China produces and saves. The result is a symbiotic relationship. As Kenneth Lieberthal describes it: 'The problem is that high American personal consumption and high Chinese personal savings are directly linked, each enabling the other. Effectively, the United States has borrowed China's savings to finance personal consumption. At the same time, China has accumulated the money to maintain high savings and makes loans to the United States by producing goods that Americans buy with their consumer dollars.'[15] This mutual dependency has created massive imbalances that both countries will have trouble unwinding. China needs to find new ways to grow without relying on American consumers who spend with borrowed money. It needs to expand its own domestic demand. The United States needs to find ways to increase its saving over the long run.[16] Over the next decades, China and the United States will be thrown together finding ways to manage their joint problems, consulting on macroeconomic adjustment policies and the wider set of economic policies. The new Strategic and Economic Dialogue, held in Washington in July 2009, is the harbinger of the new strategic partnership.

Beyond macroeconomic policy cooperation, China and the United States share a range of common interests that will draw them together in closer forms of cooperation—along with other countries in the region as well. These are global problems stemming from industrialisation and economic globalisation. Both China and the United States—as well as Japan, India and Europe—are heavily dependent on imported oil, suggesting an alignment of interest against petroleum exporting autocracies, such as Russia and Iran. These states have a common interest in price stabilisation and supply security that could become the

---

15. Lieberthal (2009).

16. See Ferguson (2008).

basis for a revitalisation of the International Energy Agency (IEA), the consumer association created during the oil turmoil of the '70s. The emergence of global warming and climate change as significant problems also suggests possibilities for alignments and cooperative ventures cutting across the autocratic and democratic divide. Like the United States, China is not only a major contributor to greenhouse gas accumulation but is also likely to be a prominent victim of climate-induced desertification and coastal flooding. China's rapid industrialisation and its consequent local and regional pollution means that it, like other developed countries, will increasingly need to import technologies and innovative solutions for environmental management. Resource scarcity and environmental deterioration pose global threats that no state will be able to solve alone, thus placing a further premium on political integration and cooperative institution building.

The United States and China also have common security interests in the promotion of stable, rule-governed societies in the developing world. There is a deep shift in the global system towards what scholars call growing 'security interdependence'. It is harder and harder for countries to achieve security without the help of others. Globalisation and technological revolutions are making it increasingly necessary to cooperate with others to achieve security. Today, where terrorists can gain access to massive violence capabilities and project them worldwide, security interdependence has taken a new leap forward. As Robert Cooper puts it: 'the world may be globalised but it is run by states. Spaces with no one in control are a nightmare for those who live there, a haven for criminals and a danger to the rest of us.' Put simply, in the coming age, there are more and more people in more places around the world who can matter to China's and America's security. The United States and China should have a growing common interest in ensuring that states in troubled parts of the world are stable and well governed.

These alignments of interests will generate incentives for China and the United States to solve their security challenges. China will need to give ground to the United States, accepting America's security presence in the region and the legitimacy of its alliance partnerships. In return, the United States will need to accept the growing Chinese leadership in the region. Opportunities for strategic bargains will be available at various moments along the shifting power trajectories and encroaching geopolitical spheres. In these circumstances, the United States can accommodate a rising China—offering it status and position within the global hierarchy—in return for Beijing accepting and accommodating Washington's core strategic interests (which presumably include remaining a dominant security provider within East Asia). China and the United States may struggle for leadership and influence in the coming decades but they will also have strong joint interests as established, status quo states in ensuring stability.

The problem with this vision of Asia's future is that it misses the global scope of America's hegemonic position. The United States occupies a commanding position at the global level for the provision of security. Its security partnerships ring the world. In Asia, it has an array of deeply institutionalised alliances and client partners. Japan, of course, sits at the centre of this American-led regional hegemonic order. The rise of China will only reinforce the usefulness of these partnerships as a hedge on future Chinese behaviour. The United States will have obligations to other Asian states. Other states in the region will resist a co-hegemonic system of regional governance. The United States and China will surely have important and expanding reasons to cooperate. But it will be only possible in a more complicated regional and global order.

Renegotiated American-led Hegemonic Order

A fourth possible future is one where the existing American-led order continues to provide a foundation for order and stability at both the regional and global level. The 'old order' evolves—perhaps it is renegotiated—but it does not fully pass away. In particular, the American-led alliance system continues to provide the basis for security cooperation across the region. India is integrated into this security order and China accommodates itself to it as well. New institutions and security mechanisms supplement the bilateral alliances, and China plays a more central role in the political and economic life of the region. But the American-led alliances continue to provide the strategic architecture for regional peace and order.

The existing order remains attractive to states in the region despite the ongoing power transition. In the first place, the alliances do a tremendous amount of 'work' in the region. As noted earlier, the US-Japan alliance provides the basis for security binding. This is what the United States and its allies pursue within their bilateral, hub-and-spoke system of security pacts. The United States makes specific security commitments to Japan, South Korea, and other regional partners, and in exchange these countries tie themselves to the United States and support its general regional strategic presence and goals. The direct benefits to the United States and its allies are obvious. But there are also indirect benefits. The United States is able to signal commitment and restraint more generally, establishing itself as the leading agent of stability and order in the region. Japan's security ties to the United States allow it to be seen within the region as a restrained great power. Japan can gain security without developing the independent military capabilities that would trigger region-wide security dilemmas.

The backbone of the American hegemonic order is its alliance system. The United States is utterly unique in the number and range of security pacts. No other great power has so many alliance ties. Russia and China have a few security agreements but they are limited and regional. In contrast, the United States has an expansive array of security relationships on a global scale. When it has taken on security partners, it has tended to keep them—even when the specific circumstances that triggered the partnership has shifted or disappeared.

More generally, the American-led regional and global order offers attractions to China as it rises. In comparative historical perspective, it is more open and rule-based and deeply institutionalised than past international orders. All international orders dominated by a powerful state have been based on a mix of coercion and consent. But the American-led hegemonic order has been distinctive in that it has been marked more by liberal than imperial characteristics. This has made it more accessible, legitimate, and durable. Its rules and institutions are rooted in and reinforced by the evolving global forces of democracy and capitalism. It is expansive. It has a wide and widening array of participants and stakeholders. In all these ways, in comparison with past international orders, it is easier to join and harder to overturn.

Several features of this American hegemonic system are particularly relevant to how China makes decisions about whether to join or oppose it. One relates to the rules and institutions of the capitalist world economy. More so than the imperial systems of the past, the liberal international order is built around rules and norms of non-discrimination and market openness—creating conditions for rising states to participate within the order and advance their expanding economic and political goals within it. Across history, international orders have varied widely in terms of whether the material benefits that are generated accrue disproportionately to the leading state or the material benefits of participation within the order are more widely shared. In the Western system, the barriers to economic entry are low and the potential benefits are high. China has already discovered the massive economic returns that are possible through operating within this open market system.[17]

A second feature of this order is the coalition-based character of its leadership. It is American led, but it is also an order in which a group of advanced liberal democratic states work together and assert collective leadership. It is not just an American order—and a reformed liberal international order would be even less dominated by the United States. But even now, a wider group of states are bound together and govern the system. These leading states do not always agree but they are engaged in a continuous process of give and take over economics, politics, and security. This too is distinctive—past orders have tended to be dominated by one state. The stakeholders in the current order include a coalition of status quo great powers that are arrayed around the old hegemonic state. This is important. Power transitions are typically seen as playing out in dyadic fashion between two countries: a rising state and a declining hegemon. This larger aggregation of democratic-capitalist states—and the resulting aggregation of geopolitical power—shifts the balance back in favour of the old order.

A final feature of the American hegemonic order is its unusually dense, all encompassing, and agreed upon rules and institutions. International order can be rigidly hierarchical and governed by coercive domination exercised by the leading state or it can be relatively open and organised around reciprocal, consensual and rule-based relations. This order has been more open and rule-based than any previous

---

17. See essays on shared American and Chinese visions of economic modernisation and global integration in Rosecrance and Guoliang (2009).

order. State sovereignty and the rule of law are not just norms enshrined in the United Nations charter. They are part of the deep operating logic of the order. To be sure, these norms are evolving, and America itself has historically been ambivalent about binding itself to international law and institutions, and at no time more than today. But the overall system is remarkably dense with multilateral rules and institutions—global, regional, economic, political and security. These institutional creations are one of the great breakthroughs of the post-war era: establishing the basis for greater levels of cooperation and shared authority and governance of the global system.

Together these features of an evolving liberal international order give it an unusual capacity to accommodate rising powers. Its sprawling landscape of rules, institutions, and networks provide newer entrants into the system with opportunities for status, authority, and a share in the governance of the order. Access points and mechanisms for political communication and reciprocal influence abound. China has incentives and opportunities to join in while, at the same time, the possibilities of actually overturning or subverting this order are small or non-existent. In addition, in the past, old international orders were ultimately overturned through hegemonic war. In the age of nuclear weapons and great power deterrence, this mechanism of historical change—thankfully—is taken away. The United States was able to build an international order because the old order was destroyed in war. But if that circumstance is not presented to China, its ability to build a new international order from the ground up is essentially impossible. And so, together, these characteristics of the American-led liberal international order have implications for how a rising China makes choices, increasing the incentive to join rather than seeking to overturn it.

It is not surprising therefore, that China has already made moves to embrace the American-led system of international rules and institutions. China's initial use of these rules and institutions has been largely pursued for defensive purposes—protecting its sovereignty and economic interests while seeking to reassure other states of its peaceful intentions by involvement in regional and global groupings. But as scholar Marc Lanteigne argues: 'What separates China from other states, and indeed previous global powers, is that not only is it "growing up" within a milieu of international institutions far more developed than ever before, but more importantly, it is doing so while making active use of these institutions to promote the country's development of global power status.'[18]

Conclusion

There are several possible pathways for Asia—some more advantageous to the United States and some less so. One possibility is that China gradually comes to dominate regional institutions, reducing American influence and the pivotal role of the US-led bilateral security pacts. This could happen if regional institutions that exclude the United States—such as ASEAN plus 3 and the SCO—emerge as serious regional entities. This is not a likely outcome. America's allies are not likely to accept this evolution in East Asian regionalism. A more likely evolution in East Asian regionalism is a growing pluralism of regional groupings and associations. The region already is marked by this multi-layered regionalism. No singular regional organisation—an 'EU of Asia'—is in the offing. There are simply too many divergent and complex problems that call for different sorts of regional mechanisms and groupings. East Asia will not follow a European pathway.

Almost certainly, the United States and China will struggle and compete for leadership within Asia. The region will become more decentralised and complex. It will not be a straight forward hegemonic order or a traditional balance of power system. It will retain and evolve aspects of both.

The challenge for the United States is not to block China's entry into the regional order but to help shape its terms, looking for opportunities to strike strategic bargains along the way. The big bargain that the United States will want to strike with China is this: to accommodate a rising China by offering it status and position within the regional order in return for Beijing accepting and accommodating Washington's core strategic interests, which include remaining a dominant security provider within East Asia. In striking this strategic bargain, the United States will also want to try to build multilateral institutional arrangements in East Asia that will tie down and bind

18. Lanteigne (2007).

China to the wider region. China has already grasped the utility of this strategy in recent years—and it is now actively seeking to reassure and co-opt its neighbours by offering to embed itself in regional institutions such at the ASEAN plus 3 and Asian Summit. This is, of course, precisely what the United States did in the decades after World War II, building and operating within layers of regional and global economic, political, and security institutions—thereby making itself more predictable and approachable, and reducing the incentives that other states would otherwise have to resist or undermine the United States by building countervailing coalitions.

References

Buzan, Barry (2004). *The United States and the Great Powers: World Politics in the Twenty-First Century.* Cambridge, U.K: Polity.

Craig, Gordon A. and Alexander L. George (1981). *Force and Statecraft: Diplomatic Problems of Our Time.* New York: Oxford University Press.

Deng, Yong (2008). *China's Struggle for Status: The Realignment of International Relations.* New York: Cambridge University Press. p. 44.

Deudney, Daniel and G. John Ikenberry (2009). "The Myth of the Autocratic Revival", *Foreign Affairs* (January/February).

Ferguson, Niall (2008). "Team 'Chimera'", *The Washington Post.* 17 November.

Fry, Greg and Jacinta O'Hagan (eds.) (2000). *Contending Images of World Politics.* New York: St. Martin's Press.

Gat, Azar (2007). "The Return of Authoritarian Great Powers", *Foreign Affairs* (July/August).

Gill, Bates and Michael J. Green (2009). "Unbundling Asia's New Multilateralism", in Michael J. Green and Bates Gill (eds.), *Asia's New Multilateralism: Cooperation, Competition and the Search for Community.* New York: Columbia University Press.

Green, Michael (2006). "Democracy and the Balance of Power in Asia", *The American Interest* (September-October).

Ikenberry, G. John (2009). "Asian Regionalism and the Future of U.S. Strategic Engagement with China", in Abraham Denmark and Nirav Patel (eds.), *China's Arrival: A Strategic Framework for a Global Relationships.* Washington, D.C.: Center for a New American Security.

———. (2008a). "The Rise of China and the Future of the West", *Foreign Affairs* 87(1): 23-37. (January-February).

———. (2008b). "The Rise of China, Power Transitions, and Western Order", in Robert Ross and Zhu Feng (eds.), *China's Ascent: Power, Security, and the Future of International Politics.* Ithaca: Cornell University Press.

———.(2008c). "A New Order in East Asia?", in Kent E. Calder and Francis Fukuyama (eds.), *East Asian Multilateralism: Prospects for Regional Stability.* Baltimore: Johns Hopkins University Press.

———. (2006). "American Strategy in the New Asia", *The American Interest* 2(1): 89-94 (September-October).

Ikenberry, G. John and Chung-in Moon (eds.) (2008). *The United States and Northeast Asia: Debates, Issues, and New Order.* New York: Rowman & Littlefield Publishers.

Jacques, Martin (2009). *When China Rules the World: The End of the Western Order and the Birth of a New Global Order.* New York: Penguin.

Kagan, Robert (2008). *The Return of History and the End of Dreams.* New York: Knopf.

Kissinger, Henry (1954). *A World Restored: Metternich, Castlereagh and the Problem of Peace, 1812-22.* Boston: Henry Mifflin Co., 1957.

Lanteigne, Marc (2007). *China and International Institutions: Alternative Paths to Global Power.* New York: Routledge.

Leonard, Mark (2008). *What Does China Want*?. New York: Public Affairs Press.

Lieberthal, Kenneth (2009). "The U.S.-China Agenda Goes Global", *Current History* (September), p. 247.

National Intelligence Council (2008). *Global Trends 2025.* Washington, D.C. p.iv.

Overhot, William H. (2008). *Asia, America, and the Transformation of Geopolitics.* New York: Cambridge University Press, Chapter Nine.

Paus, Eva, Penelope B. Prime and Jon Western (eds.) (2009). *Global Giant: Is China Changing the Rules of the Game?.* New York: Palgrave.

Posen, Barry (2009). "Emerging Multipolarity: Why Should We Care?", *Current History.* November.

Rosecrance, Richard and Gu Guoliang (eds.) (2009). *Power and Restraint: A Shared Vision for the U.S.-Chinese Relationship.* New York: Public Affairs.

Schroeder, Paul (1994). *The Transformation of European Politics, 1763-1848.* Oxford: Oxford University Press.

29

Is Conflict Inevitable between the Great Powers in Asia in 2030?

NAMRATA GOSWAMI

This chapter sets out for itself the task of answering the question: is conflict inevitable between the rising great powers in Asia in 2030? The focus of the chapter is on the conflict dynamics which can dominate relationships between the great powers in Asia in 2030, namely, the US, China, India, Japan and Russia. Identifying three significant drivers of conflict in Asia namely: nationalism and ideology, military postures (and related security dilemmas) and weak institutions, it argues that while inter-state wars are perhaps not inevitable in Asia in 2030, tensions could arise between these potential Asian great powers including the US due to uncertainty about each other's intentions, ideological leanings, aggressive nationalism and military postures, and the absence of an overarching mediating regional institution. Resource competition, the ascendency of the zero sum perspective which asserts that one country's economic and military gain is another country's loss, relative power competition, and 'prestige seeking' instead of 'security seeking' states in Asia could further lead to systemic tensions. Finally, it crafts three alternative scenarios on the nature of state relations in Asia in 2030.

Introduction

That conflict is more or less inevitable in Asia with nearly five nuclear armed countries (India, China, Pakistan, Israel and North Korea), and two others with overt nuclear capability (Japan and Iran), is somewhat suspect. As John Lewis Gaddis so perceptively wrote years ago during the Cold War period that there was something beyond bipolar conventional parity between the US and the USSR, that ensured stability and order in the international system; a factor which could even sustain China's reversal of alignments twice during the Cold War 'without any dramatic effect upon the position of the super-powers'[1] as compared to the conflict ridden atmosphere during multipolarity of the period prior to 1914. Gaddis went on to argue that this stability at the systemic level is surely not based on the inherently pacific nature of the US and the USSR who were involved in 8 to 19 conflicts respectively between 1815 and 1980.[2] Neither was it because of the strong leadership provided by the Soviet or American political class nor a result of battle weariness after two violent World Wars. This assumption stems from the fact that the US employed military force in Korea and Vietnam and the USSR in Afghanistan during the Cold War. Gaddis reached the conclusion that the 'long peace' has been really possible because of the existence of nuclear weapons since 1945 with their immense deterrent capability in the larger international system.[3]

> I am suggesting, though, that the development of nuclear weapons had had, on balance, a stabilising effect on the post war international system. They have served to discourage the process of escalation that has, in other eras, too casually led to war. They have had a sobering effect upon a whole range of statesmen of varying degrees of responsibility and capability. They have forced national leaders, every day, to confront the reality of what war is really like, indeed to confront the prospect of their own mortality, and that, for those who seek ways to avoid, is no bad thing.[4]

For futuristic studies on systemic stability, it is therefore to be hoped that nuclear weapons will keep the peace as Asian countries rise in prominence from the second half of the 20th century into the 21st century.

As in other periods of world history, the rise of Asia has led to a wholesome and inevitable shift of power and resources from the West to the East especially to countries like India and China. The National Intelligence Council's *Global Trends 2025* argues that, 'the international system—as constructed following the Second World War—will be

1. Gaddis (1986).
2. Ibid.: 121.
3. Ibid.
4. Ibid.: 123

almost unrecognisable by 2025 owing to the rise of emerging powers, a globalising world economy, an historic transfer of relative wealth and economic power from West to East, and the growing influence of non state actors.'[5] In this power transition phase, there would perhaps be opportunities for conflict, more so in Asia, given that the locus of economic and military activity will be concentrated in East Asia and the Indian Ocean region. According to a recent article by Robert D. Kaplan in *Foreign Affairs*, the Indian Ocean region will be the centre of conflict between rising powers like India and China and external powers like the US in the 21st century as they vie for dominance over one of the most viable and potent sea routes in this period of globalisation and economic inter-connectivity.[6] Worse still, given China's overt dependence on imported goods, energy resources and raw materials, to sustain the competitiveness of its economy, it may resort to armed conflict if it perceives any threat to the smooth transit of its ships in the Indian Ocean region. This is very akin to the picture that history paints of the tensions between states preceding the World Wars in Europe.

Interestingly, in this context, Aaron Friedberg in a thought provoking article, 'Europe's Past, Asia's Future?'[7] takes a position that is somewhere between the realist pessimists and the liberal optimists. The realist pessimists argue that the inherent character of inter-state relations never changes and that without the existence of an over-arching supra-national authority to resolve security issues between states, conflicts will be endemic and bloody as the dynamic of the 'security dilemma' informs state behaviour where one state's armament policy and military posture aggravates another state's fears thereby perpetuating a cycle of armament and aggressive military postures further increasing the arc of instability. The counter to this is of course to reassure a fearful state by changing one's own military posture and making, an overt and clear-cut distinction between offensive and defensive postures, if that is possible at all in military policy. (The Soviet Union under Mikhail Gorbachev is perhaps one

5. National Intelligence Council (2008).
6. Kaplan (2009).
7. Friedberg (1988).

such case in point where he reoriented the entire military posture of the Soviet Union thereby bringing about a more trusting relationship with the US.) The realist school categorically argues that inter-state relations in Asia will be afflicted by very high levels of mutual distrust, competition and conflict.[8] The rapid changes in the economic sphere in Asia are also very dangerous as they lead to further military modernisation and create a 'security deficit'. Inability to gauge each other's intentions could result in misunderstandings and worse still miscalculations about a state's policy and the audience it is targeting. China, with its authoritarian system, and great power aspiration is not only a security seeking state (for security seeking states can be reassured at some level by providing them a secure environment), but the fear is that China, as it rises to power, will question the hierarchies mostly put in place by the West, which could result in revisionist policies escalating tensions and conflict.[9] The worry is that if in response to China's rise, a policy of containment is adopted by the existing great powers, it will only result in the former's isolation, lack of incentive to change, and limited adaptability to integrate into the existing international system.[10] Realists nurture an inherently pessimistic view about Asia as being conflict-prone and tense due to several emerging power centres (India, China, Japan, Russia, unified Korea, Indonesia, and other smaller yet technologically competent countries with military potential like Singapore and Taiwan). History, according to realist interpretations, tells us that Europe faced conflicts when there was power diffusion based on multipolarity. On the other hand, the liberal optimists believe that forces like democratisation, economic interdependence, and multilateral institutionalisation will decrease the potential for conflict in Asia. Another troubling issue related to the rise of new powers, especially China, is that research in power transition points to the fact that countries in transition tend to be assertive externally. Aggressive posturing can occur also when powers are in transition from authoritarian to democratic systems (read China).[11]

---

8. Ibid.: 2.
9. Schweller (1994).
10. Shambaugh (1996).
11. Mansfield and Snyder (1995); Ibid: 2; Schweller (1994); Shambaugh (1995).

Drivers of Conflict in Asia

In this backdrop, the potential drivers of conflict in Asia amongst the rising powers like China, India, Japan, Russia and external powers like US are the following:

1) Ideology and nationalism;
2) Military postures (and related security dilemmas); and
3) Weak institutions.

Table 29.1

The Uncertainty Matrix

Drivers of Conflict		*Uncertainty Matrix (Aggregate of 10)*
Driver 1 :	Ideology and nationalism	7
Driver 2 :	Military postures (and related security dilemmas)	5
Driver 3 :	Weak institutions	4

Driver 1: Ideology and Nationalism

In terms of ranking the drivers of conflict in Asia, ideology and nationalism come first on the uncertainty matrix. By definition, ideology 'is best viewed as a belief system that explains and justifies a preferred political order for society, either one that already exists or one that is proposed.'[12] Ideology forms the basis for strategy, including the processes, institutional arrangements, and programmes necessary for the attainment of those ideological values.[13] In this context, the future of Asia is going to see a distinct division between the two ideological streams of democracy and authoritarianism. While countries like India, Sri Lanka, Bangladesh, Malaysia, Indonesia, etc., will see the forces of democratisation strengthen by 2030, China and Russia will resist such political changes because of the overt internal stabilising benefits of an authoritarian system. This includes the path to economic progress termed as 'state capitalism' which is different

12. George (2006).
13. Ibid: 2.

from the western liberal model. Unlike the neo-liberal idea of a free market with little or no state regulation, the diktat of the state in economic matters is accorded a prominent place in 'state capitalism.'[14] China, India and Russia are mostly following this model, and will perhaps do so in 2030 as well, especially after the financial crisis of 2008-09 that engulfed most of Western world as a result of its neo-liberal, non-regulatory vacuous credit system.

In terms of ideology therefore, the national ambitions of countries like Russia, China, Japan and India will dominate the future geo-political landscape of Asia. Russia would like to see itself once again as a power of eminence in the post-Soviet era. Its large supplies of gas and oil will propel it to economic, if not military prominence, in world politics. The desire for regaining prestige is a strong force within Russia as it gradually takes it place in the post-Cold War world.

The power of nationalism,[15] especially in China, Russia and Japan is strong. However, the dominant reasons for nationalism are rooted in internal power dynamics and a desire to control the immediate structure of inter-state relations at the sub-systemic level rather than as a foolish desire to subvert the international system in its entirety. It must be recognised here that countries like Russia, China and Japan are inspired by traditional great power considerations, especially in terms of honour and respect. Russia is wary of NATO and the US and is resentful of its loss of power and prestige in the game of great power relations. It is unhappy with the post-Cold War realignment and wants to revise this order based on its own nationalistic aspirations.[16]

Both Russia and China are of the view that autocracy is better than democracy especially in order to handle their vast territorial landmass inhabited by a fractious population. Both states believe that the only viable way to prosperity and stability is through an authoritarian system. The leaders of both countries are of the firm belief that democracy will disturb their internal stability. They view India's fight

14. NIC (2008): vii.
15. 'Nationalism is the doctrine that the state and the nation should be congruent...that legitimate rule is based on the sovereignty of a culturally or historically distinctive people in a polity that expresses and protects those distinctive characteristics'. See Snyder and Ballentine (1996).
16. Kagan 2007).

against naxalism and other ethnic conflicts in its border states being the result of a democratic weakness to counter dissent. There has also been resurgence in Japanese nationalism in the past few decades with increasing fear of Chinese domination given the history of mistrust between the two countries. Hence, there are calls within Japan for a re-look at Article 9 of the Japanese Constitution and the limits of the US-Japan security alliance. In contrast to the favourable international opinion on India, which due to its open democratic political system and liberal politics, is looked upon as an easy integrator into the international system despite its recent rise to power, Chinese nationalism is seen to be belligerent that could result in policies which demand a reversal of the present international system. It is argued that China is a dissatisfied state in the system and would like to challenge the status quo.[17] There are others who, however, argue that China is not going to challenge the status quo in the near future given its own limitations though security dilemmas can lead to a more aggressive military policy if it comes to its own territorial defence and maintaining its sphere of influence amongst its client states.[18]

In this regard however, it is best to remember that Chinese foreign policy gestures are mostly directed at an internal audience. Hence, they appear tough on issues of foreign policy to appear authentic to an internal audience. This is more so due to the nature of succession politics in the Chinese Communist Party (CCP) for higher leadership positions. Any conciliatory measures will leave leaders open to charges of selling out sovereignty. Hence, Chinese nationalism for the next two to three decades will be mostly a kind of 'defensive nationalism'; a reaction to its own internal instability and social unrest.[19] While the Chinese state has rapidly gone ahead with economic development and achieved high rates of growth in its GDP, it has been unable to deliver optimal public services due to rampant corruption in the CCP. Seven hundred million Chinese continue to live in the rural areas and an estimated 70 per cent of the factories are unable to meet their payroll obligations on a regular basis. Urban unemployment is growing within

17. Schweller (1994): 87
18. Johnson (2003).
19. Shambaugh (1996): 191.

China. So long as these issues continue to fester, the Chinese leadership will be pre-occupied with domestic issues. Also, internally, China is undergoing changes as the new generation of elites are no longer of the Soviet educated genre as were the older Chinese communists leaders but technocrats for whom incremental polices matter most in domestic affairs.

That Chinese nationalism is a potent driver of conflict could be perhaps an overstatement but Chinese take great pride in their state. As Lucien Pye so succinctly put it, 'China is a civilisation pretending to be a state.'[20] The CCP plays up past humiliations, and the century of shame to promote nationalistic sentiments. As is argued within China, all the past insults to the Chinese way of life were eliminated in 1949 with the Communist takeover of China. China will therefore be extremely sensitive about infringements on its 'territorial integrity and national sovereignty'. There is also a great wariness in China about excessive dependence on foreign oil. This gives rise to a nationalism that is more reactive than assertive, more insecure than secure, dismissive of others due to its own sense of weakness. This 'defensive nationalism' is reminiscent of Chinese social insecurities, and politically narrow thinking. Hence, it must be remembered that this nationalism is not a consequence of any aggressive intent but borne out of a deep sense of insecurity and lack of confidence.

Driver 2: Military Postures (and Related Security Dilemmas)

It is often argued that military postures of states could either escalate conflict between great powers or they could de-escalate tensions depending on whether a posture is defensive or offensive. While security seeking states can be handled by changing military postures, the danger is posed by states seeking greater prestige and who are dissatisfied with the prevailing international order. The crucial judgment to be made when new states rise and edge towards 'great power' status is whether they have benign or greedy intentions. The two streams of realism, offensive and defensive, offer explanations for state behaviour. Offensive realism argues that since 'uncertainty' is the most determinative constraint on state behaviour, and great powers can

20. Ibid.: 204.

never know for sure the intentions of other great powers, the only plausible policy option they have is to maximise their relative power. Defensive realism, on the other hand, argues that since states are caught up in security dilemmas, factors like military technology, geography, and assessments of the other states' intentions and motives are factored into its own policymaking.[21] While offensive realism argues for a hard core military policy to guarantee security, defensive realism argues that, 'hard line policies often lead to self-defeating and avoidable circumstances'.[22]

Within the Asian landscape, China's military modernisation and posture is looked upon with great suspicion by other states due to the nature of the political system. While many scholars argue that China is perhaps waiting for the right time to make its intentions overt in a forceful way as it is not strong enough at this point of time,[23] still others argue that China is a status quo and not a revisionist state and will therefore not try to subvert the international order as it is satisfied with the current integrative international system.[24] Yet others fear that Chinese nationalism will result in more assertive military postures. 'Naval nationalism is one example of a potentially destabilising prestige strategy.'[25] Chinese naval capabilities, at this point of time, are limited and do not allow it to dominate even its near neighbourhood of East Asia. China is aware that US maritime capabilities enable it to control the sea lanes in East Asia. China is definitely a continental power and shares borders with 14 countries including India, North Korea, Pakistan and Russia (all nuclear armed states). Despite that, China suffers from an internal bias towards its ground forces under the aegis of the People's Liberation Army (PLA). China has 300,000 troops deployed to safeguard its borders. Despite China's huge population and resources, the PLA's extensive and very costly land capabilities constrain China's maritime capability. There is therefore a re-focus in recent times on its submarine fleet which is at the heart of its maritime strategy. China has procured 12 kilo-class diesel submarines from Russia since 1992, and

21. Montgomery (2006).
22. Ibid.: 152.
23. Goldstein (2007).
24. Johnson (2003); Shambaugh (1996).
25. Ross (2006).

built twelve Song-class diesel submarines indigeneously. In 2004, it introduced an upgraded Song, which is mostly equipped with anti-ship cruise missiles.[26] Chinese nationalism impels military posturing which has led to a widespread demand for an aircraft carrier and a blue water navy.[27] Chinese nationalists are aware of the fact that China is the only permanent member of the UN Security Council which does not have an aircraft carrier.[28] Extensive coverage was thereby given to the naval procession in the East China Sea on the 60th anniversary of the Chinese navy. China also places the re-acquisition of 'lost territories' at the top of its policy agenda and views an aircraft carrier as vital to this end. The reunification of Taiwan with the mainland is a case in point. This naval expansion is also seen as a hedge against US capability to blockade any Chinese naval shipments across the Malacca Straits.

China's 2009 White Paper on Defence says that its national defence policy is aimed solely at protecting its territory and people, by creating a more technologically advanced and capable military which will enable it to conduct operations at a great distance from its borders, a goal the country hopes to fulfil by 2020.[29] China's anti-satellite and cyber policies are a part of this process. In 2007, when China launched a ballistic missile and destroyed its own satellite, raised an international alarm and questions about Chinese intentions.

China's relationship with Japan is another area of concern for the Chinese. Since the launch of the Nye initiative in 1994, Japan has taken up greater responsibilities within the US-Japan security alliance.[30] Under a revised framework of reference in 1997, it is stated that in case of conflict in the area surrounding Japan, Japan would ally with the US. The upgrading of Japan's self-defence forces enhanced insecurity levels in China with regard to a conflict with the US over Taiwan. However, things have changed in the last few years with Japan and China enjoying a robust economic relationship. China's White Paper on the issue released in 2006 categorically states that China's

26. See Goldstein and Murray (2004).

27. Ross (2006): 60.

28. Ibid.: 60-65.

29. Bajoria (2009).

30. Mochizuki (2007).

strategic priorities are solely concentrated on the region. The greatest external security threat is the possibility of Taiwanese independence with the open support of the US and the clandestine support of Japan. Hence, China's conventional forces have been trained for a short-drawn war, in the future, mostly configured along the lines of internal security, territorial defence, and limited regional offensives (read Taiwan). China's dual policy of peaceful development with obvious military modernisation is creating fears in the West and also among countries in Asia. There is also the apprehension that China's military budget may be two to three times more than the stated amount.[31]

A caveat is now in order regarding the inevitability of military conflict in 2030. Despite China's supposedly aggressive military modernisation, if one views the statistics, China's military expenditure in 2008 was $84.9 billion which accounted for 5.8 per cent of the global spend whereas that of the US was a whopping $607 billion, with a world share of 41.5 per cent.[32] The US was the top military spender in 2009 with China in 2nd place followed by France and the UK. India came 10th with a spend of $30 billion and a world share of 2.1 per cent. The pattern was the same in 2007.[33] In 2005, China spent $41 billion whereas the figure for the US was $507 billion.[34] It must be noted that the military expenditure of the US is larger than that of the next 10 powers—including China, India, France, UK, Russia, South Korea, etc.,—combined. China has also developed its nuclear arsenal, but here too the US has 50 times more warheads and 25 times more intercontinental ballistic missiles than China. The US is also far ahead in terms of technology innovation and R&D. In 2005, the US spent $330 billion on R&D, whereas China spent only $30.6 billion. Nuclear weapons are a vital part of a country's military posture. As of 2009, eight countries in the world possess nuclear weapons and out of the eight, five are in Asia (China, India, Pakistan, Israel and North Korea).

31. See Taylor and Young (2008).
32. SIPRI (2009).
33. Ibid.
34. Mochizuki (2007).

With regard to India's military posture, doctrines like 'Cold Start' *vis-à-vis* Pakistan causes alarm within Pakistan due to its obvious conventional inferiority as established by its defeat in the 1971 war with India. Significantly, in the aftermath of the December 2001 attack on the Indian Parliament by Pakistani terrorists, the Indian military launched Operation Parakram. Despite a massive troop build-up on the India-Pakistan border, the major criticism against the operation was that India lost the initiative since the armoured divisions of the Indian military's three strike corps, (I corp in Mathura, II corp in Ambala, and XXI corp in Bhopal), took nearly three weeks to reach the border between India and Pakistan because they could not be mobilised quickly enough due to the sheer volumes of men and equipment. To address this issue the Indian military formulated its 'Cold Start' doctrine in 2004. This doctrine envisages that the Indian military will 'mobilise its forces quickly and undertake retaliatory attacks in response to specific challenges posed by Pakistan's "proxy war" in Kashmir.'[35] The 'Cold Start' doctrine is a departure from the defensive

Table 29.2

World's Nuclear Forces 2009: Deployed Warheads, January 2009

Country	*Strategic Warheads*	*Non-Strategic Warheads*	*Total Deployed Warheads*
USA	2202	500	2702
Russia	2787	2047	4834
UK	160	—	160
France	300	—	300
China	186	—	186
India	—	—	60
Israel	—	—	80
Total	—	—	8392
North Korea	Conducted nuclear test explosions in October 2006 and May 2009	Not known if any nuclear weapons have been developed	

Source: SIPRI (2009): 16.

35. Ladwig (2007-08).

posturing of the Indian military and has an overtly offensive orientation. The idea behind the doctrine is to carry out quick and effective strikes within Pakistan in the face of a terrorist strike on India from Pakistan by a combined operation involving the Indian army, navy and air force. Instead of the slow moving armoured columns of the three strike corps 'Cold Start' mooted the idea of having eight smaller division-sized 'integrated battle groups' (IBGs), which would combine mechanised infantry, artillery, and armour to make them extremely effective. The air force and naval aviation would give them additional support. The movement into Pakistani territory (50 to 80 kilometres) to launch an attack would have to be completed within 72 to 96 hours from the time of the mobilisation. This would extract concessions from Islamabad and prevent the escalation of the war to the nuclear level. The recent acquisition of 145 M 777 US made ultra-light howitzers with a range of 25-30 kms by India at a cost of $650 million can be seen in the light of operationalising the 'Cold Start' doctrine.[36]

Similarly, China faces the 'Malacca Straits' security dilemma since these straits are China's lifeline and the Chinese navy is far from possessing any real time capability to confront the US in this region. The dispute over the Spratly Islands, in the South China Sea, is another emotional issue for China. John Mearsheimer believes that, 'the most dangerous scenario the United States might face in the early twenty-first century is one in which China becomes a potential hegemon in Northeast Asia.'[37] On the other hand, Zbigniew Brzezinski asserts that, 'China's leadership is not inclined to challenge the United States militarily, and its focus remains on economic development and winning acceptance as a great power', and therefore, "conflict is not inevitable or even likely.'[38] This logic is drawn from the economic rationale that the gap in GDP per capita is still too high between the two nations. The cumulative figures from 1990 to 2009, indicate that in 1990, the gap between the US and China was about $23,000, but between 2005 and

36. Rajghatta and Pandit (2010).
37. Zhao (2007).
38. Brzezinski (2005).

2009, the gap increased to $40,300. The US per capita GDP is $42,000 whereas China's is a measly $1,709.

Nevertheless, security dilemmas can be created by offensive military postures, and a change in military postures from the offensive to a more defensive mode can diffuse tensions. Incidentally, security dilemmas also arise when countries arm themselves and the intentions for these sudden armament drives are not really known or clear. And since intentions are unknown, countries gauge each other's motives from their defence procurement. In recent years, China and India have been two of the largest recipients of conventional weapons with the US and Russia being the biggest exporters followed by Germany, France and the UK accounting between them for 79 per cent of total world exports.[39] The three largest recipients of conventional weapons from 2004-2008 were China with 11 per cent of the global arms share (Russia being the main supplier: 92 per cent), followed by India at 7 per cent of the global total (Russia being the main supplier: 71 per cent), and the UAE with 6 per cent (US being the main supplier: 54 per cent). Hence, the military postures of these states can have a direct bearing for peace in Asia. India is termed as the largest single market for weapons in the future with Russia dominating as a supplier though other suppliers like France, Israel and the UK are also getting into the fray.[40]

Driver 3: Weak Institutions

A country's intentions and military postures can be gauged by others at multilateral regional or international forums. While multilateralism has been on the upward swing in Asia, regional institutions to cement multilateralism are perhaps still too weak to influence state behaviour. In this regard, the first regional institution was created in 1967 with the establishment of the Association of Southeast Asian Nations (ASEAN). Subsequently, other regional organisations came into being. These include ASEAN + 1 (ASEAN and China), ASEAN +3 (ASEAN + China, Japan and South Korea), the Asian Regional Forum (ARF), the ASEAN Vision Group, the Shanghai Cooperation Organisation (SCO), South Asian Association

39. SIPRI (2009): 14.
40. Ibid.: 15.

for Regional Cooperation (SAARC), Asia-Pacific Economic Cooperation Group, as well as a host of Track 2 non-governmental groups like the Council on Security Cooperation in the Asia-Pacific, the North East Asia Security Cooperation Dialogue, and the Shangri-La Dialogue (2010) convened by the International Institute for Strategic Studies (IISS) at Singapore in which countries like China, India and Japan are active and includes the US as an external power. China is deeply involved with ASEAN and SCO, where issues like terrorism are deabated upon. While it is a good sign that these regional organisations have been established but given their informal set up and obsessive state-centric approach, their abilities to impact any balance of power issues are limited. There is a general suspicion that both China and the US court these institutions in order to balance each other by countervailing alliances. Hence, the ASEAN is unlikely to mediate between China and the US or the SAARC between India and Pakistan.

Based on these three drivers of conflict, the three alternative scenarios on whether conflict is inevitable in Asia in 2030 are as follows.

Alternative Scenarios

Scenario One: Cloudburst

Cloudburst is a scenario where there is sudden rise in tension between states like the US, China and India in 2030 as a result of extreme forms of ideology and nationalism (Driver I), offensive military postures (Driver II), and the inability of regional institutions to mitigate tensions (Driver III). Based on a zero sum understanding of state relations in Asia, in which one state's gain is another's loss, there is an arms race, resource competition, and great power rivalry in 2030. From this perspective, the rise of China and India, more so the rise of China, is seen as a threat to the West, especially the US, as it occurs at the cost of the West's own decline. China's economic rise is seen as a direct consequence of globalisation facilitating a high level of Chinese military modernisation by 2030. Since China's economic integration with the world through the World Trade Organization (WTO), its official military budget has more than doubled—as is reflected in SIPRI figures—from 2001-2008. China has also imported huge amounts of weapons, submarines, etc., from Russia. These are of direct concern to the US Pacific Command and its allies like Japan, the Philippines and Singapore. China's aggressive posture on India's eastern border and its claims over Arunachal Pradesh are viewed by India as an affront to its territorial integrity resulting in heightened tensions on the border between the two nuclear armed neighbours. China, emboldened by a rapid military upgrade, occupies Taiwan in 2030 leading to a conflict with the US which is supported by countries like South Korea and Japan. Worse still, given the weak nature of regional organisations in Asia, there is hardly any platform where tensions as forecast in Cloudburst can be diffused in a realistic manner. China behaves like an authoritarian hegemon in Asia with little considerations for the views of other states.

Scenario Two: Rainbow

Rainbow is a scenario where multilateral cooperation triumphs in Asia thereby neutralising conflict. In 2030, the Asian countries will manage their ideology and nationalism (Driver I), ensure that their military postures (Driver II) are defensive, and undertake a proactive engagement policy negating the several military posture related security-dilemmas. Weak institutions (Driver III) like ASEAN, ASEAN+3, SCO, East Asia Summit, SAARC, etc., become stronger and support greater interdependence resulting in a positive sum view of international relations and great power interactions in 2030. As Beijing's power increases, its neighbours from Northeast Asia, Southeast Asia, South Asia, and Central Asia look to China to provide leadership on issues of vital regional security. The region increasingly views China as a status quo and not as a revisionist state. While China remains communist in ideology, it does not meddle—as it did in the '50s and '60s—in the internal affairs of Southeast Asian countries. Realisation also dawns that the border disputes with India cannot be left unresolved in the face of the growing political and economic relationship between the two countries and there is a positive momentum to the dialogue mechanism regarding the line of actual control (LAC). India also takes a leadership role in South Asia along with China and the US. While China-Pakistan relations continue to grow, China's change of policy with regard to Pakistan, observed since 1999 when it refused to help Pakistan *vis-à-vis* India in Kargil, is noteworthy and reassuring for India. China remains an exporter of goods as well as goodwill. ASEAN countries firmly integrate China into the regional fold informed by China's past behaviour during the Asian currency crisis in 1997-98 when China decided not to devalue its currency but also provided generous aid packages to the ASEAN states against the very rigid stand taken by the International Monetary Fund (IMF). This created a lasting impression in the region that China was a responsible power. China's change of policy from suspicion to engagement with multilateral regional institutions like ARF, ASEAN, and the Council for Security Cooperation in the Asia Pacific (CSCAP) makes it more responsible towards them. China also realises that its earlier suspicions that these institutions are US controlled are unfounded. The reality is that US influence is not as deep as China believed it to be and it further decreases by 2030. China utilises these multilateral forums to further its own new security concept (NSC), based on the five principles of mutual respect for territorial integrity and sovereignty, non-aggression, non-interference in each other's internal affairs, equality and mutual benefit, and peaceful coexistence. The NSC also elaborates on the need 'to conduct dialogue, consultation, and negotiation on an equal footing...to solve disputes and safeguard peace'.[41]

In this scenario, alliances with other states are looked upon in positive rather than zero sum terms for the maintenance of stability and security. By 2030, under Rainbow, US relationship with India and other South Asian, and Central Asian nations improves further. The US also comes to view China in a much more benign light and supports China's integration into the world through a proactive engagement policy. China does not behave like a hegemon but as one of the important actors in Asia taking responsibilities and rooting for multilateral cooperation.

41. Shambaugh (2004-05).

Scenario Three: Dragon Fire

In scenario Dragon Fire (rapid change), sudden geopolitical changes create a completely new scenario in Asia. First, ideology and nationalism (Driver I) as a force take a backseat as states become post-modern and start opening up borders as is the case with the European Union (EU) today. Military postures (Driver II) become less important as states enmesh their economies together propelled by stronger economic integration through mechanisms like a newly created Asian Union (AU)—in line with the EU—and a regional free trade agreement. This move is supported by a common visa regime and common currency for Asia. China and India, like France and Germany, come together for common interests and mutual benefits. India-Pakistan tensions get diffused and problem zones like Afghanistan are stabilised with vibrant democracy, education and less support for radicalism. Weak institutions (Driver III) are strengthened by the collective efforts of states and China and India take on a leadership role with US and EU support. Border disputes between India and China are resolved and Taiwan joins the mainland as there is political reform within China propelled by nationalism. The AU plays a significant role in diffusing tensions and misunderstandings between states. The US gradually retreats peacefully from Asia and becomes more of an 'off-shore' power. China behaves like a benign hegemon, and establishes symbiotic relationships with other states in the region.

Wild Cards

1. Military conflict erupts between China and the US in 2030 as China suddenly occupies Taiwan by the use of massive conventional military force. China has a blue water navy, which includes sophisticated aircraft carriers and a submarine fleet. China defeats the US in a military showdown and the latter is forced to close down its military bases in Japan, the Philippines, Singapore and Diego Garcia. US allies like Japan, South Korea and the Philippines bandwagon with China. The US retreats from Asia.

2. Facing conventional defeat with China in the Taiwan Straits and the consequent loss of position as an Asian power, the US targets China's energy lanes of communication in the Indian

Figure 29.1

Interaction between Scenarios and Drivers Propelling State Relations

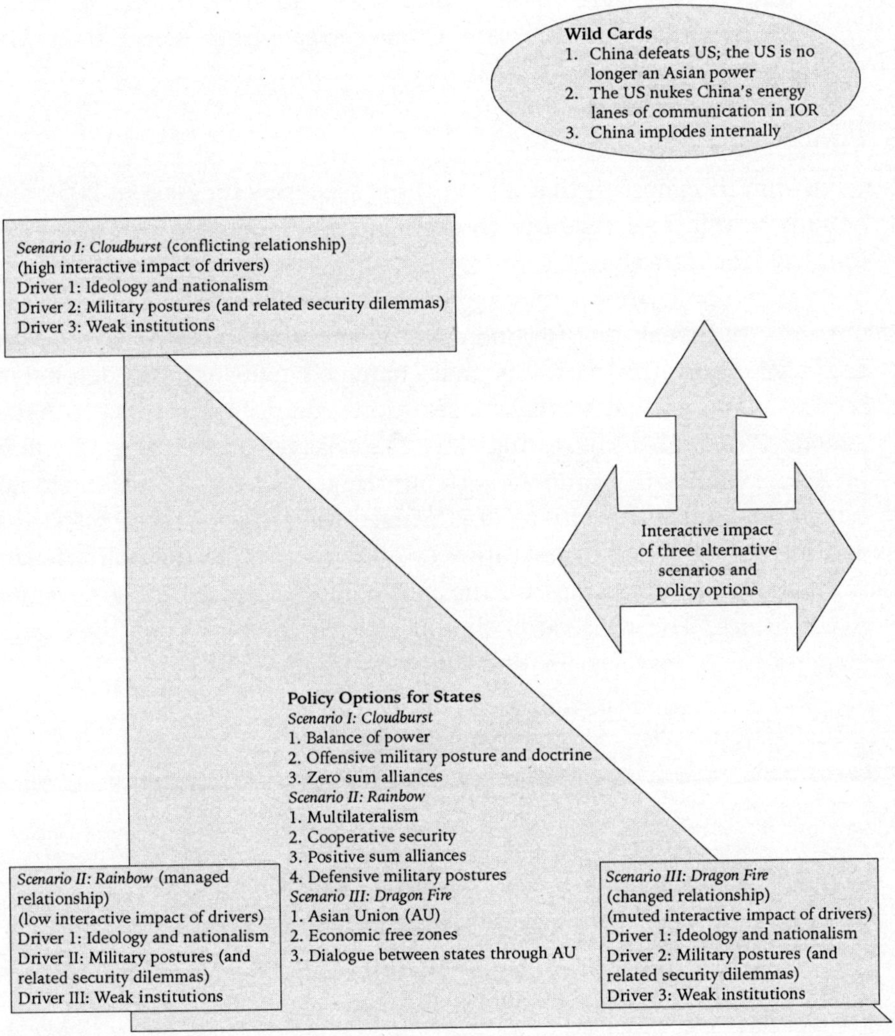

Ocean with nuclear weapons while its own missile defence shield ensures that Chinese inter-continental ballistic missiles cannot get through US air space and target US cities.

3. China implodes internally due to domestic strife and political dissent and gets divided into many smaller countries (read Soviet Union). In that case, China retreats from Asia and the US becomes stronger in Asia.

Conclusion

In sum, it is argued that all the three scenarios for Asia in 2030 are equally viable and feasible though I prefer scenario two, namely Rainbow for a prosperous and conflict-free Asia in 2030. Cloudburst informs the policymaker that aggressive nationalism, offensive military postures and weak institutions could create conflict in Asia in 2030, while Rainbow firmly states that managed nationalism, defensive military postures and stronger institutions can diffuse conflict in Asia. Dragon Fire is also interesting since it envisages an EU type of union in Asia which will guide Asian countries towards greater regional integration and prosperity by 2030. Given the range of these scenarios and the policy options they throw up, it is now up to the policymaker as to how she/he decides on the best policy practices for a peaceful Asian future. The wild cards should also be considered as they offer insights in themselves for policymaking in general.

References

Bajoria, Jayshree (2009). "China's Military Power", US: Council on Foreign Relations. At *http://www.cfr.org/publication/18459/* (Accessed on January 27, 2010).

Brzezinski, Zbigniew (2005). "Make Money, Not War", *Foreign Policy* 146: 46. (January-February).

Friedberg, Aaron L. (1988). "Europe's Past, Asia's Future?" *SAIS Policy Forum Series*. Washington DC: Johns Hopkins University. Report Number Three. October. pp.1-15.

Gaddis, John Lewis (1986). "The Long Peace Elements of Stability in the Post War International System", *International Security* 10(4): 99-142. (Spring).

George, Alexander L. (2006). *On Foreign Policy Unfinished Business*. London: Paradigm. p.1-2.

Goldstein, Avery (2007). "Power Transitions, Institutions, and China's Rise in East Asia: Theoretical Expectations and Evidence", *The Journal of Strategic Studies* 30(4 & 5): 639-82. August-October.

Goldstein, Lyle and William Murray (2004). "Undersea Dragons China's Maturing Submarine Force", *International Security* 28(4): 161-196. Spring.

Johnson, Alastair Iain (2003). "Is China a Status Quo Power?", *International Security* 27(4): 5-56. (Spring).

Kaplan, Robert D. (2009). "Centre Stage for the 21st Century Power Plays in the Indian Ocean", *Foreign Affairs*. March/April. At *http://www.foreignaffairs.com/articles/64832/robert-d-kaplan/center-stage-for-the-21st-century* (Accessed on January 21, 2010).

———. (2007). "End of History, Return of Dreams International Rivalry and American Leadership", *Policy Review*. August/September. At *http://www.hoover.org/publications/policyreview/8552512.html* (Accessed on January 5, 2010).

Ladwig III, Walter C. (2007-08). "A Cold Start for Hot Wars? The Indian Army's New Limited War Doctrine", *International Security* 32(3): 158-190. (Winter 2007/08).

Mansfield and Snyder (1995). "Democratization and War", *Foreign Affairs*, May/June, at *http://www.foreignaffairs.com/articles/50974/edward-mansfield-and-jack-snyder/democratization-and-war*

Mochizuki, Mike M. (2007). "Japan's Shifting Strategy toward the Rise of China", *The Journal of Strategic Studies* 30(4-5): 739-76.

Montgomery, Evan Braden (2006). "Breaking out of the Security Dilemma Realism, Reassurance, and the Problem of Uncertainty", *International Security* 31(2): 151. (Fall).

National Intelligence Council (NIC) (2008). *Global Trends 2025 A Transformed World*. Washington D.C. November. p.vi.

Rajghatta, Chidanand and Rajat Pandit (2010). "$ 650m US Howitzer Deal may give Army Welcome Firepower", *The Times of India*. January 29. p.11.

Ross, Robert (2006). "China's Naval Nationalism Sources, Prospects, and the U.S. Response", *International Security* 34(2): 50. (Fall).

Schweller, Randall (1994). "Bandwagoning for Profit: Bringing the Revisionist State Back In", *International Security* 19(1): 72-107. (Summer).

Shambaugh, David (2004-05). "China Engages Asia Reshaping the Regional Order", *International Security* 29(3): 60. (Winter 2004/05).

———. (1996). "Containment or Engagement of China? Calculating Beijing's Responses", *International Security* 21(2): 180-209. (Autumn).

———. (1995). "Containment Democratisation and the Danger of War", *International Security*, 20(1): 5-38. (Summer).

SIPRI (2009). *SIPRI YearBook 2009: Armaments, Disarmament and International Security*. Solna, Sweden. p.11.

Snyder, Jack and Karen Ballentine (1996). "Nationalism and the Market Place of Ideas", *International Security* 21(2): 9 (Autumn).

Taylor, Charles and Tim Young (2008). "China's Military Posture", House of Commons Library. London. pp.1-66.

Zhao, Quansheng (2007). "Managed Great Power Relations: Do We See 'One Up and One-Down?", *Journal of Strategic Studies*. August 01.

30

Asian Futures 2030

Global Strategic Trends: Alternative Scenarios

STEVE AIKEN

> The rise of India and China is changing the global balance. Together they account for about 40 percent of the world's working age population and 19 percent of the global economy in PPP (purchasing power parity) terms. On present trends, in 20 years, their collective share of the global economy will match their percentage of the global population, which is roughly where they were in the 18th Century, before European colonialism engulfed them. China's and India's trade, investments and other economic relations with the countries of East Asia and the Pacific are reshaping Asia's economic geography.[1]

Introduction

This chapter sets out an alternative view of the Asian future out to 2030. It takes as its starting point the changing circumstances that are likely to influence the global system, and the impact that they have on an increasingly interconnected and interdependent international community. The research that this study is based upon has come from detailed work by the author as part of the UK Ministry of Defence Global Strategic Trends Programme, which sets out to examine the defence and security implications that will have an impact on the UK and its key partners out to 2040.[2] Much of the work that underpins this programme has been conducted during seminars, targeted interviews held in the UK, in Europe, in the US, and during workshops held in South Africa, Japan, and at the Institute for

---

1. Speech by Lee Kuan Yew at the 37th Jawaharlal Nehru Memorial Lecture, New Delhi, November 21, 2005.
2. Development Concepts and Doctrine Centre (DCDC) (2010).

Defence Studies and Analyses (IDSA) in New Delhi. While this chapter draws on this work, the inferences drawn from it are mine alone, and should not be construed in any way as official (UK government policy or position).

This chapter will pose the scenario that the era leading out to 2030, globally, and for Asia, will be a time of considerable transition; this is likely to be characterised by instability, both in the relations between states, and in the relations between groups within states. During this time frame the world is likely to face the reality of a changing climate,[3] rapid population growth,[4] resource scarcity,[5] a resurgence in ideology, and shifts in global power from the West towards Asia.[6,7] There will be constant tensions regarding greater interdependence between states, groups and individuals and intensifying competition between them. Dependence on complex global systems, such as the global supply chains and the international market for resources, is likely to increase the risk of systemic failures.[8]

Some Drivers for Asian Futures

The distribution of global power will change. Out to 2030, the locus of global power will move away from the United States (US) towards Asia, as the global system shifts from a unipolar towards a multipolar distribution of power.[9] The hegemonic dominance of the US will fade and although they are likely to remain the pre-eminent military power, in political, economic and military terms, they are likely to be increasingly constrained as others grow in influence and

3. Ibid.: 1.
4. Ibid.: 97-107.
5. Ibid.: 114-117.
6. Drezner (2007).
7. DCDC (2010): 39-46.
8. A systemic failure is the failure of a chain of markets or institutions. It is not limited to finance, but can occur in any complex system.
9. A unipolar world has a single dominant power. A multipolar world has three or more states or alliances that dominate world politics.
10. 'The United States' unipolar moment is over. International relations in the 21st century will be defined by non-polarity. Power will be diffused rather than concentrated, and the influence of nation states will decline as that of non-state actors increases'. See Haass (2008).

confidence.[10] However, the rise of individual states, as global powers, should not be considered a certainty given the nature and magnitude of the challenges they face, nor should their eventual influence be overestimated. Instead there will be several states and institutions competing for regional and global influence, cooperating and competing within the international community in a multipolar distribution of power.

Globalisation is likely to continue, underpinned by the rapid development of global telecommunications. Politically, globalisation is likely to raise the level of interdependence between states and individuals within the globalised economy. It is likely to be an engine for accelerating economic growth, but also a source of risk, as local markets become increasingly exposed to destabilising fluctuations in the wider global economy. Economically, globalisation is likely to generate as many losers as winners, especially in the labour market. The physical manifestations of globalisation are likely to be most apparent in the globalised core, which comprises the most interdependent and economically successful regions of the world. Resources, trade, capital and intellectual property are likely to flow through this core, and rely on complex networks of physical and virtual infrastructure[11] that are likely to be vulnerable to physical disruption or cyber attack by multiple actors. Consequently, increasing dependency on this infrastructure, and the global supply chains that underpin globalisation, will leave the global, and especially the Asian, economy vulnerable to disruption. Ensuring the security of this globally distributed infrastructure is likely to be of multilateral interest.

Climate change will amplify existing social, political and resource stresses, potentially shifting the tipping point at which conflict ignites, rather than directly causing it. Extant greenhouse gas emissions will result in global temperature increases out to 2030,[12] which are likely to be unevenly distributed, irrespective of any agreement to limit future emissions. These temperature increases are

---

11. This infrastructure includes air and sea lanes and their associated ports, rail and road infrastructure, communications links, gas, oil, electricity pipelines and cables, food distribution centres, banking and finance hubs, universities and science parks, manufacturing and energy production facilities.

12. DCDC (2010): 108-110, Data taken from UK Met Office, Hadley Centre.

likely to lead to significant environmental change that may, for example, include desertification and changes to rainfall distribution patterns within the monsoon belt of the Arabian Sea and South Asia. The frequency and intensity of extreme weather events will change, possibly with severe impact on low-lying coastal regions. Rapid glacial melt, particularly in the Himalayas, may exacerbate water management problems in China, India, Pakistan and Bangladesh.

Sufficient energy, food and freshwater resources are likely to be available to sustain the growing global population and the global economy. However, distribution and access to resources will be uneven, and local and regional shortages will occur, increasing the likelihood of societal instability and of disagreement between states. Poorer states will often be unable to access the necessary resources to allow their economies to develop and their populations to prosper. The frequency, scale and duration of humanitarian crises are likely to increase. Many states, including China and India, are likely to become more dependent on food imports to feed their large and increasingly affluent populations. A shift in agricultural patterns and the distribution of grain growing areas, coupled with the rise in animal and plant diseases, is likely to disrupt food production, resulting in increased migration. However, improvements and efficiencies in agricultural production may meet much of the increased demand, given likely scientific advances that develop high-yield, disease resistant crop strains, combined with better land usage and improved irrigation. The oceans will be further exploited for protein, raising the pressure on fish stocks.

The proportion of the global population living in absolute poverty is likely to decline,[13] however, inequality of opportunity will be more readily apparent and global inequality is likely to be a significant source of grievance. Demographic trends may also fuel instability, especially in the Middle East, Central Asia and Sub-Saharan Africa. Youth bulges[14] are likely to provide a reservoir of disaffected young people. In particular, young males with limited economic prospects may be

13. DCDC (2010): 25.

14. A youth bulge is a peak on a demographic graph of median age in which the bulk of a population occurs between the ages of 15-21.

susceptible to radicalisation. However, states that experience lower birth rates and increased longevity are likely to benefit from a 'demographic dividend'.

By 2030, around 65 per cent, or six billion, of the world's population will live in urban areas, attracted by access to jobs, resources and security.[15] The greatest increases in urbanisation will occur in Africa and Asia. Up to two billion people may live in slums. Many large urban areas, especially in regions of the world suffering from poor governance, are likely to become centres of criminality and disaffection; this will lead to an increased probability of urban, rather than rural, insurgency.[16] The worst affected cities may fail, with significant humanitarian and security implications.

While strategic influence is currently concentrated in a few, great or major powers,[17] economic power is more widely spread across a range of state actors and global institutions, and in this realm, power is already multipolar. Western economic models, coupled with their relatively open societies, are likely to remain attractive influences to many individuals, especially entrepreneurs, and to some states. The US, the EU and Japan still represent around 60 per cent of world GDP but by 2030, this dominant position will have faded. Moreover, the changing distribution of power is unlikely to be simple, linear or apply to all levers of power simultaneously.

The strategic balance of military power is likely to change as Asian states close the technological gap with the West.[18] Most actors are likely to find adaptation challenging. The realignment process is likely to encompass a period of non-polarity, as states strive to realign their power to the changing strategic environment, and struggle to achieve objectives through traditional mechanisms.

15. DCDC (2010): 102-103.

16. Evans (2009).

17. The US is currently the only great power. The major powers are China, Russia, France and the United Kingdom. Japan and Germany are major economic powers. This is unlikely to change out to 2040. Powers, such as India and Brazil are likely to have achieved major power status by 2040. China may reach great power status by 2040.

18. DCDC (2010): 79-80.

How do these Drivers affect Asia out to 2030?

So given this transitional global environment what will be the likely impacts on Asia? Asia, from Pakistan in the West, to Russia in the North, to Korea and Japan in the East, coupled with the seemingly dominant power of China and India will be the home of the largest and most economically active populations. It will have, potentially, the biggest markets, centres of innovation and increasingly, the focus of new and re-emerging poles of influence. Asia is also impacted upon by other external actors, most notably the US; and in the globalised world dominated by access to, and control over, the global core, Asia is fully interconnected with many other economic, political and security interests. Asia will also have to accommodate significant areas of instability, of potential conflict and areas significantly at risk from the impact of climate change.

The Far East

Looking from East to West we first examine Japan, which will remain one of the world's largest economies, despite severe demographic challenges. Economically and militarily, it will view China as both an opportunity and a threat and this paradoxical view will drive Sino-Japanese as well as Japanese relations with the rest of Asia. It willseek to retain regional economic influence, possibly by forging and exploiting a closer relationship with the ASEAN group, both to counter Chinese influence and to prevent other emerging powers, such as Korea, taking a leading position. Japan is also a major resource importer and will face resource security issues.[19]

They are likely to gradually normalise constitutional restrictions on deploying military forces overseas and invest in its self-defence forces to dissuade and deter aggressors. Wedged between Russia, China and Korea such changes are likely to be viewed with suspicion by Japan's neighbours, given historical precedent. Japan's alliance with the US is likely to remain central to its national security, although concerns over

19. Japan has virtually no domestic oil or natural gas reserves and is the second-largest net importer of crude oil and largest net importer of liquefied natural gas in the world. Including nuclear power, Japan is still only 16 per cent energy self-sufficient. US Energy Information Administration, "Country Analysis Briefs Japan", at *http://www.eia.doe.gov/emeu/cabs/Japan/pdf.pdf.*

long-term US intentions may lead it to seek other partnerships, possibly with India, as a hedge against the rise of China.

North Korea will continue to suffer severe problems, such as energy and food distribution difficulties, while South Korea will be suffering from a rapidly ageing population. In the North, as the ruling dynasty dies out, the state will become increasingly brittle and may suffer political collapse—which is likely to result in a reunified Korea. The transition will be fraught with tension. There will be significant scope for rapid mass population movements into neighbouring states and the threat of conflict with an unstable nuclear-armed regime is likely to be of the greatest concern to the international community. Despite the substantial burden of transition, a reunified Korea, which may retain a nuclear weapons capability, as well as substantial economic and military power, is likely to become a significant force in Asia.

China

China is likely to maintain a pragmatic and supportive approach to the conduct of international relations, sharing the benefits of an international rules-based system and relying on trade in raw materials, energy and manufactured goods, to support economic development.[20] However, her current policies of non-intervention and non-interference are likely to be superseded by a more interventionist approach, as its power and influence increases. It will develop political, economic and military strategies to secure its trade and communications lanes. These strategies are likely to result in an expansion of activity and influence in resource rich regions, such as Africa, Latin America and in some parts of Asia. The Indian Ocean region, and particularly the Asian Meridian,[21] are likely to become areas of geostrategic competition.[22]

China's economic growth since 1978 has been the greatest of any large country, averaging 10 per cent per year and significantly

20. This reflects President Jiang Zemin's '16 character' guiding principle on US-China relations: 'enhance trust, reduce trouble, develop cooperation, and avoid confrontation'.

21. See Figure 30.1.

22. China practices what they style as a pragmatic 'calculative security strategy', one that emphasises the primacy of economic growth, amicable international relations combined with increasing efforts to create a more modern military, and a continued search for asymmetric strategic advantages. See Tellis and Swaine (2000).

expanding it as the leading global economy. It is the world's largest producer and consumer of steel, the second largest consumer of energy and already, by some measures, the world's second-largest economy. Its future economic development and stability will be significant for the global economy, influencing global economic demand and shaping its future political direction. Estimates of China's economic growth vary considerably. According to some it has the potential to become the world's largest economy by 2025, and double the size of the US economy by 2040.[23] However, it faces significant environmental, social, political, financial and demographic challenges that are likely to temper economic growth rates. A symbiotic economic relationship between the US and China will continue to exist. This relationship is likely to continue, although it may change in character as China's internal economic demand increases.[24]

China's continuing economic development is likely to establish it as the leading power in Asia, although it is unlikely to directly challenge the US militarily outside of this region.[25,26] War between Asian states is possible, but unlikely. The pace of change and latent tensions within the region are such that proxy conflict, rather than direct intervention is possible. China's desire for primacy in its near-abroad, allied to nationalistic impulses and historic antipathies, may result in periodic military posturing and confrontation with traditional regional rivals such as India, Japan, Korea and the US. Regional arms races, both nuclear and conventional, are possible, although efforts to prevent proliferation will continue. Potential flashpoints include Taiwan and its relationship with China, and disputes over resource rich territorial claims in adjacent seas. China is likely to represent the most capable potential adversary for the US and it will modernise its

23. Goldman Sachs (2007a).

24. China holds large amounts of US debt in the form of government bonds, and the Americans import large quantities of Chinese manufactured goods. CRS Report for US Congress, 23 January 2007.

25. Any challenge would be indirect, for example, through proxies.

26. China's 'string of pearls' strategy of 'building presence' is seen by some as an expansionist move. However, Chinese presence through the South China littorals, the Strait of Malacca across the Indian Ocean and on to the Arabian Gulf and East Africa is most likely to be concerned with securing multilateral trade and supply lines rather than a direct precursor to future expeditionary bases in countries such as Myanmar, Bangladesh, Cambodia, and along the Horn of Africa.

Armed Forces to counter perceived US, Indian and Asian threats. By 2030, it will have developed its power projection and maritime security capability and, if required, be prepared to use military force to achieve its objectives.[27]

More so than other major powers, China's future path has a wide range of possibilities, ranging from the emergence of a democratic China through to the fragmentation, or even collapse, of the state. Both are unlikely, but none can be completely dismissed. China's future will ultimately be defined by whether, and how, it manages to create a system of politics that can sustain social cohesion alongside rising prosperity.[28] Internal inequalities between a relatively prosperous, urbanised littoral region and an underdeveloped rural hinterland, and the lack of transparent and accountable governance, are likely to create tensions that may spill over into organised disorder and political violence. Alternatively, rapidly expanding urban areas may produce a diversity of political movements campaigning for greater political and social freedoms. Similarly, environmental degradation, social unrest, demographic ageing, gender imbalances, water supply difficulties, and agricultural degradation may all disrupt China's rise.[29]

The Asian Meridian

DCDC has identified the Asian Meridian (Figure 30.1) as a pivotal region that is likely to be a region of geostrategic competition.[30] It has a diverse population with large Indian and Chinese diasporas and historic links to the US and Europe.[31] The region sits astride the Malacca and Lombok Straits through which 20 per cent of global oil production is transported, including 80 per cent of China's oil imports.

---

27. China is an advocate of utilising state-led hybrid or asymmetric warfare to further its aims. This is referred in Chinese literature as 'high-tech local wars'. This is extensively detailed in Shenxing and Suping (2000). Africa is most likely to be concerned with securing multilateral trade and supply lines rather than a direct precursor to future expeditionary bases in countries such as Myanmar, Bangladesh, Cambodia, and along the Horn of Africa.
28. Stephens (2009).
29. China will have ongoing conflict, especially in the regions of Tibet and Xinjiang.
30. DCDC (2010): 66-67.
31. The Five Powers Defence Agreement links the UK, Australia, Singapore, Malaysia and New Zealand. These states agree to consult each other should a direct threat against Malaysia or Singapore occur.

Figure 30.1

The Asian Meridian[32]

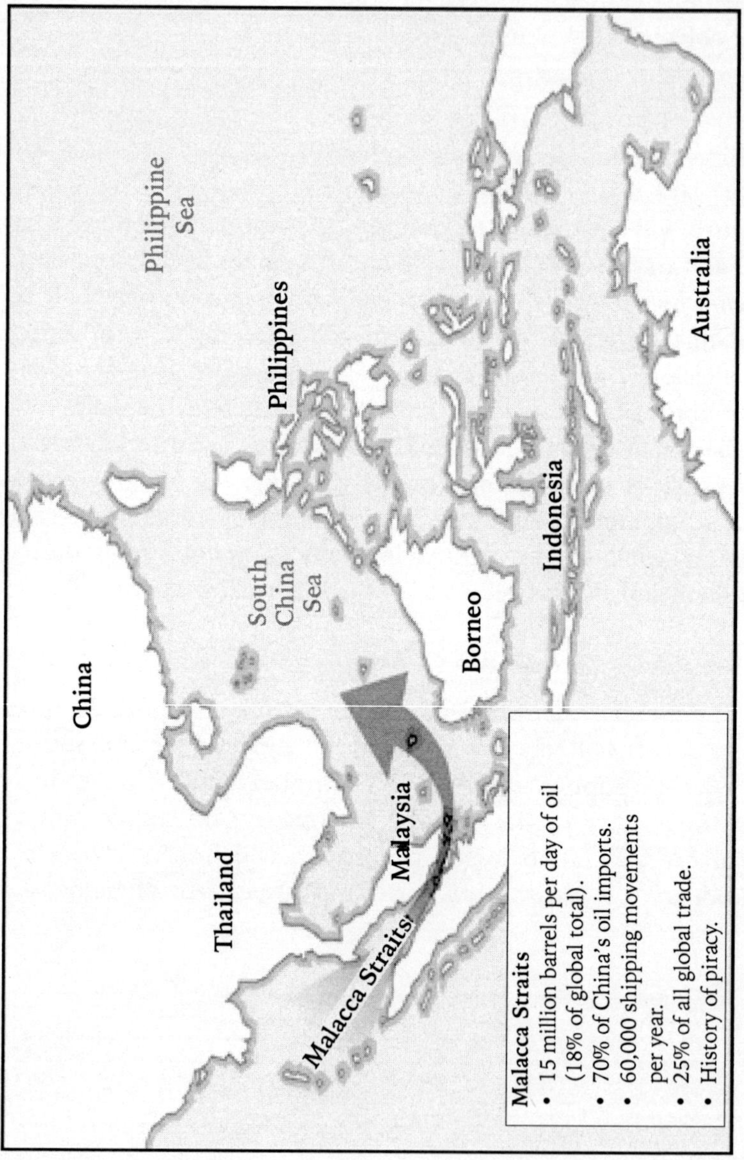

32. Is the region from Hong Kong in the North, through South East Asia into Australia. DCDC (2010): 66-67.

Over 60 per cent of global shipping travelling through these choke-points is destined for Chinese ports.[33] Similarly, Japan imports over 80 per cent of its energy needs along these routes. The importance of these choke-points is likely to grow out to 2030 placing the region at the intersection of probable Indian, US and Chinese spheres of influence. Moreover, Australia and Indonesia together account for almost half the world's coal exports and Australia in particular is a large mineral exporter.[34]

The region encompasses several states and other city states, such as Hong Kong and Singapore, that are global centres of economic and financial activity. In addition, Vietnam has a large population and is likely to continue its economic development as an important manufacturing base, becoming increasingly influential within the ASEAN region.[35] Australia, while not geographically a part of the region is also an Asian power in its own right and a centre of innovation, resource production and stability. It is likely to act as a bridge between East and West.

Islamic influences will be strong in the Asian Meridian, especially in Indonesia, Malaysia and Brunei, and amongst segments of the population in Thailand and the Philippines. Indonesia, the world's most populous Muslim majority country,[36] may experience robust economic development. However, internal problems between differing religious and ethnic groups and the effects of climate change are likely to inhibit economic and political development. Irregular activity and terrorism in support of separatism are likely and state fragmentation is possible, disrupting global trade.[37] Any disruption is likely to elicit a multinational response with China playing a significant role.

---

33. Xuegang (2008).

34. In 2007, global coal exports totalled 908 million tonnes of which Australia exported 247 million tonnes and Indonesia 187 million tonnes. Coal Portal, "World Coal Exports (Without Forecast)", at *http://www.coalportal.com/production_trade_data.cfm?data_type=Export&CFID=5583551&CFTOKEN=91771188&jsessionid=84304600833a09a727651c6b16581719462d*

35. Goldman Sachs (2007b).

36. Indonesia's population is 232.5 million. UN Population Division, 2008 medium variant. Muslim 86.1 per cent, Protestant 5.7 per cent, Roman Catholic 3 per cent, Hindu 1.8 per cent, other or unspecified 3.4 per cent (2000 census). *CIA World Factbook.*

37. Indonesia is the world's second largest exporter of coal. *BGS Mineral Profile: Coal.* March 2007.

Competition for regional influence is likely to be significant, exacerbating instability and possible disputes over resources and sovereignty. ASEAN is likely to develop its economic interconnectivity between member states but it is unlikely to emulate the EU as a supranational power in its own right. The growth in defence spending along the Meridian will continue with investment in maritime and air capabilities being substantially increased. While these forces are primarily for defensive purposes, many states in the region will be looking to use them to reinforce claims of sovereignty, both along their borders, and to further their claims in the contested exclusive economic zone (EEZ) areas.

Russia and Central Asia

Russia is an Asian power who is striving to regain its global standing in the face of domestic political, social, and demographic challenges.[38,39] Its external relations are likely to be driven by a sense of insecurity, a belief in its right to be a global power and economic factors. The near-abroad of former Soviet satellites will continue to be heavily influenced by Russian hard and soft power and is likely to remain part of a *de facto*, although largely unwelcome, Russian sphere of influence. Interference in the internal affairs of adjacent states is probable. It is likely Russia will continue to view China and Japan suspiciously and, despite membership of the Shanghai Cooperation Organisation (SCO), they will seek to deter foreign infiltration and influence, most notably from China in Eastern Siberia.

Central Asia is likely to remain prone to state weakness and instability and the resource rich area that stretches from Suez through Central and South Asia to Xinjiang has been described, by some prominent commentators, as the 'Global Balkans' of Eurasia.[40] It is an

38. Russia will continue to face pressing social challenges. High mortality rates, particularly among males, combined with low fertility rates, are likely to result in falls concentrated within the ethnic Russian section of the population. In contrast, the proportion of Russia's large non-ethnic groupings, especially Islamic groups in the southern regions, is rising and is likely to exacerbate separatist tensions. Failure to reverse this demographic trend, particularly in economically vital regions of Siberia and Russian Central Asia, may result in national decline and an inability to control its energy rich hinterland.

39. For details see Lucas (2008) and DCDC (2010): 50-51.

40. Brzezinski (2005).

area that engages the interests of many powers and the Central Asian Republics will become increasingly important centres of energy production, in particular gas. However, they are likely to be at risk of instability. Afghanistan is likely to struggle to retain stability although it may sustain sufficient stability to improve its longer term prospects.

Pakistan

Pakistan will continue to face drivers of instability. However, the institutions of state, in particular the Armed Forces and its civil society, are likely to prove resilient. In the longer-term, a dynamic intelligentsia and diaspora that mitigate ongoing instability may transform Pakistani society and the fragmentation of the state is unlikely. Pakistan's nuclear weapons are unlikely to fall into the hands of extremists or be further proliferated. However, the security of Pakistan's nuclear arsenal and its nuclear technological knowledge is likely to remain a significant concern for India and the wider international community.

India

By 2030, India is likely to have overtaken China to be the world's most populous state and is likely to prosper economically and take its place as a major, or even great power. In 1980, India's share of the global economy was slightly greater than China's, but since then its growth rate has lagged and its economy is, at present, less than half the size of China's.[41] By 2030, India is likely to reduce this gap and its economic output is likely to be of a broadly similar magnitude to China, the US and the EU. Despite poor infrastructure, problems with the educational system, and the challenges of excessive bureaucracy and corruption,[42] its economy has clear advantages over other developing economies. These include a large English speaking population, robust demographic growth, and relatively stable governance. Given its large and rapidly expanding population, India's

---

41. In 1980, China's share of the global economy at PPP rates was 2 per cent against an Indian share of 2.1 per cent. By 2007, China's share was 10.7 per cent against 4.6 per cent for India. *IMF World Economic Outlook Database 2008*.
42. Corruption Perceptions Index 2008: 3.4 (85th out of 180 countries) cited at *http://www.transparency.org/publications/gcr/gcr_2009#6.3*

output per person will remain significantly below that of other powers, although its middle class is likely to grow substantially.

India is likely to follow an 'India First' policy as it acquires political power and influence, vigorously pursuing its interests in the Indian Ocean region and along the Asian Meridian. India's influence in global affairs will increase and it is likely to become a permanent member of the UN Security Council. Its global diaspora communities, especially those involved in science, business and technology are likely to become increasingly influential. India will feel constrained and threatened by historical enmity and potential security challenges from its near neighbours, especially Pakistan and China. However, it is likely to continue its traditional aversion to alliances and maintain a desire for strategic autonomy, whilst continuing support for legitimate international security missions under the banner of the UN. However, although India will continue to invest heavily in the development of its Armed Forces, it is unlikely to be drawn into unilateral or multilateral interventions outside of the Indian Ocean region. Internally, India will continue to face complex, protracted challenges from insurgents and terrorists.[43]

India may be affected by widespread political and social turmoil in neighbouring states: many face considerable challenges, such as inequality, religious and ethnic differences and population growth. For example, religious and ethnic turmoil is likely to continue and the region is likely to remain beset by instability in governance. Similarly, an increased frequency of extreme weather events may overwhelm governance capacity and affect regional stability, especially in Bangladesh and the densely populated low-lying areas of Sri Lanka and Myanmar.

Other Actors

Other actors, such as the EU, will continue to have an influence within Asia, but primarily in the economic realm. However, the US, despite its geographical position, is an Asian power, and is likely to remain so out to 2030. The Americans will maintain a significant

43. India is currently dealing with: insurgencies in Assam, Jammu and Kashmir, Punjab, Nagaland-Khaplang; attacks from Islamic terrorist groups like Harkat-ul-Jihad-al-Islami (HuJI) and Lashkar-e-Taiba; Maoist Naxalist attacks in Eastern India; and extremist Hindu violence.

interest in Asia, through their security relationships with Taiwan, South Korea, Japan and Australia; through their own dependant territories; its economic connections, and its desire to maintain its influences and access to resources in South West and Central Asia and across the Indian Ocean region. However, the US will have to maintain this in the face of a declining proportion of global GDP.[44,45] Despite this decline, the US economy and military will still remain strong and the US will remain a politically stable great power.

Conclusion

The period out to 2030 will see the migration of power away from the West towards Asia, a process that will be driven primarily by economic factors and the changing balance of power. However, Asia will have to deal with problems of inequality, climate change, resource distribution (if not shortage) and competition with other regions of the world. Security problems will remain, with instability likely to continue in Central Asia, in Indonesia and the Philippines, and in India and China and along their borders. The challenge of maintaining access to sufficient energy and food resource for continued growth and stability will drive Asian defence and security concerns. The proliferation of WMD amongst state and non-state actors, both globally and in Asia will provide challenges for continued stability. As China and India become increasingly influential, both on the Asian and global stage they will become more involved in resolving conflict and providing leadership and direction; competition between the two, and the inter-relationships that they develop with the other Asian and global actors is likely to define the international system in the mid-century period.

44. From around 50 per cent in 1950 to 22 per cent in 2007, and although it remains three times the size of her nearest national competitor.

45. At market exchange rates, Japan is the world's second largest economy, in purchasing power parity (PPP) terms, China is second. IMF *World Economic Outlook Database 2008*.

References

Brzezinski, Zbegniew (2005). *The Choice*.

Development Concepts and Doctrine Centre (DCDC) (2010). *Global Strategic Trends out to 2040*. IVth edition. Shrivenham: Ministry of Defence. February.

Drezner, Daniel W. (2007). "The New New World Order", *Foreign Affairs*, March/April. Washington D.C.

Evans, Mike (2009). *War and the City in the New Urban Century*.

Goldman Sachs (2007a). *BRICs and Beyond*. November. New York: The Goldman Sachs Group.

———. (2007b). *BRICs and Beyond: N-11; More than an Acronym*. New York: The Goldman Sachs Group.

Lucas, Edward (2008). *The New Cold War: How the Kremlin Menaces both Russia and the West*. London: Bloomsbury

Richard N. Haass (2008). "The Age of Non-polarity", *Foreign Affairs*, May/June. Washington D.C.

Shenxing, Wang and Yang Suping (2000). "On PSYWAR in Recent High-Tech Local Wars", *Junshi Kexue (China Military Science)*. December 20.

Stephens, Phillip (2009). "Geopolitics Doesn't Travel in Straight Lines", *Financial Times*.

Tellis, Ashley J. and Michael D. Swaine (2000). *Interpreting China's Grand Strategy: Past, Present and Future*. RAND.

Xuegang, Zhang (2008). *China's Energy Corridors in SE Asia*.

Selected Bibliography

Books:

Agnew, John (2005). *Hegemony: The New Shape of Global Power*. Philadelphia: Temple University Press.

Ahmed, Akbar (2007). *Journey into Islam: The Crisis of Globalisation*. Washington DC: Brookings Institution Press.

Ali, Tariq (2008). *The Duel Pakistan on the Flight Path of American Power*. London: Simon & Schuster.

Bacevich, Andrew J. (2009). *The Limits of Power: The End of American Exceptionalism*. New York: Holt.

Barnett, Thomas P.M. (2004). *The Pentagon's New Map: War and Peace in the 21st Century*. New York: Penguin Books.

Baylis, John, Steve Smith and Patricia Owens (2008). *The Globalisation of World Politics: An Introduction to International Relations*. 4th ed. Oxford: Oxford University Press.

Bhonsle, Rahul K. (2008). *South Asia: Political, Security and Terrorism Trends*. New Delhi: Vij Books.

Brown, Harold, Joseph W. Prueher and Adam Segal (2003). *Chinese Military Power*. Washington DC: Council on Foreign Relations.

Buzan, Barry and Ole Waever (2008). *Regions and Powers: The Structures of International Security*. Cambridge: Cambridge University Press.

Chari, P.R., Pervaiz Iqbal Cheema, Stephen P. Cohen (2007). *Four Crises and a Peace Process: American Engagement in South Asia*. Washington DC: The Brookings Institution.

Cohen, Stephen P. (2001). *Emerging Power: India*. Washington DC: The Brookings Institution.

Das, Tarun, Colette Mathur and Frank-Jurgen Richter (2005). *India Rising: Emergence of a New World Power*. Singapore: Marshall Cavendish.

Development, Concepts and Doctrine Centre (DCDC) (2010). *The DCDC Global Strategic Trends Programme 2007-2040*. Shrivenham: Ministry of Defence.

De Burgh, Hugo (2006). *China: Friend or Foe?*. London: Faber & Faber.

Emmott, Bill (2008). *Rivals: How the Power Struggle between China, India and Japan will Shape Our Next Decade*. London: Penguin.

Engardio, Pete (2007). *Chindia: How China and India are Revolutionising Global Business*. New York: McGraw Hill.

Ferguson, Niall (2005). *Colossus: The Rise and Fall of the American Empire*. London: Penguin.

Ganguly, Sumit (2001). *Conflict Unending: India-Pakistan Tensions Since 1947*. New Delhi: Oxford University Press.

Gill, B. (2008). *SIPRI Yearbook 2008: Armaments, Disarmament and International Security*. SIPRI, Stockholm International Peace Research Institute and Oxford: Oxford University Press.

Goldman Sachs (2007). *BRICs and Beyond*. New York: The Goldman Sachs Group.

Guha, Ramachandra (2007). *India after Gandhi: The History of the World's Largest Democracy*. London: Macmillan.

Hackett, James (ed.) (2008). *The Military Balance: 2008*. London: International Institute for Strategic Studies.

Henshall, Kenneth (2004). *A History of Japan from Stone Age to Superpower*. New York: Palgrave.

Hughes, Christopher W. (2009). *Japan's Remilitarisation International Institute of Strategic Studies*. London: Routledge.

Kapila, Subhash (2003). *India's Defence Policies and Strategic Thought: A Comprehensive Analysis*. New Delhi: Simsid Books.

Khanna, Parag (2008). *The Second World: How Emerging Powers are Redefining Global Competition in the 21st Century*. London: Penguin.

Kumar, Nirmalya (2009). *India's Global Powerhouses: How They are Taking on the World*. Boston: Harvard Business Press.

Liang, Qiao and Wang Xiangsui (2007). *Unrestricted Warfare, China's Master Plan to Destroy America*. New Delhi: Natraj Publishers.

Lucas, Edward (2008). *The New Cold War: How the Kremlin Menaces both Russia and the West*. London: Bloomsbury.

Mahbubani, Kishore (2008). *The New Asian Hemisphere: The Irresistible Shift of Global Power to the East*. New York: Public Affairs.

Marston, Daniel P. and Chandar S. Sundaram (ed.) (2007). *A Military History of India and South Asia: from the East India Company to the Nuclear Era*. Bloomington: Indiana University Press.

Misra, Maria (2008). *Vishnu's Crowded Temple: India Since the Great Rebellion*. London: Penguin.

Mohan, Raja C. (2003). *Crossing the Rubicon: The Shaping of India's New Foreign Policy*. New Delhi: Penguin.

Muni, S.D. (ed.) (2008). *IDSA: Asian Strategic Review 2008*. New Delhi: Institute for Defence Studies and Anlayses.

Nayar, Raj Baldev and T.V. Paul (2003). *India in the World Order: Searching for Major Power Status*. Cambridge: Cambridge University Press.

Nye, Joseph S. (2009). *Understanding International Conflicts: An Introduction to Theory and History*. New York: Pearson Longman.

Overholt, William H. (2008). *Asia, America and the Transformation of Geopolitics*. Cambridge: Cambridge University Press.

Panagariya, Arvind (2008). *India: the Emerging Giant*. Oxford: Oxford University Press.

Pyle, Kenneth B. (2007). *Japan Rising: The Resurgence of Japanese Power and Purpose*. New York: Public Affairs.

Rai, Vinay and William L. Simon (2007). *Think India: The Rise of the World's Next Superpower and What it Means for Every American*. New York: Dutton.

Raj, Besant C. (2006). *Unravelling the China Miracle: A Comparative Study with India (1950–2005)*. [Unknown: *Booksurge.com*].

Sarila, Narendra Singh (2005). *The Shadow of the Great Game*. London: Constable & Robinson Ltd.

Scobell, Andrew (2007). *China's Use of Military Force, Beyond The Great Wall and the Long March*. New York Cambridge University Press.

Schofield, Victoria (2003). *Kashmir in Conflict: India, Pakistan and the Unending War*. London: I.B. Tauris.

Sen, Gautam (ed.) (2006). *Conceptualising Security for India in the 21st Century*. New Delhi: Atlantic.

Shirk, Susan L. (2008). *China Fragile Superpower.* New York: Oxford University Press.

Singh, Jasbir R.K. (ed.) (2009). *Indian Defence Yearbook 2009*. Dehradun: Natraj Publishers.

Yoshihara, Toshi and James R. Holmes (ed.) (2009). *Asia Looks Seaward: Power and Maritime Strategy.* New Delhi: Praeger Security International.

Zakaria, Fareed (2008), *The Post-American World.* London: W.W. Norton & Company.

Articles:

Bailes, Alyson J.K., Pal Dunay, Pan Gunang, and Mikhail Troitskiy (2007). "The Shanghai Cooperation Organisation", *SIPRI Policy Paper* No.17, May. Stockholm: SIPRI.

Carter, Ashton B. (2006), "America's New Strategic Partner", *Foreign Affairs* 85(4), July/August, Washington DC.

Dormandy, Xenia (2007). "Is India, or Will it Be, a Responsible International Stakeholder?", *The Washington Quarterly*, Summer. Washington.

——. (2008). "India's Key Foreign Policy Issues", Belfer Centre. August 04, cited at *www.belfercenter.org/india*

Drezner, Daniel W. (2007). *The New New World Order. Foreign Affairs*. March/April, Washington.

Economy, Elizabeth C. (2007). "The Great Leap Backwards—The Costs of China's Environmental Crisis", *Foreign Affairs*. September/October, Washington.

Hass, Richard N. (2008), "The Age of Nonpolarity", *Foreign Affairs*. May/June. Washington.

Information Office of the State Council of the People's Republic of China (2009). "China's National Defense in 2008", *Foreign Language Press.* Beijing, China.

Kamath, M.V. (2003). "Not a Superpower but an Emerging Power", *The Sunday Tribune.* New Delhi, January 26, cited at *www.tribuneindia.com/2003.*

Kaplan, Robert (2009). "Rivalry in the Indian Ocean", *Foreign Affairs.* March/April. Washington: Centre for Foreign Affairs.

Kujur, Rajat (2008). "Naxal Movement in India: A Profile", Institute of Peace and Conflict Studies (IPCS) *Research Papers* 15. September.

Ladwig, Walter C. (2007-08) "A Cold Start for Hot Wars: The Indian Army's New Limited War Doctrine", *International Security* 32(3): 158-90, Winter.

National Intelligence Council (2008). "Underpinnings of India's Economic and Political transformation; 2025", *Conference Report–NIC*, Washington, January.

Office of the Secretary of Defense (2007). *Annual Report to Congress: Military Power of the People's Republic of China 2007*. Washington: US Department of Defense.

Sharma, Raghav (2009). "India in Central Asia, The Road Ahead", Institute of Peace and Conflict Studies (IPCS). *Special Report* 63, New Delhi. January.

Singh, Manmohan (2007). "India at Sixty", *The Hindu.* New Delhi. Wednesday, August 15, cited at *www.hindu.com/af/india60*

Srivastava, Devyani and Priyashee Andley (2007). "Great Power Dynamics, India, US and China", Institute of Peace and Conflict Studies, Indian Army 15 Corps HQ, Srinagar, May.

Tellis, Ashley J. (2008), "India's Emerging Nuclear Posture", *RAND Research Brief.* Santa Monica, June.

Yew, Lee Kuan (2007). "India's Peaceful Rise", New York, *www.forbes.com.*

Journals:

US NIC (2008). *Global Trends 2025: A Transformed World.* Washington DC: National Intelligence Council, November.

Conferences/Workshops:

DCDC (2009). *Mackinder Forum 2009*, Beckett House, January 19-21.

———. (2008). *Global Strategic Trends Workshop.* IDSA, New Delhi, October 30-31

———. (2008). *Transition to a Multi-Polar World.* Workshop, Beckett House, April 30-May 1.